The Language of the Old-Okinawan *Omoro Sōshi*

# The Languages of Asia Series

*Series Editor*

Alexander Vovin (*EHESS/CRLAO, Paris, France*)

*Associate Editor*

José Andrés Alonso de la Fuente (*Jagiellonian University, Kraków, Poland*)

*Editorial Board*

Mark Alves (*Montgomery College*)
Gilles Authier (*EPHE – École Pratique des Hautes Études, Paris*)
Anna Bugaeva (*Tokyo University of Science/National Institute for Japanese Language and Linguistics*)
Bjarke Frellesvig (*University of Oxford*)
Guillaume Jacques (*Centre de recherches linguistiques sur l'Asie orientale*)
Juha Janhunen (*University of Helsinki*)
Ross King (*University of British Columbia*)
Marc Miyake (*British Museum*)
Mehmet Ölmez (*Istanbul University*)
Toshiki Osada (*Institute of Nature and Humanity, Kyoto*)
Pittawayat Pittayaporn (*Chulalongkorn University*)
Elisabetta Ragagnin (*Freie Universität Berlin*)
Pavel Rykin (*Russian Academy of Sciences*)
Marek Stachowski (*Jagiellonian University, Kraków, Poland*)
Yukinori Takubo (*Kyoto University*)
John Whitman (*Cornell University*)
Wu Ying-zhe (*Inner Mongolia University*)

VOLUME 21
The titles published in this series are listed at *brill.com/la*

# The Language of the Old-Okinawan *Omoro Sōshi*

*Reference Grammar, with Textual Selections*

*By*

Leon A. Serafim
Rumiko Shinzato

BRILL

LEIDEN | BOSTON

Cover illustration: OS 10.#534 'The Rising Pleiadis'. Found in: Hokama Shuzen 外間守善 and Hateruma Eikichi 波照間永吉, editors and authors. 2011. Teihon Omoro Sōshi [定本おもろさうし; The Omoro Sōshi, standard text]. Tokyo: Kadokawa Gakugei Shuppan, p. 329.

Library of Congress Cataloging-in-Publication Data

Names: Serafim, Leon Angelo, author. | Shinzato, Rumiko, author.
Title: The language of the old-Okinawan Omoro Sōshi : reference grammar with
    textual selections / by Leon A. Serafim, Rumiko Shinzato.
Description: Leiden ; Boston, 2020. | Series: Languages of Asia, 2452-2961 ; vol. 21 |
    Includes bibliographical references and index.
Identifiers: LCCN 2020007111 (print) | LCCN 2020007112 (ebook) |
    ISBN 9789004414693 (hardback) | ISBN 9789004414686 (ebook)
Subjects: LCSH: Omoro sōshi–Language. | Ryukyuan language–Grammar.
Classification: LCC PL886.R92 S47 2020 (print) | LCC PL886.R92 (ebook) |
    DDC 495.6/7–dc23
LC record available at https://lccn.loc.gov/2020007111
LC ebook record available at https://lccn.loc.gov/2020007112

Typeface for the Latin, Greek, and Cyrillic scripts: "Brill". See and download: brill.com/brill-typeface.

ISSN 2452-2961
ISBN 978-90-04-41469-3 (hardback)
ISBN 978-90-04-41468-6 (e-book)

Copyright 2021 by Koninklijke Brill NV, Leiden, The Netherlands.
Koninklijke Brill NV incorporates the imprints Brill, Brill Hes & De Graaf, Brill Nijhoff, Brill Rodopi,
Brill Sense, Hotei Publishing, mentis Verlag, Verlag Ferdinand Schöningh and Wilhelm Fink Verlag.
All rights reserved. No part of this publication may be reproduced, translated, stored in a retrieval system,
or transmitted in any form or by any means, electronic, mechanical, photocopying, recording or otherwise,
without prior written permission from the publisher. Requests for re-use and/or translations must be
addressed to Koninklijke Brill NV via brill.com or copyright.com.

This book is printed on acid-free paper and produced in a sustainable manner.

*To Sally Serafim and R.J. Simonds*

# Contents

**Preface** IX
**List of Figures and Tables** XI
**Abbreviations and Conventions** XII

**1 Introduction** 1
   1   What Is the *Omoro Sōshi*? 1
   2   Types of Omoro 4
   3   Versions 6
   4   Song Structure 8
   5   Overview of the Omoro Language 14

**2 Spelling System and Phonology** 18
   1   Introduction 18
   2   Reconstruction Methodology 19
   3   Suprasegmentals 37
   4   Consonants 37
   5   Processes 54
   6   Meter in Omoros 73
   7   The Question of External Evidence and Its Relation to That Presented Here 75
   8   Coda 84

**3 Lexicon** 85
   1   PJ Origin 85
   2   Loans from MJ 90
   3   Loans from Sino-Japanese 91
   4   Loans from Korean 93
   5   Origins Unknown 94
   6   *Mishōgo* (MO, Meanings Obscure) 97

**4 Nominals** 99
   1   Nouns 99
   2   Pronouns 108
   3   Numerals 122
   4   Nominal Prefixes 126
   5   Nominal Suffixes 140

# VIII

CONTENTS

**5 Adjectives** 150

1 What Is an Adjective? 150
2 Evolution of Adjectives 152
3 Functional Differences between/among Types 159
4 Functions as Modifiers, Predicates, or Noun Formatives 169

**6 Verbs** 184

1 Conjugation Types 184
2 History of Conjugation Merger: *ra-gyō yodan-ka* 229
3 Functional Split (MZ) 244
4 Development of the Gerund 249

**7 Auxiliaries** 260

1 Passive/Exalting/Spontaneous Auxiliaries: *-ari(·r)-* ~ *-uyi(·r)-* 260
2 Causative/Exalting Auxiliary: *-as-* 270
3 Negatives: *-azi* ~ *-aN* ~ *-an-* 281
4 Negative: *-adana* 288
5 The Optative/Counterfactual Auxiliary: *-(a)masyi* 296
6 Inference/Intention: *-aN, -a,* and *-am-i* 303
7 Negative Inferential/Intentional: *-umazyi* 309
8 Past: *-syi* 312
9 Perfect: *-tˣar-, -cˣyar-, -dar-, -dzyar-* 313
10 Emphatic Locative: *-ʔac°ir-u* 323
11 Progressive: *-ur-* 332
12 Progressive/Perfective: *-yaaryi* 346
13 Copula: *-yar-, -nar-* 356
14 Exalting Auxiliary Verb: *-(u)wa·r/s-* 366
15 Humilific Auxiliary: *-abir-* 385
16 Humilific Auxiliary: *tʰat°imac°ir-* 387

References 391
Index of Authors 403
Index of OS Examples 406
Index of Particles 412
Index of Linguistic and Literary Terms 414

# Preface

Many of our colleagues have given us the benefit of their input and advice during the writing, rewriting, and editing of this monograph; among them are our two anonymous reviewers, who read our manuscript with care, favoring us with solid criticism and even occasional suggestions on how to proceed. The result was a stronger monograph than would otherwise have been.

Professor Alexander Vovin, the editor of this series, was kind enough to consider our manuscript and decide to send it out for review. After the initial stage, he also made wide-ranging suggestions to improve the structure of the manuscript, which we took to heart. His frank criticisms helped us improve the work, and for that we offer our sincere thanks.

The works of the late Professor Hokama Shuzen frequently provided a beacon into some of the farther recesses of *Omoro Sōshi* meaning and structure.

We are also grateful to the following organizations for their support: the Northeast Asia Council of the Association for Asian Studies, Georgia Tech Ivan Allen College of Liberal Arts (IAC Research Funding Program) and the Okigin Furusato Shinkō Kikin.

Leon Serafim has been studying the *Omoro Sōshi* since 1975. He owes an unrepayable debt of gratitude to Professors Ikemiya Masaharu and the late Takahashi Toshizō, who, along with the great Professor Nakasone Seizen, directed the activities of the weekly-meeting Omoro Kenkyūkai [Omoro Research Society], in which he had the honor of being allowed to function as a full member. It seemed that there in Okinawa there existed—perhaps as nowhere else in Japan—the possibility for researchers from many different fields to cross-pollinate, bringing their own expertise to bear while engaging in one-at-a-time exegeses of omoros, and energetic discussions throughout.

At the same time he was introduced to the works of the giants upon whose shoulders everyone stood, including, in particular, Ifa Fuyū, Nakahara Zenchū, and of course, Hokama Shuzen.

Serafim also was allowed to join the Ryūdai Hōgen Kenkyūkai [Ryūkyū University Dialect Research Club], an undergraduate group, in their weeklong field study in 1977 in En village in northern Amami Ōshima. This, along with his later dissertation research on the dialect of Shodon, also a northern Amami dialect, formed the basis for his understanding of the earlier shape of, especially, the proto-Northern-Ryukyuan vowel system, from which the system seen in the *Omoro Sōshi* also sprang.

For six years from 1977, Serafim studied with the dean of Japanese and Korean linguistics in the United States, the late Professor Samuel E. Martin. He will always be in Professor Martin's debt for being given the privilege of studying with him.

Serafim owes an incalculable debt to his wife, Sally, who waited patiently for him to finish this manuscript so that their "retirement" together could begin. One thing that they did enjoy together, though, was their grandson's maturation in Little League baseball.

Rumiko Shinzato would like to express her deep gratitude to the late Professor Handa Ichirō, who first showed her the value of her native language, Okinawan, piqued her interest in linguistics, and instilled in her important tenets for pursuing research. His knowledge from language to literature, from people to culture, from ancient times to present, within and beyond Japan, knew no bounds. She considers crossing paths with him to be one of the greatest blessings in her life. She would like to thank her parents for passing on to her the treasure of the Okinawan heritage, including the very language analyzed in this monograph. Last but not least, she would like to express her heartfelt appreciation to her husband for his profound interest in her research, his unrelenting support and his positive and optimistic attitude during the long and grueling process of writing this manuscript. Thanks also go to her children and grandchildren for their understanding of and tolerance with her frequent withdrawals to attend to teleconferences even during family vacations.

Among the many scholars studying the Okinawan and Ryukyuan languages, we have benefitted especially from the following: Ikemiya Masaharu, Hateruma Eikichi, Shimamura Kōichi, Mamiya Atsushi, the team of Nakamoto Masachie, Higa Minoru, and Chris Drake, the Omoro Sōshi Kenkyūkai (Okinawa), Moriyo Shimabukuro, and the late Takahashi Toshizō and Uchima Chokujin. A number of linguists working in Japan, the United States, and Europe have also enlightened us through their work and their feedback, including John Bentley, Stewart A. Curry, Charles Quinn, Timothy Vance, John Whitman, and the late Maner Thorpe.

Stewart A. Curry meticulously read and critiqued an earlier draft of a chapter of the manuscript, applying his unmatched skill in formatting to it, and doing the lion's share of the indexing of the entire book.

Finally we would like to thank Chunyan Shu, Elisa Perotti, and especially Irene Jager, and the staff at Brill for catching a great number of the many errors in the manuscript.

Needless to say, all faults remaining in this monograph are ours and ours alone.

# Figures and Tables

## Figures

| | | |
|---|---|---|
| 1.1 | Textual tree of OS copies | 7 |
| 1.2 | Song structure, OS 1.#1 | 11 |

## Tables

| | | |
|---|---|---|
| 2.1 | The kana and their transliterations | 19 |
| 2.2 | The *Omoro Sōshi* Consonant System | 21 |
| 2.3 | Steps in the merger of *o and *u | 28 |
| 2.4 | \|kimo\| data | 30 |
| 2.5 | \|kumo\| data | 32 |
| 2.6 | \|koro\| data | 32 |
| 2.7 | High and mid vowel mergers (*gojūon*) | 34 |
| 2.8 | OOk /pˮu/ and /pʰu/, and OJ correspondences | 38 |
| 2.9 | OOk /pˮ/ | 39 |
| 2.10 | OOk /pʰ/ | 39 |
| 2.11 | Verb-type underlying and surface forms, with examples | 60 |
| 2.12 | Development of initial mora consonants | 74 |
| 2.13 | Chinese and Korean medieval sources and dates | 76 |
| 6.1 | Verb types, with examples and glosses | 185 |
| 6.2 | Example of table with 4G(11), *m*-type quadrigrade | 191 |
| 6.3 | Consonant- and vowel-verb subtypes | 193 |
| 6.4 | Shift from bigrade to quadrigrade | 232 |
| 6.5 | Shift from 2G to 1G verbs in pre-OOk | 233 |
| 6.6 | From lower bigrade to *r*-type neo-quadrigrade | 237 |
| 7.1 | Priestess names and (lack of) voicing marks | 286 |
| 7.2 | Effects of vowel raising 1 and vowel raising 2 | 319 |

# Abbreviations and Conventions

### Languages

| | |
|---|---|
| CoOk | (Modern) Colloquial Okinawan |
| ENJ | Early Modern Japanese |
| Lit | Literary language |
| LitJ | Literary Japanese (based on MJ; used in OS interlineations) |
| LitOk | Literary Okinawan (based on MOk) |
| MC | Middle Chinese |
| MJ | Middle Japanese |
| MOk | Middle Okinawan |
| NJ | Modern Japanese |
| Nk | Nakijin dialect of Modern Northern Okinawan |
| NOk | Modern Okinawan (Shuri, Naha) |
| OJ | Old Japanese |
| Ok | Okinawan |
| OOk | Old Okinawan (the language of the *Omoro Sōshi*), with *later* OOk being the language of the OS volumes compiled in the 17th century, and *latest* OOk referring to the language of the stone inscriptions |
| PJpc/PJ | Proto-Japonic |
| PRk | Proto-Ryukyuan |

### Texts and Resources

| | |
|---|---|
| IFZ | *Ifa Fuyū Zenshū* |
| KKKS | *Konkō Kenshū* (Hokama) |
| KKKS2 | *Konkō Kenshū* (Ikemiya) |
| KOS | *Kōhon Omoro Sōshi* |
| MYS | *Man'yō-shū* |
| NKT | *Nantō Kayō Taisei* |
| OKDJ | *Okinawa Kogo Daijiten* |
| OKRKS | *Omoro Kanshō: Ryūkyū Koyō no Sekai* |
| OS | *Omoro Sōshi* |
| RGS | *Ryūkyū Gikyokushū* |
| TOS | *Teihon Omoro Sōshi* |

## Dictionaries

| | |
|---|---|
| EOKJ | Electronic *Ōbunsha Kogo Jiten* |
| ENKDJ | Electronic *Nihon Kokugo Dai-Jiten* |
| ESKR | Electronic *Shin-Kango-Rin* |
| JDB | *Jidai-betsu Kokugo Dai-Jiten, Jōdai-hen* |
| KJE | *Kōjien* |
| NHJ | *Nakijin Hōgen Jiten* |
| NHK | *NHK Nihon-go Hatsuon Akusento Jiten* |
| ODHJ | *Okinawa Dai-Hyakka Jiten* |
| OGJ | Uemura (ed.) *Okinawago Jiten* |
| OGJ2 | Uchima and Nohara (eds.) *Okinawago Jiten* |
| OSJS | *Omoro Sōshi Jiten Sō-Sakuin*, new edition |
| RGJ | *Ryūkyūgo Jiten* |
| Sāchā | Sōshi Sāchā |
| SNKDJ | *Seisen-ban Nihon Kokugo Dai-Jiten* |
| SWEDJ | *Shin Wa-Ei Dai-Jiten* |

## Grammar Terms

### *Case and Adjunct Marking*

| | |
|---|---|
| -∅ | a way of marking locus of expected but non-appearing direct-object, indirect-object, subject, topic, or place particles, or copula |
| APP | applicative (= ditransitive / double-object) |
| APPO | appositional/appositive |
| COM | comitative: 'with', 'and' |
| DO | direct-object marker; with allomorphs -∅, -*yu*, -*Qp°a* [the latter with special usages, such as emphasis or the object of a causative] |
| GEN | genitive marker, with allomorphs -*ga*, -*gya*, -*nu* (ˣ-*nyu*) |
| INSTR | instrumental case |
| IO | indirect object marker; any dative-like particle; includes zero-marking with "indirect-object" function (i.e. -∅$_{IO}$) |
| KP | *kakari particle*, corresponding to a particular ending in *kakari musubi* (qv) |
| LOC | locative |
| PRP | purposive: -*g(y)a* |
| QT | quotative particle |
| SUB | subject, with allomorphs -*ga*, -*gya*, -*nu*, (ˣ-*nyu*) including zero-marking (i.e. -∅$_{SUB}$) |

| | |
|---|---|
| TOP | topic, with allomorphs -*wa* and -*ya*, including zero-marking (i.e. -$\varnothing_{\text{TOP}}$) |
| TRM | terminative, *until, as far as* |
| VOC | vocative |

### Conjugation Forms

| | |
|---|---|
| IZ | *izenkei*, non-subjunctive form, (definite) provisional form -*i* (cf. MR) |
| MR | *meireikei*, imperative form -*i* (cf. IZ) |
| MZ | *mizenkei*, irrealis form, subjunctive-like form -*a* |
| RT | *rentaikei*, adnominal -*u* |
| RY | *ren'yōkei*, adverbial, infinitive, nominalizer, with forms -*yi*, -*y*-, -$\varnothing$ |
| SS | *shūshikei*, sentence-ending form, with allomorphs -*u*, -*yi* |

### Conjugation Types
Verbs

| | |
|---|---|
| 2G | bigrade (name of set of verb classes) |

| NOk | OOk | P-Rk | < P-Jpc > | OJ | ‖ | NOk | OOk | P-Rk | < P-Jpc > | OJ |
|---|---|---|---|---|---|---|---|---|---|---|
| U1G$_{+P}$ | U1G$_{+P}$ | U2G | < U2G > | U2G | ‖ | (*y*)*i* | *yi* | *\*yi* | < *\*uCî* > | *ï/i* |
| U1G$_{+P}$ | U1G$_{+P}$? | U2G? | < M2G$_1$ > | | ‖ | (*y*)*i* | *yi/i* | *\*yi/\*ye/\*e* | < *\*ôCî* > | *ï/i* |
| U2G$_{-[/+]P}$ | U1G$_{-P}$ | L2G | < M2G$_2$ > | | ‖ | (*y*)*i* | *i*(, [*y*]*i*) | *\*e* | < *\*öCî* > | *ï/i* |
| U2G$_{-[/+]P}$ | U1G$_{-P}$ | L2G | < L2G > | L2G | ‖ | (*y*)*i* | *i*(, [*y*]*i*) | *\*e* | < *\*aCî* > | *ë/e* |

| | | |
|---|---|---|
| | U2G | upper bigrade (class ending in pre-OOk *\*···e*-, OOk *\*···e·r*-, and OJ *\*···ï-/···i*-, rather than OJ *···ë-/···e*-; most OJ U2G are OOk L2G [see above], but there are just a handful of true U2G in OOk, reflecting original Proto-Japonic U2G; and see just below for M2G) |
| | M2G | middle bigrade; second-largest bigrade subclass; has merged with L2G in Ryukyuan |
| | L2G | lower bigrade; largest bigrade subclass (class ending in pre-OOk *\*···e*-, OOk *\*···e·r*-, and OJ *···ë-/···e*-) |
| | PP | NOk: morphophonemic; OOk: partly morphophonemic, partly phonetically motivated; P-Rk: phonetically motivated; P-Jpc: phonetically motivated if extant; OJ: apparently non-existent |
| U1G | | upper monograde / unigrade |
| 4G | | quadrigrade (name of set of verb classes) |
| 4GE | | derivational morpheme for secondary *r*-stem; ie quadrigrade formative = ·*r*- |

ABBREVIATIONS AND CONVENTIONS                                                    XV

| KI | *k*-irregular |
| SI | *s*-irregular |

## Adjectives

| AA | affective adjective formative |
| ADJ | adjective |
| ADJ.STEM | adjective stem, such as *k°yura-* 'beautiful-' |
| AF | adjective formative |
| ADS | adjective derivational suffix |
| NDS | nominal derivational suffix |
| AV | adjectival verb / adjectival noun / adjectival nominative [three concurrent names for the same thing] |
| PA | property adjective |

## Auxiliaries

| AUX | auxiliary verb |
| EAV | exalting auxiliary verb {+(u)wa{r/s}+} |
| HAV | humilific auxiliary verb {+abir+} |
| OPT | optative |

## Other

| ADV | adverb(ial) |
| AGT | agent suffix |
| ART | abbreviated *rentai* form / abbreviated adnominal form / *tanshuku-kei gokan* |
| BE | beautifying expression |
| CAUS | causative |
| CONC | concessive |
| COP | copula: '(A) is (B)' |
| DEV | deverbal |
| DIM | diminutive |
| DSD1 | desiderative marker (1st person to self: 'I want to ...') |
| DSD2/3 | desiderative marker (1st- to 2nd/3rd-person: 'I want you to ...; I want her/him/them to ...; would that you ...; would that (s)he/they ...') |
| EP.*y* | epenthetic *y* in vowel-verb forms |
| EX | exalting, including prefixes, auxiliaries, verbs, and nouns |
| EXCL | exclamation |

| | |
|---|---|
| GER | gerund suffix, with allomorphs -*tʰi*, -*di*, -*cʰyi*, and -*dzyi* (see -GER/PRFV) |
| GER/PRFV | gerund/perfective = {-tʰee} in OOk (see GER; also G/P) |
| HMS | His Majesty's Ship [running gloss for -*tʰumyi* or -*dumyi*, signifying a royal ship] |
| HUM | humilific/humble |
| IA | inferential auxiliary |
| INF | infinitive |
| INJ | interjection |
| INT | intensifier |
| ITER | iterative |
| KM | *kakari musubi*, a kind of focusing construction |
| LK | linker (*rentai-shi*, e.g. -*na*-, -*ra*(-)) |
| MV | middle voice |
| NEG | negative morph |
| NOM | nominalizer |
| P/P | see PROG/PRFV |
| PASS | passive form |
| pass | passive function |
| PL | plural marker |
| PLN | place name |
| PN | person's name = personal noun |
| POT | potential auxiliary |
| PRFT | perfect (-*ar*-, attached to gerund {+tʰe+}) -*t°-ar*- ~ -*cy°-ar*- ~ -*d-ar*- ~ -*dzy-ar*- |
| PRFV | perfective (-*c°i*, attached to RY) *ʔar-yi-c-°-ir-u* → *ʔac°iru* (fossilized form) |
| PROG/PRFV | progressive ('be DO-ing') or perfective ('have DOne') aspect, with -*ya(a)r*-, ultimately < *(-*i*ᵣᵧ)-*ar*ₛₜₐₜ-, or -*yu(u)r*-, ultimately < *(-*i*ᵣᵧ)-worₛₜₐₜ-; also written P/P |
| PST | past: OOk -*syi* |
| | past: OJ -*kî*, -*si*, etc. |
| QP | question particle |
| RH | *ra-hen* = *ra-gyō henkaku katsuyō* 'r-stem-irregular verb(s)' = verbs of existence |
| SE | stative extension (-*u(u)(r)*-; -*a(r)*-) |
| SFP | sentence-final particle |
| SKP | sentence-final *kakari* particle |
| SOFT | softener |
| STAT | stative |
| SPON | spontaneous passive function |
| T-form | GER/PRFV-derived forms |

# ABBREVIATIONS AND CONVENTIONS

| | |
|---|---|
| TMP/CND | temporal or conditional *-ba*—also written "T/C" or "if/when" |
| VB | verb |
| VBZ | verbalizer |
| VI | intransitiv{e verb/izing suffix} |
| VPFX | verbal prefix |
| VT | transitiv{e verb or suffix/izing suffix} |
| YNQ | yes/no-question marker |

## Textual Conventions

| | |
|---|---|
| ⟨x⟩ | (between angled brackets) "x" is a conventional romanization of a piece of non-Roman script, typically OOk, but also OJ, MJ, MK, or Chinese |
| ···*x, x*··· | linguistic ellipsis |
| .../... | textual ellipsis |
| {+X} | curly brackets signifying a morphophonemic-level form |
| {r/s} | curly brackets with forward slash signifying a choice between the first and second part |
| - | at the end of a line: a regular hyphen; at the beginning of a line: a morpheme boundary—the two types of hyphens do not overlap each other in distribution, so they may be used together in any text |
| " | prefixed to a linguistic or transcriptional consonant: "the following consonant is voiced": ⟨"t⟩ = ⟨d⟩, *"t = d, X-"-tY = XdY* (in rendaku compounding) |
| ⟨"⟩ | a hiragana ditto character in the original text, delineated by angled brackets |
| ⟨" "⟩ | a double-hiragana ditto character in the original text (the horizontal version of / \ ) |
| ₎X₍ | "X" has been added by editors in the process of creating a new text out of an older text, typically in a questionable manner |
| ⟦X⟧ | "X" may be deleted during the singing of a song or recitation of a poem in order to achieve metrical congruency between verses or lines |
| ⟪X⟫ | used for dictionary headwords X |
| A → B | generally: A changes to B, but not by regular historical sound change; (in derivation) A rewrites as B; (in grammar) A precedes B; A semantically extends to B; (elsewhere) "see" |
| A ← B | (in derivation) A is a rewrite from B |
| A ↔ B | A is not the same as B, A and B are emically different |
| A :: B | A corresponds to B |
| Arch | archaic |

XVIII                                    ABBREVIATIONS AND CONVENTIONS

| | |
|---|---|
| *chōfuku* | duplicate [omoro] |
| hn | headnote (to be found in Japanese-language text) |
| *lit.* | literally |
| Lit. | Literary (e.g. Literary Okinawan, Literary Japanese) |
| MO | "meaning obscure" = *mishōgo* |
| omoro | this word is treated like an assimilated loan, with no italics: ˣOmoro, ˣ*omoro*, ˣ*Omoro*; "this omoro", "omoro scholars", "the omoro language" |

## Phonological Conventions

| | |
|---|---|
| DIG | Destruction of Incommensurate Glides ($yw \to \emptyset$) |
| X* | small raised asterisk, used to show voicing inferred from texts other than KOS, a TOS text-editing convention; see "†" |
| X* | see *word* */ morph* / segment** |
| X† | identifies a voicing mark that relies on the most liberal interpretation of the textual material, used in TOS, e.g. ⟨tu "ti† fe⟩ or ⟨tu di† fe⟩ *c°idzyi* 'acme' |
| X° | graph is definitely voiceless, as shown in TOS; not an overt TOS convention |
| *N* | non-labial mora nasal |
| *M* | labial mora nasal |
| $\mu$ | Greek letter "mu", standing for "mora"; e.g. 8$\mu$: eight moras |
| *B* | labial voiced mora obstruent |
| *G* | voiced velar mora obstruent |
| *K, Q* | voiceless velar and glottal mora obstruents |
| ˌX, ˌX | mark placed before a Progressively Palatalizable segment that irregularly fails to be Progressively Palatalized: *myi-ˌkʰanasyi-ˌkʰi* 'beloved (fossilized RT)'; *syiˌna-yi/syiˌne-e* 'obeying willingly'; -ˌnu 'GEN/SUB'; all cases are to some degree lexically/morphophonemically determined |
| *X°* | indicates phonemically non-aspirated stop or affricate (also /X'/) = [–asp] |
| *X'* | indicates phonemically non-aspirated stop or affricate (also /X'/) = [–asp] (usually written *X°*) |
| [X'] | indicates phonetically non-aspirated stop or affricate |
| [X°] | indicates phonetically non-aspirated stop or affricate |
| *V', G'* | indicates hiatus between preceding phonemic vowel or glide and following phonemic vowel or glide |
| [V'], [G'] | indicates hiatus between preceding phonetic vowel or glide and following phonetic vowel or glide |

## ABBREVIATIONS AND CONVENTIONS                                    XIX

| | |
|---|---|
| $X^h$ | indicates phonemically aspirated stop or affricate (also /$X^h$/) = [+asp] |
| [$X^h$] | indicates phonetically aspirated stop or affricate |
| [CV] | (where "C" is a voiceless stop or affricate:) the aspiration marking is unknown, or else the authors have failed to write-in the aspiration information |
| PP | progressive palatalization |
| *word* ˌ | the word/morph is unaccented/atonic |
| *wórd* | the word/morph is accented/tonic |
| *wo'rd* | the word/morph has a secondary (falling) accent |
| [wʳoˀrd] | the word/morph has a rising/falling phonetic tone |
| *\*word* / *\*morph* / *\*segment* | unattested, but reconstructed |
| °*word* / °*morph* / °*segment* | in comparisons, right or correct form or reconstruction; see below |
| ˣ*word* | in comparisons, wrong or incorrect form or reconstruction; unattested; does not exist |
| *word*\* / *morph*\* / *segment*\* | expected or predicted form, not necessarily unattested; differs from *segment*\* = small raised asterisk (see above) |

CHAPTER 1

# Introduction

## 1    What Is the *Omoro Sōshi*?

The *Omoro Sōshi* (⟨o mo ro sa u si⟩『おもろさうし』; os) is a collection of mostly shamanic songs[1] sung at ceremonial events in the Shuri (首里) court of the Ryukyuan Kingdom as well as at sacred sites throughout the Ryukyus. There are 1554 songs, or 1249, not counting duplicates (*chōfuku* 重複 omoros; Ikemiya 2015: 76). The *Omoro Sōshi* was created during the period from 1531 (Book 1), then 1614 (Book 2), to, finally, 1623 (Books 3 through 22). The motives for creating this anthology are still not certain. Ikemiya (2015: 65) hypothesizes that the first volume was sent with Prince Nakijin to Nakijin Castle (*Nakijin-jō* 今帰仁城), in the northern part of Okinawa Island, to perform the same ceremonies as at the Shuri court. For the subsequent volumes, he conjectures that their generation stemmed from the threat that the original Ryukyuan religious system might disappear under the indirect but Neo-Confucianist rule of southern Kyushu's Satsuma Clan, a rule that began in 1609, five years before Book 2.

Omoros are songs sung with a designated tune name called *fushina* (節名). According to Nakahara (1957: 55), there are 120 tune names. Of these, two tune names, *Aoriyae-ga fushi*, lit. '[To the] tune of Aoriyae' (290 omoros) and *Uraosoi-no Oya-noro-ga fushi*, lit. '[To the] tune of The High Priestess of Urasoe' (130 omoros) account for one third of all omoros with listed tune names (1957: 57).

Although it was compiled by Shuri courtiers between 1531 and 1623, some songs had already been in existence much prior to that. According to Nakahara (1957: 13–25), the *Omoro Sōshi* encompasses the following three time periods:

---

1    We call these "omoros" (with an English plural) throughout, always without italics, treating the word as a fully assimilated loan. About the NOk term, OGJ says: "*ʔumuru*₁ (N) [LitOk] ⟨o mo ro⟩. Poetry handed down in Okinawa from olden times. They are songs approximately equivalent to the *norito* of Japan, and almost all of them are[, typologically,] epic poetry. What is meant by *ʔumuru* is the omoros that were collected by the Shuri Royal Government and assembled in the *ʔumuru ʔusoosyi* ⟨o mo ro o sa u si⟩; omoros handed down by *nuuru* ('noro; shamanesses') in the countryside are called *ʔumuyi*. [Further,] *ʔomoro* is a Japanese-style pronunciation" (OGJ 555b).

© KONINKLIJKE BRILL NV, LEIDEN, 2021 | DOI:10.1163/9789004414686_002

Buraku jidai (部落時代 hamlet period):     3rd/4th–12th century[2]
Aji jidai (按司時代 Lords' period):          12th–15th centuries
Ōkoku jidai (王国時代 Kingdom period):     15th–17th centuries

Hokama (1985: 14) sees the theme of the earlier omoros to be the deities, followed by the themes of building castles, of ships, of admiration of regional lords, and finally to topics such as encomiums of the king, of his territorial expansion, trade, and his temples, or of his beautification of Shuri. Hokama sees a transition from epic to lyric poetry (*joji-shi* 叙事詩 and *jojō-shi* 抒情詩, respectively). Ifa (1975a [1924]: 27) states that the *Omoro Sōshi* in content is comparable to the Japanese *Kojiki* and *Norito* (closer to epic), and *Man'yōshū* (closer to lyric).

Shamanic songs consist of divine messages (so to speak) to people, and prayers from the people to the deities. Hokama (1985: 27; TOS 23–25) says that the former are equivalent to Miyako/Yaeyama *kanfutsï* 神口 (J *shintaku* 神託) and the latter, Miyako/Yaeyama *nigaifutsï* 願い口 (J *norito* 祝詞). He also claims that these two types of omoro have their parallels in regional shamanic songs, too: the former to *ʔumuyi* (OGJ 554b)[3] or *ʔumuri*, and the latter to *mi-seseru* [misiziʳɾi] 'exalted saying' or *o-takabe* [ʔutɑkɑbi] 'exalted praying' (Hokama 1985: 27). From the Western pragmatic point of view, it is interesting to see that the former aligns with *thinking* (or mental) verbs, while the latter, with *saying* (speech-act) verbs. Hokama asserts that between *kanfutsï* and *nigaifutsï*, the former is older and original functionally and historically. Furthermore, we might add that performing *kanfutsï*, shamans carry out dual roles: For a shaman as a deity, *kanfutsï* represents what she *thinks*, while for a shaman as a messenger, *kanfutsï* is what she *says* (Shinzato 2004).

The semantic affinity of *think* and *say* verbs is seen in the fact that the two deverbal nouns *ʔumuru* 'omoro' *lit.* '[what one] think[s]' and *sirumu* 'serumu' *lit.* 'what [one] say[s]' appear as parallel words in the OS (cf. Ikemiya 2015: 103), rephrasing each other as below:

---

2   One dominant strand of current research, however, would do away with this first period entirely, essentially beginning with the period of castle-building that has traditionally been seen as the second period. The people who were to become the Ryukyuans, in this view, would have settled the Ryukyus after an earlier people or peoples, at the beginning of the Lords' period. See Smits (2019).

3   "*ʔumu-yi*₁ 1 'thought, opinion, desire'; 2 'longing, deep attachment, love'; 3 'omoro'" (OGJ 554b). See also the discussion of *ʔumuru*₁ in the first footnote.

# INTRODUCTION

おもろ、　　　ねやが゛りや、　/ せるむ、　　　ねやが゛りや、　/
o mo ro ,　　　ne ya ga* ri ya , / se ru mu ,　　　ne ya ga* ri ya , /
ʔumu·r-u　　ni.y.agar-yi-ya　　sir-u-mu　　ni.y.agar-yi-ya
think·4GE-RT　s.r⁴-RY_NOM-TOP　say-RT-NOM　s.r-RY_NOM-TOP
とひや、⁵くさす、ˌ　　ちよわれ　/
⟨to pi ya , ku sa su , ˌ ti yo wa re　/
tʰu-pʰyak°u⁶-se-si　　c°yuwar-i⁷
10–100-years-KP　　liveₑₓ-IZ

'[I], the singer of Omoro, of Serumu, [pray for the sake of the King]. 1000 years old may [you] live [to be]!' (OS 8.#418)

The semantic affinity of *omoro* and *serumu* and the directionality of development Hokama posits from *kanfutsï* to *nigaifutsï* are also consistent with the well-known unidirectional development from mental to speech act verbs (Traugott and Dasher 1987, Shinzato 2004). As in the above song, when the two phrases *ʔumuru niiyagaryi* and *sirumu niiyagaryi* are concatenated, the sequence is always as given above, coinciding with the unidirectional development discussed here. (Length is truncated to fit into an eight-mora pattern.)

In this context, two things are of interest from the Japanese perspective. In the *Senmyō* (宣命 Imperial Edicts), the expression, *kamu-nagara* 'as (being) a deity', according to Wada (2007: 115), is to be analyzed as "a rhetorical device meaning that [the] Emperor is a Very God," corroborated by JDB (223bc ⟨ka mu na ga ra⟩). Of the 19 instances of *kamu-nagara* (out of a total of 62 edicts), 18 are connected to *think* verbs, graphically written ⟨思⟩ 'think', and ⟨念⟩ 'consider, declare', and are given the *kun* (i.e. the Japanese-language reading) of *ömöpu* 'think' as below:

天　　　下乃　公民乎　　　　恵賜比　　　　　撫賜牟　　　　正
amë-nö sita-*nö* öpo-mî-takara-*wo* utuku·si-bï-tama*p-î* nade-tamap-a*m-u tö*

---

4　s.r – sound.rise.

5　Perhaps the oddly positioned comma signals (at least the awareness of) a lengthening of the vowel of *pʰya(a)*, as in NOk *hya(a)ku,* '100' (OGJ 211b), though we see it as shortened here, along with *tʰu(u)* '10' and *se(e)* 'years', for metrical reasons (8-8-8).

6　For the aspiration we are forced to rely on the initial aspiration in the related morph [pʰyak°u] in Nakijin dialect (ROD) of present-day northern Okinawa island, which still retains an aspirated–non-aspirated distinction.

7　See discussion of *c°yuwa·r/s-* in Ch. 6 §14.3. KP ... IZ exemplifies *kakari musubi*: cf. this chapter, §5.2.1.2.

4  CHAPTER 1

奈母　随神所　　思行佐久

*namo* kamu-nagara ömöp-os-i-mês-*aku*

'As a deity, it is my intention to love and nurture my subjects' (Senmyō 1, 697 CE)

In this formulaic expression of *kamu-nagara ... ömöp-*, the word *ömöp-* embraces both 'think' and 'say' meanings, and naturally what the (ostensible) deity thought precedes what the emperor delivered verbally, thus exhibiting directionality, as 'think' → 'say'. It is no accident that the Chinese character-lexeme ⟨念⟩ *niàn* also embodied 'think' in Old Chinese, but in Modern Chinese (= NC), it means 'say' more often than it means 'think' in the sense that NC meanings of *reading out loud* or *chanting* refer to vocalizing (i.e. *saying*) the thought. Thus, the Chinese character associated with the lexeme *niàn* also shows the semantic shift from 'think' to 'say'. The Old Japanese word *kakë-m-aku*, which forms an introductory phrase for *kamï* 'god', as in *kakëmaku mo kasikôkî kamï* 'a deity too awe-inspiring for me to even dare think/state its name', also embodies both 'think'ing and 'say'ing elements (JDB 179d–180a, senses 3 and 4). These observations support Orikuchi Shinobu's claim, quoted in Hokama (1985: 19–20), that OJ *ömöpu* 'think' represented not only the meaning 'think', but also 'say'.[8]

Given the above, we concur with Hokama, that the very original meaning of *ʔumuru* < *\*omo·r-o* was 'think', representing the deity's thoughts, delivered through the mouth of the shaman—and that thereby thinking and saying were connected in the omoro text and in regional shamanic songs.

## 2　Types of Omoro

There are 22 books in the OS. Nakahara (1957: 39–50) divides them into eight groups, as below. The explanation for each omoro group below we owe to Ikemiya's (2015: 76–85) more explicit and clear expositions.

- ***Chihō omoro*** (地方おもろ) 'region-based omoros': OS 2, 5, 7, 11, 15–21.
  Of the entire OS, 725 omoro, or 46%, belong to this group. Each region reflects a historical, cultural, or political area (e.g. *Hokuzan* (北山) 'Hokuzan, Sanhoku' *lit.* 'Northern Kingdom').

---

8　Unfortunately, neither Orikuchi nor Hokama gives concrete examples. JDB, *the* OJ dictionary, does not discuss this point. It would in any case have had to be supported by the missing concrete examples in order to be so discussed. While Orikuchi and Hokama are respected throughout Japan, Ryukyuan-studies scholars probably rank among the most steeped in Orikuchian thought.

INTRODUCTION

– **Eisā omoro** (⟨ゑさ⟩ [⟨we sa⟩] おもろ) '*eisā* omoros': OS 14.
The topics in this volume are heroes or popular events. The majority of its 70 songs have no *fushina*, or tune name, which Ikemiya finds enigmatic.

Further, Ikemiya (2015: 80) disputes the conventional wisdom of connecting ⟨we sa⟩ to *eisā*, performing arts including group dances during the *o-bon* season, rituals to receive, entertain, and send away the passed-away ancestral spirits, since he thinks connecting ⟨we sa⟩ to *yeisaa‚* (OGJ 185b) is phonetically highly implausible. Rather, he expects that ⟨we⟩ should become later ⟨i⟩, i.e. (ʔ)*yi*, and, though he does not mention it, the following type, ⟨we to⟩ (OS 10, 13), has the pronunciation *ʔyii‚tu‚* in NOk, seeming to corroborate his view. However, we have seen that long mid vowels tend to stay mid rather than raise (cf. e.g. Ch. 2 § 4.5), and therefore we continue to support the original ⟨we sa⟩ = *yeisaa* hypothesis.

– **Eto omoro** (⟨ゑと⟩ [⟨we to⟩] おもろ) '(communal) labor omoros': OS 10, 13.
⟨we to⟩ (NOk *ʔyii‚tu‚* 'a shout during physical labor; a work song' [OGJ 185b]) is an interjection uttered at the time of physical labor. Both volumes are about sea travels, the difference being that volume 10 is about coastal sea travel, while volume 13 is about longer, open-ocean voyages to foreign countries. Volume 13 includes omoros about sea journeys, ships, and celestial bodies, the latter since stars guide navigators.

The question remains, however, of why *ʔyeeto* (if such it was) did raise. About the only assumption that occurs to us is that the original form was *ʔyeto*, which raised to *ʔyitʰu*, and which *then* lengthened to NOk *ʔyii‚tu‚*, with the lengthening beginning at any time that speakers saw fit to do so, since it was an onomatopoetic word. That time was anytime after the raising from short mid to short high took place.

– **Koneri omoro** (こねりおもろ) 'dance omoros': OS 9.
The omoros here relate to priestesses and their ceremonial events. This volume includes notes on *koneri*, hand movements in dance.

– **Asubi omoro** (遊びおもろ) 'ceremonial omoros': OS 12.
There are twelve omoros in the entire *Omoro Sōshi* that start off with contextualizing information (*kotobagaki* 詞書) such as time and occasion of the ceremony. Of those twelve, nine appear in this volume.

– **Meijin omoro** (名人おもろ) 'renowned singers' omoros': OS 8.
Of its 83 omoros, the first 43 belong to the singer *Omoro Neagari*, while the second 40 are part of *Akainko omoro*.[9] Neagari and Akainko are the names

---

9  ねやがり                          あかいんこ
   *ni(i)#y-aga·r-yi*                *ʔakʰa-ʔiɴ#kʰu(u)*
   [sound-**EP.y**-rise-**4GE-RY**]<sub>NOM</sub>   **PLN**-dog.sign-personage
   'Neagari'                        'Akainko'

6                                                                      CHAPTER 1

of the two famed singers, *lit.*, 'The One of the Sounds Rising' and 'The Dog-Sign Personage from Aka', or 'The Personage from Aka of the Eleventh Horary Sign (i.e. Sign of the Dog)'.

- **Shinjo omoro** (神女おもろ) 'priestesses' omoros': OS 1, 3, 4, 6.
  These omoros are paeans and benedictions directed to kings and priestesses. They signal belief in the power of words to materialize the states sung (into being, in effect) in omoros.

- **Kuji omoro** (公事おもろ) 'Shuri-court ceremonial omoros': OS 22.
  The omoros here were used for the Harvest Festival (*inaho-sai* 稲穂祭), the King's Procession to Chinen and Kudaka (*Chinen Kudaka Gyōkō* 知念久高行幸), prayers for rain (*ama-goi* 雨乞い), [congratulations on] the completion of the building of Shuri Castle (*Shuri-jō rakusei* 首里城落成), ship-launching ceremonies (*shinsuishiki* 進水式), farewells (*senbetsu* 餞別), congratulations (*shukuga* 祝賀), and coronation-ship arrivals (*kansen torai* 冠船渡来). This volume was kept under the care of the Aniya family, who were the official Omoro Conservator Family (*Omoro-Nushidori*[10] *Ke*), and, save for just one song that appears nowhere else, is a compilation of omoros from other volumes of the OS.

## 3      Versions

The Urtext of the OS was lost at the time of a fire in Shuri Palace in 1709, but the following year of 1710, it was recompiled, at which time two copies (*-bon* 本) were made, one to be kept by the Shō family (Shō-ke 尚家 in the chart below), the other by the Aniya family (Aniya-ke 安仁屋家), the officially appointed family of omoro singers. The basic difference between these two copies is that the *Aniya-bon* has so-called *kotoba kiki-gaki*, (言葉聞書) *lit.* '[things] written down heard [from] words'[11]—annotations to words—as well as commas

---

10   The J word *nushidori* is from NOk *nusyiduyi*, 'official [in the Royal Government]'. While treated offhand as Japanese, it is found in no Japanese dictionary.

11   There are several variations on this term: *kutuba ʔyeezya-gacyi* (言葉間書), *lit.* 'in-between writings [of] words', i.e. 'interlineations' (Ifa [1975a [1924]: 233]) and *kutuba mamagaki* (言葉間々書) *lit.* 'between-between writings of words' (Hokama [TOS 40–41]). According to Shimamura (2010: 525–526), researchers have been continuously using the term *kutuba ʔyeezya-gacyi* or, Japanized, *kotoba (no) aida-gaki* (言葉間書), as was originally used by Ifa, but the correct word as it appears in the Aniya-bon is *kutuba cyicyi-gacyi* or, Japanized, *kotoba (no) kiki-gaki* 'words **heard** and written' (言葉聞書), with a very similar character. Further, he believes that another reason that 聞書 is more accurate is because it aligns with KKKS' depiction of the OS as a collection of religious songs the compilers acquired aurally from *korō* 'village elders' (古老).

# INTRODUCTION

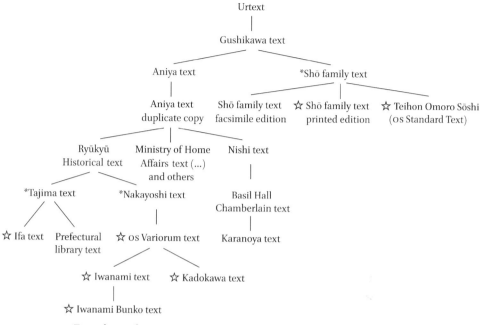

FIGURE 1.1  Textual tree of OS copies
SOURCE: BASED ON TOS P. 37

(*kugiri-ten*) and voicing-marks (*dakuten*). A year later in 1711, *kotoba kiki-gaki* were recompiled as *Konkō Kenshū* (『混効験集』, henceforth KKKS), a dictionary for reading the OS (TOS 40b). In addition, the *Shōke-bon* came to lack Books 2, 5, 15, and 19, which were later compensated for by inserting copies from the *Aniya-bon*. The *Shōke-bon* still exists, but the *Aniya-bon* does not. However, because of the completeness of the extant volumes, and because of its linguistic markings, copies generated from the *Aniya-bon*, such as the *Tajima-bon* (田島本) and the *Nakayoshi-bon* (仲吉本) have come to be used widely among Omoro researchers. The texts marked with * in Figure 1.1 are in existence today and those with ☆ are in print.

In this book, we use TOS as our base text, since it uses the Shō Family text (the closest existing text to the Urtext) as its basis, and since it points out differences between the Shō Family text and other versions (specifically those stemming from the Ryukyu Historical text), as well as variations among them in marking voicing, in graphs, and also possible copyists' errors.

8  CHAPTER 1

## 4  Song Structure

Below is an example of an omoro song (os 1.#1). For each original line, the *kana* line is given, as shown in the TOS text, followed by a line transliterating the original into our standardized romanization, followed by our reconstructed phonological representation for that line, followed by a line of short lexical and grammatical glosses.[12] Next is a more or less ordinary-English translation of the line. Thus a seven-verse omoro such as this, along with its tune information at the beginning, takes up 40 lines, followed by any flowing English version, if necessary.

OS 1.#1[13]

あおりやへが<sup>\*14</sup> ⌃<sup>15</sup>　ふし
a o ri ya pe ga<sup>\*</sup> ⌃　　pu si
*Ɂooyee-ga*　　　　*pᵒusyi*
PN-GEN　　　　　tune
[Performed to] the tune of Aoriyae

(I)　一　きこゑ　　　大ぎ<sup>\*</sup> みぎや、　　/
　　ITI ki ko we　　OPO gi<sup>\*</sup> mi gi ya ,　/
　　*kᵒyi̦ kᵒuyi*[16] *ɁuQpᵒu-gyimyi-gya*
　　famed　　　great-priestess-SUB
　　The Renowned High Priestess

---

12　The full-length grammatical glosses are available in the Abbreviations and Conventions.

13　Omoros are cited as "os [Book number].#[Omoro number in sequence from the first omoro in Book 1 right through to the last omoro in Book 22 (*tōshi-bangō*)]".

14　Appended raised small asterisks (<sup>\*</sup>) and daggers (†) in *kana*(-*kanji*) text and in our romanization of same originate in identical asterisks and daggers placed after voicing marks deployed in TOS on *kana* in the Shō-Family—and possibly other texts as well, where there are no voicing marks. In point of fact, the Shō Family text has no voicing marks at all, so for all practical purposes the TOS marks indicate emendations to the voicing marks in the KOS, the variorum edition used previous to TOS as the authority on textual questions. KOS ⟨ka⟩, TOS ⟨ka⟩, ⟨ga<sup>\*</sup>⟩, or ⟨ga†⟩.

15　The mark ⟨⌃⟩ indicates a space (more-or-less) in the original text.

16　The two parallel words *kᵒyi̦ kᵒuyi* (I) *lit.* 'heard [far and wide]' and *tʰuyumu* (II) 'resonate [far and wide]' form an interesting semantic pair in that the former takes the audience perspective (e.g. SOMEONE hears something), while the latter presents the perspective of the source (e.g. SOMETHING makes sounds).

INTRODUCTION

a. おれて、¹⁷ ∧　あすび、よわれば*　　　　/
  o re te , ∧　a su bi , yo wa re ba*　　　/
  ʔuri-tˤi　　　ʔasib-y-uwar-i-ba
  descend-GER perform-RY-EX-IZ-TMP/CND
  will descend, and when she performs [the trance dance];

b. てにが*、∧　した、　　/
  te ni ga* , ∧　si ta ,　　/
  tʰinyi-₍ᵢ₎ga ∧　syi₍ᵢ₎tˤa-Ø¹⁸
  Heaven-GEN below-DO
  [all] under heaven!

c. たいらげ*て、∧ ちよわれ　/
  ta i ra ge* te , ∧ ti yo wa re /
  tʰeera·gi-tˤi　　cˤyuwar-i
  pac·ify-GER　　beₑₓ-MR
  [o! King!,] pacify and rule over [it]!

(II)　又　　とよむ ∧　　せだ*かこが*　　　　　/ (a,b,c)
  MATA to yo mu ∧　se da* ka ko ga*　　　/
  　　　tʰuyum-u　　si-dakʰa-kʰu-ga
  　　　resonate-RT spiritual.power-high-one-SUB
  The Resounding One of High Spiritual Power

(III)　又　　しより　もり　ぐ*すく　　　/ (a,b,c)
  MATA si yo ri　mo ri　gu* su ku　　/
  　　　syiyuryi muryi gusikˤu-Ø
  　　　Shuri　　Grove　Enclosure-upon
  [Upon] the Shuri Grove Enclosure

---

17　Under the influence of Ifa's (1975a [1924]: 24) view, commas have been believed to func-
　　tion as breath markers. However, several scholars including Hokama (2012: 40–41) in TOS,
　　Shimamura (2010: 262), as well as Ikemiya (2015: 89) cast doubt on Ifa's view. Hokama
　　compared the commas with Yamanouchi Seihin's singing of omoros, and clearly they did
　　not always correspond to breath groups. Shimamura and Ikemiya both note two distinct
　　comma markings for the same song in duplicate omoros, thus casting at least some doubt
　　on the breath-group theory. Furthermore, in order for this verse to have eight moras, ʔuri-
　　tˤi ʔasib-y-uwa·r-i-ba requires shortening to ʔuri-tˤ°-asib-y-uwa·r-i-ba, thereby negating the
　　breath-group hypothesis if an attempt were made to follow it.
18　It is unknown whether the overt marking of PP was eschewed simply because it was mor-
　　phophonemically automatic—and therefore superfluous (and thus actually pronounced

10                                                                CHAPTER 1

(IV)  又    まだ゚ま   もり  ぐ゚すく              # (a,b,c)
MATA  ma da゚ ma  mo ri  gu゚ su ku          #
      *ma-dama   muryi gusik゚u-∅*
      True-Jewel  Grove  Enclosure-upon
[Upon] the True-Jewel Grove Enclosure

'I, the Renowned High Priestess, the Resounding One of High Spiritual
Power, will descend to the Shuri Grove Enclosure, to the True-Jewel Grove
Enclosure, and when I [the Sun Deity] descend and I [= Kikoe Ōgimi] do
my sacred dance, o King!, [I will grant you the power to] pacify and rule
the Kingdom!' (OS 1.#1)

As Hokama (2000a: 14b) explains, this is an "omoro of a national observance,
in which Kikoe Ōgimi, who has turned into the Sun Deity, grants to the King
the spiritual power to pacify-and-rule [*osameru*] the realm." (Taiyō-jin ni nari-
kawatta Kikoe Ōgimi ga, kokuō ni kuni o osameru reiryoku o sazukeru kokka-
teki girei no omoro.) (→ OS 3.#119)

Omoros start off with a tune name, and in this case it is ⟨a o ri ya pe ga pu
si⟩, or *ʔooree-ga fusyi*.[19] Figure 1.2 represents our structural analysis of this song.
Omoro songs consist of two main parts, which we refer to as *Body* and *Refrain*.
In this song, we have noted them by horizontal bars on top and bottom. The
body is divided into two parallel poetic couplets (*tsuiku-bu*, 対句部). In Figure 1.2, these couplets extend from the top bar vertically as I and II, connected
as "Priestess" in a darker shade of gray, and similarly, III and IV in a lighter
shade, and characterized as "Location". The terms "Priestess" and "Location" are
one-word descriptions of what these verses are about. More concretely, the first
couplet describes the deity's descending and the high priestess performing ceremonial dances. Following this, the second couplet brings in the location where
the king with the endowed spiritual power rules and pacifies the kingdom. Couplets (I, II) and (III, IV) are paraphrases of each other.

Small letters *a*, *b*, and *c* represent one free-verse refrain (*hanpuku-bu* 反復
部), and their vertical lines come together at the bottom as *Refrain* vis-à-vis

---

*as if* written *tʰinyi-gya syic゚ya* = [tʰɲigʸɑ ʃitʃ゚ɑ])—or because PP was actually actively suppressed, perhaps as a consciously archaic pronunciation practice.

19    This pronunciation is Middle Okinawan (MOk [ca. 18th and 19th centuries]), on the
      assumption that the tune name was applied at the time of the recompilation in the early
      18th century. Had it been Old Okinawan pronunciation, it would have been *ʔawuryayi*-
      *ga p゚usyi* (with an exception to Progressive Palatalization [PP] (","; cf. Ch. 2 § 5.1) marked
      before -*ga*, due to membership of *ʔawuryayi* in the lower bigrade verb class (cf. Ch. 6

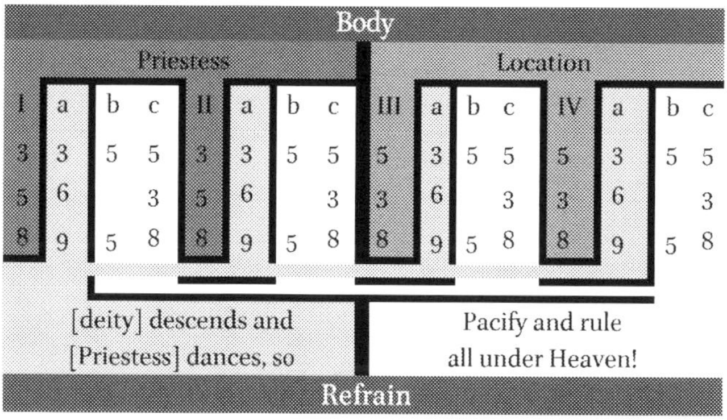

INTRODUCTION

FIGURE 1.2   Song structure, OS 1.#1

*Body* at the top. The refrain is a technique repeatedly used both in OS and in many other types of poetic literature in the Ryukyus. In this song, the refrain is semantically divided into two: the part *a*: the [deity] descends and [Priestess] dances, and the parts *b* and *c*, which can be summarized as 'pacify and rule all under heaven!'

In the text, each couplet, marked by 一 ⟨ITI⟩ (*ʔyicˤyi* 'one') or 又 ⟨MATA⟩ (*matʰa* 'again'), displays high parallelism between its lines and, typically, the same number of moras, or beats. Thus, *kˤyikˤuyi ʔupʰu-gyimyi-gya* is synonymous with *tʰuyum-u si-dakʰa-kʰu-ga*. The same applies to the other couplet, III–IV. The synonymy of the couplets serves as an important tool for decoding unfamiliar words. According to Ikemiya (2015: 130), the couplets are epic (*joji-teki* 叙事的), and consist of 8 moras. In Figure 1.2, numbers 3, 5, 8 refer to the subtotal of moras in *kˤyikˤuyi* (3 moras), *ʔupʰu-gyimyi-gya* (5) and their total (8). The refrain, on the other hand, is not necessarily made to conform to any specific metrical structure. Thus, in this song, it varies from 9, to 5, to 8. Ikemiya characterizes the refrain as lyrical (*lit.* "lyricism-like" *jojō-teki* 叙情的). It is thought to have been repeated as chant after the sung lines marked with "one" or "again" as noted above (Hokama and Saigō 1972: 611). According to Tamaki (1987: 281), only 15 songs out of 1554 in the entire *Omoro Sōshi* lack "again". Hateruma (2007a: 30–31) notes that, in what he sees as epic poetry, parallel couplets were used to advance the story line, with the omoro probably

---

§1.2.4), which almost never causes PP). (PP, briefly, usually occurs when *\*yi* is the only/final vowel in the preceding syllable; *\*yi* palatalizes, and in certain cases affricates, the initial consonant of the syllable that immediately follows it: *\*... yi-ga > ... yi-gya*.) Also note that the form predicted for MOk from that of OOk is *ˣʔooyee* rather than the widely used pronunciation *ʔooree*.

sung by a single lead singer, and the refrain chanted in a chorus by a group of singers for the purpose of building energy and power.[20]

According to Hokama and Saigō (1972: 583), Shimabukuro Zenpatsu, a musicologist, suggested (1932)[21] that the above *omoro* was recited/sung as

(I)   -(a)-(b)-(c)-   (III)
(II)   -(a)-(b)-(c)-   (IV).

Since the first half,

(I)   -(a)-(b)-(c)-   (III),

and the second half,

(II)   -(a)-(b)-(c)-   (IV),

do indeed make the biggest 'couplets' or parallels, semantically, his analysis is feasible. On the other hand, most omoro scholars (e.g. TOS [26–27], Kadekaru [2003: 162]) analyze faithfully to the couplet order, (I), (II), (III), and (IV) and regard the refrain as appearing after each couplet pair. Here, we follow the latter approach:

(I)   -(a)-(b)-(c)
(II)   -(a)-(b)-(c)

---

20  While this may be true in a great many cases, it can readily be seen that in many others the entire predicate is chanted in the refrain, in which case it is the refrain that carries the brunt of advancing the purpose or story line of the omoro. Perhaps a reformulation of Hateruma's statement is in order: The parallel couplets tell the theme and through their repetition help to build a trance-like state, while the refrains put a close to the expectation raised by the couplets, and themselves, in their own constant repetition, also help to build that desired trance-like state. While, in terms of the text that we see, the refrains may easily be omitted after their first writing—just as in the writing of Western hymn and song lyrics—the second member of the couplet cannot typically be omitted, because, while it may constitute a semantic repetition (since it is typically parallel to the first member), it is not a syllable-for-syllable repetition, and therefore needs to be written out. This would seem to be the simplest explanation for the relation between what is written and what is actually performed, and a neat encapsulation of the nature of the two types of repetition in the OS.

21  Their citation in full is: Shimabukuro Zenpatsu 島袋全発. 1932. "*Omoro Sōshi* no yomi-kata: Tendoku-hō no kenkyū" [『おもろさうし』の読み方――展読法の研究; How to read the *Omoro Sōshi*: A study of the expanded-reading technique]. In: *Okinawa Kyōiku* [「沖縄教育」; Okinawa education] (number or pages unknown).

INTRODUCTION 13

(III) -(a)-(b)-(c)
(IV) -(a)-(b)-(c),

as shown in Figure 1.2.

## 4.1 Song Structure Typology

With focus on the inclusion of the refrain after the second stanza (i.e. after the first *mata* mark) on, Tamaki (1976), quoted in TOS (28–29) divides omoros into the following three types (as above, roman numerals refer to couplets, and letters to refrains):
- *kanzen kisai* (complete delineation of refrains)
  I, a, b, c, d,
  II, a, b, c, d,
- *bubun kisai* (partial delineation of refrains)
  I, a, b,
  II, a,
- *shōryaku kisai* (total elimination of repeated refrains)
  The complete elimination of refrains becomes apparent if the song below is a duplicate omoro, say, of *bubun kisai* above.
  I, a, b,
  II,

Depending upon how the couplets appear in omoro songs, Ikemiya (2015: 129–140) observes that the majority of omoros belong to one of the two types below. Examples of A and B types are OS 1.#1 and OS 8.#418 introduced above. For the first example, the couplets are $k^{\circ}yik^{\circ}uyi$ $?up^hu\text{-}gyimyi\text{-}gya$ and $t^huyum\text{-}u$ $si\text{-}dak^ha\text{-}k^hu\text{-}ga$, appearing in Stanza 1 and Stanza 2 respectively. For the second example, the couplet $?umuru$ $niyagaryi\text{-}ya$—$sirumu$ $niyagaryi\text{-}ya$ emerges in Stanza 1.

A.  Couplets appear in two separate stanzas as (I, II) (III, IV) (V, VI)
    Stanza 1  I, a, b, c, d, e
    Stanza 2  II
    Stanza 3  III
    Stanza 4  IV
    Stanza 5  V
    Stanza 6  VI
B.  Couplets appear in one stanza (i.e. I, II in Stanza 1)
    Stanza 1  I, II, a, b
    Stanza 2  III, IV
    Stanza 3  V, VI

Ikemiya states that type A is the majority, accounting for 85% of all omoros, followed by 200 omoros of type B.

## 5 Overview of the Omoro Language

### 5.1 *Structure*

Like Japanese and Modern Okinawan, the Omoro language is essentially a verb-final language with a basic word order of SOV (Subject Object Verb). As one would expect, case marking is done with enclitic postpositions rather than prepositions. It is also an agglutinating language with auxiliaries optionally suffixed to the verb, and further extended with optional sentence-final particles (SFP).

Schematically, a default sentence structure is represented as follows:

A TOP (= topic) phrase may precede or replace the subject or direct object phrase. It actually has two major functions: (1) to delineate the thematic topic in a topic/comment construction; and (2) to delineate a choice among options, a contrastive topic. The topic particle functions similarly to Japanese in having these two functions.

A predicate consists of a verb, adjective, or copula plus optional auxiliaries, of which there may be only one, or which, when concatenated, appear in a set sequence. It should be noted, however, that the corpus of predicates is so limited in a poetic text such as this one that a full accounting of the concatenation possibilities is simply out of reach. A predicate is optionally followed by one or two sentence-final particles.

$$S_{ubject}(\text{-SUB}_{pcle}) \quad O_{bject}(\text{-DO}_{pcle}) \quad [ \quad V/ADJ/COP \quad (AUX) \quad ]_{predicate} \quad (SFP)$$

It is very common for subject and/or object marking to be omitted, frequently thus enhancing the metric regularity of the song.[22] In this manuscript, we attempted to provide the functions by affixing an overline or an empty set, a zero, to stand in for the missing particle function. This allows an overt glossing of the missing marker. Needless to say, decoding such cases may not be that straightforward but, rather, controversial in some cases. In those cases, we exercised our judgement, but made note of different interpretations by other omoro scholars.

---

22 In NOk, subjects are normally overtly marked, while direct objects and even some indirect-object-like noun phrases are not marked. In Miyako speech varieties, on the other hand, direct objects, too, are marked.

INTRODUCTION                                                                    15

5.2    *Parts of Speech*

In this monograph, we have covered the phonology in its entirety, but for the grammar, we have purposely omitted chapters for conjunctions, adverbs, and particles. As for conjunctions, they are actually difficult to isolate and therefore simply not a matter worthy of discussion; thus they are not endowed with a chapter. According to Takahashi (1991a: 18–19), the only non-controversial conjunction is ⟨ma ta⟩ (*matʰa* 'again') (see §4 above), which he attributes to omoros' poetic, non-prose, nature. In fact, almost invariably, ⟨ma ta⟩ is just part of the written apparatus for delineating the structure of any omoro, and is not really a part of the omoro itself. Likewise, there is no specific adverb chapter due to the small size of the particular lexicon, and they are treated like other lexical items individually within examples (e.g. *danyi* 'truly', *ginyi* 'really' in (OS 11.#576) in Ch. 4 §4.3).

Particles, on the other hand, are high-token-frequency items despite their relative paucity, and are an unarguably important component of grammar. But instead of allocating a chapter for the particles in a manner similar to adjectives, verbs, auxiliaries, etc., we opted for dealing with particles as they are introduced in the songs.[23] Therefore it made more sense to analyze and introduce particles in concrete song contexts. In order to compensate for this rather unconventional approach, we have provided a detailed particle index so that readers can go to specific particles of their interest to see them in context and read their description.

Of the six traditional classes of particles, this monograph includes in the index the three particle classes: **case** (格助詞 *kaku joshi*), **focus** (係助詞 *kakari joshi*), and **sentence-final particles** (終助詞 *shū joshi*). The two other particle classes, **adverbial** (副助詞 *fuku joshi*), e.g. allative -*gya*(*a*)*mi* 'as far as' and **interjectional** (間投助詞 *kantō joshi*), e.g. *ya*(*a*), are under **case** (格助詞 *kaku joshi*), and **sentence/clause-final** particles (終助詞 *shū joshi*), respectively. There is no **Conjunctive-particle** headword in the index because of inclusion of heterogeneous classes in the traditional framework (cf. Vovin [2009a: 1156]): (a) a particle (e.g. -*ba* to form [realis and irrealis] conditionals); (b) a gerund auxiliary (which may function as gerund or perfective in OOk); and (c) grammaticalized nouns (e.g. *munu* 'thing', *kʰutʼu* 'thing', either to function as a **causal** or a **concessive conjunction**). These three types of conjunctive particles are treated at a lexical level with appropriate glosses. In addition, a detailed analysis of the gerund is provided in Ch. 6 §4.

---

23    For example ⟨pa⟩ may indicate the topic marker *wa*, or direct object marker -*Qpʼa*.

16               CHAPTER 1

### 5.2.1     Case-Marking Particles

| | | |
|---|---|---|
| *-ga/-gya* | SUB | subject |
| | GEN | genitive |
| | PRP | purposive, 'in order to' |
| *-gya(a)mi* | TRM | terminative |
| *-kʰara* | ABL | from |
| *-nu/ˣ-nyu* | SUB | subject |
| | GEN | genitive |
| | DO | direct object |
| *-nyi* | LOC | locative |
| | IO | indirect object |
| | APP | applicative (= ditransitive / double-object) |
| | ADV | 'at' (time), 'by' (passive agent) |
| *-(nyi)kʰac°yi* | IO | indirect object |
| *-ǫp°a* | DO | direct object |
| *-tʰu* | COM | comitative: 'with', 'and' |
| *-di-t°i* | QT | quotative particle |
| *-yu* | DO | direct object |
| | APP | applicative (= ditransitive/double-object) |
| *-yuryi* | ABL | 'from' |

### 5.2.2     Focus Particles

| | | |
|---|---|---|
| *-du/-dzyu/-ru* | KP | *kakari particle* (cognate of OJ *-sö/-zö*) |
| *-doo* | SKP | sentence-final *kakari particle* |
| *-ga/-gya* | KP | *kakari particle* (cognate of OJ *ka*) |
| | SKP | sentence-final *kakari particle* |
| *-si/-syu* | KP | *kakari particle* (cognate of OJ *koso*) |
| | SKP | sentence-final *kakari particle* |
| *-wa/-ya* | TOP | topic |
| *-yi* | SKP | *kakari particle* (cognate of OJ *ya*) |

The *kakari* particles (KP) form the first half of the *kakari musubi* (KM) construction, an agreement phenomenon between particles and certain conjugational forms (i.e. their *musubi*), e.g. *-du/-dzyu/-ru* … RT, *-si/-syu* … IZ.

    Functionally, KM serves to focus the part of the sentence that comes prior to it, and to defocus the rest of it. KP *-du* functions similarly to a stress in English that indicates that the stressed item is what is focused on. The KP *-si* goes further, singling out the item that it attaches to as the single member of the focused

INTRODUCTION                                                                      17

class. Each KP takes different verbal endings, -*du* overwhelmingly taking -*y-ur-u* (a subcategory of RT; cf. Shinzato and Serafim 2013, Ch. 3 § 2.3), and -*si* taking -(*ir*)*i* (= IZ). The KP -*ga* takes either -(*y-ur-*)*a* (both subcategories of IA), and signifies a wondering or questioning about the marked lexeme.

For a full treatment of this syntactic phenomenon and each particle including KP -*yi*, a semantic parallel of KP -*si*, readers are referred to Shinzato and Serafim (2013).

5.2.3      Sentence-Final Particles

As the name indicates, these particles occur sentence-finally to alter the mood of the sentence (e.g. indicative, prohibitive) or to add exclamatory color.

| | | |
|---|---|---|
| *na* | SFP | question, prohibition, exclamation (according to the predicate's ending) |
| *ya*(*a*) | SFP | exclamation |
| *yo*(*o*) | SFP | exclamation |
| *do*(*o*) | SKP | exclamation |
| *yu* | SFP | exclamation |

CHAPTER 2

# Spelling System and Phonology

## 1 Introduction

In this chapter we will present our findings about the phonological system of the *Omoro Sōshi*. We base these findings on the regularities observed internally in the Ryukyuan Royal Government writers' deployment of their spelling system, including—very importantly—spelling alternations for individual words. These findings give a latticework of observed distinctions, to which phonetic detail is applied. This is done in part through knowledge of the development of the Japanese kana system and in part through knowledge of the development of the later language that came out of OOk, which is the language of the OS. It is helped in some small measure by comparison with Nakijin dialect of northern Okinawa, which retains a version of the old [± aspirate] distinction critical to understanding OOk phonology.

The crucial point in interpretation of the spelling system of the *Omoro Sōshi* is the question of whether to take the spelling at face value, that is, whether "What You See Is What You Get", i.e. whether the spelling system is a "WYSIWYG" system, and, further, what "face value" would mean.

Let us first present a simplified chart of the kana used in the OS, putting aside the question of any allographs for any one kana graph (see Table 2.1).

Note the ⟨g-⟩, ⟨z-⟩, ⟨d-⟩, and ⟨b-⟩ columns. Each one of those is in fact sometimes or always written instead (for the same word in which any of them appears) with, respectively, graphs from the ⟨k-⟩, ⟨s-⟩, ⟨t-⟩, or ⟨p-⟩ columns. For example, the word meaning 'rise' can be written either ⟨a ga ru⟩ or ⟨a ka ru⟩.[1] The first crack in the notion of a WYSIWYG system has appeared. The *assumption* is made that the word has a voiced obstruent. Indeed, sometimes an assumption is made that a word has a voiced obstruent when no voicing mark appears anywhere in any version of the OS for that word.

Looking at the chart again, let us note the ⟨p-⟩ column. We have labeled the moras as beginning with *p*, but in fact we could have labeled them with *f*, or with *h*, or with a mixture such as *h* for all except *fu*, as in the standard-Japanese Hepburn system.

---

1 In the Shō Family Text of the OS, the voicing marks are in fact never used, so the ⟨g-⟩, ⟨z-⟩, ⟨d-⟩, and ⟨b-⟩ columns in effect disappear. "⟨" marks the beginning of a graphic string, and "⟩" marks its end.

© KONINKLIJKE BRILL NV, LEIDEN, 2021 | DOI:10.1163/9789004414686_003

SPELLING SYSTEM AND PHONOLOGY

TABLE 2.1 The kana and their transliterations

| | '- | k- | g- | s- | z- | t- | d- | n- | p- | b- | m- | y- | r- | w- | N |
|---|---|---|---|---|---|---|---|---|---|---|---|---|---|---|---|
| -a | あ<br>a | か<br>ka | が<br>ga | さ<br>sa | ざ<br>za | た<br>ta | だ<br>da | な<br>na | は<br>pa | ば<br>ba | ま<br>ma | や<br>ya | ら<br>ra | わ<br>wa | ん<br>N |
| -i | い<br>i | き<br>ki | ぎ<br>gi | し<br>si | じ<br>zi | ち<br>ti | ぢ<br>di | に<br>ni | ひ<br>pi | び<br>bi | み<br>mi | – | り<br>ri | ゐ<br>wi | |
| -u | う<br>u | く<br>ku | ぐ<br>gu | す<br>su | ず<br>zu | つ<br>tu | づ<br>du | ぬ<br>nu | ふ<br>pu | ぶ<br>bu | む<br>mu | ゆ<br>yu | る<br>ru | – | |
| -e | – | け<br>ke | げ<br>ge | せ<br>se | ぜ<br>ze | て<br>te | で<br>de | ね<br>ne | へ<br>pe | べ<br>be | め<br>me | – | れ<br>re | ゑ<br>we | |
| -o | お<br>o | こ<br>ko | ご<br>go | そ<br>so | ぞ<br>zo | と<br>to | ど<br>do | の<br>no | ほ<br>po | ぼ<br>bo | も<br>mo | よ<br>yo | ろ<br>ro | を<br>wo | |

Indeed, what is the WYSIWYG assumption based on? Is the ⟨t-⟩ column *ta, ti, tu, te, to*, or is it, say, *ta, chi, tsu, te, to*? What about the ⟨s-⟩ column? Is it *sa, si, su, se, so* or *sa, shi, su, se, so*? The ⟨z-⟩ column? *za, zi, zu, ze, zo*; *za, zhi, zu, ze, zo*; or *za, ji, zu, ze, zo*? The ⟨d-⟩ column? *da, di, du, de, do*; *da, dzhi, dzu, de, do*; or *da, zhi, zu, de, do*?

The WYSIWYG assumption appears to leave the phonologization, in fact, up to the person reading the OS, as a nonce invention, never to be determined, either on the assumption that it *has* been determined, or, on the other hand, on the assumption that it *cannot* be.


## 2 Reconstruction Methodology

We lay out here what can be inferred of the phonology of the OS from internal spelling facts and from comparison with Modern Okinawan phonology.[2] Inferences center around certain key questions. Most inferences are in fact unexceptionable, such as the inference of the phoneme *a* and most aspects

---

2  In §7 we deal specifically with the question of evidence from outside the Ryukyus.

20                                                 CHAPTER 2

of its lexical distribution. Specific lexical phonological questions will be raised and answered in the process of doing other analyses, but we will lay out the basic questions here.

## 2.1    *A Preview: The os Phonological System*

As a guidepost to what follows, we offer here a view to where the reconstruction of the OOk phonological system is heading, bottom-up, so to speak.

The proto-Ryukyuan vowel system is as follows (Thorpe 1983: 31–32):

| [–back] | [+back] | |
|---|---|---|
| *i | *u | [+high] |
| *e | *o | [–high, –low] |
| | *a | [+low] |

The vowel system of OOk is as follows:

| [+front] | | [–fr, –ba] | [+ba] | |
|---|---|---|---|---|
| **[+palatal]** | **[–palatal]** | | | |
| yi(i) [⁽ʸ⁾i(ɪ)] | i(i) [ɪ(ː)] | i̇(i̇) [i̇(ː)] | u(u) [u(ː)] | [+hi] |
| ye(e) [⁽ʸ⁾e(ɛ)] | e(e) [ɛ(ː)] | | o(o) [ɔ(ː)] | [–h, –l] |
| | | a(a) [ɑ(ː)] | | [+lo] |

This is a system of eight vowels similar in its phonetic and phonemic layout to the vowel systems of many dialects of the Northern Ryukyuan Amami region, and the resemblance is more than superficial. It is also similar to the phonological system of Old Japanese, but not much stock should be put on this resemblance.

The tense high front vowel *yi(i)* is strongly palatally articulated. The front vowels *i(i)* and *e(e)* are phonetically lax, weakly fronted, and slightly lower than tense equivalents would be, and the back vowel *o(o)*, also being phonetically lax, has a slightly lower articulation than its tense equivalent would be.

The high vowels *yi(i)*, *u(u)*, and *i̇(i̇)*, are tense, but the high vowel *i(i)* is a member of the lax set. The vowel *a(a)* is not specifically tense or lax. A portion

# SPELLING SYSTEM AND PHONOLOGY

TABLE 2.2    The *Omoro Sōshi* consonant system

|  |  | Labials | Alveolars | Post-alveolars | Velars | Glottals |
|---|---|---|---|---|---|---|
| Obstruents | voiceless | $p°, p^h$ | $t°, t^h$ |  | $k°, k^h$ | $ʔ$ |
|  | voiced | $b$ [˜b] | $d$ [˜d] |  | $g$ [˜g] | $'$ |
| Affricates | voiceless | | $c°$ [ts°], | $c°y$ [ʧ°], | | |
|  |  | | $(c^h$ [tsʰ]) | $c^hy$ [ʧʰ] | | |
|  | voiced | | $dz$ [˜dz] | $dzy$ [˜dʒ] | | |
| Fricatives | voiceless | | $s$ | $sy$ [ʃ] | | |
|  | voiced | | $z$ [˜z] | $zy$ [˜ʒ] | | |
| Nasals | | $m$ | $n$ | | | |
| Glides | | $w$ | | $y$ | | |
| Moraic | nasals | $M$ [m:] | $N$ | | | |
|  | voiceless | | | | $K$ [k:k°] | $Q$ |
|  | voiced | $B$ [˜b:b] | | | $G$ [˜g:g] | |

of the tokens of *u* is from lax *\*o̖*, while the rest are from tense *\*u*. That is, there is reason to believe that *u* [u] is a merger of separate tense (originally high) *\*u* and lax (originally mid) *\*o̖*, i.e. *\*[ɔ] > \*[o̖] > [u]*. The origin of the OOk-period *o(o)* and *e(e)* is in originally long *\*oo* and *\*ee*, respectively and in the diphthongs *\*au* and *\*a'yi*, respectively. The OOk mid short *o* and *e/ye* are shortenings of long *oo* and *ee/yee* in poetic environments that call for one instead of two moras.

Table 2.2 charts the os-language consonants.[3]

In terms of place of articulation, there are labials,[4,5] alveolars, post-alveolars, velars, and glottals.[6,7] There are five articulation types, divided between

---

3   '   OOk glottal continuant; in that capacity, it determines mora structure leading to decisions on Monophthongization; also used in Japanese-language Hepburn romanization.

  ʰ   placed after an OOk voiceless stop or affricate; superscript; signals aspirate only; may be italicized.

  °   placed after aspirable consonant: signals non-aspirate.

  ○   preposed: signals preferred form; or:

      postposed: signals that a kana has been checked for voicing in TOS.

4   We hypothesize that in addition to *p°*, the sequence *Qp°* existed as well, because of words such as ⟨a pa re⟩ *ʔaQp°ari* 'awesome!' (OSJS 39a) (OS 14.#1013).

5   Concerning *w*, perhaps [labiovelar] would be a better characterization at a phonetic level.

6   The glottal continuant /'/ may be a fiction, but it is a convenient one, since it can at times function as a placeholder in a string of segments, as in *kʰuu'-yi* 'praying for', where it holds the place for {w} in {kʰuuw+yi}.

7   Moras associated with ⟨-i⟩-ending graphs are strictly-speaking Monophthongizable, because

a set of three (stops, affricates, and fricatives) that support a manner distinction between voiceless and voiced, and another set of three that have no such manner distinction. There are six moraic consonants: four obstruent and two nasal. The obstruents are further subdivided into two voiceless and two voiced.

For the oral voiceless stops and affricates, there is as well a distinction based on aspiration.

## 2.2 The pRk Mid Vowels *e and *o vs the pRk High Vowels *yi and *u

Probably the single most fraught question in OOk phonology is the status of the proto-Ryukyuan (pRk) mid vowels *e and *o, and their effects on the phonology. First we will deal with *e vs *yi, then with *o vs *u.

### 2.2.1 The pRk Mid Vowel *e and the High Vowel *yi, and the Introduction of the Archisegment *y

Proto-Ryukyuan had the vowels mid front *e and high front *yi. Questions that arise are those vowels' lexical distribution in pre-Old-Okinawan (pre-OOk) and in OOk itself, and then the reconstruction of their height and any other relevant characteristics in the os.

Let us look at spellings of OOk Progressively Palatalized (PPed) gerund forms (GER). We assume that the pRk GER was *-te, taking one of the NOk GER allomorphs -ti as our guide. Thorpe (1983: 154) independently sets up his own pRk reconstruction *te (calling forms with it "perfect participle"s), done without knowledge of the os. The os verb GER ⟨o ru ti⟩, ⟨o ro/u ti pe⟩, ⟨o ro ti we⟩ 'bringing down, lowering' occurs 64 times in the os. (Compare MJ *orosite* '(id.)'.) Of those occurrences, 59 tokens are of ⟨o ro/u ti pe⟩, 3 tokens are of ⟨o ro ti we⟩, and 2 tokens are of ⟨o ru ti⟩.

---

they have become [ʸi] early enough to feed into the First Monophthongization (M1). (See immediately below.) Those that have not Monophthongized lack the glottal "tick" /ʼ/, which functions as a glottal constriction; that tick causes *yi* to be treated as a glide-plus-vowel sequence, or, more simply, as a palatal vowel, and therefore as a candidate for Di- and Mono-phthongization. In the VGV sequence *lacking* the tick, the glide is promoted to the full consonant position, creating a VCV sequence, in which *yi* is not available for Di- and Mono-phthongization, because it occupies the Consonant slot. The result is (e.g.): *ayi = aCi → ayi* (no change); but for the sequence *with* the tick: *aʼyi = aCyi → ee*. The former form will Monophthongize during M2, which occurs probably in the 18th century or later. If the processes are viewed together, they look like this: (M1) *ayi* >1> *aʼyi* ~ *ee* >2> *ee*; (M2) *aye* >1> *ayi* >2> *aʼyi* >3> *ee*. M1 and M2 are indistinguishable using only modern Okinawan data.

# SPELLING SYSTEM AND PHONOLOGY

'bringing down, lowering'

⟨  o   ru    ti            ⟩
⟨  o   ro/u  ti   pe  ⟩
⟨  o   ro    ti   we  ⟩

The most likely phonological value that fits all cases is [ʧi]. This is because [ʧi] is the NOk form, so the form cannot have eroded to some level beyond it, and both ⟨ti pe⟩ and ⟨ti we⟩ can easily be seen as spellings that came about before a Raising, but after a PP: *oros-yi-te *[ʔɔrɔʃːt°ɛ] *⟨o ro si te⟩ > *oros-yi-cye *[ʔɔrɔʃːʧ°ɛ] *⟨o ro si ti pe/we⟩, followed by (loss of *⟨si⟩ = *syi = *[ʃː] and) Raising: *ʔoro-_-cyɪ *[ʔoro_ʧ°ɪ] ⟨o ro ti pe/we⟩ (traditional spellings) and ⟨o ru ti⟩ [ʔuruʧ°i] ʔuru-c°yi (innovative spelling). While writers were "free" to use high-vowel spelling now, in fact one reason kept them from doing so for the most part: the strong influence of tradition. The alternations A, B, and C lead to the reconstruction of, let us say, ABC, obtained through consideration of the "lowest common phonetic denominator."[8] Let us call this principle the Lowest Common Phonetic Denominator, or LCPD for short. Another principle that is derived from common knowledge about the relationship between MOk and NOk spellings and NOk pronunciation, and about the vowel-height relationship between NOk (among many other varieties of Ryukyuan) and OJ, is that the heights of the vowels in the two language groups require the inference that once Ryukyuan, too, had a distinction between high and mid vowels where now there are only high. This knowledge further requires an inference that mid vowels raised to high, variously merging or not with the pre-existing high vowels. Let us call this principle, and the historical sound-change rule that goes with it, Raising (Thorpe: 1983: 53–55).

Observe cases of use of ⟨pe⟩, ⟨we⟩, and ⟨'i⟩ after a *vowel*, as in verb forms, with the example ⟨so ro pe/we/'i⟩[9] 'put in place, unify, rule' (OJ soropë- 'put in a row; make identical' [JDB 408a]—note the independent verification of *p*, thus pJpc *p, thus pre-OOk *p as well):

⟨so ro pe⟩ :
⟨so ro pe te⟩           GER                         17 tokens
⟨so ro pe wa ⋯⟩   EX {+(u)wa·{r/s}}   5 tokens
⟨so ro pe ya ri⟩       PROG/STAT               1 token
23 tokens of ⟨so ro pe⟩ suruyi- < *sorope- VT

---

8     We thank one of our reviewers for the apt and concise phrasing.
9     ... the transcription ⟨'i⟩ signifying a vowel graph with no consonant initial.

24 CHAPTER 2

⟨so ro we⟩ :

| ⟨so ro we te | GER | 11 tokens |
| ⟨so ro we wa ···⟩ | EX {+(u)wa·{r/s}} | 2 tokens |
| ⟨so ro we ru⟩ | RT | 2 tokens |

15 tokens of ⟨so ro we⟩ *suruyi-* < *\*sorope-* VT

⟨so ro i⟩:

| ⟨so ro i te⟩ | GER | 3 tokens |
| ⟨so ro i wa ···⟩ | EX {+(u)wa·{r/s} } | 6 tokens |

9 tokens of ⟨so ro i⟩ *suruyi-* < *\*sorope-* VT

There are 47 tokens of the lexical item at issue,[10] and we propose that its phonologization is most naturally made out to be *suruyi-*, on the basis of LCPD.[11]

Again it makes sense to assume that all the forms are pronounced the same way. We know from the history of the softening of the *\*p* sound in medial position in Japanese (*ha-gyō tenko*[*-on*] ハ行転呼[音]) that before a front vowel it underwent the following

*pe* > *fe* > *we* > *ye*

(It underwent one more change in very recent times, to *'e*, i.e. a vowel with no consonantal onset.) If we apply the identical changes to Ryukyuan (cf. e.g. Thorpe [1983: 60–61]),[12] and add the equally well known Raising of mid to high vowels, we get the following:

---

10   ⟨so ro i #⟩ (3 tokens)—these are removed from the evidence because they require contextual interpretation, not morphologically based evidence, for determination of their transitivity; Hokama (2000a: 134b–135b; OS 4.#180) takes one as transitive: ⟨ma sa no , ki mo , ∧ so ro i⟩ "ma-gokoro o soroete" = "unifying their purity of heart"; and (2000a: 364b; OS 10.#546) the other two as intransitive, ⟨si mo no , YO no ∧ nu si no ∧ so ro i / a N zi˙ MATA no , a N zi˙ no , ∧ so ro i⟩ "shimo no yo no nushi, anji no naka no anji ga soroi, …" = "the southern domains' lords and the lord among the lords coming together", both based on contextual interpretation, not on morphological cues.

11   See some further discussion of *suruyi* and a proposed alternative for *yi* on p. 33.

12   "There are just a few words in which either intervocalic *\*p* or *\*Qp* should be reconstructed. The tentative choice in this study is *\*Qp*, with the consequence that no intervocalic *\*p* is posited in Proto-Ryūkyūan. In two adjective stems there must have been an alternation *\*Qp ~ \*w; this suggests that Proto-Ryūkyūan \*w may derive, in some cases at least, from an earlier intervocalic \*p. The largely adjectival nature of the \*Qp vocabulary also seems to hint that \*Q was perhaps a special expressive (emphatic?) phonological device*" [author's italics].

# SPELLING SYSTEM AND PHONOLOGY

$$*pe \; > \; *fe \; > \; *we \; > \; *ye^{13} \; > \; yi$$

and if we apply known spellings to those syllables:

| | | | | | | | | |
|---|---|---|---|---|---|---|---|---|
| $*pe$ | > | $*fe$ | > | $*we$ | > | $*ye$ | > | $yi$ |
| ⟨pe⟩ | > | – | > | ⟨we⟩ | > | – | > | ⟨i⟩ |

Let us add the changes that occurred to the syllable $*pyi$ in medial position as well:

| | | | | | | | | |
|---|---|---|---|---|---|---|---|---|
| $*pyi$ | > | $*fyi$ | > | $*wyi$ | > | $(*yi)$ | > | $yi$ |
| | | ⟨pi⟩ | > | ⟨wi⟩ | > | (–) | > | ⟨i⟩ |

Since it turns out that the medial syllables mid-vowel $*pe$ $*we$ $*ye$ and high-vowel $*pyi$ $*wyi$ $*yi$ all merge as OOk medial $yi$, with no consonantal onset:[14]

| | | | | | | | |
|---|---|---|---|---|---|---|---|
| $*pyi$ | > | $*fyi$ | > | $*wyi$ | > | $(*yi)$ | |
| $*pe$ | > | $*fe$ | > | $*we$ | > | $*ye$ | $> \; yi$ |

| | | | | | | | |
|---|---|---|---|---|---|---|---|
| ⟨pi⟩ | > | – | > | ⟨wi⟩ | | | |
| ⟨pe⟩ | > | – | > | ⟨we⟩ | $>$ | – | $> \; $⟨i⟩ |

we see that the spellings recapitulate Okinawan language prehistory, with ⟨so ro pe⟩ representing the oldest period, ⟨so ro we⟩ the next period, and finally ⟨so ro i⟩ the last period:

| | | |
|---|---|---|
| ⟨sorope⟩ | $*sorope$ | >(softening; allophony with initial $*[p^h]$)> |
| ⟨sorope⟩ | $*sorofe$ | >(merger with $*w$)> |
| ⟨sorowe⟩ | $*sorowe$ | >(Raising)> |
| | $*suruwi$ | >(glide palatalization) |
| ⟨soro/ui⟩ | $suruyi$ | 'putting together, unifying' |

---

13    There is no equivalent to ⟨ye⟩ in OS spelling (just as there is not in any but the earliest mainland Japanese kana systems), from which OOk kana spelling is derived.

14    Further, some OOk $Vyi$ in certain instances undergoes monophthongization. We treat this in §4.5, since it takes us away from the question at hand.

Therefore, as one of our reviewers posed it, "In theory, one could distinguish between *alternating* and *non-alternating*. Why not reconstruct *\*surui* instead of *\*suruyi*?" Our response to that would be as follows:

The alternating case is limited to the cases in medial position with initial ⟨p⟩, ⟨w⟩, and ⟨'⟩. Thus:

⟨pi⟩ ~ ⟨wi⟩ ~ ⟨'i⟩ ~
⟨pe⟩ ~ ⟨we⟩ ~
(⟨wi⟩ is rare, and there is no ˣ⟨'e⟩)

That means that all non-alternating ⟨Ci⟩ is always *Cyi*, and non-initial ⟨p/w/'.i/e⟩ is always *'yi*. Since specific cases of non-word-initial ⟨Ci⟩ (i.e. ⟨'i⟩, ⟨pi⟩) *do* merge with the ⟨e⟩-final graphs, that can only mean that the merger is to *high palatal*, since the ⟨i⟩-final graphs are the only ones that possess both [+high] and [+palatal] qualities. This is an invocation of the LCPD principle.

Similarly,

| | |
|---|---|
| ⟨o mo pi⟩ | *\*omopyi* |
| ⟨o mo pi⟩ | *\*omofyi* |
| ⟨o mo ˣwi⟩ | – |
| ⟨o mo i⟩ | *ʔumuyi* 'thinking' |
| ⟨o mo yo wa ru⟩ | *ʔumuyuwaru* |
| ⟨ne ga pi⟩ | *\*negapyi* |
| ⟨ne ga pi⟩ | *\*negafyi* |
| ⟨ne ga ˣwi⟩ | – |
| ⟨ne ga i⟩ | *nigayi* |
| ⟨ne ga yo wa ti pe⟩ | *nigayuwac°yi* 'exaltedly keeping praying' |
| ⟨ne ga i wa ti pe⟩ | *niga'yiwac°yi* '(id.)' |

The last two listed lexical items show that *yi* will collapse into a new syllable with a following mora starting with a vowel, a glottal stop, or a glide: *ʔumu'-yi + -uwa·r-u → ʔumu'-y-uwa·r-u* 'exaltedly thinks / feels' (os 13.#828), or *nigayiwac°yi* (os 3.#107). Thus what starts out as *\*fyi* can even become just *y*, and further, *yu* can further break down to *yi*. Interestingly, though, (*\*ye* >) *\*yi* does not break down, showing that the described changes must occur while (*\*yi* >) *\*yi* and (*\*ye* >) *\*yi* are distinct.

We have been examining medial-glide cases. Let us now turn our attention to more ordinary CV syllables, in the case where V = *\*e* or *\*yi*. Let us look at ⟨re⟩ vs ⟨ri⟩, i.e. *ri* vs *ryi*:

SPELLING SYSTEM AND PHONOLOGY

'descend(ing) (from Heaven)'
おれ ⟨o re⟩[15] : 203 tokens, including compounds
おり ⟨o ri⟩ : no tokens[16]

As the set of examples above shows, there is no confusion of the usage of ⟨re⟩ and ⟨ri⟩. This is because the vowel of the ⟨re⟩ graph and the vowel of the ⟨ri⟩ graph are different from each other. (There is no reason to assume that the distinction between ⟨re⟩ and ⟨ri⟩ is due to the consonant(s) of the two graphs, which can both safely be assumed to be [ɾ].) This means that, since ⟨ri⟩ can safely be assumed to be [ɾ⁽ʸ⁾i], then ⟨re⟩ must be something else. But what is that "something else"?

Two choices present themselves: (1) [ɾɛ], i.e. the mid-vowel choice, and (2) [ɾɪ], i.e. a high-vowel choice *that is not a palatal-vowel choice*, since that choice is blocked by the existence of ⟨ri⟩ = [ɾ⁽ʸ⁾i] in the high front palatal slot.

We have already seen that the palatalized version of the GER morpheme is occasionally written ⟨Ci⟩ as well as ⟨Ci pe⟩ or ⟨Ci we⟩, showing that the palatalized gerund alternant of verbs that 'require those alternants is with *yi*, clearly a high vowel. Let us ask, what happens if the palatal portion is taken away? That would be *c_i*, and the affricator would be missing, so *c* should be changed to *t*, giving *t_i*, i.e. *ti*, the form for e.g. ⟨o re te⟩ 'descending', with the GER morpheme *-ti* = [tɪ].

If we apply the same reasoning to ⟨re⟩ as to ⟨te⟩, then ⟨re⟩ = [ɾɪ]. Assuming for the moment that the raising seen for the front vowels applies also to the back vowels, then ⟨o re te⟩ is *ʔuriti* = [ʔurɪtɪ].

---

15    The morphology and morphophonemics of this verb are treated in Ch. 6 §1.2.2.

16    OSJS ⟨o ri po si (ya)⟩ (97c–98a): '[the deities] desiring to descend from Heaven'; OSJS believes that the word is (in its way of interpreting the writing) ⟨o ri⟩ (~ ⟨o re⟩) 'descend' (misapprehending OS spelling conventions), contravening its own KKKS citation「居度と 也」, which uses the characters ⟨居度⟩ = ⟨ORI TASI⟩ '[I/we] wish to be (present)'. In KKKS2 (1995: 288, #994) ⟨o ri po si ya⟩, Ikemiya Masaharu, the editor and compiler, says 'i-tai', i.e. '[I/we] wish to be (present)', – first person only. The character と – ⟨to⟩/⟨do⟩ is followed by an ellipsis, "*iu koto*" 'the fact (that)', i.e. *ori-tasyi-to iu koto nari* "it means '[I/we] want to be [present]'," so the subject is first-person. Interestingly, by 2000, Hokama, the junior editor of OSJS (first published in 1967), had reversed his mentor Nakahara, and himself, saying (2000a: 288b), '... *i-tai, sumi-tai* ...' = '... want to be [there], want to live [there] ...' in his free translation. The set of tokens ⟨o ri po si⟩ 8.#425, 6.#315 (KKKS 'itai'), 8.#444, 6.#337—all of which have been switched in their interpretation by Hokama 2000 from the earlier OSJS, constituted the only potential impediment to a clean sweep of over 200 tokens of ⟨o re⟩ for 'descend', with no ⟨o ri⟩ examples.

TABLE 2.3 Steps in the merger of *o and *u

| Pre-Raising | Raising: Pre-[lax]-Loss | OOk | MOk |
|---|---|---|---|
| *ku* | *ku* | *kᵒu* | *ku* |
| [kᵒu] | [kᵒu] | [kᵒu] | [ku] |
| *ko* | *kö* | *kʰu* | *ku* |
| [kʰɔ] | [kʰö] | [kʰu] | [ku] |
| *mu* | *mu* | *mu* | *mu* |
| [mu] | [mu] | [mu] | [mu] |
| *mo* | *mö* | *mu* | *mu* |
| [mɔ] | [mö] | [mu] | [mu] |

### 2.2.2 Pre-Old-Okinawan *o and *u, and the Development of Aspirated vs Plain Voiceless Stops and Affricates

In the case of the front vowels, we saw that the raising did not in itself result in merger, due to the difference in palatality of the resulting vowels. But we also note that *lack* of palatality suggests phonetic laxness, as well as aspiration in preceding aspirable consonants.[17] Under these circumstances, we hypothesize a set of changes that affected the back-vowel moras as in Table 2.3.

Had OOk, i.e. the period of the OS, been the period before Raising, then there would be essentially a one-to-one correspondence between the orthographic system and the phonology. It would be a WYSIWYG system: What You See Is What You Get. This is not the system of the OS orthography.

---

17    Regarding aspiration, Thorpe (1983: 53–55) says that pRk had phonetic aspiration in mid vowels and lack thereof in high vowels, and that as the mid vowels raised, the [±aspirate] distinction phonologized from Kudaka (an island southeast of Shuri) northwards—but not including the Shuri-Naha area. Presumably, Kudaka is a remnant of the far past in the south as well.

    We assume a dialect continuum throughout the Northern Ryukyus, and all of this area (if not, indeed, all of Ryukyuan—see Thorpe—) had the aspiration system. The Shuri-Naha area, undergoing heavy cultural pressure from outside of the Ryukyus—Japan in particular—and being the cultural, political, and commercial center, was naturally the first dialect area to lose the distinction, which also did not exist in Japanese. This is no great surprise. Thorpe, not knowing the OS, did not take it into account, and assumed that Shuri had never phonologized the distinction. The *loss* of the distinction continued into post-OS times, spreading north and south, with its contemporary border on the Okinawa mainland north of Kadena.

# SPELLING SYSTEM AND PHONOLOGY

Had OOk been the period of post-Raising but Pre-[lax]-Loss, then, despite Raising, the old {*ku ↔ *ko} distinction would still be preserved, but now as the post-raising {ku ↔ kʊ}, where a distinction of tense-/laxness would be the distinctive feature separating them. Not only that, but the old {*mu ↔ *mo}, also having been affected by Raising, would now be {mu ↔ mʊ}, again, kept distinct by tense/laxness, even though both vowels were high.

What appears to be the case, however, is that the OS orthographic system is a Post-[lax]-Loss system, in which what may once have been a {*ku ↔ *ko} distinction, having lost its vocalic distinction, either has merged its syllables or else has kept its syllables distinct, by virtue of a transformation of the formerly purely phonetic distinction of non-aspiration/pharyngeal constriction/glottal constriction of *ku [k°u] on the one hand and the aspiration of *ko [kʰʊ] on the other into a new phonemic distinction, along with every other voiceless stop and affricate pair of formerly high- and mid-vowel moras, just as noted in Thorpe (1983: 53–55). We will see that in fact they were kept apart where aspiration could play a role in distinguishing moras, just as it does in many dialects/languages of the Northern Ryukyus, starting on the central Okinawan mainland, not so far north of the Naha/Shuri area, north of Kadena, but with a holdout area east of Shuri, the offshore island of Kudaka.

As for the {*mu ↔ *mo} distinction,[18] it has to have been lost one sound-change earlier, just after the loss of the tense/lax distinction, and therefore, as we will see below, it was not distinguished in OOk. After all, nasals are not usually aspirated.

All else being equal, a raising of mid to high vowels would be expected to result in their merger, but we saw that in the case of the front-vowel moras, most {high ↔ mid} vowel mora pairs were kept distinct despite the raising because of the difference in the marking of the feature [palatal] in one or the other of the mora pair, as in e.g.:

| あみ | ⟨a mi⟩ | *ʔamyi* | [ʔamʸi][19] | [+pal] | '(fishing) net' | (OS 11.#650) ↔ |
|------|--------|---------|-------------|--------|-----------------|-----------------|
| あめ | ⟨a me⟩ | *ʔami* | [ʔamɪ] | [−pal] | 'sky' | (OS 12.#713) |

For back-vowel raisings, it might be that *o had become ʊ everywhere, thus maintaining a distinction with u. In that case, we would expect a maintenance of the mora-level distinctions in every environment. But in fact in many envi-

---

18    Some *mu does become ʍ and then ɴ, and therefore never merges with *mo.

19    This appears as the second member of two compounds, かめ、あみ ⟨ka me , a mi⟩ *kʰami-ʔamyi* 'net for catching sea-turtles' (OS 11.#650), and ざ゛ん、あみ ⟨za゛ N , a mi⟩ *zaɴ-ʔamyi* 'net for catching dugongs' (OS 11.#650).

30                                                                    CHAPTER 2

TABLE 2.4    |kimo| data

---

⟨ki mo⟩ and ⟨ki mu⟩ 'heart; liver'

⟨ki° mo⟩                          52 tokens (72.2%)
⟨ki° mu⟩                          20 tokens

⟨o gi mo⟩ (TOS) 34 tkns + 9 written w/ ⟨gi⟩ in KOS = 43 tkns w/ ⟨gi mo⟩
⟨gi mu⟩ (KOS): ∅ tokens
⟨ki" mu⟩ (inferred from TOS) 2 tokens

72 = 61% written with ⟨ki⟩    95 = 81% written with ⟨mo⟩
45 = 39% written with ⟨gi⟩    22 = 19% written with ⟨mu⟩

---

ronments the distinction no longer holds, even though elsewhere it is maintained. For example, as shown in Table 2.4, the word $k°yimu$ 'heart, mind, emotion' may be written both ⟨ki mo⟩ (the historically accurate form; 52 tokens) and ⟨ki mu⟩ (the form rendered possible because of the raising; 20 tokens).[20,21]

We expected ⟨kyi⟩ not to vary with ⟨ke⟩, since that would require a confusion of palatality, which does not occur after $k$. Thus $kyi$ was written with one graph only, as expected from the start. On the other hand, there is nothing to distinguish *$mu$ and *$mo$ after the raising, except in the very few cases where *$mu$ has first become м. Thus {*$mo$ ↔ *$mu$} > $mu$, which means that the graphemic contrast {⟨mo⟩ ↔ ⟨mu⟩} becomes the allographic alternation {⟨mo⟩ ~ ⟨mu⟩},

{*$mo$ ↔ *$mu$}    >    merged                      $mu$
{⟨mo⟩ ↔ ⟨mu⟩}      >    allographic alternation     {⟨mo⟩ ~ ⟨mu⟩}

since neither of the two old graphs has been abandoned, but rather, over time both tend to be used more and more indiscriminately. Thus there comes into being a set of allographs in which ⟨kyi⟩ does not vary, but in which ⟨mo⟩ and ⟨mu⟩ are both used, with the lesser number ⟨mu⟩ at a rate of about 28% of the total of both ⟨mu⟩ and ⟨mo⟩ after ⟨ki⟩ (or at any rate in the lexeme |kimo|).

---

20    Of course it cannot be and is not written ×⟨ke mo⟩ or ×⟨ke mu⟩, since ⟨ki⟩ and ⟨ke⟩ are kept distinguished. There is no reason to believe that the word is in origin any different than OJ $kîmô$ [kʸimʷo] 'liver; the internal organs' (JDB 246d–247a).

21    In what follows, the symbol "°" means "checked for *lack* of voicing in TOS," TOS being the final arbiter concerning voicing.

SPELLING SYSTEM AND PHONOLOGY

Now the fact is that, since there is a distinction of palatality with moras including front vowels, even moras with voiced initials (save for a predetermined set) maintain a distinction between original high-front-vowel moras *C"yi and original mid-front-vowel moras *C"e, that is, the phonological contrast {*C"yi ↔ *C"e} becomes the phonological contrast {C"yi ↔ C"i}:

phonological contrast {*C"yi ↔ *C"ē} >
phonological contrast { C"yi ↔ C"ī }

This means that there should be no allography between ⟨⁽ⁿ⁾ki⟩ and ⟨⁽ⁿ⁾ke⟩, and indeed there is none: they are kept separate. That is to say, in KOS the only allography is between ⟨ki⟩ (kyi) and ⟨"ki⟩ = ⟨gi⟩ (gyi), and that is due to a phonemic distinction, if not, as is often the case a morphophonemic one, but one that, like accent in many languages, was frequently simply not written in. On the other hand, we guess from the OJ evidence that the original back vowel of the word for 'liver (as food); heart, emotions' (OGJ 154a–155a) was o.[22] Also given our guess that the sound change from mid to high vowels was relatively recent—say, within the previous century or so—we also expect that not much slippage would have occcured in the interim, in terms of ahistorical spellings creeping in.

To show that ⟨ku⟩ and ⟨ko⟩ are kept separate, we will present two examples of large lexeme-sets that are written exclusively with, on the one hand, ⟨ku⟩, and, on the other, ⟨ko⟩. We utilized the OS database Sōshi Sāchā to find all possible combinations of syllables at issue. They are given in the orthography found in KOS.

First, ⟨ku⟩: We searched for all combinations of ⟨ku⟩, ⟨gu⟩, ⟨ko⟩, ⟨go⟩, plus ⟨mu⟩ or ⟨mo⟩, in order to find possible lexemes meaning 'cloud'. The word for 'cloud' is written as either ⟨ku mo⟩, ⟨ku mu⟩, or ⟨ku mu-⟩, or ⟨-ku mo⟩ ~ ⟨-gu mo⟩ in compounds, with no examples of ⟨ko mo⟩ or ⟨ko mu⟩, as in Table 2.5.

Clearly 100%, or 66, of the 66 tokens of 'cloud' had ⟨ku⟩, other than the members of the set with voicing, although they had ⟨gu⟩. Importantly, none had ⟨ko⟩. Note that 15% had ⟨mu⟩ instead of ⟨mo⟩, but that already has been explained. If there had been 15% ⟨mo⟩, we would be right to wonder if it had not originally been *kumu, but that is not the case.

Just as clearly, 100%, or 48, of the 48 non-voiced tokens of 'man (among men)' had ⟨ko⟩, and, importantly, none had ⟨ku⟩. We should point out that the

---

22    We can be no more precise than that, given the evidence at hand.

32　　CHAPTER 2

TABLE 2.5 　|kumo| data

'cloud' ⟨ku mo⟩ ~ ⟨ku mu⟩; ˣ⟨ko⟩ not encountered

| ⟨ko mo⟩ | ⟨go mo⟩ | | ∅ tokens |
| ⟨ko mu⟩ | ⟨go mu⟩ | | ∅ tokens |
| ⟨ku mu⟩ | ⟨go mu(-)⟩ (10/66 = 15%): | | 10 tokens |
| ⟨ku mo⟩: | ⟨ku mo⟩, ⟨-ku mo⟩, or ⟨ku mo-⟩: | | 56 tokens |

⟨-gu mo⟩: 10 tokens; rejected as evidence because of voicing

TABLE 2.6 　|koro| data

'man' ⟨koro⟩; ˣ⟨ku⟩ not encountered

⟨ko ro⟩　　48 tokens;
⟨-go ro(-)⟩　95 tokens; rejected as evidence due to voicing case of ⟨-ko⟩ ~ ⟨-ku⟩
　　　　　variation:
　　　　　⟨(-go ro) ko⟩　5 (e.g. #1088) vs
　　　　　⟨(-go ro) ku⟩　13 (e.g. #479)

Eastern Dialect of OJ has *kô-rö*[23] (JDB 314cd), the ED form of standard OJ *kô-ra* (JDB 313cd). The JDB editors note that the word is almost exclusively used toward women in ED, with just two or three exceptions. The OOk suffix ⟨ko⟩ = -*kʰu* is frequently seen in the meaning 'personage'.

Now ⟨ko⟩: We searched for all combinations of:

⟨k{o/u}r{o/u}⟩,

meaning 'man', especially an elder or a warrior male, as in Table 2.6.

Thus a clean and clear distinction is maintained between ⟨ku⟩ and ⟨ko⟩. Given the discussion above, this is not the least bit surprising. We assume that, since there is already confusion of ⟨mu⟩ and ⟨mo⟩ (i.e. "Post-[lax]-Loss"), and there is still a distinction between ⟨ku⟩ and ⟨ko⟩, then the phonology of the

---

23　The A : B / *kō* : *otsu* vowel-system conventions for Old Japanese are spelled out in fn. 24.

SPELLING SYSTEM AND PHONOLOGY
33

OS is in the period of a phonemic Aspiration distinction. Thus *kʰumu ~ -gumu* 'cloud' and *kʰuru ~ -guru* 'man (among men)'.

One last question remains: what to do about cases like ⟨-go ro k{o/u}⟩? They shouldn't exist according to the hypothesis developed here. However: Note that the form is a suffix. Then compare another unusual case where spelling does not stand in the way: the word for 'tree; wood' is *kii,* in NOk (OGJ 320a). Thus we should expect to see *-kii* or *-gii* everywhere in compounds. But the words for 'cryptomeria' and 'willow' are *sízyi* and *yanázyi*, respectively, with *-zyi* (OGJ 487b, OGJ 279a, resp.), i.e. with *\*-gyi*. Further, the combining form is not predictable: *cyáa-gi* 'Japanese podocarp' (OGJ 140), with *\*-gi* < pre-OOk *\*-ge*.

We believe that the *-kʰu* of *-guru-kʰu* < *\*-guru-kʰu* had, as a final element, recently suffered a similar fate, that is to say, that perhaps as late as the immediately preceding period, perhaps earlier, it had lost whatever distinction was keeping it apart from *\*····-kʰu*, and that that was the reason for the variation in spelling. Therefore, this case cannot be treated as an exception to aspiration keeping *kʰu* and *kʰu* distinct.[24,25]

To summarize mergers due to raising of mid to high vowels, both front and back, we present Table 2.7.[26,27]

---

24  We know that certain dialects with an aspiration distinction allow only one aspiration within a defined space through aspiration suppression after the first aspirated consonant, usually in a word, sometimes over a shorter stretch. A good example is Shodon (Serafim 1985: 23–25 [§ 2.1.3]). We have not determined whether there are dialects that do not have such a Grassmann's-Law-like constraint. For OOk, we have only externally-generated evidence on the broader question of aspiration suppression, made available through Lin's (2015; cf. § 7.4.) Chinese/Korean corpora. We have adopted, from evidence in that corpus, and from Thorpe (1983), aspiration suppression of all gerunds. According to Thorpe, in pRk, "medial *\*t* was everywhere leveled to an unaspirated consonant" (1983: 55). In addition, where Q appears or can be reconstructed as having at one time appeared in non-morphophonemic circumstances, we also assume a non-aspirated obstruent in OOk. Otherwise, we have assumed that aspiration in OOk is not suppressed in this way, not having found any information that points to such a phenomenon. It may well be that more such data will come to light.

25  Compare *#guru+kʰu* and *##si+dakʰa#kʰu##* 'Personage of High Spiritual Power = Kikoe Ōgimi', where the *#kʰu* of the latter is clearly a compounding element going together with *sidakʰa*, when compared to the former, which has already been lexicalized.

26  The chart does not include mora phonemes N < *\*no*, (perhaps also < *\*nu*, *\*myi*, *\*mu*); M < *\*myi*, *\*mu*; B < *\*bu*; G < *\*gu*; or K < *\*ku*, all but the last settling into N in NOk, and the last, into Q. Nor does it take account of the transitional *((C)ɹa,) Cɹi*, which quickly settled into *((C)wa* and) *(C)wi*.

27  That is, in a Japanese 50-syllable-chart-like framework.

34    CHAPTER 2

TABLE 2.7 High and mid vowel mergers (*gojūon*)

| | | 1 | 2 | 3 | 4 | 5 | 6 | 7 | 8 | 9 | 10 | 11 | 12 | 13 | 14 | |
|---|---|---|---|---|---|---|---|---|---|---|---|---|---|---|---|---|
| | | *ʔ∅ | *k∅ | *g∅ | *s∅ | *z∅ | *t∅ | *d∅ | *n∅ | *p∅ | *b∅ | *m∅ | *y∅ | *r∅ | *w∅ | |
| [-ba] | *[+hi] | ʔyi | k°yi | gyi | syi | zyi | c°yi | dʑyi | nyi | p°yi | byi | myi | yi | ryi | wyi? | A |
| | *[-hi] | | kʰi | gi | si | zi | tʰi | di | ni | pʰi | bi | mi | | ri | wi? | B |
| [+ba] | *[+hi] | ʔu | k°u | gu | si | zi | c°i | dʑi | nu | p°u | bu | mu | yu | ru | – | C |
| | *[-hi] | | kʰu | | su | zu | tʰu | du | | pʰu | | | | | wu | D |

## 2.3 *Vowels (Short, Long, Diphthongs)*

This is an appropriate place to point out the dual vocalic and consonantal character of the segment *y*. When we write *c°yi* [ʧʲi], we have two segments that share a "segment" between them, namely *c°y* and *yi*, but we do not write *ˣc°yyi*, since the *y* at the end of one is the *y* at the beginning of the other. In this sense, *y* has a dual consonantal and vocalic nature. The technique was used by Samuel E. Martin in Martin 1970, for the similar system of the dialect of Shodon, and continued further in Serafim 1985. We make no attempt to isolate *y* as specifically a unit of the consonant system or of the vowel system.

  The OOk vowel system is as follows:[28]

---

28 The similar OJ system has eight vowels, or, in any case, eight distinctions at the syllable level equivalent to what some scholars (such as ourselves) happen to ascribe to vowels at the phonemic level.

| A | B | C | C | C | B | A |
|---|---|---|---|---|---|---|
| î | ï | i | | u | | |
| ê | ë | e | | o | ö | ô |
| | | | *a* | | | |

The front-vowel distinctions are neutralized (= type C) after e.g. *r* (*ri* for earlier {*rî* ↔ *rï*} and *re* for earlier {*rê* ↔ *rë*}), but fully evident after e.g. *k* or *g* ({*kî* ↔ *kï*} and {*kê* ↔ *kë*} respectively). Similar statements hold for the other OJ consonants, which also affect the following "vowels." A vowel not taking part in the system of A/B distinctions is not marked with ˆ or with ¨, such as *a* or *u*, or is neutralized *i*, *e*, or *o*. Both types are designated type C. An A-type vowel that has not been neutralized is marked with a circumflex, e.g. *ê*, and a B-type, with a dieresis, e.g. *ë*. Their determination as A- or B-types is based on their function in alternations in the OJ derivational and conjugational systems.

# SPELLING SYSTEM AND PHONOLOGY

|  | [+front] | | | [−front] | | | |
|---|---|---|---|---|---|---|---|
|  | [+pal] | | [−pal] | | [−back] | | [+back] |
| [+hi] | yi(i) | [⁽ʸ⁾i(ː)] | i(i) | [ɪ(ː)] | i(i) [ɨ(ː)] | u(u) | [u(ː)] |
| [−hi, −lo] | ye(e) | [⁽ʸ⁾e(ː)] | e(e) | [ɛ(ː)] |  | o(o) | [ɔ(ː)] |
| [+lo] |  |  |  |  | a(a) [ɑ(ː)] |  |  |

The vowel *i* occurs only after the sibilants [s] and [z], in *s* [s], *c* [ts], and *z* [z], *dz* [dz], respectively, where the offglides of the affricates are essentially [s] and [z], respectively.

This system is like vowel systems in Northern Amami: there, a typical system may have seven or eight vowels, and the "extra" vowels will usually be weakly fronted, non-palatal[29] vowels, like the *[ɛ] of pre-OOk and the [ɪ] of OOk. If one looks at a map of the Northern Ryukyuan dialects, one is struck by the fact that the transition to such systems is in southern Amami, and that the transition from lack of an aspiration distinction to having one is even farther south, around halfway up the main island of Okinawa. So it appears that Shuri probably functioned as a central point from which loss of such features spread, probably by the 18th century.

By definition, no vowel-initial moras exist. What appears to be a vowel by itself is either a glottal stop plus a vowel (*ʔV* [ʔV]) or a homorganic glide plus a vowel (*yi* or *ye* or *wu* or *wo*):

*ʔV*: OOk

*ʔa*:   *ʔagaruyi* 'east' (OS 4.#198 < *\*ʔagar-u-pe* 'ris-ing-direction'; NOk *ʔagári* [ʔagaˈɾʲi] [OGJ 103b]).[30]

*ʔyi*:   *ʔyidzi-kʰu* 'brave-one' = 'soldier' < *\*ʔyidu-kʰo* (OS 3.#93); *ʔyimi* 'dream' (OS 12.#730 < *\*ʔyime* ← *\*yume*; NOk *ʔyimi,* [OGJ 254b]).

ˣ*ʔi*:   (Does not exist in glottal-initial syllables.)

*ʔu*:   *ʔukʰi-yuru* 'Uke (and) Yoro (islands)' (OS 13.#938).

*ʔyee*:   *ʔyee-cʰyi* '(one's) opposite number' (OS 6.#297 < *\*ʔaf-yi-tʰye*); NOk *ʔyee-ₜtiⱼ* 1. 'opposite number'; 2. 'the same degree of ability'. (OGJ 184b).

---

29   In the usage in this work, the sense of the term "palatal" is of phonetically having a palatal, yod-like onset to a strongly fronted vowel, save for after [ʃ] and [ʒ], where the palatal onset is indistinguishable from the preceding fricative.

30   See details in Ch. 4 § 4.2 fn. 62.

| ʔoo: | ʔoor-a-cʰyi 'fanning [it]' (OS 13.#853); cf. early MJ afur- '(it) fans'. |
| ʔayi: | ʔayi·r-u 'ripen' (OS 14.#983) > NOk ʔyée-y-u-N '(milk/pus) drips out' (OGJ 183b); cf. OJ aye- 'ripen (and fall)'. |
| ʔawu: | ʔawu-nu-tʰakʰi-ʔupʰu-nusyi 'The Great Guardian[-Deity] of Ō-no-Take' (OS 5.#237). |

'V: OOk

| yi: | yii-zukʰu ⟨···zu*···⟩[31] 'military/cargo ship' (lit. 'goodbottom', [yiːzukʰu]) < *yee-zoko ← *yee- 'good' + -"- 'COP$_{RT}$' + soko 'bottom' (OS 1.#17). |
| wu: | wuna·ryi-gamyi ⟨···ga*···⟩ 'sister-priestess' [wunaɾʲigamʲi] (OS 13.#792). (yee = [yɛː]). woo = [wɔː] ⟨wa u⟩ 'King' (OS 3.#151). |

In medial position a sequence of vowels is either a diphthong, a long vowel, or a sequence of two instances of the same vowel in different syllables, but, in the latter case, with the second vowel preceded by a rearticulation, or hiatus, shown by /'/:

diphthongs:

| a'yi | ⟨ne ga i⟩ 'praying' = niga'yi [nĩgaʲi] ~ nigee [nĩgɛː] |
| awu | ⟨a o ri ya pe⟩ '(the priestess) Aoriyae' = ʔawuryayi [ʔawuɾʲaʲi] |
| i'yi | ⟨su pe⟩ 'spiritual.power-1a' = siyi [siʲi] ʔ~ sii [siː] |
| iwu | ⟨ⁿke o⟩ 'spiritual.power-2' = giwu [gɪʷu] |
| i'yi | ⟨se i⟩ 'spiritual.power-1b' = siyi [sɪʲi] ʔ~ sii [sɪː] |
| u'yi | ⟨o mo i⟩ 'thinking (fondly of)' = ʔumuyi [ʔumuʲi] ~ ʔumii [ʔumɪː] |

long vowels:

| / | yii | ii | ïi | uu | | = | [$^{(y)}$iː | ɪː | | ïː | uː |
| | yee | ee | | oo | | | $^{(y)}$eː | ɛː | | | ɔː |
| | | | aa | | / | | | | | ɑː | | ] |

geminate vowels:
The two members of a geminate vowel are in different syllables:
/···u'u/ = /···u-u/

---

31    In Ch. 1, fn. 15, there is a discussion of the use in TOS of the raised asterisk "*" and the raised dagger "†". While NOk compounds with yii- 'good-' attach to originally voiceless-obstruent-initial items without any voicing in the compound, the opposite is true in OOk, with voiceless-initial going to voiced, as here.

SPELLING SYSTEM AND PHONOLOGY

## 3 Suprasegmentals

There can be no doubt that OOk had an accentual system, and that it gave rise to the Shuri-dialect accentual system of the 20th century that has been extensively described.[32] However, the OS materials, as far as we are aware, give no indication of accent, and therefore we are unable to reconstruct accent using those materials. Henceforth we will have nothing to say about OOk accent, though we will as a matter of course give accent data for other dialects where they are available, such as e.g. NOk (Modern Okinawan) or Modern Japanese standard dialect.

The NOk of OGJ had only an accented ↔ unaccented distinction in all the major lexical classes of its vocabulary. We show "Accented" positionally, over a specific "*V́*", even though in fact it could—as in OGJ—be shown with a suffixed accentual flag; and we show "Unaccented" with a postposed uptilt, since some speakers use this style of speech when concatenating unaccented accent phrases: "*Word⌐*".

For Length, we use Vowel Doubling "*VV*", instead of "*V:*" or "*V̄*".[33] However, length of either vowels or consonants is shown by [:] in *phonetic* brackets.

## 4 Consonants

See the chart of the OOk consonants with comments in footnotes, in § 2.1.

### 4.1 *Obstruents*

OOk consonants have five places of articulation: (1) labial (p°, pʰ, b, m, w), (2) coronal (t°, tʰ, c°, cʰ, s, d, dz, z), (3) post-alveolar (c°y, cʰy, sy, dzy, zy), (4) velar (k°, kʰ, g), and (5) glottal (ʔ, ').

### 4.1.1 Labial Stops
#### 4.1.1.1 *The Phonemes /p°/ and /pʰ/*
On the basis of the short tables immediately below, we can safely say that there is a distinction in ##- and #-initial position[34] between ⟨pu⟩ and ⟨po⟩, i.e.:

$$(\#)\#\_\_\_: \{\langle pu \rangle \leftrightarrow \langle po \rangle\}$$

with certain lexical provisos that vouchsafe the distinction.

---

32  For an overview of Ryukyuan accentual (pre)history, see Shimabukuro (2007).

33  Long *yi* is shown by doubling of the vowel nucleus: *yii*. Phonetically, [ʲiː].

34  See § 4.4 for non-initial position.

38                   CHAPTER 2

TABLE 2.8 OOk /p°u/ and /pʰu/, and OJ correspondences

| OOk | ⟨··· ū⟩ = | $\overline{°u}$ | :: | OJ | $\bar{u}$ | | |
|------|-----------|------|----|----|------|------|------|
| OOk | ⟨pūẏ{u/o}⟩ | $p\overline{°u}yu$ 'winter' | :: | OJ | $pu\underset{.}{y}u$ | '(id)' | (JDB 643c) |
| OOk | ⟨pū ru⟩ | $p\overline{°u}ru$- 'old-' | :: | OJ | $puru$- | '(id)' | (JDB 644df) |
| | | | | | | | |
| OOk | ⟨··· ō⟩ = | $\overline{ʰu}$ | :: | OJ | $o/\bar{o}/\hat{o}$ | | |
| OOk | ⟨pō si⟩ | $p\overline{ʰu}syi$- 'desire' | :: | OJ | $p\dot{o}ri\text{-}s_{SI}$- | '(id)' | (JDB 662a) |
| OOk | ⟨pō tō ke⟩ | $p\overline{ʰu}t°uk^{h}i$ 'the Buddha' | :: | OJ | $pot\bar{o}k\ddot{e}$ | '(id)' | (JDB 657ab) |

Clearly the distinction has to be one of some kind of labial stops. Languages do not typically have two kinds of voiceless labial fricative ("f") phonemes; further, we already have determined that there is a {/C°/ ↔ /Cʰ/} distinction among the phonetic-stop-initial obstruents (i.e. the stops and affricates). The natural choice, then, is a {/C°/ ↔ /Cʰ/} distinction in the labial stops, as well. Since the "o"-row *kana* typify the aspirated of the distinct segments, ⟨po⟩ should be /pʰu/. That leaves a ⟨pu⟩ :: /p°u/ correlation. These correlations closely fit the known facts of Japanese language history as well, as an OOk :: OJ correlation shows (see Table 2.8).

#### 4.1.1.2 *Evidence for* {pʰu ↔ p°u} *in OS*[35]

Boiling down the basic evidence for a {p°u ↔ pʰu} distinction, we present Tables 2.9[36] and 2.10 on page 39.[37,38]

–  /p°/ = ⟨p(u)⟩: 2 lexemes; /pʰ/ = ⟨p(o)⟩: 2 lexemes;
  /pʰ/ = ⟨p(u)⟩ ~ ⟨p(o)⟩: 1 lexeme

---

[35] This is evidence for *p···* in initial or (historically) postconsonantal position. For postvocalic position, see §4.5, "Semivowels: /y/, /w/."

[36] 01 ふ (く) ⟨pu k(u)⟩, 02 ふく ⟨pu ku⟩, 03 ふ (む) ⟨pu m(u)⟩, 04 ふな~ふね ⟨pu na-⟩ ~ ⟨pu ne⟩, 05 ふ (る) ⟨pu r(u)⟩, 06 ふさ- ⟨pu sa-⟩, 07 ふた~ふて ⟨pu ta-~ pu te-⟩, 08 ふゆ~ふよ ⟨pu yu⟩ ~ ⟨pu yo⟩.

[37] 01 ほか ⟨po ka⟩, 02 ほろめかば† ⟨po ro me ka ba†⟩, 03,04 ほし ⟨po si⟩, 05 ほてらちへ ⟨po te ra ti pe⟩, 06 ほとけ ⟨po to ke⟩, 07,08 ほう ⟨po u⟩.

[38] Concerning 02 in Table 2.10, cf. J *hono-mék-u* 'glimmer, be faintly visible'; ⟨po ro me ka ba†⟩ is found in TOS 15.#1122.

# SPELLING SYSTEM AND PHONOLOGY

39

TABLE 2.9   OOk /p°/

## /p°/: 21 morphs

|    | Morph | Gloss | ⟨pu⟩ | ⟨po⟩ |
|----|-------|-------|------|------|
| 01 | *p°uk-* | 'blow' | 27 | ∅ |
| 02 | *p°uk°u* | 'hamlet' | 38 | ∅ |
| 03 | *p°um-* | 'step, stamp' | 33 | ∅ |
| 04 | *p°una- ~ p°uni* | 'boat, ship' | 89 | ∅ |
| 05 | *p°ur-* | 'precipitate' | 14 | ∅ |
| 06 | *p°usa'-* | 'prosper' | 34 | ∅ |
| 07 | *p°utʰa- ~ p°utʰi-* | 'two' | 07 | ∅ |
| 08 | *p°uyu* | 'winter' | 07 | ∅ |
|    |       | Total | 249 | ∅ |

TABLE 2.10   OOk /pʰ/

## /pʰ/: 8 morphs

|    | Morph | Gloss | ⟨pu⟩ | ⟨po⟩ |
|----|-------|-------|------|------|
| 01 | *pʰukʰa* | 'outside' | ∅ | 04 |
| 02 | *pʰuru·mik-ʰa-ba* | 'if (the breeze) sighs' | ∅ | 02 |
| 03 | *pʰu·sy-* | 'desire' ADJ | ∅ | 07 |
| 04 | *pʰusyi* | 'star; planet' | ∅ | 05 |
| 05 | *pʰu(-)t°ir-a-c°yi* | 'lighting (it) up' | ∅ | 02 |
| 06 | *pʰut°ukʰi* | 'the Buddha' | ∅ | 04 |
| 07 | *pʰuu* | 'sail' | ∅ | 17 |
| 08 | *pʰuu* | '(grain-)ear' | ∅ | 04 |
|    |       | Total | ∅ | 45 |

Two related lexemes are found in the data, with different contexts of occurrence and with different aspiration markings.[39],[40]

| | Morph | Gloss | ⟨pu⟩ | ⟨po⟩ |
|---|---|---|---|---|
| 01 | *p ̊uu-* | 'bounti(ful)-': | | |
| | | **Total for this morph** | 15 | ∅ |
| 02 | *-pʰuu* | '-bounty' | | |
| | | ⟨po u⟩ | ∅ | 53 |
| | | ⟨po u o⟩ | ∅ | 01 |
| | | ⟨pu u⟩ | 02 | ∅ |
| | | **Total for this morph:** | 02 | 54 |

---

39    The prefixal element *p ̊uu-* (01) is a back-formation (has "calved off") from the -[*kʰa*]#*pʰuu* that means good luck, but *pʰuu* is never itself word initial. Thus the two lexemes appear in complementary slots: *p ̊uu* word-initially and ...*-pʰuu* word medially. How this came about is not clear.

      ふうよせる ⟨pū_u yo se ru⟩ *p ̄ ̊uu yu·si·r-u* 'which attracts bounty', 1 token (TOS 12.#709); ふうくに ⟨pū_u ku ni⟩ *p ̄ ̊uu-k ̊unyi* 'bountiful country', 7 tokens (TOS 2.#82, etc.); ふ(う)まわり ⟨pū_(u) ma wa ri⟩ *p ̄ ̊uu-mawaryi* 'the cape at Iheya' *lit.* 'bounty circumnavigation', 2 tokens (TOS 17.#1217, 18.#1262); ふため ⟨pū ta me⟩ *p ̄ ̊u(u)-tʰami* 'bounty, good fortune', 5 tokens (TOS 11.#560, etc.).

40    The forms of the lexeme *-pʰuu* = (02) in OOk and NOk suggest that it was borrowed twice, once before Okinawan had CwV syllables, which developed naturally in MOk, and once after. The OOk form is *kʰ_apʰuu*, and the freely occurring variant of this word in NOk is *kwafuu,* '(to happen upon) good luck' (OGJ 348a) (except for *k_afuu-syi,* 'thanks!' (OGJ 301a)). Its combining form, however, is *-gafuu*, without the *w*, probably because the forms, or at least the formant, are/is (a) holdover(s) from the older form, e.g. *yu-gáfuu* 'year of bountiful harvest' (OGJ 286a).

  –   かほう ⟨ka po u⟩ *kʰapʰuu-* 'bountiful, happiness-attracting'; ~くに ⟨~ ku ni⟩ *-k ̊unyi* 'bountiful country'; ~さうず゛゜ ⟨~ sa u zu゜⟩ *~-soozi* 'good-fortune-bringing holy-water'; ~せぢ゛ ⟨~ se di゛⟩ *~-sidzyi* 'bountiful spiritual power'; ~てだ゛ ⟨~ te da゛⟩ *~-tʰi(i)da* 'Bountiful Lord'; ~とき/時 ⟨~ to ki / TOKI⟩ *~-tʰuk ̊yi* 'auspicious time'; ~ど†し ⟨~ do†si⟩ *~-dusyi* 'bountiful year'; ~とみ ⟨~ to mi⟩ *~-tʰumyi* 'HMS Bountiful (ship name)'; ~も〻ゑらび ⟨~ mo " we ra bi⟩ *~ mumu-?yi ̩rab-yi* 'Carefully Chosen for Bounty (ship name)'; ~よせぐ゛゜すく ⟨~ yo se gu゛su ku⟩ *~-yusi-gusik ̊u* 'bounty-attracting castle'; ~よるみやがのもり ⟨~-yo ru mi ya ga no mo ri⟩ *~-yu·r-u my-aaga-nu muryi* 'Bounty-Attracting Revered Shrine';

  –   よの~ ⟨yo no ~⟩ *yuu-nu-kʰapʰuu* 'bountiful time in the world'. Cf. NOk *yu-gáfuu* 'year of bountiful harvest' (OGJ 286a); ˣ*yuu-nu-kafuu.*

## SPELLING SYSTEM AND PHONOLOGY

*(cont.)*

| | Morph | Gloss | ⟨pu⟩ | ⟨po⟩ |
|---|---|---|---|---|
| 03 | -*p°uk°uryi,* | '(part of priestess name)', | 01, | ∅, |
| | *p°uk°uryi-;*[41] | '(part of person's name)'; | 01; | ∅; |
| | *pʰukʰur-*[42] | 'gladden' VI | ∅ | 58 |
| | | **Total for this morph:** | 02 | 58 |
| | | | (0) | (58) |
| | | | | |
| 04[43] | *ʔuuk°yi-ʔup°u#dzyi,* | 'male ancestor | 02, | ∅, |
| | *ʔuuk°yi#ʔupʰu#dzyi;* | (*lit.* great great grandfather)' | ∅; | 15; |
| | *ʔupʰu-tʰaa-baru;* | '(PLN, *lit.* great paddy field)'; | ∅; | 01; |
| | *ʔupʰu-guru-t°aa* | 'the great men' | ∅ | 01 |
| | | **Total for this morph:** | 02 | 17 |

---

41　ふくりにせ ⟨pu ku ri ni se⟩: There are 2 tokens of ふくり ⟨pū ku ri⟩ *p°uk°uryi*: きみふくり ⟨ki mi pū ku ri⟩ *k°yimyi-p°uk°ur-yi* '(priestess name)' and ふくりにせ ⟨pū ku ri ni se⟩ *p°uk°ur-yi-nyii-see* 'PN' = 'person worthy of receiving a deity's grace' (OKDJ 287b, TOS 21.#1397) appear in the same song. Either aspiration was irregularly lost in these two instances, or this is a nominalization from the RY of a lost verb *\*pukur-* VI 'puff up', entirely supplanted by *\*pukure-* '(id.)' > *fúQkwi-* (OGJ 220b). (It may also be that the RY of the original verb, seen in our example *p°uk°ur-yi*, having become *p°uQkw°yi* through regular sound change, served as the base for a newly reanalyzed *r*-stem verb paradigm with stable stem [*p°uQk°wyi(·r)-*] that supplanted the now alternating stem forms of the pre-sound-change paradigm.)

42　There are 58 tokens of ほこ ⟨pō ko⟩ *pʰukʰu*⋯ 'gladden$_{VI}$': 10 of the MZ ほこら ⟨pō ko ra⟩ *pʰukʰur-a*(⋯); 4 of the GER ⟨pō ko te⟩ ほこて *pʰukʰu-tʰi*; 37 of variants of the RY form ⟨pō ko ri⟩ ほこり *pʰukʰur-y(i)*(-); 6 of the SS/RT form ⟨pō ko ru⟩ ほこる *pʰukʰur-u*; and 1 of the IZ/MR form ⟨pō ko re⟩ ほこれ *pʰukʰur-i*.

43　*#ʔupʰu-* (~ (⋯)-*ʔup°u-*): ⟨o ki o pū di⁺ ga⁺ mo ri⟩ *ʔuu|k°yi-ʔup°u#dzyi-ga muryi* 'the Great Ancestral Shrine', 1 token; ⟨o ki o pū di ga⁺ mi ya⟩ ~-*myiya* '(id.)' (both OS 21.#1394); ⟨o ki o pō di⁺ ga⁺⟩ *ʔuuk°yi#ʔupʰu#dzyi-ga* 'Great Ancestor SUB' (OS 13.#777); ⟨o ki o pō di⁺ gi⁺ ya⟩ *ʔuuk°yi#ʔupʰu#dzyi-gya* 'Great Ancestor SUB' (OS 21.#1443); ⟨o ki o pō di⁺ gi⁺ ya mo ri⟩ (OS 11.#565); ⟨o pō ta ba⁺ ru⟩ *ʔupʰu-tʰa(a)-baru* 'Ōta-baru PLN' (OS 16.#1167); ⟨ge⁺ ra pe o pō go⁺ ro ta⟩ *girayi#ʔupʰu-guru-t°aa* 'the well wrought great men' (OSJS 152b; OS 12.#694). Thorpe (1983: 60–61) suggests that there *was* a medial pRk *\*p*, but that it might have remained as a reconstructable (by the Comparative Method) medial obstruent only if it was preceded by an expressive *\*Q*. Thus pRk *\*Qp* > NOk *p* ~ *f* in medial position. Possibly our single case of ⟨o pu di⟩ may have been meant to write *ʔuQp°u-dzyi*, as against ⟨o po di⟩ *ʔupʰu-dzyi*, with lost *Q*. Nb: medial ⋯*p*⋯ only if *\*Qp*.

42                                                                    CHAPTER 2

4.1.2      Coronal Obstruents
OOk has a rich assortment of coronal obstruents. They are as follows, and are
treated below:
(1)   Stops:
       (a)   Voiceless: unaspirated: $t°$; aspirated: $t^h$; (b) Voiced: $d$:
              *T-form of r-type verb: ʔaga-t̲°i*
              *t̲ʰii* 'hand'
              *-d̲u* 'ᴋᴘ'
(2)   Affricates:
       (a)   Voiceless: $c°$, $c^h$; $c°y$, $c^hy$; subcategories:
              (i)    Unaspirated: dental/alveolar: $c°$; post-alveolar $c°y$:
                     *c̲°iru* '[musical-instrument] string(s)' (ᴏsᴊs 228c; ᴏs 14.#1044)
                     *c̲°yiryi-sabyi* 'plant rust' (ᴏsᴊs 222a; ᴏs 5.#242)
              (ii)   Aspirated: dental/alveolar: $c^h$; post-alveolar $c^hy$:
                     *c̲ʰV* none
                     *-c̲ʰyi* '-hand' [in compounds]
       (b)   Voiced affricates: dental/alveolar: $dz$; post-alveolar $dzy$:
              *ʔyid̲z̲i#k^hu* 'brave men'
              *ʔyid̲z̲yi-ru* 'to exit'
(3)   Fricatives:
       (a)   Voiceless: dental/alveolar: $s$; post-alveolar $sy$:
              *sid̲z̲i-nar-yi* '(priestess name)' (ᴏsᴊs 188d–189a)
              *s̲yima* 'district'
       (b)   Voiced: dental/alveolar: $z$; post-alveolar $zy$
              *-k^haaz̲i* '(plural marker)'
              *-z̲yu* 'ᴋᴘ' (special case of voicing of ᴋᴘ that takes ɪᴢ ending)

4.1.2.1      *The Phoneme /t^h/*
The graphs ⟨ta⟩, ⟨te⟩, and ⟨to⟩ all represent originally low or mid vowels, analo-
gous to the case of the velars (⟨ka⟩, ⟨ke⟩, ⟨ko⟩) and the labials (⟨pa⟩, ⟨pe⟩, ⟨po⟩).
While straightforward pairings of aspirated ⟨Ce⟩, a non-high-vowel set, and
non-aspirated ⟨Ci⟩, a high-vowel set, are possible for the velars and the labials,
...

| ⟨ki⟩ | ↔ | ⟨ke⟩ | ⟨pi⟩ | ↔ | ⟨pe⟩ | but | __ | ↔ | ⟨te⟩ |
| $k°yi$ | ↔ | $k^hi$ | $p°yi$ | ↔ | $p^hi$ | | | __ | ↔ | $t^hi$ |

... the graphs that are expected to fill the "__" slots for dentals/alveolars are
⟨ti⟩ and $c°yi$; they are part of a separate affricate group, which has come about
through affrication of {⟨ti⟩ = \*$t°yi$ [t°ʸi]} > {⟨ti⟩ = $c°yi$ [ʧ°i]}.

SPELLING SYSTEM AND PHONOLOGY

A parallel narrative obtains for the back-vowel grapheme set ⟨ta⟩, ⟨to⟩, and ⟨tu⟩, although this time the affricated element, while present as expected, will be lacking palatality, but have a vowel that has lost its rounding:

| ⟨ku⟩ | ↔ | ⟨ko⟩ | ⟨pu⟩ | ↔ | ⟨po⟩ | ⟨tu⟩ | ↔ | ⟨to⟩ |
|---|---|---|---|---|---|---|---|---|
| $k°u$ | ↔ | $k^hu$ | $p°u$ | ↔ | $p^hu$ | $\underline{c°ɨ}$ | ↔ | $t^hu$ |

The OOk-period ⟨tu⟩ = $c°ɨ$ is from earlier *⟨tu⟩ = *$t°u$.

Of course it hardly need be said that the three-grapheme set ⟨ka⟩, ⟨pa⟩, ⟨ta⟩ is phonemically $k^ha$, $p^ha$, and $t^ha$, respectively.

### 4.1.2.2    *The Phoneme /d/*

The only two things of any significance to say about the ⟨d···⟩-initial graphs are: (1) In all copies of the OS except TOS, which has endeavored for completeness, voicing marks are frequently left out, so that the reader of this work will see graphemic representations such as ⟨⁽"⁾ta⟩ standing for *da*. (2) As with the voiceless set ⟨ti⟩ = $c°yi$, ⟨tu⟩ = $c°ɨ$, so, too, the voiced set has etymologically high-vowel affricates: ⟨⁽"⁾ti⟩ = *ʒyi*, ⟨⁽"⁾tu⟩ = *ʒɨ*, with vowel coloration as given before.

In effect, then, for both etymological *t-* and *d-*initial sets, the moras that consisted of those consonants plus etymological *-a*, *-e*, and *-o* (i.e. *ta*, *te*, *to* > $t^ha$, $t^hi$, $t^hu$; *da*, *de*, *do* > *da*, *di*, *du*) were the only *t-* or *d-*initial moras that remained. (This is a simplified view, since new monophthongs were forming from older diphthongs that reintroduced $t^he$, $t^ho$ and *de*, *do*. Cf. § 4.5.)

### 4.1.3    Velars

OOk has a three-way distinction in the velar obstruents, and has no other velars at all. The obstruents are: $k°$, $k^h$, and $g$. The major differentiation is by voicing: $k°$, $k^h$ :: $g$; and the voiceless obstruent set, as with the other voiceless stops and affricates, is differentiated by aspiration: $k°$ [– aspirated], $k^h$ [+ aspirated].

### 4.1.3.1    *The Phonemes /k°/ and /kʰ/*

Cf. § 2.2.2. on the aspiration distinction between the voiceless velars, and the methodology for discovering it, which also applies to all the other aspirated ↔ unaspsirated pairs.

### 4.1.3.2    *The Glottal Stop /ʔ/ and the Glottal Continuant /'/*

We assume that whenever a "vowel-initial" (i.e. *a-gyō* ア行) graph is word-initial, it actually begins with a glottal stop = /ʔ/, and is differentiated from certain otherwise overlapping moras of the "w-initial" (i.e. *wa-gyō* ワ行) or "y-initial" (i.e. *ya-gyō* ヤ行) graph sets.

The glottal continuant /'/ is a sort of "ghost segment," in that its use can usually be dispensed with, with no harm done to the notation of actual words. This is similar to the use of the same consonant in OGJ, where all smooth-vowel-onset and glide-onset syllables are defined as beginning with this segment. However, other than in word-initial position the use of the segment is dispensed with. We use it mainly to distinguish cases where diphthongs are free to monophthongize, and frequently and concomitantly where *yi* sequences can trigger PP, as in the form $t^hat^hu'yi$-$c°yi$, which pairs as word-play with $t^hat^huyi$-$t°i$, both meaning 'likening' (cf. §5.1). The former word has a CGV syllable, and the latter, CV, thus blocking PP.

### 4.1.3.3     *Voiced Stops: /b, d, g/*

As has already been mentioned for *d*, all graphemes meant as voiced frequently have no voicing marks, so a set of graphs constituting that grapheme is {⟨"CV⟩, ⟨CV⟩}, and is represented by the abbreviated grapheme ⟨(")CV⟩. Thus the grapheme for *ba* is ⟨⟨は(")⟩⟩ {⟨は⟩, ⟨ば⟩} = ⟨⟨(")pa⟩⟩ {⟨pa⟩, ⟨"pa⟩}, where for ⟨"pa⟩ we normally write ⟨ba⟩.

### 4.2     *Fricatives and Affricates: Two Sets of Two* Yotsu-Gana

#### 4.2.1     The Heretofore-Introduced Phonemes /z/, /zy/, and /s/, /sy/

Four consonant phonemes are represented by the *s*-initial (*sa-gyō* サ行) set of graphs. Two sets are divided by whether their morphs can occur with voicing marks, and these can be shown with ⟨(")si⟩ = *zyi* [ʒi], and ⟨(")sV⟩ (all other vowel graphs) = *zV* (likewise). The cases that never appear with voicing marks can be assumed, barring extenuating circumstances, to represent the voiceless set, ⟨si⟩ and ⟨sV⟩, as in the above case with the voiced set:

| | [+ **voi**] | [− **voi**] |
|---|---|---|
| [+ back] | ず・す | す |
| | ⟨zu · su⟩ | ⟨su⟩ |
| [− back] | じ・し | し |
| | ⟨zi · si⟩ | ⟨si⟩ |

#### 4.2.1.1     *Phonemes /dz/ and /dzy/, and /z/ and /zy/*

It has often been claimed—e.g. Takahashi (1991a: 60–61)—that there is no /z/ ↔ /dz/ distinction in the OS, just as there is not any in NOk, and that therefore the OS language only has a *zyi* ↔ *zi* distinction. The basis for the "no-distinction"

SPELLING SYSTEM AND PHONOLOGY                                       45

argument is typically through comparison with Japanese, where it is pointed out that Okinawan has fricative spelling (i.e. *za-gyō* spelling) where Japanese historical orthography has affricate spelling (i.e. *da-gyō* spelling). What is overlooked, however, is that when Japanese orthography is left out of the picture and tokens of the same morph are compared to each other in the Okinawan spelling, that spelling is typically quite consistent, with almost no exceptions. For further discussion, see § 5.4.

### 4.2.1.2    The Phonemes /dz/ and /dzy/

The graphemes づ・つ ⟨<sup>(n)</sup>tu⟩ and ず・す ⟨<sup>(n)</sup>su⟩ are distinguished, that is, each is kept to its own set of morphs, and not intermixed with the other grapheme's morphs; therefore they constitute the ways of writing *dzi* and *zi*, respectively.

The same holds true for ぢ・ち ⟨<sup>(n)</sup>ti⟩ and じ・し ⟨<sup>(n)</sup>si⟩; therefore they constitute the ways of writing *dzy(i)* and *zy(i)*, respectively. The parenthesized (*i*) is because ⟨···i⟩ graphs are also used to write the initial part of syllables with palatal elements that are followed by vowels other than *i*, e.g. ⟨dī yā (u)⟩ *dzyoo* 'gate' (e.g. os 16.#1133) and ⟨TUKI zi yo⟩ *cᵒikᵒyi-zyu* 'none other than the moon' (os 16.#1158).

### 4.3    Nasals: /m/, /n/

The distinction between the mora-initial nasal consonants *m* and *n* can be shown quite straightforwardly:

| ⟨a ma⟩ | *ʔama* | 'far away; the sky above' |
|---|---|---|
| ⟨a ma i⟩, ⟨a ma pe⟩ | *ʔamayi* | 'with pleasure' |
| ⟨te da ga a na⟩ | *tʰi(i)da-ga-ʔana* | 'the orifice for the sun' |

### 4.4    Semivowels: /y/, /w/

The semivowels are more complex because of the converging and splitting of interpretation of graph-phoneme pairs depending on context.

Parenthetically this includes the non-initial *\*p* moras—following a very different path from the initials (treated in § 4.1.1.1)—which lenited at least to *\*w*, the ones with following front vowels continuing to *\*y*, and in many cases in the modern dialects all traces of the medial *\*p* disappearing. In the os:

| *\*pa* | *\*po* | *\*pu* | *\*pe* | *\*pyi* |
|---|---|---|---|---|
| *wa* | *wo* | *wu* | *we* | *wyi* |
| *wa* | *wo* | *wu* | *ye* | *'yi* |
| *wa* | *(w)u* | *(w)u* | *yi* | *'yi* |

46                                                                CHAPTER 2

For *y*, the correspondences are as follows:

| *y* | Initial | | | |
| --- | --- | --- | --- | --- |
| や ⟨ya⟩ | *ya | > *ya* | ⟨ya⟩ や | |
| ゑ ⟨we⟩ | *ye | > *yi* | ⟨we⟩ ゑ[44] | |
| よ ⟨yo⟩ | *yo | ⎫ | | |
| ゆ ⟨yu⟩ | *yu | ⎭ > *yu* | ⟨yo, yu⟩ よ, ゆ | |

| *y* | Medial | | | Medial  Secondary *y* |
| --- | --- | --- | --- | --- |
| や ⟨ya⟩ | *ya | > *ya* | ⟨ya⟩ や | |
| ゑ ⟨we⟩ | *ye | > *yi* | ⟨we⟩ ゑ | ⁽ʼ⁾*yi* < *ye, 'yi* ⟨pe⟩ へ; ⟨i⟩ い, ⟨pi⟩ ひ, ⟨wi⟩ ゐ[45] |
| よ ⟨yo⟩ | *yo | ⎫ | | |
| ゆ ⟨yu⟩ | yu | ⎭ > *yu* | ⟨yo, yu⟩ よ, ゆ | |

As can be seen, there is a convergence of graphs ⟨we⟩ and ⟨i⟩ on medial *yi*. Other graphs also converge on *yi* in medial position, namely ⟨pe, pi, wi⟩:

⟨we, pe ⟩ > *yi* / ⟨···V⟩___ (takes part in 2nd Monophthongization)

⟨wi, i, pi⟩ :: *'yi* / ⟨···V⟩___ (takes part in 1st Monophthongization)

The effects of this convergence can be seen everywhere in the os, as for example in the pair ⟨a ma i⟩ ~ ⟨a ma pe⟩ *ʔamayi* 'with pleasure', on a previous page.

Similarly, for *w*, the correspondences are as follows:

---

44  NOk *wikiga,* 'man' (OGJ 595a) indicates that some of the pre-OOk ⟨we⟩ :: *wi* [wɪ] correlation remained. Cf. KKKS (Kon, Jinrin) ⟨(ma) we ke ga⟩ *(ma-)wikʰi-ga* [mɑwɪkʰīgɑ] 'a man₍ₑₓ₎' [> NOk *wikiga,* '(id.)' (OGJ 595a)] → OS ⟨we ku ga⟩ *wik°uga* [wɪk°(ũ)ga] /ʔ/ *wigⁱa* [wĩg:ga] 'a man' (OSJS 370a; e.g. TOS 21.#1403); ⟨we ke ri⟩ *wikʰiryi* 'brother (as seen by sister)' > NOk *wikíyi* '(id.)' (OGJ 595b). This further suggests that those who were literate had either to learn one correlation (⟨we⟩ :: *yi*) and a list of exceptions to it (with ⟨we⟩ :: *wi*), or else simply had to learn which of the two correlations went with which word.

45  Cf. fn. 4.

SPELLING SYSTEM AND PHONOLOGY 47

| *w* | Initial | | |
|---|---|---|---|
| わ ⟨wa⟩ | :: | *wa | > *wa* |
| ゑ ⟨we⟩[46] | :: | *we | ⎫ |
| ゐ ⟨wi⟩ | :: | *wi | ⎬ > *yi* |
| を, お ⟨wo, 'o⟩ | :: | *wo | ⎫ |
| う ⟨'u⟩ | :: | *(u) | ⎬ > *wu* |

| *w* | Medial | | |
|---|---|---|---|
| わ ⟨wa⟩ | *wa | > *wa* < ⟨pa⟩ は |
| ゑ ⟨we⟩ | *we | ⎫ |
| ゐ ⟨wi⟩ | *wi | ⎬ > *yi* < ⟨i⟩ い, ⟨pe⟩ へ, ⟨pi⟩ ひ |
| を, お ⟨wo, 'o⟩ | *wo | ⎫ |
| う ⟨'u⟩ | *wu | ⎬ > *wu* < ⟨pu⟩ ふ ⟨po⟩ ほ |

For details refer back to § 2.2.1.

4.4.1      The Moras *ʔo and *wo (OOk ʔu and *wu*)
The two examples below show that the mora graphs ⟨wo⟩ and ⟨'o⟩ are used
interchangeably:

を も わ れ ゝ ⟨w̄o mo wa re "⟩ ʔ̄u mu wa ri ri (os 5.#261)
お も わ れ ゝ ⟨'ō   mo wa re "⟩ ʔ̄u mu wa ri ri (os 14.#1042)
'will (truly) be loved/ thought of'

It is clear from the modern dialects, however, that words evincing the PJ *o ↔
*wo opposition retain it intact, as can independently be verified through com-
parison with Old Japanese texts, which also retained the PJ distinction. The
reason for the interchangeability of ⟨'o⟩ and ⟨wo⟩ is that Middle Japanese had
lost the distinction before Okinawan had borrowed the script, and of course the
usage that went with it, and thus it did not have a way to distinguish between

---

46      This line does not account for the few irregular cases of ⟨we⟩ = *wi*, as in *wikʰi-ga* 'man' <
     *weke-ga*. Cf. fn. 45, and Ch. 5 § 3.2, esp. fn. 25.

its—at that time—\*[ʔɔ] and \*[wɔ], nor later OOk [ʔu] and [wu], now with ⟨'u⟩ added. (There is no ˣ⟨wu⟩ graph.) The os-internal facts are laid out in Akiyama 1975.

### 4.5 Diphthongs: Monophthongized and Stable, with Semivowels

The main point to be kept in mind about Diphthongization and following Monophthongization is that in the late OOk and early MOk periods there were two separate Monophthongizations (the First ⁀ and the Second ⁀), and that the os language of late OOk lay squarely between them. Original diphthongs that had included either or both of the high-vowel offglides \*ʸyi or \*ʸ(w)u (not what were then \*(y)e or \*(w)o), had undergone both the First Diphthongization and First Monophthongization by the os period:[47,48]

First-Diphthongization and -Monophthongization, and raising:

| | D1 | | M1 | | R | | |
|---|---|---|---|---|---|---|---|
| \*a'yi | > | \*ay | > | \*ææ | > | ee [ɛː] | > | ee |
| \*o'yi | > | \*oy | >[49] | \*wee | > | (w)ii [⁽ʷ⁾ɪː] | > | |
| \*e'yi | > | \*ey | > | \*ee | > | | | |
| \*i'yi | > | \*iy | > | \*ii~ \*iyi | > | ii ~ iyi | > | (w)ii |
| \*u'yi | > | \*uy | > | \*wyii | > | (w)yii [⁽ʷ⁾ʸɪː] | > | |
| \*yi'yi | > | \*yiy | > | \*yii | > | | | |

---

47     Concerning the alternation ii ~ iyi in the following table, the only two cases that we are aware of are ⟨se⟩, ⟨se pe⟩ sii ~ ⟨su pe⟩, ⟨su we⟩ siyi 'spiritual power', and ⟨pu we no to ri⟩ ʔpˀuyi- / ʔpˀii- / ʔʔpˀiyi-nu-tʰuryi 'rooster', lit. 'sun-ny-bird' (os 13.#820). Even if construed as pˀii-nu-tʰuryi, this word has an irregular vowel for the regular pˀyii ⟨pi('i)⟩. Perhaps the spelling was an attempt to show that irregularity; the reason for it is unknown to us. In any case this is a hapax legomenon, since the two examples of the word occur in duplicate omoros: #821 and #1544. Book 22 (##1508–1554), the final one, consists almost entirely of duplicates of omoros that have occurred in earlier books.

48     Concerning the sound changes from \*e'wu to yuu in the following table, the only examples that we know of are ⟨ke yo⟩, ⟨ke 'o⟩, ⟨ki yo⟩ (the last one occurs twice in one omoro only [os15.#68]) kʰiyu ~ kʰyuu 'today' (os 1.#19). Cf. NOk LitOk kiyu, (OGJ 320b), ColloqOk cyuu, (OGJ 171a). As for external evidence, Lin (2015: 135) has #24. Chinese Corpus 交 kiau, Middle Korean Corpus 교요, i.e. kʰjo.o 'today'—our kʰyoo [kʰʸɔː]—which is one vowel height too low, and thus lies beyond explanation with our hypothesis.

49     Probably through wey.

## SPELLING SYSTEM AND PHONOLOGY

(*cont.*)

|  | D1 |  | M1 |  | R |  |
|---|---|---|---|---|---|---|
| *\*a'wu* | > | *\*aw* | > | *ɔɔ* | } | *oo* |
| *\*o'wu* | > | *\*ow* | > | *oo* | | |
| *\*e'wu* | > | *\*ew* | > | *yuu* | } | |
| *\*u'wu* | > | *\*uw* | > | *uu* | | *(y)uu* |
| *\*i'wu* | > | *\*iyu* | > | *yuu*[50] | | |
| *\*ɨ'wu* | > | *\*ɨw* | > | – | | |

On the other hand, sequences of the sort ( *\*awe* >) *\*aye*, ( *\*awo* >) *\*awu*, having developed too late to constitute input to the historical changes that gave rise to the First Monophthongization, underwent largely identical but later development, ending up merging with the older monophthongs. So:

Second-Diphthongization and -Monophthongization:

*\*aye* > OOk *ayi* > *ay* > *ɛɛ* > *ee*, and:
*\*awo* > OOk *awu* > *aw* > *ɔɔ* > *oo*

In the latter case—the one where the diphthongal form remains—there is no dropping of graphs corresponding to offglides, while in the former, one of the two allographs contains no graph corresponding to an offglide; indeed, in the case of ⟨ya⟩ -*yoo* 'way, manner, etc.', there is no two-graph allograph at all![51]

---

50 We believe that *ʔyu-u\** 'to say' (unattested) is a result of this.

51 It is spelled only with ⟨ya⟩ and lacks an alternant ˣ⟨ya ū⟩; this still does not mean that it is *ya(a)*: OKDJ (678d–679a) gives *yoo* for the MOk pronunciation of this word. For the phonological form *yoo* we assume pre-OOk *\*yawu* < SJ *yau* ⟨ya u⟩ 様 'way, means, ….' This assumption presupposes the fortuitous lack of ⟨ya ū⟩ as an allograph of ⟨ya⟩ in the OS, though indeed it appears that monosyllables are missing such allographs more often than non-monosyllables. If ⟨ya⟩ were to have an allograph *with* the missing ⟨u⟩—i.e. ⟨ya u⟩, then that would make it a member of a type identical to ⟨ti⁽ⁿ⁾ ya (u)⟩ *dzyoo* [dʒɔ:] 'gate' (NOk *zyoo*, [OGJ 603b]; *ʔyisyí-zyoo* 'stone gate' [OGJ 262a], *ʔyísyi* 'stone' [OGJ 261a]); *ʔyic˚ya-dzyoo* ⟨i ti ya ti⁽ⁿ⁾ ya⟩ 'timber gate' [OSJS 59a, 390c], *ʔyic˚ya* 'a board, a plank, a timber' (ROD Nk /hic˚yaʳa/ [çitʃˤaʳ:] 'board, plank'), ⟨ti⁽ⁿ⁾ ya (u)⟩ (-)*dzyoo* 'gate'. Concerning OS ···c˚y···, recall that *preceding* high vowel as *well* as following high vowel suppresses aspiration; therefore *ʔyic˚ya*, not ˣ*ʔyichʸya*. *\*dzyoo* [dʒɔ:] was already in existence when the *\*… awu* of *\*##yawu##* 'way, …' transformed from a two-vowel sequence to a diphthong *\*… aw* to a monophthong

50                                                                    CHAPTER 2

The normal sequence of monophthongizations is:

(1)   with high vowels:[52]

| *ayi | | > | ee | | and |
| *au | | > | oo; | | |
| *oyi, *uyi | | > | (w)ii | | and |
| *ou, *uu | | > | uu; | | |

(2)   with mid vowels:

| *aye | > | ayi | > | ee | and |
| *awo | > | awu | > | oo; | |
| *oye, *uye | > | (ʔ)uyi | > | (ʔ)(w)ii | and |
| *owo, *uwo | > | (ʔ)uwu | > | (ʔ)uu. | |

Put together in terms of relative sequencing, it looks like this:

| | **a** | > | **b** | | > | **c** | | > | **d** | | > | **e** |
|---|---|---|---|---|---|---|---|---|---|---|---|---|
| (1) | *ayi | > | ee | [ɛː] | > | ee | [ɛː] | > | ee | [ɛː] | | |
| ii | *awu | > | oo | [ɔː] | > | oo | [ɔː] | > | oo | [ɔː] | | |
| iii | *oyi | > | *(w)ɪɪ | [(ʷ)ɪː] | > | (w)ii | [(ʷ)ɪː] | > | (w)ii | [(ʷ)ʸiː] | | |
| iv | *uyi | > | *(w)yii | [(ʷ)ʸiː] | > | { yii [ʸiː] / <br> (w)ii [(ʷ)ɪː] | | > | yii [ʸiː] / <br> (w)ii [(ʷ)ʸiː] | | | |
| v | *owu | > | *ɔɔ | [ɔː] | > | oo | [ɔː] | > | oo | [ɔː] | | |
| vi | *uwu | > | uu | [uː] | > | uu | [uː] | > | uu | [uː] | | |
| (2) | *aye | > | *ayi | [aʸɪ] | > | ayi | [aʸi] | > | ee | [ɛː] | | |
| viii | *awo | > | *awu | [aʷʊ] | > | awu | [aʷu] | > | oo | [ɔː] | | |
| ix | *oye | > | *ɵyi | [ɵʸɪ] | > | uyi | [uʸi] | > | (w)ii | [(ʷ)ʸiː] | | |
| x | *uye | > | *uyi | [uʸɪ] | | | | | | | | |
| xi | *owo | > | *ɵwɵ | [ɵʷɵ] | > | uwu | [u'u] | > | uu | [uː] | | |
| xii | *uwo | > | *uwɵ | [uʷɵ] | | | | | | | | |

---

(through Mı) ... *oo* [ɔː], therefore becoming the first coalescence of pre-existing *[ɔː] (from retained long mid vowels, such as that of *ʤyoo *[ʤɔː]) and new Mı'ed *[ɔː] (< *aw < *awu).

52   Concerning *au > oo, see ⟨ya ni⟩ and its discussion immediately above.

SPELLING SYSTEM AND PHONOLOGY

## 4.6    *Mora Segments:* /M/, /N/, /B/, /G/, /K/, /Q/

For the four voiced-mora phonemes, we assume prenasalization, because of later developments in Okinawan-language phonology, such as (⟨i n(i y)a -⟩ *ʔyin(y)a-* [ʔyĩna]/[ʔyĩɳa] >) NOk *ʔnni,* 'riceplant' (OGJ 432b) or (⟨i de⟩ *ʔyidzyi* [ʔyĩdʒi] >) *ʔnzyi,* [ʔɲ:ʳdʒi] 'exit RY' (OGJ 433a).[53]

### 4.6.1    Mora Nasals

/M/   Mora nasal phoneme, [+ labial] articulation __#(#), __[+labial], __r; we assume prenasalization (though we may not always write it in phonetic notation); the phoneme frequently occurs before /r/, where it represents a shortening of *\*mu,* but only exceptionally *\*mo;* this means that *\*(...)mor* ... retains its *m,* as in *ʔumuru* < *\*omoro* 'omoro'.

/N/   this is the "elsewhere" mora nasal phoneme, where /M/ is not to be used; we assume that, as in NOk, it acquires the articulation of its following segment, except that before vowels or in final position it may have an incomplete velar or uvular closure.

### 4.6.2    Mora Voiced Obstruents

/B/   Clearly there has to have been a distinction between at least some *\*bo* > *bu* and some *\*bu* > *B;* otherwise there would be an irregular relationship between the spelling and the later NOk phonology; an example is *\*obotu* 'Heaven' > ⟨o bo tu⟩ (not ˣ⟨o bu tu⟩) *ʔubuc°i* and *\*mabur-u* 'protect' > ⟨ma bu ru⟩ (not ˣ⟨ma bo ru⟩) *maBru;* the modern form of the latter does not exist, but, for example, Venus, the Evening Star is in NOk called *yuu-baN#maNz-y-aa* lit. 'the evening-meal protector/viewer [with desire (to eat it)]' < *\*...#maBr-y-aa;* note that *\*bo* > *bu* and *\*bu* (here) > *B;* where *\*bu* was not converted to *B,* it merged with *\*bo* as *bu,* as with the PLN ⟨ma bu ni⟩ (OS 20.#1334) *mabunyi,* NOk *mabuyi,* (OGJ 355b) < *\*maburyi* ← *\*mabunyi.*

Apparently at least *\*__u{r/t}* functioned as environments for {*\*bu > B*}, so a near-minimal pair ⟨ka bu̅ to⟩ ↔ ⟨o bo̅ tu⟩, *kʰaB̅t°u* ↔ *ʔub̅uc°i,* 'helmet' ↔ 'Heaven (Above)', respectively, was a regularity easy for OOk speak-

---

53    ⟨i na mi ne⟩ *ʔyin(y)a-myin(y)i* [ʔˀĩɳãmʸĩɲi]/[ʔˀĩɳãmʸĩnɪ] (OSJS 61c); '(Shimajiri-gun, Ōzato-son) Inamine' (TOS 14.#1037); *ʔnna-nmi,* [ʔn:nam:mi] '(Shimajiri, Ōzato) Inamine' (OGJ 432b); ⟨i de ta ru⟩ (OSJS 60c; TOS 11.#572) ~ ⟨i di pe ta ru⟩ (OSJS 57c; TOS 21.#1457) ~ ⟨i di we ta ru⟩ (OSJS 60a; TOS 21.#1457) *ʔyidzyi-t°-ar-u* [ʔˀĩdʒit°aɾu] 'which became manifest' (OSJS 60c); *ʔnzyi-₁tar-u₁,* [ʔn:dʒitaʳɾu] '(id.)' (OGJ 433a).

52                CHAPTER 2

ers to learn, but easy for later scholars to miss. Note that OOk *kʰaʙt°u* > NOk *kaɴtu,* 'hair' (vulgar) (OGJ 308b), not the modern *kabutu,* 'helmet' (OGJ 299b), a more recent re-borrowing.

/G/   The source of ɢr is *\*gur;* we therefore expect to see spellings with ⟨gu r···⟩, and indeed that is what we find; and, as expected ⟨go r···⟩ spellings lead to *gur* both in OOk and in NOk; the spelling ⟨gu r···⟩ corresponds to ɢr in OOk and to ɴgw in NOk; ɢr is phonetically [˜g:gɹ], with a voiced velar stop release, and where [ɹ] is a somewhat rounded *r,* a glide similar to American English *r,* or something like the /r/ often heard in Kabuki, Noh, or Bunraku performances; the [ɹ] is heir to both the rounding and the liquidness in the original phonological string, and it is the progenitor of the NOk *w* in this position.[54]

### 4.6.3    Mora Voiceless Obstruents

/ᴋ/   This phoneme works much the same as ɢ does, except that it is voiceless, and as such its ultimate NOk form will be (pre-OOk *\*kur* >) ᴋ°r > post-OOk ǫkw

– ⟨ma ku ra⟩ *maᴋ°ra* [mɑk:k°ɹɑ] 'pillow'

Needless to say, we expect OOk *kʰur* to be from pre-OOk *\*kor.* If it were not for the OOk ᴋ°r ↔ *kʰur* distinction, either there would exist no *kʰur* forms or no ǫkw forms in NOk. (We are ignoring possible monkey wrenches thrown into the works by considerations of vowel length.)

/ǫ/   again there is an "elsewhere" case; the main point to note about this phoneme is that it absorbs all the positional and manner features of the segment it precedes, and imparts length. It is instantiated quite sparingly outside of the realm of verbal forms. Here are two examples:

– ⟨a si⟩ あし *ʔaǫ-syi* [ʔɑʃ:ʃi] '[the time] that [we] had [our youth]' (os 7.#380)

– ⟨mo ti ti pe⟩ もちち〱 *muǫ-c°yi* [mut:tʃi] 'getting ahold of' (os 2.#69)

---

54    The word ᴋ°wa ~ -ɢwa 'child, progeny' is unusual in that it underwent its change from *\*ᴋra ~ \*-ɢra* slightly earlier than other forms did, probably due to usage frequency, and then changed its *\*r* to *w,* as the others did later. Cf. Ch. 5 §4.5: *ʔumi-i-ɢwa* 'dear children', and ⟨ku wa o mo pi⟩ *ᴋ°wa-ʔumi-i* 'love of one's child(ren)' (os 21.#1347). As one might expect from what was just stated, there are neither ⟨⁽ⁿ⁾ku ra⟩ nor ⟨ku ra⟩ spellings in this meaning.

SPELLING SYSTEM AND PHONOLOGY

## 4.7 Boundaries: Segment (Status of y), Morpheme (-, {+}), Morphotactic (-, ·), Compound (#), Word (__, ##)

Earlier in this chapter we alluded to *y*, and how it was at the same time a component of the preceding consonant, imparting palatality, and in some cases, even affrication, to it, historically at least—and a component of the following homorganic vowel. This means that not only are there the front vowels *i* [ɪ] and e [ε], but the palatally colored vowels *yi* [ʸi] and *ye* [ʸe], as well.

As for morpheme boundaries, because our general transcription attempts to dispense with too many boundaries, we have tended to use "-" as our generalized morpheme boundary marker—let us call it a morphotactic marker.

In addition, typically in Sino-Ryukyuan or Sino-Japanese compounds, we use a raised dot "·" to mark what may be only a historically extant morpheme boundary, or perhaps a psychologically real one. The raised dot will also frequently be seen as a marker of a derivational boundary within verbs or adjectives.

The typical word boundary is a space or a carriage return. When necessary, at the beginnings or in the middle of words, for clarity, we have employed "##" to mark word boundaries and "#" to mark internal word (i.e. compound) boundaries, though in other cases we have dispensed with them, as noted above.

When writing out morphophonemic-level forms—surrounded by "{}", though that is not the only use to which braces are put—we typically use {+} to mark morpheme (but not word) boundaries.

NB: Boundaries (except for word boundaries) do not necessarily coincide with mora or syllable boundaries.[55]

## 4.8 The Explanatory Status of Boundaries

While our deployment of boundaries in our transcription clearly must rely on historical information to some extent, one important exception is in the determination of some of the lexicon's internal word boundaries. The clearest example of this is the use of internal word boundaries to assure the correct interpretation of the *Yotsu-Gana* distinction. Even where there are variant forms, such as in ⟨si ma ⁽ⁿ⁾si ri⟩ ~ ⟨si ma ⁽ⁿ⁾ti ri⟩, i.e. *syimazyiryi* ~ *syimadzyiryi* 'the southernmost part of the island; Shimajiri', the fact is that this PLN consists of two parts, *syima* 'island' and *syiryi* 'back', and the compound is a rendaku form of the two elements. If an internal word boundary is retained, the output is with

---

55    Actually we do note a few cases of word-level *sandhi* in the present work.

54                                                                                                    CHAPTER 2

*dzy*, but if the boundary is demoted or lost, then the output is *zy*, explaining the
variation in the two forms. This is not a case of inability to tell apart the spelling
of ⟨⁽ⁿ⁾si⟩ and ⟨⁽ⁿ⁾ti⟩, but rather a case of variant pronunciation through variant
decisions on demotion (or not) of a compound boundary.

## 5       Processes

### 5.1      *Progressive Palatalization (PP) and Exceptions to It*

Progressive Palatalization (henceforth PP, J *kōgai-ka* 口蓋化) once, sometime
in Pre-OOk, was an entirely phonetically motivated process, in which a *preceding* phonetically highly palatal [ʸi]-sound's palatal articulation persevered until
it went all the way through the following consonant, palatalizing it.

Progressive Palatalization = PP:

... *yiC* ...    >    ... *yiCʸ*...    >    (or, conventionally, just
               ... *yiCy* ...)

Even from earliest times it appears to have caused non-palatalized (J *chokuon*
直音) and palatalized (J *yō'on* 拗音) syllables to be in free variation:

| e.g. | Pre-OOk | *\*ʔyik°ya* | ~ | | *\*ʔyik°a* 'cuttlefish' > |
| | NOk | *ʔyícya* (OGJ 244b) | ~ | | *ʔyíka* (OGJ 253b) |
| | cf. J | | | | *ika⌟* '(id.)' (no PP) |
| | | | | | |
| | Pre-OOk | *\*syit°a* | ~ | | *\*syit°ya* 'underneath' > |
| | OOk ⟨si ta⟩ | *syi⌟t°a* | :: | NOk | *syícya* (OGJ 464a) |
| | cf. OJ *sita* > | NJ *syi̥tá* '(id.)' | | | |

Note that the OOk form, *syi̥tʰa*, is not the direct precursor of the NOk form,
*syícya*.

In world languages PP is rarer than regressive palatalization, which palatalizes from right to left. Not surprisingly, Okinawan, having the less common
kind, also has the more common kind.

Palatalization of the type *CyV*, due to contraction of adjacent syllables, where
*V* is not *\*i*:

*\*kyiyora* > ⟨ki yo ra⟩ *k°yura* [k°ʸuɾa] 'beautiful' (OS 17.#1238, etc.)

SPELLING SYSTEM AND PHONOLOGY

Palatalization due to simple *Cyi* sequence:

> ⟨ki ta ta N⟩ *k°yi̧t°a#tʰaN* [k°ᵞit°ɑ#tʰɑ̃N] 'Chatan (PLN)' (OS 15.#1105, etc.); all five examples of this PLN are written without PP spelling, but a fairly straightforward set of changes to the modern [ʧɑtɑN] is inferable: *k°yit°ya#tʰaN > c°yic°ya#tʰaN > Qc°ya#tʰaN > cyataŅ* (OGJ 142b). (We assumed, for the nonce, that the aspiration distinction was very late.)

In the OOk period *k°y* and *gy* are palatalized but not yet affricated, while *\*s, \*z, \*t°, \*tʰ,* and *\*d*, in addition to the palatalization, have also acquired a post-alveolar articulation, which in the case of the stops, has led to their affrication ([ʃ], [ʒ], [ʧ°], [ʧʰ], [(d)ʒ], respectively). The voiceless members *\*c°y* and *\*cʰy*, are still stable in NOk as *cy*. The voiced affricate *ʤy* and voiced fricative *zy* had already entered into an allo-morphophonemic relationship by the time of the OS. See §5.4. By MOk, spellings show that that relationship no longer held, and that the corresponding ⟨⁽ⁿ⁾zi···⟩ and ⟨⁽ⁿ⁾di···⟩ graphs were used interchangeably.

Where there is spelling variation between non-PPed (*chokuon*) and PPed (*yō'on*) moras, we assume that the pre-OOk form had a preceding high vowel *\*yi*, and that the variation must either be free or sociolinguistically governed: in such cases, it would seem appropriate to use the exception marker "̧" to note the exceptionality. Examples:

⟨mo te⟩    *muǫt°i* ~
⟨mo ti te⟩    *muǫc°yi*    < *\*mot-°yi-te*
'grasping, holding, having', (Mamiya [2014: 170–171]),

⟨i na ku ni⟩ *ʔyi ̧ na #k°unyi* ~
⟨i ni ya ku ni⟩ *ʔyi nya #k°unyi*    'Yonaguni'

5.1.1    Exceptions to PP

In almost all cases, PP did not affect labial consonants and it did not affect consonants whose following vowel was *[u]. Since the vowel *\*/u/ is also labial, it may be that the generalization is that labiality somehow protects a consonant from PP. Whether PP affects /Cyi/ syllables is moot, since they will be affected by their own vowel in any case.

Exceptions to PP:

... *yiCu*           >    ...[ᵞɪ]*Cu*           ˣ>    PP    >    ...
... *yi*[+labial]...    >    ...[ᵞɪ][+labial]    ˣ>    PP    >    ...

That is to say, a consonant followed by *u*, or by a labial consonant, or both, is not PPable. Of course it may simply be that the labiality of both *\*u* and the *\*C* in question provides the needed generalization, i.e. [+labial]. Then, it may turn out that both *\*u* and some subset of "*\*o*" block PP, and may even ultimately lead to a determination of the [±labial] color of the A :: B (*kō* :: *otsu*) pair Proto-Ryukyuan *\*ô* :: *\*ö*.

The rounding hypothesis may help explain one other very large anomaly in the workings of PP, and that is the fact that PP has absolutely no effect on the particle ⟨-no⟩ (in only three tokens, written ⟨-nu⟩) *-nu* 'SUB/GEN', despite there being hundreds of examples of it (OSJS index 468b–472a),[56] as in:

⟨a o no te ni̱ no̱⟩ *ʔawu-nu tʰinyi̱-̱nu* 'of the blue sky' (TOS 21.#1502)

⟨ku ni̱ no u ki gu† mo⟩ *k°unyi̱-̱nu ʔuk°yi-gumu* '[our] country's floating clouds' (TOS 11.#562); and so on

The only other obvious option is to claim that there is a full word boundary between the preceding word and *\*no*, thus making PP impossible.

⟨a o no te ni̱ no̱⟩ *ʔawu-nu tʰinyi̱##nu* 'of the blue sky'

In such a hypothesis, it would help to array any other possible peculiarities of *-nu* to bolster the claim. (In NJ there *are* peculiarities of accent in attachment of the element to a preceding noun, different from other enclitics.)

Pre-OOk *\*ʔyitu* *[ʔʸɪt°u] > OOk *ʔyic°i* > NOk *ʔyíci* (OGJ 246a) [ʔʸitsi] 'when?' > ColloqOk *ʔyícyi* [ʔitʃi] (cf. NJ *ícu* '(id.)' < OJ *itu*)

pre-OOk *\*kyimo* (ˣ*kyimyo*) [because of labial *\*m* (and *\*o*?,—because OJ had type-A *ô* for this word, thought to have been rounded, or to have had a rounded onset)] 'liver; heart, fortitude'

OOk *k°yimu* (ˣ*k°yimyu*) > NOk *cyimu* (ˣ*cyimyu*) '(id.)'

OJ *kîmô* [kʸimʷo] 'liver; the internal organs' (JDB 246d–247a) > J '(animal) liver (and in set phrases)'

---

56    There are no examples of ˣ⟨-ni yo⟩ or ˣ⟨-ni yu⟩.

SPELLING SYSTEM AND PHONOLOGY

However, note that a handful of words with ?*yi* as their initial syllable, and despite being followed by a labial, still undergo PP.[57]

Irregular PP through a labial consonant:

##?*yi*[+labial] ... > ##?*yi*[+labial]*y* ...

pre-OOk ?*yima* >[despite labial \**m*]> OOk ⟨i mi ya⟩ ?*yimya* 'now' (OSJS 63b) > NOk *n*(*y*)*áa* 'already' (OGJ 399b, 421b) [##?*yi* > ∅, with *a* > *aa* and *y* > ∅]

OJ *ima* > NJ *íma*

This exception may either be lexical or else limited to cases with word-initial (\*)?*yi*. It is tempting to treat it as a metathesis of \*?*yima* > \*?*myiya* > \**myaa* > *nyaa* > *naa*, but for the fact that ⟨i mi ya⟩ = ?*yimya* (presumably not ˣ?*mya*(*a*)) is attested—OS 8.#420 and many others.

(1) a preceding etymologically non-high palatal vowel, i.e. \**ye* (\**Cye* (\*[C°ʸɛ] >) \*[C⁽ʸ⁾e]):

  – \**syer-* > \**syɪr-* > \**syi͡r-*, discussed with OS 8.#426 in Ch. 7 §9.2:
    ⟨si ra ti ya ra me⟩ *syi͡ra-c°yar-am-i* (< \**syer-as-yi-t°-ar-am-e*) 'It is ... that surely protected ....' (OS 8.#426); NOk *syirás-y-u-N* 'let know, inform' (OGJ 483a)
  and most cases of \**Vye* (\*[Vʸɛ] >) \*[V⁽ʸ⁾e], e.g.:

  – \**tatope-* > \**tatoye-* > \**tʰatʰoyɪ-* > \**tʰatʰu*⁽ʾ⁾*yi₍ᵢ₎*-
    ⟨... ta to we ti pe⟩ / ... / ... ta to we te / ...⟩
    *tʰa.t°u.ʾyi-.c°yi*              *tʰa.t°u.yi͡-.t°i*
    liken-GER/PRFV                  liken-GER/PRFV
    both: 'has likened', with purposeful manipulation (OS 1.#34)
    When the mora at issue is treated as CGV, the interpretation is ʾ*yi*, and then PP is possible, but when it is treated as CV, the interpretation is *yi*, and, since *y* is the C, PP cannot occur. The alternation here is

---

57  The one absolute prohibition is PP onto a syllable whose vowel is \**u*. Where seeming exceptions to these are found, there is always an alternative explanation that does not require the high vowel \**u* in the the syllable in the period before PP, and indeed the prohibition can function as a kind of crowbar, so to speak, to pry words apart and to discover alternative vowel colors in reconstructed forms, those alternatives giving a fuller view of the prehistory of the Proto-Ryukyuan/Pre-Ryukyuan language, and then of Proto-Japonic itself.

58                                                                                    CHAPTER 2

playful manipulation of the process. The historically accurate interpretation is the latter.

(2) a preceding long high palatal vowel, i.e. *yii*, with vocalic nucleus depalatalized (i.e. laxed) by length, i.e. *[yiː] > [yɪː]:[58]
  - ⟨... /  mi ki i do†        ... / ... / ...    mi ki do† ...⟩
    *myi(i)-k°yii-du*                      *myi(i)*[59]*-k°yii-du*
    [mʸɪ(ː)k°yɪːdu]                        [mʸɪ(ː)k°yɪːdu]
    '... [has] holy wine!' (TOS 15.#1087)
  - ⟨mi ra na⟩ *myii·r-a-na* [mʸɪːɾana] 'yes, let us look!' (TOS 14.#1031)
    ⟨mi gi ya⟩ *myi-gya* [mʸigʸa] 'in order to see' (TOS 4.#159)
    Note the disparity in PP, which we explain with a disparity in length of the stem.

  We assume that short *yi* = [ʸi] palatalizes following palatalizable consonants (= PP), while long *yii*, the length of which we assume dispalatalizes the vocalic nucleus, yielding [ʸɪː], with a palatal onset but a high front but non-palatal nucleus, shields the following consonant from PP. Thus *myi-gya* [mʸigʸa], but *myiirana* [mʸɪːɾana]. We assume paradigmatic leveling in the case of the T-forms.

  Most cases are typically inferred rather than actually observed, since the OS typically fails to note consonant quality ([± voiced]) or vowel quality ([± long]).

(3) following high vowel, i.e. *°yiC*[+hi] > *°yɪC*[+hi]:
  - 'water' ⟨su de mi du⟩ *sidi#myidzɨ|* [sidɪmʸɪdzɨ]
  Other words that are known to be subject to this same pattern (whether it be a constraint on raising of original *°ye* or a split of the periphery and nucleus of the vowel *°yi*) are lacking in the OS: *°kyɪzu* 'flaw', *°ʔyɪdu-* 'wh- ?',[60] *°pyɪru* 'garlic' (cf. *°pyi#ru* ʔ[pʸɪːru] 'day#time', paired with *°yô#ru* ʔ[yʷɔːru] 'night#time');
all depriving the PP rule of its input.

---

58  Lexical items such as ⟨a kē zu mi so⟩ *ʔa(a)kʰe͡(e)zu(u)-myi-ˌsu* 'gossamer-cloth exalted clothing', *lit.* 'dragonfly exalted clothing' (OS 13.#847), form a direct line to LitOk *ʔakezu-bani-n'-su,* '(id.)' (OGJ 110a), *lit.* 'dragonfly-wing-exalted-clothing'. The all-shortened-vowel version is used in Ryūka, while the gentry-class Shuri colloquial form of the mid twentieth century was *ʔaakēezuu,* (OGJ 99a). This and other similar examples give strong backing for there being a sprinkling of exceptions to the general rule of ⟨···e⟩ spellings aligning with high vowel pronunciations. It also provides evidence for a hypothesis that length in mid vowels impeded raising to high.

59  The form *myi(i)-* is due to the single example ⟨mi i ki yo se⟩, literally *myii-k°yi#yusi* '(the building) Miikiyose' *lit.* 'proffering holy wine' (OS 5.#229).

60  The form ⟨i ki ya⟩ *ʔyik°ya* 'how (much)?' (OS 12.#731) is present in the OS (cf. Ch. 4 § 2.1.2.3); it raises an interesting question: the form of the 'wh'-question marker before *-c°i* ('when?')

SPELLING SYSTEM AND PHONOLOGY

Note, however, that *u* appears not to allow PP under any circumstances, as in the case of \**pyi#ru* > *pyiru* 'daytime' (\**pyi#ryu*) (OS 14.#1066). Further, all of these words except \**kyɪzu* 'flaw' appear in e.g. the south-of-Kakeroma Setouchi outlier dialect of Yoro with ɪ (e.g. *mɪt* [Serafim (personal notes, 1986)]), not *yi*, suggesting that the vowel nucleus laxed. The consonant \**ky* remains palatalized in many northern Amami dialects, including e.g. the dialect of Shito'oke[61] on Kikai Island (Nakamoto [1976: 338]):

[k'idʑu] 'flaw', and others listed as well

even though everywhere else it is \**k* with a following (formerly) lax vowel (e.g. NOk Sr (\**kezu* >) *kízi* → NOk Nh ꞌ*kidʑi* [OGJ2: 84b]).

These facts show that everywhere the nuclear vowel of the first syllable must have been lax; in at least a few places (perhaps all?), this vowel lowered to the lax mid vowel \**ε*, since its reflex is indistinguishable from the reflex of that vowel; that in some dialects a velar obstruent initial \**ky* retained its palatality, but lost it in most, apparently on laxing (or lowering);

5.1.2      Interaction of PP with Gerund (GER) Morphophonemics

PP/non-PP and voicing alternations have played a crucial role in Gerund (GER) morphophonemics since prehistory. Both the reconstructed pre-OOk GER \**-tε* and the underlying OOk GER {+te} exhibit voicing alternation in their only obstruent, and PP/non-PP alternation on the very same obstruent, yielding—in OOk—a four-way consonant alternation: *t˚ ~ d ~ c˚y ~ dʑy*, or:

|         | [−voi] | [+voi] |
| ------- | ------ | ------ |
| [−PP]   | *-t˚i* | *-di*  |
| [+PP]   | *-c˚yi*| *-dʑyi*|

is a morph that is unable to cause PP, consistent with a form [ʔʲɪ], with a laxed vocalic nucleus. The allomorph of that in the case of *ʔyik˚ya* clearly is able to cause PP, so its nucleus is fully palatal. Such a situation suggests that the original form of the 'wh' question marker is \**ʔyi-*, not ˣ\**ʔye-*, since a straightforward way to link two candidate allomorphs \**ʔyi-* and \**ʔye-* is currently unavailable unless we claim that a following labial has the power to lower \**yi* to \**ye*, while a way to link \**ʔyi-* and \**ʔyɪ-* is as close as the following syllable, which has laxed the nucleus of this allomorph: \**ʔyi-tu* > \**ʔyɪ-tu* > *ʔyɪ-cɪ*.

61     This dialect, just like others in a broad region of Northern Amami, maintains a distinction between /i/ and /ɨ/=/ɪ/ after most consonants.

60　　　　　　　　　　　　　　　　　　　　　　　　　　　　　CHAPTER 2

TABLE 2.11　Verb-type underlying and surface forms, with examples

| | | | | | | |
|---|---|---|---|---|---|---|
| a | {te, GER} | → ... *t°i* | / R__ | {kʰakʰi·r, 'place'}{yi, RY}{t°e, GER} | → *kʰakʰi-t°i°* | 'placing' |
| b | | → ... *t°i* | / R__ | {tʰur, 'take'}{yi, RY}{t°e, GER} | → *tʰu-t°i°* | 'taking' |
| c | | → ... *t°i* | / (R)__ | {c°ik°aw, 'use'}{yi, RY}{t°e, GER} | → *c°ik°a-t°i\** | 'using' |
| d | | → ... *di* | / B__ | {yub, 'call'}{yi, RY}{t°e, GER} | → *yu-di\** | 'calling' |
| e | | → ... *di* | / M__ | {yum, 'read'}{yi, RY}{t°e, GER} | → *yu-di\** | 'reading' |
| f | | → ... *c°yi* | / K__ | {kʰak, 'write'}{yi, RY}{t°e, GER} | → *kʰa-c°yi\** | 'writing' |
| g | | → ...*ʣyi* | / G__ | {kʰuug, 'row'}{yi, RY}{t°e, GER} | → *kʰuu-ʣyi°* | 'rowing' |
| h | | → ...*ʣyi* | / N__ | {syin, 'die'\*}{yi, RY}{t°e, GER} | → *syi-ʣyi\** | 'dying' |
| i | | → ... *Q-c°yi\** | / IR__ | {syir, 'get to know'}{yi, RY}{t°e, GER} | → *syiQ-c°yi\** | 'getting to know' |
| j | | → *s-yi-c°yi* | / S-irr__ | {se, 'do'}{yi, RY}{t°e, GER} | → *syi-c°yi°* | 'doing' |
| k | | → *k-°yi-c°yi* | / K-irr__ | {kʰu, 'come'}{yi, RY}{t°e, GER} | → *k-°yi-c°yi°* | 'coming' |
| l | | → *ʔyi-ʣyi\** | / 'go'__ | {ʔyin-, 'go₂'}{yi, RY}{t°e, GER} | → *ʔyi-ʣyi\** | 'going' |
| m | | → *Q-c°yi\** | / T__ | {mut, 'hold'}{yi, RY}{t°e, GER} | → *muQ-c°yi\** | 'holding' |

Applying this to our list of verb subtypes in Ch. 6, we get the gerund forms in Table 2.11, with an example of each given. One caveat, however: not all verb types feature a T-form, and therefore we have had to infer a fair number of them according to rules that are inferable from the extant forms and from other sources, including NOk. We have checked all forms against OSJS, postposing raised circles for attested forms and raised asterisks for predicted forms as in Table 2.11.

If looking at the OOk form alone, a high front palatal vowel in the root may appear to jump over the consonantal segment(s) in between and PPize the GER, as in the first two examples below, but in fact close scrutiny of possible sound-change orderings shows that such a hypothesis is superfluous, and that indeed it is the immediately preceding vowel that does the PPizing. This conclusion is assured when the last example is added to the list below:

| | | | | |
|---|---|---|---|---|
| *\*syin-yi-t°e* | | 1> | *\*syiN-y-ʣye* | 2> |  *\*syiN-y-ʣye* |
| 'dying; has died' | | 3> | *\*syi-ʣye* | 4> | *syi-ʣyi* |
| | | | | |
| *\*syir-yi-t°e* | | 1> | *\*syir-yi-t°ye* | 2> | *\*syir-yi-c°ye* |
| 'getting to know; has learned' | | 3> | *\*syiQ-c°ye* | 4> | *syiQ-c°yi* |
| | | | | |
| cf. *\*mot-°yi-t°e* | | 1> | *\*mot-°yi-t°ye* | 2> | *\*moQ-c°ye* |
| 'getting a hold of' | | | | 3> | *\*muQ-c°yi* |

A potential avenue of explanation of the PP of the GER as being caused by the palatal vowel due to skipping over the immediately preceding mora and explaining the phenomenon as caused by the second mora after the preced-

SPELLING SYSTEM AND PHONOLOGY

ing, has been closed off by the fact that the *t*-type verb gerund *muQ-c°yi* is PP'ed, putting the "2nd-syllable before" hypothesis out of commission, since that syllable is back, and certainly non-palatal. It is always the preceding mora that has caused the PP, even if that mora has changed its own form in the meantime: $mo_2tyi_1te_0 > mu_2Q_1c°yi_0$.

### 5.2    *Syllabic Contraction*

We have seen that CGV moras (where G = *y*) can come about through PP. But there is another quite productive mechanism for the creation of such moras including, potentially, GwV moras, and that is Syllabic Contraction (SC). The process is quite straightforward. For whatever original cause, a word-internal mora begins with a mid or high vowel, but especially, the glides *y* or *w*. Let us look at a couple of examples, in the process getting a look at an irregularity occasioned by the borrowing and modification of the prototypical exalting verb *\*owa·r-*:

> *\*k-°yi#owa·r-* >SC> *\*k°yowar* ... >Affr> *\*c°yowar* ... >Raising> ⟨ti yo wa r···⟩ / ⟨ti yu wa r···⟩ *c°yuwar* ... 'exaltedly rules/is'

There are two irregularites in the above word, and it is well to consider that irregularities abound in words denoting some kind of politeness. What *is* regular, however, is the process of SC, yielding the form *\*k°yowar* ..., which has resulted from the merger of the vowels of *\*k°yi* + *\*o*..., initially producing *\*k°yiyo* ..., but because *i* is very short between homogeneous glides, collapsing *\*yiy* into just *\*y*, and thus resulting in the new mora *\*k°yo* ....

The two irregularities are, first, the affrication of *k°y*, of which (at this early time) this is the only example, and second, the irregularity of the verb *\*owa·{r/s}*- itself. For details, see Ch. 7 §14.5.3.

Another example of Contraction has similar, though not identical, input, but less irregular output: *\*kyiyora > k°yura* 'beauty/beautiful'. Again the input string is *\*yiyo*, and, because the *\*i* is quite short (actually a language universal for high vowels in relation to lower ones), and because the two *\*y*-s are completely identical, the loss of the intervening *\*i*, yielding a *\*yy* sequence, leads to the instant shortening of that to *y*, as it is in OOk. Let us take a look at the specific data:

| み物、 | きよら、ᴧ | あおらちゑ、 | / 國ぶ⁺さい、ᴧ | おしたて、 |
|---|---|---|---|---|
| ⟨mi MONO, | ki yo ra,ᴧ | a o ra ti we, | / KUNI bu⁺sa i,ᴧ | o si ta te,⟩ |
| *myi-munu* | *k°yura* | *ʔawur-a-c°yi* | *k°unyi-busa'yi* | *ʔusyi-tʰat°i-∅* |
| see-thing | beautiful | wave-CAUS-GER | country-bounty | -INT-raise-RY |

'waving [the banner] Beautiful Marvel / and raising up [the banner] Country Bounty' (OS 3.#89)

62                                                                                                    CHAPTER 2

Note that *k°yura* is indeed two moras long, since *myimunuk°yura* is five moras, and so is *k°unyibusa'yi*. Thus this is a case of Contraction.

### 5.2.1        Non-processual Palatalized Syllables

In addition to palatalized syllables of the type CyV where V≠ *i*, there are syllables where the palatality is part of the original syllable, typically in a borrowing, and those syllables that simply are of unknown provenance, typically in words we mark as MO, i.e. "meaning obscure".

Of the former, an example is ⟨ki ya (u)⟩ *k°/ʰyoo* 'Kyoto', 'a holy precinct', with aspiration quality unknown. The word is a SJ loan.

Of the latter type, an example is ⟨si ya na me⟩ *sya₁na₂mi₃* 'ox' (a *hapax*, metrically parallel to ⟨u ma da†⟩ *ʔu₁ma₂-da₃* 'pack-horse' [2 tokens], both therefore with three moras) (both OS 9.#506).

### 5.2.2        Palatalized *r* and—Rarely—Its Loss

In OOk the elision of *r* was in its very early stages. The changes of sequences *rya* → *'ya, ryu* → *'yu, ryo* → *'yo* were noticeably more frequent than those of *ryi* → *'yi*. Here is one of the latter:

> ⟨yo i du† ti pe⟩ *yu'-yi-dzi-c°yee* ← {yur+yi+"+cik+yi#te}
> '[the deity] has possessed [the shaman]' (OS 11.#576).

As a rule of the grammar, it was an optional elision, resorted to relatively rarely.

Contrarily, in NOk the only exception to this *r*-drop is where *r* was in the historically older environment *yi__yi*. For example the equivalent of NJ *kir-i-korós-u*, 'knife to death' is *cyir-i-kurus-y-u'-N*, [ˈʧiɾʲikuɾuʃuˈN], with *r* intact (OGJ 163a), < OOk *k°yir-yi-*. Cf. ⟨ki ri pu se te⟩ *k°yir-yi#p°usi#tʰee* 'has struck down dead' (OS 3.#103).

Here is another example with a verb that is a member of different categories in OOk and OJ: いりおとちへ ⟨i ri o to ti pe⟩ *ʔyi-r-yi#ʔutʰu-c°yi* 'shooting [a bird] down'. This is the only example of this verb, and it appears in a compound. See the fuller example in Ch. 6 §1.2.1 (14a). Takahashi (1991b: 332) notes the supposed "irregularity" of this form taking *r* in the RY form despite its being an upper monograde verb *in OJ*. He (ibid. 340) takes this as evidence that the shift from the monograde to quadrigrade (*r*-type) from OOk to NOk had been completed in this verb at this stage. He is certainly correct in this view.

Now, what about the NOk equivalent, *ʔyi-r-i-,*? We have already seen that *ˣcyi-i* 'cut-RY' in the preliminary material in OGJ was an error, and that com-

SPELLING SYSTEM AND PHONOLOGY

pounds in ROD/OGJ always gave the form with *r intact. Ditto for 'shoot-RY': the chart (OGJ 59: xiv ⊡ col. 2) mistakenly gives ˣʔyi-i, but, again, compounds in the body of both ROD and OGJ give the correct ʔyir̄-(y)i-ⱼ. Here are a couple of NOk examples for 'shoot-RY':

| | | | |
|---|---|---|---|
| ʔyir̄-cyiyuɴⱼ | 'shoot (an animal) dead', | *lit.* 'cut (down) with shots' | (OGJ 259a); |
| ʔyir̄-tubasyu 'ɴⱼ | 'fire volley after volley', | *lit.* 'let fly with shots' | (OGJ 260a). |

When we crosscheck with nouns that are known to come from *... yir̄yi, and which do not drop their *r, they do indeed accord across the board. That is, regardless of part of speech, *... yir̄yi is the only *... Vryi sequence that does not drop its *r.

### 5.3 *The Two-Mora Rule*

We first noticed the effects of this rule—and therefore the rule itself—as it applied to historical cases of the retention or loss of the segment /Q/ in word-initial position:

| 'progeny' | 'give GER' | |
|---|---|---|
| *ku ra | *##kure#te## | |
| ᴋ° ra⁶² | *##ᴋ°ri#tʼi ## | 1st possible application point |
| Q kwa | *##Qkwi#ti## | 2nd possible application point |
| | ##kwi#ti## | |

The rule did not apply in the first column because the word was not longer than two moras. In the latter case, however, it was, and the word-initial segment Q was deleted. The same rule can be seen operating synchronically in a couple of NOk verbs, namely s-y-u-ɴ 'do' and c-°y-uu-ɴ 'come'. The gerund forms of the two verbs are, respectively, Q̇-sẏi and Q̇-cẏi, while contrastive-topical forms made from the gerunds are, respectively, ∅̇-sẏe-ė and ∅̇-cẏe-ė.

### 5.3.1 Application of the Two-Mora Rule to Accent

Thorpe reconstructs Proto-Ryukyuan accent utilizing the Two-Mora Rule, although he does not call it that. The crux of it is that rising or falling tonal

---

62 We assume that OOk /r/ in the environment directly following a velar stop is in fact a glide phoneme, and as such its phonetic value is that of American English word-initial [ɹ], or something like the "r" often heard in Kabuki, Noh, or Bunraku performances.

64                                                                    CHAPTER 2

melodies on the first two moras are converted into tonic accent, and all accent
information after the second mora is thrown away in the development of the
later dialect(s):

> The melodies [+rise] and [+fall] merged in Ry. into [+accent] if their loca-
> tion features were [1st mora] or [2nd mora]. Beyond the second mora all
> accents were lost. (1983: 129)

5.3.2      Application of the Two-Mora Rule to Word Length

All independent words in OOk, just as in NOk, are assumed to obey a two-mora
constraint, that is, that they must be at least two moras in length. However,
it is also assumed that this constraint may be overridden to fit otherwise-
overlong words into the poetic meter of their particular omoro, just as in
the literary Ryūka form still used to compose and perform songs today (cf.
Ch. 6 § 2.3, "The change from *w*-stem to *r*-stem quadrigrade", for its application).

5.3.3      Application of the Two-Mora Rule to the *Yotsu-Gana* Case

Next we show that the Two-Mora Rule also applies to the solution for the *Yotsu-
Gana* distinction, as detailed just below in § 5.4.

5.4      *The* Yotsu-Gana *Distinction*

In the OS there is a distinction at the phonemic level between, on the one hand,
*zi* [zɨ] and *dzi* [dzɨ], and, on the other, *zyi* [ʒi] and *dzyi* [dʒi], as follows:

|                    | Native spelling | Transcription of spelling | Phonemicization | Most abstract |
| ------------------ | --------------- | ------------------------- | --------------- | ------------- |
| with *i* (< *\*u*) | ず ↔ づ          | ⟨zu⟩ ↔ ⟨du⟩               | *zi* ↔ *dzi*    | {Zi}          |
| with *yi*          | じ ↔ ぢ          | ⟨zi⟩ ↔ ⟨di⟩               | *zyi* ↔ *dzyi*  | {Zyi}         |

This is evidenced by the fact that the writers of the omoros maintained a nearly
perfect spelling distinction between the two sets, given certain provisos which
we will now explain.

   The phonemic form of the abstract {Z} element can be perfectly predicted
utilizing specific morpheme boundaries. If it is in the first two moras to the
right of a ## (lexical-word) or # (internal-word) boundary, it is pronounced as
an affricate:

## SPELLING SYSTEM AND PHONOLOGY

{Z} → $dz$ / #(#)$_{-1}$($_{-2}$)

eg: {ʔu-myi#tʰi-Zir-yi} → ʔu-myi#tʰi$_1$-$dzi_2$|r-yi ⟨o mi te du† ri⟩ おみてづり

'EX-EX-hand-rub-RY'

'The exalted, divine prayers' (OS 15.#1110)

This is a peculiarly apt example because it flies in the face of the known etymology in OJ *sur-* 'rub', and NOk *tii-∅ si'-yuɴ* 'to pray' (*lit.* 'to rub hands' [OGJ 472b]), which is clearly fricative in origin, but in the compound always (12 tokens) spelled as an affricate in OOk.

In every other case {Z} is pronounced as a fricative. For example:

$\overline{ʔa_1ke_2|zu_3}$#*kata* 'dragonfly#picture'

⟨a ke $\overline{zu}$ , ka ta⟩ あけず、かた

'picture of a dragonfly' (OS 9.#479); cf. OJ *akîdu* 'dragonfly', NOk *ʔaa-keezuu,* '(id.)' (OGJ 99a)

The hypothesis makes specific predictions about where internal word boundaries do or do not lie, and therefore is in principle testable. We assume that in formulating such boundaries, we mimic the unconscious processes of the writers (and of OOk language learners) themselves.

This hypothesis also sheds light on the distinction between variant spellings and pronunciations such as OS つんし ~ つち⁽ⁿ⁾ ⟨tu ɴ si⟩ ~ ⟨tu ⁽ⁿ⁾ti⟩ 'acme; top (of mountain or hill)' or あんし⁽ⁿ⁾ ⟨a ɴ ⁽ⁿ⁾si⟩ ~ ⟨a ⁽ⁿ⁾ti⟩ 'lord'. The former is related to J *tumuzi* 'whorl; whirlwind; road crossing; path' (Mamiya [2014: 75–76]), and the latter to the independent formants *\*ʔa-* 'I; my' and *\*nu(u)syi* 'master' (cf. Mamiya [2014: 72–75]), thus giving *\*ʔanu(u)syi* \*'my master' → '(my) lord'. Therefore:

$$*tu_1mu_2 \mid zyi_3 > *tu_1N_2 \mid zyi_3 > *ci_1dzyi_2 \mid$$
$$*ʔa_1nu_2 \mid syi_3 > *ʔa_1N_2 \mid zyi_3 > *ʔa_1dzyi_2 \mid$$

As can be seen from the first two columns, the bar is placed two moras to the right from the left edge of the word, clearly leaving the fricatives out of candidacy for affrication. But once ɴ and *zy* fuse, the bar is automatically placed to the right of the resulting fused segment, and that segment automatically becomes an affricate. Since both the pre- and post-fused variants continue to exist in the language right into OS times, they have not only a nasal-segment ~ no-nasal-segment variation, but in addition they have a concomitant variation in (af)frication.

This is actually one example of the workings of the Two-Mora Rule, discussed in §5.3.

Here are other examples to bolster the case for the workings of the *Yotsu-Gana* Distinction:

(1) 2nd or 3rd element of a compound is a 1-mora lexical element, where the segment is affricated:

    a. Verb root plus {RY}{#te}, yielding an affricate #$c°yi$ or (here) #$dzyi$ (T-form always with {#}):

        – __#↓ $k^huu$|#$dzyi$ Morphophonemically defined exception: all T-forms have an internal word boundary in front of them; this fits with an identical, independently derived requirement for Shodon T-forms (Serafim 1984: 125–126, 148–149); ⟨ko di† pe⟩ こぢ†へ 'row-GER(/PRFV)' i.e. 'rowing' (OS 10.#545).

        cf. __#↓ $Ɂwi-i$|#$dzyi$ ⟨o we di† pe⟩ おゑぢ†へ[63] 'following wind' (OS 10.#541)

    b. Others:

        – $s → z → dz$ __#↓ $Ɂuri$|#$dzi_1m$-$u_2$ ⟨o re du† mu⟩ おれづむ[64] 'moistening-clearing-RT' = 'early spring' (OS 2.#54) (OS 21.#1457) < *$uruw+yi''#sum+u$

(2) Element in question is a fricative, never closer than 3rd mora from left in-/ex-ternal word boundary:

    – __|↓ $syi_ir$-$a$|$z$-$i$ ⟨si ra zu⟩ しらず 'indifferent' (OS 11.#643)

(3) Full-word attachments (collocations), with 2nd word having 3 moras; the 3rd, fricative, mora is pertinent:

    – __##__|↓ $k°um$-$u$##$soo$|$\overline{zi}$ ⟨ku mu sa u $\overline{zu}$*⟩ くむさう$\overline{す}$* $k°um$-$u$##$soo\overline{zi}$[65] 'draw-RT ##clear.water' (OS 21.#1409); note that *soozi* has *$myedu$ or *$myidu$ in its prehistory, with a voiced $\overline{stop}$ (OS 7.#348) (cf. __↓ $myidzi$ ⟨mi du⟩ みづ 'water'); nevertheless, *soo*|*zi*, having the *$d/z$ element past the bar, has the phonemic element $z$, not the otherwise expected $dz$.

    – __##__|↓ $t^hat°$-$a$##$k^haa$|$zi$ ⟨ta " ka zu† ,⟩ たゝかず†, 'time.passes-IA$_{RT}$ number', i.e. 'as (the years) may go by' (OS 12.#725); NOk Vb-RT *káazi* [ka':zi] 'every time [s/t or s/o] Vb-s' (OGJ 299a); even though no length

---

63   $Ɂwi$-$i$-$dzyi$ < *$Ɂo'$-$yi$-$\overline{d}ye$ < *$Ɂow$-$yi$-$\overline{d}e$. Cf. J $o[w]$-$u$, 'follow, …'; for J -$\overline{te}$ cf. SNKDJ *te* 'wind', which cites $o$-$i$-$te$.

64   Cf. discussion in Ch. 4, §1.5 'Deverbal nouns'.

65   Apparently *soozi* lacks a NOk counterpart. OSJS (147a, ⟨ku mo sa u su⟩ 147b) glosses it with J *shimizu* '(id.)' < OJ *si-mîdu* (JDB 386cd) ~ *su-mîdu* (JDB 392cd). Cf. also 西美度 *se-mîdô* '(id.)' JDB (397d), citing MYS 3546, an Eastern OJ song. The latter (because of the mid vowel in the initial syllable) and the OOk form (because of the long mid vowel) suggest PJ *$se$-$\hat{m}edu$ > pre-OOk *$sɛwɔdzu$ > *$sɔɔzu$ > *soozi*. Spelling with ⟨sa⟩ merely mentally triggers the mid vowel pronunciation, which is conservative, and does not reflect the etymological vowel height.

SPELLING SYSTEM AND PHONOLOGY                                              67

is written, the NOk form suggests that length was there, thus putting the bar *before* the {Z}, and thus yielding *z* on the surface.

(4)    2nd mora of word is affricated:

J *z* :: O *dz*: _↓|__

-   _↓|_ *mudzi|k°yi* ⟨mu du† ki⟩ むづき *mudzik°yi* 'muzuki (= shamaness$_2$)' (OS 11.#581) (OS 21.#1506); where the etymology is opaque, as here, the word always obeys the left-of-bar rule; pre-OOk *{mo/uZuky.i/e} *pʰadzyi|m·a-t°ar-u* ⟨pa di* , ma ta ru⟩ はぢ*、またる 'start-PRFT-RT', i.e. 'that began' (OS 11.#561); pre-OOk *{Z}; cf. OJ *pazīmar-* '(id.)' (JDB 578b), with a fricative; however, also cf. OJ *patū-* 'first-, new-' (JDB 583c), with a stop

-   _↓|#__ *sidzi|#naryi* ⟨su du† na ri⟩ すづなり 'PN' i.e. '[Priestess] Suzu-nari' (OS 14.#1011); cf. MJ *suzū* '(jingle) bell', OJ *id* (JDB 387cd); pre-OOk *{suZu}

(5)    First mora of word is affricated:

-   ↓_|_ *dzyoo|ri* ⟨di† ya , pa re⟩ ぢ†や、はれ *dzyoori* [dʒoːɾɪ] 'zōri' (OS 1.#17); MJ *z* :: OOk *dzy*; pre-OOk *Z; cf. MJ *zɔɔri* (not a phonemic affricate)

-   *myi|#dzyi₁r-yi₂|#kʰyu* ⟨mi di† pe ri ki u⟩ みぢ†へりきう 'EX-announce-RY-one' i.e. '[Priestess] Mizeriko' (OS 13.#805) < pre-OOk *{myi#"s̄er+yi#ko}

(6)    The only potential counterexample to our hypothesis of the relation of phonemes to underlying forms in *Yotsu-Gana*:

-   ##↓_ / ##↓_ *dziri/ziri* ⟨du re⟩/⟨zu re⟩⁶⁶ づれ/ずれ *dziri/ziri* 'which one?'; *dz*: (OS 5.#257); ⟨zure⟩ (OKDJ 75a) (OS 13.#882) *ziri*'s only appearance, twice, is in this song; its variability is unexplained—dialectal variation?; we prefer to spell it either *dziri* or *ziri*, as it comes up, so as not to throw away data; the first mora of the word is usually affricated (6 of 8, or 75%), so the item is only quasi-irregular (1st mora of word split between 6 affricates and 2 fricatives); we do not consider this set of forms to constitute a refutation of our hypothesis

## 5.5    *Rendaku*

Rendaku is a phenomenon recognized when comparing independent morphs to bound allomorphs of the same morphemes in compounds: ##B̄## :: ##A#B'##. If the independent morph begins with a voiceless obstruent, its dependent allomorph will begin with an equivalent voiced allomorph: ##°CB## :: ##A#"CB'##. Thus, the term rendaku includes the idea of voicing in Element 2 (= B) in compounding, but at the same time, it also includes

---

66    Six tokens of ⟨⁽ⁿ⁾tu re⟩ *dziri*, three with *-ga*, three with *-nu*.

restrictions on it, specifically, Moto'ori-Lyman's Law (Vance [2005: 27–29]), which states that rendaku is blocked if the second element already has a voiced obstruent in it. Exemplifying with Japanese:

rendaku occurs:  *toki* 'time'  +  *toki*  →  *toki-°doki*  'now and then'
rendaku blocked:  *tabi* 'a time'  +  *tabi*  →  *tabi-ˣdabi/tabi-°tabi*  'often'

Here are some straightforward examples from OS:

⟨se da ka ko⟩ せだかこ *si-d̄akʰa-kʰu* (*-d̄akʰa* 'high' ← \*-*t̄ʰakʰa*) 'spiritual .power-high-**one**' (OS 1.#1)

⟨bo˚ re bo si⟩ ぼ˚れぼし *buri-b̄usyi* ([*buri-* 'assembled';] *-b̄usyi* 'star' ← \*-*p̲osi*) 'Pleiades' (OS 10.#534)

⟨we zo ko⟩ ゑぞこ *yii-z̄ukʰu* (*-z̄ukʰu* 'bottom' ← *-s̄ukʰu*) 'royal ship' *lit.* 'good-bottom' (OS 6.#325)

Here are two examples reflecting Motoori-Lyman's Law:

⟨ya ma to ta bi⟩ やまとたび (OS 10.#538) 'journey to Yamato' is not ˣ*yamatu-dabi*, but rather °*yamatu-tabi* due to the existence of the blocking voiced obstruent *b*

⟨ma pa pe ka ze⟩ まはへかぜ (OS 13.#902) 'southerly wind' is not ˣ*ma-p˚a'yi-gazi*, but rather °*ma-p˚a'yi#k̄ʰaz̄i*, due to the blocking voiced obstruent *z*

## 5.6 *Metathesis*

### 5.6.1 Introduction

A phenomenon of Vocalic Metathesis (i.e. transposition of vowels) has occurred in OOk, mostly in Sino-Japanese or Sino-Ryukyuan morphs ending in \*···*a'u* or \*···*a'yi*, but occasionally in other types of morphs—and, importantly, never automatically, though it comes closest to automaticity in the above-mentioned SJ and SR morphs. In addition, a great many of the monosyllabic morphs in which it occurs have an initial coronal consonant, such as *d*, *t*, *s*, or *r*. As far as we are aware, this phenomenon as we formulate it has never been brought up before.

Metathesis of diphthongal elements in SJ/SR morphs:

SPELLING SYSTEM AND PHONOLOGY 69

(1) *Ca'u >
 *Cu'a >
 *Cwa(a) >
 *Ca(a)

(2) *Ca'yi >
 *Cyi'a >
 *Cya(a)

## 5.6.2 Examples

*d* OOk ⟨di ya gu ni⟩ ぢやぐに (大國) *dzya('a)-gunyi* '(Our) Great Country' <
*\*dyi'a* < *\*da'yi* < 'great, grand, big'; compare ⟨da gu ni⟩ *dee-gunyi* '(id.)' (cf.
⟨⟨da i ku ni⟩⟩ (OKDJ 381a)—note that there is no ⟨⟨di ya ku⁽ⁿ⁾ ni⟩⟩ heading).

OOk ⟨mo " di ya ra⟩ *mumu-dzyara* 'the 100 chieftains' (OS 2.#47); *dzyi'ara*
<SYLLABLE CONTRACTION< *\*-dyi'ara* <METATHESIS< *\*-da'yira* ← *\*ta'yira*
(cf. J *taira* 'the Taira clan'[67]); OKDJ 673b claims that it is a "corruption" (*tenka*
転訛) of the name ⟨ta ra⟩ 'Tara/Tarō', but gives no phonological route for this
"corruption".

OOk ⟨di ya na mo i⟩ ⟨ぢやなもい⟩ *dzyanā-mii* 'Lord Jana' (OS 14.#982);
*dzyana* <(sporadic *n* < *r*)← *-dzyara* <SYLLABLE CONTRACTION< *-dzyi'ara*
<METATHESIS< *-da'yira* ←RENDAKU← *ta'yira* < ...

*t* NOk *ká·cya* 'mosquito net' < *\*...tya* < *\*...-tywa* < *\*...-tyu'a* < *\*...-tya'u* (cf.
MJ ⟨ti ya u⟩ 'hanging screen'); the composition of the word is originally
*ka* 'mosquito' and *cya* 'hanging screen'; note, however, that the word for
'mosquito' in NOk is *gaz(y)aɴ* (OGJ 190a).

The NOk word *saa·taa* 'sugar' (OGJ 452a), must have come from SJ
*\*sa#tau* '(id.)', through metathesis.

The MC and earlier forms are:

沙 Mand. shā, MC ṣa, LHan (···a < ···ai) ṣa < ṣai, OC srâi [this character ~
砂 in ESKR—both are *ping* tonal category, *ma* rhyme, given as Mandarin
*shā*] (Schuessler [2009: 216 [18–15]]);

糖 Mandarin *táng* (*ping* tone, *yang* rhyme); Schuessler does not list this
character in either of his etymological dictionaries, but all the characters
with 唐 in them (唐, 塘, {木+唐}, {虫+唐}) have exactly the same pronunciation and exactly the same *phonetic* etymology: Mand. táng, MC dâŋ,

---

67  Note the many indigenous stories of defeated Taira warriors who entered Ryukyu after the
battle of Danno'ura in 1185 (Ōkawa [Jun'ichi] (2012) [Nansō Heike ni yoru Ryūkyū/Oki-
nawa Ōchō-shi]).

LHan daŋ, OCM g-laŋ (Schuessler [2009: 77 [3–12, 700a, cde]])—the point to note is that ···ŋ stays absolutely steady throughout Chinese language history, as long as there are no suffixes to perturb it. Further, the normal development pattern of Chinese ···*aŋ* within Japanese is to ···*au*, and the typical pattern of development for *···*au* in Sino-Okinawan is for it to result in a long ···*aa*, the result of metathesis of *a* and *u*: *ta'u* > *tu'a* > *twaa* → *taa* (with loss of labial glide after a coronal or labial consonant, and with canonical lengthening to two moras in a SJ morph).

Keep in mind that there is no intrinsic reason why Okinawan should be unable to produce a sequence *a'u*, and from it, *oo*. But the word is not ˣ*saatoo*. The metathesis argument explains what happened to the rounding element *u*.

*s*  OOk ⟨ni si ya⟩ *-nyisya* '(honorific suffix)' (with Metathesis) and ⟨ni se⟩ *-nyi(i)*, *·se(e)* '(id.)' (with monophthongization₁) < *...*-sayi*

NOk ... *saa·taa*, (砂糖) 'sugar' (OGJ 452a) < *saa·tua* < *saa·tau* ← MJ ...⟨ta u⟩ ← Mand *táng*; ⟨sa⟩ *saa* results from mere lengthening of *sa*

*r*  OOk ⟨ka wa ra⟩ *kʰawara* 'Kalapa' (PLN in SE Asia) (OSJS 119c; OS 7.#356) [syllabic metathesis]; *kʰawara* < *kʰafara* < *kʰapʰara* ←METATHESIS← *kʰarapʰa* ← Indonesian *ka/elapa* 'Jakarta', the former name of Jakarta, changed initially from Kalapa to Jayakarta in 1522

NOk *zyiru*, (N) 'which one?' (OGJ 603a) [syllabic metathesis] ←META-THESIS← *zyuri* < *ʔNʣyuri* < *ʔyiʣyuri* < *ʔyidyore* < *ʔyidore* '(id.)'; cf. NJ *dore* from an Eastern-J source; cf. OJ *idure* < *idôrë*; OOk ⟨d/zu re⟩ *ʣiri/ziri* (< *ʔyɪdure*, with no metathesis) does not fit well with the vocalism of the form reconstructed from the NOk *zyiru*, suggesting that, just as with the forms in J, two competing morphs were in existence, with the *u* morph more Literary, and the *o* morph more colloquial

### 5.6.3    Details

We present here details from the processes involved with *d* (*ʣya-* ~ *dee-*), *s* (*·sya* ~ *·see*), *r* (*kawara*), *t* (*·tya* :: MJ ⟨ti ya u⟩). One important point to note here is that later changes obscure the metatheses. In part these can be ferreted out (a) through analysis of competing forms, and in part they can be seen (b) through comparison with their own allographs and with forms in the later language, either MOk or NOk.

### 5.6.3.1    d (*ʣya-* ~ dee- 'Great'); s (·sya ~ ·see 'Years of Age')

At least twice, the process occurs in morphs that also undergo different, separate sound changes, which can then be compared: i.e. in the morphemes mentioned above:

SPELLING SYSTEM AND PHONOLOGY

| dee- | <(Monophthongization)< | *dayi- | = | *dayi- | = | | *dayi- |
| dzya- [dʒɑ] | < | | | *dya- | < | *dyi₂a₁- <(Metathesis)[68]< | *da₁yi₂- |

Evidence for the pronunciation *de(e)*- [dɛː] would normally be a spelling alternation ⟨da⟩ ~ ⟨da i⟩, but here there is no ⟨da i⟩ alternant. The observed two-mora form is ⟨di ya⟩, pointing to metathesis, and to the pronunciation [dʒɑ(ː)]. This means that there are two allomorphs, one written ⟨di ya⟩ = *dzya*-, and the other written ⟨da⟩ (~ ⟨da i⟩) = *dee*-, with a missing alternant that includes ⟨i⟩.

The situation is identical with ⟨ni si ya⟩ and ⟨ni se⟩: OOk ⟨ni si ya⟩ -*nyisya* '(honorific suffix)' (OKDJ 508b; OSJS 266b) (with Metathesis) and ⟨ni se⟩ -*nyi(i),·se(e)* '(honorific suffix)' (OSJS 266b); *nyii͜see͜* 'young male person' [used in situations of reproach] (OGJ 417a) with Monophthongization (< *\*nyii*- 'two' + *\*-sayi* 'years of age' [this is also so stated by OGJ], i.e. 'young person'). Note that the spelling in the OS is with ⟨se⟩, with an ⟨e⟩ spelling being one way of writing a (typically) long front mid vowel, while ⟨sa (i)⟩ might also have been chosen.

5.6.3.2    *"O-gyaka-moi"*
To begin with, let us first look at an example of *yu-kʰ-ar-u* 'good, auspicious', the only member of the so-called *kʰaryi* conjugation (Takahashi [1991a: 13]; surely an importation from Japanese) in the OS:

| ゑ、 | け、ᴧ | よう、ᴧ | けおの、ᴧ | ゟ゚ゕ゚る゚、ᴧ | | ひに／ | ゑ、 | け、ᴧ | よう、ᴧ |
| we, | ke,ᴧ | yo u,ᴧ | ke o no,ᴧ | yo ka ru,ᴧ | | pi ni／ | we, | ke,ᴧ | yo u,ᴧ |
| yee | kʰee | yoo | kʰiwu-nu | yu-kʰ-ar-u | | p°yi-nyi | yee | kʰee | yoo |
| INJ | INJ | INJ | today-GEN | auspicious-RT | | day-LOC | INJ | INJ | INJ |
| けおの、ᴧ | | きやが†る゚、ᴧ | | ひに／ |
| ke o no,ᴧ | | ki ya ga† ru,ᴧ | | pi ni／ |
| kʰiwu-nu | | kʰyagar-u | | p°yi-nyi |
| today-GEN | | shine-RT | | day-LOC |

'Heave! Ho! Yo! On today's auspicious day! heave! ho! yo! on today's brilliant day ...!' (OS 10.#532)

---

68    Alternatively, Murayama (1981: 49) explains the palatalization here in terms of *Distanz-Palatalisierung* (German, "distance palatalization") with the *i* in *dai* palatalizing *d* by bypassing *a*, as in *dai-kuni > dyai-kuni > dʒa-kuni*. He says that *i* drops, as does *u* (in the case of *au*) after *a*, giving a number of examples.

   Shimamura (2012: 11) denies the view that *da* and *dia* come from the same source, since their usages do not overlap. Of course, in ⌐-*gunyi*, they do, but that is the only case. He also cites Nakasone Seizen, who suggests *zyoo-kunyi* 'top-country' (it should be *\*zyau >*

72  CHAPTER 2

In response to Takahashi's observation above that there is only one type (as opposed to token) of -*kʰ-ar*-, Vovin (2009a: 460) wonders if KOS ⟨ki ya ka ru⟩ ***kiya-k-ar-u*** [*sic*; but TOS ⟨ki ya ga† ru⟩ *kʰyaga·r-u*], which forms a couplet with *yu-kʰ-ar-u*, could be yet another type. However, the form ⟨ki ya⟩ = *kʰya* is actually only part of a morpheme, *kʰyaga·r-* 'to shine', related to NJ *kagar-i,* (篝) '(iron basket for holding) burning torches or a bright fire' (first attestation given in ENKDJ is OJ (MYS 19.#4156) *kagari*, in the sense of the fire in the basket, rather than the basket itself).

To explain the seemingly random PP, note NOk *tirácyaga=-y-u-N* 'teri-kaga-yaku' = 'to shine brilliantly' (VI, =*raN*, =*ti*) (OGJ 522a). Apparently the etymology is *\*tʰer-as-yi#kʰ·y·agar-* < *\*tʰer-as-* 'cause to shine' (VT) + *\*kʰaga·r-* \*[kʰãgaɾ] 'to shine' (VI), even though there is no NOk *ˣtir-ás-y-u-N* 'to illuminate [it]' (cf. NJ *terás-u,* '(id.)' [NHK]).[69] Now, note that there are many "second elements" of *rendaku* that appear to have replaced their original free forms, rather randomly from dialect to dialect, so that, for example, the free form of *\*take ~ \*-dake* '(-)bamboo' is in most Ryukyuan dialects a reflex of *\*-dake*, but in some others is a reflex of the original free form *\*take*; thus e.g. Shuri *daki*. Apparently the second element has replaced the first as a free form. Applying the same idea to the ancestor of *tirácyaga-y-u-N*, namely *\*tʰir-a[s-yi]-|kʰ·y·agar-*, we see that the "calved-off" second element of the compound (i.e. back-formation) would be *kʰyagar-*, exactly the form seen in the OOk texts.

A further problem, which is *not* metathesis (of voicing), but only appears to be, is King Shō Shin's honorific title, °*ʔu-gyakʰa-mii*, (ˣ*ʔu-kʰyaga-*; e.g. OS 5.#284) 'Exalted Shining One', with apparent velar voicing metathesis.[70]

Why the voicing reversal? The most reasonable explanation is that (a) in OOk the exalting prefix *ʔu-* voiced a following obstruent, as in the word おど の ⟨o do no⟩ *ʔu-dunu* '(imposing) building' (e.g. OS 5.#223), as opposed to free second element との ⟨to no⟩ *tʰunu* (OS 15.#1118) (NOk *ʔu-duN,* [OGJ 540b]). (b)

---

 *zyɔɔ* > *dzyɔɔ* > *dzyoo*) or *danyi-kunyi* 'true-country' (one can imagine *\*danyi* > *\*da*[∅]*yi*, etc., but with irregular intervocalic *n*-loss) as an etymon for *dzya(i)-kunyi*.

 We believe that all three of these views are rather too speculative.

69 The accent data in Martin (1987: 766, *terasu*) show that this word is accented irregularly, even in relation to NOk *tir-,* 'shine', which *does* fit the dialect-geographical accentual pattern expected of it.

70 OSJS' etymology (77ab) differs: "⟨o ki ya ka⟩ is a beautifying term shifted (*ten-jita*) [i.e. with voicing metathesis?] from *uki-agari* ['floating upward'], and means 'renowned'." (NB: *-mii* < *\*-omoyi* '-the-beloved-one'.) The only ⟨u⟩ spelling, however, is just two tokens of ⟨*u ki a ga* ri⟩ '[Captain] Uki-Agari'; all the many examples of *ʔu-gyaka* (including those referring to other persons) are with ⟨ō gi ya ka⟩. The actual literal meaning is 'The Beloved Exalted Shining One'.

SPELLING SYSTEM AND PHONOLOGY

Applying the same logic to $k^h yaga$-, the result should be non-euphonic $^x gyaga$-, and, (c) the automatic result $^x ?u$-$gyaga$-$mii$ (d) devoiced its second velar (cf. Serafim [2016: 139, 145–147] concerning Lyman's Law), (e) yielding the observed proper output $°?u$-$gyak^h a$-$mii$. (But, re (c), nb NOk $?u$-$zyága$-$muyi$ (N) [Lit.] ⟨o gi ya ga mo i⟩ 'the posthumous name of King Shō Shin' (OGJ 573b). Despite being listed in OGJ, this is decidedly a minority opinion, but represents the pre-euphonic-change version of the name; ⟨o gi $_{ya}$ ka - o mo pi⟩: $?uzyakamii$ [OKDJ 126cd].)

## 6 Meter in Omoros

### 6.1 Poetic Meter and Its Use in Determining Phonological Suprasegmentals

Let us set the stage:

As in NOk (and Standard Japanese), OOk has a distinction between *moras* and *syllables*.

A *mora* is a unit of *timing* or *meter* (think "metronome"), consisting of *one beat*: •.

A *syllable* is a unit of *phonological structure*—syllables make up the words of a language:

Distinction between syllables and moras:

NOk *neeranтaN,* 'there was no ...' $= [\overset{1}{nee}][\overset{2}{raN}][\overset{3}{taN}]$ = 3 syllables
$= [\overset{12}{••}] [\overset{34}{••}] [\overset{56}{••}]$ = 6 moras

Both NOk and OOk may have single-syllable $\#[\overset{1}{}]\#$ or multi-syllable $\#[\overset{1}{}][\overset{2}{}]\cdots\#$ words. NOk requires a minimum of two moras $\overset{12}{••}$ in any word, and this means that any one-syllable $\#[\overset{}{}]\#$ word must have two moras $\#[\overset{12}{••}]\#$, i.e. it consists of a long syllable.

As implied above, a syllable may be either one or two moras long: [•] or [••]. Both in NOk and in OOk, single-mora syllables may consist of a consonant and vowel (CV) or the *moraic* consonants (C:) N, M and Q, B, G, K.[71]

---

71  Both *N* and *Q* have mora length, and adopt characteristics of the consonant that follows them. (When *N* and *M* are word-final, they have their own place of articulation, with *N* probably uvular, i.e. [N]. *Q* is non-final only.) NOk *?aQpi,* 'that much' [?ap:ʰpi], *muQcyi,* 'holding' [mut:ʰtʃi], *mutaNtaN,* 'did not hold' [mutan:taʰN:], *?aNgwee-yii,* 'sitting cross-

74                                                                    CHAPTER 2

TABLE 2.12  Development of initial mora consonants

| NOk | < | OOk | < | Pre-OOk | Gloss |
|---|---|---|---|---|---|
| ʔ*Nzya-cyiⱼ* | < | <i di ya ti pe><br>*ʔidzya-c°yi* (OS 2.#49) | < | *\*ʔyidya-t°ye* | 'put out' |
| . . . | | . . . | | . . . | |
| *Nkée* (OGJ 435b) | < | <mu ka i><br>*Mk°ayi* (OS 13.#852) | < | *\*muk°aye* | 'greeting' |
| . . . | | . . . | | . . . | |
| --- | < | *kʰura* (⟨ko ra⟩; OS 13.#948) | < | *\*kʰora* | {'one; personage; (manly) man'} |
| . . | | . . | | . . | |
| *Qkwá* | < | *Qk°wa* (⟨ku wa⟩; OS 13.#887) | < | *\*k°ura* | 'child' |
| . . | | . . | | . . | |
| *Qcyú* | < | (*p°yic°yu*) | < | *\*p°yit°yo* | 'person' |
| . . | | . . | | . . | |

As far as we have been able to determine, the special NOk word-initial short-syllabic-mora set #ʔ*N*···, #*N*···, or #*Q*···, which are at the same time one syllable and one mora, had not yet developed in OOk, though #*M*, a precursor of #*N*, and at least one case of #*Q* had. See the accompanying Table 2.12.[72,73,74]

A two-mora syllable [··] is also called a heavy or long syllable.

The long syllables [··] have the shapes (1) CV: (i.e. CV$_i$V$_i$), (2) CV, e.g., {wuyi}, (3) CV*N*, or (4) CV*Q*···, of which the last may not occur word-finally (but it *may* occur morpheme-finally).

---

    legged' [ʔaŋːgweːʸiˤː]. *M* and *B* are labials, and *G* and *K*, velars. The velars only appear in reduced sequences from *\*k⁽ᵍ⁾ur* > *κ°r* and *\*gur* > *Gr*. Cf. e.g. ⟨ma ku ra⟩ *maκ°ra* 'pillow' ([OS 20.#1339]; NOk *maQkwaⱼ* '(id.)' [OGJ 362b]; ⟨ko ra⟩ *kʰura* 'manly man').

72   OOk *kʰura* ⟨ko ra⟩ ~ *Qk°wa* ⟨ku wa⟩ (see below); therefore *\*kora* ~ *\*kura* in pRk.

73   *Qk°wa* is an unusually early shift over from *\*κ°ra*, due to high token frequency. OOk /Q/ is not written; also, the only way to write *Cwa* is with ⟨Cu wa⟩. Further, note the NOk form *Qkwá* ~ *Qkwá-* 'progeny, child' (OGJ 445a), one of the few words left in NOk with initial *Q*. It is widely believed that this word is related to OJ *kô-ra* 'child(ren)' (JDB 313cd). We would add, however, that the Okinawan word must have undergone raising from PJ *\*kô-ra* > *\*kûra* > *\*kura* before the initial-syllable Contraction > *Qkwa*. This word may well be one of the first Contractions of this type in pre-OOk. Modern Nakijin dialect of northern Okinawa island (ROD Nk ⟨ko do mo⟩) bears this out: ⸢*k°waa*, without aspiration, and *-Qk°waa* in compounds; therefore Raising 1 probably happened before Syllable Contraction.

74   The word for 'person' (⟨pi to - no - oya⟩ 'parent of a person' [OS 5.#268]) is written only once in kana, and then it is ⟨pi to⟩. The sample is obviously not large enough from which to draw any definitive conclusions.

SPELLING SYSTEM AND PHONOLOGY 75

(1)  CV: — OOk *si(i)* 'spiritual power' (⟨se⟩ OS 3.#97), OOk *ʥyo(o)* 'gate' (⟨-di ya⟩ OS 2.#42, ⟨di ya u⟩ OS 16.#1133);

(2)  CV{wuyi} — OOk *si(i)* ~ *siyi* 'spiritual power' (⟨su pe⟩ OS 1.#6, ⟨su we⟩ OS 1.#26); OOk *yoonyi* 'like ...' (⟨ya ni⟩ OS 2.#80);

(3)  CVN — OOk *ʔaN* 'I, myself' (⟨a N⟩ OS 13.#958);

(4)  CVQ··· — OOk *muQ-cʰyi* (⟨mo ti ti pe⟩ OS 16.#1146, ⟨mo ti pe⟩ OS 2.#48) 'holding'.[75]

Apparently Q is not typically counted as a mora, nor is it written, apart from the *t*-subtype of the 4G verbal conjugation (cf. Ch. 6 §1.2).

As already explained in §2.4, the parallel verses in the OS typically have 8 moras, while those in refrains vary a great deal in their length. The commonest lengths, however, are 9 and 10 moras.

## 7 The Question of External Evidence and Its Relation to That Presented Here

### 7.1 *Aspiration, Once Again*

In what follows, our major goal is to revisit the question of the likelihood of refutation of our aspiration reconstruction, this time from the point of view of external sources, as detailed below. We believe that our hypothesis withstands this scrutiny.

### 7.2 *Sources of Reconstruction*

Up to this point, we have reconstructed the OS phonological system based exclusively on internal evidence evinced by the spelling conventions of the OS, as well as the phonological systems of surrounding dialects. External evidence, such as the documents created by Chinese and Koreans in the 15th and 16th centuries, has not in general been included, as they are beyond the scope of the present work. Nevertheless we have made one important exception.

The opposite from our approach was Lin Chih Kai's comprehensive work on the reconstruction of OOk phonology based solely on Chinese and Korean materials.[76] Here, we would like to review Lin's work and compare his reconstruction to ours.

---

75  The variant ⟨mo te⟩ should be seen as a morphologically driven non-PP, non-Q spelling, still—given the other spellings—*muQ-cˣyi.*

76  Used in this section are the following abbreviations: CC = ChiC = Chi[nese]C[orpus]; CK = prefix to a reconstructed form: Old Okinawan reconstructed by us based on LCK's Chinese and Korean corpora; KC = KorC = Kor[ean]C[orpus]; LCK = Lin Chih Kai.

76                                                                                    CHAPTER 2

TABLE 2.13   Chinese and Korean medieval sources and dates

| | Chinese sources | Korean source |
| --- | --- | --- |
| 15th C. | *Liúqiú guǎn yìyǔ*<br>『琉球館譯語』<br>*Translations by the Ryukyuan Office* | |
| Early 16th C. | *Shǐ liúqiú lù*<br>(by Chén Kǎn)<br>『使琉球錄』(陳侃)<br>*Logbook of an Embassy to Ryukyu*<br>(by Chén Kǎn) | *Haytong cheykwukki*<br>"E'umpenyek"<br>『海東諸國記』·「語音飜譯」<br>*Chronicle of the countries beyond the Eastern Sea*: 'Phonology and Translations' |
| Mid-Late 16th C. | Other *Shǐ liúqiú lù*<br>(by Kuō Rǔlín)<br>『使琉球錄』(郭汝霖) | |
| Late-16th C. | *Yīnyùn zìhǎi*<br>『音韻字海』<br>*Complete dictionary on phonological principles* | |

### 7.3     *Lin Chihkai's (2015) Reconstructions: Overview*

Lin (2015: 17) bases his reconstruction of OOk phonology on chronologically
ordered materials in Table 2.13 (translations added by Serafim and Shinzato
[S&S herafter]).

In a comparison of the LCK reconstruction with ours,[77] the following correlations are found (except for [ɪ] < *[ɛ], we pick the most evolved vowel in the
set of graphemes for the CK reconstruction):

CC-vowel–OOk-vowel correlation:

⟨i⟩     ∷   [i], [y]   ⟨ɿ⟩   ∷   [i]   ⟨əu⟩   ∷   [ʊ], [u](, [o])
⟨iəu⟩   ∷   [yuː]
⟨iɛ⟩   ∷   [ɪ]          ⟨ɿ⟩   ∷   [i]   ⟨uɔ⟩   ∷   [ʊ]
                                          ⟨u⟩    ∷   [u], [ɨ](, [ʊ])

---

77     In the process, we eliminated the following items in order to avoid anomalous compar-
       isons: 1) at least one case of mid vowel due to topicalization (*pʰicyo* 'person'); 2) anomalies
       such as ⟨t⟩ for ⟨n⟩ in CC; 3) intrusion of J forms: *kami* 'paper'; Ryukyuan forms have *b* for *m*.

SPELLING SYSTEM AND PHONOLOGY

$\langle \varepsilon \rangle$ :: [æ]      $\langle \mathfrak{o} \rangle$ :: [ɔ], [ɑ]
     $\langle a \rangle$ :: [a]   $\langle \mathfrak{v} \rangle$ :: [ɔ]
          $\langle au \rangle$ :: [ɑu̯]

KC-vowel–OOk-vowel correlation:

$\langle i \rangle$ :: [ʸi]   $\langle u \rangle$ :: [u]
$\langle ii \rangle$ :: [ɪ]   $\langle o \rangle$ :: [o][78]
$\langle jəj \rangle$ :: [ɪː]
$\langle i'u \rangle$ :: [yuː]

adjoining of two (syllabic) monophthongs yields a glide plus a long vowel, as above, and also $\langle ri'u \rangle$ :: [rʸuː]

### 7.4     *Lin Chihkai's (2015) Reconstructions: Aspiration*

Perhaps the biggest discrepancy between the LCK reconstruction and our own is that of aspiration, which is phonetic in the LCK reconstruction but phonological in ours. In the process of reviewing discrepancies, in the LCK corpora, among the forms for the same lexical item, we took the following approach: if there is aspiration marked anywhere in either ChiC or KorC, we put it in our own CK reconstruction, so that it may be dealt with systematically. This is based on the principle that information is not discarded unless and until it is shown that it is indeed not significant, that is to say, that it does not contain some aspect of the protoform to be reconstructed.[79] For example, let us look at items 14 and 15 (Table 6.1 in LCK 2015, 134), derived from the LCK corpora (see page 78).

At first glance, it appears that the LCK claim that aspiration is not phonemic in OOk is indeed the case, but closer inspection reveals a far-greater-

---

78    The large number of Korean-Corpus $\langle ((C)G)o \rangle$ where we would expect *u* rather than *o* is a real problem for our raising hypothesis. For the time being, we continue to possibly overgeneralize in claiming far more complete raising, and hope shortly to undertake a careful analysis of both the CK and the OOk data, and a much more careful comparison of the lexical items involved.

79    Here are two exceptions:
      Exception 1: where aspiration signals devoicing of a high vowel coming between two [–voi] obstruents: $^{CK*}$[pʸit͡ɕʰu] 'person' = /pyichʸu/.
      Exception 2: Rarely are the consonants we deem unaspirated written as aspirated; in the rare instances where a prenasalized obstruent is also marked as aspirated, we ignore the aspiration marking in our final ChiC- and KorC-based reconstruction, marked with the raised prefix "$^{CK}$".

78 CHAPTER 2

Entries which have Japanese cognates

| | LCK | | | S&S CK | S&S OOk | Combined OOk |
|---|---|---|---|---|---|---|
| **14. 'snow'** | | | | | | |
| | | | | *CK yuuˀkʰyi | OOkyuk°yi | *yuuˀkʰyi |
| CC: | 由乞 | iəu.khiˀ | | CK yuuˀkʰyi | | |
| CC: | 由其 | iəu.khi | | CKyuukʰyi | | |
| CC: | 由旗 | iəu.khi | | CKyuukʰyi | | |
| KC: | 유기 | ju.ki | | CKyuk°yi | | |
| **15. 'wind'** | | | | | | |
| | | | | *CK kʰadʐi | OOkkʰadʐi | *kʰadʐi |
| CC: | 嗑集 | kaˀ.tsiˀ | | CKˀkatsi | ?[kɑdʐi] | |
| CC: | 嗑濟 | kaˀ.tsi | | CKˀkaʳtsi | ?[kɑdʐi] | |
| CC: | 嗑際 | kaˀ.tsi | | CKˀkaʳtsi | ?[kɑdʐi] | |
| KC: | 칸즤 | khan.tsïi | | CKkʰanc°ïi̥ | ?[kʰɑ̃dʐɪ] | |

than chance correlation of aspiration as seen in the CK data to the claims that we have made in our present work. An example of a positive correlation is:

'rice' (28)   CKkʰumii    OOkkʰumi-sï 'Komesu' PLN      NOkkumi˩ (OGJ 331b)
(*lit.* '(the) rice(-producing) one') (OSJS 162b)

The {CKkʰu :: OOkkʰu} is perfect. The OS orthography has not caught two suprasegmental facts: (1) the long vowel of CKmii, and (2) the accent, to which it is totally blind.

There are examples of seemingly negative correlations that actually appear amenable to explanation, thus being put into the "positive" column. Let us exemplify such a correlation:

'liver' (12)   CKkʰyimu   OOkk°yimu   NOkcyimu˩ (OGJ 154–155a)

When *k and *i (*[k] and *[ʸi]) are joined together, the predicted syllable is [kʸi], without aspiration, and therefore the result is unexpected.

'(women's) inner sanctum (in the palace)'   CKuc°yi˩p°˩ara (10)    NOk——

SPELLING SYSTEM AND PHONOLOGY 79

The voicing of ₁p°₁ is not reflected in the dataset, though OKDJ (104a) says it is voiced, yielding *ʔuc°yi-bara*. Thus ₁p°₁ in this lexical item is removed from the dataset, though the word itself is retained.

'get drunk-GER' (71)    <sup>CK</sup>yuut°i    <sup>NOk</sup>wiiyuɴ˩ (OGJ 595)

The *r*-gradized-verb gerunds' morphology (Ch. 6 §2.1) shows no evidence in OS spelling of a period of *... *rt* ... or *... *tt* ... through aspiration suppression. Indeed there is no way to show a non-geminate ... *t* ... being pronounced as a non-aspirate ... *t°*.... This renders LCK's KC corpora invaluable in showing that in fact this suppression had occurred, and that already aspiration was under morphophonemic control in OOk. We can make a statement: "All GERs in OOk lack aspiration."

The CK form's root shape agrees with e.g. the Okayama gerund: *yoote*, despite the PJ form being *wep-î-të*, with root *wep-. If the OOk form is not an out-and-out borrowing from a Central or Western Japanese dialect, *wep-î-të > *wew-u-te > *yew-te > (*)yoo-te > <sup>OOk</sup>yuu-t°i.

What explains the difference in root shape between <sup>CK</sup>yuut°i and <sup>NOk</sup>wiiyuɴ˩/wii-ti˩? There appears to be no way to "back-track" to an older root form *{wiiw-} as an underlying form for CK *yuu(w)*-. Furthermore the OS spellings are no help, since they belong to ⟨we⟩, a graph which could show *ʔyi* (⟨we ra de⁺⟩ *ʔyiradi* 'choosing' [OS 3.#108]), *yi* (⟨we zo⁺ ko⟩ *yii-zuk<sup>h</sup>u* 'trading ships' [OS 1.#17]), or *wi* (⟨we ke ri⟩ *wik<sup>h</sup>iryi* 'brother(s)' [OS 14.#993]).

'good-NOM' (73)    <sup>CK</sup>yut°asya ~ <sup>CK</sup>yut°asya    <sup>NOk</sup>yutasyaɴ˩ (OGJ 293b)

<sup>CK</sup>/t°/'s aspiration has been suppressed by preceding etymological

$$*[\mathbf{V} +\mathbf{hi}]: *y\bar{u}t^{\bar{h}}a > y\bar{u}t^{\bar{\circ}}a.$$

It is assumed that this suppression cannot work with preceding etymological mid vowels (now high vowels) after raising. Note, for example, that Nakijin ˹c°yaa 'how?' < *ʔyīk̄°ya also has no aspiration, i.e. its aspiration is suppressed—although it has an aspiration distinction—and *that*, presumably by the preceding etymologically high vowel. Since part of the description is "etymologically high", it is necessarily the case that the suppression occurred before merger of the originally high and the originally mid vowels, whether that was before or after raising. If after, it follows that some feature of the formerly mid vowels still kept them distinct from the formerly high vowels, for example:

80 CHAPTER 2

[+tense] :: [−asp] vs
[−tense] :: [+asp], e.g.
[ʸi], [u] :: C° vs
[ɪ], [ʊ] :: Cʰ

Presumably, given the data at hand, the pre-raising form is *yut°a-syi-sa*, not *yota-....* Even if the adjective is related to OJ *yörö-si-*, the relation is more complex than first meets the eye.

On the other hand, there are cases of etymologically high-vowel syllables that are written as aspirated. One such example is the following:

| | | |
|---|---|---|
| 'snow' (14) | ᶜᴷyuukʰyi | ᴺᴼᵏyúcyi 'sleet' (OGJ 284b); ROD |
| | ᴼᴼᵏyuk°yi 'BE for polished rice' | recordings: no phonetic vowel |
| | (OS 12.#672) | devoicing |

The *kʰyi* of ᶜᴷ*yuukʰyi* is one of the cases of non-predicted aspiration, since ᴼᴼᵏ**kyi* should remain unaspirated *k°yi*. The CK accent on that syllable is low, coming after word-initial high, but, if ROD is any indication, both the syllables of ᴺᴼᵏ*yúcyi* remain clearly voiced, and the only voiceless sound in the word is [ʧ]. Thus we have no ready explanation for the aspiration of this sound. However, there may be a Korean-internal explanation: in Modern Korean, intervocalic /k⁽ʸ⁾/ would be pronounced [g⁽ʸ⁾], giving an output of ˣ[yugʸi]. Assuming that we can apply that Modern Korean fact to MK, we get the same output, save for the vowel length: ˣ[yu:gʸi]. Two options present themselves: the scribe might have chosen ⟨i.u.kki⟩ = [yu:k:kʸi], with a very tense, long, and completely unaspirated release. Or he could have chosen—*did* choose, in fact—⟨kʰi⟩, which lacks voicing, and probably seemed to the scribe more Okinawan-like, since tensed-consonant transcription is (almost) completely lacking in the OOk data-set.[80]

| | | |
|---|---|---|
| 'yesterday' | ᶜᴷkʰyinyuu | ᴺᴼᵏcyinuu˩ (OGJ 158a) |
| | ᴼᴼᵏ___ | |

---

80  CC ⟨iəu⟩ and KC ⟨(C)i.u⟩ both indicated vowel length, affording a more detailed look at the phonology of OOk. While NOk *yúcyi* has only a short vowel, both the Chinese and Korean data show long *yuu*. This observation can only be applied to lexical items in which the long-vowel data appear, and cannot be turned into a general statement. The general statement, if any, is that most inherent long vowels of OOk have been shortened, and do not appear in the OOk documents themselves—as many suprasegmental phenomena tend to be left out in world language writing systems.

SPELLING SYSTEM AND PHONOLOGY

Both <sup>CK</sup>*kʰyimu* and <sup>CK</sup>*kʰyinyuu* have second syllables beginning with nasals, both have historically high, palatal vowels, and both have aspirable obstruents which are indeed aspirated. We wonder if it is possible that the initial nasality of the second syllable somehow induced aspiration in the first syllable, which would otherwise have been unaspirated.

'this year' (04)   <sup>CK</sup>k°ut°usyi = [kʰų̥t°uʃi]     <sup>NOk</sup>kutúsyi [kų/ų̥tųʃị] LitOk
                   <sup>OOk</sup>kʰutʰusyi (OS 6.#298)   (OGJ 344a); Nk [ɸų̥ʳtųų'ʃị] (ROD)

<sup>NOk</sup>*kutúsyi*[81] (OGJ 344a) = tonic; if devoicing of the vowels of moras with aspirated obstruents plus high vowels before voiceless obstruents is allowed in the language, then the lack of marking of aspiration of this word is entirely explained, with the proviso elsewhere stated that a sequence of voiceless obstruents, possibly with voiceless vowels between them, acts like a consonant cluster, and deaspirates the second of the two obstruents, as well; the first obstruent can be heard either as unaspirated or aspirated under devoicing:

generalized:
(where C = voiceless obstruent, V = high vowel):
$C(\underset{\circ}{V})C^h[V, -hi] \rightarrow$
$C(\underset{\circ}{V})C°[V, -hi]$

'day(time)' (09)   <sup>CK</sup>pʰyiryu[82]          [pʸį̥ʳ]
                   <sup>NOk</sup>fíru (OGJ 240a)

The generalization above about aspiration after high vowels appearing before nasals may, given an example such as this, be expanded to include CK*r*, thus expanding the generalization from "nasals" to "sonorants". See further discussion immediately below under 'flat leather'.

'flat leather' (i.e. '(raw)hide'?)   <sup>CK</sup>pʰyiryaga   <sup>NOk</sup>___

---

81    ROD: voicing of *ku*: male speaker: [kų̥] (voiceless); female speaker [kų] (voiced).
82    The fact of the existence of this form means *pyiro̅, with PP on a non-high vowel—therefore > *pyiryo > *pyiryu. But modern dialects corroborate neither the final vowel's height nor any PP, to our knowledge. Add to that the fact that out of four examples of the word in the CC data, only one evinces *liuʔ* and the others *luʔ*, and that the only example in the KC data has no evidence of PP, either. There must be a Chinese-internal reason for the choice of *liuʔ* 陸.

82                                                                                                    CHAPTER 2

Again resonants come into the picture. Specifically concerning *r*, it seems to have had a tendency to devoice in an environment presenting all other needed elements to allow devoicing, i.e. [pʸi̥_]. This would explain the otherwise bizarre lexical alternation for the word meaning 'second-highest-ranked priestess in the land': ᴺᴼᵏ*ʔaɴsyirari̩* ~ ᴺᴼᵏ*ʔaɴsyitari̩* (OGJ 118). Note the sequences *syir* and *syit*. Two points: (1) It must have been possible for *r* to devoice in the right environment: *syir* → [ʃi̥ɾ̥]; and (2) very rarely that devoiced [ɾ̥] became [t], which is of course inherently voiceless, at least in Okinawan.

How does the latter explanation relate to 'flat leather'? The Korean spelling was ⟨pi.syaŋ.ka⟩, with ⟨sy⟩, indicating probably a voiceless [ɕʸ], which sounded sufficiently like [ʃ], the usual phonetic output of ⟨sy⟩.

'raise-INF' (67)   ᶜᴷaˀgʰiryi ~ ᶜᴷaˀgʰiˀryi   ᴺᴼᵏʔagíi

In the word for 'raise', our own reconstructed phonemic form for it is ᴼᴼᵏ/ʔagi·r·yi/ [ʔãgɪɾʸi] 'raising'. The CK aspiration is anomalous. In the Chinese corpora, the word is transcribed three ways:

an.ki?.ti        →   ᶜᴷaˀgyiˀtyi,    probably heard as [ãˀgʸiˀdʸi]
ɒŋ.kʰi?⁸³.li?   →   ᶜᴷaˀgʰyiryi,   probably heard as [ãˀgʸilʸi]
ɒŋ.kʰi?.li      →   ᶜᴷaˀgʰyiˀryi

The phonetics here mean "presumably heard by the scribes phonetically as ...." One of those ways is completely expected: a plain stop preceded by a nasal, indicating an OOk voiced stop. The other two ways, though, are not: all is the same except that the stop is aspirated: ᶜᴷn/ŋkʰ. No one believes that any kind of Ryukyuan in any period had aspirated voiced obstruents, so why the aspiration?

—   'dawn' ᶜᴷsuʳ₁tˀ₁uˀmitˀyi (LCK 90)

    ᴺᴼᵏsutumiti̩ [su̥/u̥tu̥mi̩ti̩] (OGJ 498b–499a) (phonetics from ROD); ᶜᴷ[su̥tˀu̥] making a de facto consonant cluster, thus deaspirating the [tʰ] to [tˀ]

Concerning the skewing to aspiration within the Korean data at the beginning of words, and the skewing against it in intervocalic position, if we take

---

83    Use of aspiration in ⟨kʰi?⟩ may be for Chinese-internal reasons of which we are unaware.

# SPELLING SYSTEM AND PHONOLOGY

Modern Korean (NK) as a yardstick, aspirated consonants are heavily aspirated everywhere, whereas "unaspirated" (lenis) consonants are lightly aspirated in word-initial position, and actually voiced in intervocalic or post-resonant–prevocalic position. This may lead to OOk aspirated obstruents having been heard as lenis Korean sounds initially, and as aspirated word-internally. As for OOk unaspirated obstruents, they would be even more likely to be heard as lenis (unaspirated) word-initially, because of the Korean tendency to lightly aspirate word-initial lenis obstruents, and they are likely to be heard as lenis in medial position, probably grouped together by Korean native speakers with prenasalized voiced obstruents, with only the prenasalization telling the difference to their ears.

(1)  /##CʰVCʰV/ (OOk phonemics) → (MK phonetics) [Cʰ/°VCʰV]

(2)  /##C°VC°V/ (OOk phonemics)  → (MK phonetics) ⟨C°VˣN⟩[ÇV]

(3)  /##ÇVÇᵢV/ (OOk phonemics)   → (MK phonetics) [CVNᵢ Çᵢ V]

(4)  /##ÇV̥[+hi]ÇʰV/ (OOk phonemics) →

    (a)   (MK phonetics) [if 1st C=/s/:] [##sÇV̥]

    (b)              [elsewhere:] [##ÇV̥[+hi]ÇʰV]

Put into narrative form, the above says that (1) if the OOk phonemic form is a sequence of two syllables with both of its consonants aspirated, it will find its way into Middle Korean phonetics with the first syllable either aspirated or not, and the second syllable aspirated; (2) if the two OOk syllables have unaspirated (aspirable) consonants, then they will result in written forms written in MK first syllable voiceless unaspirated and the second syllable voiced, but without prenasalization. (3) If the two Old Okinawan syllables are phonemically voiced, then in the MK output the first syllable will be written with a plain equivalent consonant, but the second consonant will be heard as a sequence of two consonants, the first consonant being a nasal ending the previous syllable, and the next consonant a plain stop or affricate, which will be phonetically voiced in that position, and together the ending nasal and the beginning phonetically voiced consonant will equal the prenasalized phonemic voiced obstruent. (4) If the first syllable of the OOk form undergoes devoicing—typically because it has an etymologically high vowel and preceding and following voiceless obstruents, then the KorC phonetic output will be one of two types: (a) if the first consonant is ᴼᴼᵏ/s/, then the output will be ⟨##sÇV⟩; or (b) elsewhere, the first syllable will still be perceived by the Korean scribe as an independent syllable, and the KorC output will be ⟨##ÇV[+hi]ÇʰV⟩.

Given the above presented data and discussion of it, we believe that we have presented sufficient justification for our own internally generated phonological hypothesis, with only minor alterations, chief of which is suppression of aspiration in all aspirable gerunds, be they original or secondarily derived through analogy. Through this procedure we have radically reduced the percentage of non-correlating items, but nonetheless, as is always the case when dealing with real-world data, there is an irreducible minimum of (to us) intractable examples of lack of correlation. Of the set of data that we attempted to correlate, first of all we excluded lexical items without aspirable obstruents (21 tokens); then we tabulated those showing perfect correlation between the CK and the OOk forms, 36.5 tokens (68%), ones not showing such correlation but nonetheless amenable to explanation, 13.5 (25%), and ones that we were unable to explain, 3 tokens (6%). Left over was a 1% rounding error.

We feel certain, in any case, that we have been able to accomplish what we set out to do despite this leftover number.

## 8    Coda

This concludes both the internally generated and externally checked spelling-phonological hypotheses and discussions in Chapter 2. The reader will find more discussions about spelling and/or phonology—especially in footnotes—throughout the rest of this work.

CHAPTER 3

# Lexicon

The lexicon of the *Omoro-Sōshi* (OS) language may be subdivided by origins into four groups: (1) PJ origin; (2) MJ loans; (3) Chinese loans; and (4) Korean loans. In addition, there are those whose (5) origins are unknown, and (6) so-called *mishōgo* (未詳語 'words the meanings of which are as yet unclear', i.e. 'Meanings Obscure' [MO]).

## 1 PJ Origin

Nouns of this group typically—though not necessarily[1]—have proven cognates in OJ substantiated by semantic and phonological correspondences. The sound correspondences of these words with OJ counterparts can all be explained by mid-vowel raising (e.g. *-kʰu* < *-ko*),[2] progressive (... *yi-k°yu* < *... yi-kyo* < *... yi-ko* < *... i-ko*) and regressive palatalization (*-busyi* 'star' < *-"-posi*), and sequential voicing (i.e. *rendaku*; see Ch. 2 § 5.5 and the previous example).[3] Examples include:

- *-kʰu(u)/-k°yu(u)* こ(う)・きよ(う)・く ⟨ko (u), ki yo (u), ku⟩ 'one/person(age)':
  - *-kʰu* < *-ko*: せだ゛かこ ⟨se da゛ ka ko⟩ *si-dakʰa-kʰu* 'spiritual.power-high–**one**' (OS 1.#1);

---

1 It is entirely possible, through presumably not common, for words to have no OJ or even any other Japonic cognates at all, but still to be Japonic. Marshaling data in favor of such cognation, however, would be impossible.
2 Three examples of *blocking* of phonological changes—two types, both apparently due to long vowel—include:
 a) *e > i* raising blocked by length:
  ʔPJ *pabêru* 'butterfly' > OJ –; > pre-OOk *paabeeruu* > OOk *pʰa(a)be(e)ru(u)* '(id.)' > LitOk *haberu/habiru* 'butterfly' (OGJ 198a); ColloqOk *haabeeruu* 'moth(; butterfly)' (OKDJ 550a) PJ *ʔukêdu* 'dragonfly'; OJ *akıdu* '(id.)' (JDB 8c); > pre-OOk *aakeezuu* '(id.)' > OOk あけ ず、かた ⟨a ke zu , ka ta⟩ *ʔa(a)ke(e)zu(u)-kata* 'picture of a dragonfly' (OS 9.#479); LitOk *ʔaakeezuu* 'dragonfly' (OGJ 99a), *ʔakezu-bani-n'su* 'summer finery (BE)' (OGJ 110a) [*-bani*: rendaku form of *háni* 'wing' (OGJ 205a); *n-su* 'clothing*BE*']
 b) raising of back mid vowel *ô > u* blocked by length: *ʤyoo* 'gate; ⌒ Avenue' (OGJ 603b; cf. OJ *tô* 'gate, door; strait' (JDB 485b–d): PP + sequential voicing of pre-OOk *too*, yielding the allomorphs *too ~ *-dyoo*; then, adoption of *dyoo* as the only allomorph), etc.
3 For a discussion of denasalization (*m > b*) in the case of a possible progenitor of *buri-* 'constellat(ing)' as *mure-*, cf. Erickson 1997.

---

© KONINKLIJKE BRILL NV, LEIDEN, 2021 | DOI:10.1163/9789004414686_004

— -*k°yu* < \*-*kyo* < \*-*ko*: たたみきよ ⟨ta ta mi ki yo⟩ *tʰat°amyi-k°yu*[4] 'noble-**one**' (OS 1.#13)

とよむ ∧    せだ\*かこが\*                    /
to yo mu ∧    se da\* ka ko ga\*              /
*tʰuyum-u     si-dakʰa-kʰu-ga*
resonate-RT spiritual.power-high-**one**-SUB
'The Resounding **One** of Great Spiritual Power' (OS 1.#1)

たゝみきよ、     / かほう ∧     よる、∧        みやが†の、    もり、∧
⟨ta " mi ki yo ,     / ka po u ∧    yo ru , ∧       mi ya ga† no ,  mo ri , ∧
*tʰat°amyi-k°yu*-∅   *kʰa·pʰuu*-∅   *yur-u*         *myi#yaga*[5]*-nu muryi*-∅
noble-**one**-VOC     fortune-SUB approach-RT look-up-GEN grove-LOC
ちよわれ    /
ti yo wa re    /
*c°yuwar-i*
reign_EX-MR
'Your Majesty [= *tʰat°ami-k°yu*], reign over Kahō Yoru Miyaga no Mori[6] Shrine!' (OS 1.#13)

— よろい ⟨yo ro i⟩ (OSJS 362b) ~ よるい ⟨yo ru i⟩ (OSJS 362a) ~ ゆろい ⟨yu ro i⟩ (OSJS 344c) *yuruyi*[7] 'armor' (cf. OSJS 362b, OKDJ 726bc, "armor imported from Yamato, serving as a symbol of power"; first attested in J in KJK, 712 CE[8])

---

4   The lexeme {kʰu} would appear long as an independent word, but exclusively appears as a quasi-suffixal element, as in these examples. We see it as short unless specifically written long (as in ⟨ki yo u⟩ [OS 13.#795, #800]), presumably attached with {#}. It can be PP'ed, because it begins with an underlyingly aspirated consonant plus high vowel < \**Co*: ··· *yi-k°yu* ← ··· *yi-k°u*; and otherwise will appear as *-kʰu*.

5   The form likely represents a metrical shortening from {myii#(ʔ)aga···}; if, on the other hand, the underlying form is the less likely {myi#(ʔ)aga···}, then *my-aaga-*.

6   Given in modern scholarly pronunciation.

7   All else being equal, this word should be ˣ*yurii*, but all else is not equal. Note that NOk has *yurúyi*, and that (1) it is diphthongal, and that (2) its accent is the reverse of NJ *yoroi*₁, suggesting relative antiquity. The best fit for OOk with these facts is *yuruyi*, as opposed to *yuru'yi*, the former signaling *uyi* = VCV, and the latter, *u'yi* = VCGV. Since we assume that in the postvocalic context it was CGV = '*yi* that led to D1 and then to M1, it follows that a postvocalic sequence not marked with the tick will not diphthongize and subsequently will not monophthongize. This is tantamount to claiming an exception to a regular sound change; blocked by \**yii*?

8   This is a culture word, as well as a word appearing in an early OJ source, so it is possible that it was borrowed again into Ryukyu after having been inherited.

# LEXICON

87

きこゑ　　大ぎﾟみぎや、　　／ あけの、　よろい、、ᴧ
ki ko we　OPO giﾟ mi gi ya ,　／ a ke no ,　yo ro i ,ᴧ
*k°yi̠k°uyi*　*ʔuQp°u-gyimyi-gya*　　*ʔakʰi-nu*　**yuruyi-∅**
famed　　　great-priestess-SUB　red-GEN　**armor-DO**
めしよわちへ、　　／
me si yo wa ti pe ,　／
*mis-y-uwa-c°yi*
wear_EX-RY-EX-GER
'The High Priestess Kikoe Ōgimi, wearing red **armor**' (OS 1.#5)

—　*buri-busyi* ぼﾟれぼし ⟨bo*⁹ re bo si⟩ 'constellation, the Pleiades' (OS 10
.#534): *buri*_VI-RY- 'gathered' (INF) < *\*-bUre-* (cf. NOk *burí-* '(id.)' [OGJ 137b]);
-*busyi* 'star' < *\*-"-posi* (cf. NOk *fúsyi* '(id.)' [OGJ 222b*f*])

ゑ、　け、ᴧ　あがﾟる、ᴧ　ぼﾟれぼし　　　　や　／
we ,　ke ,ᴧ　a gaﾟ ru ,ᴧ　boﾟ re bo si　　　ya　／
*yee*　*kʰee*　*ʔagar-u*　**buri-busyi**　　　*ya*
INT　INT　rise-RT　**constellate_RY-stars** TOP
'Eh, hey! The rising **Pleiades**!' (OS 10.#534)

Nouns in this category of PJ origin range extensively from human bodies to
clothing, animals to plants, celestial bodies to natural phenomena and terrain,
and so on.

There are nouns the meaning of which can reasonably be deduced from their
opposite number in the adjacent verse, even though phonological details have
not yet been worked out. Below are some of these nouns.[10]

---

9　Only this one token of the allograph ⟨boﾟ⟩ exists for this morph, vs at least 21 tokens written
with the allograph ⟨bu⁽ﾟ⁾⟩, supporting strongly a reconstruction of *\*bure-* *'gathered'. The
NOk form ##*buri-* [bur̥ʲi], however, suggests either *\*##bore-* or *\*buure-*, on the assumption
that *\*#būr* becomes non-observed NOk ˣ#*Nd*-, i.e. in ˣ*ʔNdi-busyi*. If mid vowel Raising and
high vowel shortening both
　　(There exists, e.g., NOk *Ndí-* 'get wet; go to ruin' [OGJ 435a], related to OJ *nure-* '(id.)'
　　[JDB 556d]. Also NOk *Nɔyari,* 'tousled appearance [of hair, yarn, ropes]' [OGJ 438],
　　related to OJ *mîdare-* [mʲĩdɑre] 'become out of place (of threadlike things); be hope-
　　lessly in love' [JDB 705ab]. Thus *\*nur ... > \*Nd ...* and *\*myid ... > \*Mdʑy ... > \*Nzy ...* suggest
　　nasal or voiced obstruent—which incorporates nasality—plus a sequence of original
　　high vowel *\*u* or *\*yi* plus *\*r* yield NOk *Nd ...* if PP is not involved, and *Nzy ...* if it is.)
occur after {*\*bur > Nd*}, then both *\*##bore-* and *\*##buure-* are possible, but the overwhelming number of ⟨bu re⟩ allograph tokens suggests a pre-OOk form *\*##buure-*.

10　There is at least one noun whose extended meaning appeared in the OS earlier than in
Japanese literature. The word *p°usyi* ふし ⟨pu si⟩ came to mean 'tune' from 'joint (of a

88    CHAPTER 3

–    ゐりちよ 〈we ri ti yo〉 *ʔyi̯r-yi-dzyi(i)* 'beautiful voices/words'[11]

| てるかはと、∧ | とご†ゑ、∧ | やりかわちへ | / |
|---|---|---|---|
| te ru ka pa to , ∧ | to go† we , ∧ | ya ri ka wa ti pe | / |
| *tʰir-u-kʰaQp°a-tʰu* | *tʰuu-guyi-∅* | *yar-yi-ˌkʰawa-c°yi* | |
| shine-RT-{well/spring}-COM | ten-voice[s]-DO | send-RY-exchange-GER | |
| てるしのと、∧ | ゐりぢよ、 | やりかわちへ | / |
| te ru si no to , ∧ | we ri di yo , | ya ri ka wa ti pe | / |
| *tʰir-u-syinu-tʰu* | **ʔyi̯r-yi-dzyii-∅** | *yar-yi-ˌkʰawa-c°yi* | |
| shine-RT-Orb-COM | **chosen-RY-voice[s]-DO** | send-RY-exchange-GER | |

'[The high priestess Kikoe Ōgimi] will exchange ten-voices with Teru Kappa [= the Sun Deity]; [the high priestess by another name, Toyomu Sedakako] will exchange [carefully] **chosen voices** with Teru Shino [again, the Sun Deity]' (OS 1.#16)

Previous analyses never mentioned the provenance of 〈ti yo〉, nor offered an explicit account of any connection of 〈we ri〉 to 〈we to〉 and 〈we i̯to〉, except for Nakahara and Hokama (OSJS 374b, 〈weri ⁽ⁿ⁾ti yo〉, 〈we ri si yu〉), which says that "it is the same etymon as *īto*, but, 〈weri̯tiyo〉 [= S&S *ʔyi̯r-yi-dzyii*] is [= refers to] words, [while] 〈weto〉 [and] 〈wei̯to〉 mean [= refer to] songs."[12] We propose that 〈weri〉 = *ʔyi̯r-yi-* (< *\*er-yi-*) is related to NJ *ér-u, er-áb-u* 'select' as *\*ʔyer-yi-* *'select(ed)*', and that 〈⁽ⁿ⁾ti yo〉 = *-dzyii* is linked to NJ *kóe ~ -goe* 'voice' < OJ *köwe* < pre-OJ *\*köwë* 'voice' in the same way as the *-gwii* in *tʰuu-gwii* in its couplet in the previous verse. The hypothesized derivation is as follows: *\*ʔyer-yi-N-kowe > *\*ʔyer-yi-gowe > *\*ʔyer-yi-goye > *\*ʔyer-yi-gyoye > *\*ʔyɪr-yi-gyoyɪ > *\*ʔyi̯r-yi-gywɪɪ > *\*ʔyi̯r-yi-dzywii → ʔyir-yi-dzyii*.[13] Just as *dzyoo* can be written 〈di

---

    bamboo)'. Quoting Serei Kunio, Shimamura (1983: 309–310) states that the tune names did not have the suffix ⁽ⁿ⁾*p°usyi* (e.g. *magaki-bushi*) until the mid-17th century in Japanese; prior to that they used the suffix *-ryū* (e.g. *Heiku-ryū*).

11    In the following discussion we will refer to *ʔyii̯tʰu* 〈we to〉 (in the title of Book 11), and 〈we i to〉 ([*hapax*], OS 8.#472; NOk *ʔyii̯tʰu*ˌ [OGJ 252b]) 'yo heave ho!', a work chant.

12    The original OSJS wording is: 「イートと語源は同じだが、『ゑりちよ』は言葉で、『ゑと』『ゑいと』は歌謡を意味する。」 "*īto to gogen wa onaji da ga,* 〈we ri ti yo〉 *wa kotoba de,* 〈we to〉 〈we i to〉 *wa kayō o imi-suru.*"

13    A minor sound change affects sequences of labio-palatalized velars, sometimes converting them into labial fricatives by the time of NOk (e.g. 〈ki ko we o po gi mi〉 *k°yik°uyi*[ *ʔuQp°u*]*-gyimyi > k°yik°ywi*[ *ʔuQp°u*]*-gyimyi > ... > NOk *cyifyí-zyiɴ* [OGJ 147b]), and at other times, as here, triggering early affrication of *gyw > dzyw > dzy*, with loss of labiality after coronals. It is not clear whether the different outcomes are due to voicing—after

LEXICON                                                                    89

ya⟩, without ⟨'u⟩ as its graphic coda in one of its allographs that takes care of
its rounding, so too can ⟨di yo⟩ be written as the allograph of ⟨di yo 'i⟩, with
the missing ⟨'i⟩ (underlyingly) taking care of the word's front-vowel articulation:

⟨di ya    'u⟩   ~   ⟨di ya⟩   ::   *dzyoo*      [dʒɔː]
(⟨di yo   'i⟩   ~)   ⟨di yo⟩   ::   *dzy{w}ii*   [dʒiː]

with {⋯} standing for a segment just deleted in that string.

–    ぢや、はれ ⟨di† ya , pa re⟩ *dzyoori* [dʒɔːɾɪ] 'sandals' (OSJS 220a)

だしきや、          うちくぎ、                  / ぢや、はれ、
da si ki ya ,      u ti ku gi ,                / di† ya , pa re ,
*dasyik°ya-∅*      *ʔuc-°yi-k°ugyi-∅*          *dzyoori-∅*
shima.misao-TOP    hammer-RY-spike-COP_SS      zōri-TOP
まわらし                           #
ma wa ra si                       #
*ma-warazyi-∅*
true-traveler's.sandals-COP_SS
'[Spiritually protecting] *dashikya*[14] [wood is made into] hammering-
spikes [for the army to drive into the new ground!] **Zōri** [are transformed
into spiritually protecting] true travelers'-footwear[15,16] [for the army!] [Let
us thereby ensure the army's victory!]' (OS 1.#17)

---

        all, if *gyw* followed the route of *k°yw*, the result would be *γβ*, a sound unknown in Oki-
        nawan.
14      Any voiceless aspirable consonant will automatically be ruled unaspirated when a pre-
        ceding vowel is etymologically high; thus the aspiration of its following consonant must
        necessarily be suppressed in this case, even though we possess no direct evidence for the
        suppression.
15      TOS has no voicing mark here, but our interpretation requires voicing.
16      Insofar as the hypothesis that we delineate here is correct, both ⟨di ya pa re⟩ *dzyo₁o₂|ri*
        and ⟨ma wa ra ["|si⟩ *ma-wa₁ra₂|zyi₃* constitute jumping-off points for successful argu-
        ments in favor of the Yotsu-Gana Hypothesis. This is because the historical origin of J
        *zoori* is *zauri*, with *z*, yet, because it comes within the purview of the first two moras,
        the OOk spelling has it "wrong", that is to say, according to OS-internal rules (1st and
        2nd moras), and the same, just in reverse, for ⟨ma wa ra ["|zi⟩, where the MJ historical
        spelling is ⟨wa ra di⟩, not ˣ⟨⋯zi⟩, again, "wrong", but obeying OS-internal rules (3rd mora
        and beyond).

90                                                                                          CHAPTER 3

The phonological form *dzyoori* [dʒɔːɾɪ][17] is related to the spelling ⟨ti ya pa re⟩ as follows: (1) The spelling ⟨ti ya⟩ is most typically the way of writing *cʲ/ʰya(a)* or *dzya(a)*. (2) The spelling ⟨···a pa⟩ may be the phonological form ···*apʰa*, ···*aba*, or ···*awa*. The ⟨···apa⟩ :: ···*awa* correspondence is due to a weakening of non-initial *\*p* to *w*, a sound change that is also found in J.[18] So, lastly, (3) the correspondence ⟨···apa⟩ :: ···*oo* is explained as due to a sound change of \*···*awa* to \*···*oo*.[19] Note, however, that the normal sound changes for Shuri are pre-OOk \*···*awa* > NOk ···*aa* and pre-OOk \*···*aawa* > NOk ···*awa*.


## 2      Loans from MJ

Abe (2009) has listed a number of OS words that she notes are not listed in JDB, but only in *JDB-Muromachi*. We have added the dates of first attestation given in NKDJ in order to give a more exact view of when they first appeared in Japanese. They are newly coined words in the period after OJ, and thus do not have their origins in PJ:

–      *p°yik-°yi-ʔyidzyi-munu* ひきいぢ*へ物 ⟨pi ki i di* pe MONO⟩ 'gift for guests'; first attested in J as ⟨pi ki i de mo no⟩ *Utsubo Mg* (宇津保物語 970–999; NKDJ).[20]

    なおが*、∧ ひきいぢ*へ、物、    / なおが*、∧ てづ*と、もの    /
    na o ga*,∧ pi ki i di* pe, MONO, / na o ga*,∧ te du to, mo no /
    *nawu-ga  p°yik°.yi.ʔyidzyi.munu  nawu-ga  tʰi-dzitʰu-munu*
    what-KP  **gift**        what-KP  keepsake
    'What (is it)?—the **gift** (that we'll give). What (is it)?—the keepsake?'
    (OS 15.#1105)

---

17    For the older-attested form [zauɾi] (934 CE), SNKDJ has the first attestation of [ʒɔːɾɪ] as 1481 CE, still before compilation of the first book of the OS.

18    See Ch. 2, §2.2.1, §4.5.

19    Just as ···*awa* → ···*oo*, so, too, ···*aya* → ···*ee*. Cf. ⟨pa ya bu* sa⟩ *pʰayaBsa* 'hawk, accipitrid' (OS 13.#919) and ⟨ko pa i, bu* sa⟩ *kʰu-pʰeeBsa* 'fast, small boat' *lit.* 'little hawk' (OS 13.#761), and NOk *fénsa* 'accipitrid' (OGJ 229a). The spelling ⟨···a i⟩ suggests ···*aya* → ···*ayi* → ···*ee*, and thus also ···*awa* → ···*awu* → ···*oo*, as well.

20    Note that *-ga* here is a question particle, related to J *ka*, and is a type of *kakari* particle, not a subject or genitive particle.

LEXICON

– *tʰumuyi* ともへ ⟨to mo pe⟩ 'comma-shape(d jewel)'; first attested in J in *Gōke Shidai* (『江家次第』1111)

| きこゑ | あおりやいや、 | / ともへ、 ∧ | | みまが†り、 ∧ |
|---|---|---|---|---|
| ki ko we | a o ri ya i ya , | / to mo pe , ∧ | | mi ma ga† ri , ∧ |
| *kˤyiˌkˤuyi* | *ʔawuryayi-ya* | **tʰumuyi-∅** | | *myi-magar-yi* |
| famed | Aoriyae-TOP | **comma.design**-DO | | three-arc-RY<sub>NOM</sub> |

かけわちへ、　/
ka ke wa ti pe ,　/
*kʰakʰi-wa-cˤyi*
hang-EAV-GER

'The high priestess Aoriyae, wearing a necklace with a crest in the shape of three **comma-shaped figures** in a circle'[21] (OS 12.#683)

## 3 Loans from Sino-Japanese

Takahashi (1991a: 40–41) has a list of about 60 Sino-Japanese words, of which about ten are, according to him, controversial as to their origins, e.g. *ʔu-soo-zi* [ʔusɔːzɪ] ⟨o sa u ze*⟩ 'thoughts'[22] [想] (OS 1.#34), or *kʰa-gwii* [kʰɑgʷɪː] 'beautiful voice' ⟨ka go† pe⟩ (OS 13.#820), ⟨ka go† we⟩ (OS 22.#1543).[23] Here are a few less controversial examples.[24]

---

21 Yoshinari and Fuku (2006: 139–140) state that the high priestess Aoriyae of the First Shō Dynasty possessed the traits of the deity of wind and rain, and that the First Shō Family's crest is *hidari mitsu-domoe* 'left[-turning] triple-comma[-shaped] crest'. In addition, they state that the King's family name Shō is written with 尚, which has three dots at the top signifying the three comma-shaped lines in the crest, and that the bottom character resembles 'turn' (回). As attractive as their hypothesis may be, we need to exercise caution here. The resemblance they point out could just as easily be an accident, and beyond proof; further it was the Chinese emperor who bestowed the family name and the character. Having said that, we nevertheless do not doubt Yoshinari and Fuku's claimed close tie between the Ryukyus and Korea.

22 Pre-OOk borrowed this Chinese morph through Japanese, probably through the Buddhist channel. After all, OOk *soo-* is more closely associated with the J Go'on ⟨sa u⟩, rather than the J Kan'on stratum, with its historical spelling ⟨si ya u⟩; Go'on morphs are (typically) more closely tied to Buddhism.

23 KKKS defines it as "*koye no yoki koto nari* (It refers to the beauty of a voice)". The interlineations give 佳声 'delightful voice' and 良い声 'good voice'.

24 The *kanji* in the parentheses below are *not* to be found in the text of the *Omoro Sōshi*, but rather are put in by us for the sake of clarity.

- *kʰa·pʰuu* かほう 'fortune, bounty' (果報);[25] cf. Ch. 2 § 4.1.1.1 fn. 40:

| 世が*ほう、ᴧ | まが*ほう、ᴧ | みおやせ | / |
|---|---|---|---|
| YO ga* po u,ᴧ | ma ga* po u,ᴧ | mi o ya se | / |
| *yu-ga·pʰuu-∅* | *ma-ga·pʰuu-∅* | *myi-ʔu-yas-i* | |
| worldly-**bounty**-DO | true-**bounty**-DO | EX-EX-give_EX-MR | |

'Please offer worldly[26] **bounty**, true **bounty**!' (OS 15.#1085)

- *siʣya* すぢや ⟨su di ya⟩ 'mortals' (衆生); NOk *sizya,* [siʳʒɑ] '(id.)' (OGJ 487a); <[27] pre-OOk *\*suʣywa* <[28] *\*suzyua* < *\*suzyau* ← MJ:

| ちにや、ᴧ | まけな、 | / | いきや ᴧある、ᴧ | すぢや、ᴧ | おて |
|---|---|---|---|---|---|
| ti ni ya,ᴧ | ma ke na, | / | i ki ya ᴧ a ru,ᴧ | su di ya,ᴧ | o te |
| *cʸinya* | *makʰina* | | *ʔyikʰʸya.ʔar-u* | *siʣya-* | *wu-tʰʸii* |
| China | MO | | what.kind-of | **mortals**-SUB | be-GER/PRFV |

| が、 | / |
|---|---|
| ga, | / |
| *ga* | |
| QP | |

'In China [tʃiɲa] Makena, what kind of **mortals** (i.e. **vassals**) were there?' (OS 19.#1300)

- *naм#ʣya* なむぢや ⟨na mu di ya⟩ 'silver' (南鐐):

---

25    While the independent word in NOk is *kwafuu,* 'good luck', with a *w*, the compound *yu-g̱áfuu* 世果報 'year of abundant harvests' is without. Judging from the fact that OSJS has only ⟨ka po u⟩, not ˣ⟨ku wa po u⟩, apparently *kwafuu,* in NOk with *w* was borrowed more recently. The time of borrowing of ...*gapʰuu* remains unknown, but it was surely before pre-OOk independently developed *kw*, *gw*, and *ʔw* sequences, since it came in with its *\*kʰw/\*gw* sequences deleted. Only later, after Ok had independently developed its own *kw*, *gw*, and *ʔw*, could *kwafuu* once again be borrowed without its *w* being zeroed out.

26    The character for the segment string *yu-*, which may be interpreted as a lexeme, *does* appear in text, as here, but is also well known as simply another way of writing the mora *yu*, in other words, as a ⟨yo⟩ allograph. Both work in this particular context.

27    Loss of *Yotsu-Gana* Distinction: cf. Ch. 2 § 5.4; *w* > ∅ /y__: cf. this chapter, fn. 13.

28    Development of *Yotsu-Gana* Distinction. Cf. Ch. 2 § 5.4; *\*u* > *\*w/\*y__V* : part of Medial *\*p* Softening (*ha-gyō tenko(-on)*), Ch. 2, § 2.2.1.

LEXICON                                                                          93

なむぢや、、∧　こが゛ね、　/　もぢ†よる、、∧　きよら　　や　/
na mu di ya , ∧ ko ga⃰ ne ,　/　mo di† yo ru , ∧ ki yo ra　　ya　/
**naм·ʣya**-∅　*kʰugani*-∅　　*muʣyur-u*-∅　*kˤyura*-∅ *yaa*
**silver**-COM　　gold-GEN　　glitter-RT-SUB beautiful SFP
'Isn't the glittering[29] of the **silver** and gold beautiful!' (OS 17.#1240)

The word *nam·ʣya* is commonly said to be a borrowing from MJ *namu·reu*
'beautiful/high-quality silver'. Presumably the borrowed protoform had *ryau*
→ *ryua* → *rywa* → *rya*, with the *r* becoming *z/ʣ* depending on *Yotsu-Gana*
rules, in this case either because it was morpheme-initial or else because it
directly followed a nasal.

## 4　Loans from Korean

To our knowledge, there has been no attempt to find any loan from Old or Middle Korean except by Vovin (2009b). There is, however, a claim by Yoshinari and
Fuku (2006: 132–140) about the influence of the belief in Yŏndŭng Halman, the
Korean god of wind and rain, on the Ryukyu kingdom by way of the Hachi-
man/Yahata creed, especially in Northwestern Kyushu.[30]

Vovin (2009b: 16) asserts that (*\*ʔayo* >) OOk *ʔayu* 'heart, liver, guts' is a
loan from Korean: MK *ǎy* 'intestines, gallbladder; bravery', Proto-Korean *\*ayo*.
In addition, he suggests (2009b: 20–21) that *gusiku* 'castle' is a loan from Old
Korean *\*kwús[ù] kwót* 'ceremonial place in Shamanism'. Further, he hypothesizes (2009b: 21–23) that (his provisionally reconstructed pre-OOk *\*siwori* [i.e.
*\*syiworyi* in our romanization] >) *syiyuryi* (> NOk *syuyi‚* 'Shuri' [OGJ 491a]) is
a loan from Middle Korean *syěWùr* [ʃəᶾβù̵l]][31] 'capital', though he cautions that
the rising accent on the first syllable, signifying a contraction of two syllables,
may throw cold water on the proposal depending on the timing of that sound
change; but we note that the OOk form is provably three moras long—as, e.g.
in the frequent pairing of the parallel ⟨si yo ri mo ri⟩ *syiyuryi muryi* and ⟨ma da

---

29　Referring to this omoro and OS 34, Shimamura (2010: 418) asserts that this word describes
　　a state suffused with metallic glittering or spiritual power radiating.

30　Yoshinari and Fuku (2006: 138) state that the relationship between the first Shō family and
　　the Hachiman/Yahata creed has been pointed out by Tanigawa (1999: 193), based on the
　　excavation in Okinawa of *ishi-nabe* 'stone pots' similar to those found on the Sonoki Penin-
　　sula, Nagasaki (Northwestern Kyūshū), and speculated about earlier by Orikuchi (1956
　　[1937]: 14–68).

31　Our interpretation of the MK phonetics, not necessarily Vovin's.

ma mo ri⟩ *ma-dama muryi*—, as is the MK form, actually *strengthening* Vovin's hypothesis linking the two.

– ʔ*ayu* あよ ⟨a yo⟩ (38 tokens), あゆ ⟨a yu⟩ (2 tokens) 'heart':

> あよ、ぢ†よく、ˆ　　げに、ˆ　あれ　　/
> a yo , di† yo ku , ˆ　ge ni , ˆ a re　　/
> *ʔayu#dzyuu-k°u　gi·nyi　ʔar-i*
> **liver**#strong-ly　tru·ly　be-MR
> 'Be[32] **gut**-strong, truly!' (OS 1.#33)

– *gusik°u* ぐすく ⟨⁽ⁿ⁾ku su ku⟩ 'holy place, place for prayer (OSJS 137c);[33] castle':

> しより　　もり　　ぐ゛すく　　　/
> si yo ri　mo ri　gu゛su ku　/
> *syiyuryi　muryi　gusik°u*
> Shuri　　Grove　**Enclosure**
> '[Upon] the Shuri Grove **Enclosure**' (OS 1.#1)

## 5　Origins Unknown

There is a handful of words whose etymologies or cognations to OJ have not yet been agreed upon among scholars.

– *tʰi(i)da* てた ⟨te ta⟩ (OS 8.#399), てだ ⟨te da⟩ 'sun' (OS 18.#1275)

---

32　This is a copular expression (cf. J *kari-katsuyō*) with interposed adverbial expression.

33　OSJS, in its discussion of the headword ⟨ku su ku⟩ (137c), cites Nakamatsu Yashū, "Kusuku-kō," and agrees with his position that the origin of the *gusuku* was as the place where the surrounding villages' tutelary deity was interred. This view would seem to accord with Vovin's etymology.

　Parenthetically, the OSJS index has only one token of ⟨gu su ku⟩ with a voicing mark, out of examples almost too numerous to count. The modern form is only with voicing. Whether voicing was original or not is rendered moot because of the possibility of the analogic spread of rendaku to the beginning of free words, as in the case of 'bamboo', *d/t⁽ʰ⁾AKI*, depending on the dialect. Nevertheless, e.g. TOS 1.#1 has ⟨si yo ri mo ri gu su ku⟩, and so on, meaning that if we trust the assigning of voicing marks by TOS, then the word has had initial *g* since the time of the first written documents.

# LEXICON

This is an important word in the *Omoro Sōshi* for religious reasons, since the Sun was worshiped as a deity, as the source of enormous spiritual energy and divine power (*tedako shisō* 'Tedako thought', e.g. Hokama 1985 and Higa 1986), and subsequently for its metaphorical use referring to kings and rulers. As for the origin of this word, there are basically three hypotheses as succinctly presented in Nakamoto (1981: 29): connection to southern external sources such as *chidaru* (Ami, indigenous language of Taiwan); to the MJ Sino-Japanese word *teNdau* 〈天道〉 *lit.* 'heaven road';[34] and to the string *\*teri-ya* 'shine-thing'. Of these three, Sanada and Tomosada (2007: 316–317) and Mamiya (2014: 39–40) support the *teNdau* origin. Note that loss of *N* can lead to compensatory lengthening of the preceding vowel (*ten* > *tee*), and that metathesis of final *au* to *ua*, frequent in pre-OOk SJ-origin morphs, will lead to dropping of the labial, leaving a short *a* (*dau* > *dua* > *dwa* > *da*). For loss of *w* after coronals, see Ch. 2 §5.6.

かみ ∧      てだ†の、    ／ まぶり、よわる、∧
ka mi ∧     te da† no ,    ／ ma bu ri , yo wa ru , ∧
*kʰamyi-∅*  *tʰi(i)da-nu*   *maвr-y-uwar-u*
deity-COM   **sun**-SUB     protect-RY-AUX_{EX}-RT
'(look!—it is the ruler over the lords,) whom the (lesser) deities and the **Sun** (Deity) deign to keep protecting.' (OS 1.#2)

よの ∧      あけて、     ／ てだの、∧   てりよる、やに              ／
yo no ∧     a ke te ,     ／ te da no , ∧  te ri yo ru , ya ni            ／
*yu(u)-nu*  *ʔakʰi-t°i*    *tʰi(i)da-nu*  *tʰir-y-ur-u-yoo-nyi*
night-SUB   break-GER      **sun**-SUB    shine-RY-SE-RT-like-ADV
'As the **sun** shines after the day breaks ...' (OS 5.#214)

—    *ʔadzyi* あぢ 〈a ⁽ⁿ⁾ti〉, あんじ 〈a N ⁽ⁿ⁾si〉 *ʔaNzyi* 'lord'

Notable hypotheses are as follows: (1) *\*ʔaruzyi* 'master' > *ʔazyi* (Ifa, cited in Mamiya [2014: 63]); (2) *\*ʔasa/\*ʔasayi* 'father' > *\*ʔasyee* > *\*ʔasyi* > *ʔazyi* > *ʔaNzyi* (Hokama [1981: 167]) and (3) *\*ʔa-ti* 'my-father' (Miyara, cited in Mamiya [ibid. 65]) based on dialectal and lexical comparisons with words with simi-

---

34    The word for 'sun' associated with this *kanji* compound is, in traditional *kana* spelling, 〈te N ta u〉 i.e. NJ *tentō*, while its other senses tend to cluster around the spelling 〈te N da u〉 i.e. *tendō* (*pace* the problem of voicing marks). However, clearly scholars who promote the view of this *kanji* compound as 'sun' mean to choose 〈te N da u〉. Mamiya (2014: 37) points out that the Rodrigues dictionary of 1603 has only 〈te N da u〉 (transliterated into *kana* from the original romanization).

lar semantics in OJ, such as *a-se* 'my dear man', *na-se* 'you, my dear husband, brother, etc.' Mamiya (ibid. 66–67) proposes a development from *\*a-nusyi* 'my-master' > *\*aɴsyi* > *ʔaɴzyi* > *ʔazyi* (S&S: strictly speaking, an unattested form in OOk). For support for his hypothesis, he points to the existence of *a-ga-nusi* 'I-GEN-master' in the MYS (5.#882); as well as parallel phonological developments of *tumusyi* 'hair whorl' > *tuᴍsyi* > *tuᴍzyi* > *cuzyi* (S&S: likewise, for this form not being attested; the OOk form is either *cᵒiʣyi* or *cᵒiɴzyi*) 'supreme position'; and *to-nusyi* 'gate guard' > *toɴsyi* > *toɴzyi* > *tozyi* (S&S: again, predicted to be OOk *tʰuʣyi*, but unattested in OS) 'wife'. Herewith, examples of *ʔaʣyi* and *ʔaɴzyi* from *Omoro Sōshi*.[35]

| しま ₍ | よせる、₍ | つゞみの、₍ | ある ₍ | あぢ / |
| si ma ₍ | yo se ru , ₍ | tu ⁿ mi no , ₍ | a ru ₍ | a di / |
| *syima-∅* | *yusir-u* | *cᵒiʣimyi-nu* | *ʔar-u* | **ʔaʣyi** |
| region-DO | attract-RT | hand.drum-DO | have-RT | **lord** |

'the **lord** who has the hand drum[36] to attract localities'[37] (OS 19.#1295)

| しより ₍ ぐ†に、なる、 | | あんじ* / |
| si yo ri ₍ gu† ni , na ru , | | a ɴ zi* / |
| *syiyuryi-gunyi-n-ar-u* | | **ʔaɴzyi** |
| Shuri-country-LOC(/COP)-STAT-RT | | **lord** |

'The **lord** {who exists in/of} the kingdom in Shuri.' (OS 10.#527)

Other noteworthy words with obscure origins include *ʔubuci* ⟨o (")po tu⟩ ([numerous tokens] ~ ⟨o bu tu⟩ [one token]) 'Deities' Home' = 'the Heavenly Home of the Deities', *nyiruya* (⟨ni ru ya⟩) 'Abode of the Deep-Earth Deities',[38] and *kanaya* (⟨ka na ya⟩) 'Eastern Celestial Home of the Deities'.[39]

---

35   For the *ʣy ~ ɴzy* alternation, and support for *ɴzy → ʣy*, see Ch. 2 §5.4.

36   The stative verb *ʔar-yi* takes DOs marked with *-nu/-ga*, not *-yu/-ɢpᵒa*.

37   Note typical DO-marking for a common transitive verb.

38   According to Hokama (1985: 54–57), *nirai* (i.e. *nyiruya* in this omoro), originally referred to *ne no kuni* 'the Deep Earth Place', where the ancestral deities stay, or where the spirits of the dead go. Therefore, it originally had a dark image, but the positivity stemming from ancestor worship gave it a brighter image, as it was believed that the ancestors would protect their living descendants. Higa (1985, "Omoro Kanshō" 14) states that the concept of *nyiruya* during the omoro era shifted from 'the Deep Earth' to 'the Easterly Sky', a sort of Utopia. Higa further adds that *nyiruya nu ʔuɢpᵒunusyi* 'Great Master of *Niruya*' arrives in *ʔayakʰu-pʰama* 'Ayako Beach (in Yonabaru)' every season (*"kisetsu no ori-me-goto ni"*) to bless the land and promise a bountiful harvest, and then returns to *nyiruya*.

39   For further exploration, readers are referred to Mamiya (2014: 81–97), which provides a good survey regarding the etymologies of these words.

LEXICON                                                                          97

## 6  *Mishōgo* (MO, Meanings Obscure)

According to Nakahara (1969 [1960]: 494), out of 5073 words used in the *Omoro Sōshi*, 20 % belong to this group. In Nakahara and Hokama (1965, "Kaisetsu [Critical outline]"), 5 % are designated as belonging to this group. Here, we list a couple of such words along with available interpretations and our evaluations of these interpretations.

– *kʰuyizyi* くひし ?'pseudo wisteria-vine' (used for making priestesses' crowns in Kudaka-Island religious ceremonies)

| せるましの、 | くひしに | / しまじりの、 |
|---|---|---|
| se ru ma si no , | ku pi si ni | / si ma zi ri no , |
| *sirumasyi-nu* | ***kʰwiizyi-nyi*** | *syima+zyiryi-nu* |
| Serumashi-GEN | ?**vine.crown**-DAT | Shimajiri-GEN |

| いくさに | / |
|---|---|
| i ku sa ni | / |
| *yi₍i₎-kʰusa-nyi* | |
| rush.grass-DAT | |

'... **into the wisteria-vine crowns** of Serumashi / into the *igusa* rushes of Shimajiri ...' (OS 1.#12)

TOS shows ⟨ku pi si⟩, with no voicing marks at all. The writing with ⟨pi⟩ cannot be taken as definitive for *pʰyi* since (1) it is word-medial, suggesting that more tokens would give *yi*, and (2) there is only one token—i.e. it is a hapax. Hokama (2000a: 181b) agrees with OSJS 144c, as does OKDJ (250c), that the word links to modern Kudaka *kuyizyi*, '*fuji-zuru modoki*' = 'pseudo wisteria-vine'. (Nevertheless, OOk *kʰwii*⋯ is more appropriate given the spelling.) The correspondence ⟨s⟩ :: /z/ is unaccounted for, but nonetheless, it seems the best choice, given the current state of knowledge. We know of no better hypothesis, that is, there is no standard opinion, for all of the above.

– *kʰusutʰipʰatʰa* こそてはた ⟨ko so te pa ta⟩ '?'

| こそてはた、ₐ | おぎも | / だ゙りじよ、ₐ | げすに、ₐ | をもわれゝ | / |
|---|---|---|---|---|---|
| ko so te pa ta ,ₐ | o gi mo | / da゙ ri zi yo ,ₐ | ge su ni ,ₐ | wo mo wa re " | / |
| ***kʰusutʰipʰatʰa*** | *ʔu-gyimu* | *daryi-zyu* | *gisi-nyi* | *ʔumuw-ari-r-i* | |
| ? | EX-liver | truly-KP | retainer-by | think-PASS-IZ | |

'[It will] truly be appreciated by [the King's] retainers in their hearts' (OS 5.#261)

Hokama (2000a: 181), while noting that there is no similar word, speculates its meaning to be 'in casual, familiar attire', but the speculated meaning nevertheless strikes one as strained. What is odd, perhaps, is that $k^husut^hi$ looks like J *kosode* 'kimono for informal occasions', and that $p^hat°a$ looks like MJ *fada* 'skin',[40] from which it is easy to see the Hokama translation attempt, though in fact we are led to a neatly "Japanese" translation—there being no $k^hu$-*sudi* in OS—and we still have the voicing problem of $k^hu(-)sut°i$ or $k^hu\#sut^hi$, not ${}^xk^husudi$. One might be tempted to save the Hokama hypothesis by an *ad hoc* attempt at treating unaspirated segments as if they are voiced, therefore $k^husu(t°{\to})di\,p^ha(t°{\to})da$. But we have not seen such an attempt at using voiceless unaspirated stops as if voiced anywhere else, and so an explanation utilizing such an attempt would suffer from the one-off nature of the explanation.

---

40    ⟨pa da†⟩ 'skin' occurs only once in the OS, in 13.#958.

CHAPTER 4

# Nominals

## 1  Nouns

### 1.1  *Characteristics*

Nouns in the *Omoro Sōshi* are probably most intriguing from the points of view of semantics and phonology. To reflect this, the current section presents three major semantic classes of nouns: place names; priestess names; and so-called *bishō-go* 'beautifying words'. The last two are especially illuminating from the point of view of metaphorical and metonymic extensions. Added to this are deverbal nouns, which are morphologically very noteworthy.

### 1.2  *Place Names*

According to Takahashi (1991b: 368–369), there are about 200 place names in the os. As merits for the use of these place names in research on the history of the Okinawan language, he states that they evince earlier phonological forms, and provide opportunities for linguists to deduce phonological changes. Some examples he provides include (521–522):

> os てぐ゛゙らん 〈te gu† ra ɴ〉 *tʰiɢraɴ* (os 16.#1164) (os 16.#1165) (os 16.#1174) :: NOk 天願 *tiŋwaɴ*,[1] ([OGJ 521a]; ENJ *teŋwaɴ* NJ *teŋaɴ*; both are Japanizations of the Okinawan PLN/PN).

---

1  He does not offer any step-by-step sound changes, unlike the following two examples. But to support his hypothesis, he lists the following pairs of forms, with the sound changes to be inferred:

    *makura* > *maqkwa* 'pillow', *mekura* > *miqkwa* 'blind person',

    *yagura* > *yaŋgwa* 'watchtower', *tuugura* > *tuŋgwa* 'cooking-quarter hut', *meɡurusu* > *miɴɡwasuɴ* 'circulate', *wogura* > *wuŋgwa* 'storage house'.

He may not run *tiŋwaɴ*, through the sound changes, but the changes are the same for the four words with the string *gur* that he gives in this footnote. However, they all lack in-between changes, which we believe are approximately: *\*teguraɴ* = \*[tʰə̃guɾã̃ɴ] > OOk *tʰiɢraɴ* [tʰĩg:ɡɹã̃ɴ] > NOk *tiŋwaɴ* [tʰĩŋ:guã̃ɴ]. The first two, with *\*kur* as input, undergo essentially the same processes (\*[kur] > \*[k·ŭr] > OOk *ɣr* [k:kɹ] > NOk *ǫƙw* [k:kụ]), except for parts associated with obstruent voicing, which also has a prenasalization component, a well understood phenomenon that is Pan-Japonic.

© KONINKLIJKE BRILL NV, LEIDEN, 2021 | DOI:10.1163/9789004414686_005

os きたたん 〈ki ta ta N〉 *k°yi̧ t°a#tʰaN* (os 12.#677) (os 13.#903) (os 15.#1104–1109) > *\*cyicyatan* *[tʃitʃatʰɑN] > *\*Qcyatan* > NOk *cyatan,*[2] (ogj 142b); NJ 北谷 <sub>CHATAN</sub> *lit.* 'north valley'.

os ぜ†りかく 〈ze† ri ka ku〉 (os 14.#1027) or 〈ze°〉 ... (os 17.#1204): pre-OOk *\*zeryik°ak°u*[3] > OOk *ziryi̧ k°ak°u* > *\*ziQk°yak°u* > Early NOk *\*ziQcyaku,* > NOk *zyiQcyaku,* (ogj 602b); NJ 勢理客; these are merely rebus graphs; nb: 〈ze〉 is not one of the *Yotsu-Gana* graphs (〈di · zi · du · zu〉), and therefore is perfectly acceptable in word-initial position.

Takahashi (ibid. 377–379) further delves into solving as place names certain mo. There follow two examples, with relevant discussion:

が†にぎ†や 〈ga† ni gi† ya〉 (os 17.#1215) (NJ 我喜屋 <sub>GA KI YA</sub>)[4]
〈ka ni ki ya〉 > *gaNzya* (like 〈ku ni ga mi〉 > *kuNzyaN* [S&S: > NOk *kúNzyaN*] 'Kunigami') > NOk Sr *gaazya,*

Takahashi hypothesizes that が†にぎ†や 〈ga† ni gi† ya〉 in the first example above refers to *gaNz(y)a* on Iheya island, as this Omoro is grouped together with other omoros of the area north of Onna. Thus it is geographically coherent with the other omoros in that volume, and the derivation from the original form to the current Shuri form, *gaazya,*, is straightforward. In Takahashi's view, omoro-period *nyi* became *N*, which further triggered a lengthening of the preceding vowel by the time of modern Shuri dialect (the well known process of Compensatory Lengthening).

いによは 〈i ni yo pa〉 (NOk 伊野波 [S&S: 〈I NO PA〉, a rebus]) (os 8.#456) 〈i no pa〉 [S&S: *ʔyi̧ nup°a*] > 〈i ni yo pa〉 [S&S: *ʔyinyup°a*];[5] Takahashi mentions that NOk forms include *nufa,*, *nuufa,*, and *nifa,*. We may add that

---

2    Note in this and in other loci where either PP or Progressive Labialization has occurred, that a shortening or loss of the vowel of the preceding mora triggers the various events, including an assimilation of the palatality / labiality to the succeeding mora. Here, Q > ∅ by 2-Mora Rule.

3    Aspiration of *\*k°a* is suppressed by preceding [+hi] *\*yi*, but PP eventually occurs anyway, being independent of Aspiration or its suppression.

4    There are two ways of writing NOk *gaazya,*, meaning that there are at least two places (ogj 187a): 我謝 〈GA ⁽ⁿ⁾SYA〉 (Nakagami, Nishihara Magiri) and 我喜屋 〈GA KI YA〉 (Shimajiri Iheya-jima). It is the latter that is associated with this word in the os.

5    In fact PP was not possible after full raising and tensing to [u]. So the latest form that was PPable was with [o], a lax, high back vowel: [ʔyinyop°a], followed by merger with [u]: > [ʔyinyup°a] = [ʔyinup°a].

NOMINALS

these forms show that the first syllable was absorbed by the following *n*, and, following Thorpe (1983: 60–61), that *p°a* < *\*Qp°a* (cf. Ch. 2 § 4.1.2, fn. 43).

As for the second instance (1991b: 381–382), Takahashi treats いにによは ⟨i ni yo pa⟩ as showing a PP, i.e. *ʔyinyup°a*. He identifies the spellings as related to three toponyms on modern Okinawa island, Inoha, a district in Tomigusuku City, as this song is placed together with the other omoros of central and southern Okinawa main island, as well as two toponyms Nyoha, one in Ōgimi Village, and the other in Motobu Town, both in the northern part of the island. Takahashi hypothesizes that the ⟨i ni yo⟩ of the OS form is a PPed form related to NOk *ʔinoo* 'back-reef moat' (RGJ 201 '(id.)') plus ⟨pa⟩ 'edge'.[6] Not only does his hypothesis contribute to the solution of a toponym puzzle, but it also allows observation of the development of culture, since the toponyms are generic. In this case we may infer that they refer to places for the establishment of villages where fishing and gathering of shellfish are possible, and where boat moorage is safe.

What follows is an example of a place name with various spellings.

NJ Chinen, NOk *cyinin* [tʃiɲiⁱʳɴ] (OGJ 157b), OOk *c°yi̯nin* : ちゑねん ⟨ti we ne ɴ⟩ (OS 18.#1278), ちへねん ⟨ti pe ne ɴ⟩ (OS 14.#1020); ちねん ⟨ti ne ɴ⟩ (OS 17.#1248)

*Chinen* refers both to the general area of southeastern Okinawa Island just next to offshore Kudaka Island, and also to Chinen Castle, about a kilometer south of Sēfā 'Utaki, which is at the cape across from Kudaka. There are 16 tokens of ⟨ti we ne ɴ⟩, 5 of ⟨ti pe ne ɴ⟩, and only 2 of ⟨ti ne ɴ⟩:[7]

| 16 tokens | 5 tokens | 2 tokens |
|---|---|---|
| ⟨ti we ne ɴ⟩ | ⟨ti pe ne ɴ⟩ | ⟨ti ne ɴ⟩ |
| *[t°ʸɛnɛɴ] | *[t°ʸɛnɛɴ] | *[t°ʸinɛɴ] |

---

6  Neither the vowel-height discrepancy (*u* vs *oo*) nor the retention or loss of the first syllable is dealt with, however. As to the former, in any case, if *\*oo* is original, and if the long vowel is shortened when *\*Qpa* is added, then the shortened vowel is subject to Raising, while the long vowel is not.

7  Judging from Nakijin as the exemplar of aspiration for Northern Ryukyuan dialects, all *cy* will

This suggests that the *[t°ʸɛnɛN] candidate should be the original one, while the three-graph ⟨ti ne N⟩ or the modern *ate-ji* spelling 知念 ⟨TI NEN⟩ implies just the opposite, that the older form is *[t°ʸinɛN]. The four-graph spelling is more historically accurate than the three- or two-graph ones, which are newer. We can connect the toponym to ⟨ti ni ya⟩ *c°yinya* 'China' (OSJS 216b), a hamlet just north of Sēfā 'Utaki, contemporary Nanjō City 南城市 (cf. Serafim [2016: 166]), hypothesizing that an assimilation to mid vowel has occurred in the penultimate syllable, along with a long-vowel shortening in the ultimate syllable (a change from super-heavy to heavy syllable) to account for an unexpected raising, this just before *N. That is:

*[t°ʸinɑ]⁸       'China [local PLN]' +
*[-ʸîN]        '[word of unknown meaning and origin]'⁹ →
*[t°ʸinɑʸîN]     >{MONOPHTHONGIZATION}>
*[t°ʸinɛ̃ːN]      >{HEIGHT ASSIMILATION}>
*[t°ʸɛnɛ̃ːN]      >{SHORTENING}>
*[t°ʸɛnɛ̃N]      >{RAISING}>
*[tʃ°ʸinĩN]       >{PALATALIZATION}> OOk
[tʃ°inĩN] *c°yinin*  >{LAX-VOWEL TENSING}> NOk
[tʃiʳɲĩN] *cyininᶦ*.

To support the above hypothesis we offer the following pair of toponyms related by the same processes, and also geographically related, both to each other and to the China :: Chinen pair: NOk *kudakaᶦ* 'Kudaka (Island, about three kilometers east of southeastern Okinawa Island)' :: *kudikiNᶦ* 'Kudeken (hamlet [not on Kudaka Island, but on the mainland, hugging the south side of the hill of Sēfā 'Utaki, which directly faces Kudaka Island])' (both OGJ 326b). Similarly:

*[k°ũdɑkʰɑ] + *[-ʸîN] →
*[k°ũdɑkʰɑʸîN] >{MONOPHTHONGIZATION}>
*[k°ũdɑkʰɛ̃ːN] >{HEIGHT ASSIMILATION}>
*[k°ũdɛkʰɛ̃ːN] >{SHORTENING}>
*[k°ũdɛkʰɛ̃N] >{RAISING}> OOk

---

    be *c°y*. For example, note even Nk *hac°yaʳa* < ... < *ʔasyit°a*, where the preceding *ʸyi* high vowel has suppressed the aspiration of unseen *ˣtʰa*.

8  Why PP does not operate on *[n] here is not clear, except to say that it became most regular in morphophonemic alternations, and least regular with *[r] and *[n].

9  Possibly *-yimu* ← *ʔumyi* 'sea'? Metathesis, while irregular, is far more common in Ryukyuan than it is in Japanese. Cf. also Miyako *iM* 'sea' (ROD 'umi').

NOMINALS

103

[kʰǔdɪkʰĩɴ] *kʰudikʰiɴ* >{LAX-VOWEL TENSING}> NOk
[kuʳdʸikʸiɴ] *kudikiɴ* (OSJS 139c ⟨ku da ka⟩ 'Kudaka'; OSJS 140b ⟨ku de ke ɴ⟩ 'Kudeken').

Serafim (2016: 164) notes that there are quite a few initial voiced obstruents in toponyms: ones with initial voiceless obstruents, 231 in OGJ, vs ones with initial voiced obstruents, 35. He accounts for voicing as calved-off (i.e. abductively derived) cases of initial obstruents of second elements of compounds where *rendaku* "sequential voicing" was applied. Here is an example (Serafim [2016: 167]).

> NOk/gani+ku/ 我如古 'Ganeko'
> ← NOk/...+ganiku/ ← NOk/kani+ku/ '1. a sandy place along the shore; 2. a horse-riding ground; 3. E[lement]2 in many toponyms', e.g. NOk/ufu+ga-niku/ 大兼久 'Ōganeku', NOk/mee+ganiku/ 前兼久 'Maeganeku', NOk/ʔucyi +ganiku/ 内兼久 'Uchiganeku'. (OGJ 307a)

He states (167) that "[i]t certainly does appear that NOk/gani+ku/ calved off, originally ... as NOk/ʔufu+/ 'Great ...' or NOk/ʔucyi+/ 'Inner ...'; such relationships are presented very revealingly in chart form by Kinjō (1974 [1938]: 168–169)."

**1.3    *Priestess Names***

Because of its religious orientation, *Omoro Sōshi* is filled with deity and priestess names. Their naming convention seems to be not random, but rather based on discernible principles. The priestess names appearing in *Nyokan O-sōshi* (1982 [1707] in Kojima, *Shintō Taikei, Jinja-hen* 52: 77–96) may be explained by the following strategies: metaphor, metonymy, and description. Using a metaphorical strategy, priestess names are compared to something outstanding such as celestial bodies (e.g. the moon or clouds), or a talisman to ward off evil.

てるつき ⟨te ru tu ki⟩ *tʰir-u-cʰikʰyi* (J 照る月 TERUTSUKI) 'shining moon' (OS 13.#850)

てるくも ⟨te ru ku mo⟩ *tʰir-u-kʰumu* (J 照る雲 TERUFUMO) 'shining clouds [reflecting the Sun's rays]' (OS 1.#16) (OS 5.#231) (OS 11.#572) (OS 21.#1457)

すづ†なり⟨su du† na ri⟩ *sidzi-nar-yi*[10] (OS 10.#524) (OS 21.#1502) (J 鈴鳴 SUZUNARI) *lit.* 'jingly-bell's sounding' [talisman to protect from evil spirits]; OSJS 188c:

---

10    This word is always written with ⟨su tu⟩ (KOS, 18 tokens) or ⟨su du⟩ (KOS, 1 token), corrected

⟨su tu—na ri⟩ '1. (name of a hand-drum) (OS 4.#187); 2. (priestess name) (OS 3.#91, OS 5.#226, OS 12.#676, OS 13.#789, OS 13.#953 [interlineation: "refers to a deity"], OS 14.#1011, OS 15.#1095, OS 15.#1096, OS 21.#1502); under this second meaning OSJS (117c, ⟨ka mi ni si ya⟩) also cites KKKS (Kon, Shingi 坤、神祇) "Parallel verse: It refers to the deity of $k^h$amyi-nyisyi ['exalted deity/priestess']"; 3. (ship name) (OS 13.#780, OS 13.#807)'

Metonymic names include extensions from priestess' belongings (the first two examples below), or place names (the last one). This is similar to "top brass" to mean highest military officers and "the Oval Office" to mean the people who work closest to the President of the United States. These two strategies (metaphor and metonymy) are identified as major mechanisms of semantic change in grammaticalization literature (cf. Hopper and Traugott [1993: 86–87]).

あお(/ふ)りやゑ(/へ/い)[11] ⟨a o(/pu) ri ya we(/pe/i)⟩ *Ɂawuryayi* (煽りやゑ AO RI YA E) '[a thing one] waves above to and fro as a parasol' → 'high-ranking priestess's ritual parasol' → 'Aoriyae [highest-ranked priestess of First Shō Dynasty]' (OSJS 22c; OKDJ 34b) (OS 4.#153)

さすかさ ⟨sa su ka sa⟩ *sas-i#k^hasa* (差笠) 'parasol thrust upward' → 'Sasu-kasa [a high-ranking priestess]' (OS 4.#173)

しより大きみ ⟨si yo ri OPO ki mi⟩ *syiyuryi Ɂup^hu-gyimyi* (voicing per TOS; 首里大君) 'great priestess of Shuri' → NJ 'Shuri Ōkimi' (OS 4.#206)

The third strategy is the description of her character, appearance, or function.

きみとよみ ⟨ki mi to yo mi⟩ *k°yimyi-t^huyum-yi* (君鳴響み KIMI TOYO MI) 'priestess-resounding' (OS 4.#208) (OS 4.#210)

きみきよら ⟨ki mi ki yo ra⟩ *k°yimyi-k°yura* (君 清 ら KIMI KIYO RA) 'priestess-beautiful' (OS 15.#1114)

---

to ⟨su du⟩ (TOS, 19 tokens). Noteworthy is the fact that there is no confusion with ⟨su⟩ or ⟨zu⟩ in writing its second mora, even though the MJ version is ⟨su z̄u⟩. For reasons for this spelling incongruity, cf. Ch. 2 §5.4.

11    Also written ⟨阿応理屋恵⟩ = ⟨A O RI YA WE⟩ in Nakijin (OSJS 22c, citing Kunigami-gun-shi 373).

NOMINALS

世ゝせきみ ⟨YO " se ki mi⟩ *yu-yusi-k°yimyi* (世寄世君) 'country-governing priestess' (OS 9.#485) (OS 11.#593)

### 1.4 *Bishō-go or Bishō-ji*

Many nouns in OSJS are classified as *bishō-go* (美称語) or *bishō-ji* (一辞), or just *bishō*. The precursors to this term were *imyō* (異名) 'alternate name' (from annotations in the Adaniya version) and *kaeshi no kotoba* (返しの詞) 'response name' in KKKS. In any case, they all express admiration, exaltation, and beautification, and perhaps for that reason the modern name *bishō(-go/-ji)* (美称語/辞 Shimamura [2010: 434]), which we translate as 'beautifying expression' = BE, was created. The *Omoro Sōshi* is especially rich in this type of usage.[12]

According to Shimamura (ibid. 410), the number of *bishō-go* for ships amounts to about 30, for an important ceremonial musical instrument, *c°idzimyi* ⟨tu du mi⟩ 'hand drum',[13] to 14 (ibid. 423), for royal umbrellas shielding from the sun, displaying power, and calling down the deities (i.e. what are called in the Japanese-language literature *ryansan*, *aori*, etc.), to 17 (ibid. 424) and edifices, to 35 (ibid. 425).

– ゑぞこ ⟨we zo ko⟩ *yi(i)-zukʰu* (J ゑ底) 'splendid ship'

| ゑぞ†こ、ʌ | かよわ、ぎ°やめ、 | / |
|---|---|---|
| we zo† ko , ʌ | ka yo wa , giʰ ya me , | / |
| *yi(i)-zukʰu-∅* | *kʰayuw-a-gyami* | |
| **good-bottom**-SUB | ply-IA-TRM | |

'As far as the **good**[14]-**bottoms** [= fine ships] may ply,' (OS 1.#17)

---

12 For example ⟨ku mo ko⟩ *k°umu-kʰu* lit. 'cloud(-like) one' (J 雲子) is an important word used 27 times. OSJS (146c) notes that it is a BE that can be paired up with ⟨ko ka ne⟩ *kʰugani* 'gold(en)', or ⟨ma TAMA⟩ *ma-dama* 'true jewel, truly jewel-like', and with meanings that span beauty, high value, splendor, or goodness. For details, see Nakasone's explanation (1987 [1976]: 264–268).

13 Cf. J *ousumí* '(id.)' < OJ *tudumî*. While it may seem superficially that the OS spelling is here in concordance with the OJ spelling, in fact it follows the rules laid out in Ch. 2 §5.4.

14 OOk *yi(i)-*: PJ *\*yë-* 'good', related to OJ *ye-* '(id.)' (*ye-si* 'good' [JDB 140cd]) and *yö-* '(id.)' (*yö-si* '(id.)' [JDB 796ab]), to pRk *\*ye-* 'id', found in e.g. NOk as the very widely used prefix *yii-* '(id.)' (OGJ 264b–268a). (Cf. NJ *i-i* < *ye-*, semi-freely alternating with *yo-i* < *yö-*.) One clear usage difference between OOk and NOk, though, is that, while NOk second elements connect with voiceless obstruents even if voicing is possible, as far as can be determined from written records, just the opposite is true for OOk, as in °*yii+zukʰu*, ˣ*yii+sukʰu* here.

106            CHAPTER 4

–   いたきよら ⟨i ta ki yo ra⟩ ~ いちやきよら ⟨i ti ya ki yo ra⟩ (*ʔyiₜtˀa-kˀyura ~*)
*ʔyicˀya-kˀyura lit.* 'board-beautiful' (板清ら) → 'splendid ship'; たなきよら
⟨ta na ki yo ra⟩ *tʰana-kˀyura* 'planking-beautiful'[15] (棚清ら) → 'fine ship';
these are examples of parallelism with different words, accentuated by
the full parallelism of the rest of each line

いたきよらは、ʌ       おしうけて       /
i ta ki yo ra pa , ʌ      o si u ke te      /
***ʔyiₜtˀ/cˀy.a-kˀyura*-Qp°*i***   ***ʔus-y-ukʰi-t°i***
**board-beautiful-DO$_{EMPH}$ push-RY-float$_{VT}$-GER**
たなきよらは、ʌ       おしうけて       /
ta na ki yo ra pa , ʌ      o si u ke te      /
***tʰana-kˀyura*-Qp°*a***     ***ʔus-y-ukʰi-t°i***
**planking-beautiful-DO$_{EMPH}$ push-RY-float$_{VT}$-GER**
'... launching[16] the boat [made] of **fine boards**,[17] launching the boat
[made] of **fine planking** ...' (OS 10.#530)

## 1.5   *Deverbal Nouns*

Deverbal nouns in the *Omoro Sōshi* come from *ren'yō* (RY) and *rentai* (RT) forms
of verbs. Here are some examples:

–   あすび˚ ⟨a su ⁽ᵐ⁾pi˚⟩ *ʔasib-yi* (RY) (OJ 遊び^{ASÔBÎ}) 'religious dancing' < あすぶ ⟨a
su bu⟩ *ʔasib-u* 'to perform religious dancing' (OSJS 35a; JDB 25bc)

おもいぐ˚わの、   あすび˚、   / み物   あすび˚、   /
o mo pi gu˚ wa no ,  a su bi˚ ,   / mi MONO  a su bi˚ ,   /
*ʔumi-ɢwa-nu*    ***ʔasib-yi***   *myii-muɴ*  ***ʔasib-yi***
EX-child-GEN     **dance-RY$_{NOM}$**  see-thing  **dance-RY$_{NOM}$**

---

15    Although seemingly a construction in which, unaccountably, the modified comes before
the modifier—something that might be said to go against Japonic constructional principles—in fact all is as it should be: the compound noun originates in a TOPIC-COMMENT
(syntactically, a SUBJECT-COPULA) sentence construction that has been nominalized
(with the "brackets" both inaudible and invisible), so that literally *tʰana-kˀyura* means '[a
thing in which] the planking is beautiful' = 'a fine/splendid ship'.

16    *ʔusyukʰit°i*: °[ʔuʃu], not ˣ[ʔusyu], i.e. the hyphens do not start the pronunciation afresh.
The reader may have noticed the spelling here, suggesting ˀ[ʔuʃiʔu], but the two verses are
embedded in a string of nine-mora verses, and taking the spellings here as outlying cases
of palatally collapsed moras, from three to two moras, makes these verses fit perfectly with
the others. Typically these spellings signal a retained boundary, which in turn signals the
start of a vowel-initial mora with a glottal.

17    "*ʔyiₜtˀ/cˀy.a-*" means "the dots signify the outer bounds, and the slash the marker of

NOMINALS

'The **performance**[18] of the beloved[19] child [of the Sun-King, who dwells in Shuri,] it is a splendid[20] **performance**.' (os 12.#663)

– てづ†り 〈te du† ri〉 *tʰi-dzir-yi*[21] (RY) (手擦り) 'rubbing the palms of one's hands together in prayer' ← *tʰi(i)-dzir-*[22] 'pray-', lit. 'hand-rub-'

やらの、 　へだ†とのが゛、 　／ おみてづ†り、 　　　／

ya ra no , 　pe da† to no ga* , 　／ o mi te du† ri , 　　　／

*yara-nu* 　*pʰida-tʰunu-ga* 　　*ʔu-myi-tʰi-dzir-yi*

PLN-GEN 　PN-lord-GEN 　　EX-EX-hand-rub-RY

'The splendid, divine **prayers** of Lord Heda of Yara' (os 15.#1110)

---

the choice, between two pronunciations, so that the pronunciation is either *ʔyi̯ tˢa-* or *ʔyic°ya-*."

18 Both OOk *ʔasib-* and its sister form in OJ, *asôb-*, descend from PJ *\*asôb-*. For the details cf. Shinzato and Serafim (2013: 154; where *ô* is written as *wo*).

19 The exalting quasi-prefix *ʔumi(i)-* is ← {*ʔumuw*+ 'love'} + {+yi 'RY'}, < *\*omop-yi*. Diphthongs that include an etymological high vowel have monophthongized by the time of the OS: from the point of view of someone looking at the texts ca. 400 years later, the diphthongal spelling :: monophthongal pronunciation is accounted for by the Monophthongization 1 sound change.

　　Here we expect *ʔumii-*, but the exigencies of meter require shortening to *ʔumi-*, as in the Ryūka song form. The first portion, then, is *ʔu₁ mi₂ ɢwa₃ nu₄*, with the mora length of ɢ (= [˜g:g], where the second [g] merely signifies a voiced velar release) not being counted by convention. This phrase is metrically parallel to *myi i₂ mu₃ N₄*.

20 NOk *mii-muN₁* [mʸi:mu'N] 'a thing to see, something interesting to see' (OGJ 375b) < OOk *myii-muN* [mʸI:muN] 'beautiful, marvelous, splendid' (OSJS 316b).

　　There are two phonological blocks against PP in the word *myii-muN*:

(1)　　Only in very constrained circumstances does PP affect a labial consonant (which is not to say that [+lab]*y*V cannot occur—it can, through the collapse of two syllables into one, which is *not* PP). In any event, it is irrelevant in *this* case. The lack of effect on a labial consonant suggests that the environment {/_C₍₊ₗₐ♭₎} served to depalatalize the preceding vocalic nucleus, thus negating the possibility of PP.

(2)　　The long-vowel allophone of /yi/, that is, of *yii*, is [ʸI:], with a non-palatal (= centralizing and/or laxing) vocalic nucleus, which is incapable of PP.

#1 has no chance to happen, since #2 blocks its ability to apply. Note that both (1) and (2) increase the number of palatal-initial vowels that are incapable of causing PP.

21 NOk *si'-y-uN₁* and NJ *súr-u* (both 'rub') show PJ *\*s*. But the OS spelling is not an example of confusion: 69 forms for 'pray' with *tii* plus *sir-* in OS use ⟨⁽ⁿ⁾tu⟩, with only one ⟨⁽ⁿ⁾su⟩. Discussion of this unexpected regularity is to be found in Ch. 2 §5.4, and discussion of *sidzi-nar-yi*, in fn. 10 in this chapter.

22 Attested in MZ (os 3.#107), and RY with the IMPFV/PROG AUX -*ur*- (os 13.#925): *tʰi(i)-dzir-y-ur-a* 'will be praying'.

108 CHAPTER 4

— おれつ゚む 〈o re ⁽ⁿ⁾tu゚ mu〉 *ʔuri-ʥim-u* (OS 13.#981) 'beginning of the moist season around March of the lunar calendar (RT)' ← おれ + すむ 〈o re + su mu〉 *ʔurii-* 'moisten' + *sim-u* 'clarify'

For the first morph, Mamiya (2014: 198) endorses Hokama's (OKDJ 173b) hypothesis: *⟨u ru pi⟩ [S&S: *\*ʔurup°yi*] > *⟨u ru i⟩ [S&S: *\*ʔuruyi*] > *⟨u ri i⟩ [S&S: *\*ʔuryii*] 'moistening'.[23] For the second morph, he (ibid. 202–203) rejects Hokama's proposal and hypothesizes its origin to be *sum-u* 'become clear' as in 'the air becomes clearer after the rain'. His rationale is that if the second segment indeed comes from *syim-u* '[ground] becomes moist' as viewed in Hokama's hypothesis, then it should be written with じ 〈zi〉 or ぢ 〈di〉, but that is not the case. Rather, Mamiya (ibid. 203–204) goes on to say, OS 10.#536 presents the expression すみ(あがて) 〈su mi (a ga te)〉 *sim-yi-(ʔaga-tʼi)* 'clearing (up)', referring to the very state he describes, that is, '[it rained and] the air became clearer'.

| | | |
|---|---|---|
| おれづ†むが、∧ | たてば゚、 | / |
| o re du† mu ga , ∧ | ta te ba゚, | / |
| *ʔuri-ʥim-u-ga* | *tʰat-°ʼi-ba* | |
| **moistening-clearing-RT-SUB** | **arrive-IZ-COND** | |

'When the early spring[24,25] arrives, ...' (OS 2.#54) (OS 21.#1457)

## 2  Pronouns

### 2.1  *Personal Pronouns*

2.1.1  First Person Pronouns: *ʔa(N)* vs *wa(N)*

There are two first person pronouns, with each having its longer form with -*N*. There is a clear difference between the two series in their token frequencies (OSJS 50a): *ʔa* (123); *ʔaN* (30), *wa* (21) and *waN* (12):

---

23  This view is not quite right, since *\*ʔuru-yi* > *\*ʔurwi-i-*, which instantly becomes *ʔuri(i)-* with a non-palatal final syllable. That syllable would be written with ⟨ro i⟩, ⟨ru i⟩, or ⟨re (i)⟩, and it is ⟨re⟩ that is chosen, apparently due to the etymological opacity of the compound. Concerning the latter point, note that this verb does not appear in OSJS, though its presumed derivative ⟨u ru wa si⟩ *ʔuruwasyi* 'beautiful' (OSJS 72b) does (6 tokens).

24  The affrication is accounted for according to the rules of Ch. 2 §5.4, as long as there is a remaining internal word boundary in this compound:
(*\*ʔurup°yi* > *\*ʔuruwyi* > *\*ʔuruyi* > *\*ʔurwii* >) *ʔurii* plus (*\*sum-* >) *sim-*,
so: *\*ʔurii-* "#sim- > *ʔuri* #zim- > *ʔuri* #ʥim-;
*\*tʰii-* "#sir- > *\*tʰi* #zir- > *tʰi* #ʥir- (*tʰii* 'hand(s)' + *sir-* 'rub' → 'pray')

25  Also おれづ゚も 〈o re du゚ mo〉 (OS 14.#994).

NOMINALS

Relative token frequencies of first-person pronoun forms:

|  | $?a(-)$ | $wa(-)$ |  |
| --- | --- | --- | --- |
| Short: ..._# | 123 | 21 | 5.9 : 1 |
| Long: ...N# | 30 | 12 | 2.5 : 1 |
| Total tokens | 153 | 33 | 4.6 : 1 |

From this, it can be deduced that $?a(N)$ is much more prevalent than $wa(N)$: 153 vs 33, or 4.6 : 1. Note, however, that the difference in their type frequencies in compounds is noticeably smaller: 14 noun types vs 6, or a ratio of 2.3 : 1, as the data below from Mamiya show (2014: 209–219).[26]

– $?a$: 14 noun types following $?a$-$ga$-, including:

あしやつ° ⟨a si ya tu°⟩ (?$?asyac°i$), probable miscopying of あしあけ ⟨a si a ke⟩ $?asyagi$ 'deity house' (OS 13.#925),

おとぢや ⟨o to di ya⟩ $?ut^hu#dzya$ 'sibling'[27] (OS 16.#1155),

おなご ⟨o na go⟩ $wunagu$ 'woman' (OS 17.#1211), etc.;

---

26   OSJS (368c) notes that the bare forms $?a$- and $wa$- appear only with the enclitics -$wa$ 'TOP' and -$ga$ 'GEN'. The appearance with genetic enclitic differs strikingly from NOk, where genetic compounding is with bare $waa$- (OGJ 587a). OS and LitOk indicate a transitional form: $wa$-$ga$-$myi$ 'oneself, I' (OS 5.#260), $wa$-$ga$-$mi$, '(id.)' (OGJ 588) → $wa$-$mi$, 'I' (OGJ 590b), the latter a newer LitOk alternant of $wanu$, 'I' (OGJ 590b), itself a LitOk equivalent of NOk $waN$, 'I' (OGJ 590b). The forms -$nu$ and -$mi$ appear unrelated.

27   According to Mamiya (119), this is the only lexical item with either $?a$-$ga$- or $wa$-$ga$-. NOk $?utu$-$zya$-$Nda$, (OGJ 571a) "(N) 'older and younger brothers, (all and any) siblings.' In former times, younger siblings (of either gender) were called $?utu$ $zya$, ..." Note that #$dzyu$ (NOk -$zya$) constitutes a single morpheme, and one attached with an internal word boundary at that; this is vouchsafed by the morpheme's beginning with $dzy$ in OOk, not ˣ$zy$. Possibly it is related to -$sya$ 'one, a person' (者), and that would explain its independent status. On the other hand, it may be a lexicalization of $?ut^hu$-$nu$#$c°ya$ 'sibling-COP#PL'—cf. $?utudzya$#$Nda$, which has grown a newer, second, plural, perceived as needed, as the compound word $?utuzya$, lost its plural semantics, presumably along with its internal word boundary: similar to J $ko$ 'child' + -$domo$ 'PL' → $ko$-$domo$ 'children' → 'child', + -$tacyi$ 'PL' → $ko$-$domo$-$tacyi$ 'children'.

– *wa*: 6 noun types following *wa-ga-*, such as:

うら 〈u ra〉 *ʔura* '(inlet-)village' (OS 13.#873),

おとぢ゚や 〈o to di゚ ya〉 *ʔutʰu#dʑya* 'sibling' (OS 17.#1181),

大ざ゚と 〈OPO za゚ to〉 *ʔupʰu-zatʰu* 'Ōzato [toponym]' (OS 6.#330), etc.

Mamiya's (2014) collocation-based study above also points to differences that are parallel to those in a study by Miura. Mamiya (2014: 220) concludes that there is a clear distinction between *ʔa-* and *wa-*: (1) *ʔa-ga* precedes nouns related to humanity/human relationship or spirit/spirituality (e.g. *ʔumi-i* 'love', (*ʔasyac'i*, a misspelling for) *ʔasyagi* 'spiritual house'), while *wa-* is combined with nouns of location and living space (e.g. *ʔura* 'bay', *k°unyi* 'country');[28] (2) structurally, *ʔa-ga* precedes a nominal clause where the observed *-ga* serves as the subject marker of the *ʔa-* to which it appends (あが゚まぶ゚る 〈a ga゚ ma bu゚ ru〉 *ʔa-ga maвr-u* 'I protect' [OS 12.#664]), but this usage is lacking with *wa-ga*. Our own study points to similar distributional characteristics: *ʔa-* has a collocational unity with deverbals such as かいなで゚ 〈ka i na de゚〉 *kʰee-nadi-* 'safeguard' (OS 12.#734) or *ʔumu-yi* 'love' (OS 14.#991), while *wa-* forms compounds with domain nouns (e.g. country, region, or terrain).[29]

| きこゑ、 | あが、 | なさいきよに、 | # |
|---|---|---|---|
| ki ko we , | a ga , | na sa i ki yo ni , | # |
| *k°yi̯k°uyi* | *ʔa-ga* | *nase(e)-kʰyu-nyi* | |
| renowned | I-GEN | father(ly)-one-IO | |

'[o give them] to **my** renowned Fatherly One!' (OS 1.#28)

| いせゑけり、ˏ | あぢ゚おそい、 | / あが、 | かいなで゚、 |
|---|---|---|---|
| i se we ke ri , ˏ | a di゚ o so i , | / a ga , | ka i na de゚ , |
| *ʔyisyi-wikʰiryi-∅* | *ʔadʑyi-ʔusii-∅* | *ʔa-ga* | *kʰee-nadi* |
| rock(like)-brother-APPO | lord-ruler-VOC | I-GEN | VPFX-safeguard |

---

28    This point is mentioned in Kadekaru as well (1987: 249–250).

29    Mamiya's analysis presented above roughly parallels Miura's (1988) following observations: *ʔa-ga* precedes a verb of emotion (= *shinjō*) (60%) (e.g. 'think (fondly) of', 'long for', 'yearn secretly for', 'pray for', 'stand and heave a(n emotional) sigh)', and the nouns associated with *ʔa-ga* are mostly emotive nouns, such as 'love', 'unrequited love', 'secret love', 'heart', 'heart/mind', etc. In contrast, (1) *wa-ga* is mostly combined with a noun (80%) indicating *possession* (= *shoyū-sei*) and *affiliation* (= *shozoku-sei*), and when it co-occurs

NOMINALS 111

たゝみきよ、
ta " mi ki yo ,
*tʰat°amyi-kʰyu-∅*
esteemed-one-VOC
'**My** Lord, the steadfast brother, the esteemed one that I safeguard ...' (OS 3.#91)

あが*、　おもひが*、　　　／こゑ∧　　　なり、いぢゑて、　　　／
a ga* ,　o mo pi ga* ,　／ ko we ∧　　na ri , i di we te ,　　／
*ʔa-ga　ʔumi-i-ga　　　kʰuyi-∅　　nar-yi-ʔyidzɨ-t°i*
I-GEN　love-RY_{NOM}-GEN　voice-SUB　resound-RY-out-GER
'**My** love's voice rang forth ...' (OS 14.#991)

Another difference, this time between *ʔaN* and *waN*, is pointed out by Kadekaru (1987: 250), in their occurrences in formulaic expressions: considering *ʔaN* first of all, the formulaic phrase あんまぶれ ⟨a N ma bu re⟩ *ʔaN-∅ maʙr-i* 'protect me' (OS 2.#86 below) accounts for 15 out of 19 instances of the entire set of tokens of *ʔaN* in the OS; and, considering *waN* next, the formulaic phrase でゝわん *di waN* 'now_{INJ} I' (OS13.#769 below) comes to eight out of all 11 tokens of *waN* found in the OS.

あん、∧　　　まぶ*て、　　／この∧と、∧　　わたしよわれ　　　／
a N , ∧　　　ma bu* te ,　／ ko no ∧ to , ∧　wa ta si yo wa re　　／
*ʔaN-∅　　maʙ-t°i　　　kʰu·nu tʰu-∅　watʰa·s-y-uwar-i*
**me/us**-DO[30]　protect-GER　this sea-DO　cross·VT-RY-EAV-MR
'(May you) protect **me/us** and let [me/us] cross this open sea!' (OS 13.#904)

あんは、∧　かみ、∧　　てづら、　／かみや、∧　あん、∧　まぶれ　　　／
a N pa , ∧　ka mi , ∧　te du ra ,　／ ka mi ya , ∧　a N , ∧　ma bu re　／
*ʔaN-wa　kʰamyi-∅　tʰidzɨr-a　　kʰamyi-ya　ʔaN-∅　maʙr-i*
I-TOP　god-IO　pray-MZ　god-TOP　**me**-DO　protect-MR
'**I** will pray to the god(s), so may the god(s) protect **me**!' (OS 2.#86)

---

with a verb, it is "of one's own concrete or direct action" (*jiku no gutai-teki chokusetsu-teki na kōdō*) (e.g. 'go', 'come', 'return', 'see', 'harvest'), and, verbs of existence ('sit', 'be', 'settle/reside').

30　Kadekaru (1987: 250) notes the non-existence of a plural form for *ʔaN*. Plural suffixes *-ra* or *-t°aa* do exist and make plural forms, but there is no ˣ*ʔaN-ra* or ˣ*ʔaN-t°aa*. On the other hand, judging from NOk *waQ-taa₁* 'we' (OGJ 591b), the expected though non-occurring form is ˣあれた ˣ⟨a re ta⟩ ˣ*ʔa·ri-t°aa*. Kadekaru conjectures that *ʔaN* in the *Omoro Sōshi* could express 'we' as well, and indeed that is more appropriate in this song's context. (OGJ 120a has *ʔaQ-taa₁*, but it is a third-person plural form, not first person.)

で、わん、、これ、、いちへ、、はりやに　　　／
de , wa n ,＾ ko re ,＾ i ti pe ,＾　pa ri ya ni　　　／
*dii* **waN**-∅ *kʰuri*-∅ *ʔyi-c°yi*　*pʰaary-an-yi*
INJ I-TOP　this-DO　say-GER　sail-NEG-YNQ
'Now, I say this, and won't I sail [the ship swiftly]!' (OS 13.#769)

おやぢ゛やう、あけて、　　／わん、、いれゝ　　　／
o ya di゛ ya u ＾ a ke te ,　／ wa N ,＾ i re "　　　／
*ʔuya-dzyoo*-∅ *ʔakʰi-t°i*　**waN**-∅ *ʔyi̦r·i·ri*
EX-gate-DO　open-GER　me-DO　enter·VT-MR
'Open the venerable gate and let **me** enter!' (OS 17.#1180)

OSJS (23ab, 49b–50a, 364c) further states that neither pronoun stem, *ʔa*- or *wa*-, stands alone, always being followed by the case marker -*ga*, or, in the case of *ʔa*-, also able to take enclitics other than -*ga*, such as -*wa* (TOP, 8 tokens), -*kara* (ABLATIVE, 1 token), -*ni* (IO, 1), and -*ya* (TOP again, 1) (cf. Mamiya [2014: 207]). This is similar to Miura's study of OJ, where, he states (1988: 11) that 85% of *a*- and *wa*- instances appear with the marker -*ga*.

In addition, OSJS (368c) claims that *ʔaN* is older than *waN*, since ⟨a N⟩ *ʔaN* is in OS and *Liúqiú Guǎn Yìyǔ* (『琉球館訳語』 *Ryūkyū-kan Yakugo* [Ryukyu-Office Dictionary of Translations]) (1487 or later, Ōtomo and Kimura [1968: 40–46]), but in *Yǔyīn Fānyì* (『語音翻訳』 *Go'on Hon'yaku* [Phonetic Translations of Words]), 1501, and other Chinese materials, only *wanu* or *waN* is used. However, the chronological order of the texts between *Liúqiú Guǎn* and *Yǔyīn Fānyì* is not without controversy (Ishizaki [2001: 55–56]). Even if the order posited by OSJS is correct, more careful text-based analyses have to be done before drawing that conclusion.

We must be careful, in any case, not to assume that forms appearing just a little earlier than their opposite number by that token acquire some special significance, such as that they are the source of the slightly later appearing form. There is not nearly enough evidence to draw such a conclusion, especially when the same temporal sequence separated by only a few years occurs in widely separated locales, as is the case in OOk and OJ.[31]

---

31 The chronology of OOk *ʔa*- vs *wa* is reminiscent of Yamada's claim that *ʔa* is older than *wa* and Vovin's successful rebuttal of that claim based on his careful analyses of texts including *Kojiki, Nihon Shoki*, and later texts.

NOMINALS 113

## 2.1.2    Second Person Pronoun: ʔu(-ga)

KKKS (OSJS 73c) treats ʔu-ga as a synonym of J ʔo-nusi 'you [to social equal or inferior]', and speculates it to be a contracted form of ʔu·nu-ga.[32] It also adds that ʔu-ga is used to refer to both the second and first person. Ikemiya (1995: 214) views ʔu-ga in the *Omoro Sōshi* as mostly a polite pronoun, and interpretable as referencing both first and second person. According to OSJS (73c–74a), in the OS, of the four tokens of ʔu-ga, two (OS 9.#491 below and OS 14.#998, which are older and come from the countryside) are still used as polite pronouns (敬称 *keishō*), while the other two, which are newer and belong to Shuri omoros, show a derogatory sense (卑称 *hishō*), such as OS 3.#96 below. Ikemiya (1995: 214), echoing OSJS (73c), notes that a derogatory second-person pronoun usage is the norm at the time of the *kumiodori*, i.e. from the beginning of the 18th century.

Despite the previous views analyzing ʔu-(ga) as a second person pronoun, we do not see convincing instances of ʔu-(ga) in OOk to substantiate such a claim, since the words in which ʔu-(ga) is claimed to appear are rather obscure in meaning, and furthermore, TOS renders almost all of the examples as voiceless *ka*, not voiced *ga*; we have almost exclusively followed TOS in our voicing interpretations for this volume, and do so here as well.

For instance, in OS 9.#491 below, interpreted as an exalting usage of ʔu-(ga) (OSJS 73c), the string of *kana* parallel to ⟨o ka° zu† ki ya ga⟩ is ⟨ma ta i ki ya ga⟩. However, while it can be broken into the pair of morphs ʔ/wukʰa- and -″{#/+}sik°ya,[33] its meaning is still unknown. The former interpretation is based on the two-word analysis of ʔu-ga + *sidzya*, but we believe the actual phonologization is ʔ/wukʰazik°ya, without voicing. (See below.) This is because the text

---

32   In the original text: 「おぬしと云心、又おのがといふを中略するか。人の上にも身の 上にも云」 "*O-nushi to iu kokoro, mata ʔu·nu-ga to iu o chūryaku suru ka. Hito no ue ni mo mi no ue ni mo iu.*" = "[It] means *o-nushi*; further, is it an abbreviation of ʔu·nu-ga? One says it both towards others and oneself."

33   The fact that there are two morphs and that the juncture point is known is shown by the two variant spellings of this word: ⟨o ka du ki ya⟩ and ⟨o ka zu ki ya⟩. The ⟨du⟩ ~ ⟨zu⟩ spelling alternation is a sign that the internal word boundary has been weakening and is variable at the time of writing. Here are the data and the reasoning for deriving the claims from them:

⟨o **ka** d̄u† ki ya⟩ ʔ/wukʰad̄zik°ya (OS 3.#97); ⟨o **ka** z̄u† ki ya⟩ (OS 3.#96, OS 9.#491) ʔ/wukʰaz̄ik°ya

According to the Yotsu-Gana Hypothesis, the spelling with ⟨⁽ⁿ⁾tu⟩ = *dzi* requires that the graph be in the first or second position after full-word or internal-word boundary. Any other boundary, or no boundary at all, will automatically result in *zi* instead, for which ⟨⁽ⁿ⁾su⟩ is used instead. This reasoning has given us an internal word boundary, but we still have no idea what the word means.

114                                                                                    CHAPTER 4

evinces only voiceless ⟨o ka°⟩ and the breaking of ⟨ma ta i ki ya⟩ as ⟨ma ta⟩ and
⟨i ki ya⟩ is untenable, as it necessitates establishing a semantic parallel of ⟨ma
ta⟩ with ⟨o ka⟩.

おか°ず†きやが、∧     まうれしや、   /
o ka° zu† ki ya ga , ∧     ma u re si ya ,   /

| | | |
|---|---|---|
| *ʔu-ga siʣya-ga* | *ma-ʔurisya* | former interpretation |
| you-GEN lineage-SUB | truly-happy | |

| | | |
|---|---|---|
| *ʔ/wukʰazik°ya-ga* | *ma-ʔurisya* | actual phonologization |
| MO₁-SUB | truly-happy | |

またいきやが、∧     まうれしや   /
ma ta i ki ya ga ,     ma u re si ya   /
*matʰa(˒ʔ)yik°ya-ga  ma-ʔurisya*
MO₂-SUB                truly-happy
'Your people[34]/MO₁ are truly happy! MO₂ are truly happy!' (OS 9.#491)

There continues a similar challenge with OS 3.#96—also ⟨o ka° du† ki ya⟩ in
OS 3.#97—both of which are taken as a derogatory usage of *ʔu-(ga)*. The voice-
lessness of ⟨o ka°⟩ is evident, and given the parallel of *ʔukʰazik°ya* with *mee-
booʣi* (derogatory term for Satsuma soldiers with shaved front hair, cf. Hokama
[2000a: 86]), it is best to interpret *ʔukʰazik°ya* as a rephrasing of 'soldiers'.[35]

---

34    This interpretation is based on two premises that are (a) often resorted to, and (b) unten-
      able:
      (1)   Any *kana* that can be voiced but is not overtly marked as voiced, can be interpreted
            as voiced or not depending on the requirements of one's hypothesis;
      (2)   *Ka-gyō yō-on* has already been merged with *ta-gyō yō-on*, as [tʃ] and [ʤy]. Therefore
            hypotheses that admit forms that require this merger can be entertained. [The only
            exception to our own "no merger" hypothesis that we know of is *°cy°uwa* ... 'to rule,
            etc.', and this has two things going for it in terms of its irregularity: (i) it is a very high-
            frequency word, and thus on the front line of new sound changes; (ii) it is *keigo*, and
            *keigo* frequently undergo semantic, grammatical, morphophonemic, phonological,
            and phonetic changes at an accelerated rate compared to lexical items in the rest
            of the language. Can such criteria be applied to save the *ʔu-ga siʣya* hypothesis?
            Apparently not. The collocation clearly is of vanishingly low frequency when com-
            pared to *cy°uwa⋯*.]
35    Ikemiya (2006: 54) differs with OSJS on the interpretation of *ʔuga*. He gives a Japanese
      translation 侵す者達をだまして *okasu mono-tachi o damashite* 'tricking the intruders'.

NOMINALS                                                                 115

あから、　　　せぢ、、　おるちへ、　　　／ まへぼ†しやよ、、
a ka ra ,　　se di ,、　o ru ti pe ,　　　／ ma pe bo† si ya yo ,、
ʔakara　　　sidʑyi-∅　ʔuru-c˚yi　　　mayi#boo#dʑya-yu
splendid.fire spirit-DO bring.down-GER　soldiers-DO

まゆわちへ　　／ ひぢゑる、　　　せぢ、、　おるちへ、　　　　／
ma yo wa ti pe ／ pi di we ru ,　　se di ,、　o ru ti pe ,　　　／
mayuwa-c˚yi　　p˚yi-dʑyir-u　　sidʑyi-∅　ʔuru-c˚yi
confuse-GER　　fire-flush.out-RT spirit-DO bring.down-GER

おかºず†きやよ、、　ゆご†ちへ　／
o kaº zu† ki ya yo ,、　yu go† ti pe　／
ʔukʰazik˚ya-yu　　yugu-c˚yi
MO-DO　　　　　　defile-GER

'Bringing the splendid fire spirit down, confusing the Satsuma soldiers, Bringing the fire (= the Sun) spirit down, defiling the *okazukya*.' (OS 3.#96)

It is of interest to note that a cognate to OJ second person *na* is not attested in
the *Omoro Sōshi*. The precursor to NOk *ʔyaa* is also absent. According to Nakasone (1987 [1976]: 240), KKKS mentions this *na* as ⟨SONO KATA⟩ 'that person', but
he found no instance of *na* in OS.[36] He further states that *ʔura* may be a polite
second person pronoun, which appears in the 15th-century Korean scholar Sin
Sukchu (申叔舟)'s *Haedong Cheguk-ki* (「海東諸国記(해동제국기)」) appendix
(1501) as 你是那裏的人 'Where are you from?' rendered in *hangŭl*, here transliterated into Yale romanization as ⟨wu la co ma phi chyu⟩, written by Nakasone
as *ura dzüma fichʻuʔ*, but more properly [uradʑʌmapʰitʃʰu]:

| | | | |
|---|---|---|---|
| Yale romanization written as | ⟨wu la | co ma | phi chyu⟩, |
| Nakasone's romanization but more properly | *ura* | *dzüma* | *fichʻuʔ*, |
| our phoneticization | [ura | dʑʌma | pʰitʃʰu] |
| OOk rendition | ʔura | dʑɨ-ma | p˚yicʰyu |
| our phoneticization | [ʔʷura | dʑɨma | pʸɨtʃʰu] |
| glossses | you | where | person |

This further developed as follows: ʔura = [ʔʷura] → [ʔʸira] > [ʔʸirʸa] > [ʔyaː] =
*ʔyaa* as the NOk non-honorific form.

────────────

36　... which is not to say that it does not exist in NOk—it can be found in scripts for Okinawan-
　　language *shibai*, and is still used by some Okinawans in their own speech.

116          CHAPTER 4

### 2.1.3      Third Person Pronoun?

As far as we could tell, no third person pronoun is found in the *Omoro Sōshi*. OSJS also lacks any such entry. However, a word of caution is in order: As the saying goes, absence of evidence is not evidence of absence.

### 2.1.4      *Wh*-Pronouns

The *wh*-pronouns co-occur with either the *kakari* particle (KP) *-ga*, or the sentence-final particle (SFP) *ga*.

–    *tʰa(a)/tʰaru* た/たる ⟨ta / ta ru⟩[37] 'who(m)?'

> たが゛、∧ とりよら、     / たが゛、∧ うちよら         /
> ta ga゛,∧ to ri yo ra ,    / ta ga゛,∧ u ti yo ra        /
> **tʰaa**-*ga* *tʰur-y-ur-a*     **tʰaa**-*ga* *ʔuc°-y-ur-a*
> **who**-KP hold-RY-SE-MZ/IA    **who**-KP beat-RY-SE-MZ/IA
> 'I wonder **who** could be holding [the drum]. I wonder **who** could be beating [it].' (OS 16.#1157)

> よろい、     / たるが、∧    きちへ、∧     にせる、     /
> yo ro i ,     / **ta ru** ga ,∧ ki ti pe ,∧   ni se ru ,    /
> *yuruyi-∅*     **tʰaru**-*ga*    *k°yi-c°yi*    *nyi-̦si-r-u*
> armor-TOP    **who**-KP     put.on-GER befit-VT-RT
> '… the armor: **whom**, putting it on, **does it** befit?' (OS 2.#60)

–    *nawu* なお(う) ⟨na o (u)⟩[38] 'what?'

> かつれんわ、∧   なおにぎ゛や、∧   たとゑる、       / やまとの、
> ka tu re N wa ,∧ **na o ni gi゛ ya** ,∧ ta to we ru ,   / ya ma to no ,
> *kʰac°irin-wa*    **nawu-nyi-gya**    *tʰat°uyi·r-u*     *yamatʰu-nu*
> Katsuren-TOP    **what**-to-KP    compare·4GE-RT    Yamato-GEN
> かまくらに、∧      たとゑる        /
> ka ma ku ra ni ,∧ ta to we ru      /
> *kʰamak°ura-nyi*    *tʰat°uyi·r-u*
> Kamakura-to      compare·4GE-RT
> 'To **what is it** that Katsuren compares? It is to Kamakura in Yamato that [it] compares.' (OS 16.#1144)

---

37    Eight tokens of ⟨ta ru⟩, five of ⟨ta⟩, 13 *in toto*, all with *-ga* '(KP)'.

38    Eleven tokens of ⟨na o⟩, one of ⟨na o u⟩, 12 in all, likely < *\*nawo* < *\*na-wo* 'what?-DO'.

# NOMINALS

— *dʑiri* づれ ⟨du re⟩[39] 'which [one]?'

あぢ゚おそいぎ゚や、 おもいぐ゚わ、 / づれの、 あぢぎ゚や、 ∧
a di゚ o so i gi゚ ya , o mo i gu゚ wa , / du† re no , a di gi゚ ya , ∧
*ʔadʑi-ʔusi-i-gya* *ʔumi-i-(Q)gwa-∅* *dʑiri-nu* *ʔadʑi-gya*
lord-lead-er-GEN dear_EX-RY-son-IO **which**-GEN lord-KP[40]
たとへる #
ta to e ru #
*tʰatºuyir-u*
compare_MV-RT
'**Which** lord compares to the lord leader's son?' (OS 5.#257)

— *ʔyicºï*[41] いつ ⟨i tu⟩[42] 'when?'

いつがキ、∧ なつ∧ たゝ しよ /
i tu ga† , ∧ na tu ∧ ta " si yo /
*ʔyicºï-ga* *nacºï-∅* *tʰatº-a* *syu*
**when**-KP summer-SUB start-IA SKP
'**When could it be** that summer starts, anyway?' (OS 7.#378)

— *ʔyikºya* いきや ⟨i ki ya⟩ 'how?; what sort of?'

いきや、∧ みちへがキ、∧ おひ、きよる /
i ki ya , ∧ mi ti pe ga† , ∧ o pi , ki yo ru /
*ʔyikºya-∅* *myii-cºyee-ga* *ʔw-ii-kº-y-uur-u*
**what.sort.of**-GEN see-PRFV-KP chase-RY-come-RY-SE-RT
'**How** has it seen (it), that it is chasing it down?' (OS 12.#731)

As the above examples show, *wh*-words in OS are rather unremarkable, as all
precede -*ga*, a question KP of new/unknown information. However, there are
two points that deserve special mention in their development to MOk and NOk.
First, a *wh*-word in OS does not precede KP -*si*, just like its counterpart OJ -*kösö*

---

39 Six tokens of ⟨⁽ⁿ⁾tu re⟩ *dʑiri*, three with -*ga*, three with -*nu* < \**ʔyedu-re*.
40 Considering the typical patterns of particle deployment in Japonic, it would seem more
reasonable to say that this example of -*gya* is a deletion, (-*gya*_SUBL) -*gya*_KP2, rather than a
fusion of two phonetically identical particles into one.
41 Recall that original high vowels are not PP-able.
42 ⟨i tu - yo ri - mo⟩ *ʔyicºï-yuryi-mu* 'more than ever' 2 tokens, ⟨i tu - ga⟩ *ʔyicºï-ga* 'when?' 3
tokens, ⟨i tu - mu⟩ *ʔyicºï-mu* ~ -M 'always, ever' 2 tokens, ⟨i tu mo⟩ *ʔyicºï-mu* '(id.)' 1 token.

118 CHAPTER 4

(Ōno 1993: 42). However, in their development to MOk, *nu(u)·ga* 'why' and *ta* 'who' came to co-occur with (*-si* >) *-si* as below. As discussed in Shinzato and Serafim (2013: 127–128), it may be the case that *nu(u)·ga-si* was already a lexicalized form (i.e. *nu(u)gasi*).

のがす　　　玉黄金　　　物思がほ　　　しちをる
***nu(·)ga(-)si*** *tamakugani* *mun.umi-gawu syi-cyor-**u***
**why-KP**　　　precious.object worried-face　do-**PROG-RT**
'Why on earth, my precious little one, are you making a worried face?' (*Chūshin Migawari no Maki*, RGS: 74)

誰がす　夜深くに　　　　殿内　　　　　　　踏入ゆす
***ta.ga-si*** *yubukaku-nyi*　*tunucyi-∅*　　　*fumiʔyiyu-si*
**who-KP** night.shadows-DAT mansion.grounds-LOC set.foot.in-NOM
名のゆらば、　　名乗れ
*nanu.yur-aba,　nanur-i!*
proclaim.self-if proclaim.self-MR
'Who on earth is it, who dares set foot on the mansion grounds? Proclaim yourself, if you dare!' (*Temizu no En*, RGS: 269)

Another interesting fact is that in NOk, *zyiru* (← OOk \**dziri*) can follow the topic (i.e. old information) marker *-ya* as in *zyiro-o* (*zyiru* + *-ya*), as pointed out in RGJ (635):

*zyiro-o* (← *zyiru* + *-ya*　) *mii.sa ga?*
which　　which + TOP　new　SKP
'Which one is new?'

Thus there is a stark contrast with NJ *dore*, which can never precede the topic marker, which indicates old information.

### 2.2　*Demonstratives*
2.2.1　　Proximal: *kʰuri/kʰunu* 'This'
In the *Omoro Sōshi*, there are 30 instances of *kʰuri* 'this (one)' and 43 of *kʰunu* 'this' (prenominal), and they are mostly, if not all, deictic. This is probably due to the fact that in this genre of literature, the immediacy of the context is critical in delivering messages to and from the deities. The examples below show *kʰuri*, *kʰunu* and the formulaic *kʰuri-∅-ru; kʰuri-∅* ....[43] In *kʰuri-ru kʰuri*, the SKP *-ru*

---

43　This set phrase is reminiscent of ***köre ya könö*** in OJ (translated as NJ *kore ga* maa 'well

NOMINALS 119

looks as if it acts like a copula, but in fact it is a Sentence *Kakari* Particle, in this case put in place after a zero-copula. We never see the Topic of the sentence, being something like a zero that signifies 'it': '[It]'s$_1$ *this*$_2$ one$_3$; *this*$_2$ one$_3$ [I tell you]!' = $k^hu_2 \cdot ri_3 \cdot \varnothing_1 \ ru; \ k^hu_2 \cdot ri_3$.

| きこゑ、 | 中ぐ゛すく、 | | / まへ、ᴧ | みれば゛ |
|---|---|---|---|---|
| ki ko we , | NAKA gu゛su ku , | | / ma pe , ᴧ | mi re ba゛ |
| *k°yi₍k°uyi* | *nakʰa.gusik°u-∅* | | *mayi-∅* | *myi·r-i-ba* |
| famed | Nakagusuku.castle-TOP | | ahead-DO | see·4GE-IZ-COND |

| みなと、 | / これど゛、ᴧ | あまみ、かねぐ゛すく | / |
|---|---|---|---|
| mi na to , | / **ko re** do゛, ᴧ | a ma mi , ka ne gu゛su ku | / |
| *myinatʰu-∅* | **kʰuri**-du, | *ʔamamyi-kʰani-gusik°u* | |
| port-COP | **this**-KP | ancient-iron$_{EX}$-castle | |

'Ah! famed Nakagusuku castle, if we look ahead, [there is] the port—***this*** is the impregnable castle of old!' (OS 14.#1006)

| この、 | 大しま、ᴧ | おれたれ、 | / |
|---|---|---|---|
| **ko no** , | DAI si ma , ᴧ | o re ta re , | / |
| **kʰunu** | *dee-syima-∅* | *ʔuri-t°ar-i* | |
| **this** | great-island-IO | descend-PRFT-IZ | |

'[It was due to the order of the deity Amamiko] that [Ogyakamoi (King Shō Shin)] descended onto **this** Great[44] Island.' (OS 5.#242)

| これる、ᴧ | これ、ᴧ | はつにしや | / |
|---|---|---|---|
| **ko re** ru , ᴧ | **ko re** , ᴧ | pa tu ni si ya | / |
| **kʰu·ri-ru** | **kʰu·ri** | *pʰac°i-nyisya* | |
| this.one-KP | this.one | first-north.wind | |

'[It]'s *this*·one; *this*·one—the first-north.wind [that we have been awaiting.]' (OS 13.#899)

---

now!' In JDB 314b), which appears sentence-initially to emphatically note the perceived objects in front of one's eyes (*ganzen no taishō o kantan to tomo ni kakunin suru*). Another formulaic expression in OOk worth mentioning is *yari kʰunu yooi* (やれ、ᴧ この ᴧ ゑ (ya re , ᴧ ko no ᴧ we)) (OS 11.#637, OS 21.#1497). This is considered a meaningless rhythmical refrain (*hayashi kotoba*) by Hokama (2000a: 425).

44 Recall that the ⟨V⟩ ~ ⟨V i⟩ and ⟨V⟩ ~ ⟨V u⟩ diphthong types are treated as already having undergone monophthongization, as opposed to the ⟨V Ce⟩ and ⟨V Co⟩, which have not. There is an alternant ⟨da† i⟩ in ⟨da† i ti⟩ *dee-c°yi* 'this, our Earth (as opposed to Heaven)' (TOS 3.#97). Positive evidence for the pronunciation of the long vowel of *dee-syima* is to be found in MOk ⟨ta i si ma⟩, in "Koyō", *kwēnya* #38.19, p. 217a [Chinen-magiri] (per OKDJ [381cd |da i si ma|]).

120  CHAPTER 4

### 2.2.2 Mesial: *ʔuri* 'That'

The mesial demonstrative in the *Omoro Sōshi* is *ʔuri*. There are 6 instances (OS 4.#159), (OS 6.#309), (OS 9.#482), (OS 11.#650), (OS 13.#822), and (OS 15.#1105), of *ʔuri*, and no instances of either ˣ*ʔu-nu* (GEN) or ˣ*ʔu-ga* (GEN). There seem to be cases where *ʔuri* could be interpreted as functioning almost like an interjection, such as OS 11.#650 below. Unlike OJ mesial demonstrative *sore*, whose usages are overwhelmingly anaphoric, the instances of *ʔuri* in the *Omoro Sōshi* are mostly, if not all, deictic. For instance, omoro literary scholars assert that OS 4.#159 (the first song below) was sung while looking at the rising Sun and obtaining spiritual power from it (Ikemiya [2006: 53], Shimamura [2015: 162]).

| こが゚ね、はなの、ᴧ | さきよれば゚、 | / あおりやゑや、 / |
|---|---|---|
| ko ga゚ ne , pa na no , ᴧ | sa ki yo re ba゚ , | / a o ri ya we ya , / |
| *kʰugani#pʰana-nu* | *sak-゚y-ur-i-ba* | *ʔawuryayi-ya* |
| golden flowers-SUB | bloom-RY-SE-IZ-T/C | Aoriyae-TOP |

| おれよ、ᴧ | みぎ゚や、ᴧ | おれわちへ | / |
|---|---|---|---|
| o re yo ᴧ | mi gi゚ ya , ᴧ | o re wa ti pe | / |
| *ʔuri-yu* | *myi-gya* | *ʔuri-wa-c゚yee* | |
| **that.one**-DO | see꜀ᴿʸ-PRP | descend ꜀ᴿʸ-AUXₑₓ-PRFVss | |

'As the golden flowers were blooming (= the sun's rays were shining through), the priestess Aoriyae (= *ʔawuryayi*) descended[45] to[46] see those = them.' (OS 4.#159)

The following omoro (OS 15.#1105) describes a situation where the lord of Urasoe has invited the lord of Chatan, along with his retainers, to a banquet at his castle (Hateruma [2007b: 54–55]), and presented him with a gift, a suit of armor. Most probably, this omoro was sung at the reception, where the armor was already prepared as a gift visible to the guest of honor, his retainers and everyone else. Thus this is a deictic usage.

| おれど゚、ᴧ | ひきいぢ゚へ、物、 | / おれど゚、ᴧ | てづと、物 # |
|---|---|---|---|
| o re do゚, ᴧ | pi ki i di゚ pe , MONO , | / o re do゚, ᴧ | te du to , MONO # |
| *ʔuri-du* | *p゚yik゚.yi.ʔyidzyi.munu* | *ʔuri-du* | *tʰi.dzit゚u.munu* |
| **that**-KP | gift | **that**-KP | keepsake |

'(What (is it)?—the gift (that we'll give). What (is it)?—the keepsake.)'
'(Silken-threaded armor. Pure-silken-threaded armor.) **That** is what the gift is. **That** is what the keepsake is.' (OS 15.#1105)

---

45  As a perfective, the morph -*cy゚ee* retains its underlying length, and thus, its original height.

46  PP'ed °-*gya*, not ˣ-*ga*, shows that *myi-* < °**myi*, not ˣˣ*myiɪ- or ˣˣ*mye(e)-*.

NOMINALS 121

The following omoro (OS 11.#650) may be interpreted as an interjectional usage, as it can in NOk. OKDJ (173) lists the *ʔuri* of this omoro as a possible, but not a decisive example of an interjectional usage. In addition Ikemiya (1987: 51) thinks it is a demonstrative with a shade of exclamatory meaning.

| こまかの、 | みおに、ˬ | / おれ、ˬ | みもん | / |
| ko ma ka no , | mi o ni ,ˬ | / o re ,ˬ | mi mo N | / |
| *kʰumakʰa-nu* | *myiwu-nyi* | *ʔuri-∅* | *myi-muɴ-∅* | |
| PLN-GEN | channel-LOC | **that**-SUB/INJ | view-thing-COP | |

'[They are casting fishing nets for dugongs and turtles] in the channel of Komaka island. **There**,[47] how splendid!'[48] (OS 11.#650)

### 2.2.3 Distal: *kʰaari* 'That'

KKKS (Kon, Gengyo), cited in OKDJ (177d) lists *kʰaari* as a distal deictic as follows:

| かあれー ˬ | 遠ふさーなり |
| ka a re " " "ˬ | TO pu sa " " " na ri |
| *kʰaari kʰaari* | *tʰuusa tʰuusa nari* |

"⟨ka a re ka a re⟩ means 'far away far away' "

OKDJ adds that "these days it is hardly used at all." We were not able to identify any instance of *kʰaari* in our search of the *Omoro Sōshi*. According to Ikemiya (1995: 269), there is a note about *kʰaari* in the Tajima Text of the KKKS (not the

---

47  According to Ikemiya (1987: 48), the word *ʔuri* had traditionally been interpreted as the verb 'descend' (e.g. OSJS 98b ⟨o re⟩ 'to descend'). But he disputes that interpretation based on his data that the verb base *ʔuri-* does not stand alone, but is always followed by suffixes or auxiliaries. Therefore, he concludes that it is impossible to take *ʔuri* here as a verb.

48  Here is Chris Drake's (1985: *Omoro Kanshō* 10) translation for the entirety of this song to give the context:

There, see, in the swift deepwater current / Between sacred Komaka and Kudaka islands
Between sacred Komaka and Kudaka islands / Throwing out nets for dugongs
Casting wide nets for turtles / Filling and filling them with dugongs
Swelling and swelling them with turtles / Pulling in numberless dugongs
Hauling up countless turtles
They eat them out on the high swells / They eat them in toward the shore
Boats rowed by the strongest-armed men
Strain prow to prow across open sea / Race churning in between long reefs.

OS) as follows: "In Shuri, they say *kaama*, in the rural areas, they sometimes say *kaari*, *ʔagata*, or the like."[49] This note refers to the language of 1895, not MOk or OOk.

The non-existence (?) of the distal demonstrative in the *Omoro Sōshi* is reminiscent of the paucity[50] of the distal demonstrative *kare* in the *Man'yō-shū* (Hashimoto [1982: 2–24–228], Quinn [1997: 65–66], Li [2002: 154], Vovin [2005: 289], Okazaki [2010: 9]). This fact does not prove the non-existence of *kʰaari* in the spoken language at the time of the OS, however. Furthermore, it does not preclude the possibility of positing it in the PJ lexicon. Just as Tajima noted its existence in regional dialects, Vovin also mentioned that |*kare*| is omnipresent in the Southern Ryukyuan dialects. We are, thus, in agreement with Vovin in positing *\*ka·rĕ*[51] as a distal demonstrative in PJ.

## 3    Numerals

There are two types of numerals, one originating in PJ, and the other borrowed from Sino-Japanese. In the example pairs below, the first and the third examples are of PJ origin and the second and fourth examples come from Sino-Japanese.

| ひとりぐ゛わの、 | / やぐ゛さぐ゛わは、ᴧ | なちへ、ᴧ | おちゑ / |
|---|---|---|---|
| pi to ri gu゛ wa no , | / ya gu゛ sa gu゛ wa pa ,ᴧ | na ti pe ,ᴧ | o ti we / |
| *p°yi̯t°u-ryi-Gwa-nu* | *yagusa-Gwa-Qp°a* | *na-c°yee(#)* | *ʔu-c°yi* |
| **one**-person-child-COP | single-child-DO | bear-PRFV | -GER |

'... having borne[52] **one** child, a single child ...' (OS 14.#983)

| てだ゛、 いちろくと | | / てにᵌ、 | てるᴧ | てだ゛と / |
|---|---|---|---|---|
| te da゛ , i ti ro ku to | | / te ni ", | te ru ᴧ | te da゛ to / |
| *tʰida* | *ʔyic°yi̯·roo-k°u-t°u* | *tʰinyi-nyi* | *tʰir-u* | *tʰida-tu* |
| sun | **first**(.born)-male-personage-COM | sky-in | shine-RT | sun-COM |

'The **first**-born[53] (= the King) of the Sun and the Sun shining in the sky—[May they stay together]' (OS 5.#212)

---

49    The original Japanese text goes 「都ニテハ、カアマ、田舎ニテハ、カアレ、アガタナド 云う事アリ。」 *"Miyako nite wa, kaama, inaka nite wa, kaari, ʔagata nado iu koto ari."*

50    There are only four instances of *kare*, three of which are written phonographically, and one logographically.

51    The vowel PJ *\*ĕ* is reconstructed when OJ has ⟨ë⟩ and pRk has *\*e*. PJ *\*ë*, on the other hand, is reconstructed when OJ has ⟨ï⟩ and pRk has (again) *\*e*.

52    NOk for the same morpheme string is *na-cyoo-cyi* 'bearing (for later)'.

53    Note that the two verses align metrically if ⟨ro⟩ is interpreted as having two moras. From

# NOMINALS

あんじ*おそいす、／ ともゝすへ、ˏ
a n zi* o so i su ,　／　to mo " su pe , ˏ
*ʔaɴzyi-ʔusi·i-si*　**tʰu-mumu-siyi**
lord-rul·er-KP　**ten-hundred**-generations　ちよわれ　／
ti yow a re　／
*cᵒyuwaar-i*
reign_EX-IZ

'It is the King, surely, who will reign a **thousand** generations!' (OS 1.#6)

ひやくさ、ぎやめ、　　／ おぎやかもいしよ、ˏ
pi ya ku sa , gi ya me ,　／ o gi ya ka mo i si yo , ˏ
**pʰyaakᵒu-see**-*gyaami*　*ʔu-gyakʰa-mii-syu*
100-**years**-TRM　　EX-shining-esteemed.one-KP　ちよわれ　／
ti yo wa re　／
*cᵒyuwaa·r-i*
reign_EX-IZ

'It is until the age of 100[54] (i.e. forever) that the Shining One[55] (= King Shō Shin) will rule.' (OS 1.#18)

In what follows, the noun *sanyi* 'number' (glossed with ⟨算⟩ [J *saɴ*, Ch *suàn*] in an interlineation (OS 5.253)) is of Chinese origin.[56] Just like *tʰinyi* 'the sky; Heaven' (天),[57] the vowel *yi* is added, it is said, for the ease of pronunciation (cf. Nakamoto [1989: 25], *Omoro Kanshō* 44). In the phrase below, *sanyi-syir-anu* 'number-know-NEG', it can mean 'indefinite number of'. It is put in parallel with the native Okinawan word *kʰa(a)zi* 'number'. Cf. NOk (-)*kaázi* 'number (of times); every (*x*-many) time(s) that ...' (OGJ 299a); NJ *kázu* 'number', *kázu-kazu* 'a large number', *kázu syirenu‿* 'untold numbers'. The latter suggests a calquing (i.e. loan-translation) relationship between OOk *sanyi syir-anu* and NJ *kázu syirenu‿*.

---

the Index of OSJS: ⟨i ti ra ko⟩ *ʔyicᵒyi-roo-kʰu*, 1 token (/roo/ :: ⟨ra (ˣu)⟩); ⟨i ti ru⟩ *ʔyicᵒyi-ru*, 1 token (shortened and raised); ⟨i ti ro⟩ *ʔyicᵒyi-roo*, 1 token (mid-V spelling taken as long mid-V); ⟨te ta i ti ro ku⟩ *tʰi(i)da-ʔyicᵒyi-roo-kᵒu*, 2 tokens; ⟨i ti ro ko⟩ *ʔyicᵒyi-roo-kʰu*, 2 tokens. Note the variability of *-kᵒu ~ -kʰu*, i.e. *-ku ~ -ko*. See Ch. 2, §2.2.2.

54　{ᵒ⟨sa⟩ (~ ˣ⟨sa i⟩)} = *-see* (OSJS 430a) is a potential but non-occurring pair of monosyllabic bimoraic graphemic units belonging to the bound morpheme *-see* 'years (of age)'. A similar one, but with a back mid vowel, is {ᵒ⟨ya⟩ (~ ˣ⟨ya u⟩)} (OSJS 496b) = *-yoo* 'way (etc.)'. A multisyllabic morpheme with occurring graphemic alternants is {ᵒ⟨na sa⟩ ~ ᵒ⟨na sa i⟩ ~ ᵒ⟨na sa fe⟩} 'father(ly one)' = *nasee* (OSJS 462), unusual because it overlaps two different alternations: {{⟨V i⟩ ~ ⟨V⟩}} and {{⟨V Ce⟩ ~ ⟨V i⟩}}.

55　One may more readily see the reason for the allomorph *-syu* by observing the roman transliteration, in effect, that {···muw+**yi**} precedes the *kakari* particle {+sŏ}, and that it is {yi} that triggers PP, resulting in *-syu*, not *-si*.

56　Schuessler (2009: 274: 25–43), MC *swân*^B/C. We do not have a source to make a decision on whether the morph is Sino-Ryukyuan or Sino-Japanese in origin.

57　Schuessler (2009: 319: 32–15), Mandarin *tiān*, MC *tʰien*.

124                                                            CHAPTER 4

さに、ᴧ        しらぬ、ᴧ    ころ⌒、                  / ... かず゛、
**sa ni,**ᴧ    si ra nu,ᴧ ko ro " ",              / ... **ka zu***,
*sanyi-∅*      *syi̯r-anu*  *kʰuru-kʰuru*              ... *kʰazi-∅*
**number-DO** know-NEG brave·man-brave·man (PL)      **number-DO**
しらぬ、        まご†ろた、          /
si ra nu,      ma go† ro ta,      /
*syi̯r-anu*     *ma-guru-t°a*
know-NEG  EX-brave·man -PL
'Many (i.e. **number** unknown[58]) soldiers ... Many true soldiers ... [pray] ...'
(OS 7.#367)


The OS uses *tsuiku* (parallel <u>verses</u>) as above and *tsuigo* (parallel <u>words</u>) as
in *sanyi* and *kʰa(a)zi*, both meaning 'number (of times)'. The combination of
the Sino-Japonic word (*sanyi*) followed by a native Okinawan word (*kʰa(a)zi*)
is reminiscent of *monzen-yomi* (文選読み), a Japanese-language strategy of
presenting a Sino-Japanese word in *on* (Chinese-based reading of *kanji*) and
its synonymous native Japanese word in *kun* (Japanese native pronunciation)
side-by-side for the purpose of reading Chinese classics. Endō (2015: 222)
explains it as follows:

> 天地玄黄 *tenchi no ametsuchi wa gwenkwau to kuroku ki nari.* ['The Heav-
> ens are dark and the Earth is yellow'—S&S] Here, *tenchi* and *gwenkwau*
> are Sino-Japanese readings for 天地 and 玄黄, respectively, while the rest
> are translations into Japanese.

The *monzen'yomi has* an '*X no Y*' or '*X to Y*' structure, where the Sino-Japanese
words X modify the native Japanese words Y.

According to Abe (2009: 144), there are 3974 pairs of *tsuiku* and *tsuigo* in
1554 songs of the *Omoro Sōshi*. She, too, sees the use of *tsuiku* and *tsuigo* in the

---

58    If not simply irregular (*syi̯r-anu*) or due to the presence of \**r*, the word meaning 'unknown'
      may come from \**syer-anu,* \**syeer-anu,* or \**syiir-anu,* with the last <u>long</u> vowel form undergo-
      ing laxing of the vocalic nucleus, \*[iː] > \*[ɪː], resulting in loss of the palatal-vowel input to
      PP. It may also be that the mark {̩} is part of the {̩+anu 'NEG'} morpheme: {̩C+anu 'NEG'}.
      If PP is never seen with negatives, this may be the most straightforward solution. It may
      even be that PP cannot operate to the right of the verb root itself (until hitting (#(#))),
      in which case the blocking of PP is not a property of the NEG morpheme, but rather, of
      the verb root itself: {ROOT̩}; and, since this is a predictable quality, it need not be writ-
      ten in: {ROOT}. (Exception: some instances of *k°yik°-uyi-* ~ *k°yik°yuyi-*, [with latter lacking
      morpheme boundary]; cf. ⟨ki ki ro⟩ 'be renowned' *k°yik°yiru* ← *k°yik°yuyiru* ← *k°yik°uyiru*.)

NOMINALS

OS as similar to *monzen-yomi* (ibid. 147) mentioned above, which became popular from the Heian through the Muromachi periods (roughly 1200–1600) in Japan. There is no doubt that they are similar, but Abe's hypothesis (ibid. 165) is simplistic in concluding that the OS was modeled after the *monzen-yomi* style. This is because *monzen-yomi* is not the only possible source for the OS literary style. Similar *tsuiku* and *tsuigo* styles were already seen as early as the *Nihon Shoki*, [The Chronicle of Japan] (7th C.), vol. 5, in an oracle (*shintaku*) in Emperor Sujin's 60th year and also in *saibara* songs, a genre of Heianperiod Japanese court music (9th C. ~; see Fuku [2013: 28–31]). In addition, Ono Jūrō, quoted in Shimamura (2010: 4) had already noted the stylistic parallels between omoro and *kweena*, orally transmitted regional songs predating the *Omoro Sōshi*. Furthermore, there is even a set of verses superficially similar to *monzen-yomi* in which the largely identical semantic pairing *k°yimu* 'fortitude, guts, heart, etc.' and *ʔayu* '(id.)' are linked in parallel. The latter word is said by Vovin (2009b: 16) to be a loan from the Silla language, the progenitor of Korean, but predating it. The OS is catholic in its use of synonymous terms in its parallel verses, and this is a sign of the generality of the phenomenon, whereas, if one wishes to link two traditions to the exclusion of others, one must search for sufficiently arbitrary traits that they share, traits not likely to be widely shared by others. Cf. Ch. 3 § 4, pertaining to the origin of *ʔayu*.

### 3.1 Against the Interpretation of yaʤyu as Involving a Number

The word *yaʤyu* [yaʤu] やちよ/やぢよ ⟨ya ti yo / ya di yo⟩ in the following song is often analyzed as the same as J *ya-ti-yo* '8000 generations'. For instance, OSJS, following Ifa (1975a [1924]: 173), glosses *yaʤyu* as 'forever' < *\*ya-ti-yo* lit. 'eight thousand generations'. However, this interpretation begs the question of why the seeming *rendaku* (*\*t > d*) between two numbers occurred. We are not aware of any other similar cases. Thus, if *yaʤyu* does mean 'eternally' as OSJS says it does, it stands as an isolated case, both semantically and morphologically. On a different account, the interlineations in the text say 'it is a *syima*.' There is a word *yaʤyukʰu* 'village headman', where the part *yaʤyu* must mean 'village', since ... *kʰu* can easily be taken as *-kʰu* '-one, -personage'; therefore the interlineation apparently intends *yaʤyu* to be interpreted as *syima* 'island/village' rather than 'forever'. Based on the foregoing, the two glosses and interpretations are given below, with the second our own preference based on the analysis above:

| | | | |
|---|---|---|---|
| やぢ゚よ、∧ | かけて、∧ | とよまさに | / |
| ya di゚ yo ,∧ | ka ke te ,∧ | to yo ma sa ni | / |
| *yadzyu(-∅)* | *kʰakʰi-t°i* | *tʰuyum-as-an-yi* | |
| eternally/islands-DO | rule-GER/PRFV | resound-CAUS-NEG-YNQ | |

'May [your] rule be known **eternally/throughout the islands**.' (OS 1.#29)

Our interpretation hinges on our knowledge of what is possible in the phonology of numbers.

## 4 Nominal Prefixes

The OS is especially rich in exalting prefixes. While in no way exhaustive, the list of high-frequency items below gives representative examples of this type of prefix. The first five, *myi-*, *ʔu(pʰu)-*, *ma-*, *kʰana-*, and *ʔuya-* are of PJ origin, and the last two, *dee-* and *dzya-* are of Sino-Japanese origin (both with the same source SJ morph). Note that the original meanings of these prefixes are not necessarily completely bleached. For instance, the prefixes *myi-*, *ʔupʰu-*, and *ma-* retain the original meanings of 'exalted', 'grand', and 'true' respectively. In turn, these have a natural correspondence with the types of nouns they modify. For instance, *myi-* tends to be used for the lord or his possessions (but also for priestesses or deities); *ʔu(pʰu)-* for titles and great and/or stone constructions; and *ma-* for qualities of jewels, wind (important for sea travel), people, etc.

The attenuation of the original meanings is highest with *myi-* and *ʔu-* (but not *ʔupʰu-* 'big, great, grand, imposing', its progenitor), and lowest with *kʰana-* 'dear-', *ʔuya-* 'parent(al)-', with e.g. *ma-* '(true-)' situating itself in the middle of this spectrum. It is probably due to this higher degree of attenuation that OSJS classifies *myi-* and *ʔu(pʰu)-* as *keishō settō-ji* 敬称接頭辞 'exalting [EX] prefixes', while it characterizes the rest as *bishō-ji* 'beautifying expressions' (BE). Within the term *bishō-ji*, OSJS also includes so-called *bishō setsubi-ji* 美称接尾辞 'beautifying suffixes', which are to be taken up in §5.3. The difference between *keishō settō-ji* 敬称接頭辞 'exalting prefixes' and *bishō setsubi-ji* 美称接尾辞 is clear, as one of prefixes vs suffixes. But one may wonder what the difference is between 'exalting' and 'beautifying'. Functionally, they are very similar, only that, as it appears from the OSJS usage, the original meanings can be more bleached in exaltation than in beautification. Thus, to avoid terminological problems, we reserve 'exalting' for all of the prefixes, which express exaltation, including *myi-*, *ʔu(pʰu)-*, *ma-*, *kʰana-*, and *ʔuya-*, while we reserve the term 'beautifying' for suffixes such as the items to be introduced in §5.3. (But we also note that

NOMINALS 127

there are Exalting auxiliaries, which can be thought of as a kind of suffix since they come after the main verb, such as Vb-*y-uwa·r-u* 'exaltedly Verb-s'; cf. Ch. 7 §14.)

### 4.1 *Exalting Prefix* myi-

Serafim (2004: 315–318) entertains the possibility of reconstructing this prefix as \**mye-*, though he believes that the most likely hypothesis is that it was \**myi-*, and that it developed an allomorph \**my\*ɪ-* under the influence of the high back vowel of the first syllable of the following morpheme. After that, no PP or reduction to *n-* occurred. He discounts the idea that it is a borrowing from OJ (318). Below are some examples:[59]

– *myi-ₖk°unyi* [mʸɪk°uɲi] みくに ⟨mi ku ni⟩ 'EX-country' (御国), an example with following high vowel

| とよむ ∧ | せだ゛かこが゛、 | / みくに | / |
|---|---|---|---|
| to yo mu ∧ | se da* ka ko ga*, | / **mi** ku ni | / |
| *tʰuyum-u* | *si-dakʰa-kʰu-ga* | ***myi-ₖk°unyi*** | |
| resonate-RT | spiritual.power-high-one-GEN | EX-country | |

'the **splendid** country of the Resounding One of Great Spiritual Power' (OS 12.#727)

– *myi-ₖkʰuyi* [mʸikʰuʸi] みこゑ ⟨mi ko we⟩ ~ みこへ ⟨mi ko pe⟩ ~ みこい ⟨mi ko i⟩ 'EX-voice' (御声)[60]

| しま、∧ | まるく、 | / みこゑしやり、∧ | おそわ | / |
|---|---|---|---|---|
| si ma , ∧ | ma ru ku , | / **mi** ko we si ya ri , ∧ | o so wa | / |
| *syima-∅* | *maru-k°u* | ***myi-ₖkʰuyi-s.yaaryi*** | *ʔusuw-a* | |
| island-DO | peaceful-ly | EX-voice-INSTR | rule/protect-MZ/IA | |

'"Let me rule the land peacefully, with my **noble** [governing] voice"'[61] (OS 1.#8)

---

59 Japanese glosses in parentheses are as found in OSJS entries for those items.
60 Also note ⟨mi ki ya u⟩ '(their) exalted faces' (OS 3.#94), with PP.
61 This is a true exception, since PP is possible. It avoids non-euphonic *kʰyuy* ..., with its sequence of palatal-labial-palatal. Cf. ⟨we ri di yo⟩ 'chosen voices', already mentioned in Ch. 3 §1.

128 CHAPTER 4

— *myi-ʔu-uni* みおうね[62] 'EX-EX-ship' (み御船)

| みおうね、ʌ | かよわ、ぎやめ、 | / せぢ、ʌ |
|---|---|---|
| mi o u ne , ʌ | ka yo wa , gi ya me , | / se di , ʌ |
| *myi-ʔu-uni-∅* | *kʰayuw-a-gyaami* | *sidzyi-∅* |
| EX-EX-ship-SUB | ply-IA-TRM | spiritual.power-DO |

| やり、やりʌ | おそは | / |
|---|---|---|
| ya ri , ya ri ʌ | o so wa | / |
| *yar-y-a(a)r-yi* | *ʔusuw-a* | |
| send-RY-CONT-RY | rule-MZ/IA | |

'"As far as my great ships may ply, let me keep[63] sending out spirit-power and rule!"' (OS 1.#17)

## 4.2 *Exalting Prefix ʔu- ~ ʔuQp°u-*

Regarding the etymon for OOk *ʔu-* and *ʔuQp°u-*, Serafim (2004: 307) states that "it is not out of the question that the Okinawans invented their own \**ʔo-* out of the pre-existing \**opo-* (probably \**öpö-*), since modern Shuri dialect possesses two frequently seen variants of 'big', *ʔufu-* and *ʔuu-*. The latter form (or its progenitor \**ʔoo-* —\**owo-*?) would only need to have shortened." This prefix is written in the OS with characters お ⟨'o⟩ and う ⟨'u⟩, syllabographs, and 御 ⟨'O⟩, a logograph. All three are pronounced the same, *ʔu-*. In some cases, only one of them is used (e.g. 御 with *gusik°u* 'castle' or *c°ik°a'yi/c°ik°ee* 'envoy', ⟨'u⟩ with ⟨ke⟩, i.e. *ʔu-kʰi(i)* 'exalted spiritual power', which together form a *hapax*).[64]

---

62 Note that this marked allomorph *-uni* is used only when there is a prefix. The unmarked allomorph *p°uni* is called for when there is no prefix (cf. Ikemiya [1987: 286]). The change *p°* > \**w* > ∅ is also seen in other polite forms such as *...-y-abir-a* 'let us humbly DO' (OSJS 338a), e.g. *kʰuu'-y-abir-a* ⟨ko ya be° ra⟩ 'let us humbly beg (the deities) for' (OS 8.#404) < \**...-yi-pʰaber-am-u* \*'...-RY-humbly.act-IA-SS'. See Ch. 6 §16 "{-abir- 'humbly DO'}". In NOk there is also another example of a polite form with a weakened initial \**pʰ*, in the word for chopsticks, *(ʔu-)me-esyi₁* < \**ʔu-myi-yasyi₁* < \**o-myi-wasyi₁* < \**o-myi-pʰasyi₁*. Cf. NJ *hásyi* 'chopsticks'. The change in the topic marker of the identical sort, \**... yi-CB-pʰa* > *... yi-CB-wa* > *e-e*, shows that the trigger is a Clitic Boundary, or in other words, the same sort of change as occurs in a cliticization.

63 For the function and development of *...-y-ar-yi*, cf. Ch. 6 §12, "...+ {-a(a)r-yi 'be(ing) DOing}".

64 The list of words that join with ⟨'u⟩ is short, as one might expect: ⟨ke⟩ *kʰi(i)* 'spiritual power', ⟨⁽ᵐ⁾sa si⟩ *-zasyi* 'an order' (← *sas-yi* 'pointing'), and ⟨mi ya⟩ *myaa* 'courtyard'. Eighteen words join with ⟨'o⟩, and 55 with ⟨'O⟩, with a great deal of overlap.

NOMINALS 129

– *ʔu-gusik°u* 御く⁽ⁿ⁾すく ⟨o ⁽ⁿ⁾k̅u̅ su ku⟩ 'EX-castle'

| しより | もり、 | ぐ*すく、 | / | なかべ† | きよら、 | 御ぐ*すく | / |
| si yo ri | mo ri, | gu* su ku, | / | na ka be† | ki yo ra, | o gu* su ku | / |
| *syiyuryi* | *muryi* | *gusik°u* | | *nakʰabi* | *k°yura* | *ʔu-gusik°u* | |
| Shuri | Grove | castle | | sky | beautiful | EX-castle | |

'Shuri castle, a beautiful,[65] **exalted** castle [in] the sky.' (OS 13.#756)

Elsewhere one can find either being used for the same word (*kʰut°u*) in one verse.

| てるかはが*、 | | おことす | / | てるしのが*、 |
| te ru ka pa ga*, | | **o** ko to su | / | te ru si no ga*, |
| *tʰir-u-kʰaQp°a-ga* | | *ʔu-kʰut°u-si* | | *tʰir-u-syi̯nu-ga* |
| Shine-{Spring/River}-SUB | | EX-message-KP | | Shine-Orb-SUB |

御ことす      /
**o** ko to su      /
*ʔu-kʰut°u-si*
EX-message-KP

'It is the message of the Shining Wellspring[66] (= the Sun Deity), it is the message of the Shining Orb.' (OS 4.#203)

Yet in other cases, only the graph お ⟨o⟩ *ʔu-* is selectively used in one member of a *tsuigo* pair (e.g. おき⁽ⁿ⁾も ~ おきむ ⟨o ⁽ⁿ⁾ki mo⟩ ~ ⟨o ki mu⟩ *ʔu-gyimu* 'your feelings', but not for its parallel word あゆ ⟨a yu⟩ ~ あよ ⟨a yo⟩ *ʔayu* '(id.)' below).

---

65   The mora *k°yu* is an example of Contraction. The reason for the lack of conservation of vowel length is unknown, however. It is similar to other contraction cases such as *c°yuwaru* 'deigns to rule', or the verbal extensions in … *C-°y-ur-u*. Note the lack of aspiration.

66   ⟨te ru ka pa⟩ ˣ~ ˣ⟨te ru ka wa⟩, that is to say, there is never a ⟨w⋯⟩-initial alternant in morpheme-internal position. Out of 75 tokens of *tʰir-u-kʰaQp°a*, 'the Sun', *all* are spelled with ⟨pa⟩. Therefore the phonological form is °*tʰir-u-kʰaQp°a*, not ˣ*tʰir-u-kʰawa*, despite the transparent semantics. While in the narrowest sense *kʰaQp°a* and *kʰawa* (the latter OSJS 119b ⟨ka wa⟩ only) mean the same, the first variant is part of a name, one with religious significance, while the second variant is merely a common noun. The second element …*-kʰaQp°a* of the noun compound has a conservative retention: in effect, … *kʰaQp°a*, < *… *kʰap°a*, just as *ʔuQp°u-* (< *ʔoQp°o ← *opo-* 'great, much, many') 'Great-' does. (It is clear, however, that *ʔuQp°u-* has by the time of NOk developed into an adnominal prefix *ʔufu-* meaning 'great, large, large number'.)

– *Ɂu-gyimu* おぎも ⟨o ⁽ⁿ⁾ki mo⟩ ~ おぎ゚む ⟨o gi゚ mu⟩ 'EX-liver/heart/guts' (御肝)

| おぎも、うちに、ᴧ | 御さうぜ゚、 | / あけど†まに、ᴧ |
|---|---|---|
| o gi mo , u ti ni , ᴧ | o sa u ze゚ , | / a ke do† ma ni , ᴧ |
| *Ɂu-gyimu-Ɂuc゚yi-nyi* | *Ɂu-soozi-∅* | *Ɂakʰi-duma-nyi* |
| EX-liver-interior-in | EX-contemplation-DO | brighten-moment-IO |

| たとゑちへ | / あよが、うちに、ᴧ | 御さうぜ゚は、 | / |
|---|---|---|---|
| ta to we ti pe | / a yo ga , u ti ni , ᴧ | o sa u ze゚ pa , | / |
| *tʰat゚u'yi-c゚yi*[67] | *Ɂayu-ga-Ɂuc゚yi-nyi*[68] | *Ɂu-soozi-Qp゚a* | |
| liken-GER | liver_EX-interior-in | EX-contemplation-DO | |

| あけだちに、ᴧ | たとゑて | / |
|---|---|---|
| a ke da ti ni , ᴧ | ta to we te | / |
| *Ɂakʰi-dac-゚yi-nyi* | *tʰat゚uyi-t゚i*[69] | |
| brighten-stand-IO | liken-GER | |

'The clarity within your heart, I will liken it to the break of day, and the tranquility within your breast, I will liken it alone to the day's first light ...' (OS 1.#34)

It is uncertain if any relative-ordering rules are deducible from the data. When both the morpheme *Ɂu-* and *myi-* co-occur, their orders of affixation seem flexible (*Ɂu-myi-*, below and *myi-Ɂu-* in OS 17 in the previous subsection above).[70]

– *Ɂu-myi-syagu* おみしやぐ 'EX-EX-liquor_EX'[71] (御神酒)

---

67 Since *-c゚yi* is a PPed syllable, the preceding syllable is palatal, thus, *'yi*. This fact is of course evidence in favor of medial ⟨we⟩ being used to write *'yi*.

68 Both *Ɂu-gyimu-Ɂuc゚yi-nyi* and *Ɂayu-ga-Ɂuc゚yi-nyi* have six moras.

69 As noted in Ch. 2, some *'yi* syllables come from C + hi-V, i.e. *\*yi*, while others come from C + mid-V, i.e. *\*ye*, and therefore post-raising [ʏi] has a hybrid status. *\*ye* was not capable of causing PP, because of the *\*e* kernel; *\*yi* was, because *\*yi* was the palatalizer par excellence. So the string *tʰat゚uyi*, coming from *\*t⁽ʰ⁾at⁽゚⁾oye*, originally did not cause PP. Therefore *\*t⁽ʰ⁾at⁽゚⁾oyet⁽゚⁾e* > *tʰat゚uyit゚i* [tʰatゝ゚uʏitゝʏɪ], with no PP. But because *\*ye* has become *yi* in OOk, and because PP is not quite dead yet as a process, it is possible to conjure *tʰat゚uyic゚yi* [tʰatゝ゚uʏitʃゝ゚ʏi] out of thin air so to speak. Here, we find two forms consciously used in the same song, so this pair is an instance of wordplay.

70 This may be an interesting contrast to a prefixation order noted in OJ liturgies as öp⁽ö⁾l- + myi- + Noun by Bentley (2001: 83). For further developments of *\*(myi-)o-myi-* and *\*(o-)myi-* into MOk, see Serafim (2004: 304).

71 Serafim (2004: 314) gives a detailed exploration of the development of this word into MOk *Ɂu-N-syaku* 'sacred wine': "*Ɂu-N-syaku B* 'sacramental wine' < *\*o-myi-syaku B*?; *\*o-myɪ-/myi-pyisakwo B*?; 'holy ladle'; 'pouring wine'; 'sacramental wine'." He states that

NOMINALS                                                                          131

かさす、　わかてだ*　　よ、　/ おみしやぐ*、ᴧ　ぬきあげ*は　　　　　　/
ka sa su ,　wa ka te da*　yo ,　/ o mi si ya gu* ,ᴧ　nu ki a ge* pa　　　　/
*k^hasasi*　*wak^ha-t^hida*　*yoo*　　*ʔu-myi-syagu-∅ nuk-°yi-ʔagi-ba*
PLN　　　　　young-lord　VOC　　EX-EX-sake-DO　offer-RY-raise_MZ-T/C
'O Young Lord of Kasasu,[72] if you raise in offer the **splendid**, grand
drinking-cup ...' (OS 21.#1428)

4.2.1        The Allomorph *ʔuQp°u-*
The longer allomorph *ʔuQp°u-* is written with 大 ⟨OPO⟩ and it appears in nouns
such as *ʔuQp°u-gyimyi* or *ʔuQp°u-nusyi* as below.

–      ***ʔuQp°u-nusyi*** 大ぬし ⟨OPO nu si⟩ ~ 大のし ⟨OPO no si⟩ 'EX-ruler' (大主)

あが*るいの、　　　　大ぬし、　　　/
a ga* ru i no ,　　　 OPO nu si ,　 /
*ʔagari-i-nu*　　　　*ʔuQp°u-nusyi*
rise-direction-GEN　EX-ruler
'The **Great** Ruler of the Rising Direction, i.e. of the East[73] (= the Sun
Deity)'[74] (OS 13.#828)

---

"***pyisakwo** originally meant 'gourd.'" But he misses the apparent fact that, largely, dialects
away from Shuri have *g*, not *k*: "Ima no hōgen de mo *misyagu*, *ʔuɴsagu* nado, dakuon
no katachi de aru [Even in today's dialects they are voiced forms, such as *misyagu* and
*ʔuɴsagu*.]" (OKDJ 630d). The change *k* > *g* occurred in J, and so it would be interesting
to find out just when the earliest forms with *g* in the J lineage are attested, in order to
verify what the earliest point in time is that *p°isago* or some later form might have been
borrowed from MJ into OOk.

72     The Lord of Kasasu was a lord of Kumejima, to the west of Okinawa island. Hateruma
       (2007d: 264) uses ⟨gasasu⟩ (our equivalent would be ˟*gasasi*) for this. We follow OSJS (107b,
       408c–490a) and the indicated (non)voicing in the appropriate TOS songs.

73     Pre-OOk *\*agar-u_RT#pe* *'ris-ing#direction' > *\*agaruye* [ʔãgaɾuyɛ] > *\*agar^(w)ee* [ʔãgaɾ^(w)ɛ:]
       (instant loss of [ʷ]) > *ʔagarii* [ʔãgaɾɪ:]. Apparently non-palatal [ɪ] arose because of
       monophthongization *before* raising. *Or*: the last element is 'sun': *\*pyi* or *\*pye*. If the latter,
       then nothing but the semantic part of the etymology changes. But if the former, then any
       element that imparts labiality to the output diphthong (an illegal sequence of either *Cwy*
       or, perhaps more narrowly, *Twy*, where *T* stands for any coronal consonant) automatically
       acts to extinguish both itself and the palatality in the output: *\*ʔagarupyi* > *\*ʔagarufyi* >
       *\*ʔagaruwyi* [···ɾuwi] > *\*ʔagarwyii* ˣ[···rẅi:] (= ˣ[···rɥi:]) → *\*ʔagarii* [···rɪ:]. This should be a
       testable claim. Why bother with this? Two responses come to mind: (1) しねりきよ ⟨si ne ri
       ki yo⟩ *syi̯niriyi-k^hyu(u)*, 'Shinerikyo', one of the two names of the Creator Deity of Okinawa,
       the other being *ʔamamyi-k^hyu(u)* 'Amamikyo' (OSJS 175b ⟨si ne ri - ki yo⟩). The pre-OOk
       form should be *\*syi̯no#ʔyir-yi#k^hoo* *'Orb Enter-ing Personage', where the "entering" "orb"
       is apparently the moon setting (Murayama [1970: 17]). (2) Our "destruction of incommen-
       surate glides" (DIG) hypothesis may help to explain the otherwise unexplainable behavior

- *ʔuQpºu-gyimyi* 大ぎみ ⟨OPO gi mi⟩ ~ 大きみ ~ ⟨OPO ki mi⟩ ~ 大君 ⟨OPO KIMI⟩ 'EX-priestess; high priestess' (大君)

  きこゑ　　大ぎ゚み
  ki ko we　**OPO** gi゚ mi
  *kºyi̧kºuyi ʔuQpºu-gyimyi*
  famed　EX-priestess
  'The Renowned **High** Priestess' (OS 1.#1)

Sometimes all three prefixes, *ʔuQpºu-, myi-*, and *ʔu-* are combined:

- *ʔuQpºu-myi-ʔu-duN* おほみおどん ⟨o po mi o do N⟩ 'EX-EX-EX-palace' (大美御殿)

  おほみおど゚ん
  o po mi o do゚ N /
  *ʔuQpºu-myi-ʔu-duN*
  **grand-beautiful-revered**-palace
  'The King's villa, (*lit.*) a **grand, beautiful, revered** palace' (KKKS2: 95)

According to OSJS (90bc), the governmental title *pʰeecºyiN* 親雲上 is said to have derived from 大やこもい ⟨OPO ya ko mo i⟩, which is composed of *ʔuQpºu-ya-kʰu* 'tribal leader' + -*mii* 'EX' (*ʔuQpºu-* is the prefix of our concern). However, to our knowledge, the set of phonological changes from the precursor of *ʔuQpºuyakʰumii* to *pºeecºyiN* has never been presented. The alternative pronunciation *pʰeekʰumii* provided a clue for us.[75] Here we venture the following derivation.

---

of the modern all-purpose exalting verb *miseeN* 'be/go/come/eat/ride/dress (etc.)', whose history requires it to have had a sequence *\*misywayiN*, with the illegal sequence *Twy*, and thus *\*misayiN* > *miseeN* in mid-20th-century male gentry speech. Yet the seemingly unexplainable forms are the one above and the gerund-derived forms: *\*misyuwacºi* > *misyoocyi* in mid-20th-century male gentry Shuri speech. Now the vanishing of the male gentry who knew this language has resulted in forms that look as if they never went through these changes: *misyeeN* and *misoocyi*! They are generated automatically, and merely phonetic.

74 A strong case has been made in many sources, most recently in Smits (2019: 196 ff.), that this Ryukyuan Sun Deity is Be(n)zaiten, and her other manifestations. We find this convincing, and have therefore changed the "Master" of our original ms to "Ruler".

75 It can be found by Googling ペークミー ⟨pe – ku mi –⟩.

NOMINALS                                                                          133

| *[ʔɔpʰɔ | ʔɔya | kʰɔ | ʔɔmɔpˈyi] | > |
| 'EX (= great) | EX-house | -one | EX (= loving)' or | |
| 'EX (= great) | EX (= parent) | -one | EX (= loving)' | |

| | *[ʔɔpʰɔʔɔyakʰɔmɔpˈyi] | > |
| | *[ʔɔːpːpˈɔ[76]ʔwaikʰɔmɔi̯][77] | > |
| | *[pːpˈɔ[78]ʔwai̯kʰyɔmɔi̯] | > |
| | *[pˈuʔweːkʰyumɪ][79] | > |
| | *[pˈuʔweːʧʰyuɴ] | > |
| | *[pˈweːʧʰyuɴ] | > |
| | *[pˈeːʧʰuɴ][80] | > |
| | Nakijin [pˈeːˈʧiˈɴ], | |
| | Shuri [peːʧiˈɴ] | = |
| | Sr *peecyiɴ* | |

The form *peekumii* did not undergo PP, nor did [moi̯] shorten to [ɴ].

## 4.3  Exalting Prefix ma-
Written with the character 圭 ⟨ma⟩, with the original meaning 'true', it grammaticalized as an exalting prefix (OSJS 293c). It attaches to a greater variety of
nouns than the first two, from ordinary people to priestesses, from jewels to gar-
ments, and from the Sun to the winds. But it seems that all relate to the authority of the Kingdom. True jewels are the symbols of authority and prosperity;
true winds ease trade-related travels, which bring wealth to the Kingdom; true
retainers serve the Kingdom.

---

76  The regular change was pre-OOk *opo- > *owo- > *oo- > ʔuu-. The form here, with the labial
    still in place, was effected through an exception to Medial Weakening brought on by gemi-
    nation of *p to *ɋp, largely in adjectives (see Thorpe [1983: 60–61], e.g. "a special expressive
    (emphatic?) phonological device. Examples include *uɋpo- ..." (ibid. 61)). The majority of
    medial *p, left ungeminated, was subject to Medial Weakening (J *ha-gyō tenko*[-*on*]), and
    either became *w/y*, or vanished entirely. For details see Ch. 2.
77  The sound change *[ʔɔya] > *[ʔwai̯] > ... > NOk [ʔɥeː] is frequent, though not predictable.
    Similarly, *[ʔɔyɔ] > *[ʔwɔi̯] > ... > NOk [ʔɥiˑ] is apparently predictable (cf. *ʔwiiz-y-u-ɴ*,
    'swim' < *oyog-...; *ʔiibi* < *ʔwiibi* < *oyobe* 'finger').
78  The change from this line to the next is due to the loss of obstruent length in initial posi-
    tion of 3-or-more-mora words, or, to put it another way, a retention of obstruent length in
    initial position of two-mora words, a regular change, part of the Two-Mora Rule. Cf. Ch. 2
    §5.3.
79  With PP, monophthongization, and then shortening.
80  The change [ʧˈu] > [ʧˈi] is irregular, but due to the palatal environment. Cf. e.g. J *syiɴzyuku*
    'Shinjuku (in Tokyo)' → *syiɴzyiku*.

– *ma-dama* ⟨ma da ma⟩ まだま 'EX-jewel' (真玉)

> まだ゚ま　　もり　ぐ゚すく　　/ (= 真玉杜城)
> **ma** da゚ ma　mo ri　gu゚ su ku　/
> *ma-dama*　*muryi gusik゚u*
> EX-jewel　grove　enclosure
> **'True-Jewel-Grove Enclosure'** (OS 1.#1)

– *ma-ʔyi̖tʰu* ⟨ma i to⟩ まいと 'EX-silk' (真糸)

> まいと、おどしの、ʌ　　　よろい / (= 真糸縅しの鎧)
> **ma** i to , o do si no , ʌ　　yo ro i　/
> *ma-ʔyi̖tʰu-ʔudusyi-nu*　*yuruyi*
> pure-silk-threaded-APPO　armor
> **'Pure-silken-threaded armor'** (OS 15.#1105)

– ma-nyisyi ⟨ma ni si⟩ まにし 'EX-North.wind' (真北風)[81]

> まにしが゚、　　　　　まねまね、　　ふけば゚、　　　　/
> **ma** ni si ga゚ ,　　ma ne ma ne , pu ke ba゚ ,　　/
> *ma-nyisyi-̖ga*　　*mani-mani*　*p゚uk゚-i-ba*
> EX-North.wind-SUB as.it.does　　blow-IZ-COND
> **'When the true North wind blows, taking its course,**[82] **....'** (OS 9.#510; OS 13.#892)

---

81 The word *nyisyi* means 'north (wind)' (as opposed to ⟨pa p/we⟩ ~ ⟨pa i⟩ *pʰayi* 'south (wind)' [OSJS 475b, 476ab ~ 474a], i.e. ⟨... V Ce⟩ ~ ⟨... V i⟩, showing *Vyi*) and its etymon in the J lineage is suggested to be *in-i-si-pê* 'leave-RY-PST-direction' = 'yore', i.e. '[place] which [we] left [long ago to come to these islands]' (OKDJ 506b; Kinjō [1970 [1950]: 260–261], citing Kanazawa Shōzaburō in *Kōjirin* (n.d.)). In the OS, *nyisyi* as an independent word also means 'north wind', trade wind from the North in the winter months; and other dictionaries, such as ENKDJ and KJE suggest 'wind' for *-si*; cf. also *-ti* '(id.)'.

82 Because the brush-written characters for *k゚u* and for repetition of two or more syllables can be difficult to tell apart—the latter takes more vertical space than the former—, in this case the word can be read either as *mani* + *k゚u* [manɪk゚u], or, interpreting the graph in question as the repetition mark, *mani* + *mani* [manɪmanɪ]. There are only two examples of this word. Literary scholars' interpretations differ on this point, Ikemiya (1987: 286) taking the former option, and all others, including TOS, taking the latter. #510 has ⟨ma ne " "⟩, and #892, ⟨ma ne ma ne⟩. Since the two omoros are duplicates, there really is no arguing it.

NOMINALS          135

When the three prefixes, *ma-*, *ʔu-*, and *myi-* are used together to modify a noun, the order of affixation is *ma-ʔu-myi-*,[83] as in the following example.

– *ma-ʔu-myi-kʰut°u* ⟨ma o mi KOTO⟩ ま御み事 'EX-EX-EX-message'

| だ*に ∧ ま、御み事る | / げ*に ∧ ま、御み事る |
|---|---|
| da* ni ∧ **ma , o mi** KOTO ru | / ge* ni ∧ **ma , o mi** KOTO ru |
| *danyi*   **ma-ʔu-myi-**ₗ*kʰutˍu-ru* | *ginyi*   **ma-ʔu-myi-**ₗ*kʰutˍu-ru* |
| truly   EX-EX-EX-message-KP | really   EX-EX-EX-message-KP |

'It is a truly **blessed, grand, reverent** message [that will be heard by the deity]; it is a wholeheartedly **blessed, grand, reverent** message [that will be heard by the deity].' (OS 11.#576)

---

83 NOk *ʔumáncyu* 'general public' (OGJ 552a) comes from *ʔu-ma-byitʰu* 'EX-EX-people'. In this coinage, the order is the expected *ʔu-ma-*. The reason that *ma-ʔu-myi-kutu* sees a reversal of those two morphemes is that 1) the order is sensitive to length, and 2) *ʔu·myi* functions as a unit; thus the raised dot instead of the hyphen. In the OS, a word of similar meaning is just *ma-⁽ᵐ⁾p°yiₗtʰu* (voicing unknown) with no *ʔu-* (⟨ma PITO⟩ [OSJS 303bc], ⟨ma pi to⟩ [OKDJ 618a]; ⟨o ma pi to⟩ [OKDJ 158b]). Looking at a modern form that is also attested in the historical record, Shuri /ʔumáncyu/ 'the common people' (OGJ 552a), note in these examples from Literary Okinawan ([OKDJ 158b] ⟨o ma pi to⟩) that the left-side *kanji* spelling in the table below is historically faithful, while the right-side one is intuitively faithful (that is, it reflects psychological reality).

| | Historically faithful | | | / | Intuitively faithful | | |
|---|---|---|---|---|---|---|---|
| Gloss | ' EX | · true | · person | / EX | · myriad | · person | ' |
| Transliteration | ⟨ O | · MA | · PITO | / O | · MAN | · PITO | ⟩ |
| Characters | ⟨ 御 | · 真 | · 人 | / 御 | · 萬 | · 人 | ⟩ |
| Phonemicization | /ʔu | · ma | · ncyu/ | / /ʔu | · maN | · (Q)cyu/ | |

These spellings suggest pre OOk */o-ma-hityo/ > OOk /ʔu-ma-Bcy°u/ [˜b:tɕ°] > MOk /ʔu-ma-ncyu/ ~ (reanalyzed) /ʔu-maN-cyu/. The OS has ⟨ma PITO⟩ = ⟨ま人⟩ (e.g. OS 305 = TOS 221; see also OSJS 303bc), without any ⟨no⟩ = ⟨の⟩ in the compound. That is of course because it was OOk /B/, not OOk /nu/, in this compound, which soon changed to MOk /M/ or MOk /N/, as is discernible from KKKS, which gives it the phonologization ⟨ma mu ti yo⟩, i.e. MOk /maMcyu/ or MOk /maNcyu/. Both OKDJ (⟨o maṗito⟩ (158b), ⟨maṗito⟩ (618a)) and Ifa Fuyū, in a note to his own brushwritten copy of the OS (cited in OKDJ ⟨maṗito⟩) agree that the word MOk /maNcyu/ is etymologically */ma-fito/ 'true people'.

136                                                                                    CHAPTER 4

## 4.4   *Exalting Prefix* kʰana-

This is written with the characters 金 ⟨KANA⟩ and かな ⟨ka na⟩, which originally meant 'iron', then extended to mean 'strong', 'great', or 'splendid' (OSJS 109).[84] The nouns modified by this prefix include architectural structures (*kʰana-gusik°u* 'iron castle', *kʰana-dzyoo* 'iron gate'), armor (*kʰana-kʰaʙt°u*[85] 'iron helmet', *kana-yuruyi* 'iron body armor'[86]), tools (*kana-pʰic°i* 'iron hammer', *kana-ma-yumyi* 'iron(-like) true-bow', *kana-mamak°yi* 'iron(-like) arrow'[87]). Examples are:

–     *kʰana-ma-yumyi* かなまゆみ ⟨ka na ma yu mi⟩ 'EX-EX-bow' (金真弓)
      *kʰana-ma(-)mak°yi* かなま〻き ⟨ka na ma " ki⟩ 'EX-EX-arrow' (金細矢)

| ゑ、 | け、 | ∧ あが°る、 | ∧ 三日月や、 | | / | ゑ、 | け、 | ∧ かみぎ°や、 |
|---|---|---|---|---|---|---|---|---|

we , ke , ∧ a ga° ru , ∧ MI KA DUKI ya ,     / we , ke , ∧ ka mi gi° ya ,
*yee kʰee ʔagar-u myi̠-kʰa#dzik°yi-ya*[88]     *yee kʰee kʰamyi-gya*
INJ INJ rise-RT three-day-moon-TOP     INJ INJ deity-GEN

かなまゆみ     / ゑ、 け、 ∧ あが°る、 ∧ あかぼしや     / ゑ、 け、 ∧
**ka na** ma yu mi   / we , ke , ∧ a ga° ru , ∧ a ka bo si ya   / we , ke , ∧
*kʰana-ma-yumyi   yee kʰee ʔagar-u ʔakʰa-busyi-ya   yee kʰee*
EX-EX-bow     INJ INJ rise-RT red-star-TOP     INJ INJ

かみぎや、   かなま〻き     /
ka mi gi ya , **ka na** ma " ki     /
*kʰamyi-gya kʰana-mamak°yi*
deity-GEN EX-EX-arrow

'Eh, hey! Ah the rising new crescent moon! / Eh hey! It's the Deity's Fine True Bow! / Eh hey! The rising Bright Planet, Venus! / Eh hey! The Deity's Fine True Arrow!' (OS 10.#534)[89]

---

84    The link between *kane* 'metal' and *-ganasyi* 'dear', to be discussed in §5.3, is discussed extensively in Ch. 5 §4.5 (**An excursus on** ⟨ka ne⟩).

85    For a discussion of *-kʰaʙt°u* for ⟨ka bu to⟩, see Ch. 2 §4.6, "Mora voiced obstruents", "/ʙ/".

86    For a discussion of 'armor', see Ch. 3 §1 fn. 7 (on *yuruyi*).

87    It *is* possible to use J *maki* (specifically *inumaki* 'J podocarp') for making bows, as an online search has shown (e.g. http://paleoplanet69529.yuku.com/topic/18701/Snakeskin-backed -osage-longbow--bamboo-backed-podocarp--sale#.WVzWqhPysUE). Thus it may be that *kʰanamamak°yi* was *kʰana-* 'strong-' *ma-* 'true' *mak°yi* 'podocarp', with *kʰana-ma-* held in common between the two parallel compounds.

88    Cf. NOk *mi-ká-zicyi* [mʸika°z⁽ʸ⁾itʃi] 'crescent/new moon' (OGJ 378a), *mí-Qka* 'three days, third day', *mí-Qcya̠* 'three days' (OGJ 380b).

89    We believe that the meaning of *ʔakʰa-* is °'bright', not ˣ'red'.

NOMINALS 137

– ***kʰana-dzyoo*** かなぢや(う)[90] ⟨ka na di ya (u)⟩ 'EX-gate' (金門)

> いし、ぢ゛やうは、ʌ たてゝ | かな、ぢ゛やうは たてゝ |
> i si , di˚ ya u pa ,ʌ ta te " | **ka na** , di˚ ya u pa ta te " |
> *ʔyisyi-dzyoo-Qpˆa tʰatˆˀi-tˀi* ***kʰana-dzyoo-Qpˆa* tʰatˆˀi-tˀi**
> EX(rock)-gate-DO erect-GER EX(iron)-gate-DO erect-GER
> 'Erecting rock-strong gates; erecting iron-strong gates …' (OS 11.#568)

## 4.5 Exalting Prefix ʔuya-

This prefix is written おや ⟨o ya⟩, but not うや ⟨u ya⟩, and originally meant 'parent(al)', 'ancestor, ancestral'.[91] This original meaning seems to be reflected in the exalting prefix, as it combines with land and possession. Examples are:

– ***ʔuya-gunyi*** おやくに ~ おやぐに ⟨o ya ⁽ⁿ⁾ku ni⟩ 'EX-country' (親国)

> みれど゛も あかぬ、 | 首里 おや国 |
> mi re do˚ mo a ka nu , | SIYO RI oya KUNI
> *myi₍ᵢ₎·r-i-dumu ʔak-°an-u syiyuryi **ʔuya-gunyi***
> observe-IZ-CONC tire.of-NEG-RT Shuri EX-country
> 'Shuri, the **Parental** Land [= the King's Capital]!, which we do not tire of gazing at.'[92] (OS 1.#7)

---

90 For a thorough discussion of *dzyoo*, see Ch. 2 § 5.6 fn. 65.

91 Ikemiya (2015: 398), however, asserts that this prefix is derived from *uya* 'gratitude' or *uya-mafu* 'to respect'. He somewhat mysteriously interprets the spelling ⟨'o⟩ as based on analogy (uya *o o-dan ni hatarakasete oya to shita mono* 'something in which they made it *oya* by setting *uya* to work as *o*'). He notes that *ʔweesyuɴ* in NOk means 'to give (HUMILIFIC)' (but not corroborable by us either in OGJ or RGJ). (Cf. the many examples of ⟨mi o ya se⟩ '(You!) humilifically (just as me) give [it] to (a superior)! (POLITE)' in the OS. We follow Torigoe [1968: 367–369] in treating this as a reflex of *myi-ʔo-yar-as-e* '[EX-EX-give-EX]ₕᵤₘ-MR', with irregular *r-elision.) If indeed *ʔweesyuɴ* is the reflex of *ʔuya*, it seems surprising that there is only one other example (see below) of the same putative case, that is, of the original vowel *u* being written with ⟨'o⟩: as in ˣ⟨u wi ta bi⟩ [—**but there is ⟨u̅ we ta bi⟩ (OS 10.#541)**—] *ʔwii-tʰabyi* 'maiden voyage' → °⟨'o pi , ta bi⟩ (OS 13.#957; cf. MJ *upi-* 'first-ever'). On the other hand, there is a handful of examples of ⟨'o⟩ → ⟨'u⟩, as in, e.g.:

⟨'o za⁺ si⟩ (OS 7.#357) *ʔu-zas-yi* '(a superior's) order' → ⟨'u za˚ si⟩ (OS 4.#195); ⟨'o wa ɾu⟩ (OS 5.#217) *ʔuwar u* 'exaltedly he' → ⟨'u wa ru⟩ (OS 17.#1248);

⟨'o mi ya⟩ (OS 11.#639) *ʔu-myaa* 'courtyard for religious events' → ⟨'u mi ya⟩ (OS 11.#565), etc.

In any case, the Ikemiya hypothesis will probably be overwhelmed by the data in favor of the string *oya* in the long run.

92 This is a favored trope within classical Japanese poetry as well, and may well be borrowed into OOk.

138 CHAPTER 4

–  *ʔuya-zakʰe* おやざ⁺かい ⟨o ya za⁺ ka i⟩ 'EX-sake' (親酒)

> なご゛、ざかい、 / おや、ざ⁺かい、ₐ きよもの /
> na go゛, za ka i , / o ya , za⁺ ka i ,ₐ ki yo mo no /
> *nagu-zakʰe-∅* *ʔuya-zakʰe-∅* *k-°y-uu-munu*
> PLN-*sake*-SUB EX-*sake*-SUB come-RY-SE-since

–  *ʔuya-dzyoo* おやぢ゛やう ⟨o ya di゛ ya u⟩ 'EX-gate' (親門)

> おやぢ゛やうₐ あけて、 / わん、 いれゝ /
> o ya di゛ ya uₐ a ke te , / wa N , i re " /
> *ʔuya-dzyoo-∅* *ʔakʰi-t°i* *waN-∅* *ʔyi̱ri-ri*
> EX-gate-DO open-GER me-DO let.enter-MR
> 'Nago *sake, sake* of long tradition[93,94]—[I] have come[95] here [with it], so,
> open the **great** gate and let me in!' (OS 17.#1180)

## 4.6  *Exalting Prefix* dee-/dzya-

The beautifying prefix *dee-/dzya-* (MOk and NOk *dee-/zya-*), spelled ⟨⁽ⁿ⁾ta⟩ and
⟨⁽ⁿ⁾ti ya⟩ (た⁽゛⁾, ち⁽゛⁾や),[96] is commonly seen as related to the Sino-Japanese
prefix (*)*dai-* 'great; large' (written 大 or 太 in *kanji*). These two variant forms
were derived in Ch. 2 §5.6, so we will repeat none of that here.

Here are some examples:

---

93  Nakahara (1957: 234) takes おや、ざ⁺かいゝ ⟨o ya , za ka i⟩ to be an alternative spelling
for *saki* [sakɪ] i.e. ⟨sa ke⟩ 'liquor', rather than *sakee* i.e. ⟨sa ka i⟩ 'border'. Hokama (1994:
155), too, takes ⟨sa ka i⟩ to be 'liquor', but he also admits the possibility of interpreting
it as 'border'. If it is the latter, he says, it refers to *sake* presented from border regions
such as Ma-Haneji (真羽地), Awa (安和), and Yabu (屋部), all of which also appear in
the succeeding verses. If what he says is true, then it is a play on words, facilitated by
the retention of the mid vowel height (i.e. consciously archaizing) and the diphthongal
spelling.

94  Diphthongal spellings for unraised (usually long) vowels: ⟨za ka i⟩ for *-zakʰe*[ʔe]; in fact
there is no way other than this to clearly differentiate even a short mid vowel; therefore
the vowel *is* probably short: *-zakʰe*.

95  The interpretation of this phrase, *k-°y-uu-munu* 'come-RY-SE-since' is due to Nakahara
(1957: 233–234) and Hokama (1994: 156). Semantically, it fits well with the MR ending in
the next verse. The vowel length here is ascribed by observation of modern forms of this
verb that suggest that the length is associated with the root of the verb itself.

96  Note that there are no ⟨⁽ⁿ⁾sya⟩ spellings, just as the Yotsu-Gana Hypothesis predicts.

NOMINALS

– *dee-kʰunyi* ⟨da*̥ ku ni⟩ だ*̥くに 'great-country/land'

だ*̥くに、ₐ　　おそうₐ　中ぐ*̥すく　　/
da*̥ ku ni ,ₐ　o so uₐ　NAKA gu*̥ su ku  /
*dee-kʰunyi-Ø　ʔusu-u　nakʰagusikʰu*
EX-land-DO　rule-RT　Nakagusuku
'[It is] Nakagusuku who/which rules the **great** land ...' (OS 2.#42)

– *dʑya-gunyi* ぢやぐ*̥†に ⟨di ya gu† ni⟩ '**big**-country/land'

ぢやぐ*̥に、　　　とよみよわれ　　　/
di ya gu*̥ ni ,　　to yo mi yo wa re　/
*dʑya-gunyi-Ø　tʰuyum-y-uwar-i*
EX-country-LOC　resound-RY-EAV-IZ
'... will resound [throughout] the Great Country!' (OS 1.#5)

The following example shows a play on words/graphics by a compiler. The *kʰunu dee-* in the first verse is written with *hiragana*-logograph, while the same word in the third verse has it in the reverse order of *logograph*-hiragana.

あまみきよが*̥、　　うざししよ、　　/ この、ₐ　大しま、ₐ
a ma mi ki yo ga*̥ ,　u za si si yo ,　/ ko no ,ₐ　DAI si ma ,ₐ
*ʔamamyikʰyu-ga　ʔu-zasyi-syu　kʰunu　dee-syima-Ø*
Amamiko-GEN　　EX-command-KP　this　great-island-LOC
おれたれ、　　　/ しねりやこが、　うざししよ、　　/ 此、ₐ
o re ta re ,　　/ si ne ri ya ko ga ,　u za si si yo ,　/ KONO ,ₐ
*ʔuri-tʰar-i　　syi̥nirya-kʰu-ga　ʔu-zasyi-syu　kʰunu*
descend-PRFT-IZ　Shineryako-GEN　EX-command-KP　this
だしま、　　　おれたれ、　　　/
da si ma ,　　o re ta re ,　　/
*dee-syima-Ø　ʔuri-tʰar-i*
great-island-LOC　descend-PRFT-IZ
'It was due to the order of the deity Amamiko herself that Ogyakamoi (King Shō Shin) descended onto this island. He and only he will govern this island forever. /May (King Shō Shin) govern this island forever! It was due to the order of [the deity] Shineryako himself [that Ogyakamoi (King Shō Shin)] descended onto this island.' (OS 5.#242)

140                                                CHAPTER 4

## 5    Nominal Suffixes

This section presents nominal suffixes, including (1) plural suffixes (*fukusū-kei* 複数形), (2) beautifying suffixes (so-called *bishō-[setsubi-]ji* 美称[接尾]辞), (3) diminutives (*shishō-ji* 指小辞), and (4) reduplicated forms / reduplications (*chōfuku-kei* 重複形).[97]

### 5.1   *Plural Suffix -ra*

The suffix -*ra* creates a plural form. It should be noted, however, that nominals without this suffix may also be interpreted as plural if the context calls for it, as below. Although there is only one suffixless ⟨a se⟩ *ʔasi* in the *Omoro Sōshi* as in OS 1.#33 below, this is clearly construed as plural. Examples are:

–   *ʔasi(i)* あせ ⟨a se⟩ 'man, men', *ʔasi-ra* あせら ⟨a se ra⟩ 'man-PL'

      首里もり、       あせは、     / つちぎりに、       きらせ       /
      SIYO RI mo ri, **a se** pa,   / tu ti gi ri ni,   ki ra se     /
      *syiyuryi-muryi*  *ʔasi-Qp°a*    *c°ic°yi-gyiryi-nyi*  *k°yi̯r-as-i*
      Shuri-Grove     **soldiers**-DO    dirt-cuttings-into  cut-CAUS-MR
      'Have our **fellows** of the Shuri Precinct cut [them] into dirt chunks.'
      (OS 1.#33)

      やへま、しま、         いづこ、     / あせら、ᴧ
      ya pe ma, si ma,       i du ko,     / a se ra, ᴧ
      *yayima-syima-∅*       *ʔyidzikʰu-∅*   *ʔasi-ra-∅*
      Yaeyama-islands-APPO soldiers-DO   **chieftain**-PL-DO
      ためやらば†、         /
      ta me ya ra ba†,     /
      *tʰami.yar-a-ba*[98]
      conquer-MZ-COND
      'If [you] send **chieftains** to conquer the Yaeyama-island soldiers, [it is [you], Great Priestess, that will govern.]' (OS 1.#36)

–   *-kʰu*     こ    ⟨ko⟩ 'man; one/personage (either gender; EX)'
   *-kʰu-ra*[99]  こら  ⟨ko ra⟩ 'man-PL' (< *-ko(-ra))

---

97    Unfortunately the same term, *chōfuku*, also refers to duplications of entire songs.

98    OSJS 213b ⟨ta me ya ra ba⟩ sees the word *tami-yar-u* 'cause to be in accord; subjugate' as composed of *tami-* 'bend' VT (cf. NOk *tami-y-u-N,* 'bend' VT, OJ *tam[ʾë]-u* '(id.)' [JDB 447bc]), and *yar-u* 'send' VT. We attempt to smooth the interpretation by seeing *tami·yar-u* as a truncated syntactic form meaning 'send to "bend"'.

99    Ifa (1975b [1924]: 517–518) asserts that the diminutive -*Qkwa* was derived from *kura*. He also

NOMINALS    141

せだかこ
se da ka ko
*si-dakʰa-kʰu*
spiritual.power-high-one_EX
'the **One** of High Spiritual Power' (OS 1.#1)

はたみ、　いくさこがｵ　　　／
pa ta mi ,　i ku sa **ko** gaᵗ　　／
*pʰat°amyi ʔyik°usa-kʰu-ga*
relative　　war-**man**-SUB
'The **soldier**, our close relative¹⁰⁰ ...' (OS 13.#962)

つる₍ⁿ₎もいの、　　　　こらがｵ、　　　／
tu ru ₍ko₎ mo i no ,　　ko **ra** gaᵗ ,　　／
*c°iru₍-kʰu₎-mii-nu　　kʰu-**ra**-ga*
splendid₍-one₎-EX-GEN man-PL-SUB
'The splendid ruler's men [launched his ship ...].' (OS 13.#948)

## 5.2    *Plural Suffixes* -t°aa,¹⁰¹ -t°ac°yi

The suffix -*t°a(a)* turns a singular noun into a plural noun. A suffix similar to this is -*t°ac°yi*, also a plural suffix as in the last of the following series of examples (OS 12.#740). These two suffixes are most probably related, but it is difficult to imagine -*t°a(a)* to be a reduced form of -*t°ac°yi*, since there is only one instance of -*t°ac°yi*, whereas -*t°a(a)* compounds are abundant. Even within this song (OS 12.#740), there are two more instances of -*t°a(a)*.¹⁰² Vovin (2005: 102) concludes that "the extreme rarity of the suffix -*tati* in the *Omoro sōshi* and absence

---

     agrees with Orikuchi Shinobu, who apparently states in his *Man'yō-go Jiten* (1976 [1919]) that the suffix -*ra* was not necessarily a plural marker originally, but was a diminutive.

100    In OSJS ⟨pa ta mī i ku sa ko⟩ (275c), Ifa Fuyū is cited as having translated the later form of this word ⟨MI KAMI PITE tu no TIKA o N pà dà Ǹ⟩ (*N-cyaN tii-ci-nu cyicya-ʔu-N-padaN*), which appeared in the MOk Kumiodori *Ōkawa Tekiuchi*, and which translates into Japanese as *soshin hitotsu no shunrui*, i.e. 'relatives with an identical ancestor'. OKDJ (541a) glosses it with the *kanji* for *fada* 'skin' and *mi(i)* 'body/self'. A big problem with the construal is that TOS has ⟨pa ta° mi⟩. We *can* say that the word refers to one's King, since it is employed as a parallel phrase to *ʔu-gyakʰa-ʔadzyi-pʰa'yi* 'His Majesty the Shining One'.

101    Nakijin *niiʳsee-t°a'a* 'the rising generation' (ROD Nk) suggests that the attachment in OOk, too, is without aspiration.

102    The last one and the succeeding six omoro belong to *k°yimyi tʰidziryi-nu mumu-gapʰuu-gut°u* 'Grand Prayer Ritual', in which King Shō Nei requested his and his predecessors' *wunaryi-gamyi* 'guardian sister-deities' to congregate and pray to heighten his spiritual power for the upcoming battle with Satsuma (cf. Shimamura [2012: 62–71]). Thus, this omoro is considered very significant. It may be for this reason that the *tʰiida-gamyi* 'Sun

of it in other Ryukyuan sources makes it highly probable that it is a loan from mainland Japanese," and we see no reason to contradict that conclusion.

—  *ʔukʰyicyʰi*[103] おきて ⟨o ki te⟩ (1) 'village head; (2) village vice-priestess', *ʔukʰyicyʰi-tʰaa* おきてた ⟨o ki te ta⟩ 'village head-PL' (OSJS 75ab)

| おきて、‸ | やりよわ | / つかい、‸ |
|---|---|---|
| o ki te ,‸ | ya ri yo wa | / tu ka i ,‸ |
| *ʔukʰyicyʰi-∅* | *yar-y-uwa-∅* | *cʰikʰee-∅* |
| **village.head-DO** | **send.off-RY-EX-MR** | messenger-DO |
| やりよわ | / | |
| ya ri yo wa | / | |
| *yar-y-uwa-∅* | | |
| send.off-RY-EX-MR | | |

'Send off the village headman! Send off the messenger [to invite the deity]!' (OS 11.#610)

| ま人たも、 | / こが*、‸ | みぼ*しや、‸ | ありよれ | / |
|---|---|---|---|---|
| ma PITO ta mo , | / ko ga*,‸ | mi bo* si ya ,‸ | a ri yo re | / |
| *ma-BCʰyu-tʰaa-mu* | *kʰuu-ga* | *myi(i)-bu-sya*[104] | *-ʔar-y-ur-i* | |
| true-person-PL-also | this-DO | see-want-AA | -VBZ-RY-SE-IZ[105] | |

'Why, even the common people are wanting to see this [fine cloth]! ...' (OS 14.#983)

---

Goddess' is selected over the plain *kʰyimyi* 'priestess', and further the plural *tʰiida-gamyi-tʰacʰyi* over the *kʰyimyi-gyimyi*. See below.

103  *ʔukʰyicyʰi* [ʔukʸiʧʰị], with [kʸị] sounding like [kʰʸ]: The NOk equivalent of this word is *ʔúQ-cyi* [ʔuˈtːʧi] 'village head' (OGJ 559b). (Another word pops up as well, *ʔucyiti,* [ʔuˈtʧịti] 'code, law' (OGJ 539b), a late borrowing, with a meaning similar to that of the J word.) For *ʔukʰyicyʰi*, there is a fair number of OOk examples, most as second members of compounds, denoting 'head of X village'. Since all *tʰi* (except for an insignificant few *tʰiⱼwᵢi*) originates in *te*, naturally it was a candidate for PP, and so: This *was* really *ʔukʰyicʰyi* with the automatically determinable PP not written (as, say, voicing frequently would not be), especially morpheme-internally. The word probably was borrowed from Japanese during state formation (the borrowing would have been early enough to be unaffected by the MJ merger {{#o [o] ↔ #wo [wo]} > {#wo [wo]}} ("the distinction between #o and #wo is neutralized by merger into #wo")—as early as 925, at the very latest by 1200 [according to a chart of sound changes in Martin [1987: 79]]), which already had well developed vocabulary for statecraft.

104  The form *bu* before *s* is from *bo* only; *bu* yields OOk ʙ before *s*.

105  For use of IZ without KP here, see Ch. 7 §6 on the bare inferential aux MZ vs IZ.

NOMINALS 143

おきてたも、 　　　／ こが*、ˆ 　きよらさ、ˆあよれ 　　　／
o ki te ta mo , 　　／ ko ga* ,ˆ 　ki yo ra sa ,ˆ a yo re 　　／
ʔuk°yicy°i-t°aa-mu 　　kʰuu-ga 　k°yurasa-ʔa-y-ur-i
village.heads-also 　　this-SUB 　beauty-VBZ-RY-SE-IZ
'... And the village headmen [exclaim,] "so beautiful!" '[106] (OS 14.#983)

—　 *kʰamyi* かみ 〈ka mi〉 'deity; priestess', *kʰamyi-t°aa* かみた 'deity-PL;
　 priestess-PL'

あんは、ˆ かみ、ˆ 　　てづら、 　／ かみや、ˆ 　あん、ˆ まぶれ 　　　／
a N pa ,ˆ ka mi ,ˆ 　te du ra , 　／ ka mi ya ,ˆ 　a N ,ˆ 　ma bu re 　／
**ʔaN-wa** 　**kʰamyi-∅** 　tʰidzir-a 　　**kʰamyi-ya** 　ʔaN-∅ 　maBr-i[107]
I-TOP 　**god**-IO 　pray-MZ 　　**god**-TOP 　me-DO 　protect-MR
'I will pray to the **god**, so may the god protect **me**.' (OS 2.#86)

やゝと、ˆ 　おせや ˆ 　　かみた 　　　／
ya " to ,ˆ 　o se ya ˆ 　　ka mi ta 　　／
*yaya.tʰu* 　ʔus-i-ya 　　kʰamyi-t°aa
gently 　　push-MR-VOC 　priestess-PL
'Push (= row) the ship gently, Priestesses.' (OS 12.#697)

—　 *tʰi(i)da-gamyi-t°ac°yi* てだかみたち 〈te da ga mi **ta ti**〉 'sun-deity-PL'

てだ*、ˆ 　かみ ˆ たち、ˆ 　とよで* 　　　／
te da* ,ˆ 　ka mi ˆ ta ti ,ˆ 　to yo de* 　／
*tʰiida-* 　-gamyi- t°ac°yi- tʰuyu-di
sun- 　　-deity-PL-SUB 　rumble-GER
'[The Hearth Deity will become immanent and] the voice of the Sun Deity
and her host will reverberate ...' (OS 12.#740)

---

106　 TOS notes that all copies except the Ifa text have 〈a yo re〉, while Ifa has 〈a (ri) yo re〉.
　　 They put 〈ri〉 in here because of (a) the Ifa text, and (b) the following, parallel 〈a ri yo
　　 re〉. We believe that this is tampering with the text. Dropping of *r* before *y* is originally
　　 a rapid-speech variant ([ʔarʸyuɾɪ] → [ʔayuɾɪ]), but also used as casual speech; seen espe-
　　 cially frequently if before *yV* other than *yi*. That is, [rʸi] → [ʸi] is far less frequent than [rʸyu]
　　 → [yu], since the palatality following [r] is less pronounced (so to speak) in [rʸi] than it is
　　 in [rʸyu].
107　 Since *bu* > B / __[+ coronal], *s, *t, and *r are all included in the generalization.

## 5.3 Beautifying Suffixes[108] (Bishō-setsubi-ji):[109] -ganasyi, -{(ʔu)/y-u}mii, *and* -(ʔu)sii

The beautifying suffixes (*bishō setsubi-ji*) to be discussed here are morphemes attached to content words to express:

| | | |
|---|---|---|
| preciousness or fondness: | *-ganasyi* | ← *kʰana·syi,* |
| love or esteem: | ... *y-umii* ~ *-Ømii* | |
| | ~ *(-nu)-ʔumii* | ←*ʔumu'-u,* and |
| protection or rule: | *-ʔusii* ~ *-Øsii* | ← *ʔusu'-u* |

§ 4 was devoted to prefixal BE; here their suffixal counterparts will be discussed. Shimamura (2010: 430) hypothesizes that, in these particular cases, the suffixal BE implies the existence of a deity in the sense that the deity 'holds dear' (i.e. *kʰana·syi*), 'loves' ((*ʔu*)*mu'-u*) or 'protects' ((*ʔu*)*su'-u*) what the BE is attached to.

– *-ganasyi*

| きこゑ、 | きみが゛なし、 | / | いづこ、しま、ᐱ |
|---|---|---|---|
| ki ko we , | ki mi ga* na si , | / | i du ko , si ma , ᐱ |
| *k°yi̧k°u'yi* | *k°yimyi-**ganasyi**-Ø* | | *ʔyidźi-kʰu-syima-Ø* |
| famed | priestess-**beloved**-ₑₓ-SUB | | soldier-ones'-land-LOC |

よりおれて、 /
yo ri o re te , /
*yur-yi-ʔuri-tʰee*
approach-RY-descend-G/P
'The famed **beloved** priestess descended onto the land of the soldiers ...'
(OS 3.#92)

The latter two have allomorphs with or without *ʔu/yu*, as in ⋯ *y-umi-i* vs *-Ømi-i* and *-ʔusi-i* vs *-Øsi-i*. For their distribution, Nakasone (1987 [1976]: 243) claims

---

108  The beautifying suffixes are typologically similar to the Japanese beautifying suffixes, such as *-sama, -saɴ, -cyaɴ,* or *-ra*. Historically they appear to originate in appositional phrases: J *Dare-dare no kata-gata* 'the personages So-and-So', where a plural takes the appositional form, as opposed to Tanaka-saɴ-tacyi 'Ms Tanaka and others'.

109  Besides these three examples, there are numerous others including *-girayi* for architecture (← *girayi·r-u* 'build'; typically with ⟨p/we⟩), *-tu(yu)myi* for ships (← *tuyum-u* 'thunder'), *-nyisya* (with metathesis) and *-nyii̧see* (with monophthongization; cf. NOk *nii̧-see,* (OGJ 417a)) for people (< *\*nyii-* 'two' + *\*-sayi* 'years of age', i.e. 'young person'), and so on.

NOMINALS                                                                    145

that the shorter form appears if the preceding vowels are anything but *yi*; and,
with *yi*, ... *y-umu'yi* is used[110] (he did not list *ʔumi-i*, however).[111] The following is
an exhaustive type-frequency list that we extracted, and his phonology-based
generalization proves accurate. We add below that list an example in an omoro
for context.

–    with ··· *y-umii*

 *tʰac°y-umii* たちよもひ ⟨ta ti yo mo pi⟩ 'PN-EX; **King** Shō Taikyū'
  (OS 5.#228)
 *tʰara'y-umii* たらひよもひ ⟨ta ra pi yo mo pi⟩ 'PN(Tarai)-EX; **Honorable**
  Tarai' (OS 20.#1353); cf. *tʰaroo-mii* たらもい ⟨ta ra mo i⟩ 'Honorable
  Tarō' (OS 16.#1157)
 *gyiɴkʰa-nar-y-umii* なりよもひ ⟨na ri yo mo pi⟩ 'PLN-become-EX; **Honor-**
  **able** Priestess of Ginka (in Nago)' (OS 17.#1185)
 *amik°u-ma-p°yary-umii* あめく、まひ、やりよもひ ⟨a me ku , ma pi , ya ri yo
  mo pi⟩ 'PLN-EX-PN-EX; Honorable Hyari from Ameku' (OS 12.#670)
 *ʔyidzyik°yi-ma-p°yary-umii* いぢˇき、まひやりよもい ⟨i di˖ ki , ma pi ya ri yo
  mo i⟩ 'splendid-EX-PN-EX; splendid Hyari' (OS 12.#670)

| あめく、 | まひやり、よもい、 | / おわるでﾅ、 |
|---|---|---|
| a me ku , | ma pi ya ri , yo mo i[112] , | / o wa ru de† " , |
| *ʔamik°u-∅* | *ma-p°yary-umii-∅* | *ʔuwar-u-dit°i* |
| Ameku-GEN | true-Hyari-esteemed$_{EX}$-SUB | come$_{EX}$-SS-QT |

---

110 In short, the rule is identical to that for use of the allomorphs of the exalting auxiliary
  {#(u)wa{s/r}- 'EX'}.
111 We also think that the selection depends upon metrical structure. For instance, we speculate that the second (*ʔu*)*mii* and (*ʔu*)*sii* in OS 11.#642 below are shortened—in the typical
  pattern of failing to say (glottal-plus-)vowel-initial moras—to keep these couplets metrically aligned, namely with seven moras: [*k°yimu-dakʰa-ʔumii*]$_{7moras}$ (the actual form in
  the various texts, save for TOS, which went too far in constructing the U₁-text) and [*ɟyima*
  *sii-nu mii*]$_{7moras}$.

  | さむだか₁の₁、 | おもい | しま‖おそいの、‖おﾊい |
  |---|---|---|
  | *k°yimu-dakʰa₁-nu₁* | *ʔumii* | *syima-‖ʔu‖sii-nu* ‖*ʔu‖mii* |
  | *k°yimu-dakʰa* | *ʔumii* | *syima-sii-nu*   *mii* |
  | liver-high₁-COP₁ | esteemed.one$_{EX}$ | country-rule-COP esteemed.one$_{EX}$ |

  'the good-hearted **esteemed one**, the country-ruling **esteemed one**' (OS 11.#642)
112 If the preceding noun ends with *yi*, then a glide *y* may be inserted as here (Takahashi
  [1991a: 42], citing Nakasone, as above). However, for the purposes of our analysis, we treat
  it as a loss of the vowel nucleus *i* (*p°yaryi → p°yary···*) and the *ʔ* of the following initial
  (*ʔumu'yi → ···umu'yi*; thus ···*yi-ʔu··· → ···y-u···*).

しらに　　　　や、/
sir a ni　　　ya , /
*syir̩-an-yi*　　*yaa*
know-NEG-QP SFP

'You mean you don't know that the true, **esteemed** Hyari of Ameku is coming?' (OS 15.#1056)

— with *-mii*

ʔyik°usa-**mii** いくさもひ ⟨i ku sa mo pi⟩ 'war-EX; **King** Eiso, great warrior king' (OS 12.#671)

ʔu-gyakʰa-**mii** ⟨o giˮ ya ka mo i⟩ おぎˮやかもい 'EX-shining-EX; **King** Shō Shin' (OS 1.#18)

ʣyana-**mii** ぢやなもひ ⟨di ya na mo pi⟩ 'PLN-EX; splendid person of Jana (i.e. **King** Satto)' (OS 14.#982)

tʰara-**mii** たらもひ ⟨ta ra mo pi⟩ 'PN(Tarō)-EX; **Honorable** Tarō' (OS 16.#1157); cf. *tʰara'y-umii*

— with *-(ʔu)mii*

ひやくさ、ぎˮやめ、　　/ おぎˮやかもいしよ、ˌ　　　　　ちよわれ
pi ya ku sa , gi ˮ ya me ,　/ o giˮ ya ka mo i si yo , ˌ　　ti yo wa re
*pʰyaak'u-see-gyaami*　　*ʔu-gyakʰa-**mii**-syu*　　　*c°yuwar-i*
100-years-TRM　　　　EX-shining-esteemed.one$_{\text{EX}}$-KP reign$_{\text{EX}}$-IZ

'For 100 years (i.e. forever), it is the Shining **Esteemed One** [= King Shō Shin] that will rule.' (OS 1.#18)

We did not find the *written* short form ⟨so i⟩ *-sii* in the *Omoro Sōshi*, though as can be seen above, metrical alignment requires hypothesizing the existence of such a form just the same. By the time of Middle Okinawan, though, there are instances of a spelled short form, as in ⟨a N si so pe⟩ *ʔaɴzyi-sii* (OKDJ 26a). In the OS there are hundreds of tokens of each of the free variants *ʔaɴzyi-ʔusii* and *ʔaʣyi-ʔusii*.

NOMINALS                                                                                                    147

– with -(*?u*)*sii*

| かみ ₍てだの、 | / | まぶり、よわる、₍ | あんじ゙おそい | / |

ka mi ₍ te da no , / ma bu ri , yo wa ru , ₍ a n zi゙ o so i /
*kʰamyi-ₜtʰiida-nu*  *maʙr-y-uwar-u*    *?aɴzyi-?usii*
deity-sun-SUB      protect-RY-EAV-RT   lord-**protector**<sub>EX</sub>
'the **King**, whom the sun deity deigns to protect' (OS 1.#2)

## 5.4    *Diminutive* -a

The suffix -*a* functions as a diminutive (cf. Takahashi (1991a: 42), Nakamoto (1987: 37), *Omoro Kanshō* 38 for a reconstructed *\*-ya*). We assume the correctness of Thorpe's (1983: 261) view[113] that the diminutive goes back to proto-Ryukyuan *\*-wa*,[114] and we further assume that this is a variant of proto-Ryukyuan and proto-Japonic *\*-ra* '(id.)'. Takahashi and Nakamoto's reconstructions with *\*y* are presumably due to the high frequency of the diminutive in the environment after *\*i*. Here are some examples:

| あかぐちやが、₍ | よいづ†き、 | / |

a ka gu ti ya ga , ₍   yo i du† ki ,            /
*?akʰa-gucʰ゚y-a-ga*   *yu-yi-dzik-゚yi*           (cf. *kʰucʰ゚yi* 'mouth')
red-mouth-**DIM**-SUB   draw.near-RY-possess-RY
'The Red-Mouthed-**One** (= the Hearth Deity) will become immanent and ...'
(OS 1.#31)

| これる、₍ | これ、₍ | はつにしや、 | / |

ko re ru , ₍  ko re , ₍  pa tu ni si ya ,        /
*kʰuri-ru*    *kʰuri*    *pʰacʰ゚i-nyisy-a-∅*     (cf. *nyisyi* 'north (wind)')
this-KP      this       first-north.wind-**DIM**-COP
'This: it's this—the First North **Wind** [that we have been awaiting].' (OS 13 .#899)

## 5.5    *Diminutive* -gama

This suffix adds the meanings of smallness in age and size, and cuteness (OSJS 115b).

---

113   "The forms ending in -*a* ... have the diminutive suffix, *\*wa* ..." [in pRk; ibid. 261].

114   Thorpe uses his reconstructed diminutive PRk *\*-wa* in eleven of his 269 Proto-Ryukyuan reconstructions (#2, #13, #44, #61, #188, #191, #209, #214, #227, #262, and #267).

148 CHAPTER 4

ほこり、 ころがた まが゙、 / ともまさり、∧ げ゙らへて /
po ko ri , ko ro ga† ma ga*, / to mo ma sa ri ,∧ ge* ra pe te /
*pʰuk°ur̥yi kʰuru-**gama**-ga tʰumu-masaryi-∅ girayi̯-t°i*
joyful men-**DIM**-SUB stern-fine-DO build-GER
'Joyful, **dear** shipwrights, having assembled the splendid-sterned Tomo-Masari
...' (OS 13.#878)

はねうち、が゙ま、∧ すだ゙ちへ、 /
pa ne u ti , ga* ma ,∧ su da* ti pe , /
*pʰani-ʔuc°yi-**gama**-∅ sida-c°yi*
wing-beat-**DIM**-DO hatch_VT-GER
'Having built our **dear**, speedy ship ...' (*lit.* 'Having hatched our little wing-
beater ...') (OS 13.#901)

## 5.6 *Reduplication*

There is a handful of reduplicated nouns in the *Omoro Sōshi*. Generally these
nouns express plurality and abundance. Besides the examples below, there
are *ʔadzyi-ʔadzyi* ⟨a di " "⟩ 'rulers' (OS 5.#273), *p°yira-p°yira* ⟨pi ra " "⟩[115] 'slopes'
(OS 2.#83), *kʰamyi-gamyi* ⟨ka mi "" "⟩ 'deities' (OS 6.#306), *k°unyi-gunyi* ⟨ku ni ""
"⟩ 'countries' (OS 10.#512), *kʰuru-kʰuru* ⟨ko ro " "⟩ 'men' (OS 1.#33), *nuru-nuru* ⟨no
ro " "⟩ 'shamans' (OS 3.#96), *syima-zyima* ⟨si ma "" "⟩ 'islands' (OS 10.#512), *tʰunu-
tʰunu* 'personages' (OS 11.#618), and *tʰoo-tʰoo* ⟨ta u " "⟩ 'flat places' (OS 2.#83).

国もちの、 はらはら、 / おぼつなよ、∧ 世、∧ そろへて /
KUNI mo ti no , pa ra pa ra , / o bo tu na yo ,∧ YO ,∧ so ro pe te /
*k°unyi-muc-°yi-nu **pʰara.pʰara** ʔubuc°i-na-yu-∅ yu -suruyi̯-tʰi*
land-hold-RY_NOM-GEN **troops** O-LK-world-DO world -align-GER
'Land-controlling legions: Obotsu, the World of Heaven, has collected [them],
...' (OS 1.#31)

きみ〜゙ゖしよ、 よしらめ、 ぬしーしよ、 よしらめ、 /
ki mi ""† " si yo , yo si ra me , nu si "" " si yo , yo si ra me , /
***k'yimyi.gyimyi-syu** yusyi̯ram-i **nusyi.nusyi-syu**, yusyi̯ram-i,*
**kimi.**priestesses-KP rule-IZ **nushi.**priestesses-KP rule-IZ
'The **kimi**-priestesses will surely rule; the **nushi**-priestesses will surely rule.'
(OS 1.#38)

---

115 Of course it may be *p°yira-byira*, but there is no direct attestation of that. The same goes
for *kʰuru-kʰuru*, *tʰunu-tʰunu*, and *tʰoo-tʰoo*. It should be noted that TOS does note voicing with the double ditto sometimes, as in the upcoming examples from (OS 1.#38) and
(OS 3.#95).

NOMINALS 149

たけ〜"*に、∧　　いのて、　／もりもりよ、∧　　いのて　／
ta ke """ " ni , ∧　i no te ,　／ mo ri mo ri yo , ∧ i no te　／
*tʰakʰi.dakʰi-nyi* ʔyi̡ nu-tʰi　**muryi.muryi-yu**　ʔyi̡ nu-tʰi
**shrines**-APP　　pray-GER　　**groves**-APP[116]　pray-GER
'[Shamanesses] praying in all shrines; [shamanesses] praying in sacred groves.
(trans. by Drake 1989: 31, *Omoro Kanshō* 55)' (OS 3.#95)

---

116　We take -*nyi* and -*yu* as applicatives, roughly meaning that the prayers are directed toward
the shrines, i.e. the groves. Historically -*yu* probably comes from *-*yo* < *-*wo*, the origin of
which is the same as OJ *wo*. The usage is admittedly semantically at the far range of the
reach of this marker. The only other option that we see is to link it to OJ -*yô*(*ri*) 'ABLA-
TIVE', but that would require setting up an etymon with just one token to take care of this
instance. In either case, the choices are not ideal.

CHAPTER 5

# Adjectives

## 1    What Is an Adjective?

In JDB, the dictionary of OJ, adjective formatives (AF) are identified using the old Kokugogaku term for adjectives, namely *keijō-gen* (JDB 33–37). The lexicographers clearly identified a category equivalent to adjectives and adjective-like lexemes[1] that did not depend on morphology. Instead it depended on a combination of semantics (description of qualities and quantities) and function (placement before a noun or at the end of a sentence, with or without an overt copula).

Traditional Japanese linguistics' view concerning the development of the adjective is twofold. On the one hand the Adjectival Formative (AF, e.g. *taka* 'high/large') came directly before the noun (phrase) described, without any morphology (i.e. derivational or conjugational suffixes) at all, and remnants of that are seen in the many AF-noun compounds left from OJ onward, e.g.:

> *taka yama* 'high mountain(s)' (JDB 413b), citing the *Norito* ceremony Minazuki no Tsugomori no Ō-Harae > *taka-yama* 'Takayama', a place name in northern Gifu Prefecture; 'Takayama', place name in Ikoma City of Nara Prefecture, in the upper reaches of the Tomio River; 'Takayama' one of the *kabane* or *uji* family names (SNKDJ)

On the other hand, the AF (again e.g. *taka*), with the help of a derivational suffix (e.g. *-si* 'SENTENCE-ENDING MORPHEME'), could be used as a sentence-final predicate:

> ... *taka-si*$_{ss}$ 'is high/large' ([JDB 409d] *taka-si*, citing NSK Tenmu 2, referring to waves)

These forms found their way back to pre-noun position, at first apparently with varying suffixes *-si* ~ *-kî*, later settling upon *-kî* 'RT' (as opposed to now clearly

---

1    Indeed they overtly stated (JDB 37a) that no category of AV (here literally translated as Adjectival Verbs = *keiyō dōshi*, also, elsewhere, Adjectival Nouns [... *meishi*]) had yet come into being in OJ. This may be interpreted as another way of saying that there was no ADJ ↔ AV distinction in the OJ period. And indeed there is good reason to believe that the same may be said of OOk, even though they are clearly distinct from each other in MOk.

© KONINKLIJKE BRILL NV, LEIDEN, 2021 | DOI:10.1163/9789004414686_006

ADJECTIVES 151

only 'ss' -*si*), and eventually fully functioning adjective paradigms mimicking verbal paradigms were born:[2]

| | |
|---|---|
| *yama taka* 'mountains: high' | *taka yama* 'high mountains' |
| *yama taka-s-î* 'mountains are high' | *taka-{ s/k}-î yama* 'high mountains' |
| *yama-sö taka-k-î* 'it is mountains that are high' | *taka-yama* 'Takayama' |
| *yama-kösö taka-k-î* 'mountains (alone) are high' | |

In effect, then, "adjectives" were once nouns that happened to be descriptive. In the process of their formation, they subsequently incorporated *ar-i*, the quintessential stative verb, onto either the ending *-sa* or the ending *-ku*—see immediately below and especially § 4.2—which eventually fused:

*-sa#ar···*    > *-sar···*;
*-ku#ar···*    > *-kar···*.

These changes resulted in the verb-like paradigms so familiar in both lineages of Japonic. They have never achieved full-scale independent status from their former forms, but rather, new forms were added to older forms, sometimes competing, sometimes not. Some of the oldest forms still exist, such as the bare stems in exclamations, first-order derivations with *-sa* and *-ku*, second-order derivations like the NJ past morpheme *-katta*. Unlike verbs, they still present quite a varied—and obvious—lineage in their paradigmatic forms, even after 1500 years. (See Frellesvig [2010: Table 12.8], *Development of the copula and adjectival copula paradigms*.) This statement holds true for both lineages of Japonic.

The question, then, is, just where on such a continuum does OOk find itself, and does it continue to develop into NOk? Clearly if the OOk descriptive-word stem (i.e. AF = *keijō-gen*) can take *-k°u* as a suffix (cognate of OJ ADJ.RY suffix *-ku*), then we can simply define that as an adjective (ADJ), and the same thing will be true for *-(k°)yi* (cognate of OJ ADJ-RT suffix *-kî*), in the few cases where it is found.

Section 2 deals with the evolution of adjectives. Section 3 discusses notable semantic differences of derivational suffixes (*-syi* and *-k°yi*). Section 4 illustrates their functions as modifiers, predicators, or noun formatives.

---

2   We put aside for the moment the development of *-kî* and *-si* themselves. Martin (1987:127) has argued for a development of OJ *-kî* and *-si* from, respectively, *-k{u#ar}-î* *'ADVERBIALIZER #STAT-RY' and *-s{a#ar}-î* *'NOM#STAT-RY'. This etymology would entail a previous round of stative extension, before the one that was just beginning in OJ.

## 2 Evolution of Adjectives

### 2.1 *Derivational Suffixes*

As pointed out above, adjectives emerged from nouns with various adjective formatives added. Here we explore such formatives.

Derivational suffixes include:

– **_-k°u_** : ⟨ku⟩ 'RY' only attaches to ADJ, by definition

⟨su we na ga* ku⟩ *siyi-naga-k°u* end-long-RY 'for a lengthy reign' (os 4.#210)

> あよが、　うちや、ᴧ　　まぢ*よく、ᴧ　　　あれ、／
> a yo ga, u ti ya,ᴧ　　ma di* yo ku,ᴧ　a re,　／
> *ʔayu-ga　ʔuc°yi-ya　ma-dzyuu³#k°u　ʔar-i*
> liver-GEN interior-TOP truly-strong-RY be-MR
> 'may your inner being be truly strong' (os 3.#93)

> とおく、ᴧ　はりやせ　　　　　／
> to o ku,ᴧ　pa ri ya se　　／
> *tʰuu-k°u　pʰa⟦a⟧∅ry-as-i*
> fast-RY　sail-VT-MR
> 'sail [it] fast!' (os 13.#971)

> わがみ、ᴧ　　　　わかく、ᴧ　　なて、　　　　　　／
> wa ga mi,ᴧ　　wa ka ku,ᴧ　na te,　　　　　／
> *wa-ga-myi-∅　wakʰa-k°u　na-t°e⟦e⟧*
> I-GEN-body-SUB　young-RY　become-GER/PRFV
> 'my body has become young[er] [and lighter, since giving birth]'[4]
> (os 5.#260)

---

3 This length is due to the newly-acquired single-syllable length—through Syllable Contraction and following Single-Syllable-Stem Lengthening—of the stem, since e.g. *c°yura-* 'beautiful' has a short Contracted syllable, and it now has a disyllabic stem, making Single-Syllable-Stem Lengthening unnecessary. In short, Contraction itself does not cause Compensatory Lengthening:

| Orig form | | Contraction | SSSL | OOk form | |
|---|---|---|---|---|---|
| *-dzi,yu- | [1,2] | > | ˣ-dzyu- | > | -dzyu,u- | [1a,1b] |
| *kyi,yo,ra- | [1,2,3] | > | c°yu,ra- | > | c°yu,ra- | [12,3] |

4 Cf. Hokama (2000a: 180–181), where he explains the folk belief linking childbirth, becoming younger, and becoming lighter.

ADJECTIVES      153

—    *-*kyi* 'RT' (?< *-*ku#ar-yi* *'-ADVERBIALIZER#STAT-RY')

-*k°yi* : ⟨ki⟩ :

| お | き | 大 | | ぢ* | ⟨o ki opo di*⟩ | (os 13.#778) |
| お | き | お | ふ | ぢ | ⟨o ki o pu di ⟩ | (os 21.#1394) |
| お | き | お | ふ | ぢ* | ⟨o ki o pu di*⟩ | (os 21.#1395) |
| う | き | お | ほ | ぢ* | ⟨u ki o po di*⟩ | (os 11.#557) |

ʔuu[5]·*k°yi*-ʔuqp°u-ʥyi 'great-"grand"-grandfather' i.e. 'ancestor'

-*yi* : ⟨we⟩, ⟨i⟩, ⟨∅⟩, in

わ か ゑ き よ う ⟨ wa ka we ki yo u ⟩ (os 13.#800)
                            = wak[h]a-yi#k[h]yuu

わ か い き よ ⟨ wa ka i   ki yo ∅ ⟩ (os 21.#1472)
                            ~ [alternātes with both above
                            and below]

わ か   き よ ⟨ wa ka    ki yo ∅ ⟩ (os 13.#789)
                            = wak[h]e[-]e#k[h]yuu 'young one'

—    ·*sa*ₙ_ds : ⟨sa⟩ '·ness' derives noun from AF

See k[h]ana·syi·ˌgi·sa below.

—    ·*syi*(-)ₐ_ds : ⟨si⟩ derivational suffix for AFs with emotional content. (This is
      discussed in more detail in § 3.)

See k[h]ana-syi·ˌgi·sa below.

—    ·*sya* : ⟨si ya⟩ portmanteau morph of {+syi '(AFFECTIVE DERIVATIONAL
      SUFFIX = ADS)'} and {+sa 'ness (NOMINAL DERIVATIONAL SUFFIX –
      NDS)'}

---

5   The morph ʔuu· is a good test case for the relation of Raising and Monophthongization (to
    long vowel) of *VwV to VV. Specifically, (a) does *owo Monophthongize to oo, or (b) does the
    same *owo first (b') Raise to *uwu (with short Vs Raising as a matter of course) and then (b")
    Monophthongize to uu? The evidence all stacks up in favor of (b)—i.e. that Raising occurs
    before Monophthongization in cases where identical vowels are on either side of the glide at
    issue—since none of the words for which we have both the OOk written forms and the NOk
    spoken forms turn out to have NOk ˟oo; rather, they have °uu, as will be seen below.

| | | |
|---|---|---|
| おみかうの、 ∧ | めづ*らしや、 | てだ* |
| o mi ka u no , ∧ | me du* ra si ya , | te da* |
| *ʔu-myi-ˌkʰawu-nu* | *midᶻira·sya*[6] | *tʰiida* |
| EX-EX-face-SUB | novel.and.beautiful·ADS.NDS_RT | sun |

'novel- and beautiful-visaged[7] Sun (= King)' (BE?) (OS 17.#1213); RT of an
adjectival relative clause (NOk *minda-sya-n,* [OGJ 379b])

– ***·ɡi*** :[8] ⟨ge[†]⟩ see OSJS 149a 'suffix attaching to stems of adjectives; ... refers
to a situation in which one makes a supposition looking from the outside'
= OBSERVATION DERIVATIONAL SUFFIX = ODS

– ***·ɡi·sa*** : ⟨ge[†] sa⟩ :

| か | な | し | げ[†] | さ |
|---|---|---|---|---|
| ka | na | si | ge[†] | sa |
| *kʰa* | *na* · | *syi* · | *ˌɡi* · | *sa* |
| intimate | | · ADS · | ODS · | NDS |

'(their/your) feeling of intimacy' (OS 12.#670)

– ***·ɡ·ar-*** : ⟨ga ···⟩ :[9]

| め | づ[†] | ら | が* | て |
|---|---|---|---|---|
| me | du[†] | ra | ga* | te |
| *mi* | *dᶻi* · | *ra* · | *ga* | - *tʲi* |
| novel | | · ODS | - GER | |

'regarding as a novelty'[10] (OS 6.#344)

---

6   We speculate, though we are unaware of any affirmative evidence, that this may be an
    example of a formerly operative broader-scale version of the so-called *karyaku-kei* 下略
    形 'apocopated form', where the RT *-ru* has been dropped before a noun, in this case, a
    noun beginning with a voiceless obstruent.

7   Compare ⟨o mi ka u no⟩ *ʔu-myi-ˌkʰawu-nu* to OS 14.#1000 ⟨mi ki ya u⟩ *myi-kʰyawu*, with
    regular PP.

8   Takahashi (1991a: 13) lists this form as, also, a derivational suffix, but it is unclear what kind
    of phonological value (i.e. voiced or voiceless) he gives to it. He says there are similarities
    as well as dissimilarities of this suffix to J ⟨ke⟩, though he fails to mention which ⟨ke⟩ he is
    speaking of.

9   Quite apart from whether it is correct to link OJ *-gë* to OJ *kë* 'sign, indication' (and the
    further question of whether *kë* is a Chinese loanword), it seems straightforward enough
    both semantically and phonologically (i.e. through the common alternation *ë ~ a*) to link
    OJ *-gë* and OJ *-ga·r-*. And such a linkage means that the nearly identical pairing in OOk
    *·gi ~ ·ga·r-* should be identified as linked in the same way, and for the same reasons. The
    OOk alternants could just as well be continuations from Proto-Japonic as they might be
    morphological-level borrowings from Japanese.

10  OSJS 324a ⟨⟨me tu ra ka te⟩⟩ says "Mezurashigatte ['regarding as a novelty']. Medete ['cher-

# ADJECTIVES

155

- **·ra** : ⟨ra⟩ "a [derivational] suffix that attaches to an adjective stem, and constitutes a [new] adjective. ⟨a ka ~⟩" (OSJS 363c);

あから
a ka ra
*ʔakʰa·ra* '[BE]'

"The habitual use of a word meaning the beauty of the state of brightly shining gradually became fixed and became a beautifying word having the meaning of beautiful or splendid. ⟨ra⟩ attaches to the stem of an adjective, and depicts a state." (OSJS 27c)

Because no examples are given, *ʔaka·ra-* is actually a bound collocation. It appears in words such as:

あからかさ
a ka ra ka sa
*ʔakʰa·ra#kʰasa* 'splendid parasol' (OS 16.#1138)

あからせぢ
a ka ra se di
*ʔakʰa·ra#sidzyi* 'splendid (invisible) spiritual power' (OSJS 27c)

It may be useful to compare *ʔakʰa-* with *ʔakʰa·ra-* connecting with a noun directly, as below.

あかぐちや
a ka gu ti ya
*ʔakʰa-guc°y-a*
bright/red-mouth-DIM
'Dear Bright/Red-Mouth / Little Bright/Red-Mouth' = 'The Kitchen Fire Deity' (OS 1.#31)

---

ishing']. Kawaigatte ['treating tenderly']." Above we have chosen the most conservative of the definitions, in terms of fit of semantics with structure. Interestingly, OSJS says that ⟨ka te⟩ has been added to the *stem* of ⟨me tu ra si ya⟩, i.e. *midzi·ra·sya*; that should mean that *-ga(r)-* has been added to *midzi·ra·syi-*, but *·syi-* is not in evidence, either directly or through PP of *-ga(r)-* to ˣ-*gya(r)-* and subsequent loss of *·syi-*. (In cases where we *know* that PP has occurred and *\*syi* has dropped, the PP spelling is always used.)

(Parenthetically, it appears that, in OJ terms, the etymology/analysis of *mëdurasyi-* is *më##[i]d[ë]#ur-a##s-i* 'eye##pop.out#SE-MZ##SI-RY', based on the U2G verb *mëdë-* 'love, etc.')

There seem to be notable semantic differences: ʔakʰa- connotes a more permanent property of the nominal it describes, while ʔakʰa·ra- implies a more transient and temporary state. 'Parasol' and 'spiritual power' both describe a 'splendid' state of being, only *contingently*, at some point in time, while 'brightness/redness' is part and parcel of the Kitchen Fire Deity. This difference parallels e.g. NJ *aka-* in *Akahata* 'Akahata' (lit. 'Red Flag', i.e. the official organ of the Japanese Communist Party) vs *aka-i hata* '(a) red flag'. In the former, the "redness" is permanently associated with Communism, while in the latter the morpheme is describing a contingent property of a specific flag. The formant OOk ʔakʰa·ra- is more similar to the contingent property in Japanese, while ʔakʰa- is closer to the permanent property expressed by *aka-* in *Akahata*.

Let us examine a couple of cases of pseudo-*ra* endings on adnominals. The first is *k°yura* 'beautiful (etc.)', the second *syira-* 'white' and a couple of words that go with it.

The lexical item *k°yura* reveals its origin in its spelling: ⟨ki yo ra⟩. Compare Early MJ *kiyo·ra* (e.g. in *Taketori Monogatari*, ca. 900) in roughly the same meaning. The MJ link of *kiyo·ra* to the adjective base *kiyo-* 'pure, limpid' (not seen in Okinawan) makes it clear that OOk *k°yura*, too, has a complex origin, not available through internal reconstruction. Presumably the origin of MJ *kiyo·ra*, as, too, *aka·ra*, was in describing something contingent and present.

It is clear that MJ *kiyo·ra* existed early enough to be borrowed into pre-OOk, but that is only a possibility, not a proof. osjs 135b says that the independent adjective stem ⟨ki yo ra⟩ *k°yura-* 'brilliantly beautiful' is used as an adnominal.[11] It goes on to say that the word has become a prefixal BE meaning beautiful, splendid, or superior:

⌒あんじ ⟨⌒ a N zi⟩ ⌒-ʔaɴzyi 'splendid lord'
⌒いちやぢや ⟨⌒ i ti ya di ya⟩ ⌒-ʔyic°ya-dzyoo 'fine plank gate'
⌒御ぐすく ⟨⌒ o gu su ku⟩ ⌒-ʔu-gusik°u 'beautiful, exalted castle'
⌒ぎみ ⟨⌒ gi mi⟩ ⌒-gyimyi 'splendid priestess'
⌒げ* ⟨⌒ ge*⟩ ⌒-gi 'splendid tree'
⌒ておりどみ ⟨⌒ te o ri do mi⟩ ⌒-tʰi-wur-yi-dum-yi 'splendid HMS Hand-
    Dance'
⌒てだ ⟨⌒ te da⟩ ⌒-tʰi[i]da 'beautiful/brilliant sun'
⌒もり ⟨⌒ mo ri⟩ ⌒-muryi 'beautiful shrine'

---

11  We may add that it is also used as a BE *suffix*: ⟨ta na ki yo ra⟩ *tʰana-k°yura* '(a large ship + BE)' ← '(the) beautifully planked (one)'.

ADJECTIVES

Now let us discuss compounds brought up by Vovin that contain *syira-* 'white (etc.)', *ʔuQp°u-* 'great, large (etc.)', and *tʰakʰa-* 'high (etc.)' and their relation to borrowing from Japanese. Vovin (2009a: 436–438) gives three examples of sequences of ADJ stem plus N, and argues against the construction having been borrowed from MJ: For one thing MJ ADJ-stem + N cases were all already compounds. Any borrowing, then, would have to have been of the compounds themselves. He admits that a few *might* have been borrowed, since identical compounds, such as *s(y)i₍ ₎ra-t⁽ʰ⁾ama*, 'white jewel', exist in both languages, on the Ryukyuan side in Ryūka and Kumiodori at any rate, even if not in OS.

He goes on to note, tellingly, that the three examples that he cites (*syi₍ra-nyisy-a* 'First North Wind', *lit.* 'white north.wind-one'; *ʔuQp°u#tʰuu* 'the wide expanse of the sea', *lit.* 'big open.sea'; and *tʰakʰa-kʰawa*¹² 'a well with a high wall where the water is drawn') have no equivalent compound in Middle Japanese. The latter certainly differs from the Japanese elements semantically, but the word is known from OJ (MYS 12.#2859) 'a river whose water level has become high because of the increase in water volume' i.e. 'a swollen river', so that Vovin's implication of the non-existence of the *phonological* word *taka-kapa* is off the mark. This does not vitiate his *argument*, however.

## 2.2 *About* katsuyō *'Conjugations'*

Post-OOk adjectives have developed through the amalgamation of *·sa* with forms of *ʔar-yi*ₛₛ 'be' as a carrier verb, to create verb-like conjugations. See OGJ (81–83) for an outline view of that set of conjugated forms in NOk. On the other hand, the only form using the more Japanese-like *····k°[u]-a···* actually to be found in OOk is ⟨yo ka ru⟩ *yu-k°-ar-u* 'good, auspicious', which has made its way into NOk (Nk) in the word $\overline{yu\,^{\text{ʔ}}k°aQ\,^{\text{r}}cyu}$ '(a member of) the gentry (class)' [with suppressed aspiration] < *\*yu-k°[u]-ar-u p°yic°yu* 'the good people'.

Due to the relatively limited variety in the adjectival data-set, we are unable to give robust paradigms for adjectives in OOk; instead we deal with the items in terms of the roots and stems proper, and with their individual suffixes (§ 4.2) and their functions in various positions (§ 4.3), which most traditional Ryukyuan linguists analyze with traditional labels such as RY, RT, or SS. (Takahashi [1991a: 12–13] notes that there are no MZ, IZ, or MR in the data.)

---

12    Mis-cited as ⟨ta ka ka pa⟩, for the actual ⟨ta ka ka wa⟩. Parenthetically, Vovin adopts the practice of using the spellings, opting out of offering phonological transcriptions (2009: xviii–xix). The distinction is not critical for his argument, however; the early MJ pronunciation would have been [takakaɸa], somewhat similar, if not identical to, [tʰakʰakʰap°a], in pre-OOk.

158　　　　　　　　　　　　　　　　　　　　　　　　　　　　CHAPTER 5

Here is an example of *yu-k°-ar-u* 'good, auspicious', mentioned above, the only member of the so-called *k°aryi* conjugation (*kari-katsuyō* カリ活用 Takahashi 1991a: 13) in the OS:

| ゑ、 | け、∧ | よう、∧ | けおの、∧ | よかる、∧ | | ひに | / |
|---|---|---|---|---|---|---|---|
| we , | ke ,∧ | yo u ,∧ | ke o no ,∧ | yo ka ru ,∧ | | pi ni | / |
| yee | kʰee | yoo(u) | kʰiwu-nu | yu-k°-**ar-u** | | p°yi-nyi | |
| INJ | INJ | INJ | today-APPO | good-**ADV-EP-RT** | | day-on | |

'Heave! Ho! Yo! On today's auspic**ious** day ...!'

| ゑ、 | け、∧ | よう、∧ | けおの、∧ | きやが†る、∧ | ひに # |
|---|---|---|---|---|---|
| we , | ke ,∧ | yo u ,∧ | ke o no ,∧ | ki ya ga† ru ,∧ | pi ni # |
| yee | kʰee | yoo(u) | kʰiwu-nu | k°yagar-u[13] | p°yi-nyi |
| INJ | INJ | INJ | today-GEN | shine-RT | day-on |

'Heave! Ho! Yo! On today's bright day ...!' (OS 10.#532)

In response to Takahashi's observation above that there is only one type (as opposed to token) of -*kʰ-ar*-, Vovin (2009a: 460) wonders if KOS ⟨ki ya ka ru⟩ ***kiya-k-ar-u*** [*sic*; but TOS has ⟨ki ya ga† ru⟩ i.e. *k°yaga-r-u*], which forms a parallel pair with *yu-kʰ-ar-u*, could be yet another type. However, the form ⟨ki ya⟩ = *k°ya* is actually only part of a morpheme, *k°yaga·r*- 'to shine', related to NJ *kagar-i⌋* (篝) '(iron basket for holding) burning torches or a bright fire' (first attestation given in ENKDJ is OJ (MYS 19.#4156) *kagari*, in the sense of the fire in the basket, rather than the basket itself).

To explain the seemingly random PP, note NOk *tirácyaga=-y-u-N* 'teri-kagayaku' = 'to shine brilliantly' (VI, =*raN*, =*ti*) (OGJ 522a). Apparently the etymology is \**tʰer-as-yi#k°y·agar*- < \**tʰer-as*- 'cause to shine' (VT) + \**kʰaga·r*- \*[kʰãgaɾ] 'to shine' (VI), even though there is no NOk ˣ*tir-ás-y-u-N* 'to illuminate [it]' (cf. NJ *terás-u⌋* '(id.)' [NHK]).[14] Now, note that there are many "second elements" of *rendaku* that appear to have replaced their original free forms, rather randomly from dialect to dialect, so that, for example, the free form of \**take* ~ \*-*dake* '(-)bamboo' is in most Ryukyuan dialects a reflex of \*-*dake*, but in some others is a reflex of the original free form \**take*; thus e.g. Shuri *daki*. Apparently the second element has replaced the first as a free form. Applying the same idea to

---

13　Aspiration-suppressed *k°ya* is in place of *kʰya* due to a preceding aspiration-suppressing high vowel. The suppression is one trace of that now-lost vowel. See below.

14　The accent data in Martin (1987: 766) show that this word (*terasu*) is accented irregularly, even in relation to NOk *tir-⌋* 'shine', which *does* fit the dialect-geographical accentual pattern expected of it.

ADJECTIVES

the ancestor of *tirácyaga-y-u-N*, namely *\*tɪr-a[s-yi]-kˑˑy·agar-*, we see that the "calved-off" second element of the compound would be *kˑyagar-*, exactly the form seen in the OOk texts.[15]

## 3  Functional Differences between/among Types

OOk adjectives appear as two distinct conjugation types: property adjectives and affective adjectives. Section § 3.1 explores their functional and semantic differences; section § 3.2 describes the derivational suffixes *·gi* and *·ga·r-* as evidentials as opposed to affective adjective types.

### 3.1  *Property* (= -kˑu) *vs Affective* (= ·syi-kˑu(-)) *Adjective Classes*
3.1.1    Two Types of Adjectives, and the Origin of *·syi*
In traditional Japanese linguistics, two subtypes of adjective conjugation are distinguished, the so-called *ku-katsuyō* ク活用 'ku-conjugation' and *shiku-katsuyō* シク活用 'shiku-conjugation' adjectives. These are the two adjective subtypes that over time have tended to conjugate more and more like verbs. Quinn (2003: 176) gives a useful description of the difference between the two classes:

> Significant semantic tendencies also help distinguish the two classes. While -*ku* adjectives routinely refer to features understood to be properties of things (entities, states and events) more or less verifiable 'out in the

---

15    A further problem: King Shō Shin's honorific title, °*ʔu-gyakˑa-mii*, (ˣ*ʔu-kˑyaga-*; e.g. os 5 .#284) 'Exalted Shining One', with velar voicing metathesis. osjs' etymology (77ab) differs: "⟨o ki ya ka⟩ is a beautifying term shifted [i.e. with voicing metathesis?] from *uki-agari* ['floating upward'], and means 'renowned'." (NB: -*mii* < \*-*omoyi* '-the-beloved-one BE'.) The only ⟨u⟩ spelling, however, is just two tokens of ⟨*u ki a ga* ri⟩ '[Captain] Uki-Agari'; all of the many examples of *ʔu-gyakˑa* (including to persons other than the King) are with ⟨o gi ya ka⟩. The literal meaning is 'The Beloved Exalted Shining One'.

   Why the voicing reversal? The most reasonable explanation is that (a) in OOk the exalting prefix *ʔu-* voiced a following obstruent, as in the word おどの ⟨o do no⟩ *ʔu-dunu* '(imposing) building' (e.g. os 5.#223), with free second element との ⟨to no⟩ *tʰunu* (os 15.#111) (NOk *ʔu-duɴ,* [OGJ 540b]). (b) Applying the same logic to *kˑyaga-*, the result should be non-euphonic ˣ*gyaga-*, and, (c) the automatic result ˣ*ʔu-gyaga-mii* (d) devoiced its second velar (cf. Serafim [2016: 139, 145–147] concerning Lyman's Law), (e) yielding the observed proper output °*ʔu-gyaka-mii*. (But, re (c), nb NOk *ʔu-zyága-muyi* (N) [Lit.] ⟨o gi ya ga mo i⟩ '[the posthumous name of King Shō Shin]' (OGJ 573b). Despite being listed in OGJ, this is decidedly a minority opinion, but represents the pre-euphonic-change version of the name. OKDJ [126cd]: under the headword ⟨⟨o gi ₍ya₎ ka - o mo pi⟩⟩: *ʔuzyakamuyi.*)

160                                                                                    CHAPTER 5

world', most -*siku* adjectives express impressions and effects that things in the world have on people, i.e. tend to refer to how things 'out there' are perceived or felt 'in here'.

Both categories have their exceptions,[16] but the above is generally recognized as a characterization that fits semantic facts with conjugational class. We will distinguish the two classes with the following English names:

*ku*-type:      "property adjectives"
*shiku*-type:   "affective adjectives"

Further, Quinn lays out the following hypothesis concerning the origin of -*si*(-):

Quinn uses examples such as \**purusatô natuka*$_{MZ}$-$s_{SH}$-$\hat{i}_{RY}$[17] "'[The] old home$_{SUB}$ [is] fondly known.' < lit. '[the] old home making [me] fond'" (181) to explain his view of how affective adjectives came into being. To him the -*a* form is an old infinitive (180), so that \**natuka*$_{MZ}$ means 'to grow fond (of)'. That verb should have its complement of case-marked nouns, though Quinn does not specify them:

[Person-SUB Place-IO natuka$_{MZ}$]

The Place *causes* the Person to 'grow fond (of it)':

[[Place$_i$-SUB  Person$_j$-IO  [Person$_j$-SUB  Place$_i$-IO  natuka$_{MZ}$  ]  s-$\hat{i}_{RY}$      ]
                                                          grow.fond    do/make
'[The Place$_i$ makes the Person$_j$ [Person$_j$ grow.fond.of Place$_i$]]'

That is a classic causative construction. If Proto-Japonic is anything like Ryukyuan, it frequently lacks SUB, DO, and IO marking, making for excellent opportunities to reorient its case structure. Furthermore, since it is also taken for granted that all noun slots except the one in the matrix SUB slot will be marked with zero = ∅, the sentence is ready to be reinterpreted:

[[Place$_i$-SUB  ∅$_j$  [∅$_j$  ∅$_i$  natuka$_{MZ}$  ]  s-$\hat{i}_{RY}$      ]
                                grow.fond    do/make
'[The Place$_i$ makes.for ∅$_j$ [∅$_j$ growing.fond ∅$_i$]].'

---

16    For instance Unger and Tomita (1983: 54) treat a class of words that are not clearly affective type in OJ, even though their stems end in ···*si*, normally considered an indicator of the affective category.

17    SH = *sa-hen* (*sa-gyō henkaku katsuyō*) = *s*-irregular conjugation = 'do'.

ADJECTIVES                                                                 161

A final lexicalization into an affective adjective finishes the process:

[Place-SUB  natuka-sî$_{SS}$           ]
            is.fondly.known
'[The Place is.fondly.known.]'

Now, why is it that the RY form is used at the end of the construction instead
of SS, the sentence-ending form expected when a verb is not stative? Quinn
explains (185) that the reason that we see a RY ending is because "(a) stativity called for an infinitival predication, and (b) the infinitive of *su* was *sî*." He
does not, however, treat the question of whether the construction had a RY ending right from the start. We believe that it acquired a RY rather than regular
verbal predicative ending at the time of its lexicalization from an embedded
construction into a flat ("pruned") adjectival construction. Thus we now modify our view of Quinn's proposal slightly, as follows:

[[Place$_i$-SUB   Person$_j$-IO  [  Person$_j$-SUB  Place$_i$-IO  natuka$_{MZ}$]  s-u$_{SS}$  ]
[[Place$_i$-SUB   $\varnothing_j$      [  $\varnothing_j$          $\varnothing_i$         natuka$_{MZ}$]  s-u$_{SS}$  ]
[Place$_i$-SUB natuka-sî$_{SS}$]

We hasten to add that this *\*s-u$_{SS}$* will never be directly observed, because it is
required by grammatical exigencies, and otherwise leaves no trace.[18]

3.1.2        Property Adjectives
Property adjectives more often than not consist of bare roots plus any associated suffixes:

たけ、$_\wedge$      たかく、     / はり$_\wedge$      ひろく、$_\wedge$      おり、あげ†て          #
ta ke ,$_\wedge$     ta ka ku ,   / pa ri$_\wedge$     pi ro ku ,$_\wedge$     o ri , a ge† te        #
t$^h$ak$^h$i-$\varnothing$   **t$^h$ak$^h$a-k°u**   p$^h$aryi[19]-$\varnothing$  **p°yi̯ru-k°u**  ʔur-yi-ʔagi-t°i
height-DO    **high-ADV**     width-DO    **wide-ADV**  weave[20]-RY-raise-G/P
'Building [the] height [of Shuri Castle] **tall-$\varnothing$** and [its] width **wlde-$\varnothing$**, [offer
up (to our sovereign) the realm-mastering rhythm!]' (OS 5.#216); cf. Hokama
(2000a: 159).

_____

18    Quinn also derives the property-adjective SS ·*syi* from the same source (180).
19    There is no genetically related word in NOk, nor is there any such word listed in OKDJ.
      Early NJ has *fari* 'crosspiece [in building construction]' (SNKDJ).
20    OSJS 97c takes this as equivalent to pre-OOk *\*op-yi* 'hoisting on one's back' + *\*age-te*

Sentences of this type work just like Japanese, with -*k°u* serving equally to indicate a clause stop and adverbialization. This is a command, without an overtly stated subject (person to whom the command is directed = the King). The two adverbialized adjective clauses are put in parallel, contrasting height and breadth, which are actually DOs of the verb as well as underlying subjects of their respective adjective clauses.

うみ、ᴧ　ちかさ、ᴧ　あもん　　　　　／
u mi , ᴧ　ti ka sa , ᴧ　a mo N　　　／
*ʔumyi-∅　c°yi̥k°a-sa　ʔa-muN*
sea-IO　near-**NOM**　STAT-because
'because [the village] is **close** to the sea' (OS 15.#1100)

Concerning *c°yi̥k°a-sa ʔa-muN* 'because [it] is close/near', note that we are looking at the starting point for the modern -*sa-N* conjugation, which is a fusion of older Ok -*sa*$_{NOM}$ '-ness' and *ʔar-* 'there to be', the latter used as a dummy verb to carry endings. Already, though, even though the forms have not fused, the semantic fusion has occurred: it does not mean ˣ'though there is proximity' (although it literally means that), but rather °'though [it] is close by, though [it] is near'. Finally, note that even in NOk this word varies in PP: *cyicya-sa-N,* (OGJ 144b) ~ *cyi̥ka-sa-N,* (OGJ 151a), and so we have taken the OOk spelling ⟨ti ka⟩ at face value = *c°yi̥k°a* rather than as morphophonemic spelling for a PPed sequence *c°yik°ya*. As expected the NJ equivalent, *cyiká-i*, has reverse tonicity: while it is accented, the NOk word is atonic. This means that the word is not a loan.

ぢ゚やなの ᴧ　よかり、しま、　　　　／
di゚ ya na no ᴧ　yo ka ri , si ma ,　／
*dzyana-nu　yu.kʰ.ar.yi-syima-∅*
PLN-APPO　**fine**$_{BE}$-village-TOP
'The **fine** village of Jana: ...' (OS 15.#1100)

The form *yukʰaryi-syima* is a *hapax*, and therefore one may legitimately raise the question of how the compilers of OSJS 347b know that *yukʰaryi* is a BE. They note, "'Fine village.' It is an item that has undergone a change from \**yoku aru*

---

'raising'. The latter is fine, but the spelling conventions do not allow ⟨ri⟩ = *yi*, and so we have suggested the alternative of weaving together a structure and raising it. The parallel word is *c°im-yi-ʔagi-t°i* 'piling up'.

ADJECTIVES                                                                           163

*syima* 'island being fine' to *\*yokaryi-syima*, and is a BE for *syima* 'village'." While
they do not directly raise the point of relationship of *yukʰaryi-* to the very common *yukʰaru-*, which is clearly a BE, they expound on the latter at some length
(347c). The sound change certainly is a one-off thing, but the environment is
right for it: [ɾ__ʃi], i.e. coronal before and palatal after. Of course, it may simply
be a scribal error for ˣ*yukʰaru*. If it is, it would have to have been in the *ur*-text,
however, since all variant texts agree on this spelling.[21]

### 3.1.2.1    *yee- 'Good'

The Pre-OOk root for 'good, auspicious, fine' could be *\*yee-* or *\*ye-*.[22] Thorpe
(1983: 108) reconstructs *\*yee-* for pRk, and we defer to his reconstruction.

Both the related *yukʰaryi-* and *yukʰaru-*, discussed briefly above, and (*\*yee-*
>) *yii-* are found only as first elements of compounds, in which they function
as BES. As mentioned elsewhere, *yukʰaru-* is found currently in one name for

---

21    A further note: NOk has an adverb *yukáyi* 'considerably' (OGJ 287a), with a prefixal variant having an adjectival meaning, *yukayi-* 'considerable' (e.g. *yukayi-muɴ* 'guite a guy'),
and what looks like a verb to go with it, *yukar-ʲ*, but with reversed accent, '(undergrowth)
grows profusely; (crops) ripen profusely'. The OOk form *yukʰaryi-* may be connected to the
NOk form *yukayi-*, regardless of the relation, then, of OOk *yukʰaryi-* to OOk *yukʰaru-*. If
they *are* related, then the verbalized adjective has been turned into a full-scale intransitive
verb, with all the possibilities implied by that change: adjectival predicates and intransitive verbal predicates may look the same if the adjectival predicates have been verbalized,
but they won't behave the same way in full-scale sentential context. To clarify, the example sentence given in OGJ for *yukayuɴʲ* 'grow profusely, ripen well' is *ʔɴni-nuʲ yuka-to-o-ɴʲ*
'the riceplants have ripened nicely'. A predicate with *-to-o-ɴ* is not possible for an adjective.

22    NOk has *yii-y-u-ɴʲ* (OGJ 265b), perhaps related to NJ *é-ru* 'get, etc.'. Clearly the J preposed
equivalent adverbial *e-* is from the same root as the J verb meaning 'get' (e.g. *e-ru*), and was
common from OJ—*ë*-Vb-MV-MZ-NEG 'not be able to ⌢' *and ë*-Vb-MV-RY-AFFIRMATIVE
'be able to ⌢' (JDB 129d–130a)—through the MJ period (though the affirmative is limited
to the earliest OJ stratum). (JDB user beware: in headwords, ⟨え|⟩ is *ë* and ⟨|え⟩ is *ye*, con-
trary to expectations. Elsewhere, a bar on the right is *kô-* or A-type, and a bar on the left is
*otsu-* or B-type, i.e. ⟨け|⟩ is *kê* [A-type] and ⟨|け⟩ is *kë* [B-type].)
    By the way, the putative irregular correspondence of PRk *\*yee-* 'get; can' and Proto-
Japanese *\*ë-* '(id.)' has remained unresolved. Conventionally one might think that either
Ryukyuan acquired a *\*y* or Japanese lost it, but it is not at all clear which, or how. One
possible solution is to have the two simply be accidental near-twins. The origin of the
Ok form would be in a lexicalized Middle Voice verb stem *\*y·ee-* 'be given', related to the
active-voice *\*y·a·r-* 'give; send', examples of the former of which are found to some extent
in OS, and the latter of which is found in the written records in abundance; both are also
in the spoken language. The origin of the J form would be in *\*ë-* 'get, receive; *undergo'
(not found as an independent morpheme in OOk, but perhaps the extension that created

the gentry class,[23] *yukaQcyu*, ← *yuk$^h$aru-*, 'BE' + *Q́cyu* 'person, people' (< *p°yic°yu* < *$*$pyityo* < *$*$pyito*). It is also found in Ryūka, where it is an independent word *yukaru*, (OGJ 287a).

– *yii-gunyi* ⟨wi gu ni⟩ 'fine country'

| めづ゛らしや、ʌ | | ゐぐ゛⁺に ʌ | いけゝゝし | / |
|---|---|---|---|---|
| me du° ra si ya , ʌ | | w͞ı gu⁺ ni ʌ | i ke " " si | / |
| *midzira·sya* | | *y͞i͞i-gunyi-∅* | *ʔyik°yi²⁴-ʔyik°yi·syi* | |
| novel.and.beautiful·AA/NDS$_{RT}$ | | fine-country-SUB | lively-lively-AA | |
| さうさしや、ʌ | | ゐぐ゛⁺に、ʌ | いけゝゝし | # |
| sa u sa si ya , ʌ | | wi gu⁺ ni , ʌ | i ke " " si | # |
| *soo#soo·sya* | | *yii-gunyi-∅* | *ʔyik°yi#ʔyik°yi·syi* | |
| happy#happy-AA/NDS$_{RT}$ | | fine-country-SUB | lively#lively-AA | |

'The **novel, fine** country is **full of life**! The **joyous, fine** country is **full of life**!' Hokama (2000a: 432a) (OS 11.#648)

– *yii-gaa* ⟨we - ga⁺⟩ 'auspicious day'

| あが゛、なさが゛、 | / ゑが⁺、ʌ | さうぜ⁺ら、ぎ゛やめや | / |
|---|---|---|---|
| a ga° , na sa ga° , | / we ga⁺ , ʌ | sa u ze⁺ ra , gi° ya me ya | / |
| *ʔa-ga nasee-ga* | *yii-gaa-∅* | *soo-zi·r-a-gyaami-ya* | |
| I-GEN father-SUB | good-day-DO | thought-do-4GE-IA-TRM-TOP | |

'my **father**[-figure], until he should consider the **auspicious** day, ...'[25] (OS 21.#1501)

---

[most] of the lower bigrades [see Ch. 6 § 2.1] in Proto-Japonic), possibly being the Middle Voice of *$*$a·r-* 'there to be; to have'. The difference in the pairs is in the presence or absence of *$*$y*.

23    Also called *samúree*, obviously related to—and borrowed from—the Japanese term *samurai*, but the term refers to women equally as it does to men, since it is the name of a class.

24    The root is written ⟨i ke⟩, and it shows just one distinct phonological form. It was originally *$*$ʔyike-* *[ʔʸik°ɛ]; it underwent PP, with subsequent raising, and then fusion of *$*$yı* to *yi*: *$*$ʔyik°e-* > *$*$ʔyik°ye-* > *ʔyik°yı-* > *ʔyik°yi-*. In that case, the spelling ⟨i ke⟩ is morphophonemic. Cf. NOk *ʔyicyi*, 'garden pond' (OGJ 246a); cf. NJ *iké* 'pond' (NHK).

25    Hokama (2000b: 415b).

ADJECTIVES

**3.1.2.2**    tʰuu- *'Fast, Speedy, Swift' (Partial Homophone of* tʰuu- ~ -duu- *'Far, Distant', Dealt with in §4.2)*

–    *tʰuu-k°u* ⟨to o ku⟩ 'speedily, quickly, fast'

> わが＊ ₍ₐ₎  うらの、₍ₐ₎  めづ゛らしや、     ／ とおく、₍ₐ₎
> wa ga＊ ₍ₐ₎  u ra no , ₍ₐ₎  me du＊ ra si ya ,  ／ to o ku , ₍ₐ₎
> *waa-ga  ʔura-nu  midʑira·syi yaa[26]  tʰuu-k°u*
> me-GEN  village-SUB  **beautiful·AA**$_{SS}$  **quickly-RY**$_{ADV}$
> はりやせ      ／
> pa ri ya se    ／
> *pʰa⟦a⟧Øry-as-i[27]*
> sail-VT-MR
> 'My village is so **beautiful**! Sail [the ship] **speedily**!'[28] (OS 13.#971)

**3.1.3**    Affective Adjectives

As pointed out briefly by Hokama (1971: 110), AFs with the *·syi(-)* extension show the emotional state of the speaker associated with the AF stem:

(OS 11.#593):
くめの、     世ゝせ、ぎ＊み、  ／ いけゝゝ、しく ₍ₐ₎      はやせ              ／
ku me no , YO " se , gi＊ mi ,  ／ i ke " " , si ku ₍ₐ₎      pa ya se            ／
(OS 21.#1480):
くめの、     世、よせぎ†み、  ／ いけゝゝ、しく、₍ₐ₎      はやせ          ₍ ／
ku me no , YO , yo se gi† mi ,  ／ i ke " " , si ku , ₍ₐ₎      pa ya se          ／
*k°umi-nu  yu.yusi.gyimyi-Ø    ʔyik°yi#ʔyik°yi· syi-k°u  pʰayas-i*
PLN-GEN  PN-VOC            **lively#lively·AA**[29]**-ADV** cause.to.flourish -MR
'O Priestess Yoyose of Kume, cause [it] to flourish **in a lively manner**!'

This adjective and *ʔuna·zyi-k°u* 'the same' are the only examples of the RY sequence ·*(")syi-k°u* in the entire OS. It can be argued that both are descriptions of impressions that might be contradicted by others, and therefore would more

---

26    There is another way to interpret ⟨me du ra si ya⟩, namely, as *midʑira·sya*, with a non-exclamatory SS. Since the song appears to require 6 moras, and since it also requires an exclamatory tone, we have chosen the form seen in our spellout of the omoro.

27    This line consists of three short metrical units of 6-6-6 moras.

28    Hokama (2000b: 130b) notes that the meaning of this omoro itself is MO, which means that its parts do not coalesce into a meaningful whole.

29    AA = affective-adjective formant; there is no property-adjective formant, since "property adjective" is the default condition.

166                                                                                          CHAPTER 5

safely be in the affective-adjective realm. It should also be noted that Quinn (2003: 177) classes reduplications, which are always affective adjectives in J, as a distinct subcategory (= (4)) of affective adjectives apart from the main subcategory (= (1)) that reports impressions.

### 3.2    ·gi (< *·ge) 'Appearing Like' and ·gar- 'Appears Like'

Here is the OSJS definition for -げ ⟨-ge⟩ ·,gi, found in the following words: (a) いちやげ ⟨i ti ya ge⟩ ʔyic°ya·gi, (b) かなしげ ⟨ka na si ge⟩ kʰana·syi·,gi, (c) みかなしげ ⟨mi ka na si ge⟩ myi#k°ana·syi·,gi: "A suffix attaching to stems of adjectives. It refers to looking at something externally, and inferring its circumstance or condition (yōsu)." (OSJS 149a)

Here is the OSJS definition for ⟨ka na si ge†⟩ kʰana·syi·gi (110b):

> ⟨ka na si ge†⟩ kʰana·syi·,gi → [OSJS 110b]: "⟨**ka na si · ke**⟩ (愛しけ) [ADJ] 'How beautiful!/Isn't [it] beautiful!'/'It is beautiful, is it not?/[It] looks beautiful.' ⟨ke⟩ [TOS ⟨ge⟩] is a suffix that attaches to the basic form of the ADJ, and speaks of the situation supposed from its outward appearance"

| おもろ、 | ねやが゛りや、 | / | おりぼ†し、∧ | | かなしげ†、 | | / |
|---|---|---|---|---|---|---|---|
| o mo ro , | ne ya ga* ri ya , | / | o ri bo† si ,∧ | | ka na si ge† , | | / |
| *ʔumuru* | *ni.y.agar.yi-ya* | | *wur-yi#bu·syi* | | *kʰana.syi·,gi* | | |
| omoro | PN-TOP | | be.present-RY#desire· AF[30] | | lovely· AF-like[31] | | |
| きよらやの∧ | | | みおどん | | / | | |
| ki yo ra ya no ∧ | | | mi o do N | | / | | |
| *k°yura·ya-nu* | | | *myi#ʔu#duN* | | | | |
| [beautiful·INT]_{NOM}-APPO[32] | | | EX#EX#building | | | | |

'[I,] Omoro-Neyagari[, present my prayer:] Oh, such a **lovely-looking**, **fine** edifice that [we] **wish** [always] to stay in! ...' (OS 8.#425)

---

30    To our knowledge kings are never first person in omoros. The verb-plus-auxiliary combination is *wur-yi-bu·syi*; here Hokama takes the subject to be the King ('We') or people in general ('we' = narrator and others). In that case *ʔumuru niyagaryiya wuryibusyi* is a unit. Our interpretation is of the "other" first person, namely the narrator, *ʔumuru niyagaryi*, since there are only two possible first-person narrators in this omoro.

31    TOS ⟨ka na si ge†⟩, KOS ⟨ka na si ke⟩ *kʰana·syi·,gi*, 'appearing lovely', with ·,gi, as with -ge in Japanese, signifying an exteriorly viewed state, i.e. not one that is felt internally.

32    In Ch. 3, end of §3, *k°yu·ra yaa* '[it] is so beautiful!' appeared as a full-fledged predicate. Now that predicate comes again in a new form, as a nominalized form turned back into a quasi-adjectival element—this time with *ya* repurposed as an intensifier—modifying another noun.

ADJECTIVES

There is only one example of いちやげ† ⟨i ti ya ge†⟩ *ʔyic°ya·ᵢgi-*, as follows:

| ゑけり、ₐ | やうらぎ*や、 | ことゞ†、 | / あんす、ₐ | いちやげ†、ₐ |
|---|---|---|---|---|
| we ke ri , ₐ | ya u ra gi* ya , | ko to ""† , | / a N su , ₐ | i ti ya ge† , ₐ |
| *wikʰi·ryi* | *yooree-gya* | *kʰut°u³³-du* | *ʔa-N-si* | **ʔyic°ya·gi-∅** |
| man·sibling | ease-GEN | matter-KP | yon-ADV-KP | **painful·seeming-ADV** |

おもい　/
o mo i　/
*ʔumi-i*
think-RY

'[praying,] "let my brother['s³⁴ ship-journey] be an easy and peaceful one," being overcome by such **heartrending** feelings.' (OS 14.#1000)

The oarsmen's rhythmic cry *yooree* is an onomatopoeticization of a hypothesized verb *\*yawara[g]·e-* 'calm$_{VT}$, soften$_{VT}$,' related to OS *yapʰarag-* or *yawarag-* 'become calm'. The word *yooree* is used, according to OSJS (333a), "apparently as a rhythmic cry [= *kake-goe*] during ship-rowing" (⟨ya u ra⟩, ⟨ya u ra pe⟩, ⟨ya u ra ya⟩ = *yooree*). There are also a related adverb (333a), ⟨ya o ra⟩ *yoora* or *yawura* 'softly, quietly, gently', and ⟨ya pa re⟩ = *yapʰar-i* 'take [it] softly, move easily along' (OSJS index 496b; Ikemiya 1987: 339 f., on omoro #728). Cf. NOk *yóoN* 'weakly; lightly; softly' (OGJ 283a).

The form *\*yapʰarage-* irregularly lost its velar—perhaps because of the onomatopoetic context—, yielding *\*yapʰaraye-*, and, through vowel raising and reduction of *\*awa* to *\*awu* (widely seen elsewhere), yielded *\*yawurayi*, a form that sometimes³⁵ allowed PP. It was at this point that it became lexically marked as a form that could optionally trigger PP, thus allowing but not necessitating *\*-ga → -gya*. After the ensuing monophthongization of *\*···ayi* to *···ee*, the word, still marked as an optional PP trigger, was free to Progressively Palatalize the following enclitic, even though the surface phonetic palatalization environment had disappeared: *yooree₍₊PP₎ + -ga → yooree₍₊PP₎-gya*.

---

33 For questions of possible second aspirate suppression in words, see Ch. 2, § 2.2.2 fn. 21.

34 The NOk form is *wikí-yi* 'brother seen from sister's point of view' (OGJ 595b), with initial *w*, so there is no doubt about the phonetics of the OOk form. There has been a long-term trend in the Okinawa area for [ui] to shift to [ii], and this trend is noticeable in the general Naha-Shuri area, as well, though to different degrees in different specific areas, and also at different speech rates. At the same time, the *yi ↔ ʔyi* distinction is being lost, and, indeed, the language itself is starting to disappear.

35 For a discussion of this type, cf. *tʰat°u( ')yi-* 'liken', discussed in Ch. 2, § 5.1.1, "Exceptions to PP," (1).

## 168

### 3.2.1 ·gar-

There appears to be only one example of the use of ···*ga(r)*···, in the lexical item *midzira·ga-t°i* 'taking care of; ...', and this means that in effect there is no class of the type {+ga·r+ 'show outward signs of V-ing'}, since a class requires at least two members. However, that does not by any means preclude analysis of the lexical item *midzira·gar-*, since there are other items that it is related to.[36]

> "⟨⟨me tu ra ka te⟩⟩ [*midzira·ga-t°i*] (珍らかて) [ADJ collocation] 'regarding as a curiosity; loving; regarding as lovable'. A form in which ⟨ka te⟩ [·*ga-t°i*] has attached to the stem of the adjective ⟨me tu ra si ya⟩ [S&S: [*midzira·sya*]].[37]
>
> [Ex] *sasyibu-∅ midzira·ga-t°i mudzik°yi-∅ kʰee-nadi-wa-c°yi* [phonetics S&S; and see below] (OS 6.#344)" (OSJS 324a)

Clearly OSJS believes in the "class of suffixes" idea, though their analysis into the two parts *midzira-* and ·*gat°i* is fine as far as it goes. And it is also obvious that they are drawing a parallel to the derivational auxiliary verb ·*gar-* of Japanese, which has exactly the same meaning that they imply but do not state that the part ·*ga-t°i* has in OOk. From their statement it is actually not clear what the term *gokan* 'stem' refers to, since it could refer either to *midzira-* or to *midzira·syi-*. If it is the latter, then there is no reasonable way to do away with ·*syi-* in the derivation, whereas if it is the former, the derivation is straightforward. Interestingly, if the former, it also starts to build an argument for an independent derivation of the complex verb within pre-OOk, since the Japanese equivalent is not ˣ*medura·gar-u* but rather °*medura·si·gar-u*. Normally it is before coronal obstruents that pre-OOk ·*syi-* 'AA' is expected to drop, but as *\*ter-as-yi#kyaga·r-u* 'shine brightly (upon)' shows, the historical sequence { *\*···syika···* > *\*···syik°ya···* > *\*···k°ya···* > ···*cya···* } is possible, but it leaves behind a trace in the form of PP, so that the remaining consonant would be (in

---

36   There are two possibilities for the relation of ·*gi* and ·*gar-*, since they must surely be related. One is that the PJ progenitor forms, *\*·gë* and *\*·gar-*, are the result of the common vowel alternation *ë##* ~ *a#C* seen in many words in e.g. OJ, such as *sakë##* ~ *saka#C* 'saké' < PJ *\*sakë##* ~ *saka#C* '(id.)'. The OOk ·*gi* ~ ·*gar-* correspondence would simply be the result of raising due to the addition of a 4GE verbalizer to *\*·gë*. The second possibility is that original *\*·gë*, again, is verbalized, but not with the verbalizer *\*·r-*, but with the verbalizer *\*·ar-yi_{ss}* 'there to be', in a common verbalization gambit throughout Japonic (pre-)history: *\*·gë* + *\*·ar-yi* → *\*·g[ë]· ar-yi* = *\*·g·ar-yi*. Because we have only one form *midzira·ga-t°i*, we cannot know which of these hypotheses is correct—in fact, only the SS would allow us to distinguish: ···*gar-u* vs ···*gar-yi*.

37   [... ie to *midzira-*.]

ADJECTIVES 169

the case at issue) OOk *gy* > NOk *zy*, and the OOk form ought to be ˣ*midzira·gya-t'i*. Thus in fact there was no \*·*syi*- in the derivation of that verb, and it looks like the two lookalikes were in fact independently derived. That is to say, OOk *midzira·gar*- is not a borrowing from Japanese.[38]

This then leaves hanging the question of why there should be only one lexical item with ·*gar*-. Perhaps a happy marriage between a loanword hypothesis and an original-word hypothesis is possible after all: Surely there was influence within the central cultural circle from the Japanese language. The OS is rife with references to Japan. We propose that *midzira*- without ·*syi*- was used by the originators of the new word, from the stock of terms available within pre-OOk itself, but that ·*gar*- was a Japanese borrowing, and that the process of word-formation was a process of calquing, i.e. loan-translation, so that in fact *medzura·syi·gar*- was used as a model for the calque, and that [*midzira*ₚᵣₑ-ₒₒₖ·garₘⱼ-]ₚᵣₑ-ₒₒₖ was created from that model.

If the emotional state or other attribution is to a third person, then ·*gi*(-) or ·*gar*- is used.

さしぶ†,ₐ　　めづ†らが˚て、　/　むづ†き,ₐ　　かいなで˚わちへ　/
sa si bu†,ₐ　me du† ra ga˚ te,　/　mu du† ki,ₐ　ka i na de˚ wa ti pe　/
*sasyibu*-∅　**midzira.ga-t˚i**　　*mudzik˚yi*-∅　*kʰe(e).nadi-wa-c˚yi*
shaman₁-DO **take.care.of-GER**　shaman₂-DO protect-AUXₑₓ-GER
'(the deity's) **taking care of** the shaman₁, protecting the shaman₂,' (OS 6.#344)

## 4　Functions as Modifiers, Predicates, or Noun Formatives

### 4.1　*Functions as a Modifier*
Functionally speaking, adjectives describe nouns. They may do so adnominally, in front of nouns:

大ごろた、ₐ　　　　　おより、　/
OPO go ro ta,ₐ　　　o yo ri,　/
*ʔuqp˚u*ₐ_ᴅⱼ-*quru-t˚aa*ₙ-∅　*ʔu-yuryi*
**great**ₐᴅⱼ-man-PLₙ-GEN　EX-sake
'for the sake of the military officers' (lit. '**great** men') (OS 3.#91)

---

38　The earliest attestation for *medzurasyigaru* given in SNKDJ is *Utsubo Monogatari* (ca. 970–999), making it a mid-Heian text.

きなわ、　　大みやに、　　　　/ きなわ、　　　ひろみやに、　　　　/
ki na wa ,　　OPO mi ya ni ,　　/ ki na wa ,　　pi ro mi ya ni ,　　　/
*k°yi̯nawa-∅ ʔuǫp°u*ADJ-*myaaN-nyi*　*k°yi̯nawa-∅ p°yi̯ru*ADJ-*myaaN-nyi*
PLN-APPO　**great**ADJ-groundN-LOC　PLN-APPO　**broad**ADJ-groundN-LOC
てだ†きよら、∧　　　　　つかい　/
te da† ki yo ra ,∧　　　　tu ka i　/
*tʰida-k°yura-∅*　　　　*c°ik°e-e*
sun-**beautiful**ADJ·SUFF·BE-DO　invite-RY
'... inviting the Beautiful Sun [= Our Lord] to the **Great** Ground, to the **Broad**
Ground, of Kinawa.'[39] (OS 15.#1126)

わなの、　　あら、かない　/ ひやくな、　　はつ、かない　/
wa na no , a ra , ka na i　/ pi ya ku na ,　pa tu , ka na i　/
*wana-nu　ʔara-kʰanee　pʰyak°u*[40]*na-∅　pʰac°i#kʰanee*
PLN-GEN　**new**-tribute　PLN-GEN　　first-tribute
'The **new** tribute from Wana, the first tribute from Hyakuna' (OS 18.#1256)

Adjectives also adverbially modify verbs. Here is an example with ⟨to ku⟩ (とく)
'fast':[41]

けお、∧ ふきよる、∧　　かぜ*や、 / とく、　　　かぜ*ど*、∧
ke o ,∧ pu ki yo ru ,∧　ka ze* ya , / to ku ,　　ka ze* do* ,∧
*kʰiwu　p°uk-°y-ur-u　kʰazi-ya*　**tʰu⟦u⟧-k°u** *kʰazi-du*
today　blow-RY-SE-RT　wind-TOP　**fast-RY**　wind-K̄P̄
ふきよる　　　　#
pu ki yo ru　　　#
*p°uk-°y-ur-u*
blow-RY-SE-R̄T̄
'The wind blowing today: *fast* indeed the wind is blowing!' (OS 8.#421)

---

39　This is NOk *cyi̯naa,* 'Kina' (OGJ 157a), written 喜名 = ⟨KINA₁⟩ in OGJ and Hokama (2000b:
207), but 喜納 = ⟨KINA₂⟩ in (OSJS 127a) (< *\*k°yi̯nawa*), both with a graph indicating *na(a)*.
Clearly the *kanji* were assigned after the loss of medial *w*. There is a different (local) place
name *cyina,* 'China', written 知名 = ⟨TI NA⟩, which is probably etymologically related to
the nearby toponym *cyiniN,* 'Chinen', written 知念 = ⟨TINEN⟩ (\**t°yi̯na* :: \**t°yi̯nen*). Cf. § 9.4
"Toponyms" in Serafim [2016: 164–169], esp. 166 (51) and 167 (57ab). See also Ch. 4 §1.2 in
the present work.

40　The choice of the aspirated *pʰya* is made on the basis of Modern Nakijin *ʼpʰyaʼk°u* '100'.
This is a Sino-Japonic morph.

41　This is related to the OJ property adjective *tô-si* '(1) sharp(-edged); (2) acute (esp. hearing);
(3) quick, nimble, alert; intense; ferocious' (JDB 493bc). See below for more discussion in
§4.2.

ADJECTIVES

| せぢこ、∧ | | なちへ、からは、 | | / わが | み、∧ |
| se di ko , ∧ | | na ti pe , ka ra pa , | | / wa ga | mi , ∧ |
| *siʣyi-ˌkʰu-∅* | | *na-cˀyi-kʰara-wa* | | *wa-ga* | *myi-∅* |
| spirit.power-child-DO | | bear-GER/PRFV-after-TOP | | me-GEN | self-SUB |

| わかく、∧ | なて、 | / |
| wa ka ku , ∧ | na te , | / |
| **wakʰa-kˀu** | *na-tˀe⌈e⌉* | |
| **young**-RY | become-PRFV | |

'After bearing the spirit-powerful child, my body/self became **young[er]**.'[42] (OS 5.#260)

Note that ADJ-*kˀu nar-* 'become ADJ[-er]' is the same construction, for adjectives with verbs of becoming or making something into something else, that is seen in NOk and throughout J language history.

| あよ、ぢｷよく、∧ | げに、∧ | あれ | / きも、ぢｷよく、∧ | | だに、∧ | あれ | / |
| a yo , diｷ yo ku , ∧ | ge ni , ∧ | a re | / ki mo , diｷ yo ku , ∧ | | da ni , ∧ | a re | / |
| *ʔayu#ʣyu⌈u⌉-kˀu* | *gi·nyi* | *ʔar-i* | *kˀyimu-ʣyu⌈u⌉-kˀu* | | *da·nyi,* | *ʔar-i* | |
| **liver#strong-ly** | tru·ly | be-MR | **liver-strong-ly** | | tru·ly | be-MR | |

'Your guts, keep them strong, truly! Your courage, keep it strong, and unwavering!' (OS 1.#33)

Here is an example of the RT form of the only property adjective with a stative-verb extension (indeed, of *either* adjective type with such an extension):

| けおの∧ | よかる∧ | | ひに | / |
| ke o no ∧ | yo ka ru ∧ | | pi ni | / |
| *kʰiwu-nu* | *yu-kˀ·ar-u* | | *pˀyi⌈i⌉-nyi* | |
| today-GEN | **auspicious**-RY·SE-RT | | day-IO | |

'on today's **auspicious** day' (OS 1.#19)

The morph *yu-*, in an adverbial form, can also modify a predicate. We give one example each of *yu-kˀu* 'good-RY' and *yu-u* '(id.)', the latter an example of so-called *u*-euphony (*u*-onbin ウ音便), with elided *k* < \**yu-kˀu* \*⌈yukˀu⌋ (< \**yo-ku*

---

42  Hokama (2000a: 181b) says that *wakʰa-kˀu na-tˀee* refers to acquiring a new life-force [J 生命力 *seimei-ryoku*] and becoming full of energy, that in archaic times they referred to childbirth as (cited in NJ) *waka-ku natte* (若くなって) 'getting young[er]' or (in NJ) *karu-ku natte* (軽くなって) 'getting lighter'.

*[yɔk°u]). There are 9 tokens of ⟨yo ku⟩, zero of ⟨yu ku⟩, 2 of ⟨yo⟩ and 1 of ⟨yu⟩ in this meaning.[43]

にし､かない､∧　　　　よせて、　　／　また、∧　　よく、∧　　まさる、　　／
ni si , ka na i ,∧　　　yo se te ,　　／　ma ta ,∧　yo ku ,∧　ma sa ru , ／
*nyisyi-kʰanee-∅　　yu·si-t°i　　　matʰa　　**yu-k°u**　masar-u*
west[44]-tribute-DO　proffer-G/P　again　　**good-ly**　excel-RT
ひが゙､かない∧　　まへ、∧　　　よせて、　　　　／　ちよわれ　　　#
pi ga° , ka na i ∧　　ma pe ,∧　　yo se te ,　　　　／　ti yo wa re　#
*p°yi̱ga-kʰanee-∅　mayi-∅　　yu·si-t°i　　　　　　c°yuwa·r-i*
east-tribute-DO　before-IO　proffer-GER/PRFV　　stay_EX-MR
'Proffer the tribute [from the] west [to our Lord]; again, proffer the tribute [from the] east, which **well** excels [it], and stay [here]!' (OS 20.#1345)

Here is an example with a euphonically changed adverbial form:

あくかべ　　　　よ、∧ よ∧　　はり、∧　　あまやかせ　　　／
a ku ka be　　　yo ,∧ yo ∧　　pa ri ,∧　　a ma ya ka se　／
*ʔak°uk°abi　　　yoo　**yu-u**　　pʰaa∅r-yi　ʔamayakʰas-i*
red.head.class　VOC　**good-ly**　sail-RY　　make.lively-MR
'Young stewards![45] sail **well** [aboard ship], and make [the country] full of life!' (OS 13.#961)

---

43　The exact song numbers are as follows: ⟨yu⟩ (OS13.#917); ⟨yu ku⟩ (none); ⟨yo⟩ (OS 13.#798; OS 13.#216) (2) 'well': ⟨yo ku⟩ (OS 8.#421; OS 11.#582; OS 20.#1345; OS 21.#1507) (and 5 others: 9 tokens); ⟨yo ku mu⟩ (OS 8.#465); ⟨yo ku mo⟩ (OS 8.#465).

44　Normally *nyisyi* is expected to mean 'north', but we agree with Hokama's (2000b: 314b) interpretation of 'west' here (i.e. the J-style interpretation), since the parallel half-couplet has *p°yi̱ga-kʰanee*, clearly 'tribute from the east', not '... from the south'.

45　The word is given a kanji gloss ⟨赤頭部⟩ (OSJS 30ab), lit. 'red head class/corporation'. SNKDJ, EKJE, and OBKJ all cite *kabu* 'head' from the MJ *kyōgen* "Sōhachi" of the late 1500s, which in turn suggests *···kʰabu-be* > *···kʰa-bi*. MJ 'turnip; head' is *kabu̱*, and NOk 'knob (of a hairpin)' is also *kabu̱* (Martin 1987: 431); *-bi* refers to social class in general.
　　A pronunciation with *kʰoobe* 'head' (← MJ *kɔɔbe* '(id.)') is possible. The graph ⟨ka⟩, after all, is an allographic spelling of *kʰoo*. OSJS cites an unnamed author who suggests ⟨waku-ko-be⟩, though they neither support nor deny the claim. Since the preceding word in #961 is *ʔuQp°u̱yakʰu*, ending in [u], the suggestion is not beyond the realm of possibility: [ʔup:uyakʰu|₁w|₁ak°uk°ɔːbɪ], with a homorganic glide [w]. In his workup of OS 14.#983, Hokama (2000b: 139) glosses ⟨a ku ka be⟩ 'young man', seemingly favoring the {wakʰa-ʔak°u-} → *waku-* allomorphic view of 'young', which would fit with the above stated view.

ADJECTIVES                                                                    173

## 4.2    *Functions as a Predicate*
Adjectives may describe through predication, at the end of a sentence:

ぐ\*すく、   おどの、∧        げ\*らへて、        / かみ、しむの、    /
gu\* su ku ,  o do no , ∧     ge\* ra pe te ,     / ka mi , si mu no ,  /
*gusik°u*     *ʔu-dunu-∅*     *girayi-, t°i*     *kʰamyi-syimu-nu*
castle        EX-building-DO  construct-GER/PRFV upper-lower-SUB
み物∧する、∧                         きよら      や  #
mi MONO∧su ru , ∧                  ki yo ra     ya  #
*myii-munu*[46]*-s-ur-u-∅*          *k°yura*      *yaa*
look-thing-do-EP-RT$_{NOM}$-TOP **beauti[ful]** !

'[I, Nabe-taru,[47] announce my omoro: He] has constructed[48] the castle [and its] buildings. Anyone who looks upon their beauty [says:] **so beautiful**[49]!' (OS 5.#244)

### 4.2.1    *tʰuu- / -duu-*
The two homophonous adjectival morphemes *tʰuu-* 'distant' and 'speedy' can be dealt with in part through context, much as, say, *red* and *read* [rɛd] can be in English. In addition, however a noun-adjective compound *ma-duu-* (*lit.* 'interval-long-') has developed specifically in the meaning of '(doing something) for a long period of time'.

Through comparison with OJ, we can clearly see that the two adjectives originated in different forms, the OJ forms being nearly identical, probably, with the forms in PJ: PJ *\*töpö-* > OJ *töpo-* 'distant' ([JDB 500cd]; cf. e.g. PJ

---

46    Also seen as *myii-muɴ(-suru)*. NOk *mii-muɴ,* 'interesting thing to see' (OGJ 375b).

47    Nabe-taru (*nabi-tʰaru*) is an omoro singer (OSJS 260b) (cf. Ikemiya [2015: 138]). His name appears in the first line of the omoro.

48    As earlier mentioned, OS 1.#34 has the GER/PRFV -*t°i ~ -c°yi* occurring on the very same bigrade verb stem, *tʰat°uyi-* 'likening X to/with Y', Ch. 2, § 5.1.1. The option of choosing V instead of CV as the final vowel in *girayi-,* is not taken here, and that is the usual case in the omoros.

49    Nakasone notes the uniqueness of *k°yura*, in the sense that there is no Ok phonological correspondent to J *kirei* (Nakasone 1987 [1979]: 192–193). He points out that OOk and NOk do not have a direct counterpart to J *utuku·si* 'cute, dear'. He also notes that no reflex of *\*kyiyora* is used in Sakishima, and that what is used instead is *kagi* < *\*kage* 'beautiful', related to MJ *kage* 'shadow; silhouette; reflection, image; a figure; light (from a heavenly body)' or *kage·rofu* 'heat haze, (a veil of) heat shimmer'. He hypothesizes that these three words, |utuku·si|—|kiyo·ra|—|kage|, reflect a chronological order from new to old, thus making the Miyako version the most conservative, then the Okinawan word, and then the standard Japanese.

*töpö·.r/s.- > OJ *töpo·.r/s.-* 'go along/through//push through'; OOk *tʰuu-* 'distant'; OOk *tʰuu·.(r)/s.-* 'go/carry through'), and PJ *tô-* 'sharp; quick-witted; ferocious; terrific' (JDB 493b), OJ *tô-* '(id.)', OOk *tʰuu-* 'early; quick; hurrying'.

It is straightforward enough to show that the two adjectives are actually homophonous. They became so after: (1) Weakening of intervocalic *\*p* to *\*w* (*\*VpV > \*VwV*); (2) Raising of short mid vowels (*\*{e,o} > {i,u}*); (3) Weakening of intervocalic *\*w* to zero (*\*{VwV} > {VØV}*); (4) lengthening of short monosyllabic roots (*##CV#(#) > ##CVV#(#)*).[50] If the changes had occurred in some other order, the observed forms in the OS would have turned out differently.

|  |  | 1 |  | 2 |  | 3 |  | 4 |  |  |
|---|---|---|---|---|---|---|---|---|---|---|
| 'distant' | *\*topo-* | > | *\*towo-* | > | *\*tʰuwu-* | > | *tʰuu-* | > | *tʰuu-* |
| 'speedy' | *\*to-* | > | *\*to-* | > | *\*tʰu-* | > | *\*tʰu-* | > | *tʰuu-* |

Here are the actual spellings, with number of tokens for each:

| spellings: | ⟨to u⟩ | ⟨to o⟩ | ⟨to⟩ |
|---|---|---|---|
| 'distant' | ⟨to u sa⟩ 5 |  |  |
| 'for a long time' | ⟨ma **do** u sa⟩ 9 | ⟨ma **do** o sa⟩ 1 | ⟨ma **do** sa⟩ 3 |
| 'speedy' |  | ⟨to o ku⟩ 2 | ⟨to ku⟩ 8 |

While the sample is small, the tokens do not interfere with each other semantically, because 'distant' appears only as *tʰuu-sa*, while *ma-duu-sa* means 'for a long period of time'. Further, the latter has the allomorph *-duu-*, with an initial voiced obstruent in place of the voiceless (and aspirated) *tʰ*. Finally, 'speedy' actually appears in the sense of 'speedily', *tʰuu-k°u*, always with *tʰ* and *-k°u*, and therefore never overlapping with the other two words.

ぎ†すゝ、ˬおてや、ちよも、　/ とうさˬおてや、ちよも　　#
gi† su ", ˬo te ya , ti yo mo , / to u sa ˬo te ya , ti yo mo　#
*gyisisi-wu.t°i#ya.cʰyoo.M*[51]　　**tʰuu-sa-wu.t°i#ya.cʰyoo.M**
PLN-LOC#even　　　　　　**far-NOM-LOC-even**
'Even in Gisusu (*zyiQsyiᵢ* [OGJ 841]), even being **far away** ...' (OS 14.#992)

---

50　There were other monosyllabic words that were already bimoraic, such as *dzyooᵢ* 'gate' (< *\*too*) (OGJ 603b). Their original mid vowels stayed mid because they were long at the time of the raising, and the raising applied only to short vowels.

51　For an analysis of *#ya-cʰyoo-M*, see Ch. 7, §13.1.

ADJECTIVES                                                                    175

とおく、∧　はりやせ　　　／
to o ku ,∧　pa ri ya se　　／
***tʰuu-k˚u***　***pʰaa∅ry-as-i***
**fast-RY**　**sail-VT-MR**
'sail [it] **fast**' (OS 13.#971)

年∧　　　　六とせ、∧　　なるぎ゛やめ、　　　／ きみ、てづ゛り、∧
TOSI∧　　　MU to se ,∧　na ru gi゛ ya me ,　／ ki mi , te du゛ ri ,∧
***tʰusyi-∅***　***mu-tʰusi-∅***　***na·r-u-gyami***　***k˚yimyi.#tʰi.ʥɨ|r̩.yi-∅***
years-TOP　six-years-IO become-4GE-RT-TRM　PN-SUB
まど゛うさ　　　　　　／
ma do゛ u sa　　　　　／
***maa-duu·sa***
**interval-distant·AA**
'Until six years have passed, o how we wait for the Kimi-Tezuri Ceremony!'
(OS 4.#202)

## 4.3　*The Adjectival Auxiliary* -bu·sya··· *'Desire'*
### 4.3.1　Desire and Point of View of Narrator
The auxiliary -*bu·sya* primarily expresses the first person's desire,[52] as shown by
the first example below.

あかの、　　おゑづ†きや、　／ うの∧時の、　　　　　　てだ゛の　／ あが゛て、∧
a ka no ,　o we du† ki ya ,　／ u no∧TOKI no ,　　　te da゛ no ／ a ga゛ te ,∧
***ʔakʰa-nu***　***ʔuyi.ʥik.˚yi-ya***　***ʔu-nu-tʰukˊyi-nu***　***tʰida-nu***　***ʔaga-t˚i***
PLN-GEN　PN-TOP　　Hare-APPO[53]-time-GEN　sun-SUB　rise-G/P
てりよる、　　　やに、　　／ おみかうの、∧　　みぼ†しや　　　　　／
te ri yo ru ,　　ya ni ,　／ o mi ka u no ,∧　mi bo† si ya　　　　／
***tʰir-y-ur-u***　***yoo-nyi***　***ʔu-myi-ₖkʰawu-nu***　***myiⅡiⅡ-bu·sya***
shine-RY-SE-RT　way-ADV　EX-EX-visage-DO　**see-desire·AA/NOM**
'Aka no Owedzuki sings this omoro: [Just] like the rising and shining at the
Hour of the Hare of the Sun[-Deity], so **do [I] desire to see** your exalted vis-
age!' (OS 8.#442)

---

52　The origin is made clear in the OJ *por-i#s[e]-* 4G-RY#'do'|ᵢₙꜰ| 'desire, wish to acquire [VT]'
　　(JDB 662a), itself ← *por-*₄ᴳ '(id.)' (JDB 662ab).
53　The NOk word for the sign of the Hare is *ʔuu,* 〈卯〉 (N), the fourth of the 12 signs. The
　　direction is east, and the time is 6 am (OGJ 571b).

176 CHAPTER 5

Takahashi points out the following omoro, which has *s*- 'do' as a collocational extension, but lacks -*uwa*··· - 'EX':[54]

| もゝと、 | ふみあが゛りや、 | / おりぼ゛しや、よ゛ |
|---|---|---|
| mo " to , | pu mi a ga* ri ya , | / o ri bo* si ya , yo ˄ |
| *mumu.tʰu* | *pºum.yi.ʔagar.yi-ya* | ***wur-yi-busya-yu*** |
| PN | PN-TOP | **be.present-RY-desire-AA/NOM-DO** |

| し、 | / |
|---|---|
| si , | / |
| *s-yi* | |
| **do-RY** | |

'Momoto Fumiagari [performs this omoro]: "[He] **wanted to be present** ...."' (OS 6.#337)

The above is the bare minimum required to show the workings of the third person usage of -*busya* as a noun—and presumably as an Adjectival RY—plus (-)*s-y(i)*- '(do as if) want(ing to)'. Below is another example of this sort, combining with the exalting auxiliary, which, needless to say, refers to other than the first person:

| きこゑ、 | うちたかが゛、 | / おはくたて、゛ | ちよわちへ、 | / |
|---|---|---|---|---|
| ki ko we , | u ti ta ka ga* , | / o pa ku ta te , ˄ | ti yo wa ti pe , | / |
| *kºyi,kºuyi* | *ʔucº.yi,tʰakʰa-ga* | *[w]upʰakºu.tʰatʰi-∅* | *cºyuwaˡaˡ-cºyi* | |
| famed | PN-SUB | PLN-IO | come_EX-G/P | |

| つぶゝみ、ごへ、 | / きゝ、ぼ゛しや、゛ | しよ、わちへ | / |
|---|---|---|---|
| tu ""† mi , go pe , | / ki " , bo* si ya , ˄ | si yo , wa ti pe | / |
| *cºidzimyi-guyi-∅* | ***kºyik-ºyi-busya-∅*** | *s-y-uwaa-cºyi* | |
| hd-v[55]-ʔGEN/ʔDO | hear-RY-desire·AA/NOM-DO | do-RY-EAV-G/P | |

'Famed Uchi-Taka [*lit.* 'Strike [the drum-note] High'] deigned to come to Ofaku-tat/ke,[56] **wanting to hear** the drum's voice ...' (OS 17.#1205)

---

54    In the *Omoro Sōshi*, addition of the verb *s*- 'do' to -*busya* was sufficient to shift the point of view of narrative from the first person's to the third person's desire. However, in NOk, *s*- 'do' itself is not enough, and an additional SE is needed. Thus, referring to the third person's psychological state, -*busya s-yo.o*_SE-*N*, with SE, must be used. Use of the desiderative -*bu·sya-N*, i.e. without SE, is permissible in a projected or hypothetical situation, e.g. 'If X, then one wants (i.e. would want) Y.' At this point, one could characterize the function of *s*- 'do' as a mere carrier of the SE, not as a point-of-view shifter. NOk:

     -*bu·sya*         -*N*    '[I] want [to DO]'
     -*bu·sya*    *s-yo-o*    -*N*    '[I] **assume** [s/he] wants [to DO]'

55    hd-v = hand-drum–voice.

56    There are questions about the graphical makeup of this word; see TOS 17.#1205 fn. 2 (p. 612).

ADJECTIVES

4.3.2    Collocations: Skewed Distribution of *-bu·sya* with *myii-* 'to See' and
         *ʔuri-* 'Descend'

As seen in the example above, *-bu·sya* readily combines with *myii-* 'to see' (17
tokens: ⟨mi po si ya⟩ (9), ⟨mi pu si ya⟩ (1) = *myii-bu·sya* '[I] wish to see'; ⟨mi ya
ri pu si ya⟩ (3) = *myii-yar-yi-bu·sya* '[I] wish to be seeing'; ⟨mi ya ke po si ya⟩
(4) = *myii-yagi-bu·sya* '[I] wish to look up to'), but also with *ʔuri-* 'to descend
(from Heaven)' (13 tokens, the next highest number). The collocational affiliation *myii-* 'to see' with *-bu·sya* is reminiscent of an OJ tendency (cf. Vovin
[2009a: 771–772]). For instance, Yoshida (1973: 1067) points out that out of 19
tokens of *-m-aku-po·si* 'wish to' in MYS, 13 are *mî-m-aku-po·si* 'wish to see' and
out of 33 tokens of *-m-aku-por-i* 'wish to', 31 are *mî-m-aku-por-i* 'wish to see' (also
see *mî-po·si* 'wish to see', the closest in form to OOk, e.g. MYS 3346 as in JDB 715a).
On the other hand, reference to desire to descend is apparently uncommon in
OJ.

    While of course it can come as no surprise that such combinations in OS are
grammatically possible, the frequency of *ʔuri-* 'descend' can be ascribed to the
religious nature of the texts.[57]

    Here is the auxiliary with *myii-* 'see-', functioning as a pre-nominal modifier
with the Genitive marker *-nu*, as below.

みやげ、ぼ†しやの、ˆ                     わかいきよ      /
mi ya ge , bo† si ya no , ˆ            wa ka i ki yo    /
*myii-yagi-__bu·sya__-nu*            <u>*wak__h__e-e#k__h__yuu*</u>
look-raise-**desire·AA/NOM-GEN**  <u>young</u>-RT-one
'the <u>young</u> one that [**we**] **wish to** look up towards' (OS 9.#491)

It can function as a predicate, as below. The example shows an amalgamation
with *ʔa*, the precursor to NOk adjective ss forms.

こが*、ˆ  きよらさ、   / こが*、ˆ  みぼ*しや、、ˆ              あよる
ko ga* , ˆ  ki yo ra sa ,  / ko ga* , ˆ  **mi bo\* si ya ,** ˆ       **a yo ru**
*k__h__uu-ga   k°yura·sa      k__h__uu-ga   __myii-bu·sya__      ʔa'-y-ur-u*
this-SUB  beauti.ful     this-DO   see_RY_-DSD1·AA/NOM STAT-RY-SE-RT

---

Hokama (2000b: 246 fn.) believes that it is meant to be ⟨o wa ta te⟩, or perhaps a scribal
error for ⟨o wa ta ke⟩, noting that it is a parallel word to the shrine name ⟨ka tu o da* ke⟩
*kac°iwu#dak__h__i*. But the latter has five moras, and "⟨o wa ta ke⟩", four. Further ⟨···ta°···⟩ is
voiceless and ⟨···da···⟩, voiced.

57  Concerning the concept of deities descending to this world, Tamaki (1991) offers a detailed
    analysis of omoros with regard to *when*, *where*, *how*, and to *whom* the deities descend.

な /
na /
*naa*
SFP
'[Lord Jana (= King Satto) is a child created by whom?] He is this beautiful! No wonder we so **wish to see** [him]!' (OS 14.#982)

Here are examples of *ʔuri-bu·sya-* (< **ore-bo·syi·sa-*) 'desire to descend (from Heaven)', functioning as a pre-nominal modifier, and as a predicate.

かゝず†、 すづ†なりや、 / おれぼ*しやの、 あめそこ、
ka " zu† , su du† na ri ya, / o re bo* si ya no , a me so ko ,
*kʰakʰa|zɨ-∅*[58] *sɨdzɨ|.nar.yi-ya*[59] ***ʔuri-bu·sya-nu*** *ʔami.sukʰu-∅*
PLN-GEN PN-TOP **descend-DSD1-AA/NOM-GEN** PLN-LOC
/ おれて、∧ おれなおさ /
/ o re te , ∧ o re na o sa /
*ʔuri-t°i* *ʔuri-nawu·s-a*
descend-GER descend-pac·ify-IA
'[I, the priestess] Suzu-Nari of Kakazu, descending to Ame-Soko, **which I wish to descend to**, let me descend and calm [it]!'[60] (OS 15.#1096)

Hokama's interpretation (2000b: 191b), is internally inconsistent: 'As for the priestess Kakazu Suzunari$_{3p}$, descending$_{3p}$ to Amesoko, which [she] wishes$_{3p}$ to descend to, || let [me] pacify$_{1p}$ the world, and make$_{1p}$ [it] calm and peaceful.'[61] To be sure, however, the passage is difficult to deal with, but we see no good reason to interpret *-bu·sya-nu* here as having a third-person subject.

かゝず†、 すづ†なりや、 / あめそこの、 こが*ね、みやに、∧
ka " zu† , su du† na ri ya , / a me so ko no , ko ga* ne , mi ya ni , ∧
*kʰakʰazɨ* *sɨdzɨ.nar.yi-ya* *ʔami.sukʰu-nu* *kʰu-gani#myaa-nyi*
PLN PN-TOP PLN-GEN [yellow-metal]$_{\text{gold·BE}}$#ground-IO

58 Concerning the vertical bars, cf. the Yotsu-Gana Hypothesis, Ch. 2 § 5.4.
59 Concerning the vertical bars, cf. the Yotsu-Gana Hypothesis, Ch. 2 § 5.4.
60 The literal meanings are: *sɨdzɨ-nar-yi* '(small.)bell-ring-ing' and *ʔami-sukʰu* 'Heaven-Bottom'. While OJ has *suzu*, the pre-OOk form is (only) apparently **sudu*, and the reason for the discrepancy is explained in Ch. 2 § 5.4.
61 "Kakazu Suzu-Nari shinjo wa, ori-tagatte-iru Ame-Soko ni orite, | yo o naoshi, odayaka ni heiwa ni shiyō."

ADJECTIVES              179

おれぼ゚しや      /
o re bo゚ si ya     /
*ʔuri-bu·sya*
descend-DSD1·AA/NOM<sub>SS</sub>
'[I,] Suzu-Nari of Kakazu, **wish to** descend to the golden<sub>BE</sub> ground(s) of Amesoko.' (OS 15.#1095)

4.3.3    Morphology: History and Comparison with Japanese

Morphologically -*bu·sya* looks a great deal like the OJ affective adjective *po·si* 'A desire B' (JDB 654cd), as mentioned above. What is remarkable about the OOk forms $p^hu·syi- \sim p^hu·sya$ and -*bu·syi-* ~ -*bu·sya* is that none of the supporting structure still visible in the case of OJ exists any more. That is to say, in OJ it is also possible to see *por-* (VT, 4G) 'wish, desire' (JDB 662ab) and *por-i s[e]-* 'want' (662a), two forms that are logically prior to *po·si* itself. However, both Japanese and Okinawan have a verb meaning 'to fall for, to fall in love with' J *hore-ru⌐* and NOk *furí-y-u-N*, and the accents agree with each other in type, both type A, suggesting that the Okinawan form is not a borrowing (for the accents, see Martin [1987: 692]).

In any case, the OJ forms allow a view of the development of the affective adjective *po·si* and its attendant syntax, which is marking an underlying DO with what would normally be a SUB case marker, from an original nominative-accusative-syntax-taking verb *por-*. While that verb itself is not available in OOk, the source must be identical.

As with the other affective adjectives, the -*sya* ending is an amalgamation of -*syi* 'AA' and -*sa* 'NOM' (cf. §2.1). From the point of view of historical comparison with Japanese, it is a cognate of *por-i s[e]-* mentioned above, i.e. PJ *\*po[r-î]·s[[e]-]î·sa* > pre-OOk *po·syi·sya* > OOk $p^hu·sya \sim$ -*bu·sya* (cf. §3.1.1, this chapter).

4.3.4   Syntax

The example below shows (Y) X-*g(y)a* $p^hu·sya$ '(Y) wants X', where X may be a reduced embedded clause.

しま、ゐりぎ゚や、ᴧ    ほしやす、   / やへま、しま、ᴧ
si ma , we ri gi゚ ya , ᴧ  po si ya su ,  / ya pe ma , si ma , ᴧ
*syima-yii·r-yi-gya*   ***$p^hu·sya$-si***   *yayima-syima-Ø*
[land-get·4GE-RY]<sub>NOM</sub>-DO DSD·AA/NOM-KP PLN-island-LOC
おわちやれ   / くに、ゐりぎ゚や、ᴧ   ほしやす、   /
o wa ti ya re  / ku ni , we ri gi゚ ya , ᴧ  po si ya su ,  /
*ʔuwa-c゚y-ar-i*   *k゚unyi-yii·r-yi-gya*  ***$p^hu·sya$-si***
go<sub>EX</sub>-PRFV-SE-IZ  [country-get·4GE-RY]<sub>NOM</sub>-DO DSD·AA/NOM-KP

180　　　　　　　　　　　　　　　　　　　　　　　　　　　　　　CHAPTER 5

きちやら、だ†け、、∧　　おわちやれ　　　　／
ki ti ya ra , da† ke , ∧　o wa ti ya re　　　／
*k°yic°yara-dakʰi-∅　ʔuwa-c°y-ar-i*
PLN-peak-LOC　　　goₑₓ-PRFV-SE-IZ
'It was [because of his] **desiring** the acquisition of [new] lands that [he] deigned to go to Yaeyama.' /
'It was [because of his] **desiring** gaining a [new] country that [he] deigned to go to Kichara (= Omoto)[62] Peak.' / (OS 21.#1409)

### 4.4　*Forming Nominal Expressions*

Nominal expressions take NOM ·*sa*, or AA/NOM ·*sya*. The following phrases are precursors to NOk adjectives in terms of the logical sequence of their formation, since they are composed of NOMINAL PHRASE + *ʔa-* 'there to be'. What is visible here is the birth of what might be called the *sari-katsuyō* or *sari* conjugation, a conjugation that came into being through fusion of ·*s(y)a* and *ʔa-* to ·*s(y)a-*, which conjugates similarly to the stative verb.

わかさ、、∧　　あし　　　　ときや、　　／
wa ka sa , ∧　a si　　　to ki ya ,　　／
*wakʰa-sa　ʔaQ-syi　tʰuk°yi-ya*
young-NOM STAT-PST_RT time-TOP
'when [we] had [our] **youth**' = 'when [we] were young' (OS 7.#380)

まみちけが*、　　　おもろ、　　／くち、　　　まさしや、、∧　　あ物、　　　／
ma mi ti ke ga* ,　o mo ro ,　／ ku ti ,　ma sa si ya , ∧ a MON ,　　／
*mamyic°yik°yi¡-ga ʔumuru-∅　k°uc°yi-∅　masa-sya　ʔa-muɴ*
PLN-GEN　　　　omoro-TOP　words-SUB certain-NOM STAT-because
'[It is] because Mamichike's omoro has **certainty** in its [predictive] words', i.e.
'[It is] because Mamichike's omoro's words are [predictively] **certain**.'
(OS 5.#264) (Cf. OSJS 140a.)

つよからど*、、∧　　かば*しや,、∧　　ある　　　#
tu yo ka ra do* , ∧　ka ba* si ya , ∧　a ru　　　#
*c°iyu-kʰara-du　kʰaba·sya　ʔar-u*
dew-more.than-KP¡ fragrant·AA/NOM STAT-RT¡
'[this dew] is¡ even¡ more **fragrant** than [ordinary] dew' (OS 14.#982)

---

62　As OSJS (126c) explains, *-dakʰi* usually means 'shrine', but can also occasionally mean 'peak', as here. An interlineation (OS 11.#558) states, "another name for Omoto Peak", the highest peak in the Yaeyama group.

ADJECTIVES 181

### 4.5 *Devolution into BE*

Beautifying expressions frequently modify nouns just as adjectives do, but they are also observed as suffixes doing the same work on the other side of their nouns, or even of their predicates. So, what criteria can be used to distinguish adjective stems themselves from adjective-stem-derived BEs? At least: (1) adjective-derived BEs have no inflection, but are purely affixal, and (2) also their semantics have shifted. Some of the beautifying expressions are descended from adjective stems, though there are also real prefixes, as well as verbs acting in modifying roles. Here is a couplet with several:

あからだ⁺け、∧          とよむ、     ／ まぎみ、きよら∧
a ka ra da⁺ ke ,∧        to yo mu ,   ／ ma gi mi , ki yo ra ∧
*Ɂakʰa·ra+dak°i*      *tʰuyum-u*     *ma-gyimyi-k°yura*
[splendid$_{ADJ}$]$_{BE}$+shrine$_N$ resound-RT   true$_{BE}$-priestess-[beautiful$_{ADJ}$]$_{BE}$
大ぬし
OPO nu si
*ɁuQp°u-nuusyi*
[great$_{ADJ}$]$_{BE}$-mistress$_N$
'[O] Ma-gimi-kiyora Ō-nushi (*lit.* **Great** mistress **True-Priestess-Beautiful**'), upon whom the **Akara** (*lit.* '**Splendid**')-Dake shrine resounds!', i.e. 'O Kikoe Ō-Gimi, upon whom the Akara-Dake shrine resounds!' (OS 9.#490)

While *ma-* 'true-' is a prefix, the three other BEs are adjective stems, two preposed, and one postposed. The forms *Ɂakʰa·ra-* and *ɁuQp°u-* are parts of names or titles, while the suffixed *-k°yura* (cf. OSJS 135c) is a more generic BE, not permanently attached to *ma-gyimyi*.

しよりもり、∧       ちよわる、        ／ おぎ゚やかもい、が゚なし、        ／
si yo ri mo ri ,∧   ti yo wa ru ,   ／ o gi゚ ya ka mo i , ga゚ na si ,   ／
*syiyuryi.muryi-∅*  *c°yuwa⟦a⟧r-u*     *Ɂu-gyakʰa-mii-gana·syi*
PLN-LOC           be.present$_{EX}$-RT   [*ADJ]$_{EX}$-shine-[VB]$_{BE}$-[ADJ]$_{BE}$
'Our **Dear** Shining Lord (= King Shō Shin), who is present in Shuri Grove' (OS 5.#230)

The suffix *-gana·syi* is a BE derived from *kʰana·syi ~ kʰana·sya*, of which, more below. In NOk this suffix is also commonly added to predicates in very flowery speech, as in:

Ɂubukun-*zyaɴsyii* Ɂwaamiseebiimi 'how are you(, my lord)?' (OGJ 536b)[63]

---

63    Under the headwords Ɂubukuɴzaɴsii(o) and Ɂubukuiganasii(o) (both *sic*).

182  CHAPTER 5

There is a suffix -⁽ⁿ⁾*kane* related to the above, which is used as a BE added to people's names, as in the following example:

なるか°ねの、ᴀ　おもいぐ゙わ、　/　しつらが゙ね、　まく°もに、　/
na ru ka° ne no , ᴀ o mo i gu* wa ,　/　si tu ra ga* ne , ma ku° mo ni ,　/
*naru-kʰani-nu* *ʔumi-i-ɢwa-∅*[64]　*syic°ira-gani-∅ ma-k°umu-nyi*
PLN-**dear**-GEN　love-RY-child-APPO　PN-**dear**-COM　[true-cloud]ₚₙ-IO
'for the sake of Naru-kane's dear children Shitsura-gane and Ma-Kumo' (OS 13 .#833) (Cf. Hokama [2000b: 52–53])

4.5.1　An Excursus on ⟨ka ne⟩
The reader will have noticed the suffix -(")$k^{(h)}$*ani* ⟨(")ka ne⟩ that is added to the male names in the preceding omoro, and the gloss 'dear'. Recall *kʰana·syi·gi* '(appearing) lovely',[65] seen previously in § 3.2, and *kʰana·sya*(-) 'dear, belovèd, beautiful'. These are related to OJ *kana-si-* 'felt deeply; (some-thing/-one) is pathetic, pitiable, dear, cute, sweet' (JDB 202bc). Thorpe (1983: 257–258) notes that nouns can be made secondarily, in an old and no longer productive pattern—but one more salient in Ryukyuan than in Japanese—by replacing final \**a* with \**e*, among just one or two other patterns of vowel replacement. Application of this statement to \**kana-* 'belovèd' yields:

\**kana-* 'belovèd' → \**kane* 'belovèdness; the belovèd'

Raising turns \**kane* into OOk *kʰani*, which is segmentally identical with *kʰani* 'metal; (esp.) gold'. Over time, the noun became the beautifying suffix *-kʰani ~ -gani*, in the process losing some of its lexical specificity, just as e.g. Japanese *sama* 'a person's form, facial features, etc.' has become a beautifying suffix *-sama* (and then *-saɴ*). This suffix *-kʰani ~ -gani* is then attached to male names.

As to what sort of male names, OSJS ⟨- ka ne⟩ (112b) gives interesting details: "(-金 [*kane* 'metal, gold']) ① metal; ② exalting suffix; ...; ③ to enclose or protect." The ellipsis expands as follows:

KKKS, Kon, Gengyo: "Words one attaches to childhood names, e.g. *taraa-gani, maci-gani*. In *Tales of Ise* it has *muko-gane*." ... In [Ifa Fuyū's] *Ryūkyū Gikyoku Jiten* (1938), it says, "when assigning child names, too, there is a uniform rule: ... for second sons and below of A(n)ji (*ʔa(ɴ)zyi* 按司 'lords')

---

64　NOk *ʔumiɴgwa⌋* '(another's) child (EX)' (OGJ 554a). Cf. Ch. 2 § 4.6 fn. 54.
65　See also Ch. 4 § 4.4 and § 5.3 for the beautifying suffix *-kʰana·syi* 'dear-, famed-'.

# ADJECTIVES

in the gentry class, they prefixed to that Ma- (*ma-* 真 'true') or Ome- (*ʔumi-* 思 'belovèd') or suffixed *-kane* (*-kani* 金 ['metal, iron, gold, money']), making their names e.g. Ma-Toku, Ma-Ikusa, or Ma-Ushi. For princes and the heirs to lordship, they then added the suffix *-"kani* to that, e.g. Ma-Ikusa-"Kane, Ma-Toku-"Kane, or Ma-Ushi-"Kane."

CHAPTER 6

# Verbs

This chapter will cover verbs with a formal, historical, and functional description. §1 presents conjugation types (consonant- and vowel-final roots and subtypes) and their conjugation forms (e.g. *mizen-*, *ren'yō-*, or *shūshi-*form). §2 explains the history of conjugation merger and shift. §3 then sheds light on the results of conjugational mergers and shift, which have a bearing on, e.g., the functional differentiation of the two *mizen* forms for the inferential auxiliary (IA). §4 delineates the morphophonemics of the verbs, including the history of the T-forms (e.g. gerunds and related forms).

## 1 Conjugation Types

As shown in the overall table below and in the set of tables introduced later in the chapter, there are three conjugational types or groups: (1) the consonant- and (2) vowel-final types and (3) the irregular group. (1) The consonant-final type includes nine different consonant-ending roots, namely *k, g, s, t, n, b, m, r,* and *w.* (2) The vowel-final verbs consist of three subtypes: upper and lower monograde (whose unextended roots end in *yi(i)* and *i(i)*, respectively) and lower bigrade (whose unextended roots end in *i*). (3) The three members of the irregular group are the so-called *k-, r-,* and *s-*irregular verbs. For more details see Table 6.1.

### 1.1 *General and* r-*stem Quadrigradization*

Before delving into the details of the verb system of the OS, let us first set up a kind of "latticework", a background against which the OS verbal system can be tracked. Useful in this regard is a rudimentary knowledge of the verbal systems of Japanese, essentially OJ, MJ, and NJ, and, in particular for the discussion here, the categorization into verb classes and subclasses, and also the categorization into the basic forms that each verb can take to carry out its functions, i.e. the already familiar MZ, RY, SS, RT, IZ, and MR.

The verb system of OJ can, very crudely, be divided into two types, and then into various smaller categories that are essentially most readily seen as irregular versions of either one or the other (or both) of the two basic types. The two types may be thought of as having a consonant-final stem or a vowel-final stem.

---

© KONINKLIJKE BRILL NV, LEIDEN, 2021 | DOI:10.1163/9789004414686_007

# VERBS

**TABLE 6.1** Verb types, with examples and glosses

Consonant-stem verbs: Quadrigrades:

| | | |
|---|---|---|
| 01. | *k*-type | eg *c°ik*- 'adheres' |
| 02. | *g*-type | eg *kʰuug*- 'rows' |
| 03. | *s*-type | eg *sas*- 'wears (a sword)' |
| 04. | *t*-type | eg *tʰat*- 'rises' |
| 05. | *n*-type | *?yin*- 'leaves' |
| 06.a. | monosyllabic *w*-type: | eg *kʰuuw*- 'beseeches' |
| 07.b. | multisyllabic *w*-type: | eg *c°ik°aw*- 'sends' |

*w*-irregulars:

| | | |
|---|---|---|
| 08.c. | multisyll: *?umuw*- 'loves' | |
| 09.d. | monosyll: *?yiw*- 'says' | |
| 10. | *b*-type | eg *?asib*- 'dances' |
| 11. | *m*-type | eg *tʰuyum*- 'resounds' |
| 12. | *r*-type | eg *mudur*- 'returns' |
| 13. | ···*yir*- *r*-subtype | eg *k°yi̯r*- 'cuts' |

Vowel-stem verbs:

Upper Monograde:

| | | |
|---|---|---|
| 14.a. | *?yi*(·*r*)- 'shoot' | |
| 14.b. | *yi*(·*r*)- 'sit' | |
| 14.c. | *myii*(·*r*)- 'see' | |

(Lower Monograde: ← 16)

Bigrades:

Middle:

| | | |
|---|---|---|
| 15.a. | ···*i*- eg *?uri*(·*r*)- 'descend' | |
| 15.b. | ···*i*- eg *?ukʰi*(·*r*)- 'launch' | |

Lower:

| | | |
|---|---|---|
| [16. | *kʰi*(·*r*)- 'kick'] | |
| 17.a. | ···*i*- eg *?akʰi*(·*r*)- 'open' | |
| 17.b. | ···*si*- *yusi*(·*r*)- 'conquer; ...' | |

Irregular verbs:

| | | |
|---|---|---|
| 18. | *k*- {kʰuⁿ} 'come' | |
| 19. | *s*- {si} 'do' | |
| 20. | *r*- eg {?ar} 'exist; have' | |

186 CHAPTER 6

Consonant-final stem  = quadrigrade  = *yodan*
Vowel-final stem  = bigrade  = *nidan*
  = monograde  = *ichidan*

As is usual in the world's languages, the irregular types are also the types of highest token frequency,[1] in particular verbs that mean:

'do' ($se_{RI}$ -)  = *s*-[column] irregular[ verb]: *sa*-[*gyō*[2] ]*hen*[*kaku dōshi*]
'come' ($kö_{KI}$-)  = *k*-[column] irregular[ verb]: *ka*-[*gyō*[3] ]*hen*[*kaku dōshi*]
'be' ($ar_{RI}$-, $wor_{RI}$-)  = *r*-[column] irregular[ verb]: *ra*-[*gyō* ]*hen*[*kaku dōshi*]

These verbs are also irregular in modern Japanese, and likewise in all stages of Okinawan language history. The *ra-gyō* 'r-column' of *ra-hen* verbs refers to the final *r* of the stem that all forms of this verb type share; they differ from ordinary *r*-type quadrigrades in that they do not distinguish RY and SS, using the ending -*i* < \*-*î* (= OOk -*yi*) for both; but because of that they distinguish between SS (with -*i*, similarly, OOk -*yi*) and RT (with -*u*, similarly, OOk -*u*), a fact that turns out to be critical for Northern Ryukyuan language history.

|  | reg *r*-type (OJ/OOk) | *r*-irreg (OJ) | *r*-irreg (OOk) |
|---|---|---|---|
| RY | *r-i/r-yi* | *r-i* | *r-yi* |
| SS | *r-u* | *r-i* | *r-yi* |
| RT | *r-u* | *r-u* | *r-u* |

In traditional Japanese linguistic terminology a *gyō* (行) is a vertical column of the 50-syllable *kana* chart, and every mora in each *gyō* has in common—at least in the earliest period of the Japanese language—the initial consonant of that mora. Thus the column *ra*, *ri*, *ru*, *re*, *rö*, and *rô* has *r* in common, and therefore a reference to the *gyō* is a reference to its initial consonant. Likewise, a *dan* (段) or *retsu* (列) is a horizontal line across the chart, and what is held

---

1  One more type is the *s/r*-irregular exalting verb *ʔuwa.s/r.-* '(exaltedly) be, do, etc.', of which, more in Ch. 7 §14. It also occurs frequently.
2  The *sa-gyō* 's-column' refers to the initial *s* that all forms of this verb share.
3  The *ka-gyō* 'k-column' refers to the initial *k* that all forms of this verb share.

VERBS                                                              187

in common among the graphs of each *dan* is their vowel, as in e.g. *'ë, kë, gë, pë, bë,* and *më*. Therefore a reference to the *dan* is a reference to its vowel, which in this case is *ë*.

A *yodan dōshi* (四段動詞) *lit.* 'a four-*dan* verb' is 'a four-vowel verb', that is to say a verb in which there is alternation among four (Modern-Japanese) vowels in its various bases. This is what in Western terminology has come increasingly to be called a quadrigrade verb, where *quadri-* is 'four' and *grade* refers to the gradation of the bases with different final vowels, i.e. to the four *vowels* involved in the set of alternations. An *r*-type quadrigrade verb (*ra-gyō yodan dōshi* = ラ行四段動詞) is one in which the invariant consonant preceding the alternating vowels (in OJ and early MJ) is *r*, and this is the "consonant" of "consonant verb"—and similarly for *k*—as follows:

–  *r*-type and *k*-type quadrigrade verbs, e.g. OJ *tör-u* 'take' and OJ *kak-u* 'scratch'

| 1 | – | MZ | *tör-ā-* | *kak-ā-* | [OOk | ⋯ *r-ā-* | [ɾɑ] | ⋯ *kʰ-ā-* | [kʰɑ] | ] |
| 2 | – | RY | *tör-ī* | *kak-ī* | [ | ⋯ *r-yī* | [ɾʲi] | ⋯ *k°-yī* | [k°yi] | ] |
| 3 | – | SS | *tör-ū* | *kak-ū* | [ | ⋯ *r-ū* | [ɾu] | ⋯ *k°-ū* | [k°u] | ] |
|  |  | RT | *tör-ū* | *kak-ū* | [ | ⋯ *r-ū* | [ɾu] | ⋯ *k°-ū* | [k°u] | ] |
| 4 | – | IZ | *tör-ē* | *kak-ē̄* | [ | ⋯ *r-ī* | [ɾɪ] | ⋯ *kʰ-ī* | [kʰɪ] | ] |
|  |  | MR | *tör-ē* | *kak-ê̄* | [ | ⋯ *r-ī* | [ɾɪ] | ⋯ *kʰ-ī* | [kʰɪ] | ] |

*Nidan dōshi* (二段動詞) *lit.* 'two-*dan* verbs', on the other hand, are 'two-vowel verbs', that is to say verbs that alternate between two vowels in the relevant parts of their bases. The increasingly common Western term is bigrade, for obvious reasons. Generally the consonant preceding the alternating vowels is ignored in the categorization. Two subtypes are recognized, upper and lower. Going vertically down the *kana* chart, we note the three middle *dan*, i.e. *ï-* (*i-*), *u-*, and *ë-* (*e-*)*dan*; *ï* (*i*) is above *u*, so those two together are an alternating pair *ï* (*i*) ~ *u*, and constitute *kami-nidan katsuyō* (上二段活用), or 'upper bigrade conjugation,' and *ë* (*e*) is below *u*, so those two together are an alternating pair *ë* (*e*) ~ *u*, and constitute the *shimo-nidan katsuyō* (下二段活用), or 'lower bigrade conjugation.'

upper bigrade conjugation $\left\{ \begin{array}{c} \ddot{\imath} \quad (i) \\ u \\ \ddot{e} \quad (e) \end{array} \right\}$ lower bigrade conjugation

188 CHAPTER 6

While NOk does have a very few—perhaps only two[4]—verbs descended from PJ upper bigrades, and while OOk surely must also have this class, descended from PJ upper bigrades, they appear to be absent in the OOk corpus, and therefore it (only) appears that all the bigrade-derived verbs of OOk are lower bigrades. We will return to this point shortly. Let us first look at OJ upper- and lower-bigrade conjugations in order to get some idea of what they are like (recall the "latticework"):

– OJ Upper bigrade verb *ör-u* 'descend' and OOk *ʔuri(·r)-* '(id.)'[5]

'descend'

| | | | pre-OJ | *ör ë - | Pre-OOk | *or e | |
|---|---|---|---|---|---|---|---|
| 1 | – | MZ | OJ | ör ī̄ - | OOk | ʔur ī̄ | ·r-a |
| | | RY | | ör ī̄ | | ʔur ī̄ | |
| 2 | – | SS | | ör- ū | | ⋯ ī̄ | ·r-u |
| | | RT | | ör- ū r-u | | ʔur ī̄ | ·r-u |
| | | IZ | | ör- ū r-e | | ⋯ ī̄ | ·r-i[6] |
| 1 | – | MR | | ör ī̄ -yö | | ⋯ ī̄ | ·r-i |

For MR ⋯*i·r-i*, note the following:

| きこゑ | 大ぎみぎや、 | / | てるかはに、ᴧ |
|---|---|---|---|
| ki ko we | OPO gi mi gi ya , | / | te ru ka pa ni , ᴧ |
| *k°yi̯k°uyi* | *ʔuǫp°u-gyimyi-gya* | | *tʰir-u-kʰaǫp°a-nyi* |
| famed | great-priestess-SUB | | shine-RT-fountain-IO |
| しられゝ | | # | |
| si ra re " | | # | |
| *syi̯r-ari·r-i* | | | |
| [know-PASS·4GE]pray-MR | | | |

'O Famed High Priestess, pray to the Sun Deity!' (OS 3.#93)

---

4 They are *sizyi-y-u-ɴ,* (related to NJ *sugí-ru*) 'exceed' and *ʔamí-y-u-ɴ* (related to NJ *abi-ru,*) 'bathe, pour water upon oneself'.

5 The forms that begin with "⋯" in this column occur in verb forms other than the one chosen for the overall chart, but they do not turn up in the OS as the specific full verb forms needed here. (For example, Takahashi [1991a: 440–446], lists no SS for |oreru| in his complete verb list.) Since the specific *endings* are instantiated in the data, however, we give the tail ends of the verbs without their full stems in order to signal the lacuna in the data, and yet give justice to the *endings'* existence.

6 Takahashi (1991a: 440–446): no IZ/MR is listed in his complete list of verbs for |oreru|. Almost all cases of IZ or MR for this verb type are built on passives, but here is the sole MR placed directly on the verb stem:

わん、いれゝ ⟨wa ɴ , i re "⟩ *waɴ-∅ ʔyi̯r·i·r-i* 'let me in!' (OS 17.#1180).

VERBS 189

– Lower bigrade verbs, e.g. *uk[ë]-u* 'launch' and *ag[ë]-u* 'raise'[7]

| | | | | | | | |
|---|---|---|---|---|---|---|---|
| 1 – | MZ | OJ *uk* $\bar{\bar{e}}$ - | OOk *ʔukʰ* $\bar{i}$ · ··· | OJ *ag* $\bar{\bar{e}}$ - | OOk *ʔag* $\bar{i}$ - | | |
| | RY | *uk* $\bar{\bar{e}}$ | *ʔukʰ* $\bar{i}$ | *ag* $\bar{\bar{e}}$ | *ʔag* $\bar{i}$ | | |
| 2 – | SS | *uk-* $\bar{u}$ | *ʔukʰ* $\bar{i}$ · *r-u* | *ag-* $\bar{u}$ | *ʔag* $\bar{i}$ · *r-u* | | |
| | RT | *uk-* $\bar{u}$ *r-u* | *ʔukʰ* $\bar{i}$ · *r-u* | *ag-* $\bar{u}$ *r-u* | *ʔag* $\bar{i}$ · *r-u* | | |
| | IZ | *uk-* $\bar{u}$ *r-e* | *ʔukʰ* $\bar{i}$ · *r-i* | *ag-* $\bar{u}$ *r-e* | *ʔag* $\bar{i}$ · *r-i* | | |
| 1 – | MR | *uk* $\bar{\bar{e}}$ *-yö* | *ʔukʰ* $\bar{i}$ · *r-i* | *ag* $\bar{\bar{e}}$ *-yö* | *ʔag* $\bar{i}$ · *r-i* | | |

For RY *ʔagī*, RT *ʔagī·r-u*, and MR *ʔagī·r-i*, note the following:

かさす、 わかてだに、 / 御みしやぐ、ᴧ ぬきあげ /
ka sa su , wa ka te da ni , / O mi si ya gu , ᴧ nu ki a ge /
*kʰasasi* *wakʰa-tʰida-nyi* *ʔu-myi-syagu-∅* *nuk°-yi-ʔagi*
Kasasu young-lord-IO EX-EX-holy.wine-DO raise-RY-**raise**<sub>RY</sub>
'[They] **will raise** the fine holy wine to the young lord Kasasu [of Kume Island], and ...' (OS 11.#608).

あげ[8]る、ᴧ つかさ、 /
a ge ru , ᴧ tu ka sa , /
*ʔagi·r-u* *c°ik°asa*
raise·4GE-RT priestess
'priestess who hoists [the sail]' (OS 13.#855).

ぬき、あげれ、ᴧ みしやぐ /
nu ki , a ge re , ᴧ mi si ya gu /
*nuk°-yi-ʔagi·r-i* *myi-syagu-∅*
raise-RY-**raise·4GE-MR** EX-holy.wine-DO
'**Raise** [it] aloft!—the exalted holy wine!' (OS 11.#586).

The last regular category is the Upper Monogrades (also frequently called the *uni*grades), which, as their name implies, have one steady vowel base throughout their paradigm. They are few in number (i.e. low in type frequency), but high in token frequency, and important as fulcrum-points for analogical change of Bigrade to Monograde:

---

7 Each of the four columns is centered on the overlined letter.

8 Since TOS neither marks this graph as voiced, nor does it discuss it, normally we would accept it as ⟨ke⟩ = *kʰi*, but Hokama (2000b: 67) convincingly treats this as ⟨ge⟩ = (for us) *gi*. Otherwise there would be no clear interpretation for the song.

– Original OOk ss forms: *k°yiru* 'to wear', *\*?ok°uru* 'to wake up'

| | | |
|---|---|---|
| *\*kyi* 'wearing' | : | *\*kyiru* 'to wear' :: |
| *\*oke* 'waking up' | : | Ø, 'to wake up' |
| where "Ø" is *\*okeru* = *\*oke·r-u* | | |

Here are two of the most important Upper Monogrades in OJ, *mî-ru* 'see' and *kî-ru* 'dress oneself':

– Upper monograde verbs in OJ, e.g. *mî-ru* 'see' and *kî-ru* 'dress oneself'

1  –  MZ  *mî̄-*   *kî̄-*
     RY  *mî̄*   *kî̄*
     SS  *mî̄-ru*  *kî̄-ru*
     RT  *mî̄-ru*  *kî̄-ru*
     IZ  *mî̄-re*  *kî̄-re*
     MR  *mî̄-yö*  *kî̄-yö*

The upper monograde (and later the lower monograde) verbs provide *the* important source for the analogical shift from both upper and lower bigrade to upper and lower monograde verbs in Japanese, and, indeed, we can say, in Japonic. In fact, the records—i.e. the OS—show that the shift to monograde happened *earlier* in Okinawan than it happened in Japanese, since it had already occurred by 1531, the earliest book of the OS, when Kyoto Japanese still had bigrades.

Now we will tabulate the verbs by class and number, and present them, each subtype in its own table, and each table followed by relevant examples from the OS. Here is a sample of how the verbs are tabulated, from the consonant type.

| | Stem | Gloss | MZ | RY | GER/PRFV | SS/RT | IZ/MR |
|---|---|---|---|---|---|---|---|
| 1) | {xxx} 2) | 3) | 4) | 5) | 6) | 7) | 8) |
| | {yyy} | | | | | | |

# VERBS

TABLE 6.2 Example of table with 4G(11), *m*-type quadrigrade

| | Stem | Gloss | MZ | RY | GER/ PRFV | SS/RT | IZ/MR |
|---|---|---|---|---|---|---|---|
| 4G (11) ···*m*- | {tʰuyum-} | 'resounds' | *tʰuyum-as*-an-yi | *tʰuyum-yi* | *tʰuyu-di* | *tʰuyum-u* | *tʰuyum-i* |
| | {tuyum-』Lit.} | 'resounds' | *tuyum-a』* | *tuyum-i』* | *tuyu-di』* | *tuyum-u*-N』 | *tuyum-i』*, *tuyum-e-e』* |

As a concrete example, see Table 6.2:

The columns in the table give,

1) the verb type ("4G") and subtype (numbers in parentheses, a total of 20; here "(11) ···*m*-"; for a detailed explanation of verb structures, cf. §2.1);

2) top row: OOk; bottom row: NOk; the root, in curly brackets, denoting a morphophonemic-level representation; all consonant-type roots, true to their name, end in consonants, though that consonant may be a hiatus consonant, ' (here, *m*);

3) a gloss, not necessarily an exhaustive listing of submeanings or connotations;

and, in what follows, *kana*-derived namings (e.g. MZ = *mizen-kei*) and analyses used in traditional grammar, shown with underlines; these do not necessarily coincide with our own analysis, which we show with hyphens; see 4) below:

4) MZ = *mizen-kei* 未然形 (*mi*- 未- 'not yet' + -*zen* -然 '-ly') = irrealis or subjunctive form; this is not a grammatical form strictly speaking, since the set of forms that it is part of do not necessarily break cleanly after the MZ:

··· *C-an* ... 'NEG'
··· *C-a* ~ *C-am*- 'IA'
··· *C-ari*- 'PASS'
··· *C-asi*- 'CAUS'
··· *C-a-ba* 'ROOT-MZ-TMP/CND' = 'if ROOT'

This last form, along with its opposite number ··· *C-i-ba* 'when ROOT' in the IZ (see below), shows that a true irrealis had taken shape before the split of Japanese and Ryukyuan from Proto-Japonic, and that therefore glossing with 'MZ' is meaningful in such cases.

MZ:  つかわれて

tu ka wa re te[9]

*c°ik°aw-**ari**-t°i*   (*underline* = MZ portion;
                        **bold** = grammatical portion)

invite-PASS-GER   (note gloss)

'being invited (by the priestess)' (OS 12.#704)

(see the chart for 4G (7) on p. 202 below)

MZ/IA:                        たゝ      かゝずゝ、

                             ta "      ka zu[†],

                        *t<sup>h</sup>at°-**a***   +   *k<sup>h</sup>azi*[10]

              time.passes-**IA/MZ**      number

'as (the years) go by' (OS 12.#725)   (see the chart for 4G (4)
                                        on p. 198 below; cf. § 3.1)

5) RY = *ren'yō-kei* 連用形 (*ren*- 連- = 'ad-' + *-yō* -用 *-verb*(*ial*)) + *-kei* -形 '-form'
   = adverbial or infinitive form;

6) GER/PRFV = gerund or perfective form, *-"Ti*, *-"Tee*, or *-"T-ar-*;

7) SS/RT, the *shūshi-kei* 終止形 (end-stop form, i.e. conclusive form) and
   *rentai-kei* 連体形 (adnominal form; *-tai* -体 'noun, nominal')

   a. SS (*-u* in all verbs except statives, where it is *-yi*, identical to the RY
      that is seen in all verb types) is the conclusive form, also commonly
      used in scholarship as the citation form; also cf. 7c just below

   b. RT (*-u* in all verb types) has two main uses:

      i)  the head of an adnominal clause, whence its name

      ii) the *musubi*, or 'binding' (mostly onto stative [auxiliary] verbs),
          of a string, the *kakari*, or 'focus', of which had been signaled by
          a *kakari* particle (KP), |do|, in a construction known as *kakari
          musubi* (KM); this is one of two subtypes of that construction

   c. in verbs, SS and RT are almost always identical, the major exception
      being with stative verbs, whose SS is with *-yi* and whose RT is with *-u*;

8) IZ/MR: *izen-kei* 已然形 (*i*- 已- 'already' + *-zen* -然 '-ly') 'realis form' and
   *meirei-kei* 命令形 (*meirei* 'an order') 'imperative'. These two merged formally from two phonologically different forms. Their history is taken up
   in § 2.3.[11] There is no allomorphy save for the form noted just before the
   next section.

---

9   Strictly speaking, the form is ⟨tu ka ∧ we , ke ∧ wa re te ,⟩, with interjections.

10  *-kazi* is a correct form according to the Yotsu-Gana Hypothesis. This is hypothesized to be
    an enclitic, not the second part of a compound, and its reflex is seen in NOk: N-*kazi* 'every
    N' (OGJ 317a).

11  See also Shinzato and Serafim (2013: 195) for more discussion of IZ and MR merger.

VERBS 193

TABLE 6.3   Consonant- and vowel-verb subtypes

|  | MZ | RY | GER/PRFV | SS | RT | IZ/MR |
|---|---|---|---|---|---|---|
| *r*-type statives |  | *C-yi* |  | *C-yi* |  |  |
| *r*-subtype |  |  | Ø-*t°i* |  |  |  |
| 1st 3 *w*-subtypes |  | '-*yi* |  |  |  |  |
| *b*- and *m*-subtypes |  |  | Ø-*di* |  |  |  |
| velar subtype: *k* | C-⁽°⁾*a* | C-⁽°⁾*yi* |  | C-⁽°⁾*u* | C-⁽°⁾*u* | C-⁽°⁾*i* |
| *s*-subtype |  |  | Ø-*c°yi* |  |  |  |
| 4th *w*-subtype |  | Ø *yi* |  |  |  |  |
| *t*-subtype |  | C-⁽°⁾*yi* | ···Q-*c°yi* |  |  |  |
| velar subtype: *g* |  |  | Ø-*dzyi* |  |  |  |
| *n*-subtype | – | – |  | – | – | – |

Table 6.3 shows the allomorphs of the various derivational morphemes with consonant and stative types:[12]

MZ -*a* [ɑ], RY -*yi* [ʸi], and IZ/MR -*i* [ɪ] do not vary at all from one root-final-consonant subtype to another. The MZ "stem" (see above) is made by affixing -*a* to the root-final consonant. Skipping the RY and GER/PRFV columns for the moment: SS differs only for the statives. Were it not for those, there would be no SS ↔ RT distinction anywhere. Except for the *r*-type stative, the SS and the RT of all consonant-type verbs is made by affixing {+[°]u} to the final consonant of the root. With {... s+u} sequences this automatically results in surface-form ... *s-i*, which is, by the way, phonemically distinct from *su*. The SS of the stative, on the other hand, is made by affixing the RY suffix;[13] throughout, the IZ/MR *i* [ɪ] is the same on all roots, though its pronunciation in the case of the 4th *w*-subtype is probably just a lengthening of the [ʔʸi] root: [ʔʸiː], i.e. {ʔyiw+i} → ʔ*yi*⁽'⁾-*i* = [ʔyiː]; the RY of all of the verb roots is made by affixing -*yi* (or its allomorph -*y*-) to the root—any variation past that point is due to morphophonemic adjustments to fit the root and the suffix together. The Gerund/Perfective suffix (actually, auxiliary) {-tee 'GER/PRFV'} evinces the greatest degree of allomorphy. See § 4.

---

12    The shading highlights differences and similarities vertically, not horizontally.

13    This distinction matters syntactically, because it allowed the distinction of SS ↔ RT to survive right into NOk, despite the loss of that distinction in all non-stative verbs—since all modern-verb SS/RT forms have been created through auxiliation with statives—and thus allowed the survival of the KM construction. Cf. Mamiya (2005: 20–22). Otherwise KM would have been lost even before the first OOk records. For KM, see Shinzato and Serafim (2013, Ch. 4).

194                                                                    CHAPTER 6

## 1.2 *Consonant-Final (Quadrigrade* = yodan [YD]) *Verbs*

The presentation that follows lays out attested examples of the above conjugation types in the same order as in the chart that they follow.[14]

First are the two velar subtypes, the voiceless and the voiced, which behave
in a similar manner:

| | Stem | Gloss | MZ | RY | GER/PRFV | SS/RT | IZ/MR |
|---|---|---|---|---|---|---|---|
| 4G (1) … *k-* | {c°ik-} | attach$_{VI,}$ possess; | *c°ik-°an* | *c°ik-°y-* | *-dzi -c°yi* (*c°i -c°yi*) | *c°ik-°u*$_{RT}$ | *c°ik-°i-*[15] |
| | {p°uk-} | blow | | | | | *p°uk-°i-* |
| | {cik-ⱼ} | attach$_{VI}$ | *cik-a*ⱼ | *cic-yi*ⱼ | *ci-cyi*ⱼ | *cic-y-u-N*ⱼ | – ? |

(1)    OOk {c°ik- 'attach' VI}; {c°ik- '(spirit) possesses' VT}; {p°uk- 'blow' VI}:

MZ:   さしぶ†の、ₐ    よ       つかんₐ
      sa si bu† no ,ₐ yo      tu ka Nₐ
      *sasyibu-nu*    *yuu-∅*  *c°ik-°an*         {c°ik+am$_{IA}$+u$_{RT}$}
      shaman-SUB      world-IO accustom$_{VI}$-IA$_{RT}$[16,17,18]
      時に
      TOKI ni
      *tʰuk°yi-nyi*
      time-IO
      'should the shaman ever become accustomed [to] the world, …'
      (OS 12.#708);

---

14    {c°ik-} and {p°uk+} are OOk, and {cik+ⱼ} is the equivalent NOk, and so on.

15    OOk *i* = [1]; NOk *i* = [ʸi]: OOk *kʰuugi* [kʰuːgɪ] 'row!', NOk *kuugi*ⱼ [kuːgʸi] '(id.)'.

16    Morpheme-final voiceless stops and affricates are not marked for the aspiration distinc-
      tion in underlying forms. All vowel-initial morphemes attach unaspirated, regardless of
      their height. The T-forms also attach unaspirated, regardless of the form of the verb root to
      which they attach. In short, all attachments are made with aspiration suppressed, whether
      it would have been so for phonetic reasons or not. So: {c°ik+aN} → *c°ik-°aN*; {c°ik+yi+} →
      *c°ik-°y(i)-*; {c°ik+yi#te*$_{GER}$*#} → *c°i-c°yi*; {c°ik+i+} → *c°ik-°i-*.

17    The double-underlined portion becomes a portmanteau (fused) morph.

18    The form *-aN* '-IA' is more archaic than *-a* '-IA'. Similar mixing of temporal levels in a single
      text is also seen in Japanese. The following is from a modern-language academic text on
      Sino-Ryukyuan language research, Ishizaki 2001: 55, 64. The first line utilizes a literary (=
      *bungo*) IA form *-n*, the second line, a modern form *-yō: soko ni arata na chiken o kuwaen to
      suru mono de aru.* '[It] is a work that seeks to add to it new information.' and: … *setsumei-
      shiyō to shita mono de aru.* '[It] is an item in which they attempted to explain … .'

VERBS                                                                      195

きかれゝ

ki ka re "

*k°yi̱ k̲-°**ari·r-i**   ← {k°yi₍₎k- 'hear' VT} : {k°yi̱ k+ari·r+i}

hear-PASS-IZ

'will (surely) be heard' (*musubi* of ⟨su⟩ -, *si* '-KP';[19] (OS 17.#1177))

RY:     つきやう、                やに

        tu ki ya u ,            ya ni

        *c°ik-°y-a'-u*          *yoo-nyi*        {c°ik+yi+ʔaw+u#yoo+nyi}

        thrust-RY-each.other-RT  appearance-ADV

        'as if[20] to thrust (their horns) at each other' (OS 9.#479)

-*yi-(ʔ)V* usually collapsed to -*y-V* in verbal concatenations.

GER:    よいづ†ちへ

        yo i du† ti pe

        *yu-yi-dzi-c°yi*                  {yur+yi_RY+"#c°ik+yi_RY+tee_GER²¹}²²

        approach-RY-become.one-GER(/PRFV)

        '(a deity) approaching and merging with (another deity)' (OS 11.#576)

SS/RT:  もいつく、ぎ*やめ

        mo i tu ku , gi* ya me

        *mii-c°ik°-**u**-gyami*            {mu°yi_RY#c°ik+u_RT#gyami}

        grow_VI-RY-attach_VI-RT-TRM

        'until he grows up (to the top of Heaven)' (OS 12.#713)

cf. NOk *mii-y-u-N*, (NEG *mii-r-aN*, GER *mii-ti*,) 'teeth/plants grow' VI (OGJ 374a);
OJ *mOy*[*e*²³]-*u* '(plants) bud, sprout'

---

19   See Shinzato and Serafim (2013: 150–155) for the allomorphy of -*si* ~ -*syu* 'KP'.

20   Recall the discussion in Ch. 2.

21   Again, a portmanteau morph.

22   Recall the rare elision of *i* before *y*. Cf. Ch. 2 § 5.2.2.

23   JDB (751a) notes an OJ form written by Yakamochi (MYS #4111) with *môi* 毛伊, i.e. *môyi*,
     which would fit best with both the spelling ⟨mo i⟩ in OS, and also explain the distinc-
     tion between NOk *mii-*, 'teeth/grass grow(s)' (OGJ 374a) :: alternative OJ *mo*[*y*]*i-* '(plant)
     buds/sprouts' on the one hand and NOk *mée-* 'burns' VI (OGJ 367b) :: OJ 毛江 *môye-* '(id.)'
     (JDB [750d–751a]). JDB points out that the reading is contested; but we counterargue:
     (1) it is a *man'yō-gana* (phonetically based) reading, not a *kundoku* (conventionalized
     Japanese) reading (of (pseudo-)Classical Chinese), and (2) it fits with an entirely sepa-
     rately derived set of facts.

IZ/MR: ふけば*
pu ke ba*
_p°uk°-i-ba_       {p°uk+i$_{IZ}$+ba}
blow-IZ-TMP/CND
'when [the north wind] blows' (OS 9.#510)

| | Stem | Gloss | MZ | RY | GER/PRFV | SS/RT | IZ/MR |
|---|---|---|---|---|---|---|---|
| 4G (2) | {kʰuug-} | 'row' | _kʰuug-as-i_ | _-kʰuug-yi_ | _kʰuu-dzyi_ | | _kʰuug-i_ |
| ⋯ _g-_ | {pʰag-} | 'assemble' | | | | _pʰag-u_$_{ss}$ | |
| | {kuug-$_{J}$} | 'rows; dozes off' | _kuug-a_$_{NJ}$ | _kuuz-yi_$_J$ | _kuu-zyi_$_J$ | _kuuz-y-u-_$_{NJ}$ | _kuug-i_$_J$, _kuug-e-e_$_J$ |

②      OOk {kʰuug- 'row' VT}

MZ: こがせ
ko ga se
_kʰuug-as-i_      {kʰuug+as$_{CAUS}$+i$_{MR}$}
row-CAUS-MR
'have them row!' (OS 10.#543)

RY: けわいこぎ
ke wa i ko gi
_kʰiwa'-yi-kʰuug-yi_      {...#kʰuug+yi$_{RY}$+∅$_{NOM}$}
compete-RY-row-RY$_{NOM}$
'rowing race' (OS 10.#515)

GER: こぢ†へ
ko di† pe
_kʰuu-dzyi_      {kʰuug+yi$_{RY}$+tee[24]}
row-GER(/PRFV)
'[their] rowing [towards us is so beautiful!]' (OS 10.#545);

---

24    On the surface this becomes a portmanteau morph that has also acquired the feature of voicing from the preceding {g}.

VERBS 197

IZ/MR: こげ†

ko ge†

*kʰuug-i* {kʰuug+i_MR}

row-**MR**

'Row!' (OS 9.#488)

(2) OOk {pʰag+ 'builds/assembles (ships)' VT}:

RY: はぎ†ちへ

pa gi† ti pe

*pʰag-yi#cy°i* {pʰag+yi_RY+ 'assembling' #te 'hand'}

build.ships-**RY**-AGTN

'shipwright' (OS 13.#905); *-c°yi* ← *-tʰi* '-hand'; cf. NOk *haz-y-ú-N* 'build (ships)' (OGJ 211a)

SS/RT: はぐ†

pa gu†

*pʰag-u* {pʰag+u_SS}

build.ships-**SS**

'will build [ships]' (OS 13.#955)

| | Stem | Gloss | MZ | RY | GER/PRFV | SS/RT | IZ/MR |
|---|---|---|---|---|---|---|---|
| YD (3) ··· s- | {sas-} | 'wear (sword)'; | *sas-a-c°yee* | | | | |
| | {nas-} | 'bear'; 'make' | | *nas-y-uwa-c°yi* | *na-c°yee* | *nas-i-na* | |
| | {kʰuug-as-} | 'make row' | | | | | *kʰuug-as-i* |
| | {nas-ⱼ} | 'bear'; 'make' | *nas-aₙⱼ* | *nas-yiⱼ* | *na-cyiⱼ* | *nas-y-u-ₙⱼ* | *nas-iⱼ*, *nas-e-eⱼ* |

(3) OOk {sas+ 'wears (sword)'}; {nas+ 'bears; creates' VT; 'makes' VT}; {kʰuug+as+ 'causes to row'}:

MZ: ささちへ

sa sa ti pe

*sas-a-c°yee* {sas+as+yi_RY#tee}

wear.a.sword-**CAUS**-(**GER**/)**PRFV**

'had [him] wear [a sword and ... had him don armor]' (OS 10.#525)

RY: なしよわちへ
na si yo wa ti pe
*nas-y-uwa-c°yi*　　　　　　　{nas+yi_{RY}#ʔuwa·s+yi_{RY}+tee}
make.into-**RY**-EAV-GER(/PRFV)
'deigning to make [him the country's brother]' (OS 9.#477)

GER: なちへ
na ti pe
*na-c°yee*　　　　{nas+yi_{RY}#tee}
make-**(GER/)PRFV**
'[she] made [the Yashiro soldiers her vassals]' (Hokama [2000a: 85])
(OS 3.#96)

SS/RT: なすな
na su na
*nas-i-na*　　　　{nas+u_{RT}+na}
create-**RT**-NEG_{MR}
'do not create [your posterity]!' (OS 10.#512)

IZ/MR: cf. ⟨ko ga se⟩

| | Stem | Gloss | MZ | RY | GER/PRFV | SS/RT | IZ/MR |
|---|---|---|---|---|---|---|---|
| 4G (4) ⋯ *t-* | {tʰat+} | 'rise' VI | *tʰat°-a* | (*yur-yi*)-*dac°-yi* | *tʰaQ-c°yi* | *tʰac°-i* (RT) | *tʰat°-i-ba* (IZ) |
| | {tat+₋} | 'stand' | *tat-a₋* | *tac-yi₋* | *taQ-cyi₋* | *tac-y-u-N₋* | *tat-i₋*, *tat-e-e₋* |

(4)　　OOk {tʰat- '(waves/clouds) rise up'}:

MZ/IA: た〉　　　　かず†、
ta "　　　　ka zu†,
*tʰat-°a*　　　+*kʰazi*,　　{tʰat+am_{IA}+u_{RT}+kʰazi}
stand-**IA/MZ** number
'as [the years] go by' (OS 12.#725)

VERBS                                                                                    199

RY:    よりだ†ち
        yo ri da† ti
        *yur-yi-dac-°yi*                    {yur+yi$_{RY}$+"#tʰat+yi$_{RY}$+∅$_{NOM}$}
        approach-RY-stand-RY$_{NOM}$ (OS 16.#1160)
        'a group of raised-platform storehouses'

GER:   たちちへ
        ta ti ti pe
        *tʰaQ-c°yi*        {tʰat+yi$_{RY}$+tee}
        rise-GER(/PRFV)
        'standing up' (OS 7.#358)

SS/RT:  たつ
        ta tu
        *tʰac°-i*          {tʰat+u$_{RT}$}
        rise-RT (identical to SS)
        '(waves/clouds) that rise' (OS 13.#809)

IZ/MR:  たてば
        ta te ba
        *tʰat°-i-ba*        {tʰat+i$_{IZ}$+ba}
        arise-IZ-TMP(/CND)
        'when [young spring] comes' (OS 2.#54)

| | Stem | Gloss | MZ | RY | GER/PRFV | SS/RT | IZ/MR |
|---|---|---|---|---|---|---|---|
| 4G (5)<br>(··· *n*-) | {ʔyin-} | *'leave' | | | *ʔyi-**dzyi*** 'going' | | |
| | {syín-}<br>{ʔń́n-} | 'die'<br>*'leave' | *syín-a* | *syín-i* [ʃi'ɲi] | *syí-**zyi***<br>*ʔń́-**zyi*** 'going' | *syin-ú-N;*<br>°*syin-ú-na* | *syín-i, syin-é-e* |

(5)    OOk
       None as independent verb
       For the following NOk form, there is no form that we have been able to
       find in the OS *as an independent verb*; however, already in the OS and
       continuing into NOk, T-based forms of {ʔyik- 'go'} (e.g. the gerund) are
       all suppletions based on *\*ʔyin-* *'leave' i.e. {ʔyin+ 'go' (suppletive allo-
       morph)} (reminiscent of English *go ~ went*, in which historically *went*
       is the past tense of the semi-obsolete verb *wend*, as in *wend one's way*).

GER: いぢ゜ゑ
i di* we
*Ɂyi-dzyi*     {Ɂyin+yi+tee}
go-**GER**(/PRFV)
'going' (OS 8.#396)

The following four tables have sequential numbers, like all the others, but these four are also serialized as (a,b,c,d), since they pertain specifically to historical *w*-stem 4G verbs. Each subtype is noted in the first square on the left part of the table.

| | Stem | Gloss | MZ | RY | GER/PRFV | SS/RT | IZ/MR |
|---|---|---|---|---|---|---|---|
| YD (6) ···*w*- (a) [mono- syll root] | {kʰuuw-} | 'appeal' | *kʰuuw-a-ba*/ *kʰwa-a-ba* | *kʰuuꞋ-y-abir-a*/ *kʰuuꞋ-yi-,ga*/ *kʰwi-i-,ga* | *kʰuu-tꞋ-ar-i* *kʰuu-tꞋi* | – | *Ɂkʰuuw-i-ba*/ *ɁkʰuuꞋ-yi-ba*/ *Ɂkʰwi-Ꞌi-ba* |
| | {kuúꞏ r-} | 'propose to her' | *kuúꞏr-aN* | *kuúꞏ-yi*/ *kwi-í-*.25 | *kuú-ti* | *kuúꞏ-yu-N* | *kuúꞏr-i* *kuúꞏr-e-e* |

(6)    OOk {kʰuuw- 'appeal'}26,27

MZ: こわば
ko wa ba
*Ɂkʰuuw-a-ba* / *Ɂkʰwa-a-ba*  {kʰuuw+a(m_{IA})_{MZ}+ba}
appeal-**MZ**-(TMP/)CND
'if you ask [for the south wind, let it be south then]' (OS 13.#928)

---

25    But cf. NOk *Ɂwi-í-Ɂnzyas-y-u-N* 'drive out, oust' (OGJ 585b), and the citation form *Ɂuú-y-u-N* 'pursue; follow; drive out' (OGJ 572a), from which latter form one would expect—all else being equal—a RY ˣ*Ɂuú'-yi*, not the attested form °*Ɂwi-í*-. Currently we know of no rule for either OOk or NOk from which to predict the correct forms (C)*uu'-yi*(-) or (C)*wi-i*(-)—though the former certainly appears to be the more conservative, and has an extra mora—and so if necessary we give both alternatives.

26    OSJS (155c) states that this verb's conjugational forms are ⟨ko⟩ (*kʰuu-*) 'ROOT', ⟨ko wa⟩ (*kʰuuw-a-*) 'MZ', ⟨ko u⟩ (*kʰuu-*) 'RY', ⟨ko we⟩ (*kʰuu'-yi-*) 'RY', and ⟨ko we⟩ (*Ɂkʰuuw-i-/Ɂkʰuu'-yi*) 'IZ'. Any attested MR would have been listed. Phonologization is the present authors'. Our own analysis is as in the following forms.

27    Also {maaw- 'dance (sweepingly); fly (in circles)'} (~ ?{moow-}) works the same way. The length is our interpretation, erring on the side of putting in too much information. Should an issue arise that shows that the form must definitely be {maw-}, then it can be corrected at that time. The same holds true for {kʰuuw-} rather than {kʰuw-}.

VERBS                                                                 201

RY:  こや、べ*ら
     ko ya , be* ra
     *kʰuu'-y-abir-a*     {kʰuuw+yi_RY+abir+am_IA}
     appeal-**RY**-HUM-IA
     'let us humbly appeal' (OS 8.#404)

     こやり、
     ko ya ri ,
     *kʰuu'-y-a(a)r·yi*     {kʰuuw+y·aar·yi}
     appeal-**RY**·STAT·RY
     'while appealing' (OS 8.#402)

     こゆ/よわちへ
     ko yu/o wa ti pe
     *kʰuu'-y-uwa-c°yi*     {kʰuuw+**yi_RY**+ʔuwa·s+yi_RY+tee}
     appeal-**RY**-EAV-GER(/PRFV)
     'appealing [for an auspicious ship name]'; both (OS 1.#38)

     こゑが*
     ko we ga*
     *kʰuu'-**yi**-ⱼga / kʰwi-i²⁸-ga*  {kʰuuw+yi_RY#ga}
     to.pray-**RY**_NOM-SUB/GEN
     '[came] to pray for [rain]' (OS 7.#391)

GER:  こうて
      ko u te²⁹
      *kʰuu-t°ee*     {kʰuuw+yi_RY+tee}
      appeal-**(GER/)PRFV**
      'having appealed [for a following wind, sail [with it]]' (OS 10.#541)

      こうては
      ko u te pa
      *kʰuu-t°i-wa*     {kʰuuw+yi_RY+tee+wa}
      appeal-**GER**-TOP
      'appealing [for it], yet [you shall not acquire it]' (OS 10.#546)

---

28  Lack of PP in ⟨ko we ga⟩ argues in favor of the form *kʰwii* (OS 7.#391, OS 22.#1546), though
    sometimes PP occurs despite the monophthongized form lacking an overt palatal vowel;
    this is a quasi-nominal.

29  This form and the following two show that the root had a long vowel.

**IZ:** こうたれ

ko u ta re

*kʰuu-t°ar-i*  {kʰuuw+yi$_{RY}$#tar+i$_{IZ}$}

appeal-PRFT-IZ

'appealed [to the deities] for [a fair south wind]' (KM) (OS 13.#902); 'it is [by praying] that [she] appealed' (*su*-type KM) (OS 13.#920)

こゑば†

ko we ba†

*ˀkʰuuw-i-ba / ˀkʰuu'-yi-ba / ˀkʰwi-i-ba*  {kʰuuw+i$_{IZ}$+ba}

appeal-IZ-TMP(/CND)

'when [one] appealed' (OS 14.#1043)

| | Stem | Gloss | MZ | RY | GER/PRFV | SS/RT | IZ/MR |
|---|---|---|---|---|---|---|---|
| 4G (7) ··· w- (b) polysyll w-stems | {c°ɨk°aw-} {ˀusuw-} | 'send; invite'; 'rule' | *c°ɨk°aw-ari-t°ɨ*[30] | *ˀc°ɨk°a'-yi/* (*ˀc°ɨk°e-e*) | *ˀusu-t°i* | *ˀusu-u* | *ˀusi-i* |
| | {cikáw-} | 'use; send' | *ciká·'-aɴ ~ ciká·r-aɴ* | *ciké-e* | *ciká-ti* | *ciká·'-yu-ɴ* | *ˀciké-e/ ˀciká-ye-e* |

(7)  OOk {c°ɨk°aw- 'send (on a mission); invite' VT}

**MZ:** つかวれて

tu ka wa re te

*c°ɨk°aw-ari-t°i*  {c°ɨk°aw+ari$_{RY}$+tee$_{GER}$}

invite-PASS-GER(/PRFV)

'being invited (by the priestess)' (OS 12.#704)

**RY:** つかい

tu ka i

'inviting [the deity to attend]' (OS 2.#63)

---

30  The actual form as seen in the omoro is as part of a rowers' chant:

⟨tu ka ∧ we , ke ∧ wa re te ,⟩ *c°ɨk°a wii kʰii warit°i*.

⟨we (, )ke⟩ is frequently inserted in the middle of words in such songs.

VERBS

つかひ
tu ka pi
$c^{\circ}ik^{\circ}\underline{a'}\text{-}\underline{yi}^{31}/\,c^{\circ}\underline{ik^{\circ}e}\text{-}e$ {$c^{\circ}ik^{\circ}aw+yi_{RY}$}
invite-**RY**
'inviting [to a ceremony]' (OS 13.#766)

かみつ°かい
ka mi tu° ka i (OS 4.#205)
かみつ°かへ
ka mi tu° ka pe (OS 12.#725)
$k^{h}amyi\text{-}c^{\circ}ik^{\circ}e\text{-}e\,/\,...\text{-}c^{\circ}ik^{\circ}\underline{a'}\text{-}\underline{yi}$ ... {$c^{\circ}ik^{\circ}aw+yi_{RY}$}
deity-invite-**RY**$_{NOM}$
'ceremony congratulating the new King on his accession, to which the
deities are invited'

つかよわ
tu ka yo wa
$c^{\circ}ik^{\circ}\underline{a'}\text{-}y\text{-}uwa\text{-}\varnothing$   {$c^{\circ}ik^{\circ}aw+yi_{RY}+\textipa{?}uwa\cdot s+i_{MR}$}
send-**RY**-EAV-**MR**
'send [your royal ship[s]]!' (OS 13.#748)

GER:   きこゑ     きみが゛なし、        / しま∧     おそて∧   ちよわれ   /
       ki ko we   ki mi ga* na si ,        / si ma ∧   o so te ∧   ti yo wa re  /
       $k^{\circ}yi\,k^{\circ}u'yi$  $k^{\circ}yimyi\text{-}\,ganasyi\text{-}\varnothing$   $syima\text{-}\varnothing$  $\textipa{?}usu\text{-}t^{\circ}i^{32}$  $c^{\circ}yuwar\text{-}i$
       famed       priestess-EX-VOC       land-DO  rule-**GER**  rule$_{EX}$-**MR**
       'O famed beloved priestess—May you **rule** the land.' (OS 6.#329)

RT:    だ゛しま、∧       おそう、∧ あぢ゛おそい  /
       da* si ma ,∧      o so u ,∧  a di* o so i   /
       $dee\text{-}syima^{33}$   $\textipa{?}usu\text{-}u$   $\textipa{?}adzyi\text{-}\textipa{?}usii$
       great-land-DO  rule-**RT**  lord-ruler
       'The lord ruler **who** rules the great land ...' (OS 22.#1524)

---

31   There are no examples of overt *rendaku* voicing marks for this word. See, e.g., the examples
     below.
32   Probably two-syllable *w*-stem T-forms developed like Eastern Japanese (e.g. Tokyo \**p* >)
     *w*-stems, that is, through \**Q*-final stems: \**?osoQ-te* > \**?oso-te*.
33   We noted in Ch. 2 §5.6, "Metathesis, Details, *d*," that, as with ⟨ya⟩ (~ ˣ⟨ya u⟩) 'way', ⟨da⟩ has
     no alternant with a vowel-only graph, in its case ⟨i⟩: ⟨da⟩ (~ ˣ⟨da i⟩).

IZ: あぢおそいしよ、∧ 天下∧                     おそい ／
a di o so i si yo , ∧ TENI SITA ∧               o so i   ／
ʔadzyi-ʔusii-syu[34]  tʰinyi-[g(y)a-]syicʲya-∅  ʔusi-i
lord-ruler-KP         heaven-[GEN-]below-DO    rule-IZ
'The lord-ruler **alone** rules [all] under heaven.' (OS 10.#518)

|  | Stem | Gloss | MZ | RY | GER/PRFV | SS/RT | IZ/MR |
|---|---|---|---|---|---|---|---|
| 4G (8) ⋯ *muw*- irreg (c) | {ʔumuw-} | 'think; feel for; love' | *ʔumuw-ari·r-i* | *ʔumu'-y-uwar-u* | *ʔumu-tˀi* | *ʔumu'-u-yoo-nyi* | – |
|  | {ʔumu'/r-ⱼ} | 'think; ...' | *ʔumu·r-aNⱼ/* *ʔuma'aNⱼ* | *ʔum·i-i-ⱼ/* *ʔumu-y-ⱼ* | *ʔumu-t-ⱼ* |  |  |

(8)    OOk {ʔumuw- (irreg) 'think; feel; consider dear; love'}

MZ:    をもわれゝ[35]
       wo mo wa re "
       *ʔumuw-ari·r-i*        {ʔumuw+ari·r+i_IZ}
       feel-**PASS·4GE-IZ**_KM (*musubi* of KM)
       'will [truly] be loved [by the common people]' (OS 5.#261)

       おもわれゝ
       o mo wa re "
       *ʔumuw-ari·r-i*        {ʔumuw+ari·r+i_MR}
       think-**PASS·4G-MR**
       'be thought of [as a long-famed lord]!' (OS 14.#1042)

RY:    おも、よわる
       o mo , yo wa ru
       *ʔumu'-y-uwar-u*   {ʔumuw+yi_RY#ʔuwa·r+u_RT}
       think-**RY-EAV-RT**
       '[everywhere that the Solar Deity] thinks [to touch]' (OS 13.#828)

---

34  {ʔosoyi-sɵ} → ʔosoyi-syɵ → ʔusuyi-syu → ʔusii-syu; if not PPed, ɵ → *i*; thus -*si* ~ -*syu*. As can be seen from the last transformation, PP operates at a more abstract level than at the surface—it thus is already a morphophonemic rule.

35  Recall that ⟨wo⟩ and ⟨o⟩ are used interchangeably, despite the retention of the /ʔ/ ↔ /w/ distinction in initial position in speech. Cf. Ch. 2 § 4.4.1.

VERBS                                                                                       205

おもいぎ゛み
o mo i gi゛ mi
*?umu'-yi-gyimyi* / *?umi-i-gyimyi* {?umuw+yi_{RY}+"#k°yimyi}
beloved-**RY**-priestess
'[our lord's] beloved priestess' (OS 11.#604)

GER:    おもて、
        o mo te ,
        *?umu-t°i*              {?umuw+yi_{RY}+tee_{GER/PRFV}}
        think-**GER(/PRFV)**
        'plotting [and scheming]' (OS 2.#47)

SS/RT:  おも、やに        / おもうやに、
        o mo ∅ , ya ni    / o mo **u** ya ni ,
        *?umu'-u-yoo-nyi*[36]      {?umuw+**u**_{RT}#yoo+nyi}
        think-**RT**-way-ADV
        '[sail the boat] just as you please (!)' (OS 13.#920) /
        '[may the King rule] as he pleases' (OS 6.#299)

|             | Stem      | Gloss | MZ                        | RY        | GER/PRFV  | SS/RT                        | IZ/MR             |
|-------------|-----------|-------|---------------------------|-----------|-----------|------------------------------|-------------------|
| 4G (9)      | {?yiw-}   | 'say' | *?y-a-ba* / *?yi'-ya-ba*  | *?yi-gya* | *?yi-c°yi* | *?y-u-yoo-nyi*               | *?yi-i*           |
| ... *i*-irreg (d) |     |       |                           |           |           |                              |                   |
|             |           |       | *?y-án* / *?yi-r-án*      | *?yi'-yi-* | *?yí-cyi* | *?y-ú-N* / *?yí-i-N* / *?yi-y-ú-N* / *?y-úu-* | *?yí-r-i* / *?yi-r-é-e* |

(9)     OOk: {?yiw- 'say' irreg}[37,38,39,40]

---

36  The option of writing a bimorphemic long vowel as if short is usually not taken, but is
    possible, as in this case.

37  Takahashi notes the change of (in effect) *$p^h$a to ya, due to the influence of *i*. All of it is
    stated without distinguishing phonology from spelling.

38  The form before the gerund is, historically, a fusion of the root *?yi- and the almost identi-
    cal RY form *-yi-, which comes between the root and the gerund in original 4G verbs. Note
    that this fusion elides *w, meaning that a gerund such as ×?yuu-t°i, a lookalike to Western
    Japanese forms, is impossible.

39  For RY, also the first element in *?yi-yar-yi-ˌsi* ⟨i ya ri se⟩ 'let's have a message passed on'
    (OSJS 64a; OS 13.#888) a merger of the verb root and RY.

40  IZ/MR: The first interpretation ('say!') is Takahashi's (1991a: 147). However, it appears to rest

MZ: いやば、

i ya ba ,

*ʔʸ-a-ba / ʔʸi'-ya-ba* {ʔyiw+a(ʔm$_{IA}$)$_{MZ}$+ba}

say-**MZ**-TMP/CND

'if [the one praying] **should** say' (OS 15.#1058)

RY: のおだにが ／ いぎや、ᴧ

no o da ni ga ／ i gi ya , ᴧ

*noo-danyi-,ga*     *ʔyi-gya*       {ʔyiw+yi$_{RY}$+ga}

what-just-KP     say$_{RY·NOM}$-PRP

'... in order **to say** just what?' (OS 14.#998)

GER: いちへ

i ti pe

*ʔyi-c°yi*            {ʔyiw+yi$_{RY}$+tee$_{GER/PRFV}$}

say$_{RY}$-**GER(/PRFV)**

'saying (it, let us have it be heard)' (OS 16.#1134)

SS/RT: いよ、やに、

i yo , ya ni ,

*ʔʸ-u-yoo-nyi*     {ʔyiw+y+ur+u$_{RT}$#yoo+nyi}

say-**RT**-way-IO

'as (they) say' (OS 8.#458)[41]

---

on a literal interpretation of ⟨pe⟩ as having (had) a vowel other than [i], e.g. [ɪ], or even interpreting the syllable as [ɸɛ] (our [p°ɛ]). However the graph ⟨pe⟩ is in a position where its only two phonetic interpretations are [bɪ]—not possible for this verb—and [yi], which in this case would be either [ʔʸi'yi] or [ʔʸi:]. Because those syllables have as their sources either the RY *-yi or the IZ/MR *-ye, both the phonetic forms are possible, not just one or the other.

41   If *ʔyu* is correctly interpreted, then it is the "shortened RT," also ← {ʔiw+ur+u$_{RT}$} = *ʔyuru*. (Cf. e.g. *k°-y-uØ-munu* 'because [the Year of the Horse] has come' and *k°uc°yi-masa·sya-aØ-munu* 'because what [he] foretells is true' [OSJS 140a].) Takahashi (1991a: 147) notes that traditionally ⟨i yo ya ni⟩ has been taken as an adverb meaning 'iyo-iyo' = 'ever more', but that there is a possibility that it means 'as (they) say' (in our phonologization, *ʔʸ-u-yoo-nyi* 'say-short.RT-as-ADV'). But Hokama (2000a: 302) (#458) translates it as 'iya ga ue ni mo', essentially the same as 'iyo-iyo' = 'ever more'. However, note the largely identical pattern in ⟨o mo (u) ya ni⟩ given in our text just above.

VERBS

IZ/MR:

　　　　　　　　　　　い〳

　　　　　　　　　i pe

　　　　　　　*ʔyi-i* [ʔ<sup>y</sup>i:]

ʔ{ʔyiw+i$_{MR}$}　/　ʔ{ʔyiw+yi$_{RY}$}

ʔ'say-**MR**　　/　ʔ'say-**RY**

ʔ'say!'　　　　/　ʔ'saying' (OS 20.#1366)

According to Hokama, the context of the omoro from which this word is extracted is that Nayo-Seri-kyo, a priestess, is behaving oddly, and saying strange, absurd things. Here is the "saying strange, absurd things" passage in the omoro:

なよせりきよ、　　　/ まきよの、かず゛、　　/ てはわ 〵　　　　い〳　 /

na yo se ri ki yo ,　/ ma ki yo no , ka zu゛,　/ te pa wa 〵　　i pe　　/

*nayu.sir.yi.k°yu-∅　　mak°yu$^{42}$-nu-k$^h$azi　　t$^h$eeQp°a$^{43}$-wa ʔyi-i*

Nayo-Seri-kyo-SUB　　village-GEN-number　　absurdity-TOP say-IZ

"Nayoseri-kyo shinjo wa takusan no buraku o mawatte wa kokkei na koto o itte [hito-bito o warawasete-iru]. [Since Nayoserikyo has gone around to many villages and muttered absurd things, [she's making people laugh].]" (Hokama 2000b: 323–324) (OS 20.#1366)

The part "... she's making people laugh" is not directly reflected in the omoro, but is Hokama's interpretive interpolation. Hokama's translation appears to take ⟨i pe⟩ as RY, unless it is meant to be seen as "itte ⟦wa⟧", in which case he may be seeing an IZ form here. As for us, we *do* see an IZ form, as in, e.g. this book, Ch. 7, § 6.4, with ···*m-i*, where it "has strong assertive tone." Our own trans-lation:

> 'Nayo-Seri-kyo, making the rounds of the villages, [constantly] giving vent to *absurdities*, ...!'

---

42　The word *mak°yu* is much discussed, and refers to a hamlet that is a consanguineal group-ing (OSJS 295c), which OSJS identifies as the earliest type of hamlet in Okinawa.

43　The NOk word *teefa$_J$* means 'joke, behaving humorously', and *teefa-a$_J$* is a 'jokester, funny person'.

|  | Stem | Gloss | MZ | RY | GER/PRFV | SS/RT | IZ/MR |
|---|---|---|---|---|---|---|---|
| 4G (10)<br>… *b*- | {ʔasïb-}[44] | 'dances' | ʔasïb-*a* | ʔasïb-*yi* | ʔasí-*di* | ʔasïb-*u* | ʔasïb-*i* |
|  | {ʔasíb-} | 'plays' | ʔasíb-*a* | ʔasíb-*i* | ʔasí-*di* | ʔasíb-*u-N* | ʔasíb-*i*,<br>ʔasíb-*e-e* |

(10) OOk {ʔasïb- 'dance'}

MZ: あすば゛*  
    a su ba*  
    *ʔasïb-a*    {ʔasïb+am}  
    dance-IA  
    '**let us** dance' (OS 14.#1005)

RY: あすび゛*  
    a su bi*  
    *ʔasïb-yi*     {ʔasïb+yi$_{RY}$+∅$_{NOM}$}  
    dance-RY$_{NOM}$  
    '**a** dance' (OS 8.#449)

GER: あすで゛*  
    a su de*  
    *ʔasí-di*          {ʔasïb+yi$_{RY}$+tee$_{GER/PRFV}$}  
    dance-GER(/PRFV)  
    'danc**ing** [a religious dance]' (OS 20.#1376)

SS: あすぶ゛*  
    a su bu*  
    *ʔasïb-u*    {ʔasïb+u$_{SS}$}  
    dance-SS  
    '**does** a religious dance' (OS 3.#90)

---

44    See Shinzato and Serafim (2013: 154) for an etymology for this word.

VERBS 209

MR: あすべ*
a su be*
*?asib-i*  {?asib+i_MR}
dance-MR
'dance!' (OS 14.#1034)

| | Stem | Gloss | MZ | RY | GER/PRFV | SS/RT | IZ/MR |
|---|---|---|---|---|---|---|---|
| 4G (11) ···*m-* | {tʰuyum-} | 'resounds' | *tʰuyum-as-an-yi* | *tʰuyum-yi* | *tʰuyu-di* | *tʰuyum-u* | *tʰuyum-i* |
| | {tuyum-ˌ Lit.} | 'resounds' | *tuyum-aˌ* | *tuyum-iˌ* | *tuyu-diˌ* | *tuyum-y-u-N,* | *tuyum-i,ˌ* *tuyum-e-eˌ* |

(11) OOk {tʰuyum- 'resounds'}[45]

MZ: とよまさに
to yo ma sa ni
*tʰuyum-as-an-yi*  {tʰuyum+as+an+yi}
resound-CAUS-NEG-YNQ
'may [you] **make** [your rule eternally] resound [everywhere]' (OS 1.#29)

RY: とよみよわれ
to yo mi yo wa re
*tʰuyum-y-uwa· r-i*  {tʰuyum+yi#?uwa · r+i}
resound-RY-EAV-MR
'deign to resound!' (OS 1.#5)

---

45  The NOk verb {tuyum-ˌ} is Literary, and forms related to it waver in shape: the toponym *timi-gusikuˌ* Tomigusuku / Tomishiro 〈豊見城〉(OGJ 520b); but the set expression *tuyumu tumigusiku* 〈とよむ豊見城〉 'the famed Tumigusiku' (OGJ 528b). The sequence *\*oyo* has frequently become *\*wii*; two roots can fruitfully be compared: *\*oyog* 'swim' > *?wiig-* and, in compounds—as in the toponym—, *\*toyom-* > *\*ˣtwiim-* > *\*tiim-* > *tim-*. The latter, *\*toyom-*, automatically lost its onglide after a coronal, and shortened. But the generalization about the fate of *\*oyo* holds for both *\*toyom-* and *\*oyog-*. There is no actively used NOk verb root *ˣti(i)m-*. The form *tumi-* appears to be a contamination from the semantically associated NJ morph *tomi-* 'rich(es)', helped along by the initial *tuyum ...* of the preceding word. The *kanji* for *timi-* are separately read TOYO-MI in NJ, and ostensibly mean 'riches-viewing'. The NJ PLN Tomishiro appears to derive from the *tumi-...* above. The OOk suffix *⁽ᵐ⁾t⁽ʰ⁾umyi* 'HMS' (*lit.* 'riches') appears not to have been involved in any of this.

GER: とよで、∧　　　　　　みもん
to yo de , ∧　　　　　　mi mo N
*tʰuyu-di*　　　　　　*myi.muN*　{tʰuyum+yi+tee}
resound-GER(/PRFV) splendid
'splendid **how** it resounds!' (OS 1.#20)

SS/RT: うらとよむ、∧　　つゞみ、
u ra to yo mu , ∧　　tu ⁿ* mi ,
*ʔura-tʰuyum-u*　*c°idzimyi-∅*　{tʰuyum+u_RT}
bays-resound-RT hand.drum-DO
'[beating] the bay-resound**ing** drum' (OS 2.#52)

IZ/MR: とよめ
to yo me
*tʰuyum-i*　{tʰuyum+i_IZ}
resound-IZ
'**it is** [our Lord] **that will** be famed' (OS 1.#33)

| | Stem | Gloss | MZ | RY | GER/PRFV | SS/RT | IZ/MR |
|---|---|---|---|---|---|---|---|
| 4G (12) | {mudur-} | 'return' | *mudur-an·yi* | *mudur-y-uwar-i* | *mudu-t°i* ···[t°ɪ] | *mudur-u* | *mudur-i* ···[rɪ] |
| ··· r- | {mudur-ⱼ} | 'return' | *mudur-aN,* | *mudu'-yi,* | *mudu-ti,* ···[ti] | *mudu'-y-u-N,* | *mudur-i,* ···[ri] |
| | {mur-} | 'leak through' | *mur-aN* | *mur-yi* 'fill(ing)' | *mu-t°i* ···[t°ɪ] | *mur-u_ss* 'fill' | |
| | {mur-ⱼ} | 'leak through' | *mur-aN,* | *mu'-yi,* | *mu-ti,* ···[ti] | | |

(12)　OOk {mudur- 'return'}

MZ: もどゞらに
mo do* ra ni
*mudur-an·yi*　{mudur+an+yi}
return-NEG·QP
'**Won't** you return?', i.e. 'We want you to return, ... .' (OS 21.#1455)

VERBS      211

RY:    もど゙りよわれ
       mo do* ri yo wa re
       *mudur-y-uwar-i*    {mudur+yi#ʔuwar·i$_{\text{IZ}}$}
       return-RY-EAV-IZ   (the IZ form is the result of KM)
       'will surely deign to return [having smitten the enemy]' (OS 11.#561)

GER:   もどて、
       mo do te ,
       *mudu-t°i*            {mudu·r+yi+tee}
       return-GER(/PRFV)
       'return**ing**' (OS 3.#91)

IZ:    もどれ
       mo do re
       *mudur-i*   {mudu·r+i$_{\text{IZ}}$}
       return-IZ
       '**will surely** return [having smitten the enemy]' (OS 10.#519)

(12)     OOk {mur- 'leak (through)'}

MZ:    もらん、
       mo ra N ,
       *mur-aN*            {mur+an}
       leak.through-NEG$_{\text{RT}}$
       '**not** penetrating [from above]' (OS 19.#1288)

       も/むらね
       mo/mu ra ne
       *mur-an-i*          {mur+an+i$_{\text{IZ}}$}
       leak.through-NEG-IZ (*musubi* of KP -*si*)
       'it's that it **doesn't** leak through' (OS 17.#1234)

RY:    もり、どころ
       mo ri , do ko ro
       *mur-yi-dukʰuru*    {mur- 'fills a container with liquid'}
       fill.up-RY$_{\text{NOM}}$-place   {mur+yi+"#tʰukʰuru}
       'where [they] fill the cups [with good wine]' (OS 10.#541)

SS: もる

mo ru

*mur-u* {mur+u$_{SS}$}

fill-SS

'fills (the cups with wine)' (OS 11.#643)

| | Stem | Gloss | MZ | RY | GER/PRFV | SS/RT | IZ/MR |
|---|---|---|---|---|---|---|---|
| 4G (13) ··· *yir-* | {k°yi̠r-} | 'cut' | *k°yi̠r-as-i* | (*myic°ya*)-*gyi̠r-yi,*[46] *k°yi̠r-yi-p°usit°i* | – | – | – |
| | {cyi̠r-ɟ} | 'cut' | *cyi̠r-aɴ,* | *cyir-i,*[47] | *cyiQ-cyi,* | *cyi'-y-u-ɴ,* | *cyi̠r-i,*\* |

(13)     OOk {k°yi̠r- 'cut'}

MZ:   きらせ

ki ra se

*k°yi̠r-as-i*        {k°yi̠r+as+i$_{MR}$}

cut-CAUS-MR

'have [them$_1$] chop [them$_2$] up' (OS 1.#33)

RY:   みちや、ぎり

mi ti ya , gi ri

*myic°ya-gyir-yi*        {+"#k°yi̠r+yi$_{RY}$+∅$_{NOM}$}

dirt-lop.off-RY$_{NOM}$

'dirt-chunks' (OS 1.#33)

## 1.3    *Vowel-Root–Final Verbs*

Unlike the consonant-final roots analyzed so far, we now turn to certain verb classes that may be categorized as having roots ending in a vowel. It will become obvious in what follows that these verbs were already on the path to becom-

---

46    *myic°ya-gyiryi*, lit. 'dirt cuttings'; *k°yiryip°usit°i* 'cutting down (an enemy)'.

47    The form given in the chart on p. 59, (xiv, イ), col. 2 of OGJ is *cyi-i,*, which would appear to have irregularly lost its *r* between two pre-raising *yi* sounds. However, with *other* preceding vowels, *ryi does* regularly lose its *r*. If it *were* to follow the pattern of *nouns*, it would be *cyiri*, and in fact a check of, e.g. ROD does show *cyiri-*, *-cyiri*, and *-zyiri* as compounding forms. Here is an example: *ʔusyí-cyiri̅-zyiri(i)*, 'hacking into small pieces; mincing' (ROD; OGJ 564b [variable accent]).

VERBS                                                                213

ing *r*-stem quadrigade verbs, i.e. *r*-consonant-final-root verbs, due to the overwhelming numerical superiority of the *r*-stem 4G's, probably far above all others combined.

The vowel-root–final verbs can be subcategorized as:
– monosyllabic-root-:
  (14 upper monograde [*yi*-type] a, b, c)
  (15 lower monograde [*i*-type])
– polysyllabic-root-:
  (16 [middle bigrade: *i*-type] a, b) and
  (17a, b) lower bigrade: *i*-type,
– irregular vowel-root verbs:
  (18) *k*-type
  (19) *s*-type
  (20) *r*-type
Each subtype is discussed below as it comes up.

1.3.1        Vowel-Root–Final Verbs (Upper Monograde)

|           | Stem | Gloss | MZ | RY | GER/PRFV | SS/RT | IZ/MR |
|-----------|------|-------|------|------|----------|-------|-------|
| (14a) *?yi-* | {?yi·r-} | 'shoot' | – | *?yi·r-yi* | – | – | – |
|           | {?yi·r-₎} | 'shoot' | *?yi·r-aN₎* | *?yi·r-i-₎*[48] | *?yi·Q-cyi₎* | *?yi·'-y-u-N₎* | *?yi·r-i₎,* *?yi·r-e-e₎* |

This verb appears to be the earliest case, as least in the OS, of a transformation
to *r*-stem 4G. We have only its RY to vouch for that, however.

(14a)     OOk {?yi·r+ 'shoot' VT}

RY:    とり、     / まわさ、だ†な、ᴧ        いりおとちへ、            /
       to ri ,   / ma wa sa , da† na , ᴧ   i ri o to ti pe ,        /
       *tʰuryi-∅*  *maw-as-adana*         *?yi·r-yi-?utʰu-c°yi*
       bird-DO   swoop-CAUS-NEG·PCPL shoot-RY-bring.down-GER
       '… not [letting] the bird circulate about, [he] shoots it down, and …'
       (OS 14.#1044);[49]

---

48    See Ch. 2 §5.2.2 for a discussion of this form and its OOk equivalent.
49    Only example of this verb. See discussion of it and the NOk *?yiri-* in Ch. 2 §5.2.2.

|  | Stem | Gloss | MZ | RY | GER/PRFV | SS/RT | IZ/MR |
|---|---|---|---|---|---|---|---|
| (14b) $yi$- | {yi-} | 'sit' | – | $yi$- | $yi$-$c°yi$ | – | – |
|  | {yí-}[50] | 'sit; settle down; stay' | $yi·r·án$ | $yi·\cdots,$ $yíi·\varnothing$[51] | $yí·cyi$ | $yi·'·y·ú·_N$ | $yí·r·i,$ $yi·r·é·e$ |

This verb has two forms, one a RY that clearly differs from (14a), and the other a GER/PRFV that undergoes PP off of the stem. What is unusual about this stem is that it stays short, except when an independent word. This conclusion is derived from the general requirement that every word have at least two moras, while the short form in compounding is derived from the facts of the NOk verb paradigm.

(14b)  OOk {yi+ 'sit' VI}

RY:  あが ∧ なさは、　　／ いきやが*、∧ いよる、∧
a ga ∧ na sa pa ,　／ i ki ya ga* , ∧ i yo ru , ∧
?a.ga  nasee-wa  ?yik°ya-ga  yi-y-ur-u
our  father-TOP  how-KP  stay-RY-SE-RT
'How is our father doing?'[52] (OS 21.#1501)

GER:  ゐちへ、∧ おわれば*、∧　　きよら　や　／
wi ti pe , ∧ o wa re ba* , ∧　ki yo ra  ya　／
yi-c°yi  ?uwa·r·i-ba  k°yura  yaa
sit-GER  stay_EX-IZ-TMP/CND  beautiful  EXCL
'[When] sitting [on his throne]—How beautiful!' (OS 5.#250);[53]

---

50  Here are other forms in OGJ (266b):
   *yi-mís-ee-N* 'o-suwari ni naru' = 'sit-EAV-CONT-SS' = '(exaltedly) sits'
   *yi-mís-ee-bir-e-e* 'o-suwari kudasaimase' = 'sit-EAV-CONT-POL-MR-POL' = 'please sit down'
   *yi-cyóo-m-i* 'sit-CONT-SS-QP' = 'Hello! (To a lower-ranked elder who is sitting)'; *lit.* 'Are (you inferior elder) sitting?'.

51  Recall the statement in Ch. 2 § 5.3.3 that all independent OOk words are assumed to have at least two moras, with the proviso that poetic meter can override that stipulation.

52  The English translation is faithful to Hokama (2000b: 415b). Two further things: (a) strangely, this omoro has no exalting forms at all; (b) it is very difficult to make out a coherent text out of the entire omoro.

53  Here is Chris Drake's translation of this song in its entirety (Omoro Kanshō 83: 21):

VERBS                                                                    215

| | Stem | Gloss | MZ | RY | GER/PRFV | SS/RT | IZ/MR |
|---|---|---|---|---|---|---|---|
| (14c) myi- | {myiꞵ-} | 'see' | *myii·ᵣr-a···* | *myii-* | *myii-c°yee* | *myii-r-u* (RT) | *myii·ᵣr-i* |
| | {NN·d-ᵣ} {miꞵ-ᵣ} | 'see' | NN·d-*aN*ᵣ | NN·z-*yi*ᵣ ~ *mii*ᵣ (Lit.)[54] | NN·*cy·i*ᵣ | NN·z-*y-u-N*ᵣ ~ *n-uu-N*ᵣ (Lit.) | NN·d-*i*ᵣ, NN·d-*e-e*ᵣ |

This verb, along with {kʰuꞵ} 'come' below, has an intrinsic floating abstract
length marker. This can be seen clearly at work in the NOk Literary form *n-
uu-N*ᵣ, where it has floated over the first morpheme boundary to lengthen the
SE {+wu+}. Note that, despite the length of the stem, it still causes PP of the
GER/PRFV.

(14c)    OOk {myiꞵ+ 'see' VT}

MZ:    くせより、ʌ              みらな            /
       ku se yo ri , ʌ         mi ra na          /
       *k°usi-yur-yi-∅*        *myii·r-a-na*
       rare-dance-RY_NOM-DO    see-MZ-DSD
       'I want to [i.e. let me] see a rare_BE dance' (OS 14.#1031)

RY:    あおりやゑや、 / おれよʌ      みぎや、ʌ   おれわちへ                /
       a o ri ya we ya , / o re yo ʌ   mi gi ya , ʌ   o re wa ti pe      /
       *ʔawuryayi-ya*      *ʔuri-yu*     *myi-gya*[55]  *ʔuri-wa-c°yee*
       Aoriyae-TOP        that.one-DO   see_RY-PRP    descend_RY-EAV-PRFV_SS
       'The priestess Aoriyae (= *ʔawuryayi*) descended to see those.'
       (OS 4.#159)

———————

        Reliable magistrate Nakamine
        Trustworthy bearer of tax tribute / a true king, this Kimishi
        the sun who rules from Shuri castle / the sun king so revered and loved
        ruling every bay and inlet / ruling everything in the country
        sitting on his throne—how beautiful
        sitting at the pinnacle—how I love to watch

54   OGJ (65) notes the significant variation in pronunciation of the Literary *ren'yō gokan*
     'adverbial stem', using the alternants *miy-abir-a*ᵣ ~ *my-aabir-a*ᵣ ~ *n-aabir-a*ᵣ to make its
     point. Clearly at some level there is a floating length marker associated with the verb stem.
     While in the Literary forms this is a vowel length marker, it becomes a marker of nasal con-
     sonant length in the colloquial variant, and thus is now defined as applying to sonorants,
     not just vowels.

55   Note discussion of the interaction of PP and vowel length in Ch. 2 §5.1.1.

GER: のう、ᴧ　みちへがⁿ、ᴧ　おひきよる　　　　　/
　　　no u ,ᴧ　mi ti pe gaⁿ ,ᴧ　o pi ki yo ru　　　　/
　　　*nuu-∅*　*myi-c°yee-ga*　*ʔuu'-yi-k°-y-uur-u*
　　　what-DO　see_RY-PRFV-KP　chase-RY-come-RY-SE-RT
　　　'[The long-billed bird:] What₂ has [it₁] seen that [it₁] is chasing [it₂]
　　　down?' (OS 12.#731)

SS/RT: かみ、しむの、　みる　　め　　#
　　　ka mi , si mu no , mi ru　　me　　#
　　　*kʰamyi -syimu-nu myii·r-u mii*
　　　high-low-SUB　　see-RT　eye(s)
　　　'the eyes of high- and low[-ranking officials] watching [the dance].'
　　　(OS 19.#1285)

IZ/MR: みれども、ᴧ　　あかぬ、　　/ 首里　　おや国　　　/
　　　mi re do mo ,ᴧ　a ka nu ,　/ SIYO RI o ya KUNI　　/
　　　*myi·r-i-dumu*　*ʔak-°an-u*　*syiyuryi ʔuya-gunyi*
　　　observe-IZ-CONC tire.of-NEG-RT　Shuri　Parent-Country
　　　'[look!, it is] Shuri, the Parental Land [= the King's Capital]!, which we
　　　do not tire of gazing at.' (OS 1.#7)

IZ/MR: あれ、ᴧ　　みれ　　よ、ᴧ きよら、ぎⁿみ　　　/
　　　a re ,ᴧ　　mi re　　yo ,ᴧ ki yo ra , giⁿ mi　　　/
　　　*ʔa·ri-∅*　　*myii·r-i*　*yoo k°yura-gyimyi*
　　　yonder·one-DO see·4GE-MR SFP beautiful_ADJ.STEM-priestess
　　　'Look at that!, o Beautiful Priestess.' (OS 13.#977)

### 1.3.2　Vowel-Root–Final Verbs (Lower Monograde)

| | Stem | Gloss | MZ | RY | GER/PRFV | SS/RT | IZ/MR |
|---|---|---|---|---|---|---|---|
| (16)<br>*kʰi-* | {kʰi-} | 'kick' | | *kʰi(·r-yi)* | | | |
| | {ki-ⱼ} | 'kick' | *kir-aɴⱼ* | *kir-i-ⱼ* | *kiQ-cyiⱼ* | *ki-y-u-ɴⱼ/*<br>*ki-y-ur-uⱼ* | *kir-iⱼ/*<br>*kir-e-eⱼ* |

The subcategory Lower Monograde is actually a historical one. "Lower" refers to
a historically low front vowel, but the vowel has since raised twice, the first time
to a (lax) mid vowel, and the second time to a lax high vowel. It has remained

VERBS 217

separate from the other monosyllabic monograde subcategory in that it has a vowel *i*, whereas the others have *yi* instead. The modern paradigm conjugates like an ··· *yir-* verb instead, even though its vowel is historically not right for it.

(16)    OOk {kʰi- 'kick' VT}

RY:     あさ、つゆは、ₐ        けり、あげ゛て、                    /
        a sa , tu yu pa , ₐ    ke ri , a ge゛ te ,              /
        *ʔasa-cʰiyu-ǫpºa*   **kʰi·r-yi-ʔagi-∅-tºi**
        morning-dew-DO kick·4GE-RY-raise-RY-GER
        '**Kick**ing up the *morning dews* ...' (OS 13.#833)

RY:     ぢ゛やなもいが゛、    /.../ けやげ゛たる、ₐ                つゆは、  /
        di゛ ya na mo i ga゛ ,  /.../  ke ya ge゛ ta ru , ₐ       tu yu pa,  /
        *dzyana-mii-ga*       ...    **kʰi-y-agi-∅-tºar-u**     *cʰiyu-wa*
        Jana-EX-SUB          ...    kick_RY-EP.y-raise-RY-PRFT-RT dew-TOP
        'The dews that Lord Jana kicked up ...' (OS 14.#982)

1.3.3    Vowel-Root–Final Verbs (Middle Bigrade[56])

|  | Stem | Gloss | MZ | RY | GER/PRFV | SS/RT | IZ/MR |
|---|---|---|---|---|---|---|---|
| (15a) ···*ri*- | {ʔuri-} | 'descend' | *ʔuri·r-an-yi* | *ʔuri-∅-wa-cºyi* | *ʔuri_RY-tºi* | *ʔuri·**ru*** (RT) | – |
|  | {ʔuri-ⱼ} | 'descend' | *ʔuri·**ra**ⱼ* | *ʔuri·**i**ⱼ* | *ʔuri_RY-ti*ⱼ | *ʔuri-y-u-N,/* *ʔuri-y-ur-u,* | *ʔuri·r-i,/* *ʔuri·r-e-e,* |

These are called "middle" for the historical reason that the final vowel of their stem is Pre-OOk *\*e*, not the OOk *i*. The OOk vowel cannot cause PP, and this is

---

56    This term was coined by Leon A. Serafim (1977: 7) to explain the correspondence-set OOk *i* :: OJ *ï*, which descends from proto Japonic (*\*ö(C)î* ﹥) *\*ö*, a mid-vowel correspondence— thus "middle"—at about the time of the split of the two lineages, leading to PRk *\*ë* (which had merged with PJ *lower* bigrade *\*a(C)î* > *\*ë*). Both lower and middle bigrades are separate from two sets of *upper* bigrade verbs. The PJ Middle Bigrades merged with the *Upper* Bigrades in the Nara official Japanese language, but with the *Lower* Bigrades in many other locales, especially in the western Japanese archipelago, and in all of the Ryukyus. Also, the obsolete term *naka nidan* 'Middle Bigrade', coined by the late-Edo-Period Kokugaku scholar Moto'ori Haruniwa, refers, in modern terms, to the Upper Bigrade conjugation, and thus the terms are in fact unrelated. (Cf. Matsumura [1971: 132bc] 'Kami Nidan Katsuyō'.)

218 CHAPTER 6

shown (almost) exceptionlessly in its gerunds. The only exception is an example of word play.

(15a)  OOk {ʔuri- 'descend' VI}[57]

MZ:  しより、　もりぐ゚すく、　　　/ きらのかず゚、ᴧ
     si yo ri，mo ri gu゚ su ku，　/ ki ra no ka zu゚，ᴧ
     *syiyuryi muryi gusik゚u-∅*　*k゚yi̗ra-nu-kʰazi*
     Shuri　grove enclosure-IO　lucky.days-GEN-number
     おれらに　　　　　/
     o re ra ni　　　/
     *ʔuri·r-an-yi*
     descend·4GE-NEG-QP
     '**May you** (= the Priestess Sasukasa) come down (= **won't you** come down?) to Shuri Grove Enclosure as many times as lucky days[58] (i.e. on every lucky day).' (OS 4.#195)

RY:  もちづ゚きや、　　/ はまが゚わに、ᴧ　　おれわちへ　　　　　/
     mo ti du゚ ki ya，/ pa ma ga゚ wa ni，ᴧ o re wa ti fe　　　/
     *muc゚yidzik゚yi-ya*　*pʰama̗.gawa-nyi*　*ʔuri-∅-wa-c゚yee*
     Mochizuki-TOP　　Hamagawa-LOC　　descend-RY-EAV-PRFV
     'The Priestess Mochizuki descen**ded** to Hamagawa ...' (OS 16.#1139)

GER:  きこゑ　　大ぎ゚みぎや、　　/ おれて、ᴧ
     ki ko we　OPO gi゚ mi gi ya，/ o re te，ᴧ
     *k゚yi̗k゚uyi ʔuQp゚u-gyimyi-gya*　*ʔuri-t゚i*
     famed　　great-priestess-SUB　descend-GER
     あすび、よわれば゚　　/
     a su bi，yo wa re ba゚　/
     *ʔasib-y-uwar-i-ba*
     perform-RY-EX-IZ-T/C
     'When the Renowned High Priestess descends **and** performs [the trance dance] ...' (OS 1.#1)

---

57  The phonology of this verb is treated at length in Ch. 2 §2.2.1.
58  Because the *yi* here does not PPize the initial consonant of the second syllable, it may have been *[k゚yɪɾɑ] < \*kyera*, or *[k゚yɪːɾɑ] < \*kyeera* or *kyüira*, i.e. not from short *\*yi*. While this case does not appear to be bimorphemic, almost all other exceptions with *yi̗r* occur with *r* morpheme-final (e.g. *ʔu-syi̗r-ari* 'prayer' [OS 13.#902]) or -initial (e.g. *myi̗r-a-na* 'let us see' [OS 14.#1031]), specifically in verb derivational or inflectional morphology. While a couple of cases of PP in these cases are known with *k゚yik゚(y)-* '[be]hear[d]', it is exceedingly rare, so its general lack may be tied to a morphophonemic exception.

VERBS 219

RT: おれる　　　かず*、　/ きみ∧　　　はやす、∧ みこい　　/
o re ru　　ka zu*, 　/ ki mi∧　　　pa ya su ,∧ mi ko i　/
ʔuri·r-**u**　　+kʰazi　　kˣyimyi-∅　pʰayas-i　myi-ˌkˣuyi
descend-**RT** number　priestess-DO praise-RT　EX-voice
'Every time [Priestess Sasukasa] descends, [there are] voices in praise
of her' (OS 11.#598)

| | Stem | Gloss | MZ | RY | GER/PRFV | SS/RT | IZ/MR |
|---|---|---|---|---|---|---|---|
| (15b) ...kʰi- | {ʔukˣi-} | 'launch' VT | ʔukˣi·r-a | ʔukˣi- | ʔukˣi-∅-tˣi | ʔukˣi·r-u (RT) | |
| | {ʔúki-} | 'launch' VT | ʔukí·r-a | ʔukí-i | ʔukí-∅-ti | ʔukí-y-u-N/ ʔukí-y-ur-u | ʔukí·r-i/ ʔukí·r-e-e |

This is just another example of a Middle Bigrade.

(15b)　OOk {ʔukˣi- 'launch, float' VT}

MZ: げ*らい、まさり、とみ、　　　　　/
ge* ra i , ma sa ri , to mi ,　　　　/
giree-masaryi-ˌtʰumyi-∅
finely.wrought-superior-large.ship-DO
おしうけらば†、　　　　/
o si u ke ra ba†,　　　　/
ʔus-yi-ʔukˣi·r-a-ba
push-RY-launch· 4GE-**MZ**-T/C
'If we launch off the finely wrought ship Masari-Tomi, ...' (OS 13.#748)

RY: ひぢやり、かた、∧　　おけわちへ、　　/
pi di ya ri , ka ta ,∧　　o ke wa ti pe ,　/
pˣyidzyaryi+kʰatˣa-∅ ʔukˣi_RY-wa-cˣyi
left-side-IO　　　　launch-**RY**-EAV-GER
'Launching [the ship] on the left side, ...' (OS 13.#917)

RT: うける　　　かず*、　/ ぢ*やぐ†にとみ、∧　おうね、　　/
u ke ru　　ka zu*, 　/ di* ya gu† ni to mi ,∧ o u ne ,　/
ʔukˣi·r-u　　+kʰazi　　dzya-gunyi-tʰumyi　ʔu-uni-∅
launch·4GE-**RT** number　great-country-HMS　EX-ship-COP

'Every time [they] set sail (*lit.* [they] **launch**), it is the exalted ship HMS Jaguni (*lit.* Great Kingdom) [which is protected by the priestess Akeshino (OSJS 218c), that [they] launch].' (OS 13.#765)

### 1.3.4 Vowel-Root–Final Verbs (Lower Bigrade)

| | Stem | Gloss | MZ | RY | GER/PRFV | SS/RT | IZ/MR |
|---|---|---|---|---|---|---|---|
| (17a) ···*kʰi-* | {ʔakʰi-} | 'open' VT | | $ʔakʰi_{RY}$ | $ʔakʰi_{RY}$-*t°i* | $ʔakʰi·r-u_{RT}$ 'dawn' VI | ....-$ʔakʰi·r-i_{MR}$ |
| | {ʔáki-} | 'open' VT, 'brighten' VI | *ʔakíra* | *ʔakî-i* | $ʔakí_{RY}$-*ti* | *ʔakí-y-u-N*/ *ʔakí-y-ur-u* | *ʔakíri*/ *ʔakíree* |

Lower Bigrades, again, are actually a historical category, since the historically previous final vowel of the stem of this category, *ë*, a low vowel, merged with the mid vowel *e* = *[ɛ], of the Middle Bigrades, creating a (let us call it) Neo-Middle-Bigrade category, which then raised all at once to a high-vowel category that was separate from the *palatal* front vowel category that already existed for monosyllables, at any rate. It is convenient to call this particular set "Lower" to distinguish the height of its original vowel, as to the "Middle" of the previous examples, even though they are synchonically members of the same ···*i*-ending category.

(17a)   OOk {ʔakʰi- 'open' VT}

RY:   たうの、みち、ᴧ        あけわちへ、         |
       ta u no , mi ti , ᴧ    a ke wa ti pe ,      |
       *tʰoo-nu, myic°yi-∅*   $ʔakʰi_{RY}$-*wa-c°yee*
       China-GEN, route-DO   open_{RY}-EX-GER/PRFV
       '[Tedokon Ōhyā][59] opened the route to China' (OS 13.#761)

GER:  おやぢ゛やうᴧ あけて、   | わん、ᴧ いれ˃        |
       o ya di* ya u ᴧ a ke te,  | wa N , ᴧ i re "      |
       *ʔuya-dzoo-∅  ʔakʰi-t°i     waN-∅ ʔyi̠ri-ri*
       EX-gate-DO    open-GER    me-DO let.enter-MR
       'Open the great gate and let me enter!' (OS 17.#1180)

---

59   This interpretation is due to Ikemiya (2015: 234).

# VERBS 221

SS/RT: よが、、 あける やに /
yo ga , ` a ke ru ya ni /
*yu-ga* **ʔakʰi·r-u** *yoo-nyi*
night-SUB **brighten·4GE-RT** similitude-ADV
"[When we humbly look upon [our lord's] face, it is as brilliant] as the dawning (*lit.* it is [as brilliant] as the night brightening)" (OS 7.#385) [trans. to J by Hokama (2000a: 268b)]

MR: おしあけれ よ、、 ぢ゙やうの、 しゆ、 /
o si a ke re yo , ` di゙ ya u no ` si yu , /
*ʔus-yi-ʔakʰi·r-i* *yoo* *dzyoo-nu* *syuu*
push-RY-**open-MR** SFP gate-GEN keeper
'Push open [the sliding doors of Sēfā Shrine], Gatekeeper!' (OS 7.#349)

| | Stem | Gloss | MZ | RY | GER/PRFV | SS/RT | IZ/MR |
|---|---|---|---|---|---|---|---|
| (17b) ···*si*- | {yusi-} | 'pull.closer, conquer' | *yusi·r-a* | *yusi*₍RY₎ | *yusi*₍RY₎-*t゚i* | *yusi·r-u* RT | *yusiri*₍IZ₎ / *yusiri*₍MR₎ |
| | {yusí-} | 'pull.closer, advise' | *yusí·r-a* | *yúsi-* | *yusí*₍RY₎-*ti* | *yusí-y-u-N* SS/ *yusí-y-ur-u* RT | *yusíri*₍IZ₎ / *yusíree*₍MR₎ |

This is another example of the Lower Bigrade subcategory.

(17b) OOk {yusi- 'pull.closer, summon; conquer' VT; 'come' VI}

MZ: やまと、 いくさ、、 よせら や /
ya ma to , i ku sa , ` yo se ra ya /
*yamatʰu-∅* *ʔyi̯kʰ゚usa-∅* *yusi·r-a* *yaa*
Japan-GEN army-DO **conquer·4GE-MZ** SFP
'Let's conquer the Yamato forces!'[60] (OS 20.#1364)

---

60 Both OSJS and Hokama (2000b: 323b) take ⟨yo se ra ya⟩ as if it meant ˣ*yusi·r-a-ba* 'if [the Japanese forces] come', but 'come' here is a real stretch semantically, and there is no sound basis for interpreting ˣ-*ya* as equivalent to -*ba* 'if'. There appears to be no softening of T/C to glides as early as OOk. Thus -*a*, while nominally MZ, is strictly speaking IA. There is no other MZ for this word.

RY: あまみきよは、、　　　よせわちへ　　　　　／
a ma mi ki yo pa , ∧　yo se wa ti pe　　　／
*ʔamamyi#kʰyu-Qpº a* **yusi-wa-cºyi**
Amamiko-DO　　　　**summon**<sub>RY</sub>-EAV-GER
'[The Sun Deity] summoned *Amamiko*, and ...' (OS 10.#512)

GER: うらうしは、、　　　よせて　　　　　　／
u ra u si pa , ∧　　yo se te　　　　　／
*ʔura-ʔura-Qpº a*　**yusi-tº ee**
village-village-DO　**gather**<sub>VT</sub>-GER.PRFV
'T[he reserve forces from t]he whole realm: [the King,] having gathered
[them] up ...'[61] (OS 1.#34)

SS: せいくさ、、　　　よせるまじ*　　　　　　　／
se i ku sa , ∧　　yo se ru ma zi*　　　　／
*si-ʔyikºusa-∅*　　**yusi·r-umazyi**
spirit-army-SUB　**allow.approach·4GE-NEG.IA**
'The spirited (= King's) army must not allow [the enemy] to approach.'
(OS 12.#721)

RT: しま、　　よせる、、　つゞみの、、　　ある、　あぢ　／
si ma ∧　　yo se ru , ∧　tu ''' mi no , ∧　a ru ∧　a di　／
*syima-∅*　**yusi·r-u**　*cºidzimyi-nu*　*ʔar-u*　*ʔadzyi*
region-DO　**attract-RT**　hand.drum-DO　have-RT　lord
'The lord who has[62] a hand-drum that gathers villages [under his con-
trol]' (OS 19.#1295)

IZ: かみゞ†ゝす、、　　　うらの、かず*、　／ いのり、やゑて、、
ka mi '''† '' su , ∧　　u ra no ∧ ka zu* , ／ i no ri , ya we te , ∧
*kʰamyi-ˌgamyi-si*　*ʔura-nu-kʰazi*　　*ʔyiˌnur-y-ayiˌ-tº i*
{priestess-priestess}-KP village-GEN-no.　pray-meet-GER

---

61　TOS (#34 n. 21) notes widespread disparities in writing "⟨u si⟩". It only makes sense, however, as a copyist's error for a *hiragana* morph ditto mark to be read out as *ʔura-ʔura* '[all
the villages in] the bays/inlets' = 'the whole realm'. OSJS (70a) and Hokama (2000a: 34–35)
simply take this compound as ⟨u ra '' ''⟩ *ʔura-ʔura*.

62　As in J, when *ʔar-* has two (not necessarily overt) structural subjects, one of which is a
functional object (here, 'drum'), it means 'have', not 'there to be'.

VERBS

よせれ　　　　　/
yo se re　　　/
*yusi·r-i*
gather·4GE-IZ
'At every village, priestesses pray together[63] and send off [the hearts of the villagers to the Kingdom's center].' (OS 6.#333)

MR:　あぢ†、かず†が、　てもち、　　　　/ 中ぐ゛すく∧
　　　a di†, ka zu† ga,　te mo ti,　　/ NAKA gu゙ su ku ∧
　　　*ʔadzyi-kʰazi-ga*　*tʰi-muc°-yi*$_{NOM}$-∅　*nakʰagusik°u*-∅
　　　lord-no.-SUB　　　hand-hold-RY-DO　Nakagusuku-IO
　　　よせれ　　　　　/
　　　yo se re　　　/
　　　*yusi·r-i*
　　　gather·4GE-MR
'Gather each[64] lord's treasure to Nakagusuku!' (OS 2.#54)

### 1.4　*Irregular Verbs*

There are three categories of irregular verbs. The first two, *k*-type and *s*-type, each have only one member (with the latter having a *z*-initial set of allomorphs used for verbalizing verbal nouns, such as *soo-zi-t°i* 'considering'). The last, the *r*-type, has several, which take a RY *-yi* SS instead of the usual *-u* SS. Tables and examples follow.

In addition there is one more irregular category, comprised of {ʔuwa{r/s}+} and {+yuwa{r/s}+}, an exalting verb and auxiliary, the latter of which is covered extensively in Ch. 7 §14.

---

63　The J translation (MJ) '*aite*' = 'together' for *-ayi-t°i*, favored by OSJS (62b) and continued by Hokama (2000a: 228b), is perhaps wrong, but a better translation does not readily present itself. The etymology of *ayi, t°i* is more likely *\*-aye-te* than *\*-ayi-te*, although the latter cannot be dismissed as a Literary holdover, just, in fact, as *aite* in the MJ texts that comes down to us is a Literary holdover, with the spoken MJ language already having split off forms that would result in Western J *oo-te*. It is, however, possible that *-ayi-t°i* is in the end the VT 'puts together', i.e. 'bundles (the prayers)'.

64　*-kʰazi-ga/nu* has now appeared a number of times, typically translated '*goto no*' = '(of) each (one)', grammaticalized from 'number', with morpheme boundary at its head having replaced word boundary, thus, through operation of YGR, having changed otherwise-occurring *dz* (*\*##|kʰadzi₂|*) to *z* (|...-*kʰazi*₂₊ₙ).

| | Stem | Gloss | MZ | RY | GER/PRFV | SS/RT | IZ/MR |
|---|---|---|---|---|---|---|---|
| (18) ⋯k- | {kʰuⁿ-} | 'come' | kʰuu- | k-°yi- | k-°yi-c°yi | k-°ur-u | k-°ur-i_{IZ}- / kʰuu_{MR}- |
| | {kuⁿ-ⱼ} | 'come' | _kuu-ⱼ_ | _c-yiiⱼ_ | Q-cyiⱼ | c-y-uu-Nⱼ/ c-y-uu-ruⱼ | kuuⱼ / kuu-waⱼ ~ k-waaⱼ |

(18)　　OOk {kʰuⁿ-[65] 'come' VI}

MZ:　　かみの、　　もゝぢやらの、　　／　おもて、ᴧ　さうぜ†て、ᴧ
　　　　ka mi no,　mo " di ya ra no,　／　o mo te,ᴧ　sa u ze† te,ᴧ
　　　　kʰamyi-nu　mumu#dzyara-nu　　ʔumu-t°i　soo+zi-t°i
　　　　North-GEN　100-lords-SUB　　　think-GER　scheme-GER
　　　　こうば†　　　　／
　　　　ko u ba†　　　／
　　　　kʰuu_{MZ}-ba
　　　　come_{MZ}-COND
　　　　'If All the Lords in the North **should** come [and attack], having considered and schemed, …'[66] (OS 2.#47)

RY:　　まはへ、ᴧ　　　　かぜ、ᴧ　　おちへ、ᴧ　きより、　　　　　　　　／
　　　　ma pa pe,ᴧ　　　ka ze,ᴧ　　o ti pe,ᴧ　ki yo ri,　　　　　　　／
　　　　ma-pʰayi-∅　　　kʰazi-∅　　ʔu-c°yi　　k°-y-uur-**yi**
　　　　true-South-APPO　wind-SUB　push-GER　come-[RY-SE-RY/SS]_{PROG}
　　　　'The true South [tail-]wind **has** come blowing.' (OS 13.#902)

---

65　The superscripted morphophonemic mark {…ⁿ…} (here part of {kʰuⁿ}) indicates a floating abstract length marker, which is free to cross morpheme boundaries when actual words are cobbled together: {kʰuⁿ+yi+wur+yi 'come+RY+SE+SS'} → k°-**y.uur.yi** in the main text below, where the length marker has crossed two morpheme boundaries to create -uur-, which would otherwise be -ur-. Compare mac°-y.**ur.yi** 'be waiting', with no mark.

66　Here is Chris Drake's translation of this song in its entirety (Omoro Kanshō 30: 13):
　　　Famed lord of Nakagusuku castle
　　　if the many chieftains in the north
　　　scheming, come and attack you
　　　use rock, use iron
　　　with your weapons drive them back
　　　widely renowned lord of Nakagusuku.

VERBS 225

GER:
さしきから、、 もだいきよ、、 きちゑ /
sa si ki ka ra ,, mo da i ki yo ,, ki ti we /
*sasyik°yi-₁kʰara* *mudee-kʰyu-∅* *k°-yi-c°yi*
Sasiki-from flourish_EX-person-SUB come-GER
'An honorable[67] personage **came** from Sashiki and ...' (OS 19.#1287)

RT:
しまが† 、 よて、、 くる、 や69に /
si ma ga† , yo te ,, ku ru , ya ni /
*syima-ga* *yu-t°i* *k°-ur-u* *yoo-nyi*
village-SUB approach-GER come-SE[68]-RT like-ADV
'As the villages **come** closer, ...' (OS 16.#1131)

IZ:
なおぢ、きよが＊、 / しよりかち、、 くれば＊、 /
na o di , ki yo ga＊ , / si yo ri ka ti ,, ku re ba＊ , /
*nawu#dzyi-kʰyu-ga* *syiyuryi-kʰac°yi* *k°-ur-i-ba*
pacify-personage-SUB Shuri-IO come-SE-IZ-COND
'If a pacifier **comes** to Shuri, ...' (OS 5.#266)

MR:
くめの、 きみはいや、 / まゑに、かち、、 よて、
ku me no , ki mi pa i ya , / ma we ni , ka ti ,, yo te ,
*k°umi-nu* *k°yiм.bayi-ya* *mayi-nyi.kʰac°yi* *yu-t°i*
Kume-GEN PN-TOP front-IO approach-GER
こう、 /
ko u , /
*kʰuu*
come_MR
'O Kimihae of Kume [Island], **approach** toward us!' (OS 11.#1409)

| | Stem | Gloss | MZ | RY | GER/PRF | SS/RT | IZ/MR |
|---|---|---|---|---|---|---|---|
| (19) ···s- | {si-} | 'do' | *εi-r-a···* | *s-yi* | *s-yi-c°yi* | *s-ir-u* (RT) | *s-ir-i* (IZ) |
| | *sV́-* | 'do' | *s-á···* | *s-yíi* | *Q-syí* | *s-y-ú-N* (SS)/ *s-y-ur-u* (RT) | *Q-syí* (MR) /∅-*syé-e* |

---

67    OSJS (325b) notes association of ⟨mo ⁽ⁿ⁾ta i⟩ as a BE with Sashiki.
68    This SE is an archaic remnant from PJ, not formed with RY within pRk.
69    See Ch. 2 §6.1 for a brief discussion of ⟨ya⟩ *yoo*.

(19)     OOk {si- 'do' VT}

MZ:     げ†お、くなべ ∧     せらに                /
        ge† o , ku na be ∧    se ra ni              /
        *giwu-k°unabi-∅*[70]   ***si·r-an-yi***
        spiritual-match-DO  do·**4GE-NEG**<sub>SS</sub>-QP
        '[Why] don't we have a spiritual match?' (OS 19.#1297)

RY:     いべの、      いのり、∧    しよわちへ、      /
        i be no ,    i no ri , ∧   si yo wa ti pe ,   /
        *ʔyibi-nu*     *ʔyi¸nuryi-∅ s-y-uwa-c°yi*
        sacred-GEN   prayer-DO   do-RY-EAV-GER
        '**Carrying** out the prayer of the sacred shrine,'[71] (OS 3.#101)

GER:    くに、うち∧しちへす、∧                    もどりよれ              /
        ku ni , u ti ∧ si ti pe su , ∧                mo do ri yo re          /
        *k°unyi#ʔuc°-yi-s-yi-c°yi-si*                *mudur-y.ur-i*
        country-strike-RY<sub>NOM</sub>-**do**-RY-GER-KP   return-RY.SE<sub>PROG</sub>-IZ
        '**Only once having** conquered the lands **shall you** be returning!'
        (OS 1.#35)

RT:     かみしもの、∧      みもの∧する、∧                きよら     や  /
        ka mi si mo no , ∧  mi mo no ∧ su ru , ∧            ki yo ra    ya  /
        *kʰamyi.syimu-nu*   *myi-munu-s-ir-u-∅*           *k°yura*    *yaa*
        [everyone-SUB      admiration-do-**SE-RT**<sub>NOM</sub>]-SUB  beautiful  SFP
        '[The **one that** everyone admires] is beautiful.' (OS 2.#59)

SS/RT:  all the ⟨su ru⟩ forms are structurally RT; there are no structurally SS
        forms

IZ:     ゆわい事、∧すれば*
        yu wa i KOTO , ∧ su re ba*
        *yuwe-e-¸gutu-s-ir-i-ba*
        celebrate-RY-event-do-**SE-IZ**-COND
        'if we do a celebratory event' = 'if we have a celebration' (OS 5.#253)

---

70    The form *k°uⁿabi-* is of course related to OJ/MJ *kurabë* '(id.)', but it is an example of *r ~ n*
      and *n ~ r* alternations, which have occurred in small numbers, and quite sporadically.

71    Recall that labials do not normally undergo PP.

VERBS 227

| | Stem | Gloss | MZ | RY | GER/PRFV | SS/RT | IZ/MR |
|---|---|---|---|---|---|---|---|
| (20) ···r- | {ʔar-} | 'exist; have' | ʔar-a- | ʔa(r)-y(i)- | ʔa-tʼee | ʔar-yi (SS) ʔar-u (RT) | ʔar-i- (IZ) ʔar-i (MR) |
| | {ʔar-ˌ} | 'exist; have' | nee(ra)-ˌ | ʔa-y(i)-ˌ | ʔa-ti(-)ˌ | ʔa-Nˌ (SS) ʔar-uˌ (RT) | ʔar-eeˌ (IZ) ʔar-iˌ/...-eeˌ (MR) |

(20)   OOk {aru 'exist' VI}

MZ:  しま世の、ˌ、       あらぎやめ、、ˌ  ちよわれ   /
     si ma YO no ,ˌ    a ra gi ya me ,ˌ ti yo wa re   /
     *syima-yu-nu*       *ʔar-**a**-gyami*   *cʼyuwar-i*
     country-era-SUB exist-**IA**-TRM   reign_EX-MR
     'May you reign throughout this epoch.' (OS 8.#279)

RY:  めづ*らしやど*、ˌ    ありよる、        /
     me du* ra si ya do* ,ˌ a ri yo ru ,     /
     *midzira-sy-a-du*      *ʔar-**y**.ur-u*
     rare-AA-NDS-KP       SE-**RY**.SE_PROG-RT
     'Rare *indeed* is it!' (OS 9.#508)

The entire form is an adjective that has been focused. In such a case the elements after the focused portion ····*du* are arrayed on a dummy stative verb, in the case of adjectives, {ar+ 'SE'} = {ar+ 'exist'}.

RY:  めづらしや、ˌ    げに、ˌ あよる        /
     me du ra si ya ,ˌ ge ni ,ˌ a yo ru     /
     *midzira-sy-a*        *ginyi*[72] *ʔa∅-y.ur-u*
     rare-ADS-NDS        truly   SE-**RY**.SE_PROG-RT
     'It is truly rare.' (OS 3.#94)

GER:  いきやる、ˌ    さうず*、ˌ        あて      が*、/
      i ki ya ru ,ˌ   sa u zu* ,ˌ        a te      ga* , /
      *ʔyikʼyar-u*     *soozi-∅*         *ʔa-tʼee*      *ga*
      what.kind.of-RT sacred.waters-SUB  have-**PRFV** SKP

---

72   This is an example of the use of adverbs in constructions that would normally have taken focus *kakari* particles, complete with RT *musubi* endings.

くもこ ∧ より、いでたる、 /
ku mo ko ∧ yo ri , i de ta ru , /
*k°umu-kʰu-∅* *yur-yi-ʔidʑyi̯-t°ar-u-∅*
golden-one-DO select-RY-out-PRFT-RT~NOM~-DO
'What kind of sacred waters[73] **did** [Kimiyoshi's deputy Terukumo] have [for cleansing] the jewel—the one she picked out?'[74,75] (OS 11.#572)

SS: ほこる、で†﹅、∧ げに、∧ あり / そこる、で†﹅、∧
po ko ru , de† " , ∧ ge ni , ∧ a ri / so ko ru , de " , ∧
*pʰukʰur-u-di-t°i* *gi-nyi* *ʔar-yi* *sukʰur-u-di-t°i*
be.glad-SS-QT-GER true-ADV STAT-SS be.overjoyed-SS-QT-GER
だに、∧ あり /
da ni , ∧ a ri /
*da-nyi* *ʔar-yi*
certain-ADV STAT-SS
'Saying [he]'s glad, [that]'s true, saying [he]'s overjoyed, [that]'s for certain.' (OS 1.#40)

RT: かぐらの、 げ†おの ∧内る、∧ かに、∧ ある、/
ka gu ra no , ge† o no ∧ UTI ru , ∧ ka ni , ∧ aru , /
*kʰagura-nu* *giwu-nu-ʔuc°yi-ru* *kʰa-nyi* *ʔar-u*
heaven-GEN [Gyō-no-Uchi]~PIN~-KP thus-ADV **be-RT**
'Heaven's Gyō no Uchi precinct it *is* that is thus.' (OS 12.#691)

IZ: たびに、∧ たつ、∧ あんは、/ くれが†てや、∧
ta bi ni , ∧ ta tu , ∧ a N pa , / ku re ga† te ya , ∧
*tʰabyi-nyi* *tʰac-°i* *ʔaN-wa* *k°uri-gat°i[76]-ya*
journey-IO leave-RT I-TOP cannot.part-COP

---

73  Recall the treatment of this word in Ch. 2 § 5.4, fn. 65, along with the Yotsu-Gana Distinction in the same section.

74  OS 21.#1457, to which this omoro is appended in slightly different spellings, has ⟨i di pe⟩ and ⟨i di we⟩ = *ʔyidʑyi-*, suggesting that the non-PP spelling was morphophonemically based. This is why we chose *ʔyidʑyi-*, not *ʔyi̯di-*.

75  The lexeme *yur-yi-ʔyidʑyi-* 'pick out' (reversal of transitivity unexplained, but cf. the use of *-owaru* (VI) 'finish' in NJ put onto verbs of either transitivity) is seen in the word in both versions of this omoro, and in *yur-yi-ʔyidʑyi-kʰu-gani* 'priceless (= carefully picked out) hairpin (*lit.* 'gold') [as worn by priestesses]'. The lexeme *yur-* 'choose; pick out' does not appear in either OGJ or RGJ; however OKDJ (725b) has MOk ⟨yori-masaru⟩ 'choose and take up in a splendid fashion' (from the Koyō [Archaic Songs]); cf. MJ *yor-* '(id.)'.

76  There is no exactly corresponding collocation that we know of in NOk, but here are two

VERBS         229

あれど゛*も、         /

a re do* mo ,      /

*?ar-i-du-mu*

SE-IZ-though-even

'Even though I who am leaving on my journey **may** find it hard to part,
...' (OS 13.#858)

MR:    あよ、ぢ†よく、∧    げに、∧    あれ   /

       a yo , di† yo ku , ∧ ge ni , ∧   a re    /

       *?ayu-dzyuu-k°u*    *gi-nyi*   *?ar-i*

       liver-strong-ADV   true-ADV   be-**MR**

       'Your will, keep it strong, truly!' = '*Do* master your fortitude!' / '*Do* stay
strong of will!' (OS 1.#33)

## 2      History of Conjugation Merger: *ra-gyō yodan-ka*

### 2.1     *Upper 2G, Middle 2G, Lower 2G in Proto-Japonic and Their Reflexes in OJ and OOk*

Just as it turns out that Old Japanese Upper Monogrades subdivide into two
categories when the uncategorizable set is put aside ...:[77,78]

---

     phonological lookalikes that have the same semantic denotation: *mac-yi-kaɴtii* 'hard to
wait' (OGJ 308b); *wakari-gatana-sa* 'hard to part' (OGJ 190a). Note that the latter is at least
overtly different from a supposed *-gata-* 'difficult to', which, however, turns out not to exist:
the equivalent form is *-guri-sya-ɴ*.

77    The OJ verb *p[i]-u* 'dry up; ebb' (JDB 629ab) is not yet an UIG verb.

78    Uncategorizable: 1a. *i-ru* 'cast (metal)' (JDB 106d); 1b. *i-ru* 'pour'; the earliest attestation is
*Ō-Kagami* (*Ōbunsha Kogo Jiten*)—we assume that it is an offshoot of *i-ru* 'cast (molten
metal)'; 2. *i-ru* 'shoot' (JDB 106d); *i-y[-e]-u* 'get shot' is a passive, and yields no further
insight; 3. *ni-ru* 'appear the same' (JDB 550cd); cf. *nOr-u* 'look (a)like' (JDB 570a; most given
examples are *nOreri*); *-nōsu* '(it is )like', an Easternism for Central *-nasu* '(id.)' (564d–565a);
the UIG verb *ni-ru* is clearly related to the 4G verb *nor- < *nör- '(id )'* (JDB 570a); 4. *ni-ru* 'boil
s/t' (JDB 550d); also *ni-y[e]-u* 'get boiled' with no separate listing, but mentioned under *iyu
= i-y[-e]-u* 'get shot' (qv); 5. *wi-ru* 'lead, take (s/o) along' (JDB 826ab) no statement is made
concerning the provenance of this verb; 6. *wi-ru* 'sit' (< *[wi-]u*) (JDB 825d–826a) 'a. sits;
b. stays; c. runs aground; d. (conscious being) exists, (cloud, mist) lays over the land'; frequently attached to RY of another verb; JDB has a discussion of a passage in the chapter
on Emperor Sujin in *Nihon Shoki* that has the form *u* that clearly has the meaning of this
verb, from which it is surmised that *wi-ru* is a shift to Upper 1G from Upper 2G *u*, i.e. from
*[wi-]u* or *[w[i-]]u* (ibid. 826a).

- With invariable A-type vowel:

 *kî-ru* [kʸiɾu] 'wear (clothing / a hat)' (JDB 249d–250a); *kî-* + *-as-u* → *kês-u* [kʸesu] 'wears_EX', but pRk *\*kos-* \*[kʰɔs] 'dress (s/o)'[79]
 *mî-ru* [mʸiɾu] 'see, look, determine' (JDB 718d–719a)

- With invariable B-type vowel:

 *mï-ru* 'revolve'; but *ta-m[ï]-u* 'revolve, rotate' (JDB 447ab; also *-damï* 'around-' [id. 447a]) shows a former and recent Upper 2G \**m[ï]-u* 'revolve, rotate' (JDB 720a *mu*); presumably related to *mö-töpor-u* 'go around; gad about' (JDB 742c), *mö-töpos-u* 'cause to go around' (JDB 742b), *mötöpos-i* 'a circular ornament' (id.), though JDB attempts no linkage with *mo-t⁽ⁿ⁾or-u* 'turn against protocol, go against; become twisted' (SNKDJ: NSK, *Nihon Ryōi-Ki*)

... so, too, Old Japanese Upper Bigrades subdivide into three subcategories[80] when the members of this group that pair up with Quadrigrades of a different transitivity are properly compared. Within Ryukyuan the PJ sets equivalent to the OJ *ï* (~ *u*) Upper Bigrades and the OJ *ï* (~ *ô*) Upper Bigrades merge into a pRk Upper Bigrade group. The third set, equivalent to the OJ Upper Bigrade group, those verbs with OJ *ï* (~ *ö*) [< pre-OJ *\*ë* (~ *\*ö*)], is comprised of one last subgroup, with a significant number of items, and this group merges with the PRk Lower Bigrades (↑UBG with LBG), as in the second of the two sets below. Let us look at the data:

1st Superset: OJ

| †††UBG | *tuk* | *ï* | - | | 'becomes used up' (VI) |
|---|---|---|---|---|---|
| | *tuk* | *ū* | - | *s-* | 'does to the utmost' (VT) |
| ††UBG | *sug* | *ï* | - | | 'goes by (a place); (time) goes by; dies; etc.' (VI) |
| | *sug* | *ō̂* | - | *s-* | 'passes (time); finishes (it); goes beyond; etc.' (VT) |

The PRk forms are the same, *\*tukï-* ~ *\*tuku-s-*, *\*sugï-* ~ *\*sugô-s-*.

---

79  About 'wear' and 'dress': cf. OSJS ⟨ko se - te⟩ *kʰu-si-tˀi* 'dressing' (OSJS 158a; OS 10.#525); NOk *kusyí-y-u-N* 'dress s/o; clothe s/o as a present' (OGJ 342a); the word is instantiated throughout Ryukyuan. More on *\*kose-*: Ch. 7 §2.4.

80  Cf. e.g. Pellard 2013, Serafim [2007: 473], Hattori 1976.
     In the discussion in this section we will distinguish among three subtypes of proto-Japonic "Upper Bi-Grade" verbs, signified by appended single, double, and triple upward-pointing arrows. (The set with the single arrow is actually UBG in (O)J only, and in fact descends from the Proto-Japonic Middle Bi-Grade verb set.) The more arrows, the rarer the number of verb pairs in the set.

VERBS 231

2nd Superset:

| †UBG | ök | *ï* | - | | 'arises₁' (VI) |
| | ök | *ȫ* | - | *r* - | 'arises₂' (VI)[81] |
| | ök | *ȫ* | - | *s* - | 'raises' (VT) |
| LBG | ag | *ë* | - | | 'raises' (VT) |
| | ag | *ā* | - | *r* - | 'rises' (VI) |

The PRk forms differ, *\*ökë-* ~ *\*ökö-s-* and *\*agë-* ~ *\*aga-r-* (i.e. PRK *\*ë, \*ë*, not OJ *\*ï, \*ë*).

Because the three- and two-arrow Upper-Bigrade classes, being so small, and semantically unimportant, are missing from the textual data, it has been commonly assumed that "all" Upper Bigrades merged with the Lower Bigrades, but if that were true, it would not be possible to account for the data readily available in the modern languages, including in Shuri. But one of the most frequent verbs in OS according to token count is 'descend', referring to deities descending to earth, and to their possessing shamans. This verb (OJ *öri-* < *\*örï-*) is invariably spelled with ⟨o re⟩ *ʔuri-* [ʔurɪ], not ⟨o ri⟩ *ʔuryi-* [ʔurʸi]. And, sure enough, it is a member of the one-arrow Upper-Bigrade subgroup OJ *ï ~ ö* < PJ *\*öî ~ ö* (cf. OJ *örȫs-*, OOk ⟨o ro su⟩ *ʔurusi* [OS 7.#357]).

### 2.2 From the Pre-OOk Verb System to the OOk Verb System

The Pre-OOk general pattern is as follows: In the paradigm of the pre-OOk bigrade and monograde verbs, several forms—those with *\*r* just before their final vowel—looked as if they were forms of quadrigrade *r*-type verbs. Because of both token and type frequency of these look-alike forms and their quadrigrade "partners", language acquirers misperceived the category of the vowel-ending stems as ending in the consonant *\*r* instead, in effect increasing the number of forms—and ultimately the membership—of the *r*-type 4G class. This has been called *ra-gyō yodan-ka* ラ行四段化 '*r*-type quadrigradization', a type of change that Anttila (1989: 196–203) refers to as an "abductive change." See Table 6.4:[82]

---

81 The Infinitive = RY of *ökör-*, i.e. *\*ökörî* (OJ *ököri*), may well be the locus of analogical change from *\*[əkəɾʸi] > \*[əkəyi] > [əkəy] = *ökï-*, with variable stem shape, either *-u(r[u/e] ...)* or *-ï(#/te/n-...)*. This may just take care of at least the *ï* (~ *ö*) set, reducing the number, both of tokens and types, of BG verbs.

82 Concerning *\*age·re* in Column 3 of Table 6.4, for "*\*ʔagere*" IZ vs MR, the MR changeover would have been facilitated if it were not to have resulted in a merger of the forms of IZ and MR right off the bat; therefore we will assume that at the time of the quadrigradiza-

232                          CHAPTER 6

TABLE 6.4    Shift from bigrade to quadrigrade

| | | Column 1 | Column 2 | Column 3 | Column 4 |
|---|---|---|---|---|---|
| | | older 2G → | newer "2G"=1G → | quasi-4G ≈ | true 4G |
| | | 'raise ...' VT | 'raise ...' VT | 'raise ...' VT | 'rise ...' VI |
| *a* | MZ | \*\**ag e₁-nu* | \**age₁-nu* | \**age·r-anu* | \**agar-anu* |
| *b* | RY | \*\**ag e₁ (-)* | \**age₁* | \**age(·r-yi)* | \**agar-yi* |
| *c* | GER | \*\**ag e₁-te* | \**age₁-te* | \**age({· **r-yi**/· **Q**}-)te* | \**aga({· **r-yi**/· **Q**}-)te* |
| *d* | SS | \*\**ag-u₂* | \**age₁·r-u* | \**age·ru* | \**agaru* |
| *e* | RT | \*\**ag-u₂ru* | \**age₁·r-u* | \**age·ru* | \**agaru* |
| *f* | IZ | \*\**ag-u₂re* | \**age₁·r-e* | \**age·re* | \**agare* |
| *g* | MR | \*\**ag e₁-ro* | \**age₁-ro/·r-o* | \**age·re* | \**agare* |

First, note the forms that had the vowel \*\**u* (that is, Column-1 *def*) instead of the vowel \*\**e* (that is, Column-1 *abcg*) of the other forms.

Bigrade verb forms with \*\**u*:

| | | Column 1 |
|---|---|---|
| | | older 2G |
| *d* | SS | \*\**ag u* |
| *e* | RT | \*\**ag u ru* |
| *f* | IZ | \*\**ag u re* |

tion, there was still a distinction between type A and B vowels; thus: PJ { \**ʔagë·r-ë* 'raise IZ' ↔ \**ʔagë·r-ê* 'raise MR'}. In terms of the orthography that we have been using, these should then be written { \**ʔage·r-ɛ* \*[ʔãgɛɾɛ] ↔ \**ʔage·r-ye* \*[ʔãgɛɾʸe]}. In broad outline we follow Thorpe [1983: 233–234] in his phoneticization of the A :: B distinction, as follows:

| | [-ro, -ba] | [-ro, +ba] | [+ro, +ba] |
|---|---|---|---|
| [+hi] | i = [ʸi] | ï (our [ɪ]) | u = [u] |
| [-hi, -lo] | e = [ɛ] | ə = [ə] | o = [⁽ʷ⁾o] |
| [+lo] | ë = [ɛ̈] | a | ö = [ɔ] |

Thorpe values: i = [i], ï = [ï], e = [e], ë = [æ], o = [o], ö = [ɔ], ə = [ə].

VERBS                                                                                                      233

TABLE 6.5    Shift from 2G to 1G verbs in pre-OOk

|   |     | Column 1 | | | → | Column 2 | | | |
|---|-----|------|---|----|---|------|---|----|---|
|   |     | older 2G | | | | newer "2G" = 1G | | | |
| a | MZ  | **ag | e | nu | | *ag | e | nu | |
| b | RY  | **ag | e |    | | *ag | e |    | ←remains in OS, but with *e [ɛ] > i [ɪ] |
| c | GER | **ag | e | te | | *ag | e | te | ←remains in OS, but with *e [ɛ] > i [ɪ] |
| d | SS  | **ag | u |    | | *ag | e | ru | |
| e | RT  | **ag | u | ru | | *ag | e | ru | |
| f | IZ  | **ag | u | re | | *ag | e | re | |
| g | MR  | **ag | e | ro | | *ag | e | ro | |

It appears from OS data, i.e. of the *Column-1bc* type, that the first reanalysis must have been that in favor of monogradization (i.e. 2G → 1G), and here high-token-frequency 1G verbs like *myi(i)-ru* 'see' or *kyi(i)-ru* 'put (clothing) on' with non-alternating bases, i.e. *myi(i)-* and *kyi(i)-*, never ˣ{*m-yi-* ~ ˣˣ*m-u-*} or ˣ{*k-yi-* ~ ˣˣ*k-u-*}, play a pivotal role. The analogy is of the proportional type, i.e. *myiite* : *myiiru* :: *agete* : ∅. Put verbally that is something like, "*myiite* is to *myiiru* as *agete* is to *blank*, and *blank* is *ageru*." Typically this will be an abductive change performed by a first-language learner, and it will occur many many times before it finally takes hold and actually becomes a new part of the living language (Anttila [1989: 196–203]).

The new set after monogradization, then, would have been as in Table 6.5.

Thorpe (1983: §7.3[238 ff.]) claims that bigrade verbs never existed in Ryukyuan. There are only two pieces of evidence to counter that claim, but they are in our estimation (barely) sufficient to do so. Those two are forms with *…ur…*, thus at least nominally assuring bigrade (*e/*u*) status, namely ⟨a tu ru⟩ *ʔa-c°-ir-u* 'that there is/are' < *that there has/have been / that there has/have come to be'[83] (OSJS 38ab), and the single instance of ⟨to yo mi yo

---

83    OSJS (38ab) may possibly be pressing semantic interpretation in what follows:

"Sonzai dōshi ⟨a ri⟩ no tanshuku-kei ⟨a⟩ ni kanryō no imi o arawasu jo-dōshi ⟨tu ru⟩ no tsuita katachi. … ⟨tu ru⟩ no imi kinō wa, kako kara no kanryō henka o arawashite-ori, kokugo no imi kinō to hobo onaji de aru."

'The form in which the auxiliary verb ⟨tu ru⟩, which expresses the meaning of completion, has attached to the abbreviated form ⟨a⟩ of the verb of existence ⟨a ri⟩. … The semantic function of [OOk] ⟨tu ru⟩ is to express a shift involving completion from the past, and is almost the same as the semantic function of th[at of th]e National Language'.

However, both OSJS ('aru') and their KKKS ("'aru' nari") sources simply gloss it as '(there to) be'.

$\overline{\text{tu ru}})^{84}$ *t<sup>h</sup>uyum-y-u-c°-ir-u* (OS 7.#371) which stand out by their singularity. The type frequency of *ʔac°iru* is just one, and the token frequency is 39. It would appear that there has been quite a semantic shift in the use of this fossilized form, which is further discussed in Ch. 7 §10. It is used as a kind of emphatic locative quasi-particle, as its use in only a single form and in the sequence Place(-*nyi*)-*ʔac°iru* strongly suggests. It should be noted that it is not the matrix verb that retains the RT irregularity, but rather the auxiliary {*#tee-}, where its old fused *{+tee#wor-} → *-*t-ur-* > -*c°-ir-*. This form predates a newer formulation, used as a perfective/progressive, using the same morpheme sequence, which becomes e.g. Nakijin -*t-ur-* [t<sup>h</sup>uɾ] and Shuri -*t-oor-*. While it is not impossible to borrow auxiliaries, which are bound forms, it appears to be somewhat less likely than borrowing independent lexical items, *unless the structures are highly congruent* (Thomason and Kaufmann [1988: 73]).

The highly significant semantic shift of *ʔac°iru* and the re-invention of a newer form from the identical pieces Nk -*tur-* / Sr -*toor-* both point to an old native bigrade form that was, through morphologization, on the point of vanishing.

Other than the one incontrovertible fossilized verb form, there is only the single type/token datum *t<sup>h</sup>uyumyuc°iru*, no matter where one looks in Ryukyuan for the existence of forms that would justify making the Ryukyuan lower "bigrade" verbs bigrade. In this case OSJS (247a) interprets the form as 'has rung out (far and wide)', i.e. with form and function directly paralleling each other.

While it is tempting to agree with Thorpe (1983: e.g. 154), who reconstructs no forms that can allow the setting up of a bigrade class separate from monograde, in the end there are two good reasons to keep the category intact: (a) as already discussed, (-*nyi*)-*ʔac°iru*, with its 39 tokens, is clearly old; and (b) OOk also preserves a clear distinction between, on the one hand, Quadrigrade and, on the other, Bigrade verb RY forms, where in the latter case there is no overt separate RY morpheme. The latter can be seen as a mere anomaly in the *r*-type Quadrigrade category—if you are a Martian linguist—but it is difficult to ignore the anomaly in the light of history, if you have a knowledge of OJ to back you up. In

---

84  The likelihood that it is a spelling mistake for ⟨to yo mi yo $\overline{\text{wa}}$ ru⟩, as has been argued, is, in our judgment, nil. This is because the brushwritten ⟨tu⟩ of this word in the TOS photographic plate (839b 371 [35ア], line 5, 2nd-to-last character) is not the wide sweeping ⟨tu⟩ of conventional *hiragana*—and the brushwritten text except for punctuation in KOS fully agrees with it (267c, line 1)—and therefore does not at all resemble the ⟨wa⟩ of conventional modern usage, nor the ⟨wa⟩ often used in OS texts, either.

VERBS                                                                              235

that case, it fits like a glove into the historical pattern of Japonic as a whole, and actually simplifies the historical enterprise, rather than complicating it. Thus we view doing away with the bigrade class within Ryukyuan as quite unnecessary. Thorpe did not have the OS data to analyze or to weigh, and we believe that when they enter the picture, they are decisive.

The formal aspect of the analogical shift from vowel verb to r-type consonant verb:

$$*... C\,\bar{e}_{\text{2G}}\text{-...} + *\cdot r_{\text{4GE}}\text{-...} \rightarrow *... C\,\bar{e}\cdot r_{\text{4GE}}\text{-...} > ... C\,\bar{i}\cdot r_{\text{4GE}}\text{-...} \quad C[\ \bar{\text{I}}\,\text{ɾ}]$$
e.g. $*or\ \bar{e}_{\text{2G}}\text{-} + *\cdot r_{\text{4GE}}\text{-...} \rightarrow *or\ \bar{e}\cdot r_{\text{4GE}}\text{-...} > ?ur\ \bar{i}\cdot r_{\text{4GE}}\text{-}a\#...$ [ʔurīɾɑ] 'might descend'

What the above pattern says is that original lower bigrade verbs—a subcategory of vowel-stem verbs—acquired a quadrigrade/consonant-stem extension. In fact there are two subtypes of this "acquisition"—one is simply a reordering of the surface structural elements of the word, with no phonetic change, as in the following example:[85]

–   ⟨a ge re⟩ *?agi·r-i*$_{\text{MR}}$ 'raise (it)!': *?age-ro*

| あかの、 | おゑづ†きや、 | / ねはの、 | おゑづ†きや、 | / この、 |
|---|---|---|---|---|
| a ka no, | o we du† ki ya, | / ne pa no, | o we du† ki ya, | / ko no, |
| ?ak$^h$a-nu | ?wii#ʣik°yi-ya | ni[i]Qp°a-nu | ?wii#ʣik°yi-ya | k$^h$u·nu |
| Aka-GEN | Owezuki[86]-VOC | Neha-GEN | Owezuki-VOC | this |

---

85   As to the upcoming reconstructed form *?age-ro*, there is no actual evidence for the pre-OOk MR form, but we assume that it is identical to the Eastern Old Japanese form in height and backness, and that the consonant is *r, not *y, which, in the case of Old Japanese -yö, is surely -yö < *-rö. Thus the EOJ form preserves an earlier shape than the Central Old Japanese form does. Thorpe's reconstruction of the Proto-Ryukyuan Imperative allomorphs, based on an examination of many dialects/languages, is quadrigrade (4G) *-e, k-liieg *ku (i.e. the bare root), and vowel ending subtypes *-ro (1983: 154).

86   The word *?wii#ʣik-°yi* is originally a description of an omoro that is specifically made in order to celebrate e.g. the completion of a public building, but eventually came to be attached to omoro singers well known for their abilities in composing and performing such omoro, as perhaps here (Nakahara [1957: 390–391]); < *?o- 'EX' + *?yipap-yi 'celebration, congratulation'. Unger (1993 [1973]) claims that the first part is composed of *?yip-ap-yi 'say-ITERATIVE/CONTINUATIVE-RY$_{\text{NOM}}$'; the rest is *-"- 'RENDAKU' + *tuk- 'attach (VI)' + *-yi 'RY$_{\text{NOM}}$', but the accent is incongruent (Martin [1987: 700]); JDB ignores such a possible analysis, though it would be obvious.

ひやし、、∧     あげ゙*れ   /
pi ya si , ∧    a ge* re   /
p゚yoosyi-∅[87]  ʔagi·r-i
rhythm-DO  **raise-MR**
'O Aka and Neha Owezuki: **raise up** this rhythm!' (OS 8.#457)

That was the case of imperatives/*meirei-kei* (MR). While their vowel *changes*, there is no segmental *addition*. Such, however, is not the case for the subjunctive/*mizen-kei* (MZ):

specifically: おれらかず、、∧                        まぶ゙*ら、   /
              o re ra ka zu , ∧                     ma bu* ra , /
              *ʔuri·r-a+kʰazi*                       *maBr-a*
              **alight·4GE[88]-IA[89]**#number.of.times   protect-IA
'Every time (a deity) should alight, let [us] protect ([you] through that deity's power)' (OS 20.#1374)

The most appropriate way to discover how bigrades became quadrigrades (that is, how *\*·r-* either was or seemed to be added to the vowel-ending stem to create a consonant-ending stem) is to see which parts of the conjugation of the two verb grades were alike. In the table below the two lines labeled "*r*-type quadrigrade" are comparands in ongoing analogical changes from bigrade to what we are here calling "*r*-type neo-quadrigrade." Convenient in this regard (while perhaps partially not actually attested) are *ʔagar-* 'rise' (VI) and *\*ʔage-* (*\*ʔage·r-*, *ʔagi·r-*) 'raise' (VT), as seen in Table 6.6.[90]

---

87   Lack of aspiration is assigned on the basis of Nk *p゚yoo'syi* (ROD, Nk).

88   "Quadrigrade extension," i.e. "YD extension."

89   In this case the IA functions as a sort of subjunctive, signaled in the translation by 'should'. See §3.2.

90   For a discussion of Japonic *\*···m-* vs *\*···ram-*, see Serafim (2007).

VERBS                                                                237

TABLE 6.6    From lower bigrade to *r*-type neo-quadrigrade

|                | MZ | RY | SS/RT | IZ/MR | GER |
|----------------|------|------|---------|---------|-------|
| *r*-type quadrigrade | *ʔagar-a* [ʔagara] | *ʔagar-yi* [ʔagarʸi] | **ʔagar-u** [ʔagaru] | *ʔagar-i* [ʔagarɪ] | *ʔagaØ-tˀi* [ʔagat˚ɪ] |
| *r*-type neo-quadrigrade | *ʔagi·r-a* [ʔagɪra] | *ʔagi·r-yi* [ʔagɪrʸi] | **ʔagi·r-u** [ʔagɪru] | *ʔagi·r-i* [ʔagɪrɪ] | *ʔagi·Ø-tˀi* [ʔagɪt˚ɪ] |
| *\*r*-type neo-quadrigrade | *\*ʔage·r-a* \*[ʔagɛra] | *\*ʔage·r-yi* \*[ʔagɛrʸi] | **\*ʔage·r-u** \*[ʔagɛru] | *\*ʔage·r-e* \*[ʔagɛrɛ] | *\*ʔage·Ø-te* \*[ʔagɛtˀɛ] |
| *\*original lower bigrade | *\*ʔage-* \*[ʔagɛ] | *\*ʔage-* \*[ʔagɛ] | **\*ʔage-ru** \*[ʔagɛru] | *\*ʔage-re₁₇/ro_{MR}* \*[ʔagɛrɛ]/···[rɔ] | *\*ʔage-te* \*[ʔagɛtˀɛ] |

## 2.2.1    Attestations

MZ:    *ʔus-yi-ʔukˀi·r-a-:*[91]

    おしうけらば†、                    /
    o si u ke ra ba†,                    /
    *ʔus-yi-ʔukˀi·r-a-ba*
    push-RY-launch·4GE-MZ-TMP/CND
    'If [Okuratsu] launches [the fine ship Masari-tomi on a journey, …]'
    (OS 13.#748)

RY:    *ʔagar-yi:*

    つみあが*り
    tu mi a ga* ri
    *cˀim-yi-ʔagar-yi*
    pile_{VT}-RY-rise_{VI}-RY_{NOM}

---

91    We recognize two subtypes of "MZ": A form such as *nar-yi-ʔagar-asi* 'cause (the sounds) to go skyward, and …' (e.g. [OS 2.#52]) is MZ in name only, since it encompasses morphemes that begin with the phoneme *a*, such as *-asi-* 'CAUS' here; the second is the *true* MZ, for which at present we can only give the example of *-a-* 'MZ' before *-ba* 'TMP/CND'. The morpheme *-ba* occurs here in the meaning 'if', but after *-i-* 'IZ' in the sense of 'when' or 'because'.

*lit.* 'a/the piling up'—name of a palace gate
'Tsumi-Agari [Gate]' (OS 12.#672, OS 15.#1085);

あがりよわちへ　　　　／
a ga ri yo wa ti pe　　／
*Ɂagar-y-uwa-cºyi*
rise-RY-AUX_EX-GER
'deigning to rise up' (OS 2.#44).

SS/RT:　　*Ɂagar-u*

あがﾟる、ᴧ　ぼれぼ*しや　　　　／
a gaﾟ ru , ᴧ　bo re bo* si ya　　／
*Ɂaga·r-u　buri-busyi-ya*
rise_VI-RT　cluster-star-TOP
'the rising Pleiades' (OS 10.#534)

あがﾟろ ᴧ あやみやに　　　　　　／
a gaﾟ ro ᴧ a ya mi ya ni　　　　　／
*Ɂaga·r-u　Ɂaya-myiya-nyi*　　　(*myiya ~ mya'a*)
rise_VI-RT radiant-ground-LOC
'the uplifting radiant ground', i.e. 'the Goeku Radiant Ground'
(OSJS 29b) (OS 14.#1001)

うちあがﾟる、ᴧ　　　なさいきよ　／
u ti a gaﾟ ru , ᴧ　　　na sa i ki yo　／
*Ɂuc-ºyi-Ɂaga·r-u　nasee-kʰyu*
beat_VT-RY-rise-RT fatherly-one
'[our] Fatherly Lord who[se name] will ring out with the beating [of
the hand-drum]' (OS 11.#631)

IZ/MR:　　*-Ɂagi·r-i-*

うちあげ†れば†、　　　　　　　／
u ti a ge† re ba† ,　　　　　　　／
*Ɂuc-ºyi-Ɂagi·r-i-ba*
beat-RY-raise·4GE-IZ-TMP/CND
'when [we] raise up the beat [of the hand drums]' (OS 9.#484)

VERBS 239

MR:     *-ʔagi·r-i*

> うちあげ†れ　　　　　　　/
> u ti a ge† re　　　　　/
> *ʔuc-°yi-ʔagi·r-i*
> beat-RY-raise·4GE-MR
> 'raise up the beat!' (OS 9.#478)

GER:    *-a'aga-t°i, -ʔagi-t°i*

> くもこいろ、　　　　　/ てりや、あがˮて、ˏ　ちよわれ　/
> ku mo ko i ro ,　　　/ te ri ya , a gaˮ te , ˏ ti yo wa re　/
> *kʰumu.kʰu-ʔyiru-∅*　*tʰir-y-a'aga-t°i-∅*　*c°yuwa·r-i*
> beautiful-color-ADV　shine-RY-rise-GER EAV-MR
> 'May you, [Priestess Sasukasa] keep shining out brilliantly!' (OS 4.#203)
> (5 moras, perhaps a rest; 5 moras, 3 moras = 6,8)

> なりとよみ、　　　　　　うちあげ†て、　　　　　/
> na ri to yo mi ,　　　u ti a ge† te ,　　　　/
> *nar-yi-tʰuyum-yi-∅*　*ʔuc°-yi-ʔagi-t°i*
> ring-RY-resound-RY_NOM-DO　beat-RY-raise-GER/PRFV
> 'striking up [the drum] Nari-Toyomi' *lit.* 'sound and resound' (OS 1.#37)

In the table before the examples, for the empty space before the gerund morpheme in the *r*-type neo-4G, i.e. *ʔagi-∅-t°i* 'raising', that space "exists" by comparison with the gerund of a true *r*-type YD, such as *ʔaga∅-t°i* 'rising'. However,
historically speaking, there have been *no* rearrangements of *any* segments, as
the phonetic gerund column shows.

### 2.3    *The Change from* w-*stem to* r-*stem Quadrigrade*
There are two subcategories of *w*-stem quadrigrades, ones with one-syllable
stems and ones with multi-syllable stems. For convenience we can call them
mono-*w*-stems and multi-*w*-stems. Mono-*w*-stems underwent an analogical
change in which their gerund stem was generalized as the stem for all other
functions as well:

| | | | | | |
|---|---|---|---|---|---|
| *\*kaw̄-u-te* | > | *\*kɔ̄ɔ-te* | > | *kʰoo-t°i* | > | *koo-ti* | 'swap/buy-GER' |
| [cf. W Japan *koo-te*] | | | | | |
| *\*kaw-yi* | → | *\*kɔɔ·r-yi* | > | *kʰoo·r-yi* | > | *koo·'-yi* | 'swap/buy-RY' |
| *\*kaw-anu* | → | *\*kɔɔ·r-anu* | > | *kʰoo·r-aN* | > | *koo·r-aN* | 'swap/buy-NEG' |
| *\*kaw-e-ba* | → | *\*kɔɔ·r-e-ba* | > | *kʰoo·r-i-ba* | > | *koo·r-e-e* | 'swap/buy-PROV' |

240                                                                                                        CHAPTER 6

Changes except those on the first line do not appear to be reflected in the os. Furthermore, it would be a mistake to overgeneralize and say that all *w*-stems underwent the same analogical change. With the exception of NOk *ʔ-y-ú-n* 'say' (< *\*ʔyiw-*), all mono-*w*-stems did undergo that analogical change, but the situation by the time of NOk with multi-*w*-stems is more complex.

Of note is that none of the multi-*w*'s that stayed multi underwent vowel lengthening or monophthongization in their stem vowel. However, apparently at random (perhaps according to token frequency) they have fallen into three classes: (1) a more conservative class that takes ····'-*an* as its negative, (2) a more innovative class that alternates between two negatives, one in ····'-*an* as above, and one in ····*r-an*, having built its negative on the quadrigrade extension (4GE) and finally (3) the most innovative one, which only takes ····*r-an*, that is, which has fully shifted to *r*-type 4G. Here are some examples:

– Subcategory (1)—Remains *w*-type 4G

   MJ *ate-gaf-u* (EOKJ) (NJ:) '1 apply (s/t) to (...); 2 allot; 3 distribute' (*Eiga Monogatari* [1028–1037]); NOk *ʔatíga|·'-y-u-n* (VT, |·'-*an*, |-*ti*) 'fix on, select, mark out; imitate, model after; slate (s/o for a position); liken (A to B)' (OGJ 127a).

   OJ *muk·ap-u* '1 face; 2 face as an enemy, oppose' (JDB 722a); NOk *nká|·'-y-u-n* (VI, |·'-*an*, |-*ti*) '1 face; 2 suffice; 3 face as an enemy' (OGJ 435b).

   OJ *negap-u* 'wish in one's heart' (JDB 558c); NOk *niga|'-y-u-n‚* (VT |·'-*an*, |-*ti*) 'ask for' (OGJ 414b).

– Subcategory (2)—Free variation between *w*- and *r*-type

   MJ *atukáf-u‚* (accent: ENHK) '1 take care of; 2 entertain; 3 use (to the fullest extent); 4 make the object of gossip; 5 find unmanageable; 6 arbitrate, intercede' (EOKJ);[92] NOk *ʔacíka|·'-y-u-n* (VT, |·'-*an* ~ |·*r-an*, |-*ti*) '1 handle; stock; use fully; 2 exploit; maltreat' (OGJ 101b). [?Or: *a[r-i-]tukap- *'be using']

   OJ *ömöp-u* '1 think (A to be B); 2 desire; 3 worry; 4 think fondly of; 5 presuppose, surmise; 6 be congenial with' (JDB 166c–167a); NOk *ʔumu'|··-y-u-n‚* (VT |·*r-an*, |-*ti*; also *ʔum-aan*[93]) 'think (that); consider; investigate; love' (OGJ 555a).

---

92    While treated in the dictionaries (EOKJ, JDB) as a separate verb, *atu·k·ap-u* (4G) '1 suffer from the heat of the sun or a flame; 2 be troubled emotionally over s/t' (JDB 29b) appears related, especially through senses 4 and 5 of the main-text *atukap-u* above. Further, the verbs are temporally in complementary distribution, with the senses of this footnote's *atu·k·ap-u* appearing only in the OJ Nara Period, and the senses of the main text's *atukaf-u* appearing in the Heian and later periods. The etymology, then, becomes transparent: *\*atu-* 'hot' + *\*-ku* 'INF [of adjectives]' + *\*-ap-* 'FREQUENTATIVE' (and 'VERBALIZER').

93    The sequence of changes is as follows: *ʔum-aan* = [ʔumɑːn] ← *[ʔumʷɑːn] < *[ʔumuwɑn]

VERBS 241

OJ *sitagap-u* 'obey' etc. (JDB 354ab); NOk *syi̯ tága*|·'-*y-u-N* (VI |·'-*aN* ~ |·*r-aN*, |-*ti*) 'obey' (OGJ 486a); appears as ⟨si ta ge ⋯⟩ in OS and in Koyō (OKDJ 321a); clearly only distantly related to OJ, since the words are members of different verb classes, even though they share *\*syitag⋯*. Thus NOk *syi̯ tága'yuN* is clearly a borrowing from Japanese, despite the free alternation in its negative forms, since only the most archaic strata evince this particular lexeme.

– Subcategory (3)—Full shift to *r*-type 4G

Early NJ *matiga*[*w*]-*u* 'cross paths' (EOKJ Jōruri *Chūshingura* 2; SNKDJ "1694"—in any case, a very recent verb); NOk *macyiga*|·'-*y-u-N̯* (VT |·*r-aN*, |-*ti*) '1 make a mistake; 2 break the rules' (OGJ 356b); this word is definitely new; cf. *baqpee-y-u-N̯* '(id.)' (OGJ 131b), an older word.

OJ *aragap-u* = NJ *araso'u* 'contest' (JDB 53b); *ʔaragaa*|·'-*y-u-N̯* (VT |·*r-aN*, |-*ti*) '1 compete, contest, resist; 2 argue' (OGJ 121a); perhaps the long *aa* is by analogy with the long *ee* of its intransitive counterpart *ʔarágee'-y-u-N* '1 (vegetables) grow grotesquely larger [accent *sic*]; 2 (human body) grows pleasingly larger or stronger-looking'.

OJ *tug·ap-u* (番) OJ (JDB 460b) ?'(one thing) follows (another)' [meaning not yet fully determined]; MJ '1 (VI) (two things) pair up (ca. 1005)'; (animals) mate (SNKDJ 1893); (VT) 2 pair (two things) up; 3 affix (an arrow to its bowstring); 4 make a solemn promise (SNKDJ 1687); 5 make preparations (SNKDJ, 13th C)'; NOk *cigáa*|·'-*y-u-N* (VI |·*r-aN*, |-*ti*) '(of work) alternate, rotate, shift back and forth'; *cigaaruu̯* 'rotation'; *cigée* 'a joint, a hinge' (OGJ 147a).

Of these the second subcategory appears to be the most abundant. In our quick search, we found three of subcategory (1), seven of subcategory (2), and four of subcategory (3). It is evident, then, that the verbs with only one full syllable in their stem in PRk—save for *\*ʔyip-* 'say'—developed a newly reshaped stem based on their diphthongized or monophthongized gerund stem, as in *\*kaw-yi-tye > ... > \*kɔɔ-te* (see later this chapter), giving new stem *\*kau-* or *\*kɔɔ-* from which all other forms sprang. However, verbs with more than one syllable in their stem had a more complex history. In any case it appears that *all* the changes that we have discussed so far, i.e. in the *w*-stems, occurred after OOk, since their reflexes are not to be found in the written data—or at least any spoken-language forms of the sort that we are discussing had not made it into the language of song yet.

---

= *\*ʔumuw-aN*. Modern Okinawan allows *Cw* sequences only if C is a velar or a glottal, so *\*[mʷ]* must have instantaneously changed to *\*[m]*: ˣ*mw* → °*m*.

242                                                                                    CHAPTER 6

The fact that the multi-syllable *w*-stems have by no means completed an analogical shift to *r*-stems even in the modern language implies that the shift to *r*-stems is a very late change. In any case, what *is* clear is that the analogical shift started with the monosyllabic stems, that it then made its way into the multi-syllabic stems, where it is in process now, but where it has not had any effect by monophthongization on the final vowel of the gerund: *ciká-ti* 'using', not ˣ*cikóo-ti* (but cf. W Japan *cukoo-te* '(id.)'). A hypothesis for the lack of monoph-thongization is presented below.

The omoro scholars Takahashi (1991a: 428–429) and Nakasone (1987 [1976]: 253) have noted that the *w*-stems' shift to *r*-stems was not in evidence in the *Omoro Sōshi*, save for the fossilized form *taboori* 'please give me' (a *hapax*), which is true, but what they did not say was that the *w*-stems were not after all mono- or bigrade verbs; therefore in actuality it is no surprise that the change did not occur to *w*-stem verbs, which are *consonant* verbs, after all, *not* vowel verbs as the mono- and bigrades are. To put it another way, there are *two r*-gradization (i.e. *ra-gyō yodan-ka*) processes, one for originally bigrade verbs, which clearly started earlier, and one for *w*-stem quadrigrades, which clearly started later, and has followed its own path. Both are morphophonemically based, and depend in part on the morphological category that they work on.

Of course there *is* also a third subclass, Subcategory 3, in ····*r-aN* only. That subclass has indeed become an *r*-stem quadrigrade group, but without any change to the final vowel of the stem, thus separating it out from the single-syllable *w*-to-*r*-stem subcategory, as explained above.

This statement ignores the special case of ColloqOk *boo·'-y-u-N,* 'snatch away' (····*r-aN*), which seemingly has split off from its LitOk sister multi-syllable *w*-stem form *ʔNbá·'-y-u-N* '(id.)' (····'-*aN*). It has gone from multi-syllable *w*-stem to single-syllable *w*-stem through analogical shift, that is, after loss of *\*ʔN* in ini-tial position before a voiced obstruent—cf. also *dak-* 'hug' < *\*ʔNdak-* < *\*ʔudak-.*[94] First comes the Okinawan-internal change, quite natural phonologically, in which the first short nasalized mora is lost, and after which the new second mora retains its full moraic weight because of being a second, not a third, mora:

| | | | | | | | | |
|---|---|---|---|---|---|---|---|---|
| *\*ʔubawīte* | > | *\*bāwīte* | > | *\*bāūtɪ* | > | *bɔ̄ɔ̄t°ɪ* | = | *boot°i* |
| *\*[ʔũbawɪt°ɛ]* | > | *\*[bawɪt°ɛ]* | > | *\*[baut°ɪ]* | > | *[bɔːt°ɪ]* | | |

---

94   OJ has *mudak-* (JDB 726b), *udak-* ([JDB 117c], [Ryōi-ki, 822]) 'embrace (person, idea)'. JDB (117c) also has an example of *idak-* from *Ruiju Myōgi-shō*, ca. 1100, but under *mudak-*, it states that the form is seen in the old readings from the *Nihon Shoki*, ca. 1000, in *Taketori Monogatari*, ca. 900, and in *Tosa Nikki*, 935. This all simply means that OJ had phonetically salient prenasalization on initial /u/.

VERBS                                                                    243

It is sometime after the loss of the first mora that a new LitOk form is borrowed, and its changes commence, in step with the multi-syllabic *w*-stems:

| | | | | | |
|---|---|---|---|---|---|
| *\*ʔŭbāwɪte* | > | *\*ʔN̄bā'ɑtɪ* | > | *ʔN̄bātˀɪ* | = *ʔN̄batˀi* |
| *\*[ʔŭbɑwɪtˀɛ]* | > | *\*[ʔmːbaːtˀɪ]* | > | *[ʔmːbatˀɪ]* | |

Interestingly both gerunds end up as three-mora forms. The shape of the syllable *ʔN* is not significant—only the fact of its existence at all is of purport, because it maintains a multi-*w* stem. Its loss, on the other hand, would force the creation of a reshaped stem on analogy with others of the sort *koo-y-u-N* :: *koo-ti* 'buy :: buying' etc.

The reverse accent of the two verbs shows that one of the two is a borrowing, and clearly that that borrowing must be the Literary form. NHK supports this hypothesis with *ubáu*, with the same "accented" category as in the LitOk accented form *ʔN̄bá'-y-u-N*, and which is the reverse of the expected unaccented *boo'-y-u-N,*, the ColloqOk form.

| | | | | | |
|---|---|---|---|---|---|
| *\*[ʔmːbawɪtˀɛ]* | *\*[ba'utˀɪ]* | [bɔːtˀɪ] | = | *bootˀi* | (OOk > NOk) |
| *\*[tˀu̥kˀawɪtˀɛ]* | *\*[tsˀu̥kˀaːtˀɪ]* | [tsˀi̥kˀatˀɪ] | = | *cˀikˀatˀi* | (OOk) |
| | | [tsi̥kati] | = | *cikati* | (Early NOk) |
| | | [tʃi̥kati] | = | *cyikati* | (Contemp NOk) |

The critical difference between the native *\*[ʔmːbawɪtˀɛ]* and (the of course native) *\*[tˀu̥kˀawɪtˀɛ]* was that the former lost its first syllable, becoming *\*[bawɪtˀɛ]*. The "Two-Mora Rule", (entertained but not named in Thorpe (1983: 129), which we discuss in Ch. 2 §5.3.1 vis-à-vis historical development of accent), is the rule in which the first two moras of a word were given extra "weight" (perhaps not a truly quantifiable or properly definable phonetic term, except perhaps in some sort of metrical-phonological scheme).[95] This led to different syllables being given weight (with ¯ over a vowel to signify a heavy mora, and ˷ under a vowel to signify a light one):

| | | | | | | | | |
|---|---|---|---|---|---|---|---|---|
| [ba | wɪ | | tˀɛ] | → | [bā | wī | | tˀɛ] |
| [tˀu̥ | kˀa | wɪ | tˀɛ] | → | [tˀṳ | kˀā | wɪ̰ | tˀɛ] |

---

95    This would, again, be included in the Two-Mora Rule.

244                                                                                    CHAPTER 6

### 3      Functional Split (MZ)

This presentation follows thematically the material presented in Shinzato and
Serafim 2013 (57–58, 71–80), but with a focus on the *Omoro Sōshi*. First comes
a discussion of the difference between the form and concept of '*mizen-kei*' (MZ
= irrealis form) and 'inferential auxiliary' (IA). Next comes a presentation of
the two inferential auxiliaries (IA), and a comparison of their form-function
relation; then their provenance; finally a comparison of similar forms in the
development of Japanese.

#### 3.1    *Difference between IA and MZ*
Superficially the IA -*a* and the MZ -*a* are the same. This is true enough in the
sentence-ending form of the IA, where the forms are indeed perfectly identical. In that case, then, why have two names for one form? Well, let us note the
following:

IZ-*ba*   -   *i*   -   *b*   *a*
MZ-*ba*   -   *a*   -   *b*   *a*
MZ        -   *a*
IA$_{SS}$  -   *a*

-IA     - IZ       -   *a*   *m*   -   *i*        'will surely ...'
{+IA    +IZ}   {   +   a   m   +   i   }

The IZ form of the IA shows that the underlying form of the IA is {+am+}, not
the same as the surface SS form of the IA, -*a*. Why, then, even have an analytical
entity "MZ" in the first place?

The most straightforward answer is that the MZ and the IZ constitute a
morphological minimal pair, since they occupy the same slot, just before the
temporal/conditional suffix -*ba* 'TMP/CND', which is construed as an irrealis
conditional, i.e. 'if', after the MZ, but as a temporal or explanatory conditional,
i.e. 'when/because', after the IZ:

やらば                          やれば[†]
ya ra ba                      ya re ba[†]
*y-ar-a-ba*                    *y-ar-i-ba*
COP-SE-**IA-TMP/CND**          COP-SE-**IZ-TMP/CND**
'(even) **if** it is' (OS 13.#898)   '**because** it is' (OS 20.#1377)

The examples are culled from the following:

VERBS                                                                   245

もゝ、あんじ、    やらばﾟ、        ／ やちよむ、、  ゑ、やれ、／
mo ", a n zi ∧   ya ra baʸ ,      ／ ya ti yo mu , ∧ we ∧ ya re , ／
*mumu-ʔaɴzyi*   *y-ar-a-ba*       -yac°yooм⁹⁶   yee   yari
hundred-lord(s) COP-SE-**MZ-TMP/CND**  -even       INJ   INJ

'Even **if** it is [a gathering of] a hundred lords—yes, indeed!' (os 11.#566)


てだﾟが、            おざし、        やればﾟ、              ／
te daʸ ga ,         o za si ∧      ya re baʸ ,           ／
*tʰililda-ga*       *ʔu-zas-yi*    *y-ar-i-ba*
sun[.goddess]-SUB/GEN EX-point-RY_NOM COP-SE-**IZ-TMP/CND**

'**because** it is the fiat of the Sun Deity' (os 3.#107)


Other MZ examples are shown below:


いぢﾟへら、かず、、  おみ、まぶてす、、      はりやせ          ／
i diʸ pe ra , ka zu , ∧ o mi , ma bu te su , ∧ pa ri ya se       ／
*ʔyidzyi·r-a-kʰazi*  *ʔu-myilil-maʙ-tʰi-si*  *pʰalalry-as-i⁹⁷*
exit·4GE-IA_MZ-times EX-look_RY-protect-GER-KP sail-CAUS-IZ(/MR)

'**every time they bid fair to** leave [port], it is surely under your protection that
[you will] have them sail!'⁹⁸ ([os 13.#746] [os 22.#1550])


げﾟらい、まさり、とみ、   ／ おしうけらばﾟ、                ／
ge° ra i ,  ma sa ri , to mi ,  ／ o si u ke ra baʸ ,           ／
*girayi*  *masar.yi-tʰum.yi-∅*  *ʔus-yi-ʔukʰi·r-a-ba*
splendid  Excel-HMS-DO          push-RY-launch·4GE-**MZ-TMP/CND**

'**if** [he] launches the splendid [craft,] HMS Excel' (os 13.#748)


---

96    The modern Shuri equivalent is -ya·cyo'oɴ (oɢJ -co 'oɴ167a), and, in Nakɪjɪn, ɪt ɪs ( ya)-c'yuɴ
      (Nakasone 1983: 279b–280a ちュン). The etymology is apparently the copular *n-i-të-pa
      uɪ-i̇-ʋü-mü *'even though it is / ... may be', with (* tö >ᴘᴘ; A/ʙɴᴇᴜᴛʀᴀʟɪᴢᴀᴛɪoɴ>) *-tʸo
      lengthening to *-tʸoo and therefore not raising in Shuri. (Parenthetically, omoro shorten-
      ing to -cyo does not result in raising, since it is a synchronic nonce phenomenon, while
      lengthening and the following suppression of raising are both diachronic phenomena.)
      For a more complete rundown on this collocation, see Ch. 7, §13.1, fn. 208.
97    If the omoro was sung with the lengths elided as shown, and the mora consonant not
      treated as a mora, then the verse is 8 moras long:
            *ʔumyimaʙt°isi pʰaryasi.*
98    ... or, 'that [they] will sail [their ship(s)]'.

246         CHAPTER 6

On examination of [aba] and [ɪba], it is obvious that it is [ba] that carries the TMP/CND meaning, and that it is [a] and [ɪ], therefore, that carry any other meaning of their respective strings. The first [a] carries the irrealis sense, thus [aba] = 'if', and the [ɪ] carries the realis or logical conditional sense, thus [ɪba] = 'when; because'. To summarize:

| [ | a | b | a | ] | | [ | ɪ | b | a | ] |
| / | a | b | a | / | | / | i | b | a | / |
| | - | a | - | b | a | | - | i | - | b | a |
| { | + | a | + | b | a | } | | { | + | i | + | b | a | } |
| 'MZ - TMP/CND' | | | | | | 'IZ - TMP/CND' | | | | |

### 3.2     *How IA Forms Have Split into Forms with Different Functions*
The plain IA morpheme may mean 'let me/us':

で*ˬ     わん、ˬ あすば*、ˬ
de*ˬ     wa N , ˬ a su ba* , ˬ
*dii*     *waN-∅ ʔasib-a*
well.then! I-SUB   dance-IA
'Well, then! **Let me/us** dance! / [**I think**] I'll dance!' (OS 14.#1005)

This is an example of the type expected in NOk for the non-extended-predicate type of IA. Note an example in NOk, also with *dii* [dʸiꞏ] '(id.)' (OGJ 176b):[99]

*dii*     *sáyi\**     *ʔyic-y-ábir-a*
well.then! I.tell.you go-RY-POLITE-IA
'well, then, **let's go!**' (\*said by a male; females will say *táyi*)

There are two (sequences of) forms that might be called IA in the OS:

てだの、ˬ   てら、ぎやめ、ˬ   ちよわれ   /
te da no , ˬ   te ra , gi ya me , ˬ   ti yo wa re   /
*tʰida-nu*     *tʰir-a-gyami*     *cˤyuwar-i*
sun-SUB     shine-IA-TRM     reign$_{EX}$-MR
'Reign as long as the sun **should/might/may** shine!' (OS 5.#272)

---

99     ... as opposed to OOk *dii* [dɪꞏ], with accent not reconstructed.

# VERBS

てるまもん、、                    てりよら          /
te ru ma mo N , ,              te ri yo ra       /
*tʰir-u-ma-muN-∅*             *tʰir-y-ur-a*
[shine-RT-true_BE-NOM]_PN-TOP shine-RY-SE-IA
'[When Biru-no Yashi-no Shī comes to (each of three named places),] (the supernaturally powerful [OSJS 239ab] priestess) Teru-Mamon **will probably/ surely**[100] be shin**ing**.' (Hokama [2000b: 166]) (OS 14.#1040)

Note the two forms and their meanings:

$tʰ$ $i$ $r$ -      - $a$ ... 'might shine, should shine, (will) probably shine' (a sort of subjunctive or irrealis sense)

$tʰ$ $i$ $r$ - $y$ - $u$ $r$ - $a$ ... 'is probably shining, will probably be shining' (inference of probability)

Note that the form with the inference of probability is, synchronically, built on the stative extension, that is to say, historically, it came into being when the IA was used more frequently, perhaps exclusively, at the end of a progressive form, as indeed the translation of this example shows. The progressive form, in turn, was built out of the RY and the stative predicate *wur-* 'there to be (animate)': *\*-yi-wur-*. The new form with inference of probability, then, came to be (*\*-yi-wur-a* >) NOk (*-y*)-*ur-a*.

Of course the form with, instead, a subjunctive or irrealis sense does *not* have the stative extension, and the IA goes directly on the root of the main verb, not on the root of the stative extension, thus (*\*-a* >) *-a*. This conserves the simple form and the old meaning.

While Okinawan and Japanese superficially appear to have followed each other closely in how they split their one IA into two constructions, a closer look reveals that the Okinawan case actually is part of a much larger generalization of epistemology/evidential marking, that is, having to do with holding back from imputing states of mind or unwitnessed actions of others in one's own speech. The main tool in this non-imputation toolkit is the use of the *ᴬ-yi-wor-* *\**'be X-ing' stative extension to keep from taking responsibility for knowledge of the mental states or the actions of second or third persons. The construction

---

100   Hokama gives a twofold translation, reflecting the hedging of a future expectation: "Teru-Ma-Mon shinjo ga **teri-kagayaite-iru no de arō**. ..., **kagayakashii koto yo**." i.e. 'The priestess Teru-Ma-Mon **will probably be shining**. ..., **oh, how brilliantly shining** she will be!' (ibid. 166b).

248          CHAPTER 6

(-*y*)-*ur-a* 'probably be X-ing' is part of that toolkit. The following are a minimal pair of IA without and with the stative extension.

大ぎ゙みよ、∧     おが゙ま    / きみ⌒"†"よ、      てづ゙ら     /
OPO gi* mi yo ,∧    o ga* ma   / ki mi ""† " yo ,     te du* ra
*ʔuQp°u-gyimyi-yu*    *wugam-a*   *k°yimyi-gyimyi-yu*    *tʰi+dʑi|r-a*
great-priestess-DO   pray.to-IA    priestess-priestess-DO   hand-rub-IA
'**Let us** address our prayers (to) the High Priestess; **let us** pray (to) the priest-esses.' (OS 3.#107)

おなりが゙み、∧      てづ゙り、よら、      /
o na ri ga* mi ,∧     te du* ri , yo ra ,      /
*wuna·ryi-gamyi-∅*    *tʰi-dʑi|r-y-ur-a*
sister·role-deity-SUB   hand-rub-RY-SE-IA
'[Now that late spring (*ʔuridʑiм*) has come,] my spirit-powerful sister **will probably be** praying [for a southerly wind (*ma-pʰayi*) to run ships—now that early summer (*wakʰanac°i*) has come].' (OS 13.#925)

A similar distinction between MZ with/without SE shown above may be seen in the OJ pair -*am*-/-*ur-am*- below (for more on this see Serafim [2007: 216–218]):

在管裳          / 君乎者       将待       /
ARI tutu mo      / KÎMÎ wo ba   MATAMU    /
*ar-i-tutu-mö*        *kîmî-wo-ba*    *mat-am-u*
exist-RY-while-even    you-DO-TOP   await-IA-SS
'Living on, **I will** keep waiting[101] for you [no one else; until the frost lies upon my long black hair].' (MYS 2.#87)

月 日       餘美都追     / 伊母      麻都良牟     曽
TUKÏ PÎ      yö mî tu tu    / i mo      ma tu ra mu    sö
*tukï-pî-∅*      *yöm-î-tutu*     *imô-∅*     *mat-ur-am-u*    *sö*
moon-sun-DO   see.go.by-RY-while    my.love-SUB   await-SE-IA-RT   SKP
'... counting the months and days, my wife **will be** wait**ing** [for me].'
(MYS 17.#3982)

---

101     The 'keep ...-ing' part comes from *aritutumö*, not from the form under discussion.

VERBS                                                                    249

## 4       Development of the Gerund

### 4.1     *Two Functions of the Gerund: Gerund and Perfective*
The PJ form of the gerund (one of the T-type morphemes)[102]—which is in origin the RY of the perfective auxiliary[103]—is *-t(-)ëë-.[104] This conveniently named "gerund" or T-type morpheme actually has had two functions throughout Okinawan language history: 1) gerund (GER), and 2) perfective (PRFV) (Hagers 2012). Very crudely put, the former parallels functionally to 'and', and the latter to 'have done / did'. In OOk, perfective use is seen in both declarative and interrogative sentences, but in NOk, the Gerund-mimicking PRFV form is limited to the context of yes-no-questions:

$$\{\text{'PRFV'}\} \rightarrow \{+\text{Ti}+\} / \underline{\quad}\{+\text{yi}\#\#\ \text{'YNQ'}\}$$

The split of the function in OOk was realized in two different forms, one, PRFV, in which {+t°ee} was realized as long -t°ee = [t°ɛ:], and in which therefore the vowel remained mid; the other, the gerund, in which {+t°ee} was realized as short (-t°e- = [t°ɛ] >)-t°i = [t°ɪ], and in which the vowel therefore was realized as a (raised) lax high vowel. It must have been long to begin with—perhaps because of its bound-word = AUX rather than suffix status—, but shortened in its new function as a gerund verbal suffix, and this shortening allowed it to raise when the raising sound change went into effect:

| Stage 1 | Functional bifurcation | Stage 2 | Shortening | Stage 3 | Raising | Stage 4 = OOk |
|---|---|---|---|---|---|---|
| *…#tee | > PRFV | *…#tee | > | *…#tee | > | …#t°ee |
|  | > GER | *…+tee |  | *…+te |  | …-t°i |
|  |  |  |  |  |  | (where $i$ = [ɪ]) |

---

102   When it is necessary to refer to the gerund/perfective and morphemes historically derived from it, we will use a new term, "T-type morpheme", so that the form-class as a whole can be specified.

103   Clearly, in terms of prehistory, the original bound word was pre-OOk *{#tɛɛ+} 'PRFV'—always bound, but possessing morphology—, and the development of the gerund out of the RY usage of this word, i.e. pre-OOk *{+tɛ} 'GER'—morphologically static—, was an instance of the de-syntacticization type of morphologization (http://www.glottopedia .org/index.php/Morphologization). This has been discussed under *r*-gradization in §2. See Ch. 7 §10 for discussion of …-c°-ir-u.

104   We assume that this PJ *-ëë- is long: *-ëë-, and speculate that it may be descended from the

250 CHAPTER 6

Here are examples of the GER use of the T-type morpheme:

| 大みづの、 | みぢよいもい、 | / おゑぢ†へ、∧ | こうて、∧ |
|---|---|---|---|
| OPO mi du no , | mi di yo i mo i , | / o we di† pe ,∧ | ko u te ,∧ |
| ʔuɢpʰu-myidʑi-nu | myi-dʑyee-mii-∅ | ʔwi-i-dʑyi-∅ | kʰu-u-t°i |
| great-water-GEN | EX-PN-EX-VOC | follow-RY-wind-DO | pray.for-RY-GER |

| はりやせ | / |
|---|---|
| pa ri ya se | / |
| pʰaary-as-i | |
| run$_{VI}$-VT-MR | |

'O Mi-Jē-Moi[105] of Ōmizu,[106] having prayed for a following wind,[107] sail [the ship]!' (OS 10.#541)

| かみの、 | もゝぢやらの、 | / おもて、∧ | さうぜて、∧ |
|---|---|---|---|
| ka mi no , | mo " di ya ra no , | / o mo te ,∧ | sa u ze te ,∧ |
| kʰamyi-nu | mumu#dʑyara[108]-nu | ʔumu-t°i | soo+zi-t°i |
| North-GEN | 100-lords-SUB | consider-GER | scheme-do-GER |

| こうば、 | / |
|---|---|
| ko u ba , | / |
| kʰuu-ba | |
| come$_{MZ}$-TMP/CND | |

'If the allied lords of the North should come [and attack], **having** considered and schemed, ...' (OS 2.#47)

---

stative RY/SS *ar-î. The other obvious option, strictly from a formal perspective, is for it to be descended from the bigrade verbalizer *[-ë-]u (cf. Whitman 2008: 166–172), in whatever form it might have had in the earliest level of PJ.

105   The duplicate (OS 13.#957) of this omoro has みてもい ⟨mi °te mo i⟩ myi-ˌdee-mii, apparently a long-mid-vowel spelling, and with highly unusual lack of voicing marking in TOS, < *myi-ˌdee-moyi; further, the alternant myi-dʑyee-mii < *myi-dyee-moyi < *myi-dee-moyi. Perhaps the precipitating difference is irregular loss in the eventual ⟨di yo i⟩ alternant of interior word boundary "#". The spelling alternation is not found elsewhere: ⟨de⟩ ~ ⟨di yo i⟩, signaling a PP-based phonological alternation dee ~ dʑyee.

106   Hokama (2000a: 360–361) identifies this as another name for pʰuru-satʰu 'Furusato'—used as a duplicate word in the same song—on the island of Yoron, just north of Okinawa Island.

107   ʔwi-i-dʑyi [ʔʷɪːdʑi] < *ʔoʼ-yi-dye < *ʔow-yi-de. Cf. J o[w]-uˌ 'follow, ...'. Note that PP in this word has to have occurred before Monophthongization, since the latter takes away the phonetic environment for the operation of the former.

108   For more on the phonology and origin of this word, see Ch. 2 § 4.6.2, p. 69.

VERBS 251

みぢや、、∧　はりやちへ、、∧　きゝや、、∧しよわ、　　　　　／
mi di† ya , ∧　pa ri ya ti pe , ∧　ki " ya , ∧ si yo wa , 　　　／
*myi-dzya-∅　pʰaary-a-c°yi　k°yik°y-as-y-uwa-∅*
EX-horse-DO　run<sub>VI</sub>-VT-GER　hear-CAUS-RY-AUX<sub>EX</sub>-MR
'Run[109] His Majesty's horses down [to find out what's on board the ships] **and** tell [His Majesty of it].' (OS 13.#749)

これど、、∧　　いちゑ、、∧　とよむ　　　　／
ko re do , ∧　i ti we , ∧　to yo mu　　　／
*kʰuri-du　ʔyi-c°yi　tʰuyum-u*
this.one-KP<sub>i</sub>　say-GER　resound-RT<sub>i</sub>
'Let *this* [song] spread [his] fame!' (Adapted from Drake, "Omoro Kanshō" 70), *lit.* 'Saying *this*, [his fame] will resound!' (OS 5.#246)

Here are examples of the perfective use of this—T-type—morpheme, three in OOk and one in NOk. It can be determined contextually as in the first example below, or structurally as in the next two examples,[110] where the yes/no question or the quotative particle follow, since these forms require the preceding form to be ss (cf. Takahashi [1991a: 11]).

たまき、、∧　　　ゑらで*、、∧　さゝちへ　　　／ ゆろい、、∧　ゑらで*、、∧
ta ma ki , ∧　　we ra de* , ∧　sa " ti pe　　　／ yu ro i , ∧　we ra de* , ∧
*tʰama-k°yi-∅　ʔyi̢ra-di　sas-a-c°yee　　　yuru⁽°⁾i-∅　ʔyi̢ra-di*
jewel-sword-DO　choose-GER　wear-CAUS-PRFV<sub>ss</sub>　armor-DO　choose-GER
こせて　　　　　　　／
ko se te　　　　　　／
*kʰu.si-t°ee*
wear.CAUS<sub>'dress'VT</sub>-PRFV<sub>ss</sub>

---

109　← {pʰaary+as+yi+tee 'run X and'}. The gerund of the verb *root* is ⟨pa tɪ pe⟩ = *pʰaa-c°yl*, with the underlying form {pʰaary+yi+tee}. Non-palatalized {r} would have led to *\*pʰaa-t°ɪ*. Note the long {aa} in the underlying form. External evidence for it comes in two forms. One is a proportional analogy: 'column'—OJ *pasira* : NOk *haaya* :: 'run(; sail)'—OJ *pasir-* : X, where solving for X gives *haay-* 'sail; run', which surfaces in the second piece of evidence, NOk *haayee̢* 'running (race)' (N) (OGJ 197a) < ... < *\*pʰasyiry-yi#ap°-yi, lit.* \*'running [with] each other', the NOk noun form a holdover from a time when the length was still present in the verb itself, which has since regularized to an ordinary r-type 4G, *ha-y-u-N₁, ha-ti̢*, (OGJ 201b) = {har+₁ 'sail; run'}, i.e. with no PP. The final {y} in the OOk underlying form is needed as a trigger for PP in T-forms.

110　Usually only context allows determination of which form is in use.

'[They] chose[111] (= GER) jeweled (= fine) swords, and had (= PRFV) [them] wear [them] [at their waist]; [they] chose (= GER) armor, and dressed (= PRFV) [them] [with it].' (OS 10.#525)

おなり、∧   だ゙ち へ、∧   ともて、   /
o na ri , ∧   da˚ ti pe , ∧   to mo te ,   /
*wuna·ryi-∅*   *da-c˚yee*   *-t˚-umu-t˚i*
sister·ly.one-DO   embrace-PRFV   -QT-think-GER
'... thinking that I **had** embraced my lover ...' (OS 12.#730)

いぢへて、で゙ゝ、∧   しられゝ   /
i di pe te , de˚ " , ∧   si ra re "   /
*ʔyidzyi[112]-t˚ee-di-t˚i syi̯r-ari·r-i*
exit-PRFV-QT-GER   [know-PASS· 4GE]pray-MR
'Though[113] [they] have left [port], let [them] pray [to the deities]!'[114] (OS 13.#798)

*ʔaɴ y-a-t˚i-i.*
thus COP-SE-PRFV-QP
'**Was** *that* it?' (OGJ 264a)

---

111   Marked *\*ʔyi̯ra···*, but historically < *\*ʔyera···* < PJ *\*ëra-*. Cf. NJ *eráb-u*.

112   See fn. 115 about the pronunciation of this lexeme. The word *ʔyidzyi̯-t˚i* is composed of {ʔyidi+ 'depart; go out'} and {+tee 'GER/PRFV'}. Normally PP is not iterative, though a handful of exceptions are known. Our lexical entry is abstract, but accords with history, treating [dʒi] as a {di} with PP due to preceding [ʸi] = {yi}. (The alternative is {ʔyi̯di+}, with an exception marker.) Since PP is not iterative, the syllable [dʒi] will not affect the next syllable, and it will remain *t˚i* = [t˚ɪ] rather than palatalizing to *c˚yi* = [tʃ˚i]. In the initial—most phonetically motivated—period of PP, perhaps it *was* iterative, a sort of palatal harmony, but if so, PP must then have become restricted to just the syllable to the right of the trigger, with a few exceptions, by the time of OOk.

113   Cf. NOk *-ɴdi'cyi* ← *-ɴ'di ʔyí-cyi* '... to( it)te' = 'saying: ...'. Also *-ɴ'di* '1 (quote:) ...; 2 in order to ...' (OGJ 435a). The initial *ɴ* of the NOk quotative particle accreted through an abductive change: quotes frequently end in the verbal ss ...(-*y-u*)-*ɴ* or adjectival ss ...(-*s-a*)-*ɴ*, or the negative ss ...-*aɴ*. The previous quotative particle *-di*, as in the OOk example here, following the forms ending in *ɴ* (after the neutralization of the *ɴ* ↔ *м* opposition) appeared to naïve speakers to be *-ɴdi* ([n:dɪ] or [n:dʸi], depending on the time of the abduction), and the underlying form was restructured, now appearing even in cases where it had not done so before (= abductive change). So: /...ɴ##di/ → /...##ɴ'di/. At an even earlier period the quotative particle was *\*-te*, without voicing, but with a mid vowel. Cf. Shinzato and Serafim [2013: 265].

114   "... funa-de shita to itte, hashitte-iru to itte shirare, kami-sama ni mamorare yo" (Hokama [2000b: 38b]).

VERBS                                                                      253

The *omoro* below (as cited in Shinzato and Serafim [2013: 253–254], and overlapping an earlier citation on p. 228 in this chapter) depicts the duties of one of
the high-ranking priestesses and her assistant, to cleanse precious jewels before
dedicating them to the King.[115] The T-form here can be interpreted as either
perfective or gerund.

きみよしが゛、　　／　さしぶ†、ᴀ　　　てるくもは、　　　／ いきやる、ᴀ
ki mi yo si ga*,　　／　sa si bu†,ᴀ　　te ru ku mo pa ,　/ i ki ya ru , ᴀ
*k°yimyi-yusyi-ga*　　*sasyibu-∅*　　*tʰiru.k°umu-wa*　　*ʔyik°yar-u*
Kyimiyoshi-GEN　　deputy-APPO Terukumo-TOP　　what.kind.of-RT
さうず゛、ᴀ　　　　あてが゛、　　　／　　　　　　くもこ ᴀ
sa u zu*, ᴀ　　　　a te ga*,　　　／　　　　　　ku mo ko ᴀ
*soo|zi-∅*　　　(A: *ʔa-t°e[e]-ga*　/　B: *ʔa-t°i-ga*)　*k°umu-kʰu-∅*
sacred.waters-SUB (A:be-PRFV-SKP　/　B:be-GER-KP) -∅golden-one-DO
より、いで゛たる　　　／ まだま ᴀ　　　　より、いで゛たる　　　／
yo ri , i de* ta ru　　／ ma da ma ᴀ　　yo ri , i de* ta ru　　／
*yur.yi.ʔyidzyi-t°ar-u*　*ma-dama-∅*　*yur.yi.ʔyidzyi-t°ar-u*
select.out-PRFT-RT　　true-jewel-DO select.out-PRFT-RT

A:　'What kind of sacred water **did** Kimiyoshi's deputy Terukumo have? (The
　　reason that I ask is) she had selected the golden jewel, the true jewel [to
　　cleanse with it].'
B:　'What kind of sacred water **does** Kimiyoshi's deputy Terukumo have, to
　　have selected the golden jewel, to have selected the true jewel [to cleanse
　　with it]?' (OS 11.#572)

The gerund/perfective already had four+four allomorphs in OOk, and *seems*, at
least, to retain that number in NOk:

---

115　As mentioned earlier, a possible variant of *ʔyidzyi-* is the non-PPed *ʔyi̯di-*; the PP involved
　　here is lexeme internal, and it should be quite automatic, thus not needing to be written
　　in. However, it usually *is* written in (as in a partially overlapping omoro, ⟨i di* we ta ru⟩ and
　　⟨i di* pe ta ru⟩ = *ʔyidzyi-tar-u* [OS 21.#1457]).
　　　　Our interpretation for *yur-yi-ʔyidzyi-* as 'select out, carefully choose' differs both from
　　Hokama 2000a (OS 11.#572) and OSJS 60c ⟨i te ta ru⟩. The complex lexical form *yur-yi-*
　　*ʔyidzyi-* is independently attested in *yur-yi-ʔyidzyi kʰugani* 'carefully selected golden one
　　[= hairpin [OSJS 360a]; = sword [OKDJ 722b]]' (⟨yo ri i di† we ko ga* ne⟩). Our SKP inter-
　　pretation in A follows Hokama's, differing from Ikemiya (1987: 224), which we give as
　　B.

| Function | [- del rel][116] | | [+ del rel] | | |
|---|---|---|---|---|---|
| | [- voice] | [+ voice] | [- voice] | [+ voice] | |
| OOk GER | *-tʲi* [tʲɪ] | *-di* [dɪ] | *-cʲyi* [ʧʲi] | *-dzyi* [dʒi] | [+hi, -long] |
| PFV | *-tʲee* [tʲɛː] | *-dee* [dɛː] | *-cʲyee* [ʧʲɛː] | *-dzyee* [dʒɛː] | [-hi, +long] |
| NOk GER | *-ti* [tʲi] | *-di* [dʲi] | *-cyi* [ʧi] | *-zyi* [(d)ʒi] | [-long] |
| PRFV(QP) | *-tii* [tʲiː] | *-dii* [dʲiː] | *-cyii* [ʧiː] | *-zyii* [(d)ʒiː] | [+long] |

However, comparison with other YNQ usages shows that the length of the perfective yes-no-question form in NOk—unlike in OOk—is actually a separate morpheme {+yi 'YNQ'}, making PRFV YNQ sequences actually allomorph fusions of {+ti+yi '+PFV+QP'}, so that the example above could be rewritten in part as:

| NOk GER | *-ti* [tʲi] | *-di* [dʲi] | *-cyi* [ʧi] | *-zyi* [(d)ʒi] | [-long] |
|---|---|---|---|---|---|
| PRFV-QP | *-ti-i* [tʲiː] | *-di-i* [dʲiː] | *-cyi-i* [ʧiː] | *-zyi-i* [(d)ʒiː] | [-long] [-long] |

Thus the number of allomorphs of the NOk gerund/perfective (GER/PRFV) morpheme has actually been reduced to four, namely *-ti(-)*, *-di(-)*, *-cyi(-)*, and *-zyi(-)*.

### 4.2 Sound Changes in Prehistory

Sometime in prehistory two general sound changes affected the shape of the gerund: 1) Progressive Palatalization and 2) Obstruent Voicing.

| Stage 1 | PP | Stage 2 | Voicing | Stage 3 |
|---|---|---|---|---|
| *-te* | > | *-te* | > | *-te* |
| | > | *-tye* | > | *-tye* |
| | | | > | *-de* |
| | | | > | *-dye* |

---

116 [del rel] is the common abbreviation for [delayed release], and distinguishes stops ([- del rel]) from affricates ([+ del rel]).

VERBS                                                                        255

Three further sound changes resulted in the forms observed in OOk:

    [- PP] [+ PP]
[- voi] *-te*     *-tye*   > AFF > *-te -cye*   > RAI > *-tɪ -cyɪ*   > PVI > *-tɪ=-tˢi  -cˢyi*=[ʧˢi]
[+ voi] *-de*     *-dye*          *-de -ʤye*           *-dɪ -ʣyɪ*            *-dɪ=-di -ʣyi*=[ʤi]
AFF= AFFrication; RAI= RAIsing; PVI= Palatalization of vowel [ʸɪ] > [⁽ʸ⁾i]

Thus the list of sound changes is, in order:
1)    Progressive Palatalization
2)    Voicing
3)    Affrication
4)    Raising
5)    Palatalization of Vowel [ʸɪ] to [⁽ʸ⁾i]
Note that 1) PP is the first, and could in fact have been a phonetic fact of PJ, as
was suggested in Shinzato and Serafim (2013: 139).

   OOk now no longer had [tˢy] or [dy] because they had been replaced by
[ʧˢ] and [ʤ], respectively, written *cˢy* and *ʣy*. The raising of [ɛ] resulted in
[ɪ], clearly different from [ʸi] in all environments; there was even a {[ʸɪ] ↔ [ʸɪ]}
distinction, and at this point *cˢyi* [ʧˢi] (e.g. *\*c̄yīk̄(y)a-sa* 'proximity' [*cˢyi₍ᵢ₎k̄ˢa-
sa* '(id.)' OS 15.#1100]) was distinct from *cyɪ* [ʧˢɪ] (e.g. *\*tac-yi-c̄yī* 'standing'
[> *tʰacˢyi-cˢyi* '(id.)' OS 7.#358]). Finally the palatalization of [ɪ] in palatal environments—*[⁽ʸ⁾ɪ] > [⁽ʸ⁾i]—meant that the formerly opposed pair {\*[ʸɪ] ↔ \*[ʸi]}
had now merged. Therefore OOk *cˢyi, ʣyi* meant only °[ʧˢi], °[ʤi], never ˣ[ʧˢɪ],
ˣ[ʤɪ].[117]

### 4.3    *Exemplification of Sound Changes in Prehistory with {···k+} and {···g+} : ····-cyi and ····-ʣyi*
K-type quadrigrades have gerunds in *-cˢyi* = [ʧˢi] (or, more precisely [ccˢi]), and
*g*-type, in *-ʣyi* = [ʤi] (or, more precisely [ɟzi]).

のすで、ˌ　はちやる　　　　　　 /
no su de ,ˌ pa ti ya ru　　　　 /
*nusi-di　　 pʰa-cˢy-ar-u*
steal-GER   wear-PRFV-SE-RT
'In fact, stealing [the sword], [she] **did** wear [it].' (OS 10.#546)[118]

---

117    We *have*, however, suggested that a later laxing of the vocalic nucleus of [ʸi] to [ʸɪ] *did* take
       place, to account for certain PP exceptions.
118    Cf. also Ch. 7 §4.1 for the same example from a different point of view.

256 CHAPTER 6

We see *pʰa-c°y-ar-u* as derived from *\*pʰak°-yi-t°[e]-ar-u*. The sequence is evidently:

$$*\cdots k°\text{-}yi\text{-}t°\cdots > *\cdots k°\text{-}yi\text{-}t°y\cdots > *\cdots k°\text{-}y\text{-}t°y\cdots > *\cdots\emptyset\text{-}t°y\cdots > \cdots\emptyset\text{-}c°y\cdots$$

The PP change may always have been present as a low-level phonetic option from the time of PJ.

| こぢ†へ ∧ | きよる、∧ | | きよら | や | / |
|---|---|---|---|---|---|
| ko di† pe ∧ | ki yo ru , ∧ | | ki yo ra | ya | / |
| *kʰuu-dzyi*[119] | *k-°y-uur-u-∅*[120] | | *k°yura*[121] | *yaa* | |
| row-GER | come-RY-SE-RT$_{NOM}$-TOP, | | beautiful | SFP | |

'Their row**ing** towards us is quite a sight to behold!' (OS 10.#545)

We see *kʰuu-dzyi* derived from *\*koog-yi-t[e]*. The sequence is evidently:

$$*\cdots g\text{-}yi\text{-}t\cdots > *\cdots g\text{-}yi\text{-}ty\cdots > *\cdots g\text{-}y\text{-}ty\cdots > *\cdots g\text{-}y\text{-}dy\cdots >$$
$$*\cdots \emptyset\text{-}dy\cdots > \cdots \emptyset\text{-}dzy\cdots$$

To put it into words in the most general way, when for whatever reason a cluster of two obstruents comes into being, the resulting cluster will take on the voicing of the first of the two. Thus:

$$*[k^y°{:}\mathrm{t\!\int}°] \text{ (to simplify, } *[k\mathrm{t\!\int}]) > *[k^y°{:}\mathrm{t\!\int}°] \text{ (more simply, } *[k\mathrm{t\!\int}]) \text{ and}$$
$$*[g^y{:}\mathrm{t\!\int}°] \text{ (more simply, } *[g\mathrm{t\!\int}]) > *[g^y{:}\mathrm{d\!\!3}] \text{ (more simply, } *[g\mathrm{d\!\!3}])$$

---

119  The length of {kʰuug+} is inferred from the NOk long-vowel root {kuug+⌐} (OGJ 346b). The modern root apparently cannot have come from a short-vowel form, and therefore—within the Okinawan lineage at least—the length is original. However, Thorpe reconstructs #179 PRk *\*kogi* with no length. Indeed only Shuri among his collection of dialects has a long vowel. Nakijin, on Motobu Peninsula in northern Okinawa Island, has /huzuʳɴ/ ([ɸu(d)ʒuʳɴ]), with a short vowel (ROD「漕ぐ」). Segmentally, Naha dialect *kuuʳzyuɴ* (OGJ2: 88a, クー「ジュン) is identical to the adjoining Shuri. Martin (1987: 711) has PJ *\*kög-*, with type B accent throughout Japonic. This accent type—low register—has sometimes been associated with first-syllable length in Shuri *nouns* (e.g. *kaagi,* 'looks; figure; shade', type 2.5, associated with low register, Martin [1987: 432], *kage*). It is not clear, however, whether the length drives the register, or vice versa.

120  The length is derived by comparison with NOk forms, e.g. **cuuru** [= our *c-y-uur-u*] '[beautiful courtesan] who is coming', under heading **cuuɴ**Ⓞ [= our *c-y-uu-ɴ,*] (OGJ 172a).

121  Also note the alliteration of all three major lexical words in this line, surely no accident. Also note the two contracted *k°y*-s.

VERBS                                                                          257

Further, one may ask if there was still a distinction between [d͡ʒ] and [ʒ] in
OOk. It is generally believed that such a distinction had been lost, and certainly
there is none such in NOk, but we believe that the merger of /d͡zy/ and /zy/ had
not yet occurred. See Ch. 2 § 5.4, p. 64 ff. for details.

Comparing the two sequences presented above, it becomes clear that they
have many overlapping points in common:

|   | 1 | 2 | 3 | 4 | 5 |
|---|---|---|---|---|---|
| K | *···*k-yi-t*··· > | *···*k-yi-ty*··· > | *···*k-yi-cy*··· > | *···*k-y-cy*··· > | *···*k-y-cy*··· > ···∅-c°y··· |
| G | *···*g-yi-t*··· > | *···*g-yi-ty*··· > | *···*g-yi-cy*··· > | *···*g-y-cy*··· > | *···*g-y-dzy*··· > ···∅-dzy··· |

A verbal statement and commentary on the sound changes affecting the velars
follows:

1   The initial consonant of the T-type morpheme progressively palatalized
    when preceded by the RY morpheme's allomorph *-yi-.[122] As to the mean-
    ing of "RY allomorph *-yi-," note that {+yi(+) 'RY'} has or had possibly three
    allomorphs: i) -yi(-), ii) *-i(?), and iii) -∅ (or a fusion of stem plus the
    zero allomorph). The particularization to *-yi in the statement reduces its
    generality in the appropriate manner, since it must only apply to the allo-
    morph with the feature specification [+ palatal] in it, i.e. the allomorph
    with y:

    a)  Before the r-gradization, *e-stem bigrade GER/PRFVs (such as *ʔage-
        ∅-te) had a zero allomorph of the RY morpheme (or, to put it another
        way, their stems themselves functioned as the RY form), and this
        allomorph had no palatalizing effect on the following GER/PRFV
        morpheme shape. Further,

    b)  r-stem quadrigrades (minus ones with the final-lexical-morpheme
        phoneme-sequence *···*yir-*) lack palatalized GER/PRFVs, having
        only the plain -tʼi GER/PRFV allomorph. We assume loss of the
        triggering *y element, either alone, e.g. *tor-yi-tye > *tor-∅i-te =
        *[tʰɔrɪtʼɛ] (the *y = *[ʸ] of *-tye = *[tʸʷɛ] is assumed to be phonet-
        ically dependent upon the preceding *phonemic* *y in the sequence

───────────────

122  It will turn out that no mention need be made of the velars at this point—that is, this rule
     applies to all verb types whose environment meets the specification of the rule.

*yi* = *[ʸi], and vanishes when its triggering environment changes) or as the entire vowel */yi/ = *[ʸi], *tor-∅-te*:

> *tor-y i-tye*
> *tor-∅ i-te*
> *tor-∅-te*
> (*tor-u-te*)

There is one further option, on the fourth row in the above table, though we do not understand how it would work from the point of view of phonological naturalness: We know that e.g. *kʰop-ˀyi-tˀye* underwent labial weakening in intervocalic position, yielding *kʰow-yi-tˀye*, with an unstable syllable *.wyi.*, and this probably quickly changed to *.wu.*, yielding *kʰow-u-tˀe*, with a newly—and automatically—de-palatalized gerund *-tˀe* from the earlier *-tˀye*. It may be at this point that a gerund built on an unstable RY allomorph, e.g. the original-*r*-stem *tʰor-i-tˀe* = *[tʰɔrɪtˀɛ], was swept in with the more stable *w*-stem *-u*$_{RY}$- allomorph[123] and became *tʰor-u-tˀe* = *[tʰɔrutˀɛ].

> *kʰop-ˀyi-tˀye*  >  *kʰow-yi-tˀye*  >  *kʰow-u-tˀe*  =  *kʰow-u-tˀe*
> *tʰor-yi-tˀye*  >  *tʰor-i-tˀe*  →  *tʰor-u-tˀe*

Thus there would have been, for consonant-stem verbs, for a time at least, a RY allomorph *-u-*.

2   A palatal(ized) consonant *ty*, *dy* became affricated *cy*, *dzy*.

3   For the velar stems (and for the *s*-stems as well—there are no *z*-stems) the vocalic core of the RY morpheme *-yi-* was lost, yielding *-y-*, when preceded by a velar verb root (ditto *s*-stem verb root) and followed by a T morpheme. Assuming that the vowel *ʸi* palatalized the preceding velar, and assuming that that palatalization was then phonologized:

> *[kˀʸi]  =  */kˀ.yi/, *[gʸi]  =  */g.yi/  >
> *[kʸˀ]  =  */kʸˀ/,  *[gʸ]  =  */gʸ/,

... so that the loss of that very same triggering vowel did *not* result in the automatic loss of the palatalization of that preceding velar,[124] then:

> *[kʰakˀʸityˀɛ]  *[kʰɔ̃ːgʸityˀɛ]
> *[kʰakˀʸitʃˀɛ]  *[kʰɔ̃ːgʸitʃˀɛ]
> *[kʰakʸːtʃˀɛ]  *[kʰɔ̃ːgʸːtʃˀɛ]
> *[kʰakʸːtʃˀɛ]  *[kʰɔ̃ːgʸːdʒɛ]

---

123   ..., since the language otherwise had not developed /i/ = [ɪ], ....

124   That "baking in" of the velar palatalization would have been most straightforward if the palatalized velars had affricated, but the sequence of changes apparently militates against such a state of affairs at the time of the changes that we are observing.

| | |
|---|---|
| *[kʰatʸːtʃ°ɛ] | *[kʰɔ̃ːdʸːʤɛ] |
| *[kʰatʃ°ɛ] | *[kʰɔ̃ːʤɛ] |
| *[kʰatʃ°ɪ] | *[kʰõ̃ːʤɪ] |
| [kʰatʃ°i] | [kʰũ̃ːʤi] |

As in the case of Japanese, the coronal obstruents underwent affrication relatively early; this is known from the Korean records. It was, however, only after Shuri's entry into its own historical era in the late 1400s that the velars underwent affrication, most likely well into the 18th or even the 19th century.[125]

4   The initial consonant of the T-morpheme voiced when preceded by a voiced obstruent (which was phonetically prenasalized) or a nasal.[126]

5   A coronal (i.e. a homorganic) palatalized consonant (i.e. [tʸː] or [ˀdʸː]) was lost before a T-morpheme (which, needless to say, was palatalized: [tʃ°] or [⁽ˀ⁾ʤ]):

---

**'scratching'  'rowing'**

---

| | |
|---|---|
| *[kʰa͞tʸːtʃ°ɛ] | *[kʰɔ̃ː͞dʸːʤɛ] |
| *[kʰa∅tʃ°ɛ] | *[kʰɔ̃ː∅dʤɛ]   after degemination |

---

These changes occurred before the changes leading to the OOk gerund of the *t*-type 4G verbs, where throughout that period the sequence remained *⋯[tʸitʸ°]⋯ or *⋯[tʃ°itʃ°]⋯, with an intact palatal vowel. This then became OOk and NOk ⋯[tʸːtʃ°]⋯ = ⋯Q-c°y⋯, as follows:

世がけ、せぢ、   ／ まわちへ、ᴧ   もちちへ、ᴧ   みおやせ   ／
YO ga ke , se di ,   ／ ma wa ti pe ,ᴧ   mo ti ti pe ,ᴧ   mi o ya se   ／
*yu-gaki-sidzyi*      *mawa-c°yi*   *muc°yi-c°yi*   *myi-ʔu-yaas-i*
world-control-s.p   turn_{VT}-GER   hold.RY-GER   EX-EX-offer-MR

'... turning and holding the spiritual power to protect and rule our world, offer it up [to His Majesty]!'[127] (OS 2.#69)

For OOk *muc°yic°yi*, we assume [mut̥ʃit̥ʃi], a form just before the geminating coalescence of the two affricates, with the vowel between them short (because high) and devoiced (because between two voiceless obstruents). The phonetics of the NOk form are [mutʸːtʃi], with the merger completed and with a voiced final mora (ROD ⟨⟨ムチュン⟩⟩).

---

125   A tip of the hat to one of our reviewers, who furnished us with Chinese data.

126   ... as it will turn out below.

127   Hokama (2000a: 61b) "... yo o hogo-shi shihai-suru reiryoku o mawashite motte tatematsure."

CHAPTER 7

# Auxiliaries

An auxiliary is defined as an inflecting form attached to a predicate form, typically a verb, an adjective, a copula, or another auxiliary, with specific grammatical and semantic functions, as laid out below. Thus, structurally it follows a predicate, but precedes a sentence-final particle. Also treated in this chapter is the copula itself.

Similar to MJ (Ōno [1968: 145–149]) and NJ (Minami [1974: 108–113]), OOk auxiliaries are also theoretically expected to be serially connected in a particular order, roughly as below:

VB + VOICE + ASPECT + NEG + TENSE + MOOD + SFP

Roughly, the order of elements may be characterized as from more objective ones, such as auxiliaries pertaining to voice or temporality, to ones indicating more subjective states, expressing the speaker's suppositions and stances (cf. Shinzato 2007). It is difficult to substantiate the above order with solid data, however, as there are few cases where multiple auxiliaries occur in sequence in the OS; this is not surprising given the nature of the OS as poetry, not prose.

## 1     Passive/Exalting/Spontaneous Auxiliaries: *-ari(·r)-* ~ *-uyi(·r)-*

In OOk, there are numerous tokens and types utilizing *-ari(·r)-*, with only two types utilizing *-uyi(·r)-*, namely *kˬyi̯ k-ˬuyi(·r)-* '(be) resounding' and *ʔub-uyi(·r)-* '[to] learn [in one's heart]'. §1.1 and §1.2 deal with *-ari(·r)-*, §1.3 covers *-uyi(·r)-*, and §1.4 gives a historical/comparative analysis.

### 1.1     *Passive* -ari(·r)-
The auxiliary {+ari·r+} forms a passive voice. For illustration, we offer the active and passive forms of the verb 'hear'. First the active: It is the RY form of the verb base: *kˬyik-ˬyi*, and takes a direct object. The preceding clause disambiguates the DO: ひやしの、 つち、 うたば†、/ ⟨pi ya si no , tu ti , ∧ u ta ba†/⟩ *pˬyoosyi-nu cˬicˬyi-∅ ʔut-ˬa-ba* 'when [← if] [she] strikes [with] the rhythmic mallet,'

© KONINKLIJKE BRILL NV, LEIDEN, 2021 | DOI:10.1163/9789004414686_008

AUXILIARIES

261

きゝ、　　かなしげ†さ　　　　　／
ki ", 　　ka na si ge† sa 　　　　／
k°yik-°yi 　kʰana·syi·gyi̯-sa
hear$_\text{VT}$-RY 　beautiful·ADS·ODS-NDS
'[when we] hear$_\text{VT}$ [it$_\text{DO}$], [it] seems [so] beautiful!' (OS 4.#182)

The passive form of the verb is made with the base plus -*ari* [ɑɾɪ], as in the example below. The word 'heard' is a modifier, 'famed', the RY of the PASSIVE 'be-ing hear-d'.

*syimu-nu　k°yi̯k-°ari　　　　　ʔyik°usa*
S.of.S-GEN　[hear-PASS$_\text{RY}$]$_\text{famed}$　army
'... the army[1] famed (*lit.* 'heard') to the South of Shuri' (OS 17.#1177)

The passive form conjugates as a L2G auxiliary. The attested forms are: -*ari* (RY), -*ari·r-i* (IZ, MR), and -*ari-t°i* (GER). There follow some examples of the passive usages in their attested conjugational forms.

In the first example below, the RY form -*ari*- is followed by another auxiliary. In the second example, however, the RY form is used to modify the head noun. This type of RY usage seems to be limited to grammaticalized prefixal usages referred to as *bishōji* 'beautifying expressions' (BE), including *tʰuyumyi*- 'resounding' (not itself a "passive") and *k°yi̯(₀)k°(y)-ari-(y)-* '(heard →) famed'.[2]

あらはゑす、ᴧ　とよみ、　　／きゝやれ、よれ　　／
a ra pa we su , ᴧ　to yo mi , 　／ ki " ya re , yo re 　／
*ʔara-pʰayi-si　　tʰuyum-yi　　k°yik°y-ari-yur-i*[3]
PN-KP　　　　　resound-RY　　hear-PASS$_\text{RY}$-SE-IZ
'It is <u>Arahae</u> who is the resounding and famed one.'[4] (OS 16.#1155)

---

1　Recall that *k°u* cannot be PPed, because *k°u < \*ku*, and moras with etymological high vowels are not PPable.

2　RY forms also appear in other very common formulaic phrases such as *ʔamayi*$_\text{RY}$-*yuu* 'peaceful-world', etc., which may be ← {##ama+'be.sweet'}{+ayi+ 'SPON'}, a lexicalized -(*a*)*yi*- word, + {##yuu## 'world, era'}.

3　Homorganic sound change of *\*w* in *\*wore* to *\*y* (i.e. to *\*yore*) to accord with a preceding *\*(y)i*.

4　"PASS" in small caps will indicate a *form*, while "pass" in lower-case will indicate a *function*, and similarly for "SPON[TANEOUS]" and "spon[taneous]", and for "EX" and "ex" for those forms and functions.

| しもの、∧ | とよみ、∧ | いくさ、/ | しもの、 | きかれ、 |
| si mo no ,∧ | to yo mi ,∧ | i ku sa , / | si mo no , | ki ka re , |
| *syimu-nu* | *tʰuyum-yi* | *ʔyik°usa* | *syimu-nu* | *k°yi̯k-°ari* |
| South.of.Shuri-GEN | resound-RY | army | S.of.S-GEN | [hear-PASS_RY]_famed |

いくさ
i ku sa
*ʔyik°usa*
army

'The army resounding to the South of Shuri, the army famed[5] (*lit.* 'heard') to the S.of.S.' (OS 17.#1177)

The two examples below show the IZ form in KM constructions, agreeing with KP forms -*zyu* and -*si*.

| だりじよ、∧ | げすに、∧ | をもわれゝ | / |
| da ri zi yo ,∧ | ge su ni ,∧ | wo mo wa re " | / |
| *daryi-zyu* | *gisi-nyi* | *ʔumuw-ari·r-i* | |
| truly-KP_KM | retainers-AGT | think-PASS·4GE-IZ_KM | |

'Indeed,[6] [the King's] heart **is** admir**ed** by his subordinates.' (OS 5.#261)

| だりす、∧ | とよみ、∧ | きかれゝ | / |
| da ri su[7] ,∧ | to yo mi ,∧ | ki ka re " | / |
| *daryi-si* | *tʰuyum-yi* | *k°yi̯k-°ari·r-i* | |
| truly-KP | resound-RY | hear-PASS·4GE-IZ | |

'Indeed, [the lord's fame] resounds and **is** hear**d** [throughout the land].' (OS 17.#1177)

Below are examples of MR. Of 73 examples of passive auxiliaries, *syi̯r-ari·r-i* 'know-PASS·4GE-MR' (33 tokens) and *yu-syi̯r-ari·r-i* 'VPFX-know-PASS·4GE-MR' (11 tokens), e.g.:

---

5 Both non-PP (the example) and PP spellings (in the following) are to be found: ⟨ki " **ya** re , i ku sa⟩ きゝやれ、いくさ *k°yiky-°ari-ʔyik°usa* '(id.)' (OS 9.#507).

6 {+sʊ 'IZ-type KP'} = -*si* ~ -*syu*: {···yi}{+sʊ} → ···*yi-syu*; elsewhere {···}{+sʊ} → ····*si*. Note the voicing discrepancy with the discussed -*zyu*. While this is not regular, it is apparently affected by a preceding nasal. What nasal? The *n* that temporally preceded the *r* of *daryi*: \**da* 'true' + \*+*nyi* + \*+*sʊ* > \**danyisʊ* > \**danyisyʊ* > \**danyizyʊ* > \**daryizyʊ* > *daryizyu*. There were, then, two changes that were possible but not exceptionless: (1) *n* > *r*; (2) *s* > *z*. Interestingly enough, the scribe did not confuse fricative ⟨si yo / zi yo⟩ -*syu*/-*zyu* (which "ties up" with -(*r*)*i*) with affricate ⟨di yo⟩ -*dzyu*, which is the allomorph for the *other* KP, {+do} = -*du* ~ -*dzyu*, which "ties up" with -(*r*)*u*.

7 Here the PP option is not taken, and the underlying form appears as-is.

# AUXILIARIES

263

| *syi̯r* - *ari* · *r* - *i* | *yu* - *syi̯r* - *ari* · *r* - *i* |
|---|---|
| know - PASS · 4GE - IZ/MR | VPFX - know - PASS · 4GE - IZ/MR |
| (33 tokens) | (11 tokens) |

count 60% of the entire number of instances. OSJS (186a) states that for the omoro composers, being known to deities and kings meant being protected and governed. In the OS, *syi̯r-ari·r-* appears in parallel with verbs meaning 'say'.[8] For instance, in the parallel verses in (OS 3.#89) below, the first verb is *yu-syi̯r-ari*, and it is coupled with the clear 'say' verb, *nu-dati·r-i* (< *nor-yi-* *'announce-RY' + *tate·r-e* *'raise-4GE-MR'), with no 'PASS' morpheme.

| 大ぎみに、ʌ | よしられ、 | / てるかはに、ʌ |
|---|---|---|
| OPO gi mi ni , ʌ | yo si ra re [re] , | / te ru ka pa ni , ʌ |
| ʔuQp°u-gyimyi-nyi | yu-syi̯r-ari·r-i | tʰiru#kʰaQp°a-nyi |
| EX-priestess-IO | [VPFX-know-PASS·4GE]speak-MR | Sun.Deity-IO |
| のだてれ | / | |
| no da te re | / | |
| nu·datʰi·r-i | | |
| state·on.high-MR | | |

'[Lower ranking priestesses:] **Speak to**[9] the High Priestess and address prayers to the Sun Deity ...!' (OS 3.#89)

| あんじおそいに、ʌ | しられゝ | / たゝみきよに、ʌ |
|---|---|---|
| aNzi o so i ni , ʌ | si ra re " | / ta " mi ki yo ni , ʌ |
| ʔaNzyi-ʔusii-nyi | syi̯r-ari·r-i | tʰat°amyi#kʰyu-nyi |
| lord-ruler_BE-IO | [know-PASS_ex·4GE]speak-MR | noble-one-IO |
| しられゝ | / | |
| si ra re " | / | |
| syi̯r-ari·r-i | | |
| [know-PASS_ex·4GE]speak-MR | | |

'**Speak humbly to** the King, **speak humbly to** the noble one ...' (OS 10.#521)

---

8 *syi̯r-ari·r-* survives into dialects of Amami as a humble form of *say* (Osada, Suyama, and Fuji'i (1980: 389) and Shigeno (2010: 8–9)).

9 Hokama (2000a: 73 [#89]) translates both ⟨yo SI ra re⟩ and ⟨NO DA te re⟩ (his text) as 'mōshi-age-yo' = 'state [to a superior]!', and adds that to do so is to be protected. In order for such an interpretation to be correct, ⟨yo si ra re⟩ should have an extra ⟨re⟩. Presumably scribal haplology is to blame for the non-existence of a second ⟨re⟩. See e.g. TOS (781: leaf 9オ), leftmost line, bottommost *kana*. We follow Hokama in our own translation.

Below are examples of GER forms of the Passive.

がぢやも、∧　　　せゝられて、　　/　ぬかこ、∧　　　せゝられて
ga di ya mo , ∧　se " ra re te ,　/　nu ka ko , ∧　se " ra re te
*gadzyamu-∅*　　*sisir-**ari-t°i***　　*nuk°a#kʰu-∅*　*sisir-**ari-t°i***
mosquito-AGT sting-PASS-GER　　gadfly-AGT　sting-PASS-GER
'〖**Being**〗stung by mosquitos, 〖and ...〗stung by gadflies ...' (OS 14.#987)

きみに ∧　　　　いしや、まれて、　/　ぬしに、∧　　　　このまれて　　　　/
ki mi ni ∧　　i si ya , ma re te ,　/　nu si ni , ∧　ko no ma re te　　/
*k°yimyi-nyi*　*ʔyisyam-**ari-t°i***　　*nusyi-nyi*　*kʰunum-**ari-t°i***
priestess-AGT love-PASS-GER　　officiant-AGT prefer-PASS-GER
'〖**being**〗loved by the priestess, 〖...〗prefer**red** by the officiant ...' (OS 3.#94)

## 1.2 Exalting -ari(·r)-

The honorific usage of this auxiliary is not as prevalent as the passive usage, as the ratio between them is 18% :: 82%. The co-occurring verbs in the honorific usage are mostly praying verbs, *ʔyi̯nur-u* and *wugam-u*. The subject of such a verb is usually a higher-ranking priestess or the King. For instance, in the examples below, it is the actions of the *k°yik°uyi ʔuQp°u-gyimyi* (OS 3.#95), the famed priestess *k°yimyi#pʰayi* of Kume-island (OS 11.#564), and the priestess of sea travel in (OS 13.#902) that are described with this exalting auxiliary *-ari·r-*. The song has been given by the priestess acting as a tutelary deity to the male sailors who are about to set sail for the North (cf. Higa [1989: 26], *Omoro Kanshō* 50).

きこゑ　　　大ぎみぎや、　　　/　とよむ ∧　　せだかこが、　　　/
ki ko we　OPO gi mi gi ya ,　/　to yo mu ∧　se da ka ko ga ,　/
*k°yi̯k°uyi ʔuQp°u-gyimyi-gya*　　*tʰuyum-u*　*si-dakʰa-kʰu-ga*
famed　　great-priestess-SUB　resonate-RT s.p.-high-one-SUB
みしま、∧　　　いのられゝ　　　　　　/
mi si ma , ∧　i no ra re "　　　　　/
*myi.syima-∅*　*ʔyi̯nur-**ari·r-i***
Shuri-DO　　pray[-PASS·4GE]ₑₓ-MR
'[O] famed priestess, the resounding one, **may you pray for** [the peace of] Shuri ...' (OS 3.#95)

AUXILIARIES                                                                                  265

げおの、　　きみはいや、　　　　　／ もゝと、ヘ　　　　てづられゝ　　　　　　　／
ge o no ,　　ki mi pa i ya ,　　　　／ mo " to ,ᴧ　　　te du ra re "　　　　　／
*giwu-nu*　　*kˣⁱyimyi#pʰayi-ya*　　　　*mumu-tʰu*　　*tʰi·dzi̧|r-ari·r-i*
spirit-GEN priestess#splendor-TOP　hundred-years pray[-**PASS·4GE**]ₑₓ-**MR**
'**May** the Priestess Kimihae (= Chinbē) **pray for** [our lord's] everlasting reign.'
(OS 11.#564)

あは、ヘ　おしられ、　　　　　　　／ おやまてす、ヘ　　　　はりよれ　　　　　／
a pa ,ᴧ　o si ra re ,　　　　　　　／ o ya ma te su ,ᴧ　　pa ri yo re　　　　／
*ʔa-Qpˣⁱa*　*ʔu-syi̧r-ari*　　　　　　*ʔuyama-tˣⁱi-si*　　*pʰaar∅-y-ur-i*
us-DO　EX-know/protect-**PASS**ᵣᵧ　pay.respect-**GER-KP**ₖₘ sail-RY-SE-IZₖₘ
'[A tail wind is blowing!] It is precisely because we are known/protected by [the
deities], because [we] venerate [them], that [we] are running along [so well]!'
(OS 13.#902)

### 1.3　*Spontaneous* -uyi(·r)-

This auxiliary is found only in two verbs, 1) *kˣⁱyi̧k-ˣⁱuyi-*, as in the High Priestess'
title (first example) and in modifiers (second example); or 2) *ʔubuyi* 'sense'.[10]
We may suspect that *kˣⁱyi̧k-ˣⁱuyi* is a loan from MJ, since it appears as an elevat-
ing prefix as in the first example, but the instances OS 21.#1454, OS 11.#577, and
OS 12.#700 preclude that possibility. In the former, *kˣⁱyi̧k-ˣⁱuyi·r-u* is a RT modifying the following noun; in the latter, it is used as a BE, an exalting suffix in the
first instance, and as at the sentence-final predicate in the second one.

きこゑ　　　　　　大ぎみぎや、　　　／ ...
ki ko we　　　　OPO gi mi gi ya ,　／ ...
*kˣⁱyi̧k-ˣⁱuyi*　　*ʔuQpˣⁱu-gyimyi-gya*
hear-**PASS**ₛₚₒₙ₋ᵣᵧ great-priestess-**SUB**
'The **famed** High Priestess ...' (OS 1.#1)

---

10　The morpheme -⁽ˣⁱ⁾*uyi*(·r)- instantiates the claimable Spontaneous functions: that means
that the functions bifurcate between the -(⁽ˣⁱ⁾*a*)*ri*(·r)- PASS and the -⁽ˣⁱ⁾*uyi*(·r)- SPON forms.
For SPON there are *kˣⁱyi̧k-ˣⁱuyi-* and *ʔub-uyi-*—and therefore a nearly perfect parallel form
\*-*oye*- in pre-OOk corresponds with -({*u/o*})*ye*- in MJ—of what must have previously
been a more robust construction, as in, for example, OJ and before. The arguments (1) *for*
borrowing may be low type frequency; and (2) *against* borrowing may be (a) extremely
high token frequency; (b) examples of phonological irregularity, suggesting old age; (c)
only passable semantic correlation of OOk *kˣⁱyi̧kˣⁱuyi*- (deverbal adjectival, BE) 'famed,
resounding' :: MJ *kikoye* (deverbal noun) 'reputation; respectability'; (d) the existence of a
certain amount of conjugation. NOk *cyifí-ziɴ* 'Kikoe Ōgimi' (OGJ 147b) shows that there
*was* a variant *kˣⁱyikˣⁱywii*-(*ʔuQpˣⁱu*-)*gyimyi*, where ···*kˣⁱyw*··· > ···*f*···. For the related DIG phenomenon, see Ch. 4 §4.2 fn. 73.

もゝする、、 とよむ、、 ／ きこゑる、、 もり ／
mo " su we ,ᴧ to yo mu ,ᴧ ／ ki ko we ru ,ᴧ mo ri ／
*mumu-siyi* *tʰuyum-u* **kˀyi̧kˀuyi·r-u** *muryi*
hundred-end resound-RT **hear-PASS**ₛₚₒₙ**·4GE-RT** grove
'The grove, which will be resounding, **famed** for many years to come'
(OS 21.#1454) (OS 11.#577)

だうの、 大や、、 きこへが、、 ／ まみや、、
da u no , ᴏᴘᴏ ya ,ᴧ ki ko pe ga ,ᴧ ／ ma mi ya ,ᴧ
*doo-nu* *ʔuQpˀu-ya* *-kˀyi̧kˀuyi-ga* *ma-myaa-∅*
PLN-GEN EX-person -hear-PASSₛₚₒₙ-SUB EX-enclosure-LOC
あすばす、、 きよら や ／ いしけなは、、
a su ba su ,ᴧ ki yo ra ya ／ i si ke na pa ,ᴧ
*ʔasib-as-i-∅* *kˀyura* *yaa* *ʔyisyikˀyinaQpˀa-∅*
dance-CAUS-RT-TOP beautiful SFP PLN-as.far.as
きこへる ／
ki ko pe ru ／
**kˀyi̧kˀuyi·r-u**
**hear-PASS**ₛₚₒₙ**·4GE-RT**
'The **famed**[11] leader of Dō [village of Kumejima]: his having [shamans] dance is so beautiful! He **resounds** as far as *ʔyisyikˀyinaQpˀa* (Ishikenaha)!' (OS12.#700)

In the following example *-yoo* 'appearance' is a noun; therefore, the preceding form has to be a RT. The actual form used, *kˀyikˀu···*, is a truncated form of the original RT form, *kˀyi̧kˀuyi·r-u*.[12]

---

11  ᴛᴏs (p. 410) states that all versions have it as ⟨ka⟩ except for the *Ifa* version, which interprets it as a voiced *ga*. ᴛᴏs also speculates that this might be a copyist error, and should be ⟨ru⟩ in accord with the other verses to maintain structural parallelism—but it reads better with *ga* than when interpreted as the parallel *ru*. Here we agree with Ifa, and take it as a subject marker *-ga*.

12  Aspiration suppression here is due to a phonological constraint. Both the *kˀyi* of *ʔyisyikˀyi-naQpˀa* and the *kˀu* of *kˀyikˀu-yoo-nyi* are not aspirated because of a rule that forces them to stay high and unaspirated because they come immediately after a historically high-vowel syllable, when otherwise we would have expected high (= raised) and aspirated (because formerly mid). Note that *kˀu* here is written with ⟨ko⟩, otherwise *kʰu*, not with ⟨ku⟩, also = *kˀu*, because an original *kʰo*'s aspiration was suppressed to *kˀo*, which did not have a separate spelling; so ⟨ko⟩ was simply kept, including after the vowel raising. The result was that for etymological mid vowels in voiceless obstruent syllables preceded by an etymological high vowel, it was normal for an *o*-column graph to be written even though in every respect the pronunciation mimicked an original voiceless-obstruent-plus-high-vowel mora.

AUXILIARIES 267

あんじおそいぎや、ˬ / おみこゑの、ˬ
a N zi o so i gi ya , ˬ / o mi ko we no , ˬ
*ʔaᴎzyi-ʔusii-gya*      *ʔu-myi#ˌkʰuyi-nu*
lord-protector-SUB    EX-EX#voice-SUB
きこやに                     /
ki ko ya ni                /
*kˢyiˌk-ˢu⟦yi·r-u⟧-yoo-nyi*
hear-P⟦ASS$_{spon}$·4GE-RT⟧-appearance-ADV
'As the lord's splendid, beautiful voice **is heard** ...' (OS 14.#992)

Another verb revealing the existence of the allomorph -$^{(°)}uyi(\cdot r)$- < *-*öyë*- in OOk is *ʔubuyi$_[$-t°i$_]$* 'being learned'. OSJS (87c–88a) claims that there was a dropped ⟨te⟩ and translates *ʔubuyi$_[$-t°i$_]$* as passive, but it does not explain the logic behind its account. It should be noted that MJ *oboye*- < OJ *ömöp-oye*- = {ömöp- 'think'}{+öyë+ 'PASS$_{spon}$'}, *and* that that is the source of the Spontaneous Passive reading.

あよがˬ うちに、ˬ おぼへ$_[$て$_]$す、      / せだかこに、ˬ
a yo ga ˬ u ti ni , ˬ o bo pe $_[$te$_]$ su ,    / se da ka ko ni , ˬ
*ʔayu-ga*   *ʔuc°yi-nyi*   *ʔub-uyi-t°i-si*        *si-dakʰa-kʰu-nyi*
liver-GEN   interior-at   learn-**PASS**$_{spon}$-GER-KP   spiritual.power-high-one-IO
しなよわ
si na yo wa
*syiˌna'-y-uwa-∅*
harmonize-RY-EAV-IZ
'its **being**, indeed, **because I feel [it] in [my] heart**, that [I] harmonize [it] with Sedakako' (OS 7.#365)

### 1.4    *Historical and Comparative Analysis*

Like OJ -*are*-/-*aye*-(~ -*öye*-)[13] ~ -*raye*- ~ -*ye*-, OOk also has two variants of the so-called passive auxiliary -*ari*(·*r*)- ~ -*uyi*(·*r*)-. As noted in Vovin (2009a: 839), OJ -*are*- is much less frequent than -*aye*- ~ -*raye*- ~ -*ye*-, but represents the apparent cognate to MJ -(*r*)*are*-. Regarding the relationship between the OJ variants, Vovin (2009a: 839) states: "The relationship between WOJ -*aye*- ~ -*raye*- ~ -*ye*- and the MJ passive suffix -(*r*)*are*- remains obscure, because there are no other

---

13    Vovin (2009a: 829) states: "...-*aye*- is assimilated to -*öye*- after the verb *ömop*- 'to think, to love.' The same allomorph -*öye*- is found after the verb *kyik*- 'to hear, to listen,' probably by analogy with *omöp*-."

cognates that exhibit the unique correspondence of WOJ -y- to MJ -r-, although it is likely that WOJ -y- is a lenited form of PJ *-r-."

Unlike OJ, the predominant auxiliary shape in OOk is -ari(·r)-, the cognate of OJ -are- and MJ -(r)are-. On the other hand, the cognate of OJ -({a/ö})ye- ~ -raye- is found as -uyi(·r)- (< *-oye(·r)- ← *-öyë-) in the fossilized exalting expressions k°yi̯k-°uyi (⟨ki ko pe⟩, ⟨ki ko we⟩ < *kyik(y)-öyë-) 'resounding' and k°yi̯k°(y)-uyi·r-u (⟨ki ko pe ru⟩, ⟨ki ko we ru⟩, ⟨ki " ro⟩ < *kyik(y)-oye·r-u), also meaning 'resounding'.[14]

| | | ... r... | | ... y... | ( | < | *... r... | ) | |
|---|---|---|---|---|---|---|---|---|---|
| "passive" | OJ | [-are-] | / | -(a)ye- | | ~ | -raye- | ~ | -öye- |
| | MJ | -(r)are- | | | | | | | |
| | OOk | -ari(·r)- | / | -ayi(·r)- | | | | | -uyi(·r)- |

In Kokugogaku (National Language Studies) literature, four terms have been used to capture the functions of this auxiliary group: *Ukemi* 受身 'Passive', *Jihatsu* 自発 'Spontaneous',[15] *Sonkei* 尊敬 'Exalting Referent Honorific' and *Kanō* 可能 'Potential'.[16,17] As diverse as they appear in these functions, a general consensus is that the Spontaneous meaning is the origin from which the other three meanings evolved (e.g. Hashimoto [1969 (1931)]). Bringing in a cross-linguistic perspective, Toyota (2011: 126) is in favor of such a path, as he sees it to be typologically the most common one, based on Greenberg's (1995: 150)

---

14  Thorpe (1983: 190) refers to the Proto-Ryukyuan forms as Middle. He claims that "Ry. actually had no specifically passive construction and the potential in a sentence like 'he can swim' was expressed by [a] completely unrelated construction ..." built on *{i}wos 'master, control' (179), expressing "agent-internal possibility / agent ability". But since OOk {+ari·r} *does* carry Passive and Honorific functions, and since a handful of instances of Spontaneous Occurrence *are* shown to have been denoted by OOk {+uyi·r+}, we have not adopted his use of the term Middle here.

15  Shibatani (1985: 827) states that "most so-called middle (medio-)passive or pseudo-passives are better understood as constructions which express SPONTANEOUS occurrence— an event that automatically occurs, or a state that spontaneously obtains without the intervention of an agent." Toyota (2011: 126), also, states that "the prototypical middle voice inherently refers to spontaneous events."

16  Whether or not to recognize -raye- in the chart above—instantiated only as one type, *i-nö ne-raye-nu* 'cannot sleep', though with several tokens—as an allomorph of the PASSIVE morpheme is controversial, as it is only attested with the verb base ne- 'sleep'. JDB (810a) clearly labels it a *Potential*, *not* a Passive. For this case see Vovin (2009: 828–829).

17  See Iwasaki (2002: 137) for a summary.

AUXILIARIES

study. He also notes that in the world's languages, it is rare for a verb of existence such as *aru* ('there to be', a stative verb) to be the progenitor of a Passive suffix (cf. e.g. Haspelmath 1990 on verbs of existence); rather, the more common source lexemes are change-of-state verbs (e.g. *become*,[18] *fall*) or motion verbs (*come* and *go*). In Japanese, however, as Toyota points out (2011: 127), the verb-of-existence source (*ar-* :: *-are-*), unexpected when looking at the origin from the world's languages, could be reconciled if the passives were derived from middles (i.e. spontaneous and potential).

The auxiliary *-ari(·r)-* in the *Omoro Sōshi* evinces both Passive and Exalting Honorific usages, but not Spontaneous or Potential. This may be somewhat surprising in comparison with OJ, because on the one hand, what were considered to be the source functions of *-(r)are-* in OJ (i.e. Toyota's Middle) are lacking, and on the other hand, his derived functions (Passive and Honorific) are predominant. The Honorific usages are generally characterized as a function developed in the early MJ period in the Japanese lineage (Yuzawa [1943: 76], Tsukishima [1969: 506]). Thus, OOk *-ari(·r)-* aligns more with MJ than OJ. However, Spontaneous, which might be expected from OJ, is attested in the *-uyi(·r)-* form (§1.3 above).[19]

To summarize, OOk forms and functions are added in chart form, together with their OJ counterparts' functions (Vovin [2009a: 828–842]):

---

18 Shinzato (2008) shows how the emergence verbs (*nar-u* 'appear/become' and *ide-k-u* 'appear') developed semantically into ability verbs in Japanese. In NOk, *na-y-u-N,* is still used as a verb denoting ability ('1. become. 2. head over. *3. is possible for [one] to [do]; [one] is able to [do]*' [OGJ 406a]).

19 Torigoe (1968: 207) considers *yapʰaru* and *tʰatʷuwaru* to be examples of Potential usage. It appears, however, that ···*ar* is part of the verbal stem, as shown in our analysis in parentheses. This is because there are NOk *yafára* and *yafáqteeN*, which show the ···*r*··· to be part of the stem. Similarly, the OOk pair {tʰatʷuw·ar+} 'compare' VI :: {tʰatʷuw·i·r+} 'compare' VT clearly shows that ···*ar-* is part of the stem.

みろく、ₐ　　みちへ、ₐ やはる、　　　　／
mi ro ku ,ₐ　mi ti pe ,ₐ ya pa ru ,　　　／
*myi·ɾukʷu-∅ myi·cʷyi　yapʰar u*　　　(S&S· *yapʰa·r-u*)
Maitreya-DO see-GER　feel.peaceful-PASS　(S&S: feel.peaceful-SS)
'Seeing the Maitreya Bodhisattva| can be soothing' (S&S: '|, one feels at peace') (OS 7.#375)
これど、ₐ　　こがね、うちに、ₐ　　たとわる
ko re do ,ₐ　ko ga ne , u ti ni ₐ　　ta to wa ru
*kʰuri-du　kʰugani-ʔucʷyi-nyi　tʰatʷuw·ar-u*　　(S&S: *tʰatʷuw·ar-u*)
this.one-KP golden_EX-interior-IO compare-PASS-RT　(S&S: compare-RT)
'[The castle in Shuri Grove,] it is *this* that compares to the Golden Enclosure (in Heaven).'
(OS 5.#239)

Functions/usages[20]

| | | Derived | | | | Source | |
|---|---|---|---|---|---|---|---|
| | | Passive | Exalting | Spontaneous | Potential | | |
| OJ | -(a/ö)y(e)- | + | - | + | + | | |
| MJ | -(a/o)y(e)- | | | (+) | | | |
| | | | | + | | -uyi(·r)- | OOk |
| | | | | | | | |
| OJ | -(r)ar(e)- | + | - | + | - | | |
| MJ | -(r)ar(e)- | + | + | + | + | | |
| | | + | + | - | - | -ari(·r)- | OOk |

## 2 Causative/Exalting Auxiliary: -as-

### 2.1 Causative -as-

The causative/exalting auxiliary -as- conjugates as a quadrigrade (4G), though some conjugational forms are missing in the OS; here are the four observed conjugations:

| | |
|---|---|
| -as-yi | RY |
| -as-i | RT, SS |
| -as-i[21] | MR |
| -a-c°yi | GER |

---

20   Adopting Vovin (ibid. 839), who states that there are no cognates of -aye- ~ -raye- ~ -ye- in MJ, the three functions are left blank, but the spontaneous function is marked as (+) because "-ye- [is] found in Middle Japanese only after the verb mi- 'to see, to look'."

21   Vovin also claims an allomorph -(a)si- (i.e. -asi- = [ɑsɪ]), but we believe that this results from a mis-analysis. The word he uses (there are a few others) is kʰuugasiya = [kʰuːɡɑsɪyɑ] 'have [them] row [it]!' The problematic point is i = [ɪ]. If it belongs to the root, then there is a causative allomorph /+asi+/ = [ɑsɪ], but if not, then /+as+/ = [ɑs]. /+i(+)/ = [ɪ] would then either belong with /ya/—actually /yaa/ = [yɑː]—or be a separate morpheme. We already know from NOk that /yaa/ is a phonologically independent sentence-final "particle" used as an interjection. Thus /+i+/ [ɪ] is a verbal suffix, and must be either IZ or MR. The form, then, is /##kʰuHg+as+ɪ#yaa/ 'row'+CAUS+MR+SFP 'have them row it!', and that means that this word gives no evidence for an allomorph /+asi+/.

AUXILIARIES                                                                            271

The examples below show it in RY, SS, RT, MR, and GER (originally RY *-yi +
*GER/*PRFV *-te) forms. In the first example below, the IO -nyi marks the indirect object = cause (AGENT of the verb tʰur- 'get'). But when tʰur-as- is fully
grammaticalized as the verb 'give', -nyi is interpreted as the IO of the *transfer*
verb 'give'. A fuller explanation follows below.

やふそ、　　　ころがま、　　/　ころがまに、ᴧ　　とらしよわ
ya pu so ,　　ko ro ga ma ,　/　ko ro ga ma ni ,ᴧ　to ra si yo wa
*yaqp°usu-∅　kʰuru-gama　　　kʰuru-gama-nyi　tʰur-as-y-uwa*
PLN-GEN　　men-DIM　　　　men-DIM-IO_{AGT}　get-**CAUS**-RY-EAV_{IA}
'[Priestess Sasukasa] will have our beloved men, our beloved men in Yafuso,
acquire [the holy eagle].' (OS 20.#1323)

いづこ、ᴧ　　　　　　なげかす　　　　な　　/
i du ko ,ᴧ　　　　　na ge ka su　　　na　　/
*ʔyidzɨ#kʰuu-∅　　nagik°-as-i　　　na*
outstanding-ones-DO　lament-**CAUS**-RT[22]　SFP_{NEG}
'Don't make the soldiers lament it.' (OS 3.#96)

もちづき、ᴧ　　　あすばす、ᴧ　　　　　　きよら　　や
mo ti du ki ,ᴧ　　a su ba su ,ᴧ　　　　　ki yo ra　ya
*muc°yi.dzik°yi-∅　ʔasib-as-i-∅　　　　k°yura　　yaa*
PN-DO　　　　　sacred.dance-**CAUS**-RT_{SUB}　beautiful　SFP
'**Having** the priestess Mochizuki perform a sacred dance is so beautiful!'
(OS 2.#50)

たう、ᴧ みやこ、　/　きや、ᴧ　かまくら、ᴧ　　かなわせ　　　　　/
ta u ,ᴧ mi ya ko ,　/　ki ya ,ᴧ　ka ma ku ra ,ᴧ　ka na wa se　　　/
*tʰoo　myaakʰu　k°yoo　kʰamak°ura-∅　kʰanaw-as-i*
China　Miyako　　Kyoto　Kamakura-DO　cooperate-**CAUS**-MR
'**Have** China, Miyako (and the other Sakishima Islands), Kyoto, and Kamakura
bend to [our] will.' (OS 6.#311)

---

22　Here we provisionally follow JDB's treatment of the OJ cognate, the purported negative sentence-final particle *na*, which states that it follows SS (JDB: 513b). The Pre-OOk
sequence is clearly *una*, so that can be treated as SS + *na*. However, in NOk 'don't write'
is *kak-u(-)na* and 'don't release (it)' is *hanas-u(-)na*, the two forms showing clearly that the
segmental sequence is Pre-OOk *... ona*. One argument then is whether the form is SS + *na*
in OOk, or whether there is a unitary suffix, Vovin's (2009a: 663–664) view: *-una* (< *-ona*)
instead of a SFP. How the OOk forms and the NOk forms are to be reconciled is not clear.

| しけうち、、∧ | あや、、∧ | あすばちへ、 | / |
|---|---|---|---|
| si ke u ti , ∧ | a ya , ∧ | a su ba ti pe , | / |
| *syik°yi-ʔuc°yi-Ø* | *ʔaya-Ø* | *ʔasib-a-c°yi* | |
| sanctum-interior-LOC | priestesses-DO | sacred.dance-CAUS-GER | |

'[Kikoe Ōgimi] **has** the [priestesses in *bingata cloth* =] *ʔaya* perform a sacred dance [within] the sanctuary.' (OS 1.#20)

| こゑかず†の、 | なりきよら | / あもと、、∧ |
|---|---|---|
| ko we ka zu† no , | na ri ki yo ra | / a mo to , ∧ |
| *kʰu'yi\|-kʰazi-nu* | *nar-yi-k°yura-Ø* | *ʔa-mutʰu-Ø* |
| sound-no.-GEN | echo-RY-fine-SUB | foot-base-DO |

| よら、しよわちへ | / |
|---|---|
| yo ra , si yo wa ti pe | / |
| *yur-as-y-uwa-c°yi* | |
| shake$_{VI}$-CAUS-RY-EAV-GER | |

'The hand-drum Narikiyora, with every beat, deigning to shake the ground at their feet, ...' (OS 10.#513)

That was, literally, 'The every-beat-y *Narikiyora* exaltedly shaking the foot-base',[23] with neither the subject nor the object marked by an enclitic, and thus potentially obscuring the grammatical relations.

The verb {tʰuras-} is worth exploring further, since it appears as a fully grammaticalized transitive verb, 'give', with which *-nyi* unambiguously marks its antecedent as the IO, the recipient. Observe the following two examples:

| かゑふたに、、∧ | おろちへ | / いづこたに、、∧ | とらちへ | / |
|---|---|---|---|---|
| ka we pu ta ni , ∧ | o ro ti pe | / i du ko ta ni , ∧ | to ra ti pe | / |
| *kʰayip°ut°a-nyi* | *ʔuru-c°yi* | *ʔyidzi#kʰu#tʰa-nyi* | *tʰur-a-c°yi* | |
| Yoron-IO | bring.down-GER | 0.#0.#PL-IO | get-CAUS-GER | |

'Invoking[24] [spiritual power] [into a shaman] in Yoron, **giv**ing it to the soldiers ...' (OS 5.#237)

---

23 The word ⟨a mo to⟩ is a *hapax* in OS, but is attested as well in the later *koyō* (*lit.* 'old songs') and Ryūka (OKDJ 42d). In its later meaning of '(constructed) embankment' it is even found in NOk (OGJ 114a): *ʔa-mutu⌟*. This is apparently a loan from MJ *a-moto* 'bright green seedlings at the outer edge of a rice nursery' (KJE); *a* 'embankment of a ricefield' (KJE), and could be composed of J elements *a* 'rice-paddy embankment' + *moto* 'base'; NOk *mu(u)tu⌟* '1 base; fount; 2 stock; capital' (OGJ 398a). However, the common word for 'leg; foot' in NOk is *f ísya* (OGJ 241), apparently related to J *hiza⌟* 'knees, lap'; it is not attested in the OS.

24 The semantic shift is: 'bring [something] down' → 'bring [something] down [from Heaven]' → 'bring [spiritual power] down [from Heaven]', i.e. 'invoke [spiritual power, which comes from Heaven]'.

# AUXILIARIES
273

| あやぎ、うまに、 | / あやぎ、くら、ˆ | かけて、 | / あやぎ、ぶち、ˆ |
|---|---|---|---|
| a ya gi , u ma ni , | / a ya gi , ku ra , ˆ | ka ke te , | / a ya gi , bu ti , ˆ |
| ʔayagyi-ʔuma-nyi | ʔayagyi-k˚ura-∅ | kʰakʰi-tˀi | ʔayagyi-bucˀyi-∅ |
| splendid-horse-onto | splendid-saddle-DO | place-GER | splendid-whip-DO |

| とらちへ | / |
|---|---|
| to ra ti pe | / |
| tʰur-a-cˀyi | |
| get-CAUS-GER | |

'Putting a splendid saddle on the splendid horse, **and giving** [him] a splendid whip ...' (OS 13.#895)

For ease of explanation, let us first use an English example for illustration:

> A has B [ₛ ~~B~~ take C ] →
> A gives C to B / A gives B C

This transition is seen in the OOk counterpart below.

> A-*nu* B-*nyi* [ₛ ~~B-nu~~ C-∅ *tur*]-*as*- 'A has B [ₛ ~~B~~ take C]'
> → 'A gives C to B' / 'A gives B C'

Using this structural illustration, the above examples can be presented as below with the missing elements filled in.

> A-nu *ʔyiʥi-kʰu-t˚aa-nyi* C-∅ *tʰur-a-cˀyi*
> 'A, giving B$_{=ʔyiʥi-kˀu-tˀaa}$ C.' (A and C are missing in the text)

> A-nu *ʔayagyi-ʔuma-nyi ... ʔayagyi-buc˚yi-∅* *tʰur-a-cˀyi*
> 'A gave B$_{=ʔayagyi-ʔuma}$ C$_{=ʔayagyi-bucˀyi}$.'

In NOk, *tur-a-cyiⱼ* works as a main verb as in the first example as well as as a secondary verb expressing a benefactive meaning of ('give' →) 'for'. The IO marker in NOk is -*ɴkayi*, not -*ni* (< OOk -*nyi*):

*A-nu   B-ɴkai tigami-∅ⱼ  turas-yu-ɴⱼ*
A-SUB B-IO    letter-DO  give-SS
'A gives a letter to B.'

*A-nu   B-ɴkai tigami-∅ⱼ  kacyi-turas-yu-ɴⱼ*
A-sub B-IO    letter-DO  write-BENEFACTIVE-SS
'A writes a letter for B.'

274                                                 CHAPTER 7

The equivalent Japanese form would be *A-ga B-ni C-o V-te-kure-*, where {+te+kure-} plays the same role as the Okinawan {+ti+turas-}.

## 2.2    *Exalting -as-*

| きや、ᴧ | かまくら、 | / かわら | / なばん、ぎやめ、 | / |
|---|---|---|---|---|
| ki ya ,ᴧ | ka ma ku ra , | / ka wa ra | / na ba ɴ , gi ya me , | / |
| *k°yoo-∅* | *kʰamak°ura-∅* | *kʰawara-∅* | *nabaɴ-gyami* | |
| Kyoto-COM | Kamakura-DO | Kalapa-COM | SE.Asia-TRM | |

| たう | / みやこ、ᴧ | そろへて、ᴧ | かなわしよわれ |
|---|---|---|---|
| ta u | / mi ya ko ,ᴧ | so ro pe te ,ᴧ | ka na wa si yo wa re |
| *tʰoo-∅* | *myaakʰu-∅* | *suruy·i-tʰi* | *kʰanaw-as-y-uwa·r-i* |
| China-COM | Miyako-DO | line.up$_{VT}$-GER | conform-CAUS$_{ex}$-EAV·4GE-MR |

'Line up Kyoto with Kamakura; Kalapa[25] with[26] other parts of Southeast Asia;[27] and China with Miyako-Sakishima, and **have** them [all] conform.' (OS 7.#356)

Another example of the exalting *-as-* is *sir-as-* [sirɑs] ~ *syi̯r-as-* [ʃirɑs] 'say$_{hum}$' (< *\*ser-as-*), and it is probably to be analyzed in pre-OOk as *\*sir-as-* 'know-CAUS/ex-', i.e. 'cause (others) to know'.[28] (Cf. NJ *syir(·)ase-ru₎* 'let know, an-

---

25    See Ch. 2 §5.6.2 for a short discussion of metathesis in this loanword.

26    OSJS 119a and Shimizu (2003: 104) state, correctly in our view, that this particle comes from *\*kiwame* 'reaching a limit' (a grammaticalization), structurally related to NJ *kiwamé-ru* 'attain; run to an extreme', and NOk *cyiwami-yu-ɴ₎* (semantically = NJ *kime-ru₎*) 'decide'; the form expected in NOk is ˣ*cyaami-yu-ɴ*, but such a verb is not to be found, so *cyiwami-yu-ɴ₎* is a J borrowing from a later period, unless *\*ki:* or *\*wa:* < *\*pa:* was originally long when not compounded. Though the accent is reversed, the noun *cywá* '(verge of) time'—related to OJ *kîpa* 'alongside; edge' (JDB 244c)—shows the same odd lack of moraic crasis as NOk *cyiwami-yu-ɴ₎* does to NJ *kiwaméru*. Martin (1987: 452) suggests a loan because of accent incongruence with other Ryukyuan languages, and because of lack of crasis, but we remain unconvinced.

27    The word is phonetically [nãbãɴ] ← SJ 南蛮 naɴ.baɴ [nãm:bãɴ:] *lit.* 'Southern Barbarians', and 'Southeast Asia' by extension. Changes such as [ãm:b] > [ãmb] > [ãb] (and eventually in MOk [ab]) were common enough in both branches of Japonic. Voiced obstruents in earlier Japonic were phonetically prenasalized; that nasality typically appeared on the vowel preceding the obstruent in question; cf. e.g. Vovin (2012).

28    Something remains to be solved about the vowel height: in the Japanese lineage *\*ê* raises to *î* when it should not in its morphophonemic context as the last vowel in a root: PJ *\*sêr-* > EOJ *\*sîr-* > OJ *sir-* 'realize' (compare [PJ *\*asôb-* >] OJ *asōb-* 'play, etc.', not ˣ*asub-*); and in Okinawan, the vowel is unstable: *syir-* ~ *sir-* ?'realize'/?'say' (< Pre-OOk *\*syir-* ~ *\*ser-* < *\*syir-* ~ *\*syer-* < PJ *\*sêr-*) (compare OOk *ʔasib-* 'do a religious dance', not ˣ*ʔasub-*). Both *i* and *yi* considered here appear to have originated in *\*ye*; the question is one of timing of changes.

AUXILIARIES

nounce, tell'.) This is a hapax and may be a play on words to connect ⟨se ra su⟩ and ⟨se ru mu⟩. Here we differ from OSJS, which does not explicitly analyze ⟨si ra su⟩ or ⟨se ra su⟩ as having any smaller constituent parts.

さしぶは、∧      おもろは、∧   せらす      /
sa si bu pa , ∧      o mo ro pa , ∧ se ra su      /
*sasyibu-wa*      *ʔumuru-Qpʰa sir-**as**-ɨ*
{*sashibu*=shamaness$_1$}-TOP omoro$_1$-DO   say-**CAUS/EX-SS**
むづきは、∧      せるむは、∧      しらす
mu du ki pa , ∧      se ru mu pa , ∧      si ra su
*mudzikʲyi-wa*      *sirumu-Qpʰa*      *syi̧ r-**as**-ɨ*
{*muzuki*= shamaness$_2$}-TOP {*serumu*= omoro$_2$}-DO say-**CAUS/EX-SS**
'The *sashibu* (= shamaness$_1$)[29] recites the *omoro$_1$*;[30] the *muzuki* (= shamaness$_2$) sings the *serumu* (= *omoro$_2$*).' (OS 11.#581) (OS 21.#1506)

Observe the following, an example of *-as-* suffixed to an adjectival form:

はたみ、     いくさこが     / 御ざけ、∧     ほしや、∧あらす、     /
pa ta mi ,     i ku sa ko ga     / o za ke , ∧     po si ya , ∧ a ra su ,     /
*pʰada.myi ʔyikʷusa.kʰuu-ga*     *ʔu-zakʰi-∅*   *pʰusya#ʔar-**as**-ɨ*
next.of.kin warrior-SUB      EX-sake-DO desire#exist-**CAUS/EX-SS**
'The soldier[ly lord]s,[31] those close by [His Majesty],[32] want fine wine.' (OS 13.#962)

---

29   The spelling is morphophonemic, with ⟨pa⟩ representing either *-wa*, in the case where PP is to be ignored, or *-ya*, in the case where PP is to operate. We adopt the former, though the evidence is essentially a tenuous WYSIWYG argument, namely, that if the writers had wanted it to be pronounced *-ya*, they would have written ⟨ya⟩. Because this is not always likely to have been the case, the ice is thin.

30   TOS fails to support using voicing in ⟨o mo ro p̄a⟩ 'omoro$_1$-DO' and ⟨se ru mu p̄a⟩ 'omoro$_2$-DO', as it might be in Kyushu dialects. Rather, emphatic DO is always written with ⟨pa⟩, and never with either ⟨wa/ya⟩ or ⟨ba⟩. The greatest likelihood is *-pʰa* or *-Qpʰa*. Given that this is emphatic, we have chosen *-Qpʰa*.

31   Also spelled ⟨i ku sa ko u⟩ (OS 11.#642), vouchsafing the length of *-kʰuu* 'one' here: *ʔyikʷusa* 'war' + *-kʰuu* '-one'. There are occasional long-vowel spellings; however, no indication of long vowel is the usual pattern.

32   We do not follow OKDJ (541a) ⟨pa d̄a mi⟩. The word is explained as literally *pʰada* 'skin' + *myi* 'body; self'. Even TOS, however, has only ⟨pa ta mi⟩. OSJS (275d–276a) cites Ifa citing *Ōkawa Tekiuchi* for ⟨O KAMI TĒ tu no TIKA o N pa da N⟩, which he apparently translates as 'relatives sharing one ancestral deity', but while the semantic connection to the OS is good, the voicing connection is unexplained.

The construction can be unified with the *-s(y)a-ar-* adjectival verbalization followed by the *-as-* exaltation marker, creating a straightforward result, as we do here:

> *\*pʰosyi-* 'desiring'
> *\*pʰosyi-* + *-sa* → *\*pʰosya* 'desire'
> *\*pʰosya* + *ar-* (verbalization) 'desire exists' = 'wants'
> *\*pʰosya* + *ar-as-* (exaltation) 'desire exists on the part of an exalted personage' >
> *pʰusya ʔar-as-* '(some exalted personage) wants (something/-one)'

## 2.3 Compound Verb myi-ʔu-ya⌈r⌉as-i < *myi-ʔo-yar-as-e

The morphophonological change that we assume here is

> \* myi - ʔo - ya     r     -a        s  - e   >
>   myi - ʔu - ya [ʔ  r̄  ]  ā̄   ʔ  ]  s  - i  .

KKKS annotates ⟨mi o ya se⟩ (みおやせ) *myi-ʔu-yasi* as *shujō ni tatematsuru mono o iu nari* "means 'to give to His Majesty'." However, since there is no *yas-* in either Ryukyuan or OJ as a verb meaning 'give', its etymon was obscure. Conversely, there is indeed *yar-* 'give' (JDB 775d) in OJ, and if we assume the existence of *\*-yar-* in the original string, then the compound *\*myi-ʔo-yar-as-e* can be connected both to OOk and to OJ, as adumbrated by Torigoe (1968: 367–369).

The overwhelming majority of the attested *myi-ʔu-ya-s-i* tokens appear as MR (214 tokens), followed by IZ (9 tokens), all of which are formally identical.

| あんの、 | かね、 ∧ぐ゙すく | / あまゑ、やり、∧ | | みおやせば゙、 | / |
|---|---|---|---|---|---|
| a N no, | ka ne, ∧gu\*su ku | / a ma we, ya ri, ∧ | | mi o ya se ba\*, | / |
| ʔan-nu | kʰani-gusik°u-∅ | ʔamayi-yaar.yi | | **myi-ʔu-yas-i-ba** | |
| we-GEN | iron-enclosure-DO | rejoice-**PROG-RY=ADV** | | EX-EX-offer-IZ-T/C | |
| すへ∧ | まさて、 | / とひやくさす、∧ | ちよわれ | | |
| su pe ∧ | ma sa te, | / to pi ya ku sa su, ∧ | ti yo wa re | | |
| siyi | masa-t°i | tʰu-p°yak°u-see-si | c°yuwar-i | | |
| forever | prosper-GER | 10–100-year-KP$_{KM}$ | rule-IZ$_{KM}$ | | |

'When I rejoicingly give the impregnable fortress to my lord, far into the future—for a thousand years!—will he rule prosperously.' (OS 5.#248)

AUXILIARIES 277

かざり、、   うちちへ、、   みおやせ       /
ka za ri ,ᴧ  u ti ti pe ,ᴧ  mi o ya se      /
*kʰazaryi-∅ ?uc-˚yi-c˚yi*   **mi-?u-yas-i**
PLN-DO      strike-RY-GER EX-EX-offer-MR
'Conquer Kasa|ri[33] and **offer** [it] [to Ogyakamoi (= King Shō Shin)]!' (OS 1.#4)

おもろよ、、   みおやせ、    / せるむよ、、   みおやせ       /
o mo ro yo ,ᴧ mi o ya se ,   / se ru mu yo ,ᴧ mi o ya se      /
*?umuru-yu[34]* **myi-?u-yas-i**    *sir-u-mu-yu*  **myi-?u-yas-i**
omoro₁-DO   EX-EX-give-MR   omoro₂-DO   EX-EX-give-MR
'[O Omoro Ne-Agari, O Serumu-Ne-Agari,] **offer up** the *omoro*, **offer up** the
*serumu* ... [[to] the Ruler of the Southern Region, [to] the Lord of Lords ...]!'
(OS 8.#411)

There is an interesting *hapax legomenon* of ⟨mi o ya se re⟩ *myi-?u-yasīr-i* in
OS, which we present in context below. Ikemiya (1995 = KKKS2: 235) takes it
as a form relatable to ⟨mi o ya su re⟩ *myi-?u-yasīr-i*, another *hapax legomenon*,
this one in KKKS. He believes that this shows a *ra-gyō-yodan-ka* 'ra-gyō-yodan-
ization' (analogical shift to *r*-type quadrigrade verb) of the conjugation, which
supposedly appeared only later in OOk history. In fact there were already ample
signs of it in the OS, as is readily seen in Ch. 6 §2. Further, it is inexplicable in
terms of that analogical shift. In the OS, there is no attested example of ⟨mi o
ya su re⟩, but only ⟨mi o ya se re⟩ below.

---

33  TOS has ruled in favor of ⟨ka sā | ri⟩, despite all books ruling against it, except the Shō-
    Family edition, which does not use any punctuation, and which therefore cannot be used
    to make a ruling in such a case. We therefore go with ⟨ka zā ri⟩ = *kʰazāryi*. However, the
    modern name *is*, after all, Kasari, and we therefore use that in our modern-form transcrip-
    tion. This PLN may seem to be a counter-example to YGH, but note that the name has the
    mora *za*, which is not involved as either input or output to YGH, which only pertains to
    original high vowels.

34  Note the form, -*yu*, of the Direct-Object enclitic, which, judging from its correspondent
    particle in OJ, *wo*, we would expect to be -*wu*, and in fact there *are* a few cases of such
    in the OS data. The other tokens coming from PJ *\*wo* are all -*yu*, regardless of the front-
    ness of their preceding vowel. This must surely be because increasingly speakers came
    to see the form -*yu* as the only morph available in the former dyad, probably because
    examples of -*yu* occurred more frequently, and younger speakers came not to realize
    the reason for the -*yu* ↔ -*wu* dyad. And besides, there were other choices, zero mark-
    ing and stress-marking, that were probably already available: a surfeit of available allo-
    morphs.

278                                                                CHAPTER 7

| しらしよ、 | みしゆ、ʌ | みおやせれ | / |
| si ra si yo , | mi si yu , ʌ | mi o ya se re | / |
| *syi̯ree-syu* | *myi-syu* | *myi-ʔu-ya[ *r-a]s·i·r-i* | |

finely.made~BE~-garment EX-garment EX-EX-give-CAUS/EX-MR

'May (the High Priestess' retainers) offer up the white garment to the High Priestess.' (OS 7.#349)

No wonder this is a one-of-a-kind form: the MR form ⟨mi o ya se⟩ = *myi-ʔu-yas-i* is being treated as if it were a new bigrade base from which a new quadrigrade *r*-stem is going to be built: → *myi-ʔu-yasir-*. By the time of KKKS, ⟨su⟩ and ⟨se⟩ both represented *si*. Perhaps this is what Ikemiya meant. This analogy ultimately went nowhere, resulting in the *hapax legomenon* seen here: → *myi-ʔu-yasi·r-i*. To review:

*myi-ʔu-yas-i*    →
*myi-ʔu-yas·i-*    →
*myi-ʔu-yas·i·r-*    →
*myi-ʔu-yas·i·r-i*

### 2.4    *Historical and Comparative Analysis*

The OOk causative auxiliary -*as*- is a cognate of Nara OJ -*as*- ~ (*a*)*se*-. Like its OJ counterparts, it also has causative and exalting usages.[35] According to Takahashi (1991a: 219), the exalting usage of -*as*- is rare due to the abundance of the exalting auxiliary, -(*u*)*war*-. However, if *myi-ʔu-yas*- 'give~pol~' can be analyzed as a contracted form of an original string \**myi-ʔu-yar-as*- '[EX-EX-give-CAUS~ex~]~hum~', a humble form meaning 'give',[36] then it boosts the number for the exalting usage of -*as*-—albeit within the humilific phrase [...]~hum~, since the number of tokens for this verb is over 200. The case of *myi-ʔu-yas*- is taken up as a separate subsection in § 2.3.

    The Gerund form always appears as -*c°yi*, but the existence of the palatalized consonant *c°y* = [tʃ°] = [ĉĉ°] assumes the existence of the vowel \**yi* in the original form, which in fact leads to a hypothesis that -*c°yi* is a contracted form of \*···*s-yi*~RT~ + \*-*te*~GER~ > \*···*s-yi-tye* > \*···*s-yi-c°yi* > \*···*s-y-c°yi* > -*c°yi*. This is just what happens to every fully lexical *s*-type quadrigrade verb.

---

35    The honorific function is recognized by Vovin (2009a: 842) for OJ -*as*-, not for -(*a*)*se*-. It is also noted in JDB for -*s-u* (=-*as*-) (380c).

36    This etymology is implicit in Torigoe's (1968: 367–369) Japanese translation of *mioyase* as *mioyarase*, i.e. lit. 'exaltedly cause to give', though he was not explicit about any diachronic changes.

AUXILIARIES       279

A causative-like transitive verb, *kʰusi-* 'dress s/o; have s/o put s/t on', related to *k°yi-* 'put on (clothing) VT'—a *hapax* in OOk but a common verb in NOk—deserves mention at this point:

| たまき、ˇ | | ゑらで、 | さゝちへ | / ゆろい、 |
|---|---|---|---|---|
| ta ma ki ,ˇ | | we ra de , | sa " ti pe | / yu ro i , |
| *tʰama-k°yi-∅* | | *ʔyi̦ra-di* | *sas-a-c°yee* | *yuru⁽ⁿ⁾yi-∅* |
| jeweled_BE-sword-DO | | choose-GER | wear-CAUS-PRFV_SS | armor-DO |

| ゑらで、 | こせて | / |
|---|---|---|
| we ra de , | ko se te | / |
| *ʔyi̦ra-di* | *kʰusi-t°ee* | |
| choose-GER | **wear.CAUS**'dress'VT -PRFV_SS | |

'[Their retainers₁] chose jeweled swords₂ and had [them₃] wear [them₂]; [they₁] chose armor₂ and had [them₃] wear [it₂].' (OS 10.#525)

*kʰusi-t°i* has an ···s··· in it, indicating a causative or transitivizer, and the stem *\*kʰose-* clearly stems from the progenitor form of *k°yi-*, itself likely analogically reshaped from the RY form, i.e. < *\*k-°yi*. Thus they both share the initial *k*···. It is not clear whether the ···*u*··· of *kʰusi-* is part of the root or part of the derivational suffix. If the latter, then it works like the passive suffix *\*-öyë- ~ \*-ayë-*, a sort of derivational vowel harmony: *\*kî-ösë-* or *\*kö-ösë*, with the first vowel dropping out. Our main point is this: While probably originally a causative construction, the verb *kʰusi-* 'dress s/o' < *\*k-ösë-* 'cause s/o to wear' is now fully lexicalized as an ordinary verb, and is not derivable from *k°yi-* 's/o wears'.

OOk does *not* seem to have a causative *auxiliary* ˣ-*syimi-*, but *does* have a causative *verb* °*syimi-* 'do_CAUS', which appears to be a cognate of the OJ *auxiliary* -*simë-* '-CAUS-'.[37] There are eight tokens of *syimi-* in OS, all of which are functionally causative, and no exalting usages are found. The attested forms include MZ, MR, and GER forms.

| かいなで、ˇ | みづ、ˇ | しめまし | / |
|---|---|---|---|
| ka i na de ,ˇ | mi du ,ˇ | si me ma si | / |
| *kʰee.̦nadi* | *#myidzi-∅* | **syimi-masyi** | |
| sacred | water-APP | **do**_CAUS·MZ-OPT | |

---

37    Vovin (2009a: 861) states: "The causative suffix -*asimey-* ~ -*simey-* is not attested in Ryukyuan per se, but the following forms from the Shuri dialect are worth attention. The causative form of the verb *s-* 'to do' in Shuri is **shimii-** ~ **shimiy-**" (cited by Vovin from other authors' text).

'[... then] we would like to **make**[38] [it] [into] sacred water [to offer to the King].'
(OS 7.#348)

きもが、　　うちに、ˎ　　おもわば　　/ きもだりよ、ˎ　　しめれ　　　　　/
ki mo ga ,　u ti ni , ˎ　o mo wa ba　/ ki mo da ri yo , ˎ　si me re　　　/
*kʸimu-ga ʔucʸyi-nyi　ʔumuw-a-ba　　kʸyimu-daryi-yu　**syimi·r-i***
liver-GEN inside-LOC think-MZ-T/C　liver-lethargy-DO **do**<sub>CAUS</sub>·4GE-MR
'If [they] should plan in [their] hearts [to attack], **cause** [them] to lose heart
(more *lit.*: "... cause a heart-loss").' (OS 3.#97)

やへま、しま、ˎ　　　いづこ、　　　　　　　/ あよ、まよいˎ
ya pe ma , si ma , ˎ i du ko ,　　　　　/ a yo , ma yo i ˎ
*yayima-syima　　ʔyidzi-kʰu-Ø*　　　　　　*ʔayu-mayu'-yi*[40]-Ø
Yaeyama-islands　{outstanding ones}[39]-AGT　liver-stray-RY<sub>NOM</sub>-DO
しめ[て]　　　/ はたら、しま　　くはら、　　　　/ きも、まよいˎ
si me [te]　　/ pa ta ra , si ma　ku pa ra ,　　/ ki mo , ma yo i ˎ
*syimi-[tʸee]*　*pʰatʸara-syima　kʸuQpʸa-ra-Ø*[41]　*kʸyimu-mayu'-yi*-Ø
**do**<sub>CAUS</sub>-[G/P]　Hateruma-island tough-PL-AGT-DO　liver-stray-RY<sub>NOM</sub>-IO
とらちへ　　　　　　　/
to ra ti pe　　　　　/
*tʰur-a-cʸyee*
take-CAUS-GER/PRFV
'[They] will have caused the mettle of the outstanding ones of Yaeyama to go
astray, and [they] will have forced the hearts of the tough men of Hateruma to
take a wrong turn.' (OS 1.#33)

---

38　The verb *syimi-* 'cause to be, make into' here is acting as if the transitive of *nar-* 'become'.
　　While J would have syntactic slots like the following: X-*ga* Y-*o* Z-*ni na·s-* 'X transforms Y
　　into-Z', probably the syntactic frame most likely to appear in OOk would be: X(-*ga/nu*)
　　Y(-*Qpʸa/-yu*) Z-Ø *syimi·r-*'(id.)'. While marking the transformed item Z with a dative par-
　　ticle is possible in both OOk and NOk, the zero marking option is preferred, just as
　　English has a minimal-marking option: '... make *it* [into] sacred water', the equivalent of
　　OOk/NOk.
39　o.o. = 'outstanding one(s)', for the example below as well.
40　... or *mayi-*(ˀ)*i-*, in the case where monophthongization is allowed to run its course.
41　NOk has *kufa-* 'hard (−object, −headed, −to get along with)' (OGJ 327b); *kufa-doori*, 'refers
　　to a person of normally strong constitution suddenly falling ill, or suddenly dying'
　　(OGJ 328ab); *kufa-y-u-N*, '... 2. relations sour; ...'; *kufa-t-o-o-N*, 'they've had a falling-out;
　　they're not on speaking terms'. For Nk forms, cf. NHJ 725a *hupʸaaʳseʹN* 'hard, tough' (491a);
　　*hupʸaa-gupʸaa-ʳtʸu* 'hard throughout' (id.).

AUXILIARIES                                                                 281

## 3        Negatives: *-azɨ ~ -aɴ ~ -an-*

### 3.1      *Allomorphs and Examples*

The OOk negative auxiliary *-azɨ* evinces a mixture of allomorphs with alternating coronal consonants, including a coronal nasal: ···*z*··· ~ ···ɴ[42] ~ ···*n*···:

OOk 'NEG' = *-azɨ ~ -aɴ ~ -an-*

The attested conjugational forms will be:

OOk NEG: there is no MZ, so:   RY:   *C-azɨ* ~
                               SS:   *C-aɴ* ~
                                     *C-an-yi*$_{QP}$[43] ~
                               RT:   *C-aɴ*[44]~
                                     *C-an-u*$_{RT}$ ~
                               IZ:   *Ca-n-i* ~

The six conjugational forms listed above are uncontroversial; here are examples of these conjugational forms:

| ふよ、ʌ | なつむ、ʌ | しらず | / なつ、ʌ | ふよむ、ʌ | しらず |
|---|---|---|---|---|---|
| pu yo ,ʌ | na tu mu ,ʌ | si ra zu | / na tu ,ʌ | pu yo mu ,ʌ | si ra zu |
| *p°uyu* | *nac°ɨ-M* | *syi̯r-az-ɨ* | *nac°ɨ* | *p°uyu-M* | *syi̯r-az-ɨ* |
| winter | summer-also | know-**NEG-RY** | summer | winter-also | know-**NEG-RY** |

| / ふよわ、ʌ | 御ざけ ʌ | もる | / なつは、ʌ | しげち ʌ |
|---|---|---|---|---|
| / pu yo wa ,ʌ | o za ke ʌ | mo ru | / na tu pa ,ʌ | si ge ti ʌ |
| *p°uyu-wa* | *ʔu-zakʰi-∅* | *mur-u* | *nac°ɨ-wa* | *syigyi-c°yi-∅* |
| winter-TOP | EX-sake-DO | serve-SS | summer-TOP | sacred-sake-DO |

---

42    Because OOk also has *M* = /M/ [+ labial], the segment *ɴ* = /ɴ/ is in fact defined as [– labial], unlike Japanese, in which the place of articulation of the segment /ɴ/ is *entirely* undefined, and takes its place of articulation from its context.

43    In the case of the two SS forms (unlike the two RT forms below), there is a clear contextual difference for the choice of either *-ɴ* (i.e. sentence-final position) or *-n-* (i.e. with following vowel). For the form of the yes/no QP in (O)Ok, see Shinzato and Serafim (2013: 80–89).

44    Note that SS and RT overlap in that both use the utterance-final form ···ɴ.

282 CHAPTER 7

もる    /
mo ru    /
*mur-u*
serve-SS

'Indifferent to winter or summer, **in**different to summer or winter, they serve good saké[45] in the winter, and sacred saké[46] in the summer.' (OS 11.#643)

とらんで†ゝ、∧    / しらんで†ゝ、∧     しられゝ       /
to ra N de† te ,∧    / si ra N de† te ,∧     si ra re re       /
*tʰur-aN-di-t°i*         *syi̯r-aN-di-t°i*     *syi̯r-ari·r-i*
catch-NEG$_{ss}$-QT-GER    know-NEG$_{ss}$-QT-GER   [know-PASS]$_{tell·EX}$-MR

'[When they ask you if you have caught turtles and dugongs,] tell them [you did] **not** catch any [turtles or dugongs], you have **not** seen any.' (OS 9.#505)

さしき、     なわしろに、    / せ∧        あらば†、      /
sa si ki ,     na wa si ro ni ,    / se ∧        a ra ba† ,      /
*sasyik°yi-∅*    *nawa.syiru*[47]*-nyi*    *si[i]-∅*    *ʔar-a-ba*
Sashiki-APPO    rice.nursery-LOC    spirit.power-SUB   exist-MZ-COND

げ†お、くなべ∧      せらに      /
ge† o , ku na be ∧    se ra ni      /
*giwu-k°unabi-∅*      *si·r-an-yi*
spiritual-match-DO   do·4GE-NEG$_{ss}$-QP

'If there exists spiritual power in Sashiki rice field, | won't [you] / [why] don't [we] | have a spiritual match [there]!'[48] (OS 19.#1297)

---

45   Note that—as with *ʔu-dunu* 'stately building'—*ʔu-zakʰi* 'fine saké' evinces the same phenomenon of *rendaku* after this EX morpheme.

46   ⟨si ge⟩ 'sacred (saké)' forms a graphemic minimal pair with ⟨si ke⟩ 'sacred (ground)'. We propose that ⟨si ke⟩ was °*syik°yi* rather than ˣ*syi̯k°i*, i.e. that PP operated freely. By the same token, if we assume that ⟨si ge⟩ is *syigyi*, then the impossibility of aspiration means that only the PP environment (which was not always trustworthy) and spelling convention would help writers opt for the historical spelling ⟨si ge⟩ over ⟨si gi⟩.

47   This word would have needed an exception mark before *\*r* before the vowel raising, though it is not now necessary. If the earlier form had been e.g. *\*syiiro* or *\*syero*, it would not have needed an exception mark before the raising, either.

48   As for ⟨-ni⟩, we hewed to the etymological analysis (-*an-yi* = NEG+QP), while OSJS (264c) opted for the synchronic reanalysis (-*a-nyi* = MZ+SFP). Note, however, that the same OSJS (266c), seems to opt for the etymological analysis in the case of ⟨-ni na⟩ 'not ...?; cannot do without ...' For instance, analyzing ⟨si na wa **ni na**⟩, they offer a diachronic-negation-based analysis: [*syinaw-a̅n-yi na* 'harmonize-NEG-QP SFP']. As for SFP -*na*, we characterize its core meaning as a 'TONE SOFTENER'.

AUXILIARIES

283

げ*らへ、　大ごろた、　　　/ さに、ᴧ　　しらん、ᴧ　　ころゝゝ　　/
ge* ra pe,　OPO go ro ta,　　/ sa ni,ᴧ　　si ra N,ᴧ　　ko ro ko ro　/
girayi-　　ʔuǫpʷu-guru-tʰaa　sanyi-∅　　syiɾ-aN　　kʰuru-kʰuru
built　　　big-man-PL　　　　number-DO know-NEG_RT man-man
'... splendid warriors, numerous (i.e. an **un**known number of) warriors ...'
(OS 1.#37)

みれども、ᴧ　　　　あかぬ、　　/ 首里　　　おや國　　　　/
mi re do mo,ᴧ　　a ka nu,　　/ SIYO RI　o ya KUNI　　/
myiₗiⱼₗⱼ·r⁴⁹-i-dumu　ʔak-°an-u　　syi#yuryi⁵⁰ ʔuya-gunyi
observe-IZ-CONC　tire.of-NEG-RT　Shuri　　Parent-Country
'[Look!, it is] Shuri, the Father Land [= the King's Capital]!, which we **do not**
tire of gazing at.' (OS 1.#7)

とまり　　　しらねど*も　　　　/
to ma ri　　si ra ne do* mo　　/
tʰumaryi-∅　syiɾ-an-i-du-mu
harbor-DO　know-NEG-IZ-KP-even
'... even though [I] don't know the harbor [well, I should be able to enter it
safely.]' (OS 13.#961)

### 3.2 *Controversial Cases (-azɨ as MZ, -azɨ as RT and -ana as RY)*

#### 3.2.1 *-azɨ as MZ*

Torigoe (1968: 179), in contrast to OSJS and Takahashi (1991a), recognizes an MZ
conjugation form *-azɨ* based on the following two examples. He analyzes what
he interprets as *cyikaw-azɨ* [*w*]*a*—not *cyikawasi* [*w*]*a*—as a conditional, meaning *kataku musubarete inai nara* 'if not tightly solidified/consolidated'. Hokama
(#824 [2000b: 49], #1074 [2000b: 182]), on the other hand, reads the same す as
*si*, not *zɨ*, and interprets it as a *plural* marker.

---

49　Because the preceding high front palatal vowel is *underlyingly* long = {yii}, the following
　　[ɾ] is not PPed. This *morphophonemic* rule requires no exception mark.

50　As a stopgap we have put in a raised hash-mark ＃ to indicate an exception to contrac-
　　tion. This may or may not have a historically sound basis. A claimed origination point
　　(Vovin 2009b: 16; cf. our Ch. 3 §4) for the name *syi#yuryi* is the name of the capital of
　　Yi Dynasty Korea, Seoul: *syewol*, *'syeʳeWul*(*h*) (Mod K *sewul*) (Yu 455a), with a long first-
　　syllable vowel.

あんじ゙、∧ げ゙す、∧　　　ちかわすﾟは、　　　　　／
a N zi゙, ∧　ge゙ su, ∧　　ti ka wa su゚ pa ,　　　　／
ʔaɴzyi　　gisi　　　　cʼyi̧kʼaw-**azi**-Qpʼa　　// cʼyi̧kʼawa-**si**-wa
lord　　　lower.official　T: pledge-**NEG**-**TMP**/**CND** // H: soldier-**PL**-**TOP**
おぎ゙も、しやり、∧　なをし、よわ　　　／
o gi゙ mo , si ya ri , ∧　na wo si , yo wa　/
ʔu-gyimu-s.y.aar.yi　nawus-y-uwa
**EX**-liver-**INSTR**　　pacify-**RY**-**EX**<sub>MR</sub>

Torigoe (T): 'Should all the lords and vassals **not** pledge [their support], will you pacify [the land], giving it all your heart?'[51]

Hokama (H): 'O lord, lower officials, soldiers,[52] put [your] hearts into pacifying [the land]!' (OS 13.#824)

Torigoe's interpretation may work for the example above, but would not work for the one below, as there is already a temporal/conditional clause *nayur-i-ba* preceding it. Interpreting it as a conditional clause creates a semantic anomaly, noted by "?" in the translation.

きこゑ、　　うらおそいに、／ しまの、　より、∧　　　　　　なよれば† 　 ／
ki ko we, u ra o so i ni , / si ma no , yo ri , ∧　　　na yo re ba† 　／
kʼyi̧kʼuyi ʔuraʔusii-nyi　syima-nu　yur-yi-∅　　nayur-i-ba
famous　　**PLN**-**LOC**　　land-**GEN** dance-**RY**<sub>NOM</sub>-**DO** dance-**IZ**-**T**/**C**
ちかわすﾟは、∧　　　　　　　　　　よりいで゙、やり ∧　　　　なおせ
ti ka wa su゚ pa , ∧　　　　　　　yo ri i de゙ , ya ri ∧　　na o se
| cʼyi̧kʼaw-**azi**-Qpʼa //cʼyi̧kʼawa-**si**-wa | yur-yi-ʔidzyi-yar.yi[53]　nawus-i
| pledge-**NEG**-**T**/**C** //soldier-**PL**-**TOP** |　dance-go.out-**RY**-**PROG** pacify-**MR**

'When [priestesses] dance island dances in Urasoe, |T:**?if they don't pledge, [they]** // H: **soldiers**| come out to dance and pacify the land.' (OS 15.#1074)

Hokama's treatment of ⟨su⟩ as a plural marker *-si* is not fully convincing, as there are no other instances of *-si* used as a plural marker except for these two examples.[54] A more plausible treatment of *-si* is to take *cʼyi̧kʼa-wa-si* as 'soldiers' based on a hypothesis of \**ti̧ ka-* 'near' (OSJS 216a) + \**-wa* 'surround-

---

51　Torigoe's original, in transliteration, is: "Teni-ga Shita no anji, gesu, chikawazu wa, o-gimo-shi-yari, naoshi-owashi, ...."

52　TOS does not give the corresponding *hiragana* a voicing mark, despite their very liberal voicing-mark policy.

53　For ⟨de⟩ interpreted as *dzyi*, see what was said in fn. 46 about ⟨si ge⟩ as *syigyi*.

54　In fact, OSJS has no entry at all for this as a plural marker.

AUXILIARIES                                                                                    285

ings' (OSJS 364b) + *-sô ~ *-si 'ones' (OSJS 187a; 199b), something like 「近曲
者」(where *-wa 「曲」 can be seen as increasingly high-tiered and exclusive levels within a castle's precinct, as easily seen, e.g. within Katsuren Castle). This
hypothesis is more believable, especially given (1) that there appears to be no
etymon *ti̯ kap- 'pledge' [except for this highly contested example of course]
in Ryukyuan, and (2) *tyi̯ ka- ~ *tyikya- 'near', while occurring in both a plain as
well as a PP'ed version in NOk (cyi̯ ka-sa-N̥ [OGJ 151a] ~ cyicya-sa-N̥ [OGJ 144b]),
occurs only as plain ⟨ti ka sa⟩ (as does ⟨ti ka wa su⟩) in OOk.

### 3.2.2    -azi as RT

Yet another form not in the list is an -azi form assigned a purported RT status.
Takahashi (1991a: 321) points out that -azi (i.e. ⟨su⟩) as in ⟨a ka su⟩ 'not tired of' is
often viewed as a RT form, as it occurs in front of nouns. For instance, the priestess name ⟨a ka su" ku ni ka , ne⟩ ʔak-°azi k°unyi-kʰani (OS 9.#486) was originally
meant to be 'Priestess Kunikane, whom we never tire of [looking at].' Similarly,
⟨a ka su" , o to" N⟩ ʔak-°azi ʔu-duN (OS 11.#579)[55] originally meant 'the exalted
building that we never tire of [looking at].' There are 11 instances of ⟨a ka su"⟩
occurring in such words as priestess names/titles or architectural structures.

With priestess names/titles:

> k°unyi-kʰani ('Kunikane', 2 tokens); k°unyi-muryi ('Kunimori', 1); k°yimyi-
> k°yura ('Kimikiyora', 1); midzi·r-asya ('Mezurasha', 3); and yar-yi-ʔusi-i
> ('Yariosoi', 2).

With architectural structures:

> ʔu-duN ('Odon / Odono', lit. 'Exalted-Personage/Structure', 2); and myaa
> ('Niwa/Miya',[56] i.e. 'a commons for religious events' 1).

A corollary to ⟨a ka su"⟩ ʔak-°azi 'not tired of' has been proposed to be ⟨ma ti
ra su⟩, assumed to be madzyir-azi 'not mixing/mixed, (just) plain, outstanding',
which is used with priestess names. (But the form is ⟨ma ti° ra su°⟩,[57] introduc-
ing an interesting wrinkle, of which more below.) Takahashi (1991a: 274–275)
speculates on the etyma of the priestess names as follows:

---

55    The voicing marks and the commas are in TOS, but not as quoted by Takahashi, and we
      have supplied the phonologizations.
56    For specifics of ⟨mi ya⟩ myaa, see Ch. 4 §4.7, fn. 64, p. 128, and fn. 91, p. 137.
57    Here a postposed raised circle on a grapheme, such as ⟨su°⟩, shows that it has been

286 CHAPTER 7

TABLE 7.1    Priestess names and (lack of) voicing marks

| | | |
|---|---|---|
| *mazyirazyi* □ | ⟨ma zi ra zi⟩ | no devoicings |
| *masyirazyi* □ | ⟨ma si ra gi⟩, | one devoicing; the spelling alternations are |
| | ⟨ma si ra zi⟩, | late, and do not warrant reconstruction to *\*dyi* |
| | ⟨ma si ra zu⟩, | or *\*gyi* |
| | ⟨ma si ra di⟩ | |
| *masyiradi* □ | ⟨ma si ra te⟩, | one devoicing; the non-affricate ⟨de⟩ spelling |
| | ⟨ma si ra de⟩ | is clearly irregular |
| *macˀyirasi* ■ | ⟨ma ti ra su⟩ | two devoicings; os, the holiest book, has the most extreme pronunciation shift, with full devoicings |

*myina-nyi-macˀyir-asi* 'everyone-with-intermingle-NEG'; that is, someone whose quality is not (merely) mingling with others, who is outstanding.

*tʰumu-nyi-macˀyir-asi* 'others-with-intermingle-NEG'; that is, someone whose quality is not (merely) mingling with others, who is outstanding.[58]

There are 18 instances of *macˀyirasi* in the *Omoro Sōshi*. They are all priestess names: '(the priestess) Machirasu'. The fact that they are so limited contextually may suggest that their final ···*asi* is a remnant of a once prevalent negative *\*···azi* form, the function of which was a RT, as Takahashi speculates. Further, scholars have generally hypothesized that the form simply is the graphic string ⟨ma ti" ra su"⟩ that has been stripped of its voicing marks, i.e. ⟨ma ti_ ra su_⟩, but nonetheless *madzyirazi*. However, it is important to note that, whatever the word may mean, phonologically it is in fact *macˀyirasi*, as the complete lack of voicing marks shows, despite the many opportunities for placing them in the available tokens (36 opportunities, none taken).

So, is that the end of the story? Apparently not: Note a set of data from OKDJ on priestess names. See Table 7.1 (□ = OKDJ 607a; ■ = OKDJ 611b).

---

checked against TOS, and that there are no instances of its appearance in the lexeme in question with a voicing mark, strongly suggesting that the phonological word has a voiceless—not a voiced—obstruent.

58    OSJS (245a) says that the meaning of ⟨to mu ni⟩ has not yet been clarified ("*mishō*"), but Takahashi appears to have made the correct interpretation as *tʰumu* < *\*tomo* 'together; a companion', perhaps 'a follower': cf. NOk *túmu* 'a follower, a retainer' (OGJ 529b). Japanese has a similar history.

AUXILIARIES                                                                287

Explanation for the above: The hypothesis that the etymology of ⟨ma ti ra su⟩ is *madyir-azu 'not mixing/mixed' → 'plainly' → 'outstandingly' is correct. The OKDJ forms show this. The reason that OS mac°yirasi exists is because there must have been a stylistic rule that speakers could devoice the obstruents of deities' and priestesses' names when those names had a common-noun origin, as a sign of their special-name status, divorced from their ordinary beginnings. Based on the foregoing argument, the analysis of -azi as RT is correct.[59]

### 3.2.3      -ana as RY

Takahashi (1991a: 219) tentatively treats the -ana in the following example (OS 13.#981) as a RY form of the negative auxiliary. Or, after segmenting off the first ... a to the preceding verb stem, the remaining -na could very well be taken as a particle: matana → mat-°a- + -na. (More on this in § 4.1 and § 4.2 in comparison with -(a)dana in OS 10.#546.)

おれづむ、ᴧ     またな、     ／ いな、ᴧ ぢやはな、ᴧ
o re du mu , ᴧ   ma ta na ,    ／ i na , ᴧ   di ya pa na , ᴧ
ʔuridzimu-∅     mat-°ana    ʔyiina    dzya#pʰana-∅
early.spring-DO wait-NEG$_{RY}$    already EX-flower-SUB
さちやる                #
sa ti ya ru              #
sa-c°y-ar-u {sak+yi+te+ar+}
bloom-PRFT-SE-RT
'Without [our] awaiting [the arrival of] spring, look!: there have already bloomed beautiful flowers!' (OS 13.#981)

### 3.3      Historical and Comparative Analysis

Yoshida (1973: 221) has noted that the OJ -(a)zu has two conjugational forms, RY and SS, of which RY was more dominant. Interestingly, in OS, the only attested form in conjugation appears as RY. Of note is that there are also special cases of -azi functioning as RT, with the priestess and building names as discussed above.

As for the nasal-based negative RT, there are two attested allomorphs: -aN and -an-u. According to Torigoe (1968: 181), there are 3 tokens of -aN and 9

---

59    We admit that, at present, we have only one case of such a phenomenon. As early as the pronunciation *[mãdʲirãzu] → *[matʲirasu], or as late as the pronunciation [mãdʑirãzɨ] → [matʃirasɨ], the change could have been effected. After the de-affrication from [ ˜dʑ] to [ ˜ʒ], the change yielded [maʃira⋯] masyira. And, apparently, the etymology was known, and the stylistic change effected, repeatedly, judging from the forms found in OKDJ.

tokens of *-an-u*. As Torigoe claims, it is surely true that *-nu* is older than *-N*, since *-nu* ~ *-N* must stem from \**-nu* alone. As for their distributions, they appear to be readily interchangeable, because this allomorphic variation is seen in duplicate omoros (e.g. *ʔak-ʰan-u* (OS 1.#7) ~ *ʔak-ʰaN* (OS 3.#125); *syi̦r-an-u* (OS 7.#367) ~ *syi̦r-aN* (OS 1.#37)).

The RY forms in the lists (§3.1.) have a *z* in them. That form is instantiated by only seven tokens (eight claimed by Torigoe [1968: 179]). Those familiar with the history of the Japanese language will readily recognize a cognate form in Japanese, *-(a)zu*, and many among them will further be familiar with the explosion of forms starting even in OJ, and greatly increasing in both token and type frequency, with the stative-extended *-(a)z-ar-*. The fact that there are so few examples in the OS, and further the fact that there are no examples at all of *z*-based negatives in the modern Ryukyuan languages, has suggested to many researchers—e.g. Vovin 2005[60]—that the form is a borrowing from the Japanese written language, and that it never "took"; thus the lack in the spoken varieties. However it appears to us just as likely, if not more so, that the form *-azi* was a lone holdover from the distant past in the OS, and that it was not borrowed. If it had been borrowed, why is it that all the forms, few though there were, had no stative extension, thus being the most archaic type. Looking at Japanese, one notices that the *z*-type negative forms have almost completely vanished also, despite their astonishing medieval efflorescence. Why should their disappearance in the Ryukyuan spoken languages be any more surprising, then? We conclude that, at the latest, \**-(a)nu-sô* 'NEG-thing/one' (Thorpe [1983: 242]; Shinzato and Serafim [2013: 209]) collapsed into \**-(a)N-zô* and then \**-(a)zu* before the split of Proto-Japonic into the Proto-Ryukyuan and Proto-Japanese lineages.

## 4    Negative: *-adana*

### 4.1    *The Negative Auxiliary Usage in* RY

The negative auxiliary *-adana* only appears in RY, as noted in Takahashi (1991a: 222). In the first example (OS 10.#546), this *-adana* (e.g. *yi̦r-adana* 'not get[ting]') occupies the same slot as *-(a)na* (*pʰak-ˀy-uwa-na*), which Takahashi

---

60    The *-azi* forms are not abundant compared to forms with *n* or *N*. Vovin (2005: 791) states that "[t]he allomorphs *-az-* and *-z-* are not attested in modern dialects, to the best of my knowledge. Thus, they probably represent loans from mainland Japanese, which is further supported by the fact that *-az-* ~ *-z* appears in the Omoro sōshi only eight times (Torigoe [1968: 179–180]). Other allomorphs are attested throughout Ryukyuan."

AUXILIARIES                                                                    289

(1991a: 219) sees as the RY of *-azi*. Takahashi considers them auxiliary verbs,
since they connect semantically to the material that they follow with a meaning of 'without ~ing'. Of note is the fact that *-adana* only has one form, and thus,
if indeed it is a *conjugational* form, it could be considered a defective auxiliary.
Or it could very well be taken as a morph recategorized into a particle (cf. §4.2).

こうては、ᴧ    ゑらだな      / こうては、ᴧ     はきよわな                   /
ko u te pa , ᴧ  we ra da na  / ko u te pa , ᴧ  pa ki yo wa na            /
*kʰuu-t°i-wa  yiᵢiᵢr-adana   kʰuu-t°i-wa   pʰak-°y-uwa-na*[61]
beg-GER-TOP  get·4GE-NEG꜀ᵣy  beg-GER-TOP  wear-RY-EX_AUX-NEG_RY
かくちへ、ᴧ     ゑたる        / のすで、ᴧ      はちやる                      /
ka ku ti pe , ᴧ  we ta ru   / no su de , ᴧ  pa ti ya ru                 /
*kʰak°u-c°yi  yiᵢiᵢt°ar-u    nusi-di      pʰa-c°yar-u*
hide_VT-GER   get-PRFT-RT   steal-GER    wear-PRFT-RT
'[She] did not get[62] [the sword], [by] begging for [it]; [she] did not wear[63] [it],
[by] begging for [it]. It is by hiding [it] that [she] got [it]; it is by stealing [it]
that [she] got [it].'[64] (OS 10.#546)

---

61    The form *pʰak°-adana* (non-honorific) could have been used, since it is metrically the
      same, so the composer consciously chose an honorific form *-uwa-*; and Hokama duly trans-
      lated it into Japanese as such: *haki-nasarazu* (Hokama 2000a: 364b).
62    Underlyingly {yii-r+}, but *yi·r-* here to fit parallel meter. NOk *yii-y-u-N,* (VT =r·aN, =ti)
      'receive; get' (OGJ 265b). Cf. *yi-y-ú-N* (=raN, =cyi) 'be seated, sit down', with short mono-
      syllabic verb stem. ... Either the two verbs represent a former time when there was a clear
      distinction between phonemically short (*yi-* 'sit') and long (*yii-* 'get') monosyllabic verb
      stems, or else the root for 'get' was vowel-ending (*\*y/w.e(e)/i(i).-*) and that for 'sit' ended
      in *\*r* (*\*w.e/i.r-* or *\*yer-*). The OJ roots are *ë-* for 'get' and *wi-* for 'sit', suggesting, contrarily,
      that the difference may have been one of original vowel height.
63    The word *pʰak°yuwana* has *-(a)na*, a variant of the preceding *-adana*, which is in paral-
      lelism to it; therefore, the negative gerund/participle is {+((ad)a)na# 'NEG_GER/PARTICIPLE'},
      though historically it may be *-(a)na < -(a)nana > -(a)dana*.
64    Yoshinari and Fuku (2006: 279–280) take this song to refer to the acts of pirates, but
      Hokama (2000a: 364b), because of the verses below preceding the lines in the example,
      takes it to be the action of a female lord, and (in his notes) therefore the queen:
      ⟨ma bo⁺ ko ri no    o na di ya ra   / su we tu gi no    o na di ya ra⟩
      *ma-bukʰur-yi-nu    wuna-dʑyara-∅  / siyi-c°ig-yi-nu    wuna-dʑyara-∅*
      [true-glad-RY]_BE-APPO female-lord-SUB  spirit-connect-RY-APPO female-lord-SUB
      'The Truly Glad Female Lord, the Spiritual-Heir Female Lord'
      (OSJS ⟨su ... ra⟩ [191c] has the identical view; see ⟨ma ... ra⟩ [306a] for amplification: Shō
      Shin's queen. ⟨ma bo⁺ ko ri⟩ is given not only as a BE for 'rich in spiritual power', but is also
      noted as the name of the female royals' quarters, perhaps thus serving as the locus for the
      'queen' view.) We may add: if indeed she were the queen, she did not have to beg for what
      she wanted or needed; she had the power to obtain it outright. On the other hand, dis-
      cussions of piracy, such as the above (also see Smits [2019: 15–59]) have gained increasing
      currency.

290          CHAPTER 7

In the next example, the square-bracketed material is the refrain (Takahashi [1991a: 267–268]), supplemented here, with (-)*dana* connecting to it, *in toto* 'dance without mistakes'. For Nakahara (1957: 211) *dana* here is a negative imperative *particle*. In a semantically similar (but morphologically somewhat dissimilar) verse (OS 9.#493), *mamig-as-i{-#}na* appears with the negative imperative form *-i{-#}na*, and Ifa, now, sees *na* in this case as, again, a negative imperative *particle*.[65]

| きみの、 | ふみあがりや、ᴧ | / ₍あすぶ゛、ᴧ | きよら | や₍/... |
|---|---|---|---|---|
| ki mi no , | pu mi a ga ri ya , ᴧ | / ₍a su bu , ᴧ | ki yo ra | ya₍ /... |
| *kˀyimyi-nu* | *pˤumyiʔagaryi-ya* | ₍*ʔasib-u-∅* | *kˀyura* | *yaa*₍ |
| priestess-APPO | PN-TOP | ₍sacred dance-RT-TOP | beautiful | SFP₍ |

| あやでᵗ、ᴧ | まめがᵗだᵗな、 | / よりて、ᴧ | まめがᵗだᵗな、 | / |
|---|---|---|---|---|
| a ya deᵗ , ᴧ | ma me gaᵗ daᵗ na , | / yo ri te , ᴧ | ma me gaᵗ daᵗ na , | / |
| *ʔaya-di-∅* | *mamig-**adana*** | *yur-yi{#ˌtʰi/-cʰyi}-∅* | *mamig-**adana**ᴿʏ* | |
| EX-hand-DO | mistake-**NEG**ᴿʏ | sway-RY-hand-DO | mistake-**NEG** | |

'Priestess (Momoto) Fumiagari: ₍[Her] sacred dance: isn't [it] beautiful!₍ [Her] hands_EX make no mistakes, [Her] swaying hands[66] make no mistakes; ₍[her] sacred dance—isn't [it] beautiful₍!' (OS 6.#339), also (OS 12.#678)

---

65    OGJ lists NOk *na* as a *suffix* (i.e. short, accentless; 399a), as does RGJ (short; 371); but OGJ2 lists it as a *particle* (again, though, short and accentless; 192a). The softener *kee* may succeed *na*, thus [na] 'don't!' or [nakɛ:] 'don't' ([OGJ 318a]; [RGJ 277]; [OGJ2 106a];).

| | NOk | | | OOk |
|---|---|---|---|---|
| | SS/RT(-)*na* | *kee* | SS/RT(-)*na kee* | -*a*_MZ*dana* |
| OGJ | ···_SS/RT-SUFF | # SFP | ···_SS/RT-SUFF # SFP | |
| RGJ | ···_SS/RT-SUFF | # SFP | ···_SS/RT-SUFF # SFP | |
| OGJ2 | ···_SS/RT # SFP | ····-SUFF | ···_SS/RT # SFP-SUFF | |
| Nakahara | | | | ···_MZ # SFP |
| Ifa | | | | ···_MZ # SFP |

Oddly, OGJ2 allows the "suffix" -*kee* (accentless, < verb form *ʔukee* 'place [it]!', OGJ2 106a; -*keʔe* ["particle"]) to attach to this "particle". This is apparently the only "particle" with an added "suffix", though SFP sequences are common. Even though *kee* < *ʔuk-ʰe-e* < *\*ok-e-wa* 'place/put-MR-SOFT', a verb form, it has apparently grammaticalized with *na* to *na*(-)*kee*. If *na* is indeed a SFP, then *kee* has grammaticalized into a SFP, and then *na kee* = *na*_SFP *kee*_SFP. If -*na* is still a *suffix*, then -*na kee* = -*na*_SUFF *kee*_SFP. The suffix *na*, along with *kee*, is now grammaticalizing into a SFP, and its wavering causes even lexicographers to disagree. Grammatically, *na* apparently exists in a neutralization position between "suffix" and "particle".

66    The difference between an example like ⟨i ri ti pe⟩ いりちへ *ʔyiryi-cˀyi* 'entering' (OS 5.#223) and ⟨yo ri te⟩ よりて *yur-yi#ˌtʰi* / *yur-yi#cʰyi*, seen above, is in the relationship

# AUXILIARIES 291

The following two omoros lead to different interpretations of *-da(na)* depending upon the perception of the purport of the word *ciyu* 'dew' in the examples: (a) negative and ominous or (b) positive and auspicious. If it is (a), then, of the two offered interpretations below, the RY interpretation of *-dana* (= a) prevails (cf. Takahashi [1991a: 265]), but if it is (b), then the wish interpretation (= b) is preferable (cf. Kadekaru [2003: 74–78]).

おうね、、　くらなみ、、　　ようつゆ、　　/ かけら、だ†な、、
o u ne ,ˆ　ku ra na mi ,ˆ　yo u tu yu ,　/ ka ke ra , da† na ,ˆ
ʔu-uni-∅　kʰura-namyi-∅　yuu-cʰiyu-∅　　kʰakʰi-r-*adana*
EX-ship-DO dark-waves-GEN night-dew-DO　cover·4GE-NEG$_{RY}$
はりやせ　　　　　/
fa ri ya se　　　/
pʰary-as-i
sail-CAUS/VT-MR

(a)  RY reading: 'Sail[67] the splendid ship,[68] not splashing[69] up the night froth[70] of the dark waves.'

(b)  Wish reading: 'The splendid ship: sail [it] on the dark waves, because [I] wish [for you] to splash the night froth [upon it].' (OS 13.#808)

---

between the spelling and the morphological structures involved. The verbal structure ʔyir-yi-cʰyi is tightly bound in a rule-governed complex of a morphophonemic paradigm, and thus is always spelled out fully in its most phonetic form. On the other hand, noun compounds may even be nonce compounds, and, as such, speakers may be much less attentive to the phonetic details of the compounding. Thus even a PPed form may not be written out with PP spelling. Note, e.g. ⟨te⟩ ~ ⟨ti pe⟩, the two in the same omoro, in parallel lines (OS 11.#584, ⟨i (")te "⟩ ~ ⟨i (")ti pe te⟩), but clearly pronounced ʔyidzyi-tʰi 'emerging'.

As in the case of e.g. ···yikʰyi written as ⟨···i ke⟩ (OS 11.#648) (cf. Ch. 5 § 3.1.2), so too, ···yi-cʰyi may still be written ⟨···i te⟩, since it is ⟨···i ti⟩ that ought to indicate ···yi-cʰyi, without aspiration. Nevertheless, PP may not apply if internal word boundary blocks it, making the case slightly different from the ···yikʰyi one.

67  Ikemiya (1987: 320) explains this verb's history as follows: From ⟨pa si ra se⟩, ra palatalized to become rya, then si dropped, leaving pʰarya···,··· , i.e. *pʰasyira···> *pʰasyirya···> pʰaⱷrya··· = pʰarya···. However, assuming that it did what the word *pʰasyira 'pillar' did (NOk haaya, [OGJ 197a]), then it should have at least an underlying form {pʰaary+ 'run; sail'}, with a long vowel as compensatory lengthening

68  The EX word ʔu-uni gives us a window into a time before rendaku became the norm in EX words with ʔu-: *o-pʰune > *o-wune > ... > ʔu-uni. If the compounding had always had rendaku, it would have been *o-bune > ˣʔu-buni.

69  Torigoe (1968: 192) analyzes ⟨ta na⟩ phonemically as tana and morphologically as ta + na 'SS of perfective auxiliary, OJ tari cognate + SFP'. However, his analysis begs the question as to why all eight examples of ta occur with na. Further, given the existence of -dana as a negative auxiliary in Amami dialects, it is more plausible to interpret this, at least in its origin, as a negative auxiliary.

70  The words ⟨yo u tu yu⟩ (2 tokens) and ⟨a sa tu yu⟩ 'morning dew' (1 token) are spelled only

| | | |
|---|---|---|
| みぢ†へりきうが*、∧ | もぢ†よる | / ふなさき、∧　　つよ、∧ |
| mi di pe ri ki u ga*,∧ | mo di† yo ru | / pu na sa ki,∧　tu yo,∧ |
| *myi-ʣyir-yi-kʲyu-ga* | *muʣyuru-∅* | *pʲuna-sakʲyi-∅ cʲiyu-∅* |
| EX-announce-RY-one-APPO | blinding beauty-VOC | ship-prow-IO　dew-DO |
| つけだ†、∧　　はりやせ | / | |
| tu ke da†,∧　pa ri ya se | / | |
| *cʲikʲi-da*[71]　*pʰaᴵaᴵry-as-i* | | |
| put_MZ-NEG_RY　sail-CAUS-MR | | |

(a) RY reading: 'O blinding beauty [Priestess] Mizeriko—run[72] the prow [through the waves] without getting the froth [upon it].'

(b) Wish reading: 'O blinding beauty [Priestess] Mizeriko—run the prow [through the waves], putting the [spirit-powerful] froth [upon it]!' (OS 13.#805)

As Kadekaru notes, four out of eight tokens of *cʲiyu* are concentrated in the volume concerning trade missions. She also notes (77–78) that of 40 tokens of *pʰary-as-i* 'sail [it]!', 37 instances converge on that volume. Further, she claims that instances of *pʰary-as-i* are combined with positive factors, such as sailing with a tail wind, sailing protected by spiritual power, sailing calmly and smoothly, racing with the winging birds, and so on. She argues that the two instances of *cʲiyu* shown above would be the only exceptions from that tendency, if indeed *cʲiyu* is interpreted as something negative. However, utilizing a 'wish' interpretation of -(a)da(na)—which has been independently hypothesized and strongly supported by both written records in post-omoro literature and by dialectal evidence throughout the Ryukyu archipelago[73]—allows, in turn, the interpretation of *cʲiyu* to be simplified, with only a positive connotation. Thus she concludes that the two omoros above should have a 'wish' reading. To support this "positive interpretation" view, she also brings in folk

---

with ⟨tu yu⟩, and all other 8 instances of the word are spelled ⟨tu yo⟩, outnumbering the ⟨tu yu⟩ spelling. The examples with ⟨tu yu⟩ appear only as second elements of two-element noun compounds, in complementary distribution with all examples of ⟨tu yo⟩. There must have developed a temporary distinction between *cʲuyo* ⟨tu yo⟩ and *cʲuyu* ⟨tu yu⟩, the latter the newer form used only as second element in noun compounds, then with a merger after general raising, as *cʲiyu*, with the two *spellings* in their observed distributions.

71　The *na* of -(a)da(na) is missing. The first vowel is automatically dropped.

72　This is a refrain, the part of the omoro noted for irregular meter. Assuming, however, that it is broken into two groups of six moras each, then the long *aa* of /pʰaary-as-i/ should shorten to *a*, giving *pʰaryasi*.

73　For written records cf. e.g. OKDJ (472bc) ⟨na⟩ ···*aᴵdaᴵna*, and for modern Ryukyuan evidence, Nakasone (1983), Matsumoto (1986) and Sawaki (2009).

AUXILIARIES 293

medicine (2003: 81), noting that traditionally, people stepped on morning dew hoping for it to cure beriberi. Given the independent evidence above about the positivity of dew (i.e. spiritual power, *pʰaary-as-* occurring only with positive factors, and curative power in folk medicine), it seems therefore that the wish interpretation is more appropriate.

OSJS (202b) describes *-da* (our *-(a)da*) in the second example as a truncated form of *-dana* (our *-(a)dana*). Takahashi (1991a: 274) supports that account, citing the following near-identical examples.

あまの　　　みぢ†へりきよが†、　　　／しないとみ、ᴧ
a ma no　　mi di† pe ri ki yo ga†,　　／ si na i to mi,ᴧ
*ʔama-nu*　　*myi-ʣyi|r-yi-kʰyu-ga*　　*syi̧ ne-e-r̩ tʰumyi*[74]
Heaven-GEN EX-announce-RY-one-SUB　harmonize-RY-HMS
まぢ†ら、だ†なᴧ　　めより[75]　　　／
ma di† ra , da† na ᴧ me yo ri　　／
*maʣyi̧ r-adana*　　*mii-yur-yi*
blinding-**ly.NEG**　　be.visible_RY-SE-SS
'[The Priestess] Mizeriko from Heaven [says]: HMS Shinai is seen as far-and-above [any others].' (OS 13.#879)

きみおそい、ぎ†みの、　　／まぢ†ら、だ†ᴧ　　めより　　　／
ki mi o so i , gi† mi no ,　　／ ma di† ra , da† ᴧ me yo ri　　／
*k°yimyi-ʔusii-gyimyi-nu*　　*maʣyi̧ r-ada*　　*mii-yur-yi*
priestess-ruler-priestess-SUB　mixing-**ly.NEG** be.visible_RY-SE-SS
'The high priestess looks outstanding[76] (*lit.* does not mix with others).' (OS 9.#480) (OS 11.#595) (OS 21.#1462)

### 4.2 Sentence-Final Particle: Rhetorical Question (hango) *or Wish* (ganbō)

The following examples are all interpretable either as a negative rhetorical question or a wish. In the former case, the speaker presents a situation, and questions its validity for the sake of affirming it, as in: 'Is the situation (= Sentence) not the case?' → 'Of course it is the case.' If the situation involves deities, kings, or priestesses, the interpretation takes on a further implication as follows: 'Will the situation (= Sentence) not be the case?' → 'If it is not the case(, it

---

74　There appear to be no PPed tokens of *-tʰumyi*, i.e. ˣ-*cʰyumyi*, so it blocks PP: {+r̩tʰumyi}.

75　Notice *mii-* [mɪː] for what ought to be *myi-yi-* [mʸiʸyi]; apparently *mii-* < \**mee-* < \**myee-* < \**myi-ye-*.

76　In the preceding omoro (OS 13.#879), the same phrase appears as *maʣyi̧ r-adana mi-yur-yi*. Thus, this *maʣyi̧ r-ada* is considered a variant of *maʣyi̧ r-adana*.

will not do).'[77] → 'Of course it will be the case [with the aid of a powerful entity]' → 'May that be the case.' What has occurred historically is a reinterpretation (an abduction) of the sequence. The point of origin, ····-(*a*)*dana*, has been split into ····-(*a*)## plus ##*dana*: the result is a two-fold recategorization: (1) the *mizen-kei* (= subjunctive form) of the verb is now a free-standing word, not just a conjugational form; (2) the new *dana* is a free-standing sentence-final particle, clearly distinct not only semantically but also morphologically from the form that gave it its birth. These recategorizations are reflected in the second glosses.

いちよかゝゝ、ヘ　ころた、　　/ あやの、　　　　みやし、ヘ
i ti yo ka " " , ∧　ko ro ta ,　　/ a ya no ,　　　mi ya si , ∧
ʔyic°yuʔ#kʰakʰa kʰuru#tʰa-∅　ʔaya-nu　　　myi-yoosyi-∅
MO.superior?$_{ADJ}$ man-PL-SUB　beautiful$_{EX/BE}$-GEN　EX-rhythm-DO
うちよわちへ、　　　/ かみは、ヘ　　まただ†な /
u ti yo wa ti pe ,　　/ ka mi pa , ∧　ma ta da† na /
ʔuc-°y-uwa-c°yi　　kʰamyi-wa　mat-°adana　or mat°a dana
beat-RY-AUX$_{EX}$-GER　deity-TOP　wait-NEG$_{RY}$　wait$_{MZ}$ SFP
RhQ: '[Superior men] are beating the beautiful rhythms[78] [for the deities], and so, of course the deities are tarrying [i.e. delaying leaving for the other world, i.e. prolonging their stay]!'
Wish: '[Superior men] are beating the beautiful rhythms [for the deities]. May/Let the deities tarry [i.e. stay longer]!' (OS 11.#596)

げらゑ*、　すづ†なりぎ*や、　/ やゝの、　き[よ]ら、ヘ　しよれど*も、
ge ra we* , su du† na ri gi* ya , / ya ya no , ki 『yo』 ra , ∧ si yo re do* mo ,
girayi　　sidzinaryi-gya　　yaya-nu　k°yura-∅　s-y-ur-i-du-mu
BE$_{ADJ}$　　PN-SUB　　　EX-APPO　dance-DO　do-RY-SE-IZ-KP-even
/ あが*ヘ なさと、　　　/ みこゑ、ヘ　　あわさだ†な　/
/ a ga* ∧ na sa to ,　　/ mi ko we , ∧　a wa sa da† na /
ʔa-ga　naseei̯-tʰu　　myi-kʰuyi-∅ ʔawas-adana　or ʔawasa　dana
I-GEN　father-INSTR　　EX-voice-DO　chorus-NEG$_{RY}$　chorus$_{MZ}$ SFP
RhQ: 'Priestess Suzunari is dancing beautifully—of course she will sing together with my Father.'
Wish: 'Priestess Suzunari is dancing beautifully—may she sing together with my Father!' (OS 14.#1011)

---

77　Cf. Matsumoto's (1986: 870) use of Japanese *nomanakereba* for Kikai dialect *numadana* 'if [you] don't drink', i.e. 'you must drink', to translate some instances of *dana*.

78　*myi-yoosyi* ← *myi-* 'EX' + *p°yoosyi* (⟨pi ya si⟩ 'rhythm' [OSJS 285a]). For the phonological process, see Ch. 4 § 4.1 fn. 62. Also: possibly *myoosyi*.

AUXILIARIES                                                                               295

あまみや、　みるやにや、　／よざ†け、ᵥ　もらゝゝと、　　／きみが*、ᵥ
a ma mi ya ,　mi ru ya ni ya ,　/ yo za† ke ,ᵥ　mo ra mo ra to ,　/ ki mi ga* ,ᵥ
ʔamamyi.ya myiruya.nya　　yuu-zakʰi　mura.mura-tʰu　k°yimyi-ᵢga
PN(deity)　　PN(deity)　　EX-saké　ful-ly　　　　priestess-GEN
まぶ*り、ᵥ　　せだ†な、　／
ma bu* ri ,ᵥ　se da† na ,　/
maʙr-yi　　si-**dana**　or si　　***dana***
protect-NOM do-NEG$_{RY}$　do$_{MZ}$ SFP

RhQ: 'Serving *saké* to our ancestral deities, Amamiya and Niruyanya. Of course
they'll protect our priestess.'
Wish: 'Serving *saké* to our ancestral deities, Amamiya and Niruyanya. May they
protect our priestess!' (OS 21.#1401)


### 4.3    *Issues Concerning the Categorization of* -adana

As noted in Takahashi (1991a: 222), there is only one conjugational form of
*-adana*, RY; thus OKDJ (398a) treats it as a conjunctive particle (接続助詞 [*se-
tsuzoku joshi*]), but OSJS (209c) classifies it as either an auxiliary (助動詞 [*jo-
dōshi*]) or a sentence-final particle (SFP = 終助詞 [*shū-joshi*]).

As discussed in the preceding sections, especially in § 4.2, here we take its
starting point to be a defective auxiliary rather than a conjunctive particle,
and also list any other SFP usages as rhetorical question (*hango* 反語), or wish
(*ganbō* 願望), which we consider to be reanalyses or recategorizations of this
auxiliary. This also means that the MZ form of the verb preceding the new SFP
now can have the status of an independent word.[79]


### 4.4    *Historical and Comparative Analysis*

There are 19 tokens and 14 types (excluding duplicate omoros, but including
two cases of *-(a)da, c°ik°i-da* and *madzyir-ada*, both noted in footnotes below)
of the auxiliary *-adana* in the *Omoro Sōshi*. There is no remnant of this in NOk,
but it is reportedly used in Amami dialects (Matsumoto [1986: 867–888]), and
also in Sakishima dialects ([OSJS: 209c], Sawaki [2009: 84]).

The cognation of the OOk *-adana* and [Old Japanese] Eastern Dialect [ED]
is suggested by Thorpe (1983: 241–242) as follows:

> In Ry [S&S: our Proto-Ryukyuan] and ED, on the other hand, the inflection
> of negatives was based on the negative participle: *{a}da (Ry), and {a}na

---

79    Of course a *seeming* (i.e. formally identical) MZ already exists as an independent word,
      but only incidentally having the same form, since it is actually the IA of the verb, and in
      fact has an origin distinct from the MZ.

(ED). The n̲ of the latter looks very much like a contamination with *{a}nu (a suffix not attested in eighth century ED material). Thus one finds in ED senana 'not doing, without doing,' and kŏnani 'not coming, without coming,' in Ry. respectively *seda(na) and *kŏda(na).[80]

Thorpe notes that his idea is built on Hōjō's original suggestion of cognation, but differs from Hōjō's in that Hōjō does not view *na* as a dynamic locative, but rather as an exclamatory particle.[81] As noted in Matsumoto (1986: 879), Nakijin has MZ + -ɴna, which parallels the function of Amami -*dana*, having both negative-RY and wish meanings. This also lends support to Thorpe's proposal.

## 5 The Optative/Counterfactual Auxiliary: -(*a*)*masyi*

### 5.1 The Optative -(a)masyi

The optative auxiliary -(*a*)*masyi* (perhaps < *-am-a·syi *'IA-MZ·AA') expresses the speaker's wish or desire, or in limited cases, counter-factuality of the proposition.[82]

Below are the only verbs that this auxiliary attaches to, i.e.:[83]

あらまし

a ra ma si

ʔar-amasyi

be_INANIMATE-OPT (OS 11.#557, [OS 21.#1409][84])

'may [it] be so!'

---

80   S&S: But cf. OKDJ 472bc ⟨na⟩ ···*ana* (2) "attaching to MZ," showing that PRk, too, had a form *-ana 'NEG_RY'.

81   Vovin (2012: 99) has a different view for the final -*na* element: "The EOJ form in V-(*a*)*n-a-na* functionally corresponds to WOJ V-(*a*)*n-u-ni* 'because/when not doing V'. It is likely to consist etymologically of the negative suffix -*an*-, EOJ-specific attributive -*a*- and EOJ-specific dative-locative case marker -*na*. Since verbal and nominal morphology do not mix in OJ, EOJ locative -*na* cannot follow the negative *-(*a*)*na*- directly, and there must be some intermediate nominalizing morpheme. I believe that this morpheme is EOJ-specific and a rare attributive in -*a*..."

82   Although OSJS (298a) lists its core meanings as 'future', 'inference', and 'intention', 'optative (wish to V)' and 'counter-factual conditional (would (have) V (-ed))', it is unclear from the short description in OSJS if a common thread runs through these meanings, and, if so, what that is. Semantically, they belong to the irrealis domain.

83   This form is secondary to -*bu·sya* 'wish (to)' in token- and lexical frequency. That form, the more common one, already treated in Ch. 5 § 4.3, has led to the NOk desiderative.

84   Bracketed omoro numbers are duplicate omoros.

# AUXILIARIES

297

かが*、おらまし
ka ga*, o ra ma si
*ka[a]ga[a]-**wur**-amasyi*
shine<sub>ROOT</sub>-SE-OPT (OS 17.#1211)
'[we] want [her] to be shining'[85]

しめまし
si me ma si
***syimi**-masyi*
do<sub>CAUS</sub>-OPT (OS 7.#348)
'may [they] make [it] so!'

すへまし
su pe ma si
***siyi**-masyi*
place-OPT ([OS 11.#559] [OS 21.#1411], [OS 21.#1455])
'[they] would like to place [it]'

せまし
se ma si
***sii**-masyi*
do-OPT ([OS 17.#1222]; [OS 18.#1252])
'[we] wish to do; let [us] do'

{ぬ/の}ば*まし
{**nu/no**}ba* ma si
***nub**-amasyi*
extend-OPT ([OS 11.#557, twice] [OS 21.#1409, twice])
'[they] wish to extend'

---

85   OSJS (104bc) says that ⟨ka ga*, o ra ma si⟩ is composed of the stem of ⟨ka ga* ya ku⟩, to
which is added the MZ of ⟨o ri⟩, i.e. ⟨o ra⟩, and then the optative auxiliary verb ⟨ma si⟩;
putting it all together: ⟨ka ga* + o ra + ma si⟩. It does not explain how a verb should come
to lose half of its stem, leaving only ⟨ka ga*⟩ to carry the meaning of 'shine'. The explanation
comes clearly into view upon examining OKDJ (181, 182), and upon further considering, of
all things, the early-modern Okinawan word for 'movi[ing] pictur]e'. Let us examine the
last first: the word is *kaagaa-wudu-yi, lit.* 'silhouette-danc-ing'. The form *kaagaa-* refers to
the effect of throwing light upon a form, and then having it fall upon a background. OKDJ,
under |kaga-wori| (181b), suggests a link to *ka#ga* 'day#day' (i.e. 'shine-shine'), and also
eschews a connection to -*yak*-, opting instead for three verbs of existence, giving |kaga-
wori|, |kaga-ar-as-u|, and |kaga-kiyowar-u| as the basic underlying forms for the observed
forms. See also Ch. 5 § 2.2 for further discussion of 'shine'.

298        CHAPTER 7

with a total token frequency of 6, excluding any duplicate omoro. Because there is no reflex in any modern Ryukyuan dialects (Vovin [2009a: 820]), this must be a loan from MJ.

Its only conjugated form attested in the *Omoro Sōshi* is ss. The auxiliary -(*a*)*masyi* appears in the collocational patterns of:

> *N ya-tʻi-ya* ...-(*a*)*masyi* 'N COP-GER-TOP...-(*a*)*masyi*'

and

> *V-tʻi-ya* [...-*amasyi*] 'V-GER-TOP [...-*amasyi*]'.

An example of the noun-plus-copula pattern above is:

おぼ゚つだ゙け、ᴧ あつる、 / すで゙る、ᴧ で゙うみづ゙よ、 /
o bo* tu da† ke , ᴧ a tu ru , / su de† ru , ᴧ de† u mi du* yo , /
*ʔubucʻi-dakʰi-∅* *ʔa-c-°ir-u* *sidi·r-u* *dʑyoo-myidʑi-yu*
Heaven-shrine-LOC STAT-PRFV-SE-RT purify·4GE-RT pure-water-DO
かみぎ゙や、 きも ᴧ やてや、 / いづこ、しま、ᴧ
ka mi gi* ya , ki mo ᴧ ya te ya , / i du† ko , si ma , ᴧ
*kʰamyi-gya* *kʻyimu* *ya-tʻi-ya* *ʔyidʑi#kʰuu#syima-∅*
deity-GEN heart COP-GER-TOP brave-one(s)-land-LOC
おろちへ、 / かいなで゙、みづ゙、ᴧ しめまし /
o ro ti pe , / ka i na de* , mi du* , ᴧ si me ma si /
*ʔuru-cʻyi* *kʰee.nadi#myidʑi-∅* **syimi-masyi**
let.descend-GER holy-water-IO **do**$_{\text{CAUS.MZ}}$**-OPT**

'**May [they]** hand down the water in Heaven's Shrine—because it is the [very] heart of the deities—to the Land of the Brave Ones, and **have it become** the [King's] holy water!' (OS 7.#348)

The clauses with *ya-tʻi-ya* and with *V-tʻi-ya* structurally constitute conditional clauses.[86] However, as noted in Takahashi (1991a: 223), if these phrases are interpreted as counterfactual conditionals, then the sentence would not make much sense: "If it had been the deities' intent, we would have had it become the [King's] holy water. [But since it wasn't, we did not do so.]" Similarly, the *counterfactual* meaning of OS 11.#559 below would be "If it had been the world of our ancestors, they would have served hundreds of jars of sake,"[87] which Taka-

---

86    An exception to this is the counterfactual usage discussed in §5.2.

87    Translating from the original text: "From the point of view of Classical Japanese grammar,

# AUXILIARIES

hashi (1991a: 223), at least, does not consider to be an appropriate meaning for a shamanistic song, though not stating why. Takahashi agrees with OSJS (336c)'s interpretation of *N + ya-tºi-ya* as causal, i.e. 'because it is N' and hence, gives it an optative interpretation.

うきおほぢ゛が゛、　　　　　世、ハ　やてや、　　　／ もゝ、が⁺めむ、ハ
u ki o po di⁺ ga⁺ ,　　　yo , ʌ　ya te ya ,　　／ mo " , ga⁺ me mu , ʌ
ʔuu·kºyi#ʔuqpºu#ʤyi-,ga[88]　*yuu*　**ya-tºi-ya**　　*mumu-gami-*M
great·AA-grand-father-GEN　world　COP-GER-TOP　hundred-jar-even
すへまし　　　／
su pe ma si　　／
*siyi-masyi*
**prepare-OPT**

ˣ'Had it been the world of our ancestors, they would have served hundreds of jars of *sake*' (COUNTERFACTUAL) → °'Its being the world of our ancestors, we will → expect to → want to serve hundreds of jars of *sake* (OPTATIVE).' (OS 11.#559)

Omoro scholars in general are in accord that this example means 'wish to'. For instance, the *optative* interpretation is offered in Shimamura (2012: 120–121) as 'Since it is the ancestral world, we would like to serve hundreds of jars of sake.'[89] See the same optative interpretation for OS 17.#1211 below, also recognized by Hokama (2000b: 248), and for OS 17.#1222 and OS 21.#1409 below, and by Nakahara (1957: 247 and 1957: 416, respectively).

てるよもひ、が゛なし、　　／ あが゛、おなご、ハ　やてや、　　　／ うちちへ、、ハ
te ru yo mo pi , ga⁺ na si ,　／ a ga⁺ , o na go ʌ　ya te ya ,　　／ u ti ti pe , ʌ
*tʰiru-y-umii-ganasyi-∅* ₈μ　*ʔa-ga-wunagu*　**ya-tºi-ya** ₈μ　*ʔuc-ºyi-cºyi* ₃μ
[shine-sun-BE-BE]PN-SUB　I-GEN-lady　COP-GER-TOP　beat-RY-GER
かが゛、おらまし　　　　　／
ka ga⁺ , o ra ma si　　　／
*kaagaa-wur-amasyi* ₈μ
**shine-STAT-OPT**

---

〈ya te ya〉 means 'if [it] were / had been' and 〈ma si〉 may be considered to mean 'would have DONE'" (223).

88　Cf. our Ch. 5 (§ 2.1): *ʔuu·kºyi-ʔuqpºu-ʤyi* 'great-great-grandfather' i.e. 'ancestor'.

89　In the original text: "Because [it] is the ancestral world, [we] wish to place many jars of holy wine." ("Shigen no yo de aru kara, ōku no mi·ki-game o suetai." Shimamura [2012: 120–121]).

'Since Priestess Teru-Hi-Omoi-Ganashi[90] is our [beloved/respected] lady, **may [she] shine** along with the beat of [our] drums.' (OS 17.#1211) (Assume $\text{?uc°yic°yi}$ is extrametrical, as if $\text{?uQc°yi}$.)

たかかわの、　　みづ*の、　/ よこす 〜　　もの、〜　やてや、　　　/
ta ka ka wa no ,　mi du* no , / yo ko su 〜　mo no , 〜 ya te ya ,　　　/
t$^h$ak$^h$a-k$^h$awa-nu myidzi-nu　　yuk$^h$us-i　munu　**ya-t°i-ya**
high-well-GEN,　water-SUB　channel-RT thing　COP-GER-TOP
のきあげ*、みづ*、　　/ かいなで*、みづ、〜　　　せまし　　#
no ki a ge* , mi du* ,　/ ka i na de* , mi du* , 〜　se ma si　　#
nuk°yi-?agi#myidzi-∅　k$^h$ee-nadi#myidzi-∅　**si-masyi**
thrust-raise-water-DO　VPREF-safeguard-water-IO　**make-OPT**
'Since the high-walled well's water is channeled water, **we would like to** make the scooped-up water the safeguarding-ritual water.' (OS 17.#1222)[91]

くむ　　さうず*　　や、ちよむ、　　/ みちゑ、〜　いぢ*へ、〜 いき、〜
ku mu　sa u zu*　ya , ti yo mu ,　/ mi ti we , 〜 i di* pe , 〜 i ki , 〜
k°um-u　soo|zi　ya-c$^h$yoo-M　　myi-c°yi　?yi-dzi　?yik°yi[92]-∅
draw-RT　clear.water COP-CONC-even　see-GER　go-GER　breath-DO
のば、まし　/ くだ†る　　　つぢ†　や、ちよむ、　　/ みちへ、〜
no ba , ma si / ku da† ru　　tu di†　ya , ti yo mu ,　/ mi ti pe , 〜
**nub-amasyi**　k°u-dar-u　c°idzi　ya-c$^h$yoo-M　myi-c°yi
**extend-OPT**　step-PRFT-RT summit COP-CONC-even　see-GER
いぢ*へ、〜 あよ、〜　のば、まし　#
i di* pe , 〜 a yo , 〜　no ba , ma si #
?yi-dzi　?ayu-∅　nub-**amasyi**
go-GER　heart-DO extend-**OPT**

---

90　OSJS links ⟨te ru pi yo mo pi ga na si⟩ to this one, without overtly hypothesizing any phonological relationship, and saying that it refers to a high-status person. It is OKDJ (446c)
that equates them by listing them as spelling alternatives for the same word. Probably
*teru#pyi#?o··· >LOSS OF INTERNAL WORD BOUNDARIES, INTERVOCALIC VOICELESS
LABIAL LENITION> *teruwyiyo··· > *teruyiyo··· > *teruyo··· > t$^h$iruyu···.

91　This song refers to part of the O-Ara-Ori (?u-?ara-?uri), the ritual associated with the ini-
tiation of Kikoe Ōgimi, in which she visits a series of sacred sites before reaching Sēfā
?Utaki. This song refers to the ceremonial ritual at Oyakawa, Yonabaru-chō, where her
forehead is wet with sacred water taken from the well there (cf. Nakahara 1957: 246–247).
It is reminiscent of Christian baptism.

92　The word in NOk is ?yiicyi, 'breath; breathing' (OGJ 250). By contrast, 'go-RY' is ?yíc-yi
(OGJ 246a) and 'go-GER' is ?ń-zyi (OGJ 249a), a suppletion from *?yin- *'leave'.

AUXILIARIES     301

'**May you** go and see[93] even if it be [as little as] the beautiful clear water, and feel at peace [*lit.* extend your breath]; **may you** go and see even the summit[94] you stepped on, and feel at peace [*lit.* extend your heart].' (OS 21.#1409)[95]

Here is the only possible example of *V-t°i-ya* (not *N + ya-t°i-ya*):

なかち、     あやみやに、     / みればず、∧     きも、∧
na ka ti ,     a ya mi ya ni ,     / mi re ba† , ∧     ki mo , ∧
*nakʰac°yi-∅*     *ʔaya-myaa-nyi*     *myii·r-i-ba*[96]     *k°yimu-∅*
PLN-APPO     BE$_{EX}$-courtyard-LOC    see·4GE-IZ-when    heart-SUB
はゑてや、     / もゝがずめも、∧     すへまし     /
pa we te ya ,     / mo " ga† me mo , ∧ su pe ma si /
*pʰayi-t°i-ya*     *mumu-gaami-M*     *siyi-masyi*
effloresce-GER-TOP    hundred-jar-even    place-OPT
'Since [our] hearts effloresce, observing within the courtyard of Nakachi, || we would like to serve hundreds of jars [of sake].' (OS 21.#1455)[97]

### 5.2    *Counterfactual -*(a)*masyi*

Below is an example interpretable as counterfactual.

うきおほぢ*が*、∧     おわにや、     / ゑん、げらへ、∧
u ki o po di* ga* , ∧     o wa ni ya ,     / we N , ge ra pe , ∧
*ʔul⟦u⟧·k°yi#ʔuQp°u#ʣyi-ga*    *ʔuwa-⟦a⟧n-y-a ... [ɲa]*    *wiN-∅ girayi-∅*
great·AA-grand-father-SUB    be$_{EX}$-NEG-IZ-T/C    residence-TOP build-SUB
あらまし     #
a ra ma si     #
*ʔar-amasyi*[98]
STAT-**CF.COND**

---

93    This is an errand construction; in NOk it would be *NN-cyi, ʔyic-y-ú-N* 'go and see' in the order opposite from English.

94    NOk *cíʣyi* 'summit' (OGJ 165a). Nb: ⟨tu di |⟩ = *c°iʣyi* ~ ⟨tu N | zi⟩ = *c°iNzyi*: YGH; cf. Ch. 2 §5.4.

95    We followed the OSJS main text for *k°um-u-soozi* (OSJS 145a) and *k°u-dar-u c°iʣyi* (OSJS 140a).

96    Note the minimal pair *myii-* 'see' :: *mii-* 'be visible/seen'.

97    TOS notes that the last line of the omoro cited here and the preceding lines may originate in different omoros. And yet both lines consist of 10 moras.

98    Cf. *ka(a)ga(a)-wur-amasyi* above. The pattern is rare, and is probably best handled structurally as TOPIC + DEVERBAL SUBJECT + VERB in *-amasyi* form, functioning as if TOP + MAIN VERB + SE-*amasyi*.

302                                            CHAPTER 7

'If [you] had not had[99] [your] ancestors [in Kumejima] (*lit.* in the state when [you] had no ancestors [in Kumejima]), [you] could have built [your] house[100] [here in Yaeyama].' (OS 21.#1409) (cf. Nakahara [1957: 414])

### 5.3    *Historical and Comparative Analysis*

The OJ counterpart *-amasi* has three patterns (cf. Yoshida [1973: 388–402]) as below, with examples:

–   Pattern 1: **Sentence-final** usage in the collocational pattern of 'hypothetical/question ...*-amasi*', expressing **counterfactuality** (CF.COND):

妻毛      有者      採而      多宜麻之
TUMA-*mö*   AR-A-*ba*,    TUM-Î-TE   *tagë-masi*
wife-even   have-MZ-if,   pick-RY-GER   partake$_{MZ}$-CF.COND
'If [I] but had a wife, I would pick [it/her] and partake [of it/her].' (MYS 2.#221) [play on sound sequence *tum ...*],

–   Pattern 2: **Sentence-final** usage without collocation, expressing an exclamatory *wish*:

花        有     時尔    相益物乎
PANA-∅     AR-U   TÖKÎ-*ni*   AP-A-*masi*-MÖNÖ-*wo*
flower-SUB   be-RT   time-at   meet-MZ-CF.COND-although-EXCL
'[I] would have wanted to meet [with you] when [mandarins] had been blooming [not when their oranges had fruited].' (MYS 8.#1492),

–   Pattern 3: **Sentence-medial** usage, expressing a modal-like meaning *'should-, supposed to be'*.

---

99   We see here special rules for a seeming fast-speech or colloquial form of the exalting negative conditional *Ɂuwaanya*. We assume, but do not attempt to show, that the form has long *aa*, due to dropped *s*, from one of the two bases /Ɂuwa·s-/ (therefore from /Ɂuwa·s+a+/) of the exalting main verb 'exist, go, come', the other being /Ɂuwa·r-/. We would further expect ⟨ne ba⟩, but get a reduced ⟨ni ya⟩ instead, showing overall *Ɂuwaanya* < \**Ɂowa·s-a-n-e-ba* 'if there did not exist'.

100   Its relation to OJ/MJ is unclear. Nakahara (1957: 416) suggests 院, pre-NJ SJ *weɴ* /kan'yō-on *wiɴ*, later *yeɴ*/*iɴ*, resp. 'lge bldg w/ surrounding fence (etc.)'. Schuessler (2009: 269) has Mandarin yuàn, MC jwänᶜ, Late Han wanᶜ, and Minimal OC wens.

AUXILIARIES

| 萬代尓 | 國 | 所知麻之 | 嶋 | 宮 | 波 | 母 |
|---|---|---|---|---|---|---|
| YÖRÖZU-YÖ-*ni* | KUNI | SIR-AS-***Amasi*** | SIMA-∅ | MÎYA | *pa* | *mö* |
| m-g-t[101] | country. | know-EX-**should**$_{RT}$ | bank-GEN | palace | SFP | SFP |

'The palace on the bank, which **should** govern the country through many generations.' (MYS 2.#171)

In OOk, Yoshida's first pattern above seems to be more predominant than the other two. However, the OOk patterns are used in an optative rather than a counterfactual meaning, as shown in §5.1 and §5.2. In addition, OOk -(*a*)*masyi* only occurs sentence-finally, not followed by any sentence-final particles. This is different from OJ -(*a*)*masi*, which, according to Yamada (1954: 282–283) and Vovin (2009a: 673), occurs frequently before the conjunction *mönö*(-*wo*). Yamada (284) also claims that -(*a*)*masi* (i.e. -(*a*)*m-a·si*) is the adjective version of -(*a*)*m-u* (see §6 and Ch. 6 §3), where the latter is more verb-like.

## 6      Inference/Intention: -*aₙ*, -*a*, and -*am-i*

The auxiliary -*a*(*ₙ*) (underlying form {+am}) can denote either inference or volition. If the subject is first person, then it conveys the speaker's intention, while it expresses inference if it is third person. This auxiliary has two attested overt conjugational forms, SS -*aₙ* and IZ -*am-i*. In addition, there is also the covert RT/SS form -*a*, without the final nasal, which is phonologically identical to the MZ of the preceding verb stem. The history and functions of this truncated form were discussed at length in Ch. 6 §3.

### 6.1     *Inference/Intention* -*aₙ* *in* SS
Compared to the RT/SS -*a*, the SS -*aₙ* is attested only in five examples, as shown below. It is clear that this is a remnant of the original *\*-am-u* > -*aₙ*, and the precursor to the final -*a*. Here are all the examples of this auxiliary in SS:

いみやは、ᴧ　せめてᴧ　うたん、　　　／
i mi ya pa ,ᴧ　se me teᴧ　u ta N ,　　　／
*ʔyimya-wa*[102] *simi-t°i*　*ʔut-°aₙ*
now-TOP　　attack-GER conquer-IA
'Now, **let us** attack and conquer [them].' (OS 2.#45)

---

101    m-g-t = myriad-generation-through.
102    The only exception to PP of *m* is when it follows #*ʔyi*, for reasons unclear.

| | | | |
|---|---|---|---|
| あせら、、 | ため やらば†、 | / おきなます、、 | |
| a se ra , ∧ | ta me ya ra ba† , | / o ki na ma su , ∧ | |
| *ʔa-si-ra-∅* | *tʰami yar-a-ba* | *ʔuk°yi-namasi-∅* | |
| I-elder.brother-PL-GEN | sake COP-MZ-T/C | deep.sea-mincemeat-APP | |

すもらん、          /
su mo ra N          /
*sim-u·r-aN*
make$_{CAUS}$·4GE-IA

'If [it] is for the sake[103] of [our] soldiers₁, **let us** have [them₁] keep making [the enemy] into offshore mincemeat [in sea battle].' (OS 1.#36)

Nakahara (1957: 232) states that ⟨su mo ra N⟩ (phonologically *simuraN*) is a mistake for ⟨si me ra N⟩ (*syimiraN*). Here, we agree with him partially because of other example(s) of ⟨o ki na ma su si me te⟩ ... *syimi-t°i* 'having [them₁] make [them₂] into *ʔukºyi-namasi*' (OS 3.#93). Concerning *\*syimuraN*, we believe that it started as

*\*syim[e        #w]or-am-u*
*\*make.into$_{CAUS.RY}$    #STAT-IA-SS/RT*

and went through a vowel-loss and vowel shift following labials, as below:

  *\*syim[e#w]or-am-u*
>  *\*syim[]ōr-am-ū* (after vowel-loss)
>  *\*syimūr-aм-∅* (after vowel-shift).[104]

---

103 The phrase *tʰami yar-a-ba* is somewhat diputable. On the one hand, the phrase can be separated as the noun ⟨ta me⟩ *tʰami* 'sake', and the copula {yar+} *yar-yi* '[A] is [B]'. On the other, there is a verb *\*tame-* 'bend [it]', found in *koyō* (= old songs) and in the modern language. It refers to the physical bending of materials used in construction: *tamí-y-u-N* (OGJ 509b). For that verbal construal, see Nakahara [1957: 226], Ikemiya [2006: 39], and Higa Minoru in Omoro Kanshō 9. However, within the OS itself, all 17 examples of *tʰami* are glossed by OSJS and clearly understood as meaning '(for the) sake (of)'. The two claimed exceptions turn out not to be material:

 (1) three duplicate tokens of what is actually *madzyirada miiyuri* 'is seen as not mixing' = 'is seen as unparalleled' ([OS 9.#480] [OS 11.#595] [OS 21.#1462]), and

 (2) the one hapax *here*: *tʰami yaraba*, in other words 'for the sake of'

 While a meaning of 'bending' or 'twisting' can be eked out of the hapax, a perfectly ordinary glossing of 'if it is for the sake of' can also be obtained. That leaves no reason at all for the defense of the 'bend/twist' hypothesis. We believe that the scholarship that takes the latter view has been led astray.

104 Note the loss of the *second* of the two vowels in the case of the exalting honorific:

AUXILIARIES                                                                                305

## 6.2    *Inference/Intention* -aN *in* ss: *Controversial Cases*

Here are some controversial examples, which some scholars take as instances
of negation rather than as inference.

なさいきよが*、　　おせぢ*、　　　　　／　もゝあぢ*、ᴧ
na sa i ki yo ga*, o se di*,　　　　　／　mo " a di*,ᴧ
*nasee-kʰyu-ga*　　*ʔu#sidzyi-∅*　　　　*mumu-ʔadzyi-∅*
father-one-GEN   EX-spiritual.power-APP   hundred-lord-SUB
たちあわん　　　　　　　／
ta ti a wa N　　　　　　　／
*tʰac-°yi-ʔaw-aN*
stand-RY-harmonize-IA
'By dint of our father's spiritual power, a great many (*lit.* hundreds of) lords **will**
be in attendance.' (OS 6.#310)

Takahashi (1991a: 224) points out the possibility of interpreting this as a negative auxiliary. Noted for his caution, he says "There is also the possibility that it
is the ⟨N⟩ of negation," without further explanation. We hazard a guess that his
vacillation hinges on the interpretation of the bare noun phrases *nasee-kʰyuu-*
*ga ʔu-sidzyi-∅* and *mumu-ʔadzyi-∅*. Here is our attempt at a Negative interpretation: 'By dint of our Father's spiritual power, hundreds of lords will not stand
in our way.' However, note the existence of the NOk word *tac-yi-ye-e,* 'attendance (for directing, inspecting, etc.)', which weakens a negative-interpretation
argument. Thus, we are in favor of the inference interpretation presented above
in our translation.

なつたなし、ᴧ　　　やれば†、　／はだ†、からむ、ᴧ　　さわらん　　　／
na tu ta na si,ᴧ　　ya re ba†,　／ pa da†, ka ra mu,ᴧ sa wa ra N　　／
*nac°i-tʰanasyi*　　*yar-i-ba*　　*pʰada-kʰara-M*　　*sawar-aN*
summer-kimono   COP-IZ-T/C   skin-ABL-even   touch-IA/NEG
つしやの、　　たま、ᴧ　やれば†、　／くびゝからむ、ᴧ　　さわらん　　　#
tu si ya no,　ta ma,ᴧ ya re ba†,　／ ku bi* ka ra mu,ᴧ sa wa ra N　　#
*c°isya-nu*　　*tʰama*　*yar-i-ba*　　*k°ubyi-kʰara-M*　　*sawar-aN*
bead-GEN   jewel   COP-IZ-T/C   neck-ABL-even   touch-IA/NEG
'Since [it] is a summer kimono, [it] **will** (not) even touch skin. Since [it] is a
beaded necklace, [it] **will** (not) even touch the neck.' (OS 13.#958)

---

*…ē#ōwa··· > ... >···ī-∅wa···. The rule may be sensitive to the relative lengths of the two
morphemes: -wūr- has only one vowel, whereas -ʔūwā··· has two.

Scholars' interpretations are divided on this song. Takahashi (1991a: 224) and OSJS (171b) take ⟨sa wa ra N⟩ as including the inference/intention auxiliary, as does Vovin (2009a: 811–812), but with a hortative sense: 'because [it] is a summer garment, **let [us] touch** through the skin, ...'. Ikemiya (2006: 43), on the other hand, analyzes it as including a negative auxiliary. 'Because it is a short-sleeved ordinary piece of attire, it will not even touch the skin; because they are round beads, they will not even touch the neck.' The context for this omoro is so opaque that no final decision can firmly be made as to whether it has IA or NEG in it.

### 6.3    *Inference/Intention -am-i (IZ) in KM Constructions*

The IZ form of the auxiliary in the following omoro occurs as a *musubi* form of the KP -*si* or its palatalized variant -*syu*, of which there are quite a few tokens in the *Omoro Sōshi*. Below are just a few examples out of 260+ (Uchima [1994: 101]) such examples in addition to (OS 1.#36) introduced earlier.

| せ、いくさ、∧ | おしたてば†、 | / 大ぎ゛みしよ、∧ | 世しらめ | / |
|---|---|---|---|---|
| se , i ku sa ,∧ | o si ta te ba† , | / OPO gi* mi si yo ,∧ | YO si ra me | / |
| si-ʔyik°usa-∅ | ʔus-yi-tʰat-°i-ba[105] | ʔuQp°u-gyimyi-**syu** | yu-syi ̯r-**am-i** | |
| s.p-army-SUB | push-RY-rise-IZ-T/C | EX-priestess-**KP** | world-rule-**IA-IZ** | |
| せひやく、∧ | おしたてば゛、 | / せだ゛かこす、∧ | 世しらめ | / |
| se pi ya ku ,∧ | o si ta te ba* , | / se da* ka ko su ,∧ | YO si ra me | / |
| si-pʰyaak°u-∅[106] | ʔus-yi-tʰat-°i-ba | si-dakʰa-kʰu-**si** | yu-syi ̯r-**am-i** | |
| s.p-100-SUB | push-RY-rise-IZ-T/C | s.p-high-one-**KP** | world-rule-**IA-IZ** | |

'When the spirit-powerful hundreds [of the army] set forth, **it is** our Great Lord **who will surely** rule the land. When the hundreds set forth, **it is** the One of High Spiritual Power **who will surely** rule the land.' (OS 1.#31)

| うら∧のかず*、 | きみぶ†∖しよ、∧ | まぶ゛れ | / |
|---|---|---|---|
| u ra ∧ no ka zu* , | ki mi ゛"† " si yo ,∧ | ma bu* re | / |
| ʔura-nu kʰaazi | k°yimyi-gyimyi-**syu** | *mabur-i* | |
| village-'s number | priestess-es-**KP** | protect-**IZ** | |

... ...

---

105    This is the VI of a pair: *ʔus-yi#tʰat-°i-ba* VI 'when one sets out' :: *ʔus-yi#tʰat°i-r-i-ba* VT 'when someone sends one off'. There is another set as well, with the meaning 'if', where the suffix -*ba* attaches to the MZ of either the VI or VT: *ʔus-yi#tʰat°-°a-ba* :: *ʔus-yi#tʰat°i-r-a-ba*.

106    The form is *pʰyaak°u*, not *\*pʰyak°u*. Cf. NOk *hya(a)ku* (OGJ 211b), and note that the meter is nine syllables throughout these four verses. Choice of aspirated rather than non-aspirated initial is based on Nakijin ⌈*pʰyaʼk°u* (ROD「百」).

AUXILIARIES           307

しよりもり、       きみゞ†ゝしよ、ˬ     まぶら゚め      /
si yo ri mo ri ,    ki mi ᵐᵗ " si yo , ˬ    ma bu˚ ra me   /
*syiyuryi-muryi*    *k˚yimyi-gyimyi-syu*   *mabur-am-i*
Shuri-grove     priestess-es-**KP**     protect-**IA-IZ**

'**It is** the priestesses of the inlet villages **who are to** protect [the ship in its voyage]; ... **it is** the priestesses of the Shuri sacred grove, **who will surely** protect [it].' (OS 13.#853)

The following example piques our interest because it includes a lexicalization of the contracted form *-si* + *ʔar-am-i* '**KP** + there.to.be-IA-IZ' → *-sarami* [sɑɾɑmı] (> LitOk *-sa'rami* [sɑ'ɾɑmʸi] [OGJ 460a]) and its own contraction *-sa'mi* [sɑ'mʸi] (OGJ 456b–457a)), now the only remnant of this construction in MOk and NOk (the latter mostly though not entirely Literary in usage).[107]

たくだる、ˬ       げ゚すの、ˬ    うちやり、ˬ      さらめ       /
ta ku da ru , ˬ      ge˚ su no , ˬ   u ti ya ri , ˬ     sa ra me     /
*tʰakºu-dar-u*     *gisi-nu*    *ʔuc-ºy.aar-yi*     *sarami*
strategize-PRFT-RT   retainers-SUB   conquer-PROG-RY   will ⟦have⟧ surely

'[O Your Majesty, ]your retainers who strategized **will certainly** have conquered [the enemy].' (OS 6.#314)

### 6.4    *Inference/Intention -am-i (IZ) in Non-KM Constructions*

There are some IZ examples occurring without the KP, such as the first example (OS 21.#1411) below. They make a stark semantic contrast with the following IA(/MZ) example (OS 21.#1451).[108] The sequence *-am-i* (IZ) has strong assertive tone, while *-a* (superficially a MZ) indicates vacillation on the part of the speaker.

---

107   The usually perspicacious OGJ has in this case missed the opportunity to link the two modern particles, perhaps because their meanings are not quite the same: *sa'rami* 'surely must be/DO', *-sa'mi* 'sure is/DOES (...), I tell you!'. RGJ (456, 461) does point out the relationship, as does OKDJ (310d, 312ab). The latter points to poetic-metrical considerations for the shortened form *-sami*. It also considers the included verb to be the copula *yar-*, though *ºy can in fact *not* be explained phonologically, while *ʔar- 'there to be', without *ºy, *can* be.

108   Here, the form *mac-ºy-ur-a* is presented as a lookalike for the MZ of *mac-ºy-ur-yi*. However, more accurately, it is to be analyzed as the IA *mac-ºy-ur-aN* (= {+am+u} RT/SS) minus ···N by a morphophonemic deletion.

| あやみやの、 | 大ご†ろ、 | / あまこ、∧ | あわちへ、∧ |
|---|---|---|---|
| a ya mi ya no , | OPO go† ro , | / a ma ko ,∧ | a wa ti pe ,∧ |
| ʔaya-myaa-nu | ʔuQpᵒu-guru-∅ | ʔamakʰu-∅ | ʔawa-cᵒyi |
| splendid_BE-enclosure-'s | big-men-SUB | eyes-DO | lock-GER |

| もどˀらめ、 | / |
|---|---|
| mo doˀ ra me , | / |
| mudur-**am-i** | |
| return-**IA-IZ** | |

'The elders at the splendid enclosure **will (surely)** lock eyes and return.'
(OS 21.#1411)

| おにの、 | きみはゑや、 | / やほう、∧ | ひちへ、∧ |
|---|---|---|---|
| o ni no , | ki mi pa we ya , | / ya po u ,∧ | pi ti pe ,∧ |
| ʔunyi-ˌnu | kᵒyimyi-pʰayi-ya | ya-pʰuu-∅ | pᵒyi-cᵒyi |
| supernatural-APPO | priestess-south.wind-TOP | jib-sail | pull-GER |

| まちよら | / |
|---|---|
| ma ti yo ra | / |
| mac-ᵒy-ur-**a** | |
| wait-RY-SE-**IA** | |

'Spiritually powerful Kimi-Hae (= Chinbē), pulling on the small sail: **could** she be waiting [for an auspicious wind]?' (OS 21.#1451)

## 6.5 *Historical and Comparative Analysis*

The difference between the OOk IZ -*am-i* and "MZ" (actually SS/RT) -*a(N)* parallels the OJ IZ -*am-ë* and SS/RT -*am-u* forms, respectively. The SS/RT expresses the speaker's uncertainty, while the IZ conveys the speaker's certainty (Shinzato and Serafim [2013: 273–276]).

1.
| 吾 | 背子乎 | 何處 | 行目 | 跡 | 辟竹之 |
|---|---|---|---|---|---|
| *WA[-GA]* | *SEKÔ-wo* | ***IDUTI*** | *YUK-**Am-ë*** *tö* | | *SAKÎ-TAKË-nö* |
| I-GEN | love-SUB | **where** | go-**IA-IZ** QT | | split-bamboo-like |

| 背向尒 | 宿之久 | 今思 | 悔裳 |
|---|---|---|---|
| *SÖ-GAPÎ-ni* | *NE-si-ku* | *IMA-si* | *KUYASI-mö* |
| back-facing-ADV | sleep-PST_RT-NOM | now-EMPH | regrettable-SFP |

'[I] regret even now [our] having slept back to back, like two pieces of split bamboo, thinking, **where would** my husband go? (He would not go anywhere.)' (MYS 7.#1412)

AUXILIARIES 309

2.  吾　　勢枯波　　　　何所　行良武 ...　　　隠乃
    WA[-GA] se-kô-pa　　　IDUKU YUK-Ur-am-u ...　NABARI-nö
    I-GEN　male-lover-TOP　**where**　go-SE-IA-RT　　hidden-GEN
    山乎　　　　　　今日香　越等六
    YAMA-wo　　　　　KÊPU-ka　KÔY-Ur-am-u
    mountains-through today-KP cross-SE-IA-RT
    '[I] **wonder where** [my] love is traveling. [I] **wonder** if it is today that [he]
    is crossing over the mountains [that are hidden like seaweed in the off-
    ing].' (MYS 1.#43)


## 7　　Negative Inferential/Intentional: -*umazyi*

### 7.1　*The Auxiliary* -umazyi

There are six tokens of this negative inferential/intentional auxiliary, all occurring sentence-finally in collocation with ⟨yo se ru⟩ *yusi·r-u*···. Here are some
examples:

だ*しま、ᴀ　　あるぎ*やめも、　　/ せいくさ、ᴀ
da* si ma ,ᴀ　　a ru gi* ya me mo , / se i ku sa ,ᴀ
*de-syima-∅　　ʔar-u-gyami-mu　　si-k°usa-∅*
EX-island-SUB exist-RT-TRM-even　spirit-army[109]-SUB[110]
よせるまじ*　　　　　/ だ*くに、ᴀ　　　　あるぎ*やめも、　　/
yo se ru ma zi*　　　/ da* ku ni ,ᴀ　　　a ru gi* ya me mo , /
*yusi·r-umazyi　　　　　de-k°unyi-∅　　　ʔar-u-gyami-mu*
{let.draw/.near·4GE}-NEG.IA　EX-country-SUB　exist-RT-TRM-even

---

109　Metrically it is either *si-* or *sii-*, and either -*k°usa* and -*pʰyak°u* or -*ʔyik°usa* and -*pʰyaak°u*
　　on the succeeding lines, all possible metric outcomes. Eight moras per line being gener-
　　ally preferred, and the couplets both before and after these being clearly with eight moras
　　per line, our two lines are then with *si k°usa* 'spirit army' and *si pʰyak°u* 'spirit hundred(s)'.
　　(The form -*k°usa* 'army' is regularly elided *ʔyik°usa*, and *sii* and *pʰyaak°u* may optionally
　　be shortened. Cf. also NOk *hya(a)ku,* 'hundred' [OGJ 211b].)
110　The verb *yusi·r-u* is transitive, and thus Hokama (2000a: 475) takes *si-k°usa* as a direct
　　object; however, it is more appropriate to take it as a subject in this case, because *si-k°usa*
　　and *ʔyik°usa* differ in that the beautifying prefix *si(i)-* 'spirited' makes the former the king's
　　army, while the lack of same makes the latter the enemy's army. This is evident in the last
　　song of this section (OS 20.#1332). If it is the king's army, it is more logical to treat it as the
　　subject: "the king's army will not let [them] approach."

310 CHAPTER 7

せひやく、ᴧ　　よせるまじ*　　　　　/
se pi ya ku , ᴧ　yo se ru ma zi*　　　　/
*si-pʰyakᵒu-∅　yusi·r-umazyi*
spirit-army-SUB let.draw.near.4GE-NEG.IA

'As long as [this] great land exists, the spirited army **will not** allow [the enemy] to approach. As long as [this] great country exists, the spirited hundreds **will not** let [the enemy] approach.' (OS 12.#721)

しよりもりぐ*すく、　　　　　/ くもかぜ†す、ᴧ
si yo ri mo ri gu* su ku ,　 / ku mo ka ze† su , ᴧ
*syiyuryi muryi gusikᵒu-∅　　kᵒumu-kʰazi-si*
Shuri Grove Enclosure-TOP　clouds-winds-KP
よりそへ、　　　　　　　/ のちが*、　すゑ、　 / せくさ、ᴧ
yo ri so pe ,　　　　　/ no ti ga* , su we ,　/ se ku sa , ᴧ
*yur-yi-si-i*[111]　　　　*nucᵒyi-ga sii-∅　　si-kᵒusa-∅*
{approachᵥᵢ-RY-alignᵥᵢ-IZ}　lives-GEN end-TRM　spirit-army-SUB
よせる、まじ*　　　　/
yo se ru , ma zi*　　　/
*yusi·r-umazyi*
let.draw.near· 4GE-NEG.IA

'Shuri Grove Enclosure, it is the clouds and winds that hover over [it]; [until] the end of our lives,[112] our spirited army will not let [the enemy] approach.' (OS 13.#757)

やらざ* もり、ᴧ　いしらご*は、ᴧ　　おりあげ*て、　 / ともゝ
ya ra za* mo ri , ᴧ　i si ra go* pa , ᴧ　　o ri a ge* te ,　/ to mo "
*yaraza　muryi　ʔyisyi-ra-gu-ɋpᵒa　ʔuryi-ʔagi-tᵒi　　tʰu-mumu*
Yaraza　Grove　stone-LK-DIM-DO　weave-raise-GER　ten-hundred

---

111　The phonological form is *yuryisii*; this concerns the interpretation of ⟨···o pe⟩ in a *w*-type verb ending as either RY ···(*w*)*i-i* or IZ ···*uy-i*. The spelling with ⟨pe⟩ makes clear the possibility of two morphophonemic interpretations: {{yur+yi#suw+yi} 'VB+RY#VB+RY'} → *yur-yi-si-i* (with Monophthongization 1, which occurs before OOk), where the second of the two verb bases ends with a RY that suspends the clause, meaning 'and'; and {{yur+yi#suw+i} 'VB+RY#VB+IZ'} → *yur-yi-suy-i*, where the second verb base ends with an IZ that closes a clause focused with the KP {+si 'KP'}, attached to the noun {kᵒumu+kʰazi 'clouds and winds'}. The choice is entirely by contextual interpretation, since the written form is identical.

112　The word *nucᵒyi* may invite one other interpretation. OSJS (272b) glosses this omoro with 'later', but the semantics do not fit. Since the phonology passes muster and semantics is in favor of 'life', we favor that interpretation.

# AUXILIARIES

すへ、、せいいくさ、、　よせる、まじ　　　　　　　／
su pe ,ₐ se i i ku sa ,ₐ　yo se ru , ma zi　　　　／
*siyi*　*siyi-ʔyik°usa-∅*　*yusi·r-**umazyi***
ending　spirit-army-SUB {let.draw.near·4GE}-**NEG.IA**

'... building up the stones of Yaraza-Mori [Fort] / for ten hundred generations, our spirited army will not let [the enemy] approach.' (OS 13.#763)

いしやら、よの、ぬしの、　　　／ げ゛らへ、たる、、　御ぐ゛すく　　／ いくさ、、
i si ya ra ,　yo no , nu si no ,　/ ge゛ ra pe , ta ru ,ₐ o gu゛ su ku　/ i ku sa ,ₐ
*ʔyisyara*　*yu-nu-nuusyi-₁nu*　*girayi-₁t°ar-u*　*ʔu-gusik°u-∅*　*ʔyik°usa-∅*
PN　world-'s-ruler-SUB　build-PRFT-RT　EX-castle-SUB　army-DO

よせる、まじ†　　　　　／ かたき、、　よせる、まじ†　　　　／
yo se ru , ma zi†　　/ ka ta ki ,ₐ　yo se ru , ma zi†　　　　/
*yusi·r-**umazyi***　　　*kʰatak°yi-∅*　*yusi·r-**umazyi***
{let.draw.near·4GE}-**NEG.IA**　enemy-DO　{let.draw.near.4GE}-**NEG.IA**

'[This is] the castle that the worldly ruler in Ishāra[113] built. [It] **will not** let the [enemies'] army approach; [it] **will not** let the enemies approach.' (OS 20.#1332)

## 7.2　*Comparison with OJ*

Because of the fact that the appearance of this auxiliary is limited to just one verb, the construction shown in the examples may have become fossilized by this time, along with *yusi·r-*, as a set phrase, presumably from an earlier more varied set of usages. The only attested conjugation form is SS, while there is no formal distinction between SS and RT in OOk except in *r*-irregular (i.e. stative) verbs, of which there are no examples in this case. Noting the paucity of occurrences, Nakasone (1987 [1976]: 109) assumes that *-umazyi* is a MJ loan from the post-Heian word. Similarly, Vovin (2009a: 695) suggests a loan from MJ due to its formal similarity to MJ *-umazi* and the absence of any reflex in NOk or any other modern dialects. We might add that the sound change from OJ *-umasizi* to post-OJ *-umazi* is irregular, and the likelihood of the same irregular sound change occurring independently in etymologically related lexical items in two different languages is slight enough to discount, barring independent evidence. Thus the sound change happened only once, in OJ, and then *-umazi* was borrowed in its post-sound-change form into Shuri dialect.

All the OOk examples above are interpretable as negative inference/intention, holding *-umazyi* in common with the affirmative inferential auxiliary

---

113　This is modern *ʔyisyaara₁* (OGJ 262a, 828a), in Ishibaru Aza in Mabuni Village, Shimajiri-gun (southern Okinawa Island), designated in units current at the time of original publication of OSJS (55b).

-*a(m)*-. Vovin (2009a: 692) notes that "[i]n sharp contrast to Middle Japanese, where -umazi can have the functions of a negative debitive, a negative probability, and a negative potential, the WOJ suffix -*umasiNsi* is predominantly attested in the function of a negative potential." This suggests that OOk usages are more in line with MJ -*umazi* usage.

## 8 Past: -*syi*

The past tense auxiliary -*syi* appears only in RT, and only twice in the same song (Torigoe [1968: 193], Takahashi [1991a: 226], [OSJS: 432b]), and further only with the supporting stative verb *ʔa*- acting as a verbalizer of only one adjective base, namely *wakʰa*- 'young'. In other words, there is a fossilized expression *wakʰa-sa ʔaQ-syi tʰukʰyi-ya* 'when I was young'. As Vovin (2005: 935) views it, this *hapax legomenon* is most likely a loan from MJ.[114]

| わかさ、、 | あし | ときや、 | / たまきや、、 | | ゑらで*、、 |
|---|---|---|---|---|---|
| wa ka sa , ₍ | a si | toki ya , | / ta ma ki ya , ₍ | | we ra de* , ₍ |
| *wakʰa-sa* | -*ʔa(Q)-syi* | *tʰukʰyi-ya* | *tʰama#kʰyi₍i₎-ya* | | *ʔyi̯ra-di* |
| young-ness | -STAT-PST$_{RT}$ | time-TOP | jeweled$_{BE}$-sword-TOP | | choose-GER |
| さちや物、 | | / ひやくさ、、 | | なてからは、 | / |
| sa ti ya MONO , | | / pi ya ku sa , ₍ | | na te ka ra pa , | / |
| *sa-cʰya-munu* | | *pʰya₍a₎kʰu-see-∅* | | *na-tʰi-kʰara-wa* | |
| wear-PRFT-CONC | | hundred-years.old-APP | | become-GER-after-TOP | |
| こがね、すへ、 | つきやり、 | / 御まへ、 | | かゞ、おらに | / |
| ko ga* ne , su pe ₍ | tu ki ya ri , | / o ma pe , | | ka " * , o ra ni | / |
| *kʰugani-siyi-∅* | *cʰik-ʰy.aaryi* | *ʔu-mayi-∅* | | *kʰaga-wur-anyi* | |
| BE-spirit-SUB | attach-PROG | EX-front-LOC | | shine-STAT-DSD1 | |
| わかさ、、 | あし | ときや、 | / よろい、、 | | ゑらで*、、 |
| wa ka sa , ₍ | a si | to ki ya , | / yo ro i , ₍ | | we ra de* , ₍ |
| *wakʰa-sa* | -*ʔaQ-syi* | *tʰukʰyi-ya* | *yuru̯yi*[115]-∅ | | *ʔyi̯ra-di* |
| young-ness- | -STAT-PST$_{RT}$ | time-TOP | armor-TOP | | choose-GER |
| きちや物、 | # | | | | |
| ki ti ya MONO , | # | | | | |
| *kʰyi-cʰya-munu* | | | | | |
| wear-PST-NOM | | | | | |

---

114   While the OOk version appears only in the one form -*syi*$_{RT}$, the MJ auxiliary, generally (but not always) attaching to RY forms, appears as -*ki*$_{SS}$, -*si*$_{RT}$, and -*sika*$_{IZ}$ (cf. EOKJ -⟨ki⟩). The details are quite complex. See also JDB (236b–d).

115   The NOk word is *yurúyi* (OGJ 291b); for discussion, cf. Ch. 3 §1 fn. 7.

# AUXILIARIES

'While I chose swords and wore them when I was[116,117] young,
> After reaching 100 years, I wish to be brimming[118] in supernatural power,
> shining brightly before the King.
While I chose armor and wore it when I was young,
> [After reaching 100 years, I wish to be brimming in supernatural power, shining brightly before the King.]' (OS 7.#380)


## 9 Perfect: -*t°ar*-, -*c°yar*-, -*dar*-, -*dzyar*-

### 9.1 Perfect -Tar-

This Perfect -*Tar*- describes an event that happened/started sometime in the past with its effect continuing to the present. It is comparable to English *have ~en*, or *have been ~ing*. The perfect auxiliary has four allomorphs, spelled as follows:

| | | | | | |
|---|---|---|---|---|---|
| ⟨ta r···⟩[119] | = | -*t°ar*- | or | -*dar*- | , |
| ⟨da r···⟩ | = | | | -*dar*- | , |
| ⟨ti ya r···⟩ | = | -*c°yar*- | or | -*dzyar*- | , and |
| ⟨di ya r···⟩ | = | | | -*dzyar*- | . |

The third and fourth lines are the PPed allomorphs of the more basic, unpalatalized, forms; in addition the Voiceless :: Voiced distinction operates in exactly the same way as with the Gerunds/Perfectives -*t°i* ~ -*c°yi* ~ -*di* ~ -*dzyi*. We will henceforth use the cover term -*Tar*- to refer to all of these allomorphs. There are 67 instances of Plain -*t°ar*- and -*dar*-, and 65 tokens of Palatalized -*c°yar*- and -*dzyar*-.

This auxiliary has three attested forms: MZ, RT and IZ. The SS form, in our view, is contested, as will be discussed presently.

---

116 The form was probably *ʔaQ-syi* < *ʔar-yi-syi*. OOk appears to have had the segment *Q*, not present in mora counts in most instances, and never written. A mora count check is not possible in this song, since the verse is simply repeated, with perfect parallelism.

117 The form *waka-sa-ʔaQ-syi* is actually a specific example of the earlier form of the modern *waka·s-a-ⱼ* 'be young' < *waka·sa ʔar*- 'be young' ← *waka·sa-∅_SUB ʔar*- 'there is youth', with the stative acting as a verbalizer. Cf. NOk *waka·s-a-N,* 'be young; be inexperienced'. Note the senses of inexperience and long experience compared in this omoro.

118 For more on this, see §12, "The progressive/perfective -*yaaryi*."

119 ⟨ta r···⟩ and ⟨ti ya r···⟩ in KOS can represent both voiced and voiceless allomorphs, but only voiceless ones in TOS.

314                                                                CHAPTER 7

## 9.2    *Perfect -Tar- in MZ*
Let us first show the only example of a MZ form for each allomorph.

ぬすと、     みやす、   ∕ かくと、みやす、ʌ     とたらめ        #
nu su to ,   mi ya su ,   ∕ ka ku to , mi ya su , ʌ   to ta ra me        #
*nusi-t°u*[120]   *#mya(a)-si*   *kʰak°u-t°u#mya(a)-si*   *tʰu(Q)-t°ar-am-i*
steal-person -cat-KP         hidden-person-cat-KP take-**PRFT-IA-IZ**
'Surely it is the thieving cat, the hidden cat, that must've taken[121] it.'[122]
(OS 20.#1366)

かみ、   てだ*す、ʌ   しら、ちやらめ ʌ      #
ka mi ,   te da* su , ʌ   si ra , ti ya ra me ʌ      #
*kʰamyi tʰida-si*      *syi̥ ra-c°yar-am-i*   (< *syer[123]-as-yi-tar-am-e*)
deity   sun.deity-KP protect$_{EX}$-**PRFT-IA-IZ** know-EX-RY-PRFT-IA-IZ
'It is the deity—the sun deity—that surely protected [the kingdom].'
(OS 8.#426)

## 9.3    *Perfect -Tar- in RT*
The examples below are glossed with our interpretation of the forms, that
is, as RT. This is because one can easily argue that these examples are all
RT forms, expressing exclamation ([OS 13.#747], [OS 13.#981]) and explanation
([OS 9.#491], [OS 10.#546]). For exclamation/explanation as RT functions, see
Onoe (1982: 12–13) and Sakakura (1993: 264–265). In fact Hokama (2000ab)
always appears to opt for the RT interpretation, insofar as we have been able
to see, for instance, supplementing an exclamatory particle *-zo* (OS 13.#747), or
using the nominal predicate endings *-no da* (OS 13.#747) and *koto da* (OS 13.#981)
in his J translations.

---

120   NOk *nusu-du̥* 'thief, burglar, robber' (OGJ 427a). Note the incongruity in voicing between
      OOk *nusi-t°u* and NOk *nusu-du̥*. Also, see the note below on OOk *nusim-* 'steal'.
121   NOk Naha *tuQ-ta-N* 'took' (OGJ2: 185a) vs Shuri *tu-ta-N̥* '(id.)' (OGJ 528b) suggests a gemi-
      nate obstruent.
122   Hokama (2000b: 323b–324b) translates it as *totta no de arō ka* 'could it be that [it] took
      [it]?', but in fact the use of noun + KP *-si* with VB + IA in IZ form—i.e. VB-*am-i* is
      a statement of surety *that*, not of wondering *if*. Cf. Shinzato and Serafim (2013: 274–
      275).
123   The verb is likely related to NOk *syirás-y-u-N* 'let know, inform' (OGJ 483a), an accented
      verb, so the initial-syllable vowel was short, leading to the conclusion that lack of PP is
      due not to *yii* = *[yɪː] but rather to *ye* = *[yɛ].

AUXILIARIES                                                          315

おしぢ*へたる、                     ゑ、    /
o si di* pe ta ru ,               we ,    /
*ʔus-yi-ʤyi̯-t°ar-u*                yee
push_VT-RY-go.out_VT-PRFT-RT INJ[124]
'[The King's boat] is [now] pushed out [to sea]! Huzzah!' (OS 13.#747)


わかいきよ、ᴧ              いきやて、          みちやる、ᴧ     / したたりやよ、ᴧ
wa ka i ki yo ,ᴧ         i ki ya te ,      mi ti ya ru ,ᴧ   / si ta ta ri ya yo ,ᴧ
*wakʰe-e#kʰyu-∅*          *ʔyik°yaa-t°i*[125]   *myi-c°yar-u*      *syi̯t°a+t°arya-yu*
young-RT-person-IO encounter-GER gaze-PRFT-RT    full.cheeks-DO
みちやる        #
mi ti ya ru       #
*myi-c°yar-u*
gaze-PRFT-RT
'Did we encounter and gaze at the young lord! Did we see [his] full cheeks!'
(OS 9.#491)


いな、ᴧ ぢやはな、ᴧ       さちやる          #
i na ,ᴧ  di ya pa na ,ᴧ   sa ti ya ru       #
*ʔyiina   ʤya#pʰana-∅   sa-c°yar-u*
already EX#flower-SUB bloom-PRFT-RT
'[Without awaiting [the arrival of] spring,] [look!:] there have already[126]
bloomed [great-big-]beautiful flowers!' (OS 13.#981)


In the following example, both forms are used. Note here the automatic PP and
Contraction of *pʰa-c°yar-u ← pʰak-°yi-t°yar-u ← pʰak-°yi-t°ar-u.*


かくちへ、ᴧ     ゑたる        / のすで、ᴧ      はちやる        /
ka ku ti pe ,ᴧ  we ta ru      / no su de ,ᴧ   pa ti ya ru      /
*kʰak°u-c°yi   yi[i]̯-t°ar-u    nusi-di       pʰa-c°yar-u*
hide_VT-GER     get-PRFT-RT    steal-GER[127]  wear-PRFT-RT

---

124   OSJS (369a) says that this word is used when one is exclaiming, for example, as with a
      cry while rowing, and that it is also used as a rhythmic refrain when singing omoros. We
      assume a relation to NOk '-*yii* (OGJ 264b), which attaches, however, to MZ = IA, and appar-
      ently emphasizes volition and adds a feeling of warmth toward one's interlocutor, who is
      either an equal or an inferior.

125   Originally a compound verb *\*ʔyik-yi#ʔaw-* 'go and meet', related to NOk *ʔyicyá(a)-y-u-N*
      'happen upon; meet; reach(; have sexual relations)' (OGJ 245a).

126   The length of *yii* means a lax vowel nucleus, undoing the power of PP. Cf. NOk *ʔyii̯na̯*
      '(id.)' (OGJ 252a).

127   Whether the first syllable is *nu* or *N* is a point of contention. The OOk form *nusim-* suggests

'[[She] did not get [it] [by] begging for [it]. [She] did not wear [it], [by] begging for [it].] It is by hiding [it] **that** [she] got [it]; it is by stealing [it] **that** [she] got [it].' (OS 10.#546)

As in the examples below, the collapse of the syllable *ri* (e.g. *\*syi̯r-ari-tʰˈaru* → *syi̯r-aQ-tʰˈar-u*)—which carries the sense of RY—to Q in the preceding PASS morpheme (due to the effects of the T-type allomorph *-tʰˈar-u*) is regular, and is shared with NOk:

| あだ*にやも、˄ | しらたる、 | きもあぐみ、˄ |
|---|---|---|
| a da* ni ya mo , ˄ | si ra ta ru , | ki mo a gu mi , ˄ |
| *ʔadanyiya-mu* | *syi̯r-aQ-tʰˈar-u* | *kʰˈyimu-ʔagum-yi-∅* |
| PLN-also | know-PASS-**PRFT-RT** | [heart-long for-RY<sub>NOM</sub>]<sub>BE</sub>-SUB |
| しらたる、 | / | |
| si ra ta ru , | / | |
| *syi̯r-aQ-tʰˈar-u* | | |
| know-PASS-**PRFT-RT** | | |

'Adaniya[128] **was** another well known one! Kimu-Agumi **was** a well known one!' (OS 2 #66)

---

*\*nuu̯su̯m-* 'steal', with *\*uu > u* (vowel shortening in first syllable in most verbs, needed to block ˣ{*\*nu > ɴ*}) and *\*u > i / s__*. NOk is *nusim-ⱼ* (OGJ 427a), suggesting *\*nosom-*, with *\*no > nu* and *\*so > su*. The NOk form probably represents an analogical remodeling to the pattern CVᵢCVᵢC-, working off of the first (= *u*) of the two vowels of OOk, since the second, *i*, cannot be combined with *n*. Thus ˣˣ*nosom-* is a ghost reconstruction. As for the OOk form, on the one hand atonal accent may suggest original, lost, first-syllable length (*nus⋯ⱼ < \*nuus⋯ⱼ*), and, on the other, a reason is needed to account for the form not having become ˣ*nsim-*. Since this has been spelled only twice, once in the verb with °⟨no⟩ and once with °⟨nu⟩ and no times with ˣ⟨ɴ⟩, the OOk syllable seems indeed to be °*nu*, not ˣɴ. The remodeling appears to have occurred after OOk. Thus, we opt for OOk *nu*.

128 According to Hokama (2000a: 59b), *ʔadanyiya* is a personal name, and *kʰˈyimu-ʔagumyi* is a title of respect for him. In other settings, they can be names of shrines (cf. Hokama [2000a: 59b], OSJS [⟨ki mo a ku mi⟩, 131c], [⟨a ta ni ya⟩, 35c]). Shimizu (2003: 234–235), whose view we favor, takes the latter tack, but identifying *kʰˈyimu-ʔagumyi* as BE.

The NOk equivalent (not the NJ equivalent Adaniya) *ʔadaɴna⌡* (OGJ 103a) is four moras long, suggesting that the form retained the mora *nyi* (from *nyii?*—see below) long enough to maintain its mora count, or else that the word was influenced by the separate *ʔadaɴⱼ* (but note also *ʔadani⌡* '(id.)'!—both OGJ 102b). The fact of the existence of a variant with *ni* in NOk suggests pre-OOk *\*adanyii⌡*.

The reason for the odd placement of *-mu* in the first, not the second, verse is that *ʔadanyiya* is only four moras, while five are required to fit the pattern of the first part of the next verse. The addition of *-mu* fills the bill. Thus: 5μ-5μ. Note that the next part of each verse is also five: *syi.ra.Q.tʰˈa.ru* = 5μ.

AUXILIARIES 317

あおり、くもの、　　　　　あんじ＊、　／ ぢやぐに〻
a o ri , ku mo no ,　　　a n zi＊ ,　 ／ di ya gu ni 〻
ʔawur-yi-k°umu-nu　　　ʔanzyi-∅　dzya-gunyi-∅
[scud-RY-cloud]ᴮᴱ-APPO lord-TOP　great-country-LOC
しらたる　　　　　　　　　／
si ra ta ru　　　　　　　／
syi̱ r-aQ -t°ar-u
know-PASS-**PRFT-RT**

'My, how well known the Lord of the Scudding Clouds is throughout the great
country! [After all, it's precisely after conquering [the enemy] that he returns!]'
(OS 10.#519)

あまみや、〻　　　はぢ＊、またる、　　／ しより、もり、　ぐ＊すく、　　　　／
a ma mi ya , 〻　　pa di＊ , ma ta ru ,　／ si yo ri , mo ri , gu＊ su ku ,　　　／
ʔamamyiya-∅　　pʰadzyim·a-t°ar-u　syiyuryi-muryi gusik°u-∅
Amamiya(.era)-IO start·VI-**PRFT-RT**　Shuri-grove　enclosure-TOP
'The Shuri Grove Enclosure that began[129] in the Amamiya era: ...' (OS 22.#1516)

きこゑ　　大ぎ＊みぎ＊や、　　／ おしやたる、〻　　せいくさ、　／
ki ko we　OPO gi＊ mi gi＊ ya ,　／ o si ya ta ru , 〻　se i ku sa ,　／
k°yi̱k°uyi ʔuQp°u-gyimyi-gya　ʔusya-t°ar-u　si-ʔyik°usa
famed　　great-priestess-SUB　send.off-**PRFT-RT** spirit-army
'the spirited army[130] that the Famed High Priestess has sent'[131] (OS 11.#561)

Below are examples in which RT was used in **a relative clause with a nominal
head.** The majority of the RT examples belong to this usage.

くすぬきの、　　　　みおうね、　／ おしうけ、たる、〻　みおうね、　／
ku su nu ki no ,　　mi o u ne ,　／ o si u ke , ta ru , 〻 mi o u ne ,　／
k°usinuk°yi-nu　　myuuni　　ʔusyukʰi-t°ar-u　myuuni
camphor.wood-APPO EX.EX.ship　launch-**PRFT-RT** EX.EX.ship

---

129　See Ch. 2 §5.1 'The *yotsu-gana* distinction' for a phonological explanation of this word.

130　Apparently the two verses are designed to fit into an 8–8 moraic pattern. We shortened *sii-*
　　⋯ in this context to obtain the best fit, using Ryūka metrics as our guide. Omoro metrics
　　differ greatly from the canonical Ryūka 8-8-8-6 pattern, however.

131　OSJS (81b) says, for ⟨osi-ya-taru-se-ikusa⟩, "[it] means 'army that [she] sent.'" Concern-
　　ing ⟨osi-ya-taru⟩, it assumes a citation form ⟨osi-yaru⟩ [i.e. *osyí-yar-* 'VPFX-send'], citing
　　an interlineation ([OS 21.#1456], a duplicate of [OS 11.#561]) with a gloss 押寄ル ⟨OSI YO
　　ru⟩ 'PREF-go.by/approach', meaning 'send' in this context. Thus the form has short *a*, not
　　long *aa*. We mention this because a NOk lookalike with *aa* has an unrelated main verb:
　　ʔus(y)áa-ta-N ← ʔus(y)áa-y-u-N 'merge VI' (OGJ 566b) < *osyí-ap- or *osyí-ap-ʰar-.

318            CHAPTER 7

'The great, majestic ship[132] [made] of [fine] camphor-wood,[133] the great, majestic ship **that** [they] launched[134] [into the sea].'[135] (OS 13.#891)

| しより、ᴧ | おわる、ᴧ | てだ*こが*、 | / | げ*らへたる、ᴧ | ゑぞ†こ、 | / |
|---|---|---|---|---|---|---|
| si yo ri , ᴧ | o war u , ᴧ | te da* ko ga* , | / | ge* ra pe ta ru , ᴧ | we zo† ko , | / |
| *syiyuryi*[136]-∅ | *ʔuwa·r-u* | *tʰida-kʰu-ga* | | *girayi,-t°ar-u* | *yii-zukʰu* | |
| Shuri-LOC | dwell<sub>EX</sub>-RT | Solar-One-SUB | | build-**PRFT-RT** | good-bottom[137] | |

'The fine ship **that** the Sun's Offspring dwelling in Shuri built [—isn't it splendid!].' (OS 13.#758)

| ぢやなもひや、 | / | たが*、ᴧ | なちやる、ᴧ | くわ | が†、 | / |
|---|---|---|---|---|---|---|
| di ya na mo pi ya , | / | ta ga* , ᴧ | na ti ya ru , ᴧ | ku wa | ga† , | / |
| *dzyana-mii-ya* | | *tʰaa-ga* | *na-c°yar-u* | *ʔk°wa*[138]-∅ | *ga* | |
| Jana-BE-TOP | | who-SUB | create-**PRFT-RT** | child-COP<sub>RT</sub> | SKP | |

'Lord Jana (= King Satto)[: he] is the progeny **that** *who* bore?' (OS 14.#982)

---

132 The loss of word boundary after exalting compounding elements (*myi-ʔ*)*u#* (> *myi-ʔu*∅), results in word-initial \**#p* falling into word-medial position, i.e. >∅ *p*, resulting in weakening to *w* (>∅) (cf. Ch. 2 §2.2.1, i.e. *ha-gyō tenko(-on)* ハ行転呼音); thus \**o#pune* > \**opune* → \**owune* > \**ʔuwuni* > *ʔuuni*. Further, constant double-exalting joining of *myi-* and *ʔu-* > NOk *myu(u)- ~ n(y)u(u)-*. A canonical eight moras in the verses yields *myuuni* here. Note that this gives evidence for earlier compounding of *ʔo-* with a non-voiced following obstruent, as opposed to regular OOk compounding of *ʔo-* with voiced: ⟨o do no⟩ *ʔudunu* 'edifice' (e.g. [OS 5.#223]) See also Ch. 2 §5.6 'O-gyaka-moi'.

133 OS spellings for 'tree' are normally ⟨ke⟩ as in (4) below. On rare occasions, a ⟨ki⟩ spelling shows up, including the one at issue here and (OS 10.#538) (only two instances) as in (1). This spelling difference is preserved as *kii vs. cyi* in NOk. Similar spelling and phonological differences hold in the case of compounds (2) and (3) vs. (5). The two different outcomes in NOk are explained in terms of what Serafim (2008: 84–88) calls Vowel Raising 1 and Vowel Raising 2 as in Table 7.2 in the text.

134 NOk does not have a morpheme-for-morpheme equivalent word, but does have *ʔukí-y-u-N* 'float VT' (OGJ 550a). OKDJ (133a) takes the portion OOk *ʔus(-)yi-* to be an intensifying prefix, while OSJS says nothing about it. The spelling ⟨o si u ke⟩ probably represents *ʔusyukʰi-* [ʔuʃukʰɪ], if in fact both verses, being parallel, had eight moras. Cf. *ʔusya-* [ʔuʃa] in the previous example. Both are examples of the use of meter to determine Syllable Contraction.

135 This omoro is made up of modified noun phrases, including a phrase suggesting a blessing of its voyage.

136 This word, NJ /syuri/, is always OOk *syiyuryi* (3 moras), not MOk *syuyuyi* (3) ⟨⟨si yo ri - te N - ga na si⟩⟩ (OKDJ 340d), or the NOk *s(y)uyi,* (2) (OGJ 491a). In this omoro, for example, its parallel word is ⟨gu su ku⟩ *gusik°u* 'castle', clearly with three moras.

137 'Good bottoms' are large ships that only the most powerful governments could hope to send out for trade.

138 Cf. Ch. 2 fn. 73 for details on *ʔk°wa* and its sound changes.

## AUXILIARIES

**TABLE 7.2** Effects of Vowel Raising 1 and Vowel Raising 2

| | | Vowel Raising 1 | | Vowel Raising 2 | |
| --- | --- | --- | --- | --- | --- |
| | (1) | (2) | (3) | (4) | (5) |
| Phonological change | | ··· -*k˚yi* < \**···kyii* < \**···kee* | ··· -*k˚yi* < \**··· kyii* VR1 < \**···kee* | *kʰii* VR2 < \**kee* | -*gi(i)* < \**ge* |
| Spelling | ⟨ki⟩ | ⟨gi⟩ | ⟨gi⟩ | ⟨ke⟩ | ⟨ke⟩ |
| Example | camphor-wood | Yagi, *lit* 'Eight Trees' | Japanese cedar | tree/ wood | Japanese zelkova tree |
| OS example | ⟨ku su nu k̄ɪ⟩ (OS 13.#891) (OS 10.#538) | ⟨ya gi⟩ (OSJS 333c) | ⟨sugi⟩ (OSJS 333c) | ⟨ke⟩ (OS 13.#792) | |
| OS phonetic | *k˚usɨ-nu-k̄˚yɪ* | *yaa-gyi* | *sɨ-gyi* (OS 21#1404) | *kʰii* (OS 13.#792) | |
| NOk (Shuri) | *kusū-nu-cyi,* '(id)' (OGJ 342b) | *yaazyi,* [PLN] (OGJ 272a) | *sízyi* (OGJ 487b) | *kii,* (OGJ 320a) | NOk *cyaá-gi*; 'J podocarp' (< \**keya-ge* [OGJ 140ab]); |
| Supplementary notes | *sɨ̄* (OOk) → *°sū*, *×sɨ̄* (NOk analogical fix) | | | | Shodon *khyáá#gi(i)* 'black pine' < \**keya#ge* (Serafim 1985: 22n12, 34, 47) |

The following are examples in which RT functions to **nominalize a sentence**. There are a fair number of examples of this kind.

すざべ、　大ざ*とが*、　　／　かぢ*、∧　とたる、∧
su za be , OPO za* to ga* , / ka di* ,∧ to ta ru ,∧
*sɨiza-bi* *ʔuQp˚u.zatʰu-ga* *kʰadzyi-∅* *tʰuQ-t˚ar-u-∅*[139]
elder PN-GEN/SUB rudder-DO maneuver-**PRFT-RT**$_{\text{NOM}}$-SUB

こまさ　　よ、／
ko ma sa yo , /
*kʰuma-sa* *yoo*
skill-NOM$_{\text{SS}}$ SFP

---

139  The development, OOk < pre-OOk, is \**tʰuQ-t˚ar-u* < \**tor-i-t-ar-u* < \**tor-yi-te-ar-u/o* = RT. For ···*Q-t˚ar-*, cf. Ch. 2 § 4.6.3 "Mora voiceless obstruents".

'Oh, what skill our elder, Ōzato, [displays in] maneuvering the rudder!'[140]
(OS 13.#750)

| | | | |
|---|---|---|---|
| きみが゚なし、ᴧ | みちやる、ᴧ | まさり、 | / |
| ki mi ga* na si , ᴧ | mi ti ya ru , ᴧ | ma sa ri , | / |
| k°yimyi-ᵧganasyi-∅ | myi-c°yar-u-∅ | masar-yi-∅ | |
| priestess-beloved-DO | see-PRFT-RT_NOM-SUB | prosper-RY | |

'Those who have seen the beloved priestess will be the better for it; ...'
(OS 6.#319)

The RT form appears as a *musubi* for KP -*ga* (other-directed question) and KP
-*du*.

| | | | | |
|---|---|---|---|---|
| てるくもは、 | / いきやる、ᴧ | さうず*、 | あてが*、[141] | / |
| te ru ku mo pa , | / i ki ya ru , ᴧ | sa u zu* , | a te ga* , | / |
| tʰiru.k°umu-wa | what.sort-RT | soozi-∅ | ʔa-t°i-**ga** | |
| Terukumo-TOP | | sacred water-SUB | STAT-GER-KP | |
| くもこᴧ | より、ᴧいで゚たる、 | / まだ゚まᴧ | より、いで゚たる | # |
| ku mo ko ᴧ | yo ri , ᴧ i de* ta ru , | / ma da* ma ᴧ | yo ri , i de* ta ru | # |
| k°umu.kʰu-∅ | yur.yi-ʔyidzyi̯-*t°ar-u* | ma-dama-∅ | yur.yi-ʔyidzyi̯-*t°ar-u* | |
| golden.one-DO | select-out-PRFT-RT | true-jewel-DO | select-out-PRFT-RT | |

'What kind of sacred waters does [Kimiyoshi's deputy] Terukumo have, [to
cleanse] the selected golden (jewel), the selected true jewel?' (OS 11.#572)

| | | | |
|---|---|---|---|
| ねやが゚り | よ、 | / わらてる、ᴧ | いぢ゚やる | / |
| ne ya ga* ri | yo , | / wa ra te ru , ᴧ | i di* ya ru | / |
| ni(i)yagaryi | yoo | wara-t°i-**ru**[142] | ʔyi[143]-**dzyar-u** | |
| PN | INJ | smile-GER-KP | go-PRFT-RT | |

---

140   Chris Drake's translation of this song in its entirety is presented below. (*Omoro Kanshō* 17)
      The old helmsman Ōzato, / how delicate his hands on the tiller—
      we ask the great shamaness / to move his ship with wind from the south
      old master Ōzato, / how finely he works his tiller
      on the Kōchi, come back at last, / leaving sleeves of wake in the reefs.

141   For interpretation alternatives, see Ch. 6 §4.1. Two functions of the gerund: gerund and
      perfective.

142   The enclitic -*du* sometimes lenited to -*ru*, but its PPed counterpart -*dzyu* (according to
      the Two-Mora Rule: #*dzyu*, because of the affricate °*dzy* instead of fricative ˣ*zy*) could not,
      because only *d* functioned as input to the lenition rule {*d* → *r*}. This *d*-to-*r* lenition is now
      extremely widespread in NOk dialects.

143   This *ʔyi*- is an allomorph of a suppletive root {ʔyin+ 'go'} (< *ˣleave') of {ʔyik+ 'go'}, used

AUXILIARIES 321

'Neyagari, he **has** gone, smiling. [= O Neyagari: smiling, is [how he's] gone.]'
(OS 8.#430)

## 9.4 *Perfect* -Tar- *in* IZ

Here are examples of IZ -*t°ar-i* and -*dar-i*, which appear as *musubi* of KP -*si* or
its PPed allomorph -*syu*.

はつにしやす、ˇ　まちよたれ　　　　　　／
pa tu ni si ya su ,ˇ　ma ti yo ta re　　　／
*pʰac°i-nyisy-a-si*　*mac-°y-u-t°ar-i*
first-north-er-**KP**　await-RY-SE-**PRFT-IZ**
'**It was** the first north wind itself **that** they awaited.' (OS 13.#899)

大ぬしが˙、　　　　このみす、　　　／ゑぞ†こ、　　／みおうね、ˇ
OPO nu si ga˙ ,　　ko no mi su ,　　／ we zo† ko ,　／ mi o u ne ,ˇ
*ʔuQp°u-nu₍u₎syi-ga kʰunum-yi-si*　*yii-zukʰu-∅*　*myuuni-∅*
great-master-**GEN**　plan/liking-RY-**KP**　good-bottom　EX.EX.ship-**DO**
このだ˙れ、　　　　／
ko no da˙ re ,　　／
*kʰunu-dar-i*
construct-**PRFT-IZ**
'**It was** to **none other than** the plan/liking of the great master[144] **himself that**
they buil**t** the large ship.' (OS 13.#831)

## 9.5 *Historical and Comparative Analysis*

OOk -*Tar*- is often compared to OJ -*tar-i* [tari] 'PRFT' (Vovin 2005: 974) due to the
similarity in their composition, since both are built on the gerund/perfective[145]
(= GER/PRFV) morpheme (*)-*te* + one of the two major existential verbs (= RH;
OJ -*ar-i*, OOk -(*ʔ*)*ar-yi* 'there to be'). One major difference is that the expected SS
form -*Tar-yi*\* seems to be lacking in OS,[146] though -*Tar-u* evinces sentence-final

---

for suffixing T-initial-forms. It is also worth noting the homonyms: *ʔyidzyi*, either *ʔyi-dzyi*
{ʔyin₁yi₍RY₎#te} 'go GER/PRFV' or *ʔyidzyi* {ʔyidi₍R₎ 'oxit RY'}

144　OSJS (⟨OPO nu si⟩ (2), p. 89c) speculates that this is King Shō Chū, Shō Hashi's son.

145　This is approximately equivalent to English 'have DOne'.

146　Torigoe ("TK," 1968: 186–187) considers the following to be an example of SS:
やりおそいは、ˇ　たかˇべて ˇ　／まはゑ、かぜˇ、ˇ　こうたれ　　　　　　／
ya ri o so i pa ,ˇ　ta ka be te ˇ　／ ma pa we , ka ze˙ ,ˇ　ko u ta re　　　／
*yar.yi.ʔusi.i-Qp°a*　*tʰakʰabi-t°i*　*ma#pʰayi#kʰazi-∅*　*kʰuu-t°ar-i*
priestess.name-**DO**　worship-**GER**　true₍BE₎-south-wind-**DO**　beg.for-**PRFT-SS**^**TK**/IZ^**S&S**
'[She] worshipped Yariosoi, and begged for the True South Wind' (ibid.; Hokama [2000b:

usages, which Takahashi (1991a: 230, 235) considers ss forms (§ 9.3). Because of this, it is unclear if this auxiliary in fact conjugated as *r*-irregular (RH = *ra-gyō henkaku* [ラ行変格]) or as *r*-type quadrigrade (*r*-type 4G = *ra-gyō yodan* [ラ行四段]), i.e.:

| | RH | *r*-type 4G | Status of the 2 hypotheses |
|---|---|---|---|
| MZ | *-Tar-a* | *-Tar-a* | ← Same |
| SS | *-Tar-yi** | *-Tar-u** | ← Different |
| RT | *-Tar-u* | *-Tar-u* | ← Same |
| IZ | *-Tar-i* | *-Tar-i* | ← Same |

If one subscribes to the latter view, then the ss forms *-Tar-u* represent the spread of the RT form into the ss territory, a process that is seen for example in MJ.[147] Interesting at this juncture is the existence of the form *-c°ya-M*, which indicates the initial emergence of the NOk ss form.

---

93b]: *ma-hae-kaze o kōta no da* 'in fact, [we] begged [her] for a true south wind') (OS 13.#902)

The reason that TK took ⟨ko u ta **re**⟩ to be ss is because (a) he believed that this is a form with **ryi**, and (b), because it comes at the end of the sentence, making the stative's "···*r -yi*" a ss form. However, we take the same graph to represent ···*r-i* = IZ, because (1) IZ was capable of appearing sentence-finally without being triggered by **KP** *-si*, and (2) because there exists a similar song with similar wording, which *does* contain **KP** *-si*, as below:

| ゑひやの∧しが゛、 | ふなやれ、 | / たかへてす、∧ |
|---|---|---|
| we pi ya no ∧ si ga゛, | pu na ya re , | / ta ka be te su , ∧ |
| *ʔyip°ya.nu.syii.ga* | *p°una-yari* | *tʰakʰabi-tʰi-si* |
| Iheya.no.Shī.'s | ship-sailing[.song] | worship-GER/PRFV-KP |
| こうたれ、 | / | |
| ko u ta re , | / | |
| *kʰuu-t°ar-i* | | |
| beg-PRFT-ssTK/IZS&S | | |

'A ship-sailing [song] by Iheya no Shī: "[Oshi-Waki-no-Oya-Noro] begg**ed**, through wor-ship **no less**."' (OS 13.#920)

Cf. Hokama (2000b: 102b): *kami o agame-uyamatte koso kaze o kōta no da* '... precisely by revering the deities **did** [she] beg for the wind'.

147 Vovin (2009a: 974) says that, "[g]iven the high frequency of the form *-itar-* ~ *-tar-* in Classi-cal Japanese and the Ryukyuan form's almost exact resemblance to the Classical Japanese form, we are most likely dealing with a loan here." However, in fact there is a four-way allomorphy in the ···*t*··· portion, i.e. ···*t*··· ~ ···*d*··· ~ ···*cy*··· ~ ···*dzy*···, the typical Okinawan allomorphy for T morphemes, and in addition the portion *-ar-*, a stative extension, is just as common in Ryukyuan as it is in Japanese, surely because it was common in the proto-

AUXILIARIES     323

| あかか、が†い | / たまか、が†い ∧ | おとちやむ / |
|---|---|---|
| a ka ka , ga† i | / ta ma ka , ga† i ∧ | o to ti ya mu / |
| ʔakʰa-kʰagee-∅ | tʰama-kʰagee-∅ | ʔutʰu-c°ya-M |
| bright-thread.ball-TOP | round-thread.ball-TOP | lose-PRFT-SS |

'The bright[148] thread-ball,[149] the round thread-ball [the priestess] lost [them].'
(OS 20.#1366) [this omoro continues in § 9.2, p. 314]

## 10     Emphatic Locative: -ʔac°ir-u

### 10.1    Why the Label "Emphatic Locative"?

We label the auxiliary *ʔac°ir-u* the Emphatic Locative (EMPLOC) for its obliga-
tory inclusion of location words and its semantics of added emphasis, distinct
from the source verb *ʔar-yi* 'there is; one has'. Because of the formal resemblance to a part of the paradigm of OJ *-t-u* 'PRFV', one may expect this auxiliary
to be characterized as Perfective. While we do not deny its cognate relationship to OJ *-t-u* (more on this in § 10.5), its OOk counterpart came to be more
restricted syntactically and more specialized semantically.

First, syntactically, all 39 instances take the pattern below:

     Location (-*nyi*) + -*ʔa-c°-ir-u* + Noun

The locution -*ʔac°ir-u* forms a relative clause that includes the location word,
optionally marked by the locative particle -*nyi*. (This "missing locative marker"
is quite common in Okinawan syntax in all periods.) Second, its head nouns are
highly restricted to symbols of power, such as *c°irugyi* '(fine) sword', *myi-ˌkʰusyi*
('(august personage's) waist' →) 'long-sword',[150] (the location of the longsword

---

      language. A further note: these forms are seen not only in the culture center, but exist in
      fact in all Ryukyuan dialects. The likelihood of borrowing drops dramatically in the case
      of a piece of morphology shared by all dialects. Therefore, we believe that arguments for
      borrowing are in fact vitiated.

148    According to Nakahara (1957: 154), this word could be interpreted either as *ʔa-ga* 'I-GEN'
      or *ʔuyu*, a parallel word of *tama* 'ball'. Since *wa* instead of *ʔa* is more commonly used for a
      possessor (cf. Ch. 4 § 2.1.1), we opted for the one-morpheme interpretation, i.e. 'bright'.

149    The word ⟨ka ka i⟩ (our *kʰage(e)*) is interpreted by Nakahara ([1957: 154] [his spelling, not
      ours]) as beads priestesses wear around their neck. The basis of his interpretation comes
      from an *omori* in Kunigami (northern Okinawa), elicited by Shimabukuro Genshichi, with
      the same apparent theme. But we do not agree with Nakahara, despite the fact that the
      Kunigami *omori* has the same theme as in this omoro.

150    This is a metonymic shift in meaning. The word *kusyi* is/was not the native word for 'waist',
      but the point remains valid, since native OOk speakers (presumably of high status) had

324 CHAPTER 7

at the august personage's waist), *pʰayaʙsa* 'falcon; (Royal Ship) Falcon' or *wasyi* 'eagle', both references to spiritual protectors in voyages, which also are frequently points of analogy for speedy ships themselves; or *ma-gani* 'true metal', i.e. 'magnetite', a rare and valuable substance. Thus, we adopt the label Emphatic Locative for this locution.

## 10.2 ʔac°ir-u vs. ʔar-yi

The form *ʔac°ir-u* marks a stark contrast with the verb of existence and of possession, *ʔar-yi*. Below is a list of the patterns the RT form *ʔar-u* participates in, from higher to lower frequency:

a. *kʰa·nyi* 'like this' / *gi·nyi* 'indeed' + *ʔar-u* (19 tokens)
   *kʰa·nyi ʔar-u* '[It is the Royal Ship of Heaven Kagura no Te-Yori-Tomi] that is thus.' (OS 3.#139)
b. Adjective stem + *-s(y)a* + *ʔar-u* (6 tokens)
   *kʰana-sya-ʔar-u* '[it is (the citizens of) Mishima (= Shuri) and Yoshima (= Naha) that he] is thought of fondly [by]' (OS 13.#785)
c. Subject + *ʔar-u* (9 tokens)
   *dee-k°unyi-∅ ʔar-u-gyami-*M 'As long as [this] great land exists[, we will not allow (the enemy's) spirited army to approach.]' (Cf. §7.1; [OS 12.#721])
d. *ʔar-u* + Noun (7 tokens)
   *siyi-∅ ʔar-u k°unyi-k°yura-ga* '[The Priestess] Kuni-Kiyora, full of spiritual power' (OS 16.#1156)
e. Loc(*-nyi*) + (Subject$_{\text{NEW-INFO}}$ +) *ʔar-u* /(Subject$_{\text{TOP}}$ +) Loc(*-nyi*) + *ʔar-u* (2 tokens)
   *gusik°u-∅ ʔu-duN-∅ gira°yi-ˌt°i* / *kʰagura-nu gi°wu-nu-ʔuc°yi-nyi ʔar-u* '[His Majesty] built the castle building / and it [= the building] is[, indeed,] in the Heavenly Spiritual Precinct.'[151] (OS 4.#158)
f. Loc(*-nyi*) + Subject + *ʔar-u* + Noun (2 tokens)

The last pattern (f), as follows, resembles the pattern that (*-nyi*)-*ʔac°ir-u* 'EMPLOC' takes. However, there is a difference, since *ʔar-u* in (OS 19.#1295) is

---

the wherewithal to construct the word from at least one foreign lexical item. The word *mi-kosyi* also occurred in Japanese, with the meaning 'EX-waist', but the metonymy to 'EX-sword' is purely an Okinawan invention.

151 If OOk *ʔar-* is anything like NJ *ar-*, there will be two alternative slots for the grammatical subject, either at the beginning of the sentence for presupposed information (as here), or just before the verb for newly introduced information, equivalent to a 'there to be' reading in English. In the former case, it is also possible that the subject has been "extruded" (Martin [1975: 621–622]) to noun head of its relative clause, but (here) not mentioned, since it would be understood.

AUXILIARIES

used in a sense of possession rather than existence as in (OS 2.#53) (and all other examples of -ʔac°ir-u).

さしき、　よりやげの、　もりに、　／ しま∧　　よせる、∧
sa si ki ,　yo ri ya ge no ,　mori ni ,　／ si ma ∧　　yo se ru , ∧
sasyik°yi　yuryagi-nu　　muryi-nyi　syima-∅　　yusi·r-u
PLN　　　PLN-APPO　　grove-LOC　island-DO　rule·4GE-RT
つゞみの、∧　　ある∧　　あぢ　／
tu ''' mi no , ∧　a ru ∧　a di　／
c°iʣi|myi-nu　　ʔar-u　ʔaʣyi|
hand.drum-DO　have-RT　lord
'... the lord who has a hand-drum in the grove of Sashiki Yoriyage [with its magical power] to rule the island ...' (OS 19.#1295)

中ぐ゛すく、　　　　　ねぐ゛に、　　／ ねぐ゛に、∧　　あつる、∧
NAKA゛gu su ku ,　　ne gu⁺ ni ,　／ 〈ne gu⁺ ni , ∧　a tu ru , ∧
nakʰagusik°u　　　　nii-gunyi　　nii-gunyi　　-ʔac°ir-u
Nakagusuku.castle_PLN　root-country　root-country　-EMPLOC-RT
はやぶ゛さ、　　／
pa ya bu゛sa ,　／
pʰayaʙsa
falcon(ship)[152]
'Nakagusuku, the root country; [the Royal Ship] the Falcon, **in** the root country ...'[153] (OS 2.#53)

Given the above, we stand by the label Emphatic Locative for ʔac°ir-u. Having said that, in the offing are questions of what the history of the form is and what

---

152　Cf. OJ payabusa (JDB 596d–597a) 'falcon (class *Accipitridae*, Asiatic sparrow hawk)'. Birds such as OOk pʰayaʙsa 'falcon' (> *pʰayiᴍsa > MOk *feeɴsa* > NOk *féɴsa* '(id.)' [OGJ 229a]), *wasyi* 'eagle' 〈〈wa si〉〉 (OSJS 367a) etc. in OS metaphorically refer to royal ships, traveling easily as they do over water and possessing a fierce nature and (cf. OSJS 367a) traits as spiritual birds. See Higa ("Omoro Kanshō" 51), Hokama (1985: 148), and Hateruma (2007c: 235). OGJ *féɴsa* quotes KKKG: "(pa i ɴ ɢa) taka no ɢōmyō [〈pa i ɴ sa〉 *feeɴsa* generic term for hawks]." CoOk 'hawk' is, however, *taka,* (OGJ 506a).
　　　Note also the key fact that the collapse of *bu before *s to ʙ assured that *bu and *bo would not merge in that position.
153　Hokama (2000a: 54b): "Nari-todoroku Nakagusuku wa neguni (kuni no chūshin) de aru. Neguni ni aru Hayabusa (senmei) de Tokunoshima, Amami Ōshima o hogo-shi shihai-shite hiki-yoseyo." 'Resounding Nakagusuku is the center of the country. Draw Tokunoshima and Amami Ōshima nearer by protecting and ruling them, with [the Royal Ship] Hayabusa, which is at the country's center.'

the variations in its syntax and usage are.[154] At this point, we have to leave these questions for future research.

## 10.3    *ʔacᵒïr-u in RT*

Here are some examples from the RT forms.

| はび†ら、ₐ | あつる、ₐ | みこし、 | / ねぐ†に、ₐ | あつる、ₐ |
|---|---|---|---|---|
| pa bi† ra ,ₐ | a tur u ,ₐ | mi ko si , | / ne gu† ni ,ₐ | a tur u ,ₐ |
| *pʰabyi̠ra-* | *Ø-ʔa.c.ᵒïr-u* | *myi-̠kʰusyi* | *nii-gunyi-* | *Ø-ʔa.c.ᵒïr-u* |
| PLN | -EMPLOC-RT | EX-longsword | root-country | -EMPLOC-RT |

| つるぎ*、 | / |
|---|---|
| tu ru gi* , | / |
| *cᵒïrugyi* | |
| sword | |

'The longsword, **at/in** Habira [village], the sword, **at/in** the root country.'
(OS 20.#1335)

| しまじ*りに、ₐあつる、 | / つしやこの、 | まが†ね、 | / |
|---|---|---|---|
| si ma zi* ri ni ,ₐa tur u , | / tu si ya ko no , | ma ga† ne , | / |
| *syima\|+zyiryi-nyi-ʔacᵒïr-u* | *cᵒïsya.kʰu-nu* | *ma-gani* | |
| PLN-LOC-EMPLOC-RT | magnet-GEN | true_BE-metal | |

'The true magnetic[155] metal (existing) in Shimajiri.' (OS 21.#1493)

---

154    Shimizu (2003, v.1: 218) notes that *-ʔacir-u*, i.e. [ʔatsiɾu], the expected later form of *-ʔacᵒïr-u*, does not appear in Ryūka at all. In his view, it is difficult to think that auxiliaries completely disappear in the transition from omoro to Ryūka, and thus this leads him to say that it was probably a loan or a copy of Japanese usage in the omoro period.

155    Three strikes against this being *zyi-syakᵒu* (cf. NJ *zyí·syaku* '(id.)' < MJ *zyi·syaku*): 1) The actual OOk word begins with an affricate, since ⟨tu⟩ requires *cᵢi*, but the word that had been proposed as its point of origin has to be SJ-derived, and the candidate SJ form is ⟨zi si ya ku⟩ = *zyi·syaku* = [ʒiʃaku], with *\*zi > zyi*, i.e. with [ʒi], not *\*di > dʑyi* = [dʑi]. 2) Again for the first graph, TOS has a *voiceless* obstruent ᵒ⟨tu⟩, not ˣ⟨du⟩, and we only trust a determination of obstruent voicing with, minimally, TOS *overtly* showing a voiced obstruent. 3) The third graph is ⟨ko⟩, not ⟨ku⟩, and, with only a scattering of exceptions, ⟨ko⟩ and ⟨ku⟩ are distinguished in spelling (but not necessarily ⟨go⟩ and ⟨gu⟩, which are voiced graphs, and therefore cannot be distinguished by whether the transition between C and V is [ʰ] = aspirate, showing *\*o*, or [ᵒ] i.e. [ ] {nothing} = non-aspirate, showing *\*u*, since only voiceless stops and affricates can evince the relevant distinction).

    Our guess is that the original hypothesis is right in seeing this as magnetic metal, almost certainly meteoritic in origin, and probably splattered and/or misshapen into globules or nodules, at least to some extent, from the heat of atmospheric entry. These are the *\*tusya-ko > cᵒïsya-kʰu* 'bead-ones' → *cᵒïsyakʰu* 'magnets'.

AUXILIARIES                                                                                    327

## 10.4  *Another Purported Token of* -c°ir-u

There is possibly only one ordinary verb used with -c°ir-u, a single token,
tʰuyum-y-u-c°ir-u 'has resounded' as below (however, see Ch. 6 §2.2, fn. 84 for
a possible scribal mistake). All other purported allomorphs turn out to be just
that, "purported", not really admissible as actual evidence for the existence of
allomorphy, and therefore, not really admissible as evidence for a true, conjugated auxiliary in OOk.

天ᴧちよく、ᴧ        とよみ、よつる、        ／世のᴧ        つぼ゛に、ᴧ
TENIᴧ ti yo ku,ᴧ  to yo mi, yo tu ru,     ／ YO noᴧ    tu bo°ni,ᴧ
tʰinyi-c°yuu-k°u  **tʰuyum-y-u-c°ir-u**    *yuu-nu*    *c°ibunyi-∅*
Heaven-strong-ly  **resound-RY-SE-PRFV-RT**  official-GEN gift-APP
みしやご゛、   ／
mi si ya go°,  ／
*myi-syagu*
EX-sake
'[It is] the official gift, the exalted sake,[156] which resonates all the way to Heaven'
(OS 7.#371)

One purported example in which |Tu| is attached to a verb other than Ɂar-yi, in
this case in a supposed allomorph -dzir-u, is the following.

せなは、   おきて、     ／なつ、   みづ†る、ᴧ                            かに、ᴧ
se na pa,  o ki te,     ／ na tu,  mi dzi†ru,ᴧ                          ka ni,ᴧ
*sinapʰa-∅* *Ɂuk°yi̱tʰi-∅*  *nac°i-∅* *myi-dzir-u* (< *myic-°yi-c-°ir-u) *kʰa·nyi*
PLN-GEN    officer-TOP   summer   fill-**PRFV-RT**                    that·ADV
ある    ／
a ru    ／
*Ɂar-u*
exist-RT
'The officer of Senaha, he is as spirited as the **full** arrival of the summer.'
(OS 13.#814)

---

156  This *gu*, with voiced °g, not with a voiceless obstruent, i.e. ˣk°u, explains the significant
     variation in spelling, with ⟨ku⁽ⁿ⁾⟩ (29 tokens) and ⟨ko⁽ⁿ⁾⟩ (5 tokens). Most purely in the case
     of velar-initial syllables, a back-vowel raising leaves no trace in the preceding consonant
     when that consonant is voiced, since the only possible trace is one of [± aspirated], which
     occurs only after voiceless stops and affricates. Since it is °myi-syagu, not ˣmyi-syak°u, the
     spelling is likely to accumulate a smattering of errors as time goes on, i.e. {⟨mi si ya ku⁽ⁿ⁾⟩}

328                                                                                    CHAPTER 7

The form ⟨mi du⁺ ru⟩, seen in the KOS text as ⟨mi tu ru⟩, *appears* to allow
for an interpretation *myic°iru*. This in turn would seem to mean 'has filled'.
Now, what is required for that interpretation is {myic+yi+c°ir+u}, which seems
appropriate, assuming the intransitive base. This would give an intermediate
*myic-°yi-c°ir-u*, and the ultimate output could be *miQ-c°ir-u*, with Q unwritten.
Unfortunately for the hypothesis, however, the form has a voicing mark in TOS,
meaning that it is actually *myidⱬiru*, making all of the above argumentation
moot. The only interpretation left is to see the form as *myidⱬi-ru* 'water-KP',
where -*ru* is the softened allomorph of {+du}, and which is seen a fair number
of times independently in the OS text. Thus the text will read, "it is the summer
water that is like that", even though this reading is difficult to contextualize
in the omoro. We have been led to the conclusion, however, by the evidence
itself.

Below are three alleged perfective SS cases. In the first example, Nakahara (1957: 194) and Higa (Omoro Kanshō 84) take *kʰiwayic°i* as an interjection, and OSJS (154c) is inclined to, as well, but labels it "MO. Apparently a
*hayashi-kotoba*" = a meaningless word of musical accompaniment. However,
Takahashi (1991a: 236) notes that Kamida Sōei (quoted originally in Nakasone
[2009 [1988–1997]: 5]) interprets it as ⟨ki po [p]i tu⟩ (presumably *k°ywi-i-c°i*
< *\*kyipop-yi#t-u*) 'has escalated the fighting spirit/has become more compet-
itive'.

| みるやにや、、ᴧ | よなれ、がⁿみ、、ᴧ | やれば*、 | / けわいつ | / |
|---|---|---|---|---|
| mi ru ya ni ya ,ᴧ | yo na re , gaⁿ mi ,ᴧ | ya re ba*, | / ke wa i tu | / |
| *myiruya#nyaa* | *yu₍u₎.nari-gamyi* | *yar-i-ba* | *kʰiwe-e-c-°i* | |
| PN-personage | wise-priestess | COP-IZ-COND | b.h.s.c.[157]-RY-**PRFV-SS** | |

'If the Miruya personage is a wise priestess, [with her help,] we would be spiritually capable.' (OS 11.#627)

The form ⟨ke wa i tu⟩ occurs only in two omoros, and one is a duplicate of the
other. Thus it is in effect a *hapax*. Although the portion ⟨ke wa i⟩ occurs repeatedly elsewhere, with a total of 12 tokens, in the meaning 'competing/competi-

---

> {⟨mi si ya ku⁽ⁿ⁾⟩ (~ ⟨mi si ya ko⁽ⁿ⁾⟩)}, since all the spellings are ways of writing [mʸiʃã̃gu].
And we will not necessarily know which is the correct etymological vowel, except through
other means. In this case, Serafim (2004: 314) has discussed the option of *\*myi-pyisago*
'EX-[drinking-]gourd' > *\*myi-wyisyago* > *\*myiisyagu* > *myisyagu* as the source, though the
token count suggests just the opposite. Cf. Ch. 4 § 4.2, fn. 71.

157    b.h.s.c. = be highly spiritually capable.

AUXILIARIES                                                                     329

tion, bracing oneself',[158] $k^h iwa$-°$yi$-$c$°$i$ cannot be viewed as built on the disyllabic $w$-type verb stem $k^h iwa$-°$yi$ ← {$k^h i_1 wa_2 w$+$yi$},[159] since regular morphophonemic processes known from disyllabic $w$-verb roots should yield a non-
existent:

—      *$k^h iwa'$-$u$-$c$-°$i$ → *$k^h iwooc$°$i$ → $^x k^h \overline{iyoo}c$°$i$

(cf. ⟨i ki yo i⟩ $?yik$°$\overline{yoo}yi$ '(humble) invitation' (OSJS 52b) ← *$?yik$-$yi$ + $?aw$-$yi$
$lit.$ 'going + meeting'), the latter an interlineation glossing the word literally

Given the above, it is difficult to link ⟨ke wa i⟩ and ⟨ke wa i tu⟩. Thus, we follow
OSJS, and regard $k^h iwa$-°$yi$-$c$°$i$ as MO.

As for the following, second, example, Hokama (2000a: 134b) conjectures
that $myi$ $ric$°$ina$ is a place name, Idesuna, right by Tonaki Island, while Tori-
goe (1968: 183) sees it as |mire-tsu-na| 'see-PRFV-SFP', presumably $myir$-$yi$-$c$-°$i$-$na$
'see-RY-PRFV-SS-SFP',[160] on the assumption that he believes the graph ⟨re⟩ is
pronounceable as $ryi$, be it inherently or by PP:

| くめ、 | げ゛すに、ᶺ | きﾞやせ | / | かき、ᶺ | となき、ᶺ | みれつ |
|---|---|---|---|---|---|---|
| ku me , | ge゛ su ni ,ᶺ | ki " ya se | / | ka ki ,ᶺ | to na ki ,ᶺ | mi re tu |
| $k$°$umi$ | $gisi$-$nyi$ | $k$°$yik$°$y$-$as$-$i$ | | $k^h ak$°$yi$ | $t^h unak$°$yi$ | $myir$-$yi$-$c$-°$i$ |
| PLN-GEN | official-IO | listen-CAUS-MR | | PLN | PLN | see-RY-**PRFV-SS** |

な、 #
na , #
$na$   (Torigoe's
SFP   analysis)
'Have the Kume officials listen to you! (= Tell the Kume officials!) Have they seen
[to] (i.e. taken care of) [the people of] Kaki (= Aguni) and Tonaki?' (OS 4.#179)

Apparently Torigoe has assumed that the verb meaning 'see' has developed a
4GE alternative RY form, but in fact, putting aside the form in question here,

---

158    They are (OS 6.#332) (twice); (OS 10.#520); (OS 11.#627); (OS 12.#703) (3 times); (OS 13.#788);
       (OS 13.#865) (twice); (OS 19.#1284); and (OS 21.#1488).
159    OJ has $kîpop$- '(id.)' (JDB 245d), and pRk is likely *$kepap$-, suggesting PJ *$kêp|ö/a|p$-.
160    The form $myi$ $ric$°$ina$ (or $myiryic$°$ina$) precedes $?uk$°$yi$ $t$°$i$ (or $?uk$°$yic$°$yi$) 'official' in
       (OS 8.#443) and (OS 14.#1037), in which $na$ seems to be functioning as a linker. OSJS (321c)
       says flatly that ⟨mi re tu na o ki te⟩ means 'Medoruma (village) official'. In the current
       example, $na$ appears not to have the same linking function.

330  CHAPTER 7

which cannot function as its own supporting evidence, there appear to be no such forms in the *Omoro Sōshi*. Further, as the modern GER/PRFV *NN-cyi,* shows, even the present-day verb, the RY of which is *NN·z-yi, < \*myii·r-yi*, has no GER/PRFV form *ˣNN-z-yi-cyi,* or even *ˣN(N)·Q-cyi,*.

Thus the likelihood of ⟨mi re tu na⟩ being evidence for the existence of a perfective *V-c-i···* (where V is not *ʔa*) is slim, thus obliterating the possibility of this example of *···ci···* as a perfective auxiliary. Rather, it is more likely to be a toponym, perhaps "Idesuna", the one that Hokama suggested, though the phonological correspondences remain highly questionable.

The next example is especially controversial. The first interpretation is due to Torigoe (ibid. 183), and the second is due to Hokama (2000a: 317).

大ぎ†みぎや、   いぞ†こ   / こげ†ˏ つな、ˏ   やぢ†よく   /
OPO gi† mi gi ya ,   i zo† ko   / ko ge†ˏ tu na ,ˏ   ya di† yo ku   /
*ʔuꞯpºu-gyimyi-gya   yii̠·zukʰu-∅   kʰuug-i-c-ºi-na   yadzyukºu*
great-priestess-GEN boat-DO   row-RY-**PRFV**-SS-SFP village.wives
'You've rowed the High Priestess' boat [well], wives of the fishing village.' (Based on Torigoe's interpretation)

*ʔuꞯpºu-gyimyi-gya   yii̠.zukʰu-∅ / kʰuug-i   cºina-ya   cºyuu-kºu*[161]
great-priestess-GEN ship-DO   / row-MR rope-TOP strong-ly
'Now! Row the High Priestess' ship! [Tighten] the rope with force.' (Based on Hokama's interpretation) (OS 9.#488)

Torigoe's interpretation does not hold. The guadrigrade verb *kʰuug-* 'row' had T-forms beginning like this: *kʰuu-dzy···*. No *g*-type 4G form descending from *\*-t-u* exists, so we do not know what the output of a joining of *\*koog-yi-* and *\*-t-u* would look like. It may even have been *kʰuug-yi-c-ºi*, but the datum cannot argue for the conclusion. In any case, we would have expected some sort of merger of the consonants of *···gyit···*, but none is in evidence.

Hokama's interpretation requires a phonological form *cºyuu-kºu*, but the actual form is *dzyuukºu*, requiring either that the word for 'strongly' be com-

---

161   There is a verse where this word appears with a clear voiced initial consonant as in ⟨ko ke tu na ya d̄i yo ko⟩ (OS 10.#523). If it is indeed a voiced consonant, it seems difficult to take this as an adverb meaning 'forcefully'.

   The ⟨ko⟩ of ⟨ya di yo ko⟩ alternates with ⟨ku⟩, thus looking like the morph ⟨ko⟩ (~ ⟨ku⟩) 'personage', where the alternation is found in third or later moras. They may well be the same etymon, but, even so, the entire phrase is still largely opaque etymologically.

AUXILIARIES                                                                       331

pound-internal, or that it not mean 'strongly' at all. In addition, a post-palatal topic particle -*ya* is hypothesized in the wrong phonological environment, not a likely scenario.

The gist of the argumentation above is that no plausible hypothesis exists to "crack the code" in this omoro, and therefore the ⟨tu⟩ in question cannot be considered data in support of a hypothesis concerning GER/PRFV allomorphs and their suffixation in OOk.

The end result is that, except for the one word *t<sup>h</sup>uyum-y-u-c-°ir-u*, which is also only one token, the only allomorph of the GER/PRFV morpheme other than |-Ti| is the -*c-°ir-u* of *?a-c-°ir-u*, used only in N[ɲi?atsiɾu] = (N$_{LOC}$(-*nyi*)-*?a-c-°ir-u*) suggesting a fossilized, lexicalized -*?ac°ir-u*. Thus it is very likely that the only cognate GER/PRFV allomorphs of OJ -*t-u* that are left in OOk are |-Ti| and |-Tee| (i.e. Gerund/Perfective), with any other forms in OOk already out of the picture.

### 10.5 *Historical and Comparative Analysis*

At first glance, a seeming auxiliary -*c-°i* formally corresponds to the OJ L2G perfective -*t-u* = {#të+u 'GER/PRFV+SS'}. Just like OJ -*t-u*, but unlike any other OOk auxiliaries, it seems to conjugate as lower bigrade.[162] (If the GER/PRFV is taken into the picture, then we see that historically the form being treated here and the GER/PRFV are part of a now-fossilized paradigm. See Ch. 6 § 2.2.) But that seems to be the extent of the relation between the two.

The OOk -*c-°i* overwhelmingly appears in the RT form *?a-c-°ir-u* (39 tokens), suggesting its status as a fossilized form. It seems that the internal synchronic structure of the word [?ats°iɾu] has undergone a shift: the prenominal verb-plus-perfective combination must have been analogically remodeled to an emphatic locative quasi-particle–quasi-verb, like this, for which arguments continue below:

(-*nyi*) *?a-c-°ir-u*    '(-LOC) exist$_{RH}$-PRFV-SE-RT' →
(-*nyi*)-*?ac°ir-u*    '(-LOC)-EMPLOC-RT'

---

162    Nakasone (2009 [1988 1997]: 4 5) notes that there are no other examples of the lower bigrade conjugation for this word (and, by implication, one other, *t<sup>h</sup>uyum-y-u-c-°ir-u* 'echoes far and wide') in SS = -*u*, RT = -*uru*, or IZ = -*ure*, and thus he casts doubt on a commonly held hypothesis that the word in question, ⟨a tu ru⟩ = *?ac°iru*, is from *\*?ar-yi-t-ur-u* 'exist$_{RH}$-RY-PRFV-SE-RT', i.e. *\*{?ar+yi#te#wur+u 'RH+RY#GER/PRFV$_{RY}$#RH+RT'}. On the RH verb *?ar-*, there are likely 2 (3) forms of "-*c-°i*" [OSJS 384b]: RY (= GER *?a-t<sup>h</sup>i* [3 tokens], PRFV *?a-t<sup>h</sup>ee* [4]) and RT *?a-c-°ir-u* → (-*nyi*)-*?ac°ir-u*. That is to say, depending on one's treatment of ⟨a tu ru⟩ (both diachronic and synchronic), "-*c-°i*" either does or does not have allomorphs and therefore conjugation.

332                                                                 CHAPTER 7

Furthermore, unlike OJ *-t-u*, *ʔa-c-°ir-u* does not refer to the past, but rather, to a state continuing into the present.[163] Because of this, it may be a misnomer to call it perfective, which refers to an event in the past. Interesting in this regard is Yamada Yoshio's view ([1938: 398], quoted in Yoshida [1973: 527]), which states that the essential function of *-t-u* is to express confirmation of an event or state, and that the perfective aspect is secondary, as something certain necessarily entails something complete, objectively speaking. Torigoe (1968: 183) echoes a similar view in stating explicitly that *ʔa-c-°ir-u* is not perfective (though without any arguments for that view), but rather that it adds an emphasis such as 'surely', 'no doubt', or the like. We remain content to hew to our previously stated position, which is the commonly accepted one.

## 11    Progressive: *-ur-*

### 11.1    *The Progressive:* -ur-: *Overview*

This auxiliary (AUX), *-ur-* '-SE-' attaches to the RY form of the verb and functions as a Stative Extension: $\{V_{RY}+ur_{SE.AUX}+\}$. The verb+SE expresses Progressive Aspect, and, with certain verbs, Perfective (Resultative) Aspect. This auxiliary is comparable to Standard J *-Te*$_{GER}$*-i*$_{SE}$- and central and western Japanese dialectal *-y*$_{RY}$*-or*$_{SE}$-. A comparative analysis is taken up in §11.7.

For this auxiliary there are the following spellings:

⟨**yo** ri/ru⟩:    *-y-u.r-yi/r-u*    260 tokens
⟨**yu** ru⟩:      *-y-ur-u*        5 tokens
⟨**yo** ra⟩:      *-y-ur-a*        10 tokens 'probably is V-ing'
⟨**yu** ra⟩:      *-y-ur-a*        ∅ tokens

Some representative verbs from high to low frequency include:[164]

---

163    The only *ar-i-t-u* example in the *Man'yō-shū* (17.#4011) clearly refers to a past event:
須太久　舊江尓 /　　平等都日毛 /　　　　　伎能敷毋　　安里追
*sudak-u* PURU-ye-ni    *wotötupî-mo*            *kînöpu-mo*    *ar-i-t-u*
flock-RT old-river-LOC the.day.before.yesterday-too yesterday-too exist-RY-**PRFV-SS**
'[The duck] was at the river where [other ducks] flocked the day before yesterday, and yesterday, too.'

164    The appended RY suffix is put in to show context, and is not part of the morpheme in question.

AUXILIARIES                                                                 333

| | | | |
|---|---|---|---|
| *s-y-* 'do' | (95) | *tʰir-y-* 'shine' | (11) |
| *pʰaar∅-y* 'run, sail' | (19) | *tʰac-°y-* 'stand' | (11) |
| *ʔar-y-* 'exist' | (18) | *tʰuyum-y-* 'resound' | (10) |
| *mudur-y-* 'return' | (15) | *k-°y-* 'come' | (10) |

This auxiliary conjugates as RH. The attested conjugational forms include
-(*y*-)*ur-a̅* (MZ), -(*y*-)*ur-yi̅* (RY/SS), -(*y*-)*ur-u̅* (RT),[165] and -(*y*-)*ur-i̅* (IZ).

## 11.2    *Progressive in IA/MZ: (-y)-ur-a*

Here are some examples of the Progressive in its IA/MZ form. Note that the
forms *tʰur-y-ur-a* and *ʔuc-°y-ur-a* appear in concordance with the KP -*ga*, forming a KM construction, and, strictly speaking, are not MZ, but rather the formally
identical IA.[166] Furthermore, there are many more examples of -*y-ur-a*, as Inference, with Progressive SE, than of -*a* alone, as Intention, without Progressive
SE.

たらもいや、 / とくらしや、 / あまへ、よら、 /
ta ra mo i ya , / to ku ra si ya , / a ma pe , yo ra , /
*tʰaraa-mii-ya*    *tʰuk°ura-syii-ya*    *ʔamayi-y-ur-a*
PN-EX-TOP        PN-EX-TOP        rejoice$_{RY}$·EP.*y*-SE-MZ$_{IA}$
ほこり、よら、 /
po ko ri , yo ra , /
*pʰukʰur-yi-y-ur-a*
take.pride-RY·EP.y-SE-MZ$_{IA}$[167]
... ...
たが*、ʌ とりよら、 / たが*、ʌ うちよら、 /
ta ga* , ʌ to ri yo ra , / ta ga* , ʌ u ti yo ra , /
*tʰaa-ga tʰur-y-ur-a*        *tʰaa-ga ʔuc-°y-ur-a*
who-KP hold-RY-SE-MZ$_{IA}$    who-KP beat-RY-SE-MZ$_{IA}$

---

165   Takahashi (1991a: 183) lists -*ur-u* as a SS form. The examples he lists attach to the exclam-
      atory particle *na*, involve the adverb *gi-nyi* 'truly', or are interpretable contextually as
      exclamatory sentences. Thus, we take -*ur-u* to be a RT form. For a similar discussion con-
      cerning -*t-ar-u*, see § 9.3.

166   For a detailed analysis and explication of both Okinawan and premodern Japanese KM,
      cf. Shinzato and Serafim (2013: Ch. 2).

167   EP.*y* is dealt with in detail in § 11.6.

'Tara-moi—Tokura-shī[168]—**must be** rejoicing and proud[169] ... . **I wonder** who
**could be** holding [the drum]. **I wonder** who **could be** striking [it].' (OS 16.#1157)

てるまもん、、∧    てりよら   /
te ru ma mo N , ∧    te ri yo ra   /
*tʰir-u-ma-muN-∅*    *tʰir-y-**ur-a***
[shine-RT-true~BE~-NOM]~PN~-SUB shine-RY-**SE-MZ**~IA~
'[The goddess] Teru-Ma-Mon **is probably** shining [there].' (OS 14.#1040)

おにの、  きみはゑや、  / やほう、、∧ ひちへ、、∧
o ni no ,  ki mi pa we ya ,  / ya po u , ∧ pi ti pe , ∧
*ʔunyi-ˌnu*  *k°yimyi-pʰayi-ya*  *ya-pʰuu-∅ p°yi-c°yi*
supernatural-APPO priestess-south.wind-TOP jib-sail-DO pull-GER
まちよら  /
ma ti yo ra  /
*mac-°y-**ur-a***
wait-RY-**SE-IA**
'Spiritually powerful Kimi-Hae (= Chinbē), pulling on the small sail, **could** [she]
**be** waiting [for an auspicious wind]?' (OS 21.#1451)

---

168 The OSJS view of ⟨to ku ra si⟩ as an **ADJ**, 'joyful, festive' (241c) has been superseded by
the view that this is a **PN** with a rank marker, as we treat it here. Cf. Hokama (2000b:
222b) and OKDJ (453b). Now, is it *tʰuk°ura-syii* or *tʰuk°ura-syi*? In OS 17.#1207, the only
other example of the use of the same name, the parallel word to *tʰuk°urasyi(i)* (4 or
5 moras) is *wakʰa-mac°i-ga* 'Wakamatsu-SUB', with five moras. In the present song the
parallel to *tʰuk°urasyi(i)ya* (5 or 6 moras) is *tʰara(a)-mii-ya* 'Tar|ā|-Moi-TOP' (NOk Tarā
[OKDJ 408ab]), with 5 or 6 moras.

| *syii* hypothesis | | | | | | | *syi* hypothesis | | | | | |
|---|---|---|---|---|---|---|---|---|---|---|---|---|
| *tʰa* | *ra* | *a* | *mi* | *i* | *ya* | | *tʰa* | *ra* | *mi* | *i* | *ya* | |
| *tʰu* | *k°u* | *ra* | *syi* | *i* | *ya* | ○ | *tʰu* | *k°u* | *ra* | *syi* | *ya* | ○ |
| *wa* | *kʰa* | *ma* | *c°i* | *ga* | | | *wa* | *kʰa* | *ma* | *c°i* | *ga* | |
| *tʰu* | *k°u* | *ra* | *syi* | *i* | | ○ | *tʰu* | *k°u* | *ra* | *syi* | .... | × |

The *syii* hypothesis works in both omoros, while the *syi* hypothesis works only in one.
Therefore -*syii* is the correct choice. It also accords (not surprisingly) with the length of
the corresponding NOk word, *syíi* (OGJ 468b).

169 Likely not contracted in order to have the parallel verbs fit the same five-mora frame. The
*kutō-ten* (comma) is suggestive.

AUXILIARIES                                                                                            335

## 11.3    *Progressive in RY and SS:* (-y)-ur-yi

The RY and SS forms are formally identical. One difficulty in distinguishing RY from SS is that a verse could be interpreted either as two juxtaposed clauses (i.e. RY), or as two complete paratactic sentences (i.e. SS). But even with this challenge, -*y-ur-yi* below may be glossed as RY, since we prefer to interpret the two events (ships coming closer *and* day breaking) as concurrent = RY, rather than sequential = SS (i.e. ships come closer *and then* the day breaks—it just doesn't make sense that the ship's arrival would prompt the day to break):

| せりよさの、 | はつき | / はへき、おり、∧ | あけより | # |
|---|---|---|---|---|
| se ri yo sa no , | pa tu ki | / pa pe ki , o ri , ∧ | a ke yo ri | # |
| *siryiyusa-nu* | *pʰacʰik°yi-∅* | *pʰaa-yi#k-°yii-**wur-yi*** | *ʔaki·y-**ur-yi*** | |
| PN-GEN | Hatsuki-SUB | run-RY-come-RY-SE-RY | day.break·EP.y-SE-SS | |

'[As] [the ship] Hatsuki[170] from Seriyosa[171] (i.e. Okinoerabu) **is** aproach**ing**,[172] the day **is** break**ing**.' (OS 13.#940)

In the next example (OS 11.#564), semantically it is feasible to interpret the first two -*y-ur-yi* clauses (standing and sitting) as modifying (i.e. RY usage) the last i.e. main verb, depicting the anxious manner of *waiting*. The combination of these three verbs (i.e. 'stand-sit-wait') as a sequential unit appears in three omoros (additionally: [OS 21.#1395], [OS 21.#1483]).

---

170   OSJS (⟨se ri yo sa - no - pa tu ki⟩ 198b) はつき ⟨pa tu ki⟩ and Hokama (2000b: 111–112) suggest that this is actually an error for はこき ⟨pa ko ki⟩「端漕ぎ」 *ha-kogi* 'rowing along the deep outer edges (of the reef)', and Hokama cites (OS 13.#937) ⟨pa ko gi†⟩ *pʰaa-kʰuug-yi* '(id.)' to bolster it, where indeed it is related to *siryiyusa* and has *gyi*. Hokama notes *haa, paa* 'edge' which we do not find in NOk sources, but there is ⟨pa⟩ (OKDJ 529d), which appears in Ryūka in the collocation *yama-nu fa(a)* 'edge of the mountain', a collocation identical to one in Japanese. In any case, while that word has *g*, the word in our present omoro has *k*, thus breaking the connection. The end result, then, is that the second graph is likely not miswritten, and we have *pʰacʰik°yi*.

171   This word (also written ⟨se ri yu sa⟩) is the four-mora *siryiyusa* and not a three-mora ˣ*siryusa* ([OS 10.#554], [OS 13.#868]): it is put in parallel with e.g. ⟨ka i/we pu ta⟩ *kʰayip°ut°a* 'Yoron Island', ⟨a su mo ri⟩ *ʔasimuryi* 'Asumori Shrine' at Hedo Point in northernmost Ok[inawa] Is[land], ⟨a ka ma ru⟩ *ʔakʰamaru* 'Akamaru' in Kunigami, northern Ok Is, ⟨ka na pi ya bu°⟩ *kʰana-p°yaʙ* (four moras) 'Kana-Byōbu Shrine' in Nakijin, and ⟨sa ki yo da°⟩ *sak°yi-yuda, lit.* 'cape/jutting branch' i.e. 'Cape Zanpa' in Central Okinawa, this latter also with purposely averted syllable contraction.

172   With *pʰaarØ-*, occasionally *r* drops before *yi*, and this is such a case: {pʰaary+yi+} →(degemination)→ *pʰaar-yi-* →(r-drop)→ *pʰaa'-yi-*. It is, however, very rare for these *r*-derived *ayi* diphthongs to monophthongize to *ee*, right to the present day. Nonetheless one known case is NOk *ʔu-n-cyee⌋* 'my humble borrowing' < *\*ʔu-n-cʰyayi* < *\*o-myi-kar-yi lit.* 'EX-EX-borrow-RY_NOM', not accidentally, a polite form. Cf. Serafim (2004: 304).

| あやみやの、 | ころた、 | / たちより、ᴧ | ゐより、ᴧ |
|---|---|---|---|
| a ya mi ya no , | ko ro ta , | / ta ti yo ri ,ᴧ | wi yo ri ,ᴧ |
| *ʔaya-myaa-nu* | *kʰuru+t°aa-Ø*[173] | *tʰac-°y-ur-yi* | *yi-y-ur-yi* |
| EX-courtyard-GEN | man/soldier+PL-SUB | stand-RY-SE-RY | sit_RY-EP.*y*-SE-RY |

| まちより | # |
|---|---|
| ma ti yo ri | # |
| *mac-°y-ur-yi* | |
| wait-RY-SE-SS | |

'The men in the [Lord's] courtyard, [while] standing and sitting, are awaiting [his procession].' (OS 11.#564)

Examples of the SS form -*y-ur-yi* (formally identical to the RY form) are given in what follows. The first example shows the joining of -*y-ur-yi* with an instantaneous verb, expressing the Perfective aspect (cf. §11.7 for the perfective interpretation). Contextually, it is more appropriate to read it as SS, as what follows this verse is "so let the King know of the ship's arrival". The second example shows the SS form unambiguously as it precedes a quotative particle.

| おや、おうねや、ᴧ | はちへ、ᴧ | きより、 | / |
|---|---|---|---|
| o ya , o u ne ya ,ᴧ | pa ti pe ,ᴧ | ki yo ri , | / |
| *ʔuya-ʔu-uni-ya* | *pʰaa-c°yi* | *k-°y-uur-yi* | |
| EX-EX-ship-TOP | run-GER | come-RY-SE-SS | |

'The Lord's great ship has sailed back.' (OS 13.#749)

| いぢ゚へて、 | で†ゝ、ᴧ | しられゝ | / はり、より、 | で†ゝ、ᴧ |
|---|---|---|---|---|
| i di゚ pe te , | de† " ,ᴧ | si ra re " | / pa ri , yo ri , | de† " ,ᴧ |
| *ʔyidzyi̠-t°ee*[174] | *di-t°i* | *syi̠r-ari·r-i* | *pʰaarØ-y-ur-yi* | *di-t°i* |
| depart-PRFV | QT-GER | know-PASS·4GE-MR | sail-RY-SE-SS | QT-GER |

| しられゝ | / |
|---|---|
| si ra re " | / |
| *syi̠r-ari·r-i* | |
| know-PASS·4GE-MR | |

'[O sailors, pray to the Shuri Priestess, [that is,] to the Great Priestess;] let it be known that [the ship] departed; let it be known that [it] is sailing.' (OS 13.#798)

---

173 Nk -*t°aa* (NHJ 219a) ~ -*c°yaa* (ibid. 263b) 'PLURAL'.

174 See Ch. 6 fnn. 107, 112, 115 on *ʔyidzyi̠-t°ee*.

AUXILIARIES

## 11.4 *Progressive in* RT: (-y)-ur-u

The RT form -*y-ur-u* appears in the relative clause, S-pronominal (headless relative clause), exclamatives, and KM (cf. Shinzato 2011).

### 11.4.1 Relative Clauses

けお、∧ ふきよる、∧ 　まにしや、　　　　　/
ke o ,∧ pu ki yo ru ,∧ 　ma ni si ya ,　　　　/
*kʰiʼwu　p°uk-°y-**ur-u**　　ma-nyisyi-₁ya*
today　blow-RY-SE-RT　true-North.wind-TOP
'The True North Wind (that **is**) blow**ing** today ...' (OS 11.#618)

あまみやから、∧ 　とよみよる、　　　/ ちへねん、もり　　城、　　　　/
a ma mi ya ka ra ,∧ 　to yo mi yo ru ,　 / ti pe ne N , mo ri　GUSUKU ,　/
*ʔamamya₍ a₁-kʰara　tʰuyum-y-**ur-u**　　c°yi₍niN[175]　muryi　gusik°u*
ancient.time-since　resound-RY-SE-RT　PLN　　　grove　enclosure
'The Chinen Grove Enclosure, which **has been** echo**ing** since ancient times.'
(OS 14.#1022)

### 11.4.2 Nominalized Sentence

These Nominalized Sentences, occur with *k°yura* 'beautiful'. Note here that *k-°y-**uur-u*** is interpreted as denoting progressive aspect (cf. [OS 13.#749] above for the perfective interpretation of the same verb).

しより、　いちやしが、　　　　　　/ こぢ†へ∧　きよる、∧
si yo ri , i ti ya si ga ,　　　　　 / ko di† pe ∧ ki yo ru ,∧
*syiyuryi　ʔyic°ya.syii-ga*　　　　　*kʰuu-dzyi　k-°y-**uur-u**-∅*
PLN　　　[dear-personage_EX]_PN-SUB/GEN　row-GER　come-RY-SE-RT-SUB
きよら　　や /
ki yo ra　ya 　/
*k°yura　yaa*
beautiful SFP
'Isn't the row**ing** of Icha-shī of Shuri towards us beautiful!' (OS 10.#545)

うきはたの、　　　/ なおれよる、∧　　　　きよら　　や /
u ki pa ta no ,　 / na o re yo ru ,∧　　　ki yo ra　ya 　/
*ʔuuk°yi#pʰat°a-nu　nawuri-y-**ur-u**-∅　k°yura　yaa*
big-banner-SUB　　swing-EP.y-SE-RT-SUB beautiful SFP
'Isn't the swing**ing** of the big banner [in the winds] beautiful!' (OS 13.#797)

---

175　Or *c°yinyiN*, if PP has operated and, as typical, no spelling trace is put in.

### 11.4.3 Exclamatives

Exclamatives here are defined as a sentence ending in RT, and expressing the speaker's/writer's exclamation. When RT is used as an exclamative, it often cooccurs with the adverb *ginyi* 'truly' as in the first example, or exclamatory SFP as in the second example.

みぢ*へりきよが*、　　　　　／　げ*に、∧ はりよる、　　　／
mi di* pe ri ki yo ga* ,　　　／ ge* ni , ∧ pa ri yo ru ,　　／
*myi.dzyir.yi.kʰyu-ga*　　　　　　**gi·nyi**　　*pʰa(a)r-y-**ur-u***
[EX-announce-RY-one]ₚₙ-SUB/GEN　**tru-ly**　sail-RY-SE-RT
'[Priestess] Mizeriko[176]['s ship] is truly sail**ing** [well]!' (OS 13.#770)

ぢやなもひや、　　／ たが*、∧　なちやる、∧　　くわ　　が†、　　　　／ こが*、∧
di ya na mo pi ya , / ta ga* , ∧　na ti ya ru , ∧　ku wa　ga† ,　　　／ ko ga* , ∧
*dzyana.mii-ya*　　*tʰa(a)-ga* na-c°yar-u　　Qk°wa　∅-ga　　　kʰu·ga*
Lord.Jana-TOP　　who-SUB create-PRFT-RT child　COPʀₜ-SKP　this·GEN
みぼ*しや、∧　　　　あよる　　　　な　／
mi bo* si ya , ∧　　a yo ru　　　na　／
*myi-bu-sy-a*　　　*ʔa'-y-**ur-u***　　*naa*
see-DESI-AA-NOM　COP-RY-SE-RT　SFP
'Lord Jana (= King Satto) is a child created by whom? (He is this beautiful! No wonder the people) **are** want**ing** so much to see him!' (OS 14.#982)

### 11.4.4 KM Constructions

In the following KM construction, OOk KP -*du* (~ -*dzyu* ~ -*ru*), cognate with OJ KP -*sö/-zö*, calls for RT in the *musubi*. Thus, for the OOk root *p°ur-* 'fall (of rain)', RT *p°ur-y-**ur-u*** instead of SS *p°ur-y-**ur-yi*** is used.

---

176　This priestess name appears in two different types of spellings: ⟨mi **di** p/we ri ki yo⟩ for the affricate *dzyi* [~dʒi] and ⟨mi **ze** ri ki yo⟩ for the fricative [~zɪ]. Historically, both versions derive from *{myi+N+ser+yi#kʰo} >→ *myi-ͺzir-yi-kʰyu* ~ *myi-dzyir-yi-kʰyu* lit. 'EX-announce-RY-oneₐₙᵢₘₐₜₑ', i.e. 'the Exalted Announcer', with pre-OOk verbal element *ser-* 'announce'. We believe that the variations have resulted from variations in the tightness of the compounding and the loss of N when the phonological process of sequential-voicing and PP applied. Since N precludes PP, the fricative version was realized when N was still present in the sequence, while the affricate version emerged when N was lost. The relative occurrence of the two alternants is ⟨⁽ⁿ⁾se⟩ 4 :: ⟨⁽ⁿ⁾ti p/we⟩ 18, which, while lopsided, is still statistically significant. This distinction looks just like the *ʔaɴzyi* :: *ʔadzyi* 'lord' distinction, save for one thing: in the case of *myiziryikʰyu*, the nasal has dropped—and PP is lacking, which is explained by the double consonant of *···ɴz. We can no more explain the doublet of *ʔaɴzyi* :: *ʔadzyi* than of *myiziryikʰyu* :: *myidzyiryikʰyu*, but that does not make them any the less real for it.

AUXILIARIES                                                                                                  339

しより、∧　　ふる、∧　あめや、　/ すで†みづ゜ど゜、∧　　ふりよる　　　　　/
si yo ri ,∧　　pu ru ,∧ a me ya , / su de† mi du゜ do゜,∧ pu ri yo ru　　/
*syiyuryi-∅　p゜ur-u　ʔami-ya　sidi-myiʒi-du　p゜ur-y-ur-u*
PLN-LOC　fall-RT　rain-TOP　birth-water-KP　fall-RY-SE-RT
'The rain falling on Shuri: **it is** water of rebirth **that is falling**.' (OS 7.#386)

In the following KM construction, the KP question particle *-ga*, cognate with
OJ KP *-ka*, connects with a RT form in the *musubi*. The last two verses in
the next example respond to the first two questions. In these responses, KP
emphatic particle *-si*, cognate with OJ *-kösö*, requires an IZ ending, which is
exactly the requirement in OJ as well (for more on KM, see Shinzato and Serafim 2013).

のう、∧　　みちへが†、∧　おひきよる、　　　　　　/ いきや、∧　みちへが†、∧
no u ,∧　　mi ti pe ga† ,∧ o pi ki yo ru ,　　　　/ i ki ya ,∧　mi ti pe ga† ,∧
*nuu-∅　myi-c゜yee-**ga**　ʔu(u)'-yi-k-゜y-ur-u　　ʔyik゜ya-∅ myi-c゜yee-**ga**
what-DO　see-PRFV-KP　chase-RY-come-RY-SE-RT　how-ADV　see-PRFV-KP
おひ、きよる　　　　　　/ きみ、∧　　　　みちへす、∧
o pi , ki yo ru　　　　/ ki mi ,∧　　　mi ti pe su ,∧
*ʔu(u)-yi-k-゜y-**ur-u**　　k゜yimyi-∅　myi-c゜yee-**si**
chase-RY-come-RY-SE-RT　priestess₁-DO see-PRFV-KP
おひきよれ、　　　　　/ ぬし、∧　　　みちへす、∧
o pi ki yo re ,　　　　/ nu si ,∧　　mi ti pe su ,∧
*ʔu(u)-yi-k-゜y-**ur-i**　　nu₍u₎syi-∅　myi-c゜yee-**si**
chase-RY-come-RY-SE-IZ　priestess₂-DO see-PRFV-KP .
おひきよれ、　　　　　　#
o pi ki yo re ,　　　　　#
*ʔu(u)-yi-k-゜y-**ur-i***
chase-RY-come-RY-SE-IZ
'[The long-billed bird:] What **has it** seen **that** it is chasing [it] down? How **has
it** seen [it], **that** it is chasing it down? **It is precisely because** it has seen the
*kyimyi*-priestess that it **is** chasing it down. **It is precisely because** it has seen
the *nuusyi*-priestess that it **is** chasing it down.' (OS 12.#731)

## 11.5　*The Progressive in IZ: (-y)-ur-i*

The IZ form *(-y)-ur-i* is used in KM (*si ... IZ*) as in the example directly above
and one below, and is also used in *realis* conditionals forming *when*-clauses
(last two examples below).

あはれ、　かなし、　きみはゑ、　　　　　／くに、うち∧
a pa re ,　 ka na si ,　 ki mi pa we ,　　　 / ku ni , u ti ∧
ʔaqp°ari　 kʰanasyi　 k°yimyi#pʰayi　　　 k°unyi#ʔuc-°yi-∅
awesome cherished priestess-south.wind　 country#strike-RY<sub>NOM</sub>-DO
しちへす、∧　　もどりよれ　　　／
si ti pe su , ∧　 mo do ri yo re　 /
s-yi-c°yi-s*t̲*　　 mudur-y-**ur-ī̲**
do-RY-GER-K̲P̲ return-RY-SE-IZ̲
'Awesome, cherished [Priestess] Kimi-Hae (= Chinbē)!—only once having conquered the lands **will you return**.' (OS 1.#35)

こが゚ね、　　はなの、∧　　さきよれば゚、　　　　／あおりやゑや、／おれよ∧
ko ga゚ ne ,　 pa na no , ∧　 sa ki yo re ba゚ ,　 / a o ri ya we ya , / o re yo ∧
kʰugani　　#pʰana-nu　 sak-°y-**ur-i**-ba　　 ʔawuryayi-ya　　 ʔuri-yu
golden　　 flowers-SUB bloom-RY-SE-IZ-T/C Aoriyae-TOP　　 that.one-DO
みぎ゚や、∧　おれわちへ　　　　　／
mi gi゚ ya , ∧　 o re wa ti pe　　 /
myi-gya　　 ʔuri-wa-c°yee
see<sub>RY</sub>-PRP　 descend<sub>RY</sub>-AUX<sub>EX</sub>-PRFV<sub>SS</sub>
'When golden flowers **bloom**, the priestess Aoriyae has [figuratively] descended to see them.' (OS 4.#159)

ゑ、　け、∧　あさど゚れが゚、∧　　しよれば゚[177]　　／ゑ、け、∧
we ,　 ke , ∧　 a sa do゚ re ga゚ , ∧　 si yo re ba゚　　 / we , ke , ∧
yee　 kʰee　 ʔasa-duri-ga　　　 s-y-**ur-i**-ba　　　 yee　 kʰee
INJ　 INJ　 morning-calm-SUB do-RY-SE-IZ-T/C　 INJ　 INJ
ようど゚れが゚、∧　　しよれば゚　　／
yo u do゚ re ga゚ , ∧　 si yo re ba゚　 /
yuu-duri-ga　　 s-y-**ur-i**-ba
evening-calm-SUB do-RY-SE-IZ-T/C
'Once the morning calm **has fallen**; once the evening calm **has fallen**, …'
(OS 10.#531)

---

177　This and its twin in the next line are very frequent in the *Omoro Sōshi*, totaling 40 tokens.
　　 Literary scholars' interpretations differ on these phrases. Hokama (2000) takes it as Pro-
　　 gressive, while *Omoro Kanshō* 33 sees it as Perfective and translates it as *asa nagi ni naru
　　 to* 'once the morning calm (be)comes'.

AUXILIARIES                                                                341

## 11.6    *Historical Analysis of Allomorphic Variations*

The AUX *-ur-* '-SE-' has allomorphic variations as below:

| U1G: | *m* | *yi-y-u* | *r-* | (⟨m | **i yo** | r⋯⟩ | 'is looking' | [OS 20.#1346]) |
|------|-----|----------|------|------|----------|------|--------------|----------------|
| L2G: | *gira* | *yi-y-u* | *r-* | (⟨ge*ra | **pe yo** | r⋯⟩ | 'is building' | [OS 14.#1051]) |
| L2G: | *Ɂakʰ* | *i-y-u* | *r-* | (⟨ak | **e yo** | r⋯⟩ | 'has dawned' | [OS 13.#906]) |
| 4G: | *tʰi* | *r-y-u* | *r-* | (⟨te | **ri yo** | r⋯⟩ | 'is shining' | [OS 3.#91]) |

At the level of spelling, the term "allomorphic" seems a misnomer, as the same ⟨yo⟩ is used for the three different classes of verbs. However, at the morpho-phonemic level, their origins are revealed to be different.

First, with vowel verbs (1G), a "euphonic" *y* appears at the head of the SE *-ur-*, yielding *-yur-*. Historically this results from the conversion of the back glide *w* seen in the independent stative verb *wur-* 'there to be [animate]' to the front glide *y*, due to the influence of the preceding front vowel of the stem of the vowel verb:

$w \rightarrow y \ / \ \{V\,[+\text{front}]\}$ __
(a back glide becomes front when preceded by a front vowel)

which functions as its (older) RY form:

1G: *\*myi*RY- 'see_RY' + *\*-wur-* 'there to be' > *myi-yur-*[178]

Second, with consonant verbs, the SE appends to the RY suffix that has been affixed to the verb base, and that suffix's fuller form is *-yi(-)* (i.e. V_base-*yi-* + *-ur-* → V_base-*y-ur-*). As can be seen, *-yi-* gets shortened to the *-y-* allomorph before *-ur-* (⋯C-*y-ur*⋯):

4G: *tʰir-yi-wur-* > *\*tʰir-yi-yur-* > *tʰir-y-ur-* (⟨te ri **yo** r⋯⟩ [OS 3.#91])

---

[178]  Recall that phonemically high long vowels have phonetically lax nuclear vowels. Thus *myi-* 'see' will have [mʸi] (with a short, tense, high, front, palatal vowel) while *myii* will have [mʸiː] (with a palatal onset, but with a lax [iː]). Also recall that PP cannot bridge a non-palatal divide. Thus any changes within the 'see' paradigm that required palatalization must have occurred before the lengthening of the stem. (Since there *are* such forms, and since the verb has a long stem in NOk, it stands to reason that the stem started out short but then lengthened. This would mean that the floating length mark /ⁿ/ in the case of this lexical item developed in historical times, and was not present in pre-OOk like {kʰuⁿ+ 'come'} < *koⁿ+.)

342                                                                                                                    CHAPTER 7

What the above shows is two different historical processes leading to the same output: the epenthetic *y* for vowel verbs and the base-generated, contraction-modified *y* (*yi+-wur → yi+yur → yur*) for consonant verbs. Two claimed exceptions to this generalization are *pʰaa'-yi-k-ˀyi-'wur-yi*[179] 'run~RY~-come-RY-SE-SS' (see [OS 13.#940], §11.3) and *myi-'wur-i-ba* 'see~RY~-SE-IZ-COND' (OS 10.#512), according to Takahashi (1991a: 186). The first simply results from non-application of the contraction rule, showing that, at that time and in the language of song, contraction—while almost exceptionless—was still optional. The second shows the same thing, but not by lack of application of contraction, since there is none to begin with: the point to notice in this case is that, just as in the preceding example, a hiatus has been allowed to keep the process from moving forward, and in this case that process is the euphonic change from *w* to *y*. We show the hiatus with an apostrophe (') instead of our customary hyphen.

Etymologically, Serafim (2007: 216–217) hypothesizes that there *was* a PJ stative extension *\*-ur-*, but that the SES of Ryukyuan represent a second iteration of invention of stative extensions within Japonic; this second iteration is the *\*-wor-* historically underlying the SES in the Ryukyuan lineage.

Morphophonemically, there was a choice between utilizing or not utilizing a SE, and such a choice influenced the conjugational paradigm. For instance, OOk evinces two MZ conjugational forms, one without the stative extension, and the other built on it (cf. Ch. 6 §3). Functionally, the former conveys a volitional sense, while the latter expresses inferential meanings. Furthermore, it is the latter, the one with the incorporated SE, that agrees with the KP *ga*.

### 11.7   *Comparison with Kindaichi's Japanese Verb Classification*

Takahashi (1991a: 182) states that this auxiliary denotes ongoing actions, but that sometimes, it can also express result (i.e. Perfective) when used in conjunction with *shunkan dōshi* 'instantaneous verbs' (in the sense of Kindaichi 1950 in relation to J verbs). Since Kindaichi Haruhiko's taxonomy of NJ verbs is relevant to OOk SE -(*y*)*ur*-(*yi*), we shall briefly summarize his analysis. He divides J verbs into four groups, depending on their suffixation patterns—or lack thereof—of the J SE -*i-ru*, the animate verb of existence,[180] to their gerund, as below:

---

179   ← {pʰaay+yi+...}.
180   It is shorn of its animacy as a stative extension, however.

# AUXILIARIES

| | | | |
|---|---|---|---|
| *jōtai dōshi* | 'stative verbs', | e.g. *ár-u* | 'exist [inanimate]' |
| *keizoku dōshi* | 'continuation verbs', | e.g. *tabé-ru* | 'eat' |
| *shunkan dōshi* | 'instantaneous verbs', | e.g. *syin-u⌐* | 'die' |
| *dai 4 rui* | 'Type 4', | e.g. *sobié-ru* '(mountains) tower'[181] | |

Very roughly, stative verbs do not co-occur with the auxiliary verb *-i-ru*, a stative *extension* (SE) in our terminology, which when used independently is a stative *verb*. In contrast, Type 4 always requires the suffixation of *-i-ru*. Combined with *-i-ru*, continuation verbs denote ongoing activities, e.g. *tábete-i-ru* 'be eating', while instantaneous verbs denote results, e.g. *syinde-i-ru⌐* 'has died, is dead' but not 'is (in the process of) dying'.

| *jōtai dōshi* | *keizoku dōshi* | *shunkan dōshi* | *dai-4-rui* |
|---|---|---|---|
| 'stative verbs' do not take *-iru* states | 'continuation V' can take *-iru* ongoing activities | 'instantaneous V' can take *-iru* results | 'type-4 verbs' require *-iru* |

Now, applying these concepts to OOk, and taking concrete examples from the OS, we show the difference between Continuation and Instantaneous verbs below. The first example, with the Continuation verb {mat+ 'wait'} → *mac-*, expresses the Progressive Aspect, while the Instantaneous verb {kʰuⁿ+ 'come'}[182] → *k-* in the second example denotes the Perfective Aspect.

| にし | 道や、ᴧ | ぢ゚ちやなおもいぎ゚や、ᴧ | まちより | / |
|---|---|---|---|---|
| ni si | MITI ya ,ᴧ | di゚ ya na o mo i gi゚ ya ,ᴧ | ma ti yori | / |
| *nyisyi* | *-myic°yi-ya* | *dzyana\|-ʔumi.i-gya* | *mac-°y-ur-yi* | |
| north | -road-TOP | PLN-love.RY_NOM-SUB | wait-RY-SE-SS | |

'[If I go by] the north road, my love in Jana will **be waiting** for me.' (OS 14.#996)

---

181  Kindaichi's classification overlaps with Vendler's (1957: 147) classification, based on English, derived from the different aspectual characteristics when the use of *be ...-ing* occurs or does not occur: *jōtai dōshi* (Vendler's stative); *keizoku dōshi* (activity/accomplishment); *shunkan dōshi* (achievement). Kindaichi's Type 4 appears to be Japanese-specific. OOk data do not seem to evince this class.

182  Recall that the superscripted morphophonemic mark {ⁿ} indicates a floating abstract length marker (cf. Ch. 6 fn. 54).

| てが゛ねまる、 | / しま∧ | かねて、∧ | きより | / |
|---|---|---|---|---|
| te ga\* ne ma ru , | / si ma∧ | ka ne te ,∧ | ki yo ri | / |
| *tʰi.gani.maru-∅* | *syima-∅* | *kʰani-t°i* | *k-°y-**uur**-yi* | |
| [hand-iron-BE]ₚₙ-TOP | island-DO | conquer-GER/PRFV | come-RY-SE-SS | |

'[The army, led by the sword] *Te-Gane-Maru*,[183] (has) conquered the island and **has** come (back).' (OS 8.#420)

There are some notable differences between J and OOk. First of all, contrary to Kindaichi's classification of Japanese verbs, the stative verb *ʔar-yi* in OOk ranks third highest in the list of verbs co-occurring with *-(y)ur-*, as listed in §11.1. One might expect that stativizing an already stative verb would be superfluous. However, it is not unheard of outside of Tokyo Japanese. For instance, Osaka dialect has *i-te-ru* 'ANIMATE STATIVE + GER + SE', and Kyushu dialect, *at-te-iru* 'INANIMATE STATIVE + GER + SE' (e.g. *kaigi at-te-iru* 'there is a meeting going on' [an interview with a linguist, Shinohara Akiko in http://blog.rkbr .jp/fukayaiki/]). In these two cases, the SE may be turning these stative verbs into non-stative verbs, thereby expressing a transient meaning (cf. English *He is funny* vs *He is being funny*). In the case of OOk, the combination may show a transitional stage from the pre-OOK verb paradigm to a new stative-extension-based verb paradigm. Takahashi (1991a: 186) suggests that the NOk SS form *ʔa-N* may embody SE in its developmental stages, just as OS data show.

Here are examples of *ʔar-y-ur-yi*, *ʔar-y-ur-u*, *ʔar-u-yur-u*, and *ʔa'-y-ur-u*.[184]

| きど†かさに、 | / けさ、げ゛らへ、∧ | ありより | / |
|---|---|---|---|
| ki do† ka sa ni , | / ke sa , ge\* ra pe ,∧ | a ri yo ri | / |
| *k°yi̯dukʰasa-nyi* | *kʰisa-girayi-∅* | *ʔar-y-**ur**-yi* | |
| PLN-LOC | ancient-building-SUB | exist-RY-SE-SS | |

'**There stands** a building from of old in Kijoka.'[185] (OS 13.#968)

---

183   The omoro makes a play on *kʰani-* 'conquer' and a rendakued equivalent *-gani-* 'iron', referring to the sword blade.

184   Additional examples are: *ʔaryi-* ([OS 9.#508], [OS 11.#628], [OS 15.#1079], [OS 21.#1434], [OS 21.#1456]), *ʔaru-* (OS 13.#785) and *ʔa-* ([OS 3.#94], [OS 14.#982]). Sometimes a variation is seen within one song as well (*ʔaryi-yur-i* and *ʔa'-yur-i* [OS 14.#983], though that only represents *r*-drop, seen elsewhere as well).

185   NJ *kijoka* 喜如嘉, NOk *cyizyuka̯* (OGJ 166a); OOk *k°yi̯dukʰasa* is a variant of ⟨ki di yo ka sa⟩ *k°yidzyukʰasa* '(id.)', apparently a mere stylistic variant, but, as expected, showing that the original form is with \**do*, therefore pre-OOk \**kyidokasa*. The etymology is unknown to us.

AUXILIARIES                                                                345

めづ゛らしやど゛、∧        ありよる        / おもかしやど゛、∧
me du* ra si ya do*, ∧   a ri yo ru     / o mo ka si ya do*, ∧
*midzira-sy-a-du*      *?ar-y.ur-u*        *?umukʰa-sya-du*
rare₁-AA-NDS-KP       COP-RY.SE_PROG-RT   rare₂-AA.NDS-KP
ありよる          /
a ri yo ru        /
*?ar-y.ur-u*
COP-RY.SE_PROG-RT
'[This here] **is** truly rare; it **is** rare indeed.'[186] (OS 9.#508)


いしけ、なは、        まみやに、        / けさ、げ゛らへ、、∧
i si ke , na pa ,     ma mi ya ni ,    / ke sa , ge* ra pe , ∧
*?yisyik°yi-naaQp°a* *ma-myaa-nyi*       *kʰisa-girayi-∅*
[Ishike-Naha]_PLN     true-courtyard-LOC  splendid-building-SUB
あるよる          #
a ru yo ru        #
*?ar-yi-yur-u*
exist-RY-SE-SS
'**There is**[187] a splendid building in the courtyard of Ishike[188]-Naha.'
(OS 13.#785)


めづらしや、、∧                     げに、∧ あよる            /
me du ra si ya , ∧                    ge ni , ∧ a yo ru         /
*midzira-sya*                        *gi·nyi*  *?a'-y-ur-u*
novel.and.beautiful-ADS.NDS_RT tru·ly  **be**-RY-SE-RT
'Beautiful and novel is what it truly **is**!'[189] (OS 3.#94)

---

186    These are adjective extensions.

187    Noting that all the text versions have it as ⟨a ru yo ru⟩, TOS (457c n. 1, #785) nonetheless
       suggests that it may be an error, and that the correct form should be ⟨a ri yo ru⟩. On the
       other hand, it may be that the omoro writers are signaling that this RY is not to be abbre-
       viated from ···r·yi- to ···r y , but that the syllable is to remain ···r-yi- Since a ⟨ru⟩ = *ru* SS or
       RT cannot actually be elided with a following ···*yu*, it is one way of doing that. This is our
       preferred explanation, though the ultimate answer remains open.

188    The English gloss is given in, essentially, its proto-form *?yisyike *[?ⁱiʃik°ɛ]. PP gives
       *[?ⁱiʃikʸɛ], then Raising, *[?ⁱiʃikʸɪ], then Tensing = Merger, [?ⁱiʃikʸi] = OOk *?yisyik°yi*. We
       assume that ⟨···i Ce⟩ (where C would be aspirated) yields ···*yiCyi*. The preceding high vowel
       has dampened aspiration.

189    This is an example of an adjective in a verbally predicated form, but "infixed" with an
       intensive adverb *gi·nyi* that also triggers KM in the stative predicate.

346          CHAPTER 7

Secondly, the instantaneous verb {kʰuⁿ+ 'come'} in its {+wur+ 'SE'} form *k-ʾy-uur-yi* 'come-RY-SE-SS', can also denote progressive aspect, as below.

おゑぢへ、 かぜ*ᴧ　おちへ、ᴧ きより　　　　　 /
o we di pe , ka ze*ᴧ　o ti pe ,ᴧ ki yo ri　　　　 /
*ʔwii#dzyi　kʰazi-∅　ʔu-cʾyi　k-ʾy-**uur-yi***
follow-ing　wind-SUB　push-GER come-RY-SE-SS
'The following wind **is** push**ing** (i.e. is blowing) and coming toward us.'
(OS 13.#902)

## 12     Progressive/Perfective: *-yaaryi*

### 12.1    *Takahashi's Analysis: 10 Functions of* -yaaryi

The defective auxiliary *-yaaryi* is attested in OOk only in the RY conjugational form, *-yaaryi*ᵣᵧ.[190] Semantically, Takahashi (1991a: 175–177) ascribes to it the following ten meanings: (1) iterative action, (2) progressive action with respect, (3) intensification, (4) state of mind, (5) location of activity, (6) complementary actions, (7) means, (8) instrument, (9) cause, and (10) purpose. However, as will be argued shortly, not all of these meanings are intrinsic to *-yaaryi*, but rather they are contextually derived. Here are examples for each meaning Takahashi lists with his Japanese wordings in parentheses. Below we will gloss *-yaar-* as PROG or PRFV.

(1)    Action occurring iteratively (*dōsa no keiki* [継起])

いと、ᴧ　　　　ぬきやり、　　　　 / なわ、ᴧ
i to ,ᴧ　　　　nu ki ya ri ,　　　 / na wa ,ᴧ
*ʔyi̧ tʾu-∅　nuk-ʾyaaryi*　　　　nawa-∅
silk.thread-DO push.through-**PROG-RY**　rope-DO

---

190   Takahashi (1991a: 179–180) lists one example that may be taken either as SS or RY:
     ...げ*らへて、 / げ*らへ、やり、　　 / おもひぐ*わの　 / 御ため /
     ge*ra pe te ,　/ ge* ra pe , ya ri ,　/ o mo pi gu* wa no　/ o ta me /
     *girayi̧-tʾi　　girayi-ᵈyaaryi　　ʔumii-gwa-nu　　ʔu-tami*
     build-GER　　build-PROG-?RY/?SS　dear-child-GEN　EX-sake
     Hokama (2000b: 69b): "[Erabu-jima, hanare-jima ni iru chōrō-tachi ga, ōki na gusuku o] tsukuri ni tsukutte, [kore mo ryōshu-sama no] omoi-go no o-tame [de aru yo.]" '[The elders on Erabu island, on the offshore island,] built and continued to build [the Great Castle, and this is] for the sake of the [feudal lord's] dear son!' (OS 13.#859)

# AUXILIARIES

ぬきやり　　　　　／
nu ki yari　　　　／
*nuk-°yaaryi*
push.through-**PROG-RY**
'[What a beautiful hawser it is!] [It is being made by] **continually** pushing silken thread[191] through, **continually** pushing ropes through ...' (OS 11.#632) (OS 12.#711) (OS 21.#1470) (OS 21.#1492)

(2) Progressive of action with exaltation (*dōsa no keizoku no sonkei*), with {c°yuwa·r+}

| げ*す、 | ／ま人、ˬ | すだ*しやり、ˬ | ちよわれ　／ |
|---|---|---|---|
| ge* su , | ma PITO ,ˬ | su da* si ya ri ,ˬ | ti yo wa re　／ |
| *gisi-∅* | *ma-Bcʰyu-∅* | *sid·as-**yaaryi*** | *c°yuwar-i* |
| retainer-DO | EX-people-DO | nurture·CAUS-**PROG**RY | be-MR |

'May he [= the King] **keep** nurtur**ing** his retainers and the people, and reign!' (OS 6.#305)

(3) Intensification (*kyōi*)

| しよりもり、ˬ | げ*らへて、 | ／げ*らへ、やり、　／ |
|---|---|---|
| si yo ri mo ri ,ˬ | ge* ra pe te , | ／ge* ra pe , ya ri ,　／ |
| *syi#yuryi-muryi-∅* | *girayi,-t°i* | *girayi-**yaaryi***[192] |
| [PLN-grove]PLN-DO | build-GER | build-**PROG**RY |

| おぎ*やかもいに、ˬ | みおやせ　　　　／ |
|---|---|
| o gi* ya ka mo i ni ,ˬ | mi o ya se　　　　／ |
| *ʔu-gyakʰa-mii-nyi* | *myi-ʔu-ya-s-i* |
| EX-shining-esteemed.oneEX-IO | EX-EX-give-EX-MR |

'Build Shuri grove [castle]—**keep** build**ing** [it until it's finished]!—and present it to O-Gyaka-Moi (= King Shō Shin)!' (OS 5.#240)

---

191 According to Nakahara (1957: 249), ⟨i to⟩ (NOk *ʔyi̯tu̯*, which now means 'silk'), ⟨na wa⟩ (NOk *naa̯*, which now means 'rope'), and ⟨tu na⟩ (NOk *cina̯*, which now also means 'rope'), are used synonymously. OKDJ (77b) notes that ⟨i to⟩ implies relation of the Lord to his subjects. Hokama (2000a: 632b) notes the apparent folk belief that invested in the ropes and threads used to make the hawser was a supernatural power.

192 This structure with reduplicated verb is reminiscent of *kʰayu-yi-kʰayu-tʰi* 'plying to and fro' (OS 14.#996); cf. 4G(7), p. 202.

348                                                             CHAPTER 7

(4)   State of mind (*shinri jōtai*)

       あんの、　かね、ʌ　ぐ゚すく　　　　　/　あまゑ、やり、ʌ
       a N no ,　ka ne , ʌ　gu゚ su ku　　　/　a ma we , ya ri , ʌ
       *ʔaN-nu　kʰani　　-gusik°u-∅*　　　　*ʔamayi-yaar-yi*
       we-GEN iron　　-enclosure-DO　rejoice-PROG-RY=ADV
       みおやせば゚、　　　　　/
       mi o ya se ba゚ ,　　　/
       *myi-ʔu-ya-s-i-ba*
       EX-EX-give-EX-IZ-T/C
       'When we rejoicingly present our strong (i.e. Shuri) castle [to the King]
       ...' (OS 5.#248)

(5)   Attaching to {##wur+}, and meaning 'being at ...', it expresses location
       where activity is carried out (*dōsa no okonawareru basho*)[193]

       かわはんた、ʌ　　　おりやり、　　/ こゝはんた、ʌ　　みれば゚　　　　/
       ka wa pa N ta , ʌ　o ri ya ri ,　/ ko si pa N ta , ʌ　mi re ba゚　　　/
       *kʰawa#pʰaNt°a-∅　wur-yaaryi　kʰusyi#pʰaNt°a-∅　myii-r-i-ba*[194]
       river-cliff-LOC　be-PROG~RY~	back-cliff-LOC　see-4GE-IZ-T/C
       'When we view the rear[195] cliff, being [at] the well's edge, ...' (OS 11.#571)

(6)   Concurrent actions: 'on the one hand, ...; on the other, ...' (*ryōmen*)

       おろす、ʌ　　　　かみや、　/ いづこ、ʌ　　　　　　やしなやり、　　/
       o ro su , ʌ　　　ka mi ya ,　/ i du† ko , ʌ　　　ya si na ya ri ,　/
       *ʔuru·s-i　　kʰamyi-ya　ʔyidʑi#kʰu-∅　yasyi̧na-yaaryi*
       descend·VT-RT deity-VOC　outstanding-ones-DO nurture-PROG~RY~

---

193  He asserts that this "corresponds to" the etymon for the NOk deverbal postnominal
     enclitic *-wuti* 'at' (← -∅ wu-ti 'be-ing [at]-'). They *do* both share {wur+}.

194  We assume that the vowel of ⟨mi⟩ was long, and, as such, had a laxed nucleus: [mʸɪ:]; how-
     ever, it may also have been *myi·ry-i-ba* [mʸiɾʸiba], with the scribe not bothering to write
     an "obvious" PP. (With respect to *-ba*, recall that PP does not normally operate through
     labials, nor does it normally operate iteratively.)

195  KOS (noted in TOS 11.#571, n. 3) speculates that ⟨ko "⟩, the form accepted by both KOS and
     TOS, may be a scribal error for ⎣ ⟨si⟩, and we interpret it as ⟨si⟩ as well. Nakahara (1957:
     368) interprets *kʰawa-pʰaNt°a* as the Southern part of Aguni Island, and *kʰusyi-pʰaNt°a* as
     the northern edge of Kumejima Island, the two of which are situated opposite each other
     divided by an expanse of water. Nakahara takes *kʰusyi-pʰaNt°a* to refer to Kasasu Waka-
     Anji( Young Lord Kasasu)'s own castle (*kyojō* 居城). We accept this interpretation at face
     value; it is in any case a *hapax*. Cf. NOk *háNta* '(1) edge; (2) cliff('s edge)' (OGJ 206b).

AUXILIARIES                                                                349

あぢ\*おそいよ、∧ まぶ\*れ、    /
a di\* o so i yo ,∧ ma bu\* re ,   /
Ɂadʑyi-Ɂusii-yu    maвr-i
lord-ruler-DO      protect-MR
'O deity we called to [i.e. made] descend [to the earth]—may you **keep**
nurtur**ing** soldiers and also protect our Lord Ruler!' (OS 7.#372)

(7)    Means (*hōhō, shudan*)

うしあや、たて、∧    とりやり、        / ぬり、てぼ†こ、∧
u si a ya , ta te ,∧   to ri ya ri ,      / nu ri , te bo† ko ,∧
Ɂusyi-Ɂaya-tʰat°i-Ø tʰur-**yaaryi**        nur-yi-tʰii-bukʰu-Ø
bull-BE-shield-DO   take.up-**PROG**ᴿʏ  paint-ʀʏ-hand-halberd-DO
とりやり、        / いちやぢ\*や、∧ せめつけて、            /
to ri ya ri ,       / i ti ya di\* ya ,∧  se me tu ke te ,          /
tʰur-**yaaryi**       Ɂyic°ya-dʑyoo-Ø simi-c°ikʰi-tʰi
take.up-**PROG**ᴿʏ  wood-gate-DO  attack-repeatedly-GER
かなぢ\*や、∧    せめ、つけて        #
ka na di\* ya ,∧   se me , tu ke te      #
Ɂkʰana-dʑyoo-Ø simi-c°ikʰi-tʰi
iron-gate-DO    attack-repeatedly-GER
'Tak**ing** up beautiful bull[-painted] shields, tak**ing** up painted hand-hal-
berds, [our army] will lay into [the enemy's] wooden gates, will lay into
[their] strong gates.' (OS 21.#1446)

(8)    Attaches to the form *s-* 'do-', meaning NJ '-o-shite', denoting instrument or
means (*zairyō, shudan*)[196]

みこゑ     しやり、∧  おそわ          /
mi ko we   si ya ri ,∧  o so wa          /
myi-ˌkʰuyi s-**yaaryi** Ɂusuw-a
EX-voice   do-PROG rule/protect-IA
'[Because the Famed High Priestess has calmed it,] may you rule [the land
peacefully], **by** [your] august [governing] voice.' (OS 1.#8)

---

196   He notes (1991a: 177) that in this case, *s-yaaryi* developed into NOk *-saayi* 'by (means of)
      ⌣'. (We may add that this occurs after the Monophthongizations) We hypothesize *-saani*

(9) Cause, reason (*gen'in, riyū*)

あめ ₍ₐ₎　ふりやり、₍ₐ₎　すみあが゚て　　／くれ ₍ₐ₎　ふりやり、₍ₐ₎
a me ₍ₐ₎　pu ri ya ri , ₍ₐ₎ su mi a ga゚ te　／ ku re ₍ₐ₎　pu ri ya ri , ₍ₐ₎
*ʔami-∅　pʰur-yaar-yi sim-yi-ʔaga-t°ee　kʰuri-∅　pʰur-yaar-yi*
rain-SUB　fall-**PRFV**ᵣᵧ　clear-RY-up-PRFV　rain-SUB fall **PRFV**ᵣᵧ
すみあがて　　　　／
su mi a ga te　　　／
*sim-yi-ʔaga-t°ee*
clear-RY-up-PRFV
'The rain **has** fall**en**, so the sky has cleared up, the showers **have** fall**en**, so the sky has cleared up' (OS 10.#536)

(10) Purpose (*mokuteki*)

あが゚、なやり、₍ₐ₎　おれわちへ、　　／ やし、なやり、₍ₐ₎
a ga゚ , na ya ri , ₍ₐ₎ o re wa ti pe ,　／ ya si , na ya ri , ₍ₐ₎
*ʔagana-yaaryi ʔuri-wa-c°yi　　yasyiₙ na-yaaryi*
nurture-**PROG**ᵣᵧ descend-EX-GER　rear-RY-**PROG**ᵣᵧ
おれわちへ　　　　#
o re wa ti pe　　　#
*ʔuri-wa-c°yi*
descend-EX-GER
'Descending [**in order**] **to** nurture [the soldiers], descending [**in order**] **to** rear [the soldiers] ...' (OS 1.#37)

### 12.2　*What Unites the 10 Functions?*

Takahashi's extensive array of functions is informative, but may at the same time obfuscate an important generalization. In our view these multiple layers of meaning can reasonably be reduced to the core meaning of Progressive/Perfective. To this end, (1) 'iterative action' and (2) 'progressive action with respect' are self-explanatory as Progressive. Additionally, (3) 'intensification' results from the reduplication of the same verb with *-y-aar-yi* (e.g. *girayi-t°i girayi-yaaryi* 'build and keep building ...!' above). Not surprisingly, repetitive aspect adds an emphatic tone, and expressing a repetition of the same action aligns with the Progressive aspect. Furthermore, (4) 'State of mind' is dictated

---

'(id.)' < *\*s-yaaryi*, as well, through *r ~ n* alternation, which is sporadic and relatively rare, and which stabilizes the syllable structure.

AUXILIARIES 351

by the verb that comes before -*yaaryi* (e.g. *ʔamayi-yaaryi* 'rejoicingly' above), and the state by definition is an ongoing thing, just like the Progressive aspect. Similarly, in his (5) 'location' category, -*yaaryi* is combined with the stative verb *wur-yi*, yielding the 'being at' reading, or ongoing state (e.g. *kawa-pʰaɴtᵒa-∅ wur-yaaryi* 'being at the river-cliff' above).[197]

His (6) 'complementary actions' depicts complementarily one agent's concurrent activities in progress (e.g. *yasyi̯na-yaaryi* 'keep nurturing … and [complementarily] …' above). Both (7) 'means' and (8) 'instrument or means' categories share durativity, which is in line with Progressive aspect.[198]

His (9) 'cause, reason (*gen'in, riyū*)' is pragmatically induced through implicature. That is, the first clause *ʔami-∅ pᵒur-y-aar-yi* delineates the rain falling, and the second clause *sim-yi-ʔaga-tᵒi* indicates the clearing of the sky. Putting these clauses together, the hearer's mind seeks a relevance or a connection between them, and, as a consequence, the 'cause' implicature arises (Grice 1975, Traugott and Dasher [2002: 34–40]):

{There is continual rain.} {The sky has cleared up.}      >
{There being continual rain, the sky has cleared up.}      >
{Because of the continual rain, the sky has cleared up.}

Similarly, the (10) 'purpose' reading emerges as it is the most natural reading to connect the two clauses *ʔagana-yaaryi* 'nurture [the soldiers]' and *ʔuri-wa-*

---

197    Recall that location is frequently zero-marked. This makes it easy for a new (here, Dynamic-)Locative marker to develop from the verb governing the locative phrase: $X\text{-}\emptyset_{\text{LOC}}$ *wur-yaaryi*ᵣᵧ → *X-wuryaaryi*ₗₒ꜀. Given that background, if we change *wuryaaryi* to *wutᵒi* (see §12.4 for -*(y)aar-(yi)* :: -*tᵒi*), then we have NOk syntax, where the verbal clause ending in *wutᵒi* is not at all a verbal clause any more, and thus *wutᵒi* does not mark the clause as a stative-verb clause; rather, it is now part of a larger-scale active-verb clause, built as if out of the pieces of the current omoro, marking the place where *action* occurs, that is, *seeing*:

    OOk: *kʰawa-pʰaɴtᵒa-∅ wur-yaaryi, kʰusyi-pʰaɴtʰa-∅ myi·ɾ-i-ba* 'When we view the rear cliff, being [at] the well's edge, …'

    NOk: *kaa-haɴta-wuti kusyi-haɴta ɴɴ-d-e-e* 'When we view the rear cliff at the well's edge, …'

198    As for the distinction between his 'means' and 'instrument or means' categories, it really amounts to how those two sets turned out in later Okinawan. The category (7) 'means' utilizes lexical verbs, while the category (8) 'instrument or means' crucially appends onto the specific dummy-verb to create a set phrase:

    *s-yaaryi* '*lit*. doing continually' → -*syaaryi*ᵢₙₛₜ 'by means of'

The example for the lexical-verb type is:

    *nur-yi-tʰi-bukʰu-∅ tʰur-y-aar-yi* '**taking** up painted hand-halberds'

above; for the set-verb type,

    *myi·ᵢkʰuyi s-y-aar-yi* '**by** [your] august [governing] voice'.

*cʲyi* '[deities] descending'. In essence, *-yaaryi* is describing the act of nurturing which would expectedly last some span of time, in other words, Progressive.

## 12.3    *The Progressive/Perfective Aspectual Dyad*

In some cases, it is difficult to pinpoint whether a given *-yaaryi* is Progressive or Perfective. For instance, in the following song, the auxiliary *-yaaryi* has been taken to be, on the one hand, a Progressive auxiliary 'be DOing' in OSJS (52b and 341a), and a Perfective auxiliary 'have DOne' by Hokama (2000a: 27b).[199]

| あおて、ᴧ | いきやり、 | / かたき、ᴧ | ひぢめ、わちへ | / |
|---|---|---|---|---|
| a o te ,ᴧ | i ki ya ri , | / ka ta ki ,ᴧ | pi di me , wa ti pe | / |
| ʔoo-tʲi | ʔyik-ʲyaaryi | kʰatʲakʲyi-∅ | pʲyidzyimi-wa-cʲyee | |
| join(.in.battle)-G/P | go-RY-P/P-RY | enemy-DO | subjugate_RY-EAV-G/P | |

'Going against the enemy in battle, [she] has subjugated [them].' (OS 1.#25)

Here is another example:

| かな、かぶ†と、ᴧ | きやり | / かな、よろい、ᴧ | きやり | / |
|---|---|---|---|---|
| ka na , ka bu† to ,ᴧ | ki ya ri | / ka na , yo ro i ,ᴧ | ki ya ri | / |
| kʰana-kʰaʙtʲu-∅ | kʲyii-**yaar-yi** | kʰana-yuruyi-∅ | kʲyii-**yaar-yi** | |
| EX-war.helmet-DO | don-P/**P-RY** | EX-armor-DO | don-P/**P-RY** | |

'[The Lord] **has donned** / **is wearing** a beautiful helmet, and beautiful armor' (OS 21.#1446)

## 12.4    *The Parallelism of -yaaryi_{RII} and Gerunds*

The Progressive/Perfective aspectual dyad also connects to an interesting note offered by Takahashi (1991a: 177), which states that the auxiliary *-yaaryi* alternates in some verses with a Gerund. For instance, in the first example, the Progressive *-yaaryi* in *pʲyik-ʲyaaryi* is in a parallel construction with the Perfective gerund *-tʲi* in *sagi-tʲi*. The Progressive comes first, the Gerund, second. In the second examples, the paired words are *tʰu-tʲi* and *tʰur-yaaryi* in the Gerund-Progressive order. In the OS, items in parallel structures indicate structural/grammatical and semantic/functional equivalencies.

---

199    In the present context, it appears to be functionally Perfective, i.e. to mean 'have DOne'; a discrepancy in the authorities' interpretation of the lexical meaning is most probably due to the fact that Progressive/Perfective are two sides of the same coin. And, there are no native speakers to instruct us on the fine points!

AUXILIARIES

353

まこ、∧　　　ひきやり、　　／ かちや、∧　　さげて、　　／
ma ko ,∧　　pi ki ya ri ,　／ ka ti ya ,∧　sa ge te ,　／
*makʰu-∅　 p°yik-°yaaryi　kʰac°ya-∅　 sagi-t°i*
curtain₁-DO　draw-PROG_RY　curtain₂-DO lower-GER
'By drawing the curtain₁,[200] lowering the curtain₂,[201] [we will invite the lord].'
(OS 20.#1367)


大ぎ†みが゛、∧　　　なおさ、∧　とて、∧　　　おれわちへ、　　　／
OPO gi† mi ga゛,∧　　na o sa ,∧　to te ,∧　　o re wa ti pe ,　　／
*ʔuQp°u-gyimyi-¸ga　nawusa-∅ tʰu-t°i　 ʔuri-wa-c°yi*
great-priestess-SUB　ritual-DO　choose-GER descend-EAV-GER

...
くにもりが゛、∧　　　時∧　　とりやり、∧　　　おれわちへ　　　#
ku ni mo ri ga゛,∧　　TOKI∧　to ri ya ri ,∧　o re wa ti pe　　#
*k°unyi.muryi-¸ga　tʰuk°yi-∅ tʰur-yaaryi　 ʔuri-wa-c°yi*
PN-SUB　　　　　time-DO　choose-PROG_RY descend-EAV-GER
'The Great Priestess [= Ō-Gimi] descended, choosing the ritual [for the prosperity of the King]; Kunimori [= Ō-Gimi] descended, choosing the date.'[202]
(OS 13.#864)


Takahashi (1991a: 181) hypothesizes that the vicissitudes of *-yaaryi* and the
Gerund show mutual influences: he says that the former had no sentence-
final form, and indeed we see none. In contrast, the latter had both, which we
agree is true, as GER/PRFV. Further, he says that the usage of *-yaaryi* declined,
though we know from heavily used NOk forms *-yaani* and *-saani* that it did not

---

200　This word for 'curtain' (幕, J *makú*) (and its parallel *kʰac°ya*, too) is a *hapax legomenon*,
　　and is surely a borrowing from MJ (NOk *ma(a)ku*, [OGJ 360a]). Probably OOk speakers,
　　sensitive to phonetic aspiration, heard this Sino-Japanese word as either [makṵ] (which
　　sounds aspirated) or [makʰṵ] (NJ is [maʳkʰṵ]), and therefore assigned a phonemicization
　　/makʰu¸/ = ⟨ma ko⟩ to it, also making it seem either that this was an example of literate
　　OOk speakers' indifference to ⟨u⟩- and ⟨o⟩-tier spelling distinctions (only partially true,
　　and not true after *k*), or that the word had come up from Proto-Japonic *\*makö*, both highly
　　unlikely. The spelling, while only a single instance, is due to borrowing.
201　NOk *kácya* 'mosquito net' (OGJ 299b); *kácya fic-y-ú-N* 'kaya o tsuru' = 'pull [*lit.* hang] a
　　mosquito net' (the latter, also 232a, under *fic-y-ú-N*). Nakijin *haʳc°yaaʔ pʰiʳc-°y-u-N* '(id.)'.
　　(We assume OOk *c°y* on the basis of the Nakijin form, and on assumption of ... *c°ya* ←
　　... *c°ywa* ← ... *c°yua* ← ... *c°yaũ* ⟨蚊[ka]帳[tyau]⟩—recall the Metathesis Rule) OSJS (108c)
　　points out that OOk ⟨ka ti ya⟩ = *kʰac°ya* meant a sort of curtain, not the modern mosquito
　　net.
202　This is a parallel construction, as is typical; *ʔupʰu-gyimyi* and *k°unyi.muryi* (*lit.* 'country-
　　defender') are just two ways of referring to the same person.

354                                                                    CHAPTER 7

decline. He claims that when it did, the Gerund came to take its place sentence-medially, but that in turn led the Gerund's sentence-final usage to its demise. Certainly he is correct in stating/implying that the perfective uses of the |Te|-form became circumscribed, now used only with yes/no perfective questions, but otherwise replaced with NOk-*ta*- 'PRFV' < OOk -*t*-°*ar*-. But without a consideration of the latter, and perhaps of more, the picture may not be complete. This is beyond the scope of our investigation.

### 12.5    *Historical and Comparative Analysis*

The Progressive/Perfective -*yaaryi* is both functionally and structurally similar to OJ -*êr-i* [yer$^y$i] < Early OJ -*êr-î* 'has DOne' < \*-*î#ar-î* \*'there.to.be$_{RY}$'; the OOk form -*yaaryi* '?is DOing / ?has DOne' is also from \*-*î#ar-î* \*'there.to.be$_{RY}$'; the two auxiliary verbs have probably been created independently.[203] The OOk form -*yaaryi* is the progenitor of NOk -(*y*)*aayi* ~ -(*y*)*aani* 'having DOne ...; DOing ..., and then ...'.[204]

One might wonder if one reading over the other is predictable. The auxiliation has three parts: (1) the verbal root preceding the auxiliary itself, which embodies aspectual characteristics of continuation of a state, or of a change of state (cf. *keizoku dōshi* 'activity verbs' [*lit.* 'continuity verbs'] vs. *shunkan dōshi* 'achievement verbs' [*lit.* 'instant(aneous) verbs']); (2) the RY morpheme (including its zero allomorph = {+∅}), which provides a *quasi-nominal* character (e.g. *infinitive*); and (3) the dependent verb \*-*ar*$_{RH}$- 'there.to.be', which, being a stative, provides stativity secondary to the main verb, if any. Typically, Continuative-RY-*ar*- gives Progressive interpretation (first example below), while Change-of-State-RY-*ar*- gives Perfective (i.e. resultative) interpretation (second example).[205]

---

203   As one of our perceptive reviewers put it, "To bolster the case for OOk -*yaaryi* being an independent creation, one could cite the verb I just used (*being*—an approximate English analogue to stative verb + RY) as an auxiliary. Stative verb + RY equivalent is not a typologically unusual combination. The case for inheritance or borrowing would be stronger if a morpheme sequence had few if any parallels in other languages. This contrasts with the case of \**owas*- on p. 353 which is unlikely to have arisen independently in OOk and MJ."

204   Recall two facts about *r* that explain its shape in this set of NOk alternants: a) \**r* can *sporadically* change to *n*; and b) OOk *ryi regularly* becomes the NOk moraic *yi* [$^y$i] when in post-vocalic position.

205   This is a very simplistic view. As the predictability of the gerund + *i-ru* construction between Progressive and Perfective aspects has been debated to this day since the inception of Kindaichi's hypothesis (cf. §11.7, this chapter), this is not a facile task for OOk -*yaar*$_{RH}$-. For instance, *p°ur*- '(rain) fall' is a continuative verb, but *ʔami-∅ p°ur-y-aaryi*

AUXILIARIES    355

しま、∧    まるく、∧    / みこゑしやり、∧    おそわ    /
si ma ,∧    ma ru ku ,∧    / mi ko we si ya ri ,∧    o so wa    /
*syima-Ø    maru-k°u    myi-,kʰwii-s-**yaaryi**    ʔusuw-a*
island-DO peaceful-ADV    EX-voice-do-RY-**PROG**<sub>RY</sub> rule-MZ/IA
'[Because the Famed High Priestess has calmed it,] may you rule the land peacefully, **by** [your] august [governing] voice.' (OS 1.#8)

くもは∧    きやり、    / こが゚ねじ†ま、∧    はちへ、∧おわちへ    /
ku mo pa ∧ ki ya ri ,    / ko ga* ne zi† ma 、∧    pa ti pe ∧ o wa ti pe    /
*k°umu-wa    k°-**yaaryi**    kʰugani-zyima-Ø    pʰa-c°yi-ʔuwa-c°yi*
clouds-TOP come-**PRFV**<sub>RY</sub>    EX-island-ALLATIVE sail.fast-EX-GER
'[Responding to the priestesses' prayers for wind], the clouds [pushed by the winds] **have** come, and [the fine ship] will sail [any time now, here,] to the golden<sub>BE</sub> island [pushed by the same winds] …' (OS 22.#1545)

Vovin (2009a: 1085) characterizes an OJ AUX -*yar*<sub>YD</sub>- as a 'directive auxiliary' indicating "that the action expressed by the main verb is directed at a certain object (or goal) located some distance from the agent." He further states that this -*yar*- is "a rare auxiliary, attested only in the *Man'yōshū* (and predominantly in the later texts) and in the Norito". In addition, he notes (2009a: 1086) that there is no attestation in Eastern OJ, and that, to the best of his knowledge, it is only otherwise attested in Old Ryukyuan (our OOk). As a result, he suspects the OOk AUX -*yaaryi* to be a loan from Classical Japanese. The OJ -*yar*- that Vovin points out as related to the supposed -*yar*- of OOk is in fact a fictive relation; the OOk "-*yar*<sub>YD</sub>-" is actually -*y-aar*<sub>RH</sub>- ← *yi*<sub>RY</sub>-*ar*<sub>RH</sub>-, and is an independently arrived at construction that, rather, structurally mimics the OJ -*êr*- [yer], not because of one-to-one semantics (the semantics are similar but not the same), but rather because of one-to-one lexical match. The fact of perfect lexical match (stative *\*ar*- + RY *\*-î*) but not perfect semantic match is what gives

---

'rain-SUB fall-PROG/PRFV<sub>RY</sub>', i.e. 'the rain has fallen, and …' expresses a PRFV rather than a PROG meaning. (See Takahashi's category (9) in §12.1) The same applies to the example below where the continuative verb *ʔyi,rab*- 'choose' induces a PRFV reading:
ゑが、∧    ゑらびやり、∧    おれわちへ、    /
we ga ,∧    we ra bi ya ri ,∧ o re wa ti pe ,    /
*yii,-ga-Ø    ʔyi,rab-**yaaryi**    ʔuri-wa-c°yi*
auspicious-day-DO choose-**PRFV**<sub>RY</sub> descend-EX-GER
'[Kikoe Ōgimi,] having chosen an auspicious day, descended … .' (OS 3.#110)
Suffice it to say that the level of the aspectual analysis for OOk -*yaaryi* is just as challenging as the -*te-iru* construction in Japanese, but with the added difficulty that there are no native speakers to consult to clear up ambiguities.

356 CHAPTER 7

-*yaar*- away as a lookalike rather than as something that comes down to both languages from Proto-Japonic.

## 13   Copula: -*yar*-, -*nar*-

The term copula here is used to refer to a part of speech that has both auxiliary- and verb-like attributes, expressing the meaning of '(A) is (B)'. Allomorphs of the so-called defective copula, such as -*nu*, i.e. the genitive particle '-GEN' (< *-$n_{COP}$-$o_{RT}$) and the adverbial particle -*nyi* 'ADV', (< *-$n_{COP}$-$yi_{RY}$) are not included in this section, but are treated as particles, plain and simple. The grammaticalized OOk -*n-ar*- < *-*n-yi* *'COP-RY' + *ar*- 'DUMMY$_{RH}$' is included.

There are two copulas[206] in the OS: *-y-ar-yi-* * and *-n-ar-yi-* *.[207] Their etymological and possible allomorphic relationship aside (to be discussed in § 13.3), in what follows, the copulas *-yar-yi* and *-nar-yi* are discussed as separate entities.

### 13.1   *Copula:* -yar-

This auxiliary has the attested forms *-yar-a*- (MZ), *-yar-i*- (IZ), and *-ya-t°i* (GER). Below are some examples of MZ forms (*yar-a*-) followed by the Temporal/Conditional particle *-ba*.

| も〻、あんじ*〻 | やらば、 | やちよむ、 | ゑ〻 | やれ、 | / | とよむ、 |
|---|---|---|---|---|---|---|
| mo ", a N zi*〻 | ya ra ba , | ya ti yo mu , | we〻 | ya re , | / | to yo mu , |
| *mumu-ʔanzyi* | *yar-a-ba* | *ya-c°yoo-mu* | *yee* | *yari* | | *tʰuyum-u* |
| hundred-lord | COP-MZ-CND | COP-CONC-even | INJ | INJ | | resound-RT |

| あぢ*おそい | / |
|---|---|
| a di* o so i | / |
| *ʔadzyi-ʔusii* | |
| lord-ruler | |

'Even if[208] it be [among] many lords, yea!, huzzah!, [it is our] resounding Lord Ruler!' (OS 11.#566)

---

206   Vovin (2009a: 549) states that the copula *to* is attested once (OS 13.#854) in OOk. However, it is unclear which *to* he is referring to. Torigoe (1968: 166) regards ⟨ku me ta ra⟩ (OS 13.#900) as *kume-t-ar-a*($N_{1A}$) 'Kume-COP-DUMMY-IA', but OSJS (145b) points out that it is a place name. He also takes ⟨ni se ta re⟩ (OS 20.#1383) to be *nyi(i), se(e)-tar-i* 'ruler + copula *-taryi* in IZ'. However, there are 7 other instances of ⟨ni se ta re⟩, none of which can be given the gloss Torigoe proposes. In contrast, OSJS (266b) analyzes it as *nyi, ·si-tare* 'be appropriate' + auxiliary *-tar*$_{PRFT}$-*i*$_{IZ}$. Here we follow OSJS's accounts in both cases.

207   These forms are presented here in RY for consistency with the other sections, but they are not actually attested as RY.

208   Hokama (2000a: 381b), following OSJS (336bc), translates this portion *-ya-c°yoo-mu* as 'de

AUXILIARIES

The context of the omoro below is to celebrate the completion of a new ship here personified as *waɴ* 'me', speaking to its "parent"/owner, who is anxious to send it off on its maiden voyage.

おや、ˌ やらばＴ、　　でＴˀ、　/ わん、　はりやせ　　　/
o ya ,ˌ ya ra baＴ ,　deＴ " ,　/ wa ɴ ,　pa ri ya se　　/
*ʔuya*　　**yar-a-ba**　　*di-t°i*　　　*waɴ-∅ pʰaary-as-i*
parent　**COP-MZ**-T/C　QT-GER　　me-DO　sail-CAUS-MR
'Saying "If indeed I **am** your parent[, I would do thus]", send me off [to sea]!' (OS 13.#898)

The following are examples of IZ in KM constructions (OS 17.#1148, OS 14.#995) and with the Temporal/Conditional particle -*ba* (OS 8.#454, OS 16.#1167):

しつらいす、/ ことなおし、がＴみ ˌ　　　　　やれ　/
si tu ra i su ,　/ ko to na o si , gaＴ mi ˌ　ya re　/
*syic°iree-si*　　*kʰut°u-nawus-yi-gamyi*　　**yar-i**
PN-**KP**　　　　thing_DO-correct_VT-RY-deity　COP-**IZ**
'**It is** Priestess Shitsurai, **none other, who is** the deity [to bring happiness and peace to the world] correcting [wrong] things.' (OS 16.#1148)

にしだＴけに、ˌ　　　　　　　　　　おわる、　　　/ たけの、
ni si daＴ ke ni ,ˌ　　　　　　　　o wa ru ,　　/ ta ke no ,
*nyisyi-ˌdakʰi-nyi*　　　　　　　　*ʔuwa·r-u*　　*tʰakʰi-nu*
{west/north}-{shrine/peak}-LOC　exist_EX·4GE-RT　shrine-GEN

---

sae mo' = 'even (if) only, even (if) as little as'. Modern Shuri is -*ya#cyo'oɴ* '(id.)' (OGJ 167a), and Modern Nakijin is -*yac°yuɴ* '(id.)'. The clitic compound -*c°yoo-mu* '-CONC-even' is related to OJ -*tö-mo* '(id.)'. Clearly there was a PP trigger that subsequently vanished in pre-OOk. The pre-OOk Copula construction is ultimately *\*n(-yi_i)(-t(y_i)ee)(-pa) ## ar-yi* \***'COP-RY(-GER)(-T/C) ## STAT-SS**. As e.g. JDB notes (504b), OJ -*tö-mo* attaches to the SS of verbs, and of course the SS of a stative is the same as the RY, namely -*ʔ*, so e.g. *ar-i-tö-mo* 'even if it be' (504c). Applying this to OOk

　　*\*…ar-yi#too-mo → \*…ar-yi-cyoo-mo → \*…aQ-c°yoo-mu → \*…a-c°yoo-mu*

The graph ⟨mu⟩ alternates with ⟨mo⟩ in about equal numbers, so this is the clitic -*mu* 'even'. The fact that the members of the graphic pair ⟨mo⟩ ~ ⟨mu⟩ alternate as they do suggests that the scribes knew it was a separate morpheme.

　　There is another concessive, -*du-mu*, but it attaches to IZ, just as its correspondent, -*dö-mo*, did in OJ. JDB avoids etymologically linking this concessive to -*tö-mo*, though it tentatively links the latter to the quotative -*tö*. We, too, will treat -*c°yoo-mu* and -*du-mu* as unrelated.

よきが†なししよ、　　　／くめの、　しま、が†み　やれ、　／
yo ki ga† na si si yo ,　　／ ku me no , si ma , ga† mi ya re ,　／
*yuk°yi-₎ganasyi-**syu**　　*k°umi-nu　syima-gamyi　**yar-i***
[snow-beloved_EX]_PN-**KP**　　**PLN-GEN**　island-deity　**COP-IZ**

'The Deity Yoki-Ganasi,[209] residing in/on the Western[210] Shrine/Peak is indeed the [tutelary] deity of Kume Island.' (os 13.#955)

The following examples illustrate the IZ form in the temporal/conditional clause and concessive clause.

あかの、　おゑづ†きや、　／しまの、　　　よた、ᴧ　やれば*、　／
a ka no ,　o we du† ki ya ,　／ si ma no ,　　yo ta ,ᴧ ya re ba* ,　／
*ʔakʰa-nu　ʔwiidzik°yi-ya*　　*syima-nu　yutʰa　**yar-i-ba***
**PLN-GEN** Owezuki-**TOP**　　Island_BE-**GEN** Yuta　**COP-IZ-T/C**
だ†にる、から、ᴧ　きより　　　　／
da† ni ru , ka ra ,ᴧ ki yo ri　　　／
*danyiru-kʰara　k-°y-uur-yi*
**PLN**-from　　　come-**RY-SE-SS**

'**Since** Owezuki (= Singer)[211] Aka[212] **is** the Island[213] Yuta,[214] he has come from Daniru (= Niruya,[215] the paradise beyond the sea).' (os 8.#454)

---

209　Both tokens in os of 'Yoki-Ganashi' appear in this omoro, spelled with 〈yo〉. Both osjs and Hokama (2000b: 119–120) apply the kanji 〈雪〉 'snow' (OJ *yukî* [JDB 777d–778a]). Hokama assumes the pronunciation *yuki*, apparently based on the assumption that this is a case of "omoro spelling," i.e. historically mistaken spelling due to the merger of high and mid vowels. While this is a real but less common phenomenon than assumed, it is applied here to explain the spelling 〈yo〉 for assumedly historically correct 〈yu〉, given the OJ spelling. 〈yo ki〉 meaning 'pure; white' occurs relatively frequently, with only a few 〈yu〉 used instead of 〈yo〉, implying that *\*yokyi* is the correct older form, regardless of its original meaning.

210　The meaning here is 'West(ern)' instead of the expected 'North(ern)' (note *nísyi* 'north' (OGJ 420a), and *nisyi-buc-yi*, '(winter's) north wind' (OGJ 420a)). This is because *nyisyi-₎dakʰi* is in parallel with *p°yi₎ga-dakʰi* 'Eastern Shrine/Peak' in the same omoro, where *p°yi₎ga- ~ p°yigya-* can only mean 'east', or be the P(L)N 'Higa'. Some idea of the complication of direction terms may be gotten from the following: NOk *fízya* 'Higa (PLN)'; *ʔyíri* 'west' (OGJ 258b) < *\*ʔyir-u-pʰe* 'enter-RT-direction', i.e. the direction you face to see the sun enter the earth; *ʔagári* 'east' (OGJ 103b) < *\*ʔagar-u-pʰe*, i.e. the direction you face to see the sun rise out of the earth ( *\*agaryi \*'east' > ˣʔagayi*); *ʔagari-kata₎* ([OGJ 103b] in Shuri:), *fizya-hoo₎* ([OGJ 242a] in the countryside:) 'eastern direction'.

211　See a discussion of this word in fn. 86 in Ch. 6 §2.2 on song (os 8.#457).

212　osjs (27a) treats Aka (NOk *ʔaka₎* 'Aka_PLN' [OGJ 107a]) and its aligned word, Neha (NOk *nifa₎ ~ nu(u)fa₎* 'Nyoha_PLN' [OGJ 415a]), as synonymous, pointing to the singer's place of birth, near present-day Sobe, Yomitan Village, in central Okinawa.

213　This is a beautifying usage, according to Hokama (2000a: 300b).

214　In present-day Okinawa, a *yuta* is a female shaman. Given that, a suspicion might arise as

AUXILIARIES        359

てだ†が、      おざし∧      やれば*、    /   首里もり、∧
te da† ga ,     o za si ∧     ya re ba* ,   /   SIYO RI mo ri , ∧
*t*ʰ*iida-ga*     *ʔu-zas-yi*     **yar-i-ba**     *syiyuryi-muryi*
Sun.deity-GEN   EX-order-RY<sub>NOM</sub>   COP-IZ-T/C    PLN-grove-TOP

ふさて、      /
pu sa te ,     /
*pº usa-tºi*
prosper-GER

'As [it] **is** the order of the Sun deity, Shuri grove will prosper, and ...' (OS 3.#107)

おなご、あんじ、∧ やれどむ      /
o na go , a N zi , ∧ ya re do mu    /
*wunagu-ʔaɴzyi*    **yar-i-duм**
female-lord      COP-IZ-CONC

'**Even if** [it] **is** a female lord ...' (OS 10.#535)

The next example is controversial.

これど*、∧    だ*にの、∧    まてだ*、∧    やれ    / つくしちやら、
ko re do* , ∧   da* ni no , ∧   ma te da* , ∧   ya re   / tu ku si ti ya ra ,
*kʰuri-du*     *da·nyi-nu*    *ma-tʰi(i)da*   *yar-i*[216]   *cºikºusyi#cʰyara-∅*
this-KP      true-GEN     true-Sun     COP-IZ    (sword.name)-DO

---

      to whether the gender of Aka no Owezuki is male or not. However, it should be pointed out that a *yuta* is indeed a kind of shaman, but has no official status in the Royal hierarchy, and thus is not required to be female. Thus Aka no Owezuki can be—and is—male in this omoro. As for other shamanic figures, *nuuru* (*nuru*, [OGJ 293a, 426b], *nuuru*, [OGJ 428]) are part of the Royal Government's religious hierarchy, and are exclusively female. For more information on *yuta* (e.g. becoming *yuta*, practicing as *yuta*, and a historical survey of *yuta* in Okinawan society), see Katō (1983: 779–780).

215    Regarding the *hapax* ⟨ta⁽ⁿ⁾ ni ru⟩, two hypotheses are presented (OKDJ 399b): (1) OSJS suggests ⟨ta⟩ is a beautifying-like word, and ⟨ni ru⟩ corresponds to ⟨ni ru ya⟩; (2) To Nakasone Seizen (1987 [1979]: 283–293) ⟨da ni ru⟩ means 'the true place', and from that it came to mean 'the ideal land beyond the sea'. We might add one more possibility: *\*nyiruyu →* *\*nyiruda → danyiru*. The word *\*nyiruya* is recognized in OS often in parallel to *kanaya*, both of which mean the ideal land beyond the sea. In NOk, the pairs *.g/n.iree-ka'nee*, and *nirayi-ka'nayi* (OGJ 420a and 419b resp.) are used, but Nakamoto was the first to note that there is no *\*nyi rayi* in OS. For the comprehensive survey of the hypotheses to date, see Mamiya (2014: 81–97). As for the ultimate origin, Nakamoto (1990: 887) hypothesizes *\*myi* 'earth' + *\*-ro* 'GEN' + *\*ya* 'house', presumably the earthly house from which the sun emerges, but that is in the realm of pure conjecture.

216    This is an irregular KM, with *-du* ... IZ where *-du* ... RT is the norm, probably because of

360 CHAPTER 7

はきよわちへ、　　/.../ たま、あしぢ゙や、　　ふみ、よわちへ　　#
pa ki yo wa ti pe, /.../ ta ma, a si di* ya, pu mi, yo wa ti pe #
*pʰak-°y-uwa-c°yi* *tʰama-ʔasyi#ʣya-∅ p°um-y-uwa-c°yi*
wear-RY-EAV-GER jewel-high#clog-DO step-RY-EAV-GER
'This is indeed the true Sun (= King)! ... wearing [his sword] Tsukushi-Chara,
wearing [his] bejeweled_BE clogs.' (OS 6.#324) (OS 22.#1525)

Ifa (1975a [1924]: 168) takes the first verse as part of the KM construction, where
the KP *du* is irregularly bound with IZ. On the other hand, Takahashi (1991a:
242) takes it as MR. Likewise, Uchima (1994: 152) analyzes *yar-i* as MR, but the
KP *du* as bound with the noun *tʰiida* (i.e. 'this *is* the true Sun. Be [that]!').

Yet on another account, Torigoe (1968: 164) takes the *du* (or *doo*) not as a KP
but as an interjectional particle, thus subsequently discerning -*yari* as SS.

The verses that follow the presented line iterate how kingly lord appears,
wearing the precious sword and footgear, *affirming* the status of the lord as the
*true* King, rather than *imploring* the lord to *be* the true king (i.e. Uchima's and
Takahashi's MR account). Because of the overt kingly elements in Ifa's version,
we favor his KM account, which stresses the already existing kingly countenance.

On the other hand, Torigoe's account is actually impossible, since the
spelling ⟨ya rē⟩ can only be construed as either MR or IZ. For it to be either
SS or RY, the spelling has to be ⟨ya rī⟩.

The following are examples of the Gerund of *ya-t°i* < \**yaQ-t°i* < \**yar-u-te* <
\**yar-yi-te* 'COP-RY-GER'. (This historical development ignores the question of
the evolution of the copula root itself.)

かみぎ゙や、　きも ₍ₙ₎　やてや　　　/ いづこ、しま、
ka mi gi* ya, ki mo ₍ₙ₎ ya te ya / i du† ko, si ma,
*kʰamyi-gya k°yimu ya-t°i-ya ʔyiʣi#kʰu-syima-∅*
deity-GEN heart COP-GER-TOP brave-one-island-LOC
おろちへ、　　/
o ro ti pe, /
*ʔuru-c°yi*
bring.down-GER
'As [it] is the deity's will (*lit.* heart/liver), [we] have brought [it (= the purified
water from Heaven)] down to the soldiers' island (i.e. Shuri), and ... .' (OS 7.#348)

---

-*du* and *danyinu* being used together. A doubled number of assertive elements made what
would have been straight *du*-type KM closer to *si*-type, in effect a more focused type.

AUXILIARIES                                                                361

うきおほぢ゛が゛、　　　　　世、ˎ　やてや、　　　/ もゝが゙めむˎˎ
u ki o po di* ga*,　　　　　YO,ˎ ya te ya,　　　/ mo " ga† me mu,ˎ
ʔuu·kˍyi#ʔuQpˍu-dzyi-ˌga　yuu　ya-tˍi-ya　　　mumu-gami-M
great·AA#grand-father-GEN world COP-GER-TOP　hundred-jar-even
すへまし　　　/
su pe ma si　　/
siyi-masyi
prepare-OPT
'Its being the world of our ancestors, we will → expect to → want to serve hundreds of jars [of *sake*].' (OS 11.#559)[217]

## 13.2　*Copula?:* -n[-]ar-

On the assumption, for the time being, that the form *nar-* to be discussed here
is a copula, *-n-ar-* is a contracted from of #*n-yi#ar-* '#COP-RY#STAT-'. Attested
forms include *-n-ar-u* (RT), *-n-ar-i* (IZ) and *-n-ar-i* (MR). By some accounts, this
is classified as a copula, but we will dispute that analysis while examining the
hypothesized copula examples below.

しより、ぐ゙゙に、なる、　　　　　　あんじ゛、/
si yo ri , gu† ni , na ru ,　　　　a N zi*,　 /
syiyuryi-gunyi-**n-ar-u**　　　　ʔaNzyi
Shuri-country-**LOC(/COP)-STAT-RT** lord
ぐ゛すく、ぐ゙゙に、なる、　　　　　　あんじ゛ /
gu* su ku , gu† ni , na ru ,　　　a N zi*　/
gusikˍu-gunyi-**nar-u**　　　　ʔaNzyi
castle-country-**LOC(/COP)-STAT-RT** lord
'The lord **who is in** Shuri, the lord **who is in** the castle.' (OS 11.#527)

OKDJ (⟨na ri⟩ 497ab) interprets the instances in this song as Location-*nar-u* ←
Location-*nyi ar-u*, not copular, and Hokama (2000a: 349b) glosses them with
"*no*" = 'of', an interpretation not at odds with OKDJ. To the extent that he chooses
a non-copular interpretation, we concur. There is no reason to attempt a copula
interpretation.

In the next song below, Hokama (2000b: 146b) ignores the copula interpretation, giving it the interpretation of 'become' instead.

---

217　See §5 of this chapter for further discussion of this song for *ʔuu·kˍyi#ʔuQpˍu-dzyi* and *siyi-*
　　*masyi*.

| ひる〵 | なれば†、〵 | | きも | か、よい〵 |
|---|---|---|---|---|
| pi ru〵 | na re ba†,〵 | | ki mo | ka , yo i〵 |
| *p°yiru-∅* | ***nar-i-ba*** | | *k°yimu-∅* | *kʰayu'-yi*[218] |
| daytime-APP | (COP/)become-IZ-T/C | | heart-SUB | commune-RY |

| かよて | / よる〵 | なれば†、〵 | | いめ |
|---|---|---|---|---|
| ka yo te | / yo ru〵 | na re ba†,〵 | | i me |
| *kʰayu-t°i* | *yuru-∅* | ***nar-i-ba*** | | *ʔyimi-∅* |
| commune-GER | nighttime-APP | (COP/)become-IZ-T/C | | dream-SUB |

| か、よい〵 | かよて | / |
|---|---|---|
| ka , yo i〵 | ka yo te | / |
| *kʰayu'-yi* | *kʰayu-t°i* | |
| commune-RY | commune-GER | |

'When **[it] is** daytime / When day **comes**, [our] hearts commune; When **[it] is** nighttime / when night **comes**, [our] dreams commune.' (OS 14.#996)[219]

Hokama's account accords with our own view:

| ひる ... | / よる ... | なれば†、〵 |
|---|---|---|
| piru... | / yoru ... | na re ba†,〵 |
| *p°yiru-* | *yuru-* | ***nar-i-ba*** |
| daytime-APP | nighttime-APP | **become-IZ-TMP/CND** |

'When it **becomes** day, ... / when it **becomes** night, ...'

| にし〵 | こわば、〵 | にし〵 | | なれ | / はゑ〵 |
|---|---|---|---|---|---|
| ni si〵 | ko wa ba ,〵 | ni si〵 | | na re | / pa we〵 |
| *nyisyi-∅* | *kʰuuw-a-ba* | *nyisyi∅/-∅ /-∅* | | ***nar-i*** | *pʰayi-∅* |
| North.wind-DO | ask-T/C | N.wind∅/-SUB/-APP | * | | South.wind-DO |

| こわば、〵 | はゑ〵 | | なれ | / |
|---|---|---|---|---|
| ko wa ba ,〵 | pawe〵 | | na re | / |
| *kʰuuw-a-ba* | *pʰayi∅/-∅ /-∅* | | ***nar-i*** | |
| ask-TMP/CND | S.wind∅/-SUB/-APP | * | | |

---

218 Concerning the choice of the form *kʰayu'-yi* over the otherwise inferrable *kʰayi-i*, note modern LitOk *kayu-yi,,* (OGJ 301b) almost identical to the OOk form. There may be two reasons for this: (1) *kʰayu-* was retained due to pressure from other identical forms in the paradigm, and (2) Japanese may have had a hand in retaining the diphthong intact. (The verb may be a borrowing, since a correspondence of atonic accent in both languages is anomalous for direct genetic relation.)

219 Ifa sees this as one of the 56 love songs (1975a [1924]: 91), "rare" in the OS.

AUXILIARIES                                                                   363

'Should [the priestess] pray for the North Wind, **may {it.be(come)//
there.be}**[220] the North Wind. Should [the priestess] pray for the South Wind,
**may {it.be(come)//there.be}** the South Wind.' (os 13.#928)

While all three senses seem possible, (a) the first sense (i.e. copular 'be') is
not the only sense, so it is not necessary to choose it, since two other senses
are available; and (b) the second sense (i.e. locative '(may) there be'), while
seeming natural in English, feels somewhat strained in Japanese. All in all,
the third sense, '(may [it]) become', seems the most likely, perhaps in OKDJ
(499ab)'s definitions (1), (2), or (5) of ⟨na ru⟩ 【成る・為る】 : "(1) things and
events come about as an effect; (2) to change [over] to some thing or state;
...; (5) to reach a time or state". In any case, again, there appears to be no
need to accept this item as an example of a purported copula *"nar-yi"*. Indeed,
Occam's Razor, the rule against multiplying entities unnecessarily, certainly
dooms the Copula hypothesis, since it simply is not needed to explain any
of the examples. The only reason that it is even possible to entertain it is
that there is no SS form to certainly decide for or against it on strictly formal
grounds.

What follows is the final claimed example of an *n*-based copula, an item
cited by Vovin (2009a: 536) and adapted here:

| いによはの、 | おきて、もち 〟 | なる | # |
|---|---|---|---|
| i ni yo pa no , | o ki te , mo ti 〟 | na ru | # |
| *ʔyinyupʰa-nu* | *ʔuk˚yic˚yi-muc-˚yi* | ***nar-u*** | |
| Inyoha-GEN | governing-hold-er | COP-RT<sub>NOM</sub> | |

'**the one who is** Administrator of Inyoha' (os 8.#456)

The entire omoro is laid out below with the copula interpretation. The numbers
on the text (left) and their translation (below) match:

| ITI | 1 | *ʔakʰa-nu-kʰu* | *ʔuyidzik˚yi-ya* |
|---|---|---|---|
| | | Aka-GEN-one | Oyezuki-VOC |
| | 2 | *ʔyisyi-kʰani-nu* | *yoo-nyi* |
| | | rock-metal-GEN | like-ADV |
| | 3 | *ʔ(u-)nuc˚yi*[221]-∅ | *c˚ig-y-uwa·r-i* |
| | | EX-life-DO | pass.on-RY-EAV·4GE-MR |

---

220    *= COP/become/ttb-MR.

221    The spelling をのち ⟨wo no ti⟩ is a *hapax* for ⟨we no ti⟩ or ⟨i no ti⟩, the latter the most

| MATA | 4 | *niiQpˤa-nu* | *ʔuyidžikˤyi-ya* |
|------|---|-------------|-------------------|
|      |   | Neha-GEN    | Oyezuki-VOC       |
| MATA | 5 | *ʔyinyuQpˤa-nu* | *ʔukˤyicˤyi-muc-ˤyi **nar-u**-∅* |
|      |   | Inyoha-GEN  | governing-hold-er COP-RT-IO |

1 The Oyezuki, the one from Aka [addresses ...]
4 The Oyezuki of Neha [= Aka] [addresses ...]
5 ... the one who is Administrator of Inyoha:
3 "Continue [your] exalted life!
2 [Long,] like rock or metal!"

There appears to be one other option besides a copula interpretation:

MATA  *ʔyinyuQpˤa-nu*  *ʔukˤyicˤyi-muc-ˤyi*-∅  **nar-u**-∅
Inyoha-GEN  g'ship-hold-er-APP  become-RT$_{NOM}$-IO
'to the one who will become ☐ A. of I.'

In other words, 'Pass on exalted life, [long,] like rock or metal, to the one who will become Administrator[222] of Inyoha.' This seems like a perfectly straightforward interpretation, though it involves two "zeroes" in the OOk phrasing, as marked by the squares above, in the post-major-word slots: (1) 'to-the.one.who-will.become'; (2) 'become ∅-Administrator'.

---

plentiful. Why are we faced with the highly unusual ⟨wo⟩, which seems to replace *ʔyi* of *ʔyi̱nucˤyi* (< *ʔyi̱notyi*) 'life(-force); (long) life', and which normally writes *ʔu* or *wu*? There are two equally palatable answers:

a) The first is that ⟨wo⟩ writes *ʔu*, and is the EX prefix, attached to the word, but with the glottal- (i.e. vowel-)initial syllable of *ʔyi̱nucˤyi* dropped; while by no means universal, the phenomenon is also seen elsewhere in OS.

b) The second appears to lie with NOk *nucyi̱* '(id.)' (OGJ 423b), the colloquial form equivalent to LitOk *ʔyinucyi̱*. The pre-OOk high-vowel moras *ʔyi* and *ʔu* tend, in word-initial position, to trace the following weakening path (where *N* stands for "nasal" or "(phonetically) prenasalized voiced obstruent"): *ʔyiN/ʔuN → ʔNN → ʔN → N*. (This weakening path is also a sequence of decreasing politeness.) This is seen in e.g. *ʔyiméɴseen* (OGJ 254b) → *ʔɴméɴseen* → male-gentry *ʔméɴseen* (OGJ 352) → ColloqOk *ménsyeen* (OGJ 368b) 'come/go/be', in e.g. the commonly seen and heard expression of welcome, ColloqOk *ménsoore(e)* (gentry-speech *ʔméɴsyooree*). The upshot: ⟨wo no ti⟩ is a one-off spelling of *ʔnucˤyi*, a form on its way to what would become the ColloqOk *nucyi̱*.

222 OKDJ gives two LitOk pronunciations under ⟨o ki te⟩ (124d–125b): non-PPed *ʔucyi̱ti* (likely a hypercorrection based on spelling, like English ['ɔftɪn] for the historically correct ['ɔfn:] 'often') and PPed *ʔuQcˤyi* (cf. NOk [obsolete] *ʔúQcyi* [OGJ 559b]). The form here is pur-

# AUXILIARIES

Assuming this interpretation, the need for an *n*-based copula in OOk evaporates.

## 13.3 Historical and Comparative Analysis

What if the two copula forms OOk *-yar-yi-* and OJ *nar-i* are related? If they are not, what would be the progenitor for OOk *-yar-yi-*? Torigoe (1968: 163) asserts that they are related because of the change from OJ copula *n(-i )ar-i* to *yar-i* (i.e. in the Kinki region) in the Muromachi period (1336–1573), and further, because of *yar-i*'s present-day existence in the Kinki area dialects. Handa (1999: 224), like Torigoe, sees the NOk copula *-ya-yi-*—most likely descended from OOk *-yar-yi-*—as related to the copula *ya* in the Kinki dialects.

Vovin (2009a: 528–529) notes that in OJ, the uncontracted form of the copula, *ni ar-*, is more frequent than the contracted one, *nar-*, but by MJ, the contracted one is the norm. In OOk, only the contracted form is claimed to be attested. Vovin (536) and Shimizu (2003: 115) speculate that OOk *naryi* may be a loan, though we have shown that in fact this alleged *n*-copula did not in fact exist in texts. We believe, however, that—of course—pre-OOk had its own copula, and, unsurprisingly, it was either similar or identical to the *n*-initial copula of the Japanese lineage. Note, however, that the initial \**n* had disappeared before the advent of written records, as explained below.

The pre-OOk reconstruction is \**n-yi#ar-* or \**n-yi#te#ar-*, with either choice leading to \*{*yár-* 'COP[ULA]'}.[223] In later Okinawan, there occurred some sort of contamination involving the almost identical topic particle and its allomorphs, allowing hybrid forms such as the sentence *ʔaraɴ* '[It] is not [so]', with

---

posely written as non-PPed, appearing thus in at least 27 tokens. OOk ⟨o ki te⟩ is a loan from MJ *okite* 'regulation', and is apparently monomorphemic, thus most naturally written without PP spelling, regardless of PP pronunciation. Non-PP spellings for PPed forms in case of \**Ce* syllables are especially common, such as:

(a) ⟨i se⟩ ~ ⟨i si⟩ *ʔyisyi* 'superior, splendid (etc.)'; BE ([OSJS 55c]; in e.g. [OS 3.#91]) ?< 'rock(-like)' (Ch. 4 §2.1.1); (b) ⟨i si ke na pa⟩ *ʔyisyik°yi#napʰa* 'Ishike-Naha (PLN)' (§1.3 in [OS 12.#700], §11.7 in [OS 13.#785]); (c) ⟨si ke u ti⟩ *syik°yi#ʔuc°yi* 'sanctum interior' (§2.1 in [OS 1.#20]); (d) ⟨si ge ti⟩ *syigyi#c°yi* 'sacred sake' (§3.1 in [OS 11.#643]); (e) ⟨yo ri i de⟩ *yur-yi#ʔyidzyi-* 'coming out [to dance]' (§7.1 in [OS 19.#757]); (f) ⟨i ke i ke oi⟩ *ʔyik°yi#ʔyik°yi·syi* 'full of life' (Ch. 5 §3.1.2 in [Hokama 2000a: 432a] [OS 11.#648]); (g) ⟨ma mi ti ke⟩ *mamyic°yik°yi* 'Mamichike (PN)' (Ch. 5 §4.4: [OS 5.#264] [OSJS 484c]).

On the other hand, a single PPed token exists of a lookalike word:

⟨o ki t̄i p̄e ta te⟩ *ʔuk°yi#cʰyii-tʰatˀi*, 'small fishing craft', *lit.* 'offshore-hand(=mast-)erect' [OSJS 75a].

223 Compare the accentuation of *ʔa-ɴ* (atonic), just the opposite of *yá-ɴ* (tonic), suggesting that the accent of the copula is due to the copula core morpheme itself, thus, prelimilarily, \**nV́-* 'COP' (tonic), with the accent of the following morpheme(s) being effaced.

no {ya+} 'COP' morpheme on the surface.[224] There *is* a *nar-* allomorph of the copula *as a surface form* in MOk, and that is a borrowing from MJ, and it is shortlived, appearing only in Ryūka and Kumiodori, and not in OOk at all.

## 14 Exalting Auxiliary Verb: *-(u)wa·r/s-*

The form *-(u)wa·r/s-* may be characterized as an Exalting Auxiliary Verb (EAV); since it happens to have a sister Verb that is largely identical, but functions as a Verb. The auxiliary function is derived historically from the main-verb function; this is a common occurrence both in Ryukyuan and in Japanese. The EAV elevates the subject of the sentence, and thus turns an ordinary Verb into one expressing respect directed toward its grammatical subject. In the OS these subjects are deities, priestesses, kings, or lords. The EAV attaches to the RY of the main verb, as detailed below. It is usually referred to as |owaru|:

> *-(u)wa·r-* ~
> *-(u)wa·{s}-* ~
> *-(u)wa(-)*

It is probably no exaggeration to say that this is the most important auxiliary both in its token frequency and in its semantic indispensability in the religious contexts of the OS. It appears in an extremely common lexicalized verb compound *c°yuwar-* 'exaltedly be' in OS (§14.2), is preserved in NOk *miseeN*, 'exaltedly do/eat/say' (§14.3), and evinces its trace in the NOk softener *wa* (§14.4). It is also illuminating in a historical and comparative analysis with its OJ/MJ counterparts OJ *öpömasu* >MJ> *opasu* > *ofasu* > *owasu* (§14.5). This section also touches upon the honorific *taboo·r/s-* 'deign to give' (§14.6).

### 14.1 *Allomorphs and Examples*
Here are examples of the allormorphs *-(u)wa·r-* and *-(u)wa·{s}-*. Their historical development and comparative analysis with their OJ and MJ counterparts are discussed fully in §14.5.

---

224 Now typically affirmative sentences with a final copula in NOk end with X##{ya}+ {?ar}+{m}, whereas in the negative, the {ya} morpheme is treated the same as a topic/contrast marker: X+{ya}##{?ar}+{an}. So: *syimucyi yaN* '[It]'s a book.' *syimucyee araN* '[It] isn't a book.'

AUXILIARIES                                                                    367

### 14.1.1    Fuller Examples of -(u)wa·r-

MZ:    おぎ゚やかもいしゆ、∧　さしよわめ
       o gi* ya ka mo i si yu , ∧    sa si yo wa me
       *ʔu-gyaka-mii-syu*          *sas-y-**uwa**-m-i*
       EX-shine-EX-KP             wear-EAV$_{MZ}$-IA-IZ
       '[The True Sword in the Palace Confines], it is The Shining One himself
       who will **deign** to wear [it].' (OS 12.#660)

RY:    あおりや、∧　とりよわり　　　／ ておりや、∧
       a o ri ya , ∧   to ri yo wa ri      / te o ri ya , ∧
       *ʔawur.yi-ya*   *tʰur-y-**uwa·r**-yi*    *tʰi-wur-yi-ya*
       *ryansan*-TOP  take-RY-**EAV·r**-RY  hand-bend-RY$_{NOM}$-TOP
       とりよわり　　　　　／
       to ri yo wa ri     /
       *tʰur-y-**uwa·r**-yi*
       take-RY-**EAV·r**-RY
       '… **deign**ing to take up the *ryansan*[225] (= the cooling( ones)), **deign**ing to
       take up the folding fans (= the hand-bend(ings)), [the priestesses will fill
       each warship with spiritual power as it is completed and launched] … .'
       (OS 1.#38)

RT:    かみ∧てだの、　／ まぶり、よわる、∧　　　あんじ゚おそい ／
       ka mi ∧ te da no , / ma bu ri , yo wa ru , ∧  a N zi* o so i   /
       *kʰamyi-tʰiida-nu*   *maʙr-y-**uwa·r**-u*   *ʔaɴzyi-ʔusii*
       deity-sun-SUB        protect-RY-**EAV·r**-RT lord-ruler
       '[Look!—it is] the Ruler over the Lords, whom the Sun Deity deigns to be
       protecting.' (OS 1.#2)

---

225  In premodern-Ryukyu historical studies these specially constructed Chinese-style para-
     sols are called *ryansan*. The word to be found in OGJ (447b) is *ránsaɴ*, glossed as 'parasol
     carried above the King's palanquin, usually *ʔu-ránsaɴ*'. The characters associated with it
     are 〈涼傘〉, which in J are pronounced *ryōsan*, referring to a (*lit.* 'cool[ing]') parasol. In reli-
     gious studies they, along with the folding fans, are thought to be places for the deities to
     alight. At the time of the compilation of OSJS, it was not yet well understood that 〈ri〉 and
     〈re〉 were distinguished, and so the compilers of this mid-20th-century dictionary mis-
     takenly believed that 〈te o ri〉 was the same as 〈te ni o re〉 'heaven-alighting' (〈〈teori〉〉
     [OSJS 230b]). This has since been corrected in newer works: cf. OKDJ 〈〈te-wori〉〉 (446d),
     or Hokama ([2000a: 40b, 41b, 42b] [OS 1.#38]), but the interpretation of a place where
     spiritual power is gathered has remained.

In the above case it seems reasonable to assume that the original Progressive meaning (cf. functions of SE *-ar-* in *-(y)a(a)r-(yi)* as Progressive Aspect marking in §12) is still operative, even though formally it is no different from the others.

RT:   ひやくさ、ᴧ        なるぎ*やめむ、      / おもかわり、ᴧ
      pi ya ku sa ,ᴧ     na ru gi* ya me mu ,   / o mo ka wa ri ,ᴧ
      *pʰyakºu-see-∅*    *nar-u-gyami-M*         *ʔumu-kʰawar-yi-∅*
      100-years.old-APP  become-RT-until-even    face-change-RY_{NOM}-DO
      しよわるな                    /
      si yo wa ru na                /
      *s-y-uwa·r-u-na*
      do-RY-EAV·r-RT-NEG_{MR}
      '[O Exalted Lord Ruler, Exalted Fatherly One!—] deign not to change your visage even unto the age of 100 years!' (OS 7.#363)

IZ:   てにの、     いのり、      しよわれば*、              /
      te ni no ,   i no ri ,      si yo wa re ba* ,           /
      *tʰinyi-nu*   *ʔyi̜nur-yi-∅ s-y-uwa·r-i-ba*
      heaven's     pray-er-DO    do-RY-EAV·r-IZ-TMP
      'since [she] has deigned to perform the prayer[226] to heaven, ...' (OS 1.#4)

---

226   This omoro includes two words that represent different strains in spelling or pronunciation. One is *ʔyinyupʰa* 'Inoha', a place name, which has an overtly spelled PP of *n*, otherwise relatively rare. The other is ⟨i no ri⟩, which we have transcribed as *ʔyi̜nur-yi*, a deverbal noun to which is appended a reverbalization with *s-* 'do'. Interestingly, a Buddhist priest named Taichū who had spent time in Ryukyu before the Satsuma invasion of 1609 recorded some omoro performances, and the word in question was transcribed as ⟨i ni yu ri yu wo wa re ba⟩, probably *ʔyinyur-y-uwa·r-i-ba* (or ...*-ywo(o)wariba*), with PP, not with an exception to it (Ikemiya [2015: 190–192], citing Taichū's *Ryūkyū Shintō-ki*). Relatively few *n-* and *r*-initial moras are written as PPed, despite being in a PP environment. Why would they not be written out with PP spelling if they undergo it? There is no more difficulty writing PP spelling for these than for any other moras. We have written the exception marker throughout, awaiting enlightenment. [Possibly, coronal sonorants are *automatically* PP'ed in the appropriate environments, making them psychologically non-salient, whereas the "elsewhere" cases are more "noticeable", and therefore psychologically salient, thus more susceptible to PP spelling conventions.]

AUXILIARIES                                                                    369

MR: いしかねの、　　　やに、　/ をのち、ᴧ　　　　つぎˮよわれ　　　　　　　/
i si ka ne no ,　　ya ni ,　/ wo no ti ,ᴧ　　tu giˮ yo wa re　　　　/
ʔyisyi-kʰani227-nu yoo-nyi　ʔ(u-)nucˮyi-∅228 cˮig-y-**uwa·r**-i
rock-metal-GEN　like-ADV　(EX)-life-DO　continue-RY-**EAV·r**-MR
'Deign to continue your life (long), like rock or metal!' (OS 8.#456)

14.1.2　　　Examples of -uwa·{s}-

きこゑ、　　大ぎˮみぎや、　　　/ おぼつ　ゑが、ᴧ
ki ko we ,　OPO giˮ mi gi ya ,　/ o bo tu　we ga ,ᴧ
kˮyi̜kˮuyi ʔuQpˮu-gyimyi-gya　ʔubucˮi　yii-gaa-∅
famed　　great-priestess-SUB　Heaven₁ auspicious-day-DO
とりよわす、　　　/ ... とよむ、　　　せだˮかこが、　/ かぐˮら
to ri yo wa su ,　/ ... to yo mu ,　se daˮ ka ko ga ,　/ ka guˮ ra
tʰur-y-**uwa·s**-i　　　tʰuyum-u　　si.dakʰa.kʰu-ga　　kʰaɢra
take-RY-**EAV·s**-SS　renowned-RT Sedakako_PN-SUB　Heaven₂
ゑが、ᴧ　　　　　とりよわす。
we ga ,ᴧ　　　　to ri yo wa su 。
yii-gaa-∅　　　　tʰur-y-**uwa·s**-i
auspicious-day-DO take-RY-**EAV·s**-SS
'The Famed High Priestess [= Kikoe Ōgimi, i.e.], the Renowned Sedakako [=
the One of High Spiritual Power], will **deign to** divine the auspicious day for
the Obotsu Heaven, [that is,] for the Kagura Heaven.' (OS 3.#88)

We know of no explanation for the round period ⟨。⟩ seen after the second verse-
pair, and therefore we have ignored it. The parallel words ʔubucˮi and kʰaɢra
both refer to Heaven, very important words in this religious text.
　　The next two examples do not really directly show the existence of {s}, but
it is ascertainable from the PP'd -t of the gerund {tˮee} (cf. §14.5).

たちよわちへ、　　　　　/
ta tɪ yo wa ti pe ,　　　/
tʰac-ˮy-**uwa**-cˮyi
set.off-**EAV-GER**(/**PRFV**)
'[Kikoe Ōgimi] **deigned to** set off (to battle), and ...' (OS 1.#25)

―――――――
227　The interlineation here says, "Chōmei no koto nari." = "It refers to long life." This is a *hapax*.
228　For discussion of this form, see fn. 221.

| | | | |
|---|---|---|---|
| ¹きこゑ | あおりやい、 | / ²おれて、、 | あすび*、よわれば†、 / |
| ki ko we | a o ri ya i , | / o re te , ^ | a su bi* , yo wa re ba† , / |
| k°yi̥k°uyi | ʔawuryayi | ʔuri-t°i | ʔasib-y-**uwa·r**-i-ba |
| famed | Aoriae | descend-GER(/PRFV) | dance-RY-**EAV·r**-IZ-T/C |

| | | |
|---|---|---|
| ³ひやし、、 うちちへ、 | / ⁴きみよ、、 | |
| pi ya si , ^ u ti ti pe , | / ki mi yo , ^ | |
| p°yoosyi-∅ ʔuQ-c°yi | k°yimyi-yu | |
| rhythm-DO beat-GER(/PRFV) | priestess-DO | |

| | | |
|---|---|---|
| ぶ†れよわせ | / ⁵とよむ、 | あおりやへや、 / |
| bu† re yo wa se | / to yo mu ^ | a o ri ya pe ya , / |
| buri·y-**uwa·**₁**r/s-a**₁s-i | tʰuyum-u | ʔawuryayi-ya |
| gather_vı-EP.y-**EAV·**₁**r/s-CA**₁US-MR | resound-RT | Aoriae-TOP |

| | | |
|---|---|---|
| ⁶玉なるし、、 とりよわちへ | # | |
| TAMA na ru si , ^ to ri yo wa ti pe | # | |
| tama.nar.u.syii-∅ tʰur-y-**uwa**-c°yi | | |
| Tamanaru.shī-DO take-RY-**EAV**-GER(/PRFV) | | |

'¹,⁵Famed, Renowned [Priestess] Aoriae, ²when you **deign to** descend [from Heaven] and dance—⁶**deign**ing **to** take (up) (the hand-drum) Tama-Naru-Shī [= BE-resound-one_BE] and ³beat the rhythm—⁴**deign to** cause the priestesses to dance together!' (OS 12.#686)

The complete omoro of the above is presented below in order to give the appropriate context for understanding the form ⟨bu† re yo wa se⟩ *buriyuwasi*.²²⁹ The omoro appears to beseech the priestess Aoriaye, the highest priestess in the land—before the advent of the office of Kikoe Ōgimi in the Second Shō Dynasty—to ritually descend to the holy ground and to lead the assembled priestesses in dancing, using the named hand-drum Tama-Naru-Shī, lit.

---

229  A secondary point, this one about the main lexical theme of *buri·y-uwa·s-i*: a L2G verb such as this should have the predicted form *buri-wa·s-i**, not found in texts. The verb root literally means 'gather vı', not 'gather and dance' or 'dance together': The *buri-* of *buri·y-uwa·s-i* is claimed to mean just 'dance' in OSJS (290a), even though *kanji-kana*-glossed with 群れ 'gather vı'; Hokama (2000a: 455b) glosses it 'have [them] *dance together*'. A compound *bure-ma{w}*- 'gather and dance' numbers 14 tokens. Just one token, ₁₁*ʔasib-yi*₁₁-*buri -may*₁-*i-ba*₁ 'when they dance and dance-together' (OS 7.#370), suggests that {buri#maw+} is treated as a single lexical entity. For the unusual form of the lexical root/compound, two possibilities arise: a) the ur-scribe accidentally dropped the ⟨ma⟩ of ⟨pu⁽ᵐ⁾ re ma̅ yo wa se)*, and all later copyists faithfully followed; or b) since the post-asterisked term has a double meaning, the other one being 'causing [the] massed [priestesses] to lose their senses', dropping *ma* was an intentional taboo deformation. In any case, the word is a *hapax*.

AUXILIARIES                                                                    371

'Jewel(-like) Resounding [Animate] One'.

As is usual in omoros, the song uses parallelism: cf. 1‖5 and 3‖6. In addition, as usual, the omoro is divided into body and refrain portions, albeit a bit unusually: Verses 2 and 4 are meant to be repeated as refrains:

| k°yi̠k°uyi ʔawuryayi | 1 | Famed Aoriae, |
| *ʔuritʰ°i ʔasibyuwariba* | *2* | *When you deign to descend and dance,* |
| p°yoosyi ʔuQc°yi | 3 | Beating the rhythm, |
| *k°yimyiyu buriyuwa['a]si* | *4* | *Deign to cause the priestesses to dance together!* |
| tʰuyumu ʔawuryayiya | 5 | (The) renowned Aoriae |
| *ʔuritʰ°i ʔasibyuwariba* | *2* | *When you deign to descend and dance,* |
| tʰamanarusyii tʰuryuwac°yi | 6 | Deigning to take up (the hand-drum) Tama-Naru-Shī, |
| *k°yimyiyu buriyuwa['a]si* | *4* | *Deign to cause the priestesses to dance together!* |

The EAV appears appended to three verbs, giving the examples *ʔasib-y-uwa·r-i-ba* 'when/because you dance', *tʰur-y-uwa-c°yi* 'deigning to take (up); having deigned to take (up); deigned to take (up)', and of course the verb that we wish to focus on: ⟨buᵗ re yo wa se⟩ *buri·y-uwa·₍r/s-a₎s-i*, our attempt to show two candidate surface phonetic forms [burɪyuwɑsɪ] and [burɪyuwɑːsɪ], differing only in the choice of either short [ɑ] or long [ɑː], and the possibility that they come either from an underlying form (and presumably historically earlier form as well)

{buri+(maw+yi+)uwa·r+as+i 'assemble'+EAV·r+CAUS+MR} or
{buri+(maw+yi+)uwa·s+as+i 'assemble'+EAV·s+CAUS+MR},

where the only difference is an extension {·r+} or {·s+} on the {+EAV+} root. More exactly, the candidate historical forms are either *\*bure#maw-yi#opʰa·r-as-e* or *\*bure#maw-yi#opʰa·s-as-e*. If this form is very old, then the reconstructions are fictions based on the song's context, and actually what you *get* is what you *see*: *\*bure#opʰa#se-∅* \*'assemble#deign#do-MR'. This seems satisfactory save for one problem, namely, that it lacks an overt causative morpheme. Perhaps it did not need one, since it would otherwise have appeared as ˣ-(*y*-)*uwa*(*a*), with a dropped consonant. We can say that one consonant will always drop in the MR, and so if the phoneme ···s··· appears, it is the ···s··· of the causative, not of the EAV root extension.

372                                                                                    CHAPTER 7

**14.2** *The Lexicalized Compound* c°yuwar- *'Exaltedly Be'* < *k-yi-owar-*
*'Deign to Come'*

Forms such as ちよわれ = ⟨ti yo wa re⟩ = *c°yuwar-i* come from *\*k-yi-* 'come-RY'
+ *\*-owar-e* '-EAV-MR' (← *\*owa[s-u]r-* 'exaltedly come/be/go'), through palatalization and affrication of the velar. Elsewhere in OS, the velar-plus palatal
sequence *\*ky* remains unaffricated until after the OOk period. Thus, this is an
exceptional case, since e.g. the *k*-type 4G verb RY is always ···*k-°yi*, never ˣ···*c-°yi*.
The exalting verb form *c°yuwar-i*_MR 'be, if it please you!' (← *c°yuwar-* ~ ... 'exaltedly be') is a typical example of formal irregularity in the formation of exalting
verbs, at least in Okinawan and Japanese, and such irregularity is probably to
be found in other languages as well.

The form (etc.) then extended its meaning from 'come + exaltedly be' to
'exaltedly be (/come/go)'. (Cf. NJ *iraQsyár-u* and *-te-iraQsyar-u* for a similar
semantic extension):[230]

'come and exaltedly be'      >
'be coming'                  >
'exaltedly be (/come/go)'

Here are some examples of MZ, RT, IZ, and MR.

まぶ*り、よわば*、        / もゝすゑ、ᴧ    ちよわれ        /
ma bu*ri, yo wa ba*, / mo " su we,ᴧ ti yo wa re  /
*maBr-y-uwa-ba*          *mumu-siyi*   *c°yuwa·r-i*
protect-RY-EAV_MZ-T/C    100-endings   **reign**_EX·r-MR
'If (i.e. given that) [the Sun Deity] **deigns to** protect [the Sovereign_i], may [he_i]
**honor us by reigning** for 100 generations!' (OS 11.#617)

Given the form *maBr-y-uwa*_MZ-*ba*_T/C in this verse, the default interpretation is
the conditional 'if'. However, because the deity's protection is assured in the
preceding verse ('none other than the Shining Well will protect you'), it is more
appropriate semantically to interpret it as 'given that'. Indeed, when the same
verse appears near the end of the omoro, it takes the IZ form (*maBr-y-uwa·r-i*
*-ba*), that is, the easily understood 'because' interpretation.[231]

---

230   It is not unusual for the verbs of *coming-being-disappearing*, i.e. 'come-be-go', to form a
      natural class. These unaccusative verbs are not found in transitive-intransitive dyads, and
      they often trigger a syntactic inversion (e.g. in English 'there appeared SUBJECT'). For more
      on this class of verbs, see Shinzato (2010).

231   The only written difference between them is the ex- or in-clusion of れ ⟨re⟩, raising a sus-

AUXILIARIES                                                                    373

The following is a very late-appearing usage of RY + -*c°yuwa*··· as an EAV similar in meaning and usage to the earlier-developed RY + -(*u*)*wa*···.

きこゑ、　　せのきみや、　　／ いのり、やり、ᴧちよわば†、　／
ki ko we ,　se no ki mi ya ,　／ i no ri , ya ri , ᴧ ti yo wa ba† , ／
*k°yi͵k°uyi　sinuk°yimyi-ya　　ʔyi͵nur-yaar-yi-c°yuwa-ba*
famed　　　Se.no.Kimi-TOP　　pray-PROG-**RY-EAV**-T/C
'If the famed Se-no-Kimi **deigns to** keep praying, ...' (OS 3.#88)

The form -*yaar-yi*- (§ 12) is the Progressive, while the form -*c°yu-wa*- adds exaltation. In the OS almost all examples of *c°yuwa*··· are main verbs, but in the
language of the stele inscriptions, some of which actually predate the OS, but
which postdate the OS language in form and usage, it occurs only as EAV (Oshiro
[1987: 48–49]).

まだま、もり、ᴧ　　　　ちよわる、　／ てだが†、　　　ませ、ᴧ
ma da ma , mo ri , ᴧ ti yo wa ru , ／ te da ga† ,　　ma se , ᴧ
*ma.dama.muryi　　c°yuwa·r-u　　tʰiida-ga　　ma-sii*
Madama.Mori_{PLN}　　**dwell**_{EX}**·r**-RT　　sun-SUB/GEN true_{BE}-s.p[232]
うきゆ、ぐ†も、　　　／
u ki yu , gu† mo ,　／
*ʔuk°-y-u-gumu*
float-RY-SE-cloud
'... the Sovereign [lit. 'the True-Spiritual-Power-Floating-Clouds-of-the-Sun']
who **deigns to dwell** [at] Madama-Mori [= the Castle where Madama-Mori
Shrine is] ...' (OS 3.#90)

ひやくさ、ぎ*やめ、　　　　／ おぎ*やかもいしよ、ᴧ　　ちよわれ　　／
pi ya ku sa , gi* ya me ,　　／ o gi* ya ka mo i si yo , ᴧ ti yo wa re　　／
*pʰyaak°u-see-gyaami　　ʔu-gyakʰa-mii-syu　　c°yuuwa·r-i*
100-years-TRM　　　　　　EX-shining.one-EX-KP rule_{EX}**·r**-IZ
'For 100 years (i.e. forever) the Shining One [= King Shō Shin] is who **will deign
to rule**.' (OS 1.#18)

---

        picion that the difficulty in interpretation stems from the ur-scribe's having accidentally
        dropped ⟨re⟩ in this verse, but not in the other.
232    s.p = spiritual.power.

374                                 CHAPTER 7

**14.3**    *OOk |mesiyowaru| 'Deign to Do/Eat/Drink/Wear/Put on (etc.)' > NOk
miseeN, 'Exaltedly Do/Eat/Say'*

Another compound incorporating the OOk auxiliary -*uwar/s*- is the NOk exalting verb *miseeN,* [mʸisɛːn] 'exaltedly say/do/eat' (OGJ 381b; the sense 'eat$_{EX}$' is
(was) used toward older commoners by gentry-class speakers).

The parallel NOk EAV -*mis(y)e'eN* ~ -*Ns(y)e'eN* is built off of the independent
verb \**mes-yi-owar/s*-,[233] present in OS as only an independent verb |mesiy-
owaru| *mis-y-uwar/s*-. Only two forms appear in the text, ⟨me si yo wa ti pe⟩
(17 tokens) and ⟨me si yo wa re⟩ (one token).

あけの、       よろい、ʌ   めしよわちへ、           /
a ke no ,     yo ro i ,ʌ  me si yo wa ti pe ,     /
ʔakʰi-nu     yuruyi-∅  **mis-y-uwa-cʲyi**
fine$_{BE}$-APPO  armor-DO  **wear**$_{EX}$-RY-EX-GER/PRFV
'[Kikoe Ōgimi,] **deign**ing **to put on** the fine armor, ...' (OS 1.#5)

うまが゚なし、ʌ    めしよわれ   /
u ma ga゚ na si ,ʌ me si yo wa re  /
ʔuma-ganasyi-∅  **misyuwa·r-i**
horse-BE-DO     **ride**$_{EX}$**·r**-MR
'[O Nikuke-sha,] **deign to ride** [your] fine horse!' (OS 16.#1138)

Interestingly, even before the writing of the first *Omoro Sōshi* book in 1531, there
were already a handful of stele inscriptions that reflected an already newly
developed later form of exalting language. More specifically, there appeared
an EAV -*misyuwar/s*- (Oshiro [1987: 48–49]). Reflecting the fact that the OS
language—which had only had a full verb usage, and not yet developed such
an EAV—, and the received wisdom that main verb usage is older than the auxiliary verb usage (Traugott and Dasher 2002), it follows that the OS language
was highly conservative, while the stele language reflected more closely the
language of actual aristocratic speech. After that, too, there proceeded mas-
sive changes in form. The alternant with {s} is part of the morphophonemic-
form base for e.g. gerunds, something already familiar because of the use of
\**owa·r/s*-:

---

233    The origin of \**mes-u* is apparently in MJ *mes-u* < OJ *mês-u.* (Cf. also JDB [734c–735a] *mês-
u.*) SWEDJ explains the form as originally the exalting form of *mi-ru* 'see'. It had already
developed a whole array of other meanings even in OJ, and included the meanings seen
in OOk by the time of at least the 1200's.

# AUXILIARIES

{mis+yi+uwa·s+yi+tʰee} → *mis-y-uwa-cʰyi*.

The {s} never actually appears in the output form.

Here is a short example: In the OS one finds forms interpretable as *misyuwar-* ~ ... meaning 'exaltedly be/come/go', and which are a combination of earlier *\*mes-yi-* 'exaltedly see (etc.)' + *\*owar(/s)-*. The former form *\*mes-* is widely seen even in NJ, in examples such as *o-ki ni mes-u* 'it appeals to you' (cf. Shakespeare's *As You Like It*, translated as *O-Ki ni Mesu Mama*), or in the now-homely word *mesyi* = *meshi* 'cooked rice; a meal'. In the stele inscriptions these forms, while written in omoro orthography, are attached to verb RY, and have become EAVs, in other words, what omoro language uses just *-(u)war(/s)-* for, and their form is now the male gentry-class NOk, e.g. ...-*misee-N* (~ ...-*Nsee-N*) / ...-*misyoo-cyi* (~ ...-*Nsyoo-cyi*). One still sees the *\*-owar(/s)-* forms in Ryukyuan languages and dialects that are relatively far from the old Shuri/Naha cultural center, typically as:

*-oor(/s)-*.

The old omoro forms have been superseded by descendants of the newer *-misyuwa* ... as the new exalting auxiliaries, and in addition the independent *ʔuwa* ... have disappeared, as well. The old morphemes still exist in modern Okinawan in highly modified forms:

− *misyoo-cyi* 'exaltedly be-ing, etc.' < ... < *mis-y-uwa-cʰyi* < *\*mes-yi#owas-yi-te*

− *-misyoo-cyi* ~ *-Nsyoo-cyi* 'exaltedly V-ing' < ... < (same)
  Contemporary Shuri *misoo-cyi, -misoo-cyi* ~ *Nsoo-cyi*

− *misee-N* < ... < *\*mes-yi#owar-yi#wo-mu* '... (sentence-ending form)'
  Contemporary Shuri *misyee-N* < ... < (same)

Let us now return to our starting point, *cʸyuwa* ...: Along with the forms given just above, it exists, at least as a form in OGJ (537b):

> *ʔu-cyee-yi-miseʔe-N*, "To exaltedly deign to be/go/come. ... Honorific language used in reference to the nobility. The ordinary honorific language of gentry-class people to each other is *ʔmeNsee-N*."

The word, if it were actually to have existed long ago with the components represented in the present-day form, is as follows, with coordinate structures over time indicated:

| | | | | | | | | | | | | |
|---|---|---|---|---|---|---|---|---|---|---|---|---|
| * o | + k - | yi + owa | r - | yi + | wor - | yi + | mes - | yi + | owar - | yi + | wor - | u + mo |
| * ʔu - | c | ˚y wa | y | y | - yi + | mis | y | wa | y - | y | | u - N |
| * ʔu - | c | y | ee | | - yi - | mis | | ee | - | yi | | - N |
| ʔu - | | cyee | | | - yi - | | | misee | | | | - N |

Of course, such a full form probably never existed. Rather, it is more likely that ʔu-cyee-yi- and -misee-N were put together at a later date, and that before that each had its own parallel history.

### 14.4 Pre-OOk EAV + IA: *-(o)was-a > NOk wa 'Softener'

As seen below, what appears to be the bare root of the EAV (i.e. -uwa below) is functionally a MR. OSJS (99a) only gives it in its entirety as functionally an imperative, simply glossing it as J -tamae 'deign to ...!'.

| おれて、₍ | おれ、なふしよわ | / |
|---|---|---|
| o re te , ₍ | o re , na pu si yo wa | / |
| ʔuri-tʰee | ʔuri-nawus-y-uwa | |
| descend-GER/PRFV | descend-do.again-RY-EAV_MR | |

'Having descended, deign to descend again!' (OS 1.#24)

OKDJ ([173 cd] [specifically for this word]; [145 a–d] [for |ofaru|]) says that it is not clear whether the form should be reconstructed as having *···wara or *···wasa. However, while s-dropping is otherwise documented, r-dropping before MOk is not.[234] We believe that its most likely source is the pre-OOk EAV with added IA: *-(o)was-a, followed by dropping of *···s··· to *-(o)waʹa, and shortening of the vowel sequence to *-(o)wa, and mid vowel raising to -(u)wa.

An example in NOk of an IA used as an indirect imperative form is díi numa, 'well, then, let's (you) drink! [MOTHER TO CHILD]'. The form -wa survives today in attenuated form as the Softener of the direct MR: kak-i 'write-MR' + -wa 'SOFT' → kak-i-wa ~ kak-e-e 'write-MR, won't you?'. The odd attachment to MR instead of RY may be due to abduction based on Lower Bigrade-type verbs, with stems ending in pre-OOk *···e > OOk ···i > NOk (non-palatalizing) ···i: pre-OOk *ore-w(as-)a 'descend-MR' > OOk ʔuri-wa. This would have been NOk ˣʔuri-wa ~ ˣʔure-e but for reanalysis, which resulted in the development of the new "SOFTENER" attached to the M̄R̄ of any form, therefore ʔuri-ri, + -wa = ʔuri-re-e, 'descend, won't you?'

---

234 But cf. *myi#o-yar-as- > myi-ʔu-yas- 'proffer_HUM', likewise an honorific form.

AUXILIARIES                                                                    377

## 14.5 Historical and Comparative Analysis

### 14.5.1 The Origin of OOk EAV

The auxiliary allomorphs come from *ʔuwa·r-* ~ *ʔuwa·{s}-*, an independent verb with a meaning similar to *c-°y-uuwa·r-* ~ *c-°y-uuwa·{s}-* 'deign to be/come/go'.[235] It must be a borrowing from Heian-period Japanese, since it is widely accepted that the early Mid Heian form *owa#s(e)-* ~ *owa#s-ur-* (*s*-irreg = SI) is from Early Heian *ofas-* [oɸas] 'to exaltedly be, to deign to be' (actually considered to be two competing paradigms during a transition period, one 4G and the other SI).[236] The important point that underlies this assumption is that the MJ word is believed to have come from OJ *öp⟨ö⟩-* 'great' + *[i-]mas-* 'exaltedly is'.[237] The likelihood that both Japanese and Okinawan would have independently *irregularly derived* (\*)owas- is just too slim to countenance a reconstruction of ×\*öpö#(i)mas- back into Proto-Japonic, and to then assume that that word gave birth to the reflexes in both MJ and OOk. This means that the word is a borrowing into pre-OOk from MJ. Since we have good reason to derive MJ *ofa#se-*<sub>SI</sub> from OJ *öpö-* 'great(ly)' and *(i-)mas-*<sub>4G</sub> 'deign to be', the MJ form is new, and then there is no reason to suppose that the OOk form is any more ancient than the MJ form, and every reason to believe that it was borrowed as a *Kulturwort* from Japan, a polity that even in the OS already figured in omoros as a place that Ryukyuans saw themselves competing with culturally.

The origin within Okinawan is pre-OOk *\*owa#s(e)-*<sub>SI</sub> ~ *owa#s-ur-*<sub>SI</sub>, a borrowing of *ofas-*<sub>4G</sub> ⌐ *ofa#s(e)-*<sub>SI</sub> ~ *ofa#s-ur-*<sub>SI</sub> 'exaltedly be' in MJ (EOKJ ⟨o pa su⟩), eventually harking back to OJ *\*öpö-[i]mas-*<sub>4G</sub> 'greatly-be<sub>EX</sub>'[238] (*s*-type 4G). There

---

235   For *c(-)°y(-)uuwa·r/s-*, we normally dispense with the first two hyphens, since the word clearly has undergone an irregular sound change *\*[k°ʸu] → [tʃ°u]* showing psychological merger of the morphemes into a new single one, as detailed below.

236   ENKDJ explains *ofas-* approximately as follows:

   (|owasu|, ⟨Word history⟩): (1) it was used since the Heian Period, and gradually overwhelmed |imasu|, which had been in use since the Nara Period. ... (2) Etymologically it is not clear whether its direct ancestor was *ofo-mas-u*, *of-as-i-mas-u*, or *ofo-mas-i-mas-u*. (3) The conjugation, in terms of usage, is identical to SI: MZ *ofase-*, RY *ofasi-*, RT *ofasuru*, and IZ *ofasure*. Apparently OJ *i-mas-*, while in MJ retaining RY *i-mas-i*, shifted the rest of its conjugation to L2G.

   It is important to note that an *s*-type conjugation that is all L2G, except for just RY 4G, is identical to SI, that is, it *is* SI. Thus *ofas-*, with *(i)-mas-* forming its conjugating end, turned out to be SI.

237   There are, in fact, one or two cases to support this hypothesis, as alluded to in the previous note. Presumably [oɸomasu] > [oɸoṃasu] > [ofoŋ̃asu] > [oɸuŋ̃asu] > [oɸuŋasu] > [oɸasu].

238   There is an OJ form *öpö-mas-i-mas-u* (JDB 161d) ← *öpö-* 'great(ly)(-)' (JDB 155d–156a) + *mas-i-mas-u* 'be<sub>EX</sub>-RY-EAV-SS' = 'deign to exaltedly be' ([JDB 675a–b]; other OJ forms are: *mas-*

378  CHAPTER 7

was also *öpö-mas-i-mas-$_{4G}$, but this appears as MJ ofas-i-mas-$_{SP}$ so it is not the direct progenitor of the Okinawan form.

| OJ | → | MJ | → | pre-OOk | → | OOk |
|---|---|---|---|---|---|---|
| *öpö-(i-) | | ofas-$_{4G}$ | | *owa#s$_{[}(e)_{]}$⁻$_{SI}$ ~ | | ʔuwa·{s}- |
| mas-u$_{4G}$ | | ofa-se-$_{SI}$ | | *owa#$_{[}$s-u$_{]}$r-$_{SI}$ | | ~ ʔuwa·r- |

-(u)wa·{s}-
~ -(u)wa·r-

Among the OOk reflexes, the first two are main verbs; and the last two are auxiliaries. Within the auxiliaries, there are four allomorphs with distinctive features being -r vs. -s in the stem consonants as well as non-existence vs. existence of -u in the first syllable. In the next two sections, we explain the genesis of the -uwa- vs. -wa- and -(u)war- vs. -(u)was- allomorphs.

14.5.2    The Allomorphs: -uwa-, -uuwa-, and -wa
The keeping or dropping of the vowel u of the OOk EAV -(u(u))wa···[239] depends upon the historical phonology/synchronic morphology of the preceding verb: succinctly put, u stays if the verb it attaches to is 4G or U1G,[240] but drops if it is any other type of verb, including L2G, as below. Below are illustrations of allomorphic differences in the three verb types:

| 4G | tʰac°-y-uwa-c°yi | 'standing' (OSJS 208b) |
|---|---|---|
| | stand-RY-EAV-GER/PRFV | |
| U1G | my-uuwa-m-i | 'do protect (← see)' (OS 21.#1396) |
| | see-EAV-IA-IZ | |
| L2G | tʰat°i-wa-c°yi | 'erecting' (OSJS 209b) |
| | erect-RY-EAV-GER/PRFV | |

---

'exist/go/come$_{EX}$(-RY)-EAV' [JDB 675d–676b]; mas(·e)-u 'cause to deign to sit/go/come' [JDB 676b]; i-mas-u 'exaltedly be/go/come(-RY)-EAV' [JDB 100bcd], i-mas(e)-u 'cause to exaltedly be(-RY)-EAV'; suffixal verb 'I humbly do/say ...' [JDB 100d–101a]).

239   At this point we assume the Floating-Length-derived form -uuwa-, based largely on the behavior of the Floating-Length root {ku"-$_{J}$} in NOk, where there is no Float in kuu-N$_{J}$ 'not come', or kuu-wa$_{J}$ 'come!' (the latter no relation to -uuwa- above). However there is also kw-aa$_{J}$, with Float, for the same meaning as kuu-wa$_{J}$. Other forms with Float include c-y-uu-N$_{J}$ '(citation form)' and c-y-aabir-a$_{J}$ 'excuse my entry', where Float is required. All forms, OGJ 172a.

240   Also included are the irregular short-vowel monosyllabic root s(i)- 'do' (see below), with RY s-y(i)-, exalting form s-y-uwa···, (no floating length marker), and the special exalting verb c°yuuwa···, 'deign to be/go/come', discussed below. It is based on {kʰu"+} 'come'.

AUXILIARIES

The difference between the first two verb types and the third is that historically, 4G or U1G have the high vowel \*···*yi*-, which in this environment became ···*y*-, but L2G verbs have the mid vowel \*···*e*-, which eventually changed to -*i*. Fuller expositions with step by step derivations follow below, with concrete examples.

The difference in vowel height between \*···*yi*- and \*···*e*- is a crucial factor in determining which one of the two distinct syllabic contractions -*uwa* (< \*-*owa*) undergoes in its affixation. The two such changes laid out below are well-known within Japonic. The first sound change collapses the high vowel *yi* of the first syllable into a glide *y*. The second sound change starts with a sequence of two *mid* vowels (*e* and *o* in ···*e#owa*···), and elides the second vowel (*o*) entirely. These two sound changes applied largely to 4G and L2G verbs, respectively:

Syllabic contractions:

(1)    4G: $Cy_1V_1$V_1$ → $Cy_1V_2$ ( \*···$y\bar{i}$#owa··· > \*···$\underline{y}$-owa··· )

(2)    L2G: $CV_1$V_2$ → $CV_1\emptyset$ = $CV_1$ ( \*···$e$#$\overline{owa}$··· > \*···$e$-$\emptyset wa$··· )

Needless to say, both changes occurred before the (second) vowel raising ( \*$o$ > $u$, \*$e$ > $i$).

In contrast, in the case of the U1G verbs, the root (*Cyi*-), after development of an epenthetic *y* (*Cyi·y*-), was abbreviated (to *Cy*-), just as in the 4G verbs, and—in the case of the Floating Length subtype—a further sound change of Float of length to the next syllable occurred. All epenthetic *y*s were swept up at the same time in particular environments and then deleted, no matter their provenance:

*myi*$^{\prime\prime}$- +   *ʔuwa*··· →   *myi·y-u*$^{\prime\prime}$*wa*··· → *myiyuuwa*··· → *myuuwa*···
see-        EAV        see·EP.*y*-EAV[241]

To put it another way, $^{x}$···*yiiy*···—as opposed to $^{\circ}$···*yiy*···—cannot function as input into the syllabic collapse.[242] Cf. *t*$^{h}$*ac-*$^{\circ}$*y-uwa-c*$^{\circ}$*yi* 'standing' above, the immediate precursor (and the phonological underlyer) of which is \**t*$^{h}$*ac*$^{\circ}$*-yi·y-uwa-c*$^{\circ}$*yi*.

---

241    NOk has distinct Common and Literary forms for 'see', e.g. the LitOk form *n*(*y*)-*uu*-*N*, 'see' (OGJ 428a) < *my-u*$^{\prime\prime}$-*M*, which results through regular sound change from *myi*$^{\prime\prime}$-*yo-mu* (no *r* to block Float), and *NN·z-y-u-N*, (OGJ 437a) < \**M*$^{\prime\prime}$·*r-y-u-M*, the result of regular sound change from an analogically remodeled root \**myi*$^{\prime\prime}$·*r-yi#yo-mu*, with analogically placed *r* blocking the Float sound change.

242    A word of warning is in order, however: in NOk, an alternative ss to the usual

380 CHAPTER 7

If there is no Floating Mark, there is no lengthening in a following syllable due to it.

Let us now show step-by-step derivations of the three groups with concrete examples.

### 14.5.2.1 4G = Consonant-Stem Verb and Similar Verb Types

In this verb group, the linkage to a following Verb or Auxiliary requires an intervening RY morpheme, pre-OOk *-yi-: *VB$_{4G}$-yi-VB/AUX. Thus the Exalting Auxiliary Verb (EAV) {+(u)wa·r/s+} connects in the following way, with the following sound changes:

| pre-OOk | *...C-yi$_{RY}$#owa ... | = | |
|---|---|---|---|
| | *...C-yi#owa ... | > | weakening of word boundary[243] |
| | *...Cyiyowa ... | > | contraction and raising |
| OOk | ...C°yuwa ... | = | sequence without morpheme boundaries |
| | ...C°-y-uwa ... | = | sequence with morpheme boundaries |

たちよわちへ        | < *tʰac°-yi- + ʔuwa-c°yi
⟨ta ti yo wa ti pe⟩ | < *tat-yi + owa-s-yi#tee
tʰac°-y-uwa-c°yi    | stand-RY-EAV#GER/PRFV
'[the High Priestess] has deigned to set off (to war), and ...' (OS 1.#25)

### 14.5.2.2 U1G = Upper Monograde Verbs

Upper Monograde Verbs (U1G) come in two varieties for our purposes, namely those with and those without a Floating Length Mark (V)$^{H}$. The FLM occurs only in monosyllabic verb roots, and crosscuts the categories of U1G and monosyllabic irregulars; for example:

| | [+FLM] | [−FLM] |
|---|---|---|
| [+U1G] | {myiʰ+} 'see' | {kyi+}[244] 'don' |
| [−U1G] | {kʰuʰ+yi+} 'come' | {si+yi}[245] 'do' |

---

NNZ-y-u-N$_J$ 'see SS' is n-uu-N$_J$ (< n-y-uu-N$_J$), suggesting that the OOk underlying form for 'see', like 'come', had a floating length mark: {myiʰ+}+{+uwa·r+}+{+i} → my-uuwa·r-i* 'please deign to look after us!' (OSJS 320c). So NOk n-uu-N$_J$ (OGJ 428a) ← {myiʰ+wu+m}.

243 Includes growth of epenthetic homorganic glide *y.

244 Cf. ⟨ki ti pe⟩ 'donning' (OSJS 126b).

245 Cf. ⟨se da na⟩ si-dana 'wanting to do' (OSJS 194a) and ⟨si ti pe⟩ s-yi-c°yi (OSJS 173bc).

AUXILIARIES

| pre-OOk | *CV$^{\text{II}}$-yi$_{\text{RY}}$#owa ... | | = | *CV$^{\text{II}}$-yi#owa ... |
| | weakening of word boundary[246] | | > | *CV$^{\text{II}}$yiyowa ... |
| | Contraction, Raising, and Float[247] | | > | Cyu$^{\text{II}}$wa ... |
| OOk | sequence without morpheme boundaries | = | | Cyuuwa |
| | sequence with morpheme boundaries | | = | C°-y-uuwa ... |

14.5.2.3    *L2G* = *Lower Bigrade Verbs*

Now when the sequence is of an etymologically non-high vowel—the typical case is L2G, i.e. with stem-final pre-OOk *e* > OOk *i*—followed by the exalting auxiliary (EAV), there is no intervening separate RY morpheme *-yi-*, since the stem of the first verb itself (e.g. ?uri$_{\text{RY}}$- 'descend' or kee-nadi$_{\text{RY}}$- 'caress') fulfills that RY role:

| pre-OOk | *...Ce$_{\text{RY}}$#owa ... | > word-boundary weakening |
| | *...Ce$_{\text{RY}}$ -owa ... | > Mid-Vowel Drop |
| | *...Cewa ... | > Vowel Raising |
| OOk | ...Ciwa ... | |

おれわちゑ
⟨o re wa ti we⟩
*?uri-wa-c°yi* <
*\*ore#wa·s-yi#te*[248]
descend$_{\text{L2G,RY}}$#EAV·s-$_{\text{RY}}$#GER/PRFV$_{\text{RY}}$
'deigning to descend' ([OS 21.#1489]; Nakasone [1987 [1976]: 71])

かいなでわる
⟨ka i na de wa ru⟩
*k$^h$ee-nadi-wa·r-u* <
*\*kak-yi#nade#wa·r-u*
scratch-RY#stroke$_{\text{L2G,RY}}$#EAV·r-RT
'whom [she] deigns to protect' ([OS 1.#13]; Nakasone [1987 [1976]: 71])

---

246    Includes growth of epenthetic homorganic glide *\*y*.

247    We assume Float of Length after Raising, yielding *uu*; if the order is reversed then the result is *oo*. The already mentioned *n-uu-N,* 'see' < *\*myi$^{\text{II}}$-wo-mu* suggests that Raising First is the correct approach.

248    *?uri-* < *\*ore-* is a regular L2G verb in PRk—unlike its equivalent *öri-* (< *\*örï-*) in OJ, an U2G verb—and is, in any case, a vowel-stem verb.

382                                                                                    CHAPTER 7

14.5.3    The Allomorphs -(u)war and -(u)was
Within Okinawan, the newly imported exalting honorific developed two stems,
(1) an older stem *owa·s- (cf. MJ ofas$_{4G}$- → owas$_{4G}$- ~ owa#s(e)$_{SI}$- → owa#s(e)$_{SI}$-),
and (2) a newer one *owa·r$_{4G}$- (presumably from *owa#s(e)·ur$_{SI}$- through dropping of *s and vocalic metathesis as below):

$$*\cdots wasur\cdots > *\cdots wa'ur\cdots > *\cdots wu'ar\cdots > *\cdots wwar\cdots > *\cdots war\cdots^{249}$$

The final *s of *owa·s··· is indirectly ascertainable, though not actually visible,
in the gerund form:

*owa·s-yi-te
*owa·s-yi-tye       >   Progressive Palatalization
*ʔuwa·s-yi-cˇ°yɪ    >   Short Mid Vowel Raising and Glottal Phonologization
ʔuwa      -cˇ°yi    >   Post-Palatal ɪ-Palatalization; syi-Dropping

As one of its sources the gerund alternant -cˇ°yi has tokens that follow the s-stem
verbs, and, just as in the s-stem verbs, the s in the case of ʔuwa·s- is dropped
after leaving its consonantal trace in the Progressive Palatalization and voiceless affrication of cˇy in the gerund.[250] An s-stem example from os: おろち(へ)
= ⟨o ro ti (pe)⟩ = ʔuru-cˇ°yi [ʔuɾutʃ°i] 'letting down, causing to alight' ← *oros-yi-te
'(id.)'. Other gerund alternants for other conjugation types are -ʥyi [ˇʤi], -tʰi
[ˇtʰɪ], and -di [ˇdɪ].[251]
   On ⟨··· i wa ···⟩: There is one other case of ⟨··· i wa ···⟩ that appears to be an
exception to the pattern we have shown here: ねがﾞいわちへ ⟨ne ga* i wa ti pe⟩
'deigns to keep beseeching [the deities through the shaman]' (os 3.#107). The
phonologization is indeed niga'yiwac°yi. However, yi here is not strictly speaking just a RY form; rather, it is an early example of the usual later change of yu
to yi, seen for example in NOk stilted pronunciation tuyuN, ~ ColloqOk tuyiN,

---

249   The *su hypothesis is supported by words such as NOk saa·taa, 'sugar' (OGJ 452a), pre-
      sumably from *sa#tau ← Sino-Japanese. As hypothesized in Ch. 2 §5.6.2, "Examples," "t,"
      this may be the result of metathesis of a and u: *ta'u > *tu'a → *twa → taa (labial glide loss
      after coronal/labial consonant, and lengthening to two moras in a SJ morph).
250   The sound change is not just a morphophonemic one, but is seen also in nouns, with
      no discernible morphological trigger: *asyita *[ʔaʃɪt°a] > *asyitya *[ʔaʃɪt°ya] > *ʔasyicya
      *[ʔaʃɪtʃ°a] > OOk ʔac°ya *[ʔatʃ°a] ([osɟs 38a] ⟨a ti ya⟩) > NOk ʔacya, [ʔaˤtʃa] (OGJ 101a)
      'tomorrow'; cf. NJ asyitá, [ʔaˤʃɪta⁽ⁿ⁾] 'tomorrow'.
251   Historically (putting aside a few details): *···k/s-yi-te > ···-c°yi; *···g/n-yi-te > ···-ʥyi; *···r/w-
      yi-te > ···-tˇ°i; *···b/m-yi-te > ···-di. A proposed alternant, say, *owa·k- instead of *owa·s- would
      simply be out of the question.

AUXILIARIES                                                                    383

'take' (OGJ 528b). Thus *niga'-y-uwa-c°yi* is actually the regular form for this verb
({nigaw+yi+uwa·s-yi-tee}), and there is no irregularity.

## 14.6    OS ⟨ta bo† u⟩ and ⟨ta bo° re⟩

OS has two *hapaxes*, ⟨ta bo† u⟩ and ⟨ta bo° re⟩.[252] While OSJS (210c)[253] treats
both as examples of the later *taboo·r/s-* 'deigns to give',[254] OKDJ convincingly
distinguishes the two, giving a different meaning for the first, and accepting
the meaning of the second as it is given in OSJS.

These are two completely unrelated roots, and at least three words:

– NOk *tabú'-* 'accumulate, store, save, keep in reserve' ([OGJ 503b]; related to
  MJ *tabaw-* ~ *kabaw-* 'cover, hide from view'), NJ *kabáw-* 'protect, provide
  cover for, speak up for; favor (one's injured limb)' related to OS ⟨ta bo† u⟩
  *tʰabu'-u*, our *\*tabow-*. OKDJ (|ta bo pu| 403c) takes care of this *hapax*, as
  'accumulate (etc.)', and therefore as unrelated. However, that leaves ⟨ta bo°
  re⟩. We believe this is the unusual spelling of *o*-tier-for-*oo*-pronunciation of
  *tʰaboori* [tʰãbɔːɾı], probably by this point without any internal morphology
  other than the final MR: *tʰaboor-i*.

– NOk *taboo·r/s-ı* 'bestow, deign to give' < ?\**tab-y-owa·r/s-* / ?\**tabe#wa·r/s-*.
  No tokens evince an RY allomorph *-y-*, suggesting that regularly formed L2G
  *\*tabe-* and the regular following EAV allomorph for L2Gs, namely *\*-wa·r/s-*,
  have linked to make up the word.

– OKDJ (401 cd) |tabi-ofaru| '1. higher-ranking personage bestows s/t upon a
  lower-ranking person; 2. humbly receive; be given by an exalted personage'.
  OKDJ (401 cd) uses a ghost headword |tabi-ofaru|, glossing it as the hon-
  orific form for both giving and receiving. MOk: *tabocyi* 'deigning to give',
  *tabo(o)ri/tamori* 'please give'. EAV on a GER: 'DO for me/us'. NOk: [OGJ 503b]:
  *taboo-y-u-N,* VT = *·r-aN,* = *·∅-cyi* '(superior) gives (to inferior).' Only MR
  *taboori* 'please give (to me/us)' is used. In poetry: *tabori*.

– NOk *tabí-y-u-N* (OGJ 503a) < *\*tabe·r-* [Lit.] 'tamawaru' = '1. humbly receive;
  be given by an exalted personage; 2. bestow'.[255,256]

---

252   ⟨ta po u⟩     (OSJS 445c)     = ⟨ta bo† u⟩     (TOS 11.#567);
      ⟨ta po re⟩    (ibid.)         = ⟨ta bo° re⟩    (TOS 8.#447).

253   ⟨ta po · u⟩ 'tamau' = '(a superior) gives (to an inferior)'; ⟨ta po · re⟩ 'tamaware' = 'please
      confer (upon me)'.

254   NOk ([OGJ 503b], *taboo-y-u-N,*; NEG *taboo·r-aN,*; GER *taboo-cyi,*) has a fossilized *taboo·r-i,*
      'please give to me', or, appended to a preceding verbal Gerund, 'please DO for me'. The GER
      clearly shows *\*owa·s-*, because of *-cyi*, not *-ti*.

255   The reversed polarity of *tábi-* here, while dependent on a translation of the meanings of
      OGJ's gloss of J *tamawaru*, is crucial for the etymology of *tʰaboo·r/s-*, since it must literally
      mean 'exaltedly bestow': *\*tabe-[o]wa·r/s-*.

256   The J root *tab-* 'deigns to give' is from earlier (and concurrent) *tamap-*, with the second *a*

384 CHAPTER 7

The compilers of OKDJ have erred in putting certain spellings under the wrong headword: At issue are the examples under headword |tabi-ofaru| (401 cd) in word-shape sections that contain |···-mesiofa···| in them. These should be moved to the word-shape sections under |tabu| (402d–403a). The words at issue have diphthongal spellings, such as ⟨bo i⟩ for *bi*, while the ones under |tabu| have monophthongal spellings, e.g. ⟨be⟩ for *bi*, that being the only difference between them. Thus, for example, under different headwords are different spellings of the same word, *ʔu-tabi-misyoor-i* 'please give (me/us)' as, in the first instance, ⟨o ta bo i me si ya u re⟩, and in the latter, ⟨u ta bi mi si ya u ri⟩.

The spelling ⟨ta boᵗ u⟩ is a separate verb, according to OKDJ (403c):

たが、　ためが、ʌ　たぼᵗう、　　/ たが、　　ためが、ʌ　よしも　　　　/
ta ga ,　ta me ga , ʌ ta boᵗ u ,　/ ta ga ,　ta me ga , ʌ yo si mo　　/
*tʰaa-ga*　*tʰami-ga*　**tʰabu'-u**　　*tʰaa-ga*　*tʰami-ga*　*yusyim-u*
who-GEN benefit-KP store.up-RT　who-GEN benefit-KP persevere-RT
おもいぐ*わの、　　ためす、　/ きみよしぎ*や、　ためす　　#
o mo i gu* wa no ,　ta me su ,　/ ki mi yo si gi* ya , ta me su　#
*ʔumi-ɢwa-nu*　　*tʰami-si*　　*k°yimyi.yusyi-gya* *tʰami-si*
love-RY-child-GEN benefit-KP　Kimiyoshi-GEN　benefit-KP
'For whom do we lay in [the treasures]? For whom do we persevere? For [our] beloved child[257]—none other; for Kimiyoshi—none other ... .' (OS 11.#567)

Cf. |tabopu|[258,259] (OKDJ 403c) 【貯う】 VB OS 'preserve; save up; use sparingly'; |yosimu| *yusyim-y-u-N* 'stop' VI/VT (OKDJ 710ab); (OGJ 503b): *tabú'-y-u-N*

---

zeroed out and *mp* > *mb* > *ᵐb* > *b*. We show VmVp-: *tamap-* 'bestow', for the case of succeeding ···*amap*···, and *ömöpö-ye-* 'to come to mind'. The former gives NJ *tabe-* 'eat' ('have bestowed on one') and the latter, *oboe-* 'learn (by heart); learn; experience; come to mind'.

| t | A | m | A | p | - | | ö | m | ö | p | ö | - | y | e | - | |
|---|---|---|---|---|---|---|---|---|---|---|---|---|---|---|---|---|
| t | A | m | | p | - | | ö | m | | p | ö | - | y | e | - | |
| t | A | | ᵐb | - | → | | ö | | ᵐb | | ö | - | y | e | - | → |
| t | a | | b | - | | | o | | b | | o | - | y | e | - | |

This type of sound change has happened on a number of occasions.

257　The NOk form is *ʔumi-ŋgwa⌟* '(your) beloved child' (OGJ 554a), showing that a geminate obstruent is there, but lacks formal written expression. OOk Vɢw [V̆g:w] > NOk Vŋgw [V̆ŋ:gw]. Cf. Ch. 2 §4.6 "/ɢ/", esp. fn. 54.

258　Cf. ENKDJ |taba·u| ⟨tabapu⟩ i.e. *taba'-u* 【庇・貯・惜】 VT *p//f/w*-type 4G '(1) To put away with great care. To store away. Or, to not want to take out (to [be]grudge, be stingy/tight-fisted, unwilling to give/pay, to hold back). (2) (Usually in the form *inocyi / mi o tabau*) to aid in keeping others from harm. = *kabau*. (3) To not make public, to not show openly.' Both *taba'-u* and its cousin *kaba'-u* make their appearance in the Kamakura period or later.

259　How does pre-OOk *\*tabow-* relate to MJ *tabaw-*? The word is a late-enough borrowing from MJ to pre-OOk to have been borrowed after the commencement of monophthon-

AUXILIARIES

VT = ·*r-aN*, =-*ti*. 'accumulate, save up, preserve, keep in reserve'. (OGJ 292b–293a): *yusyim-y-u-N,* VI =*m-aN*, =-*di* '(id.)'.

## 15 Humilific Auxiliary: -*abir*-

The Humilific Supplementary Verb -*abir*- is most probably a loan from MJ -*i#faber*- '-RY-HAV-' with a phonological change of *\*f > \*w > y* after *\*yi* (cf. OSJS [338a] [⟨- ya pe ra⟩], Takahashi [1991a:174]),[260] and loss of initial *y* through analogy. This attaches to the RY of the verb. As already pointed out by Takahashi (ibid.), the only attested form is MZ/IA.

Here is the exhaustive set of attested examples, which express, in sequence, inference (one example), volition, and hortation (two examples each):

ゑぞにやの、　　　うちや、　　／　あまへ、やべ°ら　　　　／
we zo ni ya no ,　u ti ya ,　／ a ma pe , ya be˚ ra　　／
*ʔyii̯zu-nyaa-nu　ʔuc˚yi-ya　ʔamayi·y-abir-a*
PN-personage-GEN house-TOP　rejoice_RY·EP.*y*-HSV-IA
ほこり、やべ°ら　　　／
po ko ri , ya be˚ ra　／
*pʰukʰur-y-abir-a*
celebrate-RY-HSV-IA
'The Eiso[261] household[262] **must be** rejoicing, [they] **must be** celebrating.'[263] (OS 5.#289)

---

gization of MJ ···*au*··· > ···*ɔɔ*···. Thus SS and RT *tabau* > *tabɔɔ* and GER *tabaute* > *tabɔɔte*. These would become pre-OOk *\*tabo-o* ~ *\*tabo-u* and *\*taboo-te*, respectively, and, after the raising, probably *tʰabu-u* and *tʰabuu-tʰi*, respectively. (Were it not for the effects of paradigmatic leveling, the forms might have turned out to be °*\*tʰabu-u* and ˣ*\*tʰaboo-tˀi*.) R-gradization would eventually yield *tʰabu·r-u* and *tʰabu-tʰi*, and the observed OGJ forms *tabúyuN, tabúraN, tabúti*.

260　The initial change, a shift from internal word boundary "#" to morphological boundary "+" (conventionally written "-" in running text), is probably irregular, but the following change, softening of *\*p* to *w* (and then possibly to *y*/zero) is phonologically determined. This is the well known *ha-gyō tenko(-on)* 'change of pronunciation of the *h* column consonant [in medial position]'. The reinterpretation of the historically initial *y* as either a preceding EP.*y* or an RY morpheme is a further twist.

261　According to OSJS (371a), this word refers to a powerful lord who lived in Iso village in Urasoe. They note that *Chūzan Seikan*, a chronicle, has this person as *Eiso-ō* 'King Eiso' (1229–1299). In NOk, *ʔyiizu,* (N) 'Iso (伊祖)' (OGJ 253a). Nakagami—Urasoe-magiri (828b). As already noted, long *yii* has developed a non-palatal nucleus that prevents PP.

262　The interpretation of this word affects the interpretation of the whole sentence. Hokama (2000a:199b) takes it as 'era', while OSJS ⟨we zo ni ya no u ti⟩ (371c) gives 'house' and, under

だ\*しま、∧　　　　まぶ\*りやべ\*ら　　　／
da\* si ma , ∧　　　ma bu\* ri ya be\* ra　／
*da-syima-∅*　　　*maʙr-y-**abir-a***
great_BE-island-DO protect-RY-**HAV-IA**
'[We][264] **shall** protect the Great Island.' (OS 7.#362)

すへの、　　　　　　ちな、∧　うるわし、　　／ こやり、∧
su pe no ,　　　　　ti na , ∧　u ru wa si ,　／ ko ya ri , ∧
*siyi-nu*　　　　　*c°yi̧na-∅*　*ʔuruwasyi-∅*　*kʰuu'-yaar-yi*
spirit.power_BE-GEN rope-SUB beautiful-ss　pray-**PROG-RY**
うちや、べ\*ら　／
u ti ya , be\* ra　／
*ʔuc-°y-**abir-a***
make-**HAV-IA**
'Ropes[265] imbued with spiritual power are beautiful. We **shall** make[266] ropes, praying for [the deities' favor].' (OS 8.#402)

おもろ、たね、∧　こや、べ\*ら　　　　　　／
o mo ro , ta ne , ∧　ko ya , be\* ra　　　　／
*ʔumuru-tʰani-∅*　*kʰuu'-y-**abir-a***
omoro-seeds-DO pray.for-RY-**HAV-IA**
'Let us pray for the omoro-seeds (= inspiration for omoro?[267]).' (OS 8.#404)

---

⟨u ti⟩ (66b), gives 'household', citing an interlineation from this song. The Hokama version would go into English as '[The people in] the Eiso era must be rejoicing; [they] must be celebrating'. In this interpretation, the humilific takes the stance of the humble common people vis-à-vis the ruler. In the OSJS interpretation, the humilific takes the stance of the members of the household, who are naturally socially below the head of the household, who is, of course, also the ruler of the realm.

263　Here the HSV *-abir-* is performing two functions: (1) the addition of humilification and (2) progressive aspect to the sentence. Thus the translation using 'be V-ing'.

264　Kikoe Ōgimi and the Solar Deity are cooperating in the protection of the Land, and Kikoe Ōgimi speaks for both of them, using her own humilific stance vis-à-vis the King, to state that they will protect the Great Country. That is why the use of *-abir-* is called for here.

265　The spelling ⟨ti na⟩ for proto-Japonic \**tuna* 'rope' is phonologically irregular, since it requires interpretation as *c°yi̧na*, not only with the "wrong" vowel ˣ*yi* for °*i*, but also, if indeed with phonological *yi* (and we are not sure that that is the case), having a high front palatal vowel that does not cause PP. Thus it may be irregular on two counts.

266　The verb in the meaning of 'make' is reserved for corded items.

267　Hokama (2000a: 279b).

AUXILIARIES

まにし、∧           こや、べ゛ら           / おいちへ、∧
ma ni si ,∧        ko ya , be° ra        / o i ti pe ,∧
*ma-nyisyi-∅*      *kʰuu'-y-abir-a*       *ʔwi-i-cʰyi(i)-∅*
BE-North.wind-DO pray.for-RY-**HAV-IA**  follow-RY-wind-DO
こや、べ゛ら           /
ko ya , be° ra        /
*kʰuu'-y-abir-a*
pray.for-RY-**HAV-IA**
'Let us pray for the North Wind, let us pray for a tail wind.' (OS 13.#775)

As noted above, the only attested form for this auxiliary in OS is MZ. This is
rather puzzling given the fact that its successor in MOk, e.g. in Kumi Odori,
and in NOk has robust and full conjugational forms. At this point, this puzzle
has to be left for future research.

## 16      Humilific Auxiliary: *tʰat°imac°ir-*

This humilific auxiliary is attested only twice, and twice only because of duplicate omoro. According to Shimizu (2003: 120), there is not even one instance of
⟨ta te ma tu r[e ba]⟩ in Ryūka. Further, in NOk, no form phonologically corresponding to it is used. These statements concur with OKDJ (396d), which has
the lexical item occurring only in OS. Therefore, we agree with Vovin's (2009a:
1038–1039) account as follows:

> However, because there are no cognates in the modern dialects, and
> because even the distribution in Old Ryukyuan is limited, not to mention
> the fact that *tatematur-* is widely used as a humble auxiliary in Middle,
> but not in Western Old Japanese, O[ld ]R[yukyuan] *tatematur-* is better
> treated as a loan from Middle Japanese.

Here is the example:

きこゑ     大ぎ゛みぎ゛や、       / いのり、∧たてまつれば゛、   / まん、
ki ko we   OPO gi° mi gi° ya ,    / i no ri ,∧ ta te ma tu re ba° , / ma N,
*k°yi̧k°uyi* *ʔuQp°u-gyimyi-gya*   *ʔyi̧nur-yi-tʰat°imac°ir-i-ba*   *maN*
famed      great-priestess-SUB    pray-RY-**HAV**-IZ-TMP/CND    myriad

| まん ∧ | あすら、まん ∧ | ちよわれ / |
|---|---|---|
| ma n ∧ | a su ra , ma n ∧ | ti yo wa re / |
| *maN* | *ʔasira-maN* | *c°yuwar-i* |
| myriad | numberless-myriad | reign$_{\text{EX}}$-MR |

'When the Renowned Great Priestess **offers** prayers, may [the King] reign [over the Kingdom] forever!' ((OS 1.#14) (OS 3.#132), with slight spelling differences)

OSJS treats ⟨ta te ma tu re ba⟩ as an auxiliary verb: ⟨- ta te ma tu re pa⟩ (209a) and ⟨i no · ri - ta te ma tu re - pa⟩ (62b), glossing the latter as 'upon offering up prayers, upon humbly praying'. It is possible to view ⟨i no ri⟩ = *ʔyi̠nur-yi(-)*[268] as either a deverbal noun (without the parenthesized hyphen) meaning 'prayer'—in which case it would be seen as marked with -∅ '-DO' and followed by a full verb *tʰat°imac°ir-i-ba*, ie, 'when (one) offers up prayers'—or as the RY form of a verb—in which case it is followed by a humilific auxiliary *-tʰat°imac°ir-i-ba*, i.e. 'when (one) prays abjectly/humbly':

| *ʔyi̠nuryi* | - ∅ | *tʰat°imac°ir* | - *i* | - *ba* |
|---|---|---|---|---|
| prayer | - DO | offer$_{\text{HUM}}$ | - IZ | - TMP/CND |

'when (one) offers up prayers'

| *ʔyinur* | - *yi* | - *tʰatʰimac°ir* | - *i* | - *ba* |
|---|---|---|---|---|
| pray | - RY | - HSV | - IZ | - TMP/CND |

'when (one) prays abjectly/humbly'

Both make sense, and indeed mean the same thing. In favor of the *noun ʔyinur-yi* is the placement of both a comma and a space between it and the following

---

268     The *verb ʔyi̠nur-* has a large set of forms (OSJS 62): *ʔyi̠nu-tʰ°i*$_{\text{G/P}}$, *ʔyi̠nur-an*$_{\text{NEG}}$-*yi*$_{\text{QP}}$, *ʔyi̠nur-a*$_{\text{MZ}}$-*ba*$_{\text{T/C}}$, *ʔyi̠nur-am*$_{\text{1A}}$-*i*$_{\text{1Z}}$, *ʔyi̠nur-ari*$_{\text{PASS}}$-, *ʔyi̠nur-u*$_{\text{RT}}$, *ʔyi̠nur-i*$_{\text{1Z}}$-, and *ʔyi̠nur-y(i)*$_{\text{RY}}$-VB. The phonological strings *···*yi̠no*··· and *···*yinu*··· have merged (> ···*yi̠nu*···) in OOk. But the word is always written with ⟨no⟩, despite Sāchā's 58 tokens. It is reconstructible as *\*ʔyi̠nor-*, just as expected from OJ *inör-* (JDB 90a). *\*n* and *\*r* are largely written as if immune to PP, and graphic exceptions are typically due to metathesis instead—but not so for *ʔyinyupʰa* < *\*ʔyinyopa* ← *\*ʔyinopa* 'Inoha (PLN)'. (Recall also the earlier discussion in fn. 221 suggesting that ⟨i no⟩ = *\*yino* is *always yinyu*, regardless of non-PP spelling.) Four words meaning 'pray' include *ʔyi̠nur-*, *wugam-*, *niga(w)-*, and *kuu(w)-*, the latter two being requests. While OGJ says *ʔyi̠nu-y-u-N*$_{J}$ is "new," it obviously is not. Further, it reverses the accent of Tk *inór-u*: it is a pRk word or an old loan. Martin (1987: 697, 737) suggests PJ *\*i-* 'VPFX' + *nör-*$_{\text{A}}$ 'declare; scold' (cf. *nör-öp-*$_{\text{A?}}$ 'curse', NOk *nurá-y-u-N* 'scold' [also OGJ 426a], perhaps originally reformulated on the basis of *nurá'-ari-y-u-N* 'be scolded' ← *\*nurwa'-ari-* ← *\*nuruw-ari-* ← *\*norow-are-*).

AUXILIARIES

word. However, all other instances of the noun *-ʔyinur-yi* are as second members of tight (without *-nu-*) or loose (with *-nu-*) [six-mora] compounds:

| | |
|---|---|
| *ʔyibi-**nu**-ʔyi̯ nur-yi* | 'prayers at the central precinct of the shrine' (OSJS 63a) |
| *siN-**nu**-ʔyi̯ nur-yi* | 'a thousand (i.e. a great many) prayers' (OSJS 199b) |
| *cʰïk°asa-ʔyi̯ nur-yi* | 'the *tsukasa*-priestess prayers' (OSJS 223a) |
| *tʰinyi-**nu**-ʔyi̯ nur-yi* | 'prayers to the deities residing in Heaven' (OSJS 236bc) |
| *myi-syima-ʔyi̯ nur-yi* | 'the Three-Precincts/Exalted-(Is)land prayers' = prayers for the prosperity of Shuri (OSJS 311c) |

... suggesting that in fact the view of *ʔyi̯ nur-yi*-$_{VB}$ + *-tʰat°imac°ir*-$_{HAV}$, i.e. of *-tʰat°imac°ir-* as a HAV, is the correct one.

# References

Abe Minako 阿部美菜子. 2009. "*Omoro Sōshi* no gengo nendai" [『おもろさうし』の言語年代; What historical stage of Japanese is the *Omoro Sōshi* vocabulary most similar to?]. In: Takahashi Osamu et al., eds., *Okinawa Bunka wa Doko kara Kita ka* [Where did Okinawan culture come from?], 133–190. Tokyo: Shinwasha.

Akiyama Noriko 秋山紀子. 1975. "Omoro Sōshi no gotō 'o' to 'wo' no kana-zukai oyobi hyōki-hō" [『おもろさうし』の語頭「お」と「を」の仮名遣い及び表記法; On orthography and spellings of ⟨o⟩ and ⟨wo⟩ in the *Omoro Sōshi*]. *Chi'iki Bunka Kenkyū* [Studies of regional cultures] 1: 7–12.

Anttila, Raimo. 1989. *Historical and Comparative Linguistics.* Amsterdam: John Benjamins.

Bentley, John. 2001. *A Descriptive Grammar of Early Old Japanese Prose.* Leiden: Brill Academic Publishers.

Endo, Mitsuaki 遠藤光暁. 2015. "Language contact between Chinese and Japanese: Peculiarity of Japanese in the manner of accepting Chinese." In: Wang, William S-Y., and Chaofen Sun, eds., *The Oxford Handbook of Chinese Linguistics*, 215–225. Oxford: The Oxford University Press.

ENKDJ, see Shōgakukan Kokugo Jiten Henshūbu

EOKJ, see Matsumura et al., eds. 2008.

Erickson, Blaine. 1997. "Another source of M ~ B variation in Japanese." *Japanese/ Korean Linguistics* 6: 143–159. Stanford: CSLI.

ESKR. See Kamata et al.

Frellesvig, Bjarke. 2010. *A History of the Japanese Language.* Cambridge: Cambridge University Press.

Fuku Hiromi 福寛美. 2013. '*Omoro Sōshi*' to Gun'yū no Seiki: Sanzan Jidai no Ō-tachi [『おもろさうし』と群雄の世紀――三山時代の王たち; The *Omoro Sōshi* and the era of the rival leaders: The kings of the Sanzan era]. Tokyo: Shinwasha.

Greenberg, Joseph H. 1995. "The diachronic typological approach to language." In: Masayoshi Shibatani and Theodora Bynon, eds., *Approaches to Language Typology: A Conspectus*, 145–166. Oxford: Oxford University Press.

Grice, H. Paul. 1975. "Logic and conversation." In: Peter Cole and Jerry L. Morgan, eds., *Speech Acts. Syntax and Semantics* 3, 41–58. New York: Academic Press.

Hagers, Steven. 2012. "The perfective use of *-ti* in Shuri Ryukyuan." Paper proposal for the 22nd Japanese/Korean Linguistics Conference.

Handa Ichirō 半田一郎. 1999. *Ryūkyūgo Jiten* [Dictionary of Ryukyuan]. Tokyo: Daigaku Shorin.

Hashimoto Shinkichi 橋本進吉. 1969 (1931). "Joshi, Jodōshi no Kenkyū" [助詞・助動詞の研究; Studies of particles and auxiliary verbs]. In: Hattori Shirō, Ōno Susumu,

Sakakura Atsuyoshi, and Matsumura Akira, eds., *Hashimoto Shinkichi-hakushi Chosaku-shū* 8, *Kōgi-shū* 3. Tokyo: Iwanami Shoten.

Hashimoto Shirō 橋本四郎. 1982. "Shiji-go no shi-teki tenkai" [指示語の史的展開; The historical development of deictics]. In: *Kōza Nihongogaku* 2: 217–240.

Haspelmath, Martin. 1990. "Grammaticalization of passive morphology." In: *Studies in Language* 14: 25–72.

Hateruma Eikichi 波照間永吉, ed. 2007. *Ryūkyū no Rekishi to Bunka* [琉球の歴史と文化 The history and culture of Ryukyu]. Tokyo: Kadokawa Shoten.

Hateruma Eikichi 波照間永吉. 2007a. "*Omoro Sōshi* e no izanai" [おもろさうしへの誘い; Invitation to the *Omoro Sōshi*]. In: HERRB, 1–13.

Hateruma Eikichi 波照間永吉. 2007b. "*Omoro Sōshi* kara nani o yomi-toru ka" [『おもろさうし』から何を読み取るか; What insight do we gain by reading the *Omoro Sōshi*?]. In: HERRB, 43–73.

Hateruma Eikichi 波照間永吉. 2007c. "*Omoro Sōshi* no shōchō hyōgen to hiyu hyōgen" [おもろさうしの象徴表現と比喩表現; Symbolic expressions and metaphorical expressions in the *Omoro Sōshi*]. In: HERRB, 217–242.

Hateruma Eikichi 波照間永吉. 2007d. "Omoro Kanshō: Gasasu no waka-teda" [おもろ鑑賞——ガサスの若てだ; An omoro exegesis: The young Sun Prince of Gasasu]. In: HERRB, 264–266.

Hattori Shirō 服部四郎. 1976. "Nihongo to Ryūkyū-go" [日本語と琉球語; Japanese and Ryukyuan]. In: Ifa Fuyū Seitan Hyakunen Kinenkai, eds., *Okinawa-gaku no Reimei* [沖縄学の黎明; The dawn of Okinawan studies], 7–55. Tokyo: Okinawa Bunka Kyōkai.

HERRB. → Hateruma Eikichi, ed.

Higa Minoru 比嘉実. 1986. "Ryūkyū Ōkoku, ōken shisō no keisei katei: Waka-teda kara teda-ko e" [琉球王国・王権思想の形成過程～若太陽から太陽子へ～; The process of formation of the Ryukyuan Kingdom and of the ideology of royal authority: From *Waka-teda* to *Teda-ko*]. In: Shimajiri Katsutarō, Kadena Sōtoku, Toguchi Shinsei San-sensei Koki Kinen Ronshū Kankō I'inkai, eds., *Kyūyō Ronsō*, 771–802. Naha: Hirugisha.

Hokama Shuzen 外間守善 and Saigō Nobutsuna 西郷信綱, eds. 1972. *Omoro Sōshi* [『おもろさうし』; Book of *Omoros*], Nihon Shisō Taikei [Series on Japanese Thought], vol. 18. Tokyo: Iwanami Shoten.

Hokama Shuzen 外間守善 and Tamaki Masami 玉城政美, eds. and authors. 1980. *Nantō Kayō Taisei* 1, *Okinawa-hen jō* [南島歌謡大成 1 沖縄篇上; Treasury of the songs of the Southern Isles, 1, Okinawa volumes, A]. Tokyo: Kadokawa Shoten.

Hokama Shuzen 外間守善 and Hateruma Eikichi 波照間永吉, eds. and authors. 2011. *Teihon Omoro Sōshi* [定本おもろさうし; The *Omoro Sōshi*, standard text]. Tokyo: Kadokawa Gakugei Shuppan.

Hokama Shuzen 外間守善, ed. 1995. *Okinawa Kogo Daijiten* [沖縄古語大辞典; Comprehensive Dictionary of Old Okinawan], Tokyo: Kadokawa Shoten.

# REFERENCES

Hokama Shuzen 外間守善, ed. and annot. 2000ab. *Omoro Sōshi* [おもろさうし; The *Omoro Sōshi*]. Iwanami Bunko, yellow series, 2 vols.: 142-1, 142-2. Tokyo: Iwanami Shoten.

Hokama Shuzen 外間守善. 1970. *Konkō Kenshū: Kōhon to Kenkyū* [混効験集・校本と研究; The *Konkō Kenshū*: Variorum text with interpretation]. Tokyo: Kadokawa Shoten.

Hokama Shuzen 外間守善. 1971. *Okinawa no Gengoshi* [沖縄の言語史; A linguistic history of Okinawa]. Tokyo: Hōsei Daigaku Shuppankyoku.

Hokama Shuzen 外間守善. 1981. *Okinawa no Kotoba* [沖縄の言葉; The language of Okinawa]. Nihongo no Sekai [日本語の世界; The world of the Japanese language], 9. Tokyo: Chūō Kōronsha.

Hokama Shuzen 外間守善. 1985. *Omoro Sōshi* [おもろさうし; The *Omoro Sōshi*]. Shirīzu Koten o Yomu, vol. 22. Tokyo: Iwanami Shoten.

Hokama Shuzen 外間守善. 1994. *Nantō no Kamiuta Omoro Sōshi* [南島の神歌『おもろさうし』; Songs of the Southern Islands: The *Omoro Sōshi*]. Tokyo: Chūō Kōronsha.

Hokama Shuzen and Saigō Nobutsuna 外間守善・西郷信綱, eds. and comps. 1972. *Omoro Sōshi* [おもろさうし; The *Omoro Sōshi*]. Nihon Shisō Taikei 18. Tokyo: Iwanami Shoten.

Hopper, Paul J., and Elizabeth Closs Traugott. 1993. *Grammaticalization*. Cambridge, England: Cambridge University Press.

Ifa Fuyū 伊波普猷. 1935. *Ryūkyū Gikyoku Jiten* [琉球戯曲辞典; Dictionary of Ryukyuan Kumiodori]. Tokyo: Kyōdo Kenkyūsha.

Ifa Fuyū 伊波普猷. 1974 [1929]. *Kōchū Ryūkyū Gikyokushū* [校註琉球戯曲集; Collection of Ryukyuan dramas, collated and annotated] In: Hattori Shirō, Nakasone Seizen, and Hokama Shuzen, eds., *Ifa Fuyū Zenshū*, vol. 3. Tokyo: Heibonsha.

Ifa Fuyū 伊波普猷. 1975a [1924]. *Ryūkyū Seiten Omoro Sōshi Senshaku* [琉球聖典『おもろさうし』選釈; A selection and interpretation from the Ryukyu sacred book the *Omoro Sōshi* [The Book of Omoros]], *Ifa Fuyū Zenshū*, vol. 6, 27–207. Tokyo: Heibonsha.

Ifa Fuyū 伊波普猷. 1975b [1935]. "Omoro Ochibo Shū" [おもろ落穂集; Gleanings from among the Omoro]. In: *Ifa Fuyū Zenshū*, vol. 6, 462–520. Tokyo: Heibonsha.

Ikemiya Masaharu 池宮正治. 1987. "Ma-Naban e" [真南蛮へ; To Siam]. In: OSKS, 319–326.

Ikemiya Masaharu 池宮正治. 1987. "Misaki iku fune" [岬行く船; Ship coursing past the capes]. In: OSKS, 53–58.

Ikemiya Masaharu 池宮正治. 1987. "Shō Nei ōhi no ure'i" [尚寧王妃の愁い; The despair of Shō Nei's queen]. In: OSKS, 285–292.

Ikemiya Masaharu 池宮正治. 1987. "Tama o susugu" [玉を濯ぐ; Purifying the jewels]. In: OSKS, 222–228.

Ikemiya Masaharu 池宮正治. 1987. "Yaura yaura kaze yo" [やうら やうら 風よ; Softly, softly, o wind!]. In: OSKS, 337–343.

Ikemiya Masaharu 池宮正治. 1987. "Zan o toru" [人魚を獲る; Catching dugongs]. In: OSKS, 47–52.

Ikemiya Masaharu 池宮正治. 1995. *Ryūkyū Kogo Jiten Konkō Kenshū no Kenkyū* [琉球古語辞典『混効験集』の研究; A study of the dictionary of the Old Ryukyuan language, the *Konkō Kenshū*]. Tokyo: Dai'ichi Shobō.

Ikemiya Masaharu 池宮正治. 2006. "*Omoro Sōshi* ni okeru reiryoku no shosō to hyōgen: Reiryoku wa fukashi ka" [『おもろさうし』における霊力の諸相と表現――霊力は不可視か; Various aspects of, and expressions for, spiritual power in the *Omoro Sōshi*: Is spiritual power invisible?]. *Nihon Tōyō Bunka Ronshū* 12: 33–57.

Ikemiya Masaharu 池宮正治. 2015. *Ikemiya Masaharu Chosakushū, 1: Ryūkyū Bungaku Sōron* [池宮正治著作集・1――琉球文学総論; A collection of the works of Ikemiya Masaharu, 1: Survey of Ryukyuan literature]. Tokyo: Kasama Shoin.

Ishizaki Hiroshi 石崎博志. 2001. "Kango shiryō ni yoru Ryūkyū-go kenkyū to Ryūkyū shiryō ni yoru Kanwa kenkyū ni tsuite" [漢語資料による琉球語研究と琉球資料による官話研究について; On Ryukyuan language studies by Chinese materials [*sic*]]. *Nihon Tōyō Bunka Ronshū* [日本東洋文化論集; Human Science. Bulletin of the Faculty of Law and Letters, University of the Ryukyus, Department of Human Sciences] 7: 55–98.

Iwanami Shoten 岩波書店, eds. 2006. *Kōjien* [広辞苑第六版; The *Kōjien*, a Japanese language dictionary, 6th Edition], electronic edition in Casio EX-word Dataplus 8, XD-U 18000. Tokyo: Ōbunsha.

Iwasaki, Shoichi. 2002. *Japanese*. Amsterdam: John Benjamins.

JDB. See Jōdaigo Jiten Henshū Iinkai, eds.

Jōdaigo Jiten Henshū Iinkai 上代語辞典編集委員会, eds. 1967. *Jidaibetsu Kokugo Daijiten, Jōdai-hen* [時代別国語大辞典・上代編; A periodized comprehensive dictionary of the Japanese language: Old Japanese], Tokyo: Sanseidō.

Kadekaru Chizuko 嘉手苅千鶴子. 1987. "An mabute kono to watashiyoware." [我守て此の海渡しよわれ; (May you) protect us and let us cross this ocean]. In: OSKS, 247–253.

Kadekaru Chizuko 嘉手苅千鶴子. 2003. *Omoro to Ryūka no Sekai: Kōkyō-suru Ryūkyū Bungaku.* [おもろと琉歌の世界――交響する琉球文学; The world of omoros and Ryūka: Ryukyuan literatures in harmony] Tokyo: Shinwasha.

Kamata Kunihiko, Yasuda Naoko, and Taishūkan, eds. 2011–2013. Electronic *Shin-Kango-Rin*, 2nd ed. [新漢語林]. Tokyo: Taishūkan Shoten.

Katō Masaharu 加藤正春. 1983. "Yuta" [ゆた; *Yuta* shamans]. In: ODHJ, 779–780.

Kenkyūsha 研究社, eds. 2008. (*Tegaki Taiō*) *Shin Wa-Ei Daijiten* (手書き対応) 新和英大辞典 [New Comprehensive Japanese-English Dictionary, with handwriting lookup] 5th ed. Tokyo: Kenkyūsha.

Kindaichi Haruhiko 金田一春彦. 1950. Kokugo dōshi no ichi bunrui [国語動詞の一分類; One categorization of the verbs of Japanese]. *Gengo Kenkyū* 15: 48–63.

KJE, see Iwanami Shoten 2006.

REFERENCES

Kinjō Chōei 金城朝永 (1974 [1944]), "Naha hōgen gaisetsu" [那覇方言概説; An outline of the Naha dialect], In: T. Ōfuji and S. Hokama, eds., *Kinjō Chōei Zenshū* 1, *Gengo・Bungaku-hen* [金城朝永全集 1 言語·文学篇], 1–150. Okinawa: Okinawa Taimususha.

Kinjō Chōei 金城朝永 (1970 [1950]). "Kita o nishi to yobu hanashi: Hōi to kaze no Ryūkyūgo" [北を西と呼ぶ話：方位と風の琉球語; About calling 'north' *nishi* (J 'west'): Ryukyuan words having to do with compass directions and the winds], In: Ōfuji Tokihiko and Hokama Shuzen, eds., *Kinjō Chōei Zenshū* 1, *Gengo・Bungaku-hen* [金城朝永全集 1 言語・文学編], 258–261. Okinawa: Okinawa Taimususha.

KKKS = Hokama 1970.

KKKS2 = Ikemiya 1995.

Kojima Yōrei 小島瓔禮 (Shintō Taikei Hensan-kai), eds. 1982. *Shintō Taikei: Jinja hen* (*Okinawa*). [神道体系・神社編 (沖縄); Survey of Shintō: Shrines (Okinawa)] Tokyo: Seikōsha.

KOS, see Nakahara and Hokama, eds. and comps. 1967 [1978].

Li Changbo 李長波. 2002. *Nihongo Shiji Taikei no Rekishi* [日本語指示体系の歴史; History of the Japanese deictic system]. Kyoto: Kyōto Daigaku Gakujutsu Shuppankai.

Lin, Chihkai. 2015. *A Reconstruction of Old Okinawan: A corpus-based approach*. PhD Dissertation, University of Hawai'i.

Mamiya Atsushi 間宮厚司. 2005. *Miruya, amamiya, obotsu* no gogen [ミルヤ、アマミヤ、オボツの語源; The etymologies of the words *miruya, amamiya*, and *obotsu*]. *Hōsei Daigaku Bungakubu Kiyō* 50: A71–A90.

Mamiya Atsushi 間宮厚司. 2014. *Okinawa Kogo no Shinsō: Omoro-go no Tankyū* [*Zōho Ban*] [沖縄語の深層　オモロ語の探求 [増補版]; The deepest strata of the Okinawan language: An investigation of the *omoro* language [Enlarged edition]]. Tokyo: Shinwasha.

Martin, Samuel E. 1970. "Shodon: A Dialect of the Northern Ryukyus." *Journal of the American Oriental Society*, 90.1: 97–139.

Martin, Samuel E. 1975. *A Reference Grammar of Japanese*. Tokyo: Tuttle.

Martin, Samuel E. 1987. *The Japanese Language Through Time*. New Haven and London: Yale University Press.

Matsumoto Hirotake 松本泰丈. 1986. "Amami hōgen no ⁻*dana* no yōhō no oboegaki" [奄美方言の⁻ダナの用法の覚書; Some thoughts on the usages of ⁻*dana* in Amami dialects]. In: Matsumura Akira Kyōju Koki Kinenkai, eds., *Matsumura Akira Kyōju Koki Kinen Kokugo Kenkyū Ronshū*, 867–882. Tokyo: Meiji Shoin.

Matsumura Akira 松村明. 1971. *Nihon Bunpō Daijiten* [日本文法大辞典; A comprehensive dictionary of Japanese grammar]. Tokyo: Meiji Shoin.

Matsumura Akira 松村明, Yamaguchi Akiho 山口明穂, and Wada Toshimasa 和田利政, eds. 2008. *Ōbunsha Kogo Jiten* 旺文社古語辞典, 10th ed., electronic edition in Casio EX-word dataplus 8, XD-U 18000. Tokyo: Ōbunsha.

Minami, Fujio 南不二男. 1974. *Gendai Nihongo no Kōzō* [現代日本語の構造; The structure of Modern Japanese]. Tokyo: Taishūkan Shoten.

Miura Sukeyuki 三浦祐之. 1988. *Kodai-go o Yomu* [古代語を読む; Reading the ancient language]. Tokyo: Ōfūsha.

Murayama Shichirō 村山七郎. 1970. "Shinateru·Terushino kō" [しなてる・てるしの考; A consideration of ⟨sinateru⟩ and ⟨terusino⟩]. *Kokugogaku* 82: 16–28.

Murayama Shichirō 村山七郎. 1981. *Ryūkyū-go no Himitsu.* [琉球語の秘密; The secrets of Ryukyuan]. Tokyo: Chikuma Shobō.

Nakahara Zenchū 仲原善忠. 1957. *Omoro Sōshi Shinshaku* [『おもろさうし』新釈; New interpretations from the *Omoro Sōshi*]. Naha: Ryūkyū Bunkyō Tosho.

Nakahara Zenchū 仲原善忠. 1969 [1960]. "Omoro kenkyū shigo" [おもろ研究私語; Personal notes on omoro studies] (*The Ryūkyū Shinpō*, September 19–23), reprinted in *Nakahara Zenchū Senshū* 2:483–492. Naha: Okinawa Taimususha.

Nakahara Zenchū 仲原善忠 and Hokama Shuzen 外間守善, eds. and comps. 1978 [1965]. *Kōhon Omoro Sōshi* [校本おもろさうし; *Omoro Sōshi*, variorum edition]. 4th printing. Tokyo: Kadokawa Shoten.

Nakahara Zenchū 仲原善忠 and Hokama Shuzen 外間守善, eds. and comps. 1978 [1967]. *Omoro Sōshi Jiten · Sōsakuin* [おもろさうし辞典・総索引; Dictionary and comprehensive index of the *Omoro Sōshi*], 2nd ed. Tokyo: Kadokawa Shoten.

Nakamoto Masachie 中本正智. 1976. *Ryūkyū Hōgen On'in no Kenkyū* [琉球方言音韻の研究; Studies in Ryukyuan-Dialect phonology]. Tokyo: Hōsei Daigaku Shuppankyoku.

Nakamoto Masachie 中本正智. 1981. *Zusetsu Ryūkyūgo Jiten.* [図説琉球語辞典 Linguistic atlas of Ryukyuan]. Tokyo: Kinkeisha.

Nakamoto Masachie 中本正智. 1990. *Nihon Rettō Gengo-shi no Kenkyū.* [日本列島言語史の研究; A Study of the linguistic history of the Japanese archipelago]. Tokyo: Taishūkan.

Nakamoto Masachie 中本正智, Higa Minoru 比嘉実, and Chris Drake クリス・ドレーク. 1984.10–1993.01. *Omoro Kanshō: Ryūkyū Koyō no Sekai* [おもろ鑑賞　琉球古謡の世界; Omoro exegeses: The world of old Ryukyuan songs]. In *Gekkan Gengo* 13.10–22.1. Part of series *Okinawa-go no Susume*. Tokyo: Taishūkan.

Nakasone Seizen 仲宗根政善. 1983 *Nakijin Hōgen Jiten* [今帰仁方言辞典; A dictionary of Nakijin dialect]. Tokyo: Kadokawa Shoten.

Nakasone Seizen 仲宗根政善. 1987 [1976]. "Omoro no sonkei dōshi *owaru* ni tsuite" [おもろの尊敬動詞「おわる」について; On the omoro exalting verb |owaru|]. Reprinted in: Nakasone Seizen, *Ryūkyū Hōgen no Kenkyū* [琉球方言の研究; Studies in the Ryukyuan dialects], 238–263. Tokyo: Shinsensha.

Nakasone Seizen 仲宗根政善. 1987 [1979]. "Nakabe kiyora o-gusuku" [なかべきよら御城; The fine castle in the beautiful sky]. Reprinted in: id., *Ryūkyū Hōgen no Kenkyū*, 283–293. Tokyo: Shinsensha.

Nakasone Seizen 仲宗根政善. 2009 [1988–1997]. Omoro-go kō [おもろ語考; Thoughts on the omoro language]. *Okinawa Bunka (Nakasone Seizen Sensei Seitan Hyaku-nen Kinen Shinpojiumu)* [沖縄文化(仲宗根政善先生生誕百年記念シンポジウム); Okinawan Culture (A Symposium Commemorating the Hundredth Anniversary of Professor Nakasone Seizen's Birth)] 42.2: 1–53.

NHK Hōsō Bunka Kenkyū-jo NHK 放送文化研究所, eds. (n.d.) *NHK Nihon-go Hatsuon Akusento Jiten* [NHK 日本語発音アクセント辞典; The NHK Japanese pronunciation and accent dictionary], electronic version, in Casio EX-word Dataplus 8 (XD-U18000). Tokyo: Casio.

NKT, see Hokama and Tamaki, editors and authors. 1980.

ODHJ, see *Okinawa Dai-Hyakka Jiten*.

OGJ, see Uemura Yukio, ed. 1963.

OGJ2, see Uchima and Nohara, eds. 2006.

Ōkawa Jun'ichi 大川純一. 2012. *Nansō Heike ni yoru Ryūkyū Okinawa Ōchō-shi* (jō-kan).[南走平家による琉球沖縄王朝史上巻; A history of the Ryukyu/Okinawan courts founded by southward-fleeing Taira-clan families (vol. 1)]. Tokyo: Fuji Denshi Shuppan.

Okazaki Tomoko 岡崎友子. 2010. *Nihongo Shijishi no Kenkyū* [日本語指示詞の研究; A Study of Japanese demonstratives]. Tokyo: Hitsuji Shobō.

OKDJ, see Hokama Shuzen, ed. 1995.

OKRKS, see Nakamoto Masachie, Higa Minoru, and Chris Drake.

Omoro Kenkyūkai おもろ研究会, eds. 1987. *Omoro Seikashō* [おもろ精華抄; The quintessence of omoro studies]. Naha: Hirugisha.

Ōno Susumu 大野晋. 1968. "Nihon-jin no shikō to jutsugo yōshiki" [日本人の思考と述語様式; Japanese people's thought and their predication patterns]. *Bungaku* 36.2: 25–36.

Ōno Susumu 大野晋. 1993. *Kakari Musubi no Kenkyū* [係り結びの研究 A study of *kakari musubi*], Tokyo: Iwanami.

Onoe Keisuke. 1982. "Bun no kihon kōsei: Shiteki tenkai" [文の基本構成：史的展開; Basic structure of sentences: Historical development]. In: Morioka Kenji 森岡健二, ed., *Kōza Nihongogaku* [講座日本語学 Course in Japanese linguistics], Tokyo: Meiji Shoin.

Orikuchi Shinobu 折口信夫. 1956 [1937]. "Ryūkyū kokuō no shutsuji" [琉球国王の出自; The roots of Ryukyuan kingship]. In: *Orikuchi Shinobu Zenshū*. Tokyo: Chūō Kōron-sha.

Orikuchi Shinobu 折口信夫. 1976 [1919]. *Man'yōshū Jiten* [『万葉集』辞典; A dictionary of the *Man'yōshū*], in *Orikuchi Shinobu Zenshū* [折口信夫全集; The complete works of Orikuchi Shinobu], 6. Tokyo: Chūkō Bunko.

Osada Suma 長田須磨, Suyama Nahoko 須山名保子, and Fuji'i Misako 藤井美佐子, eds. 1980. *Amami Hōgen Bunrui Jiten* [奄美方言分類辞典; A semantically classified dictionary of an Amami dialect], 2. Tokyo: Kasama Shoin.

Oshiro, Tokiko. 1987. *Aspects of Semantic Change in Honorific Verbs of the Okinawan Language*. Unpublished Ohio State University MA thesis.

OSJS, see Nakahara and Hokama, eds. 1975.

OSKS. See Omoro Kenkyūkai, eds. 1987.

Osterkamp, Sven, comp. 2007. Sōshi sāchā [双紙サーチャー Sōshi searcher, v0.3 [20070124]]. Electronic search tool, to be used with Takahashi Toshizō's bare *Omoro Sōshi* text.

Ōtomo Shin'ichi 大友信一 and Kimura Akira 木村あきら. 1968. *Nihonkan Yakugo: Honbun to Sakuin* [『日本館訳語』——本文と索引——; The *Rìběnguǎn Yìyǔ*: Text and index] Kyoto: Rakubunsha.

Pellard, Thomas. 2013. "Ryukyuan perspectives on the Proto-Japonic vowel system." *Japanese/Korean Linguistics* 20: 81–96. Stanford: CSLI.

Quinn, Charles J. 1997. "On the origins of Japanese sentence particles *ka* and *zo*." In: J. Haig and H. Sohn, eds., *Japanese/Korean Linguistics* 6: 61–89. Stanford: CSLI.

Quinn, Charles J. 2003. "From verb infinitive to formant/ending: -*si* in early Japanese adjectives." In: Patricia M. Clancy, ed., *Japanese/Korean Linguistics* 11: 175–188. Stanford: CSLI.

RGS (*Ryūkyū Gikyokushū*), see Ifa Fuyū. (1974 [1929]).

Sāchā, see Osterkamp 2007.

Sakakura, Atsuyoshi 阪倉篤義. 1993. *Nihongo Hyōgen no Nagare* [日本語表現の流れ; The flow of Japanese expression through time]. Tokyo: Iwanami Shoten.

Sanada Shinji 真田信治 and Tomosada Kenji 友定賢治. 2007. *Chihōbetsu Hōgen Gogen Jiten* [地方別方言語源辞典; Dialect etymological dictionary by region]. Tokyo: Tōkyōdō.

Sawaki Motoei 沢木幹栄. 2009. "Ryūkyū hōgen no hitei o arawasu setsuji no ikeitai ni tsuite" [琉球方言の否定を表わす接辞の異形態について; On the suffix meaning negation in Ryūkyū dialect [*sic*]]. *Jinbun Kagaku Ronshū Ningen Jōhō Kagaku-hen* 43: 77–85.

Schuessler, Axel. 2009. *Minimal Old Chinese and Later Han Chinese: A Companion to Grammata Serica Recensa*. ABC Chinese Dictionary Series. Honolulu: University of Hawai'i Press.

Serafim, Leon A. 1977. *The relationship of pre-Japanese and proto-Japanese*. Unpublished ms.

Serafim, Leon A. 1985. *Shodon: The Prehistory of a Northern Ryukyuan Dialect of Japanese*. Tokyo: Hompo Shoseki Press.

Serafim, Leon A. 2003. "When and from where did the Japonic language enter the Ryukyus?—A critical comparison of language, archaeology, and history." In: Alexander Vovin and Toshiki Osada, eds., *Perspectives on the Origins of the Japanese Language*, 463–476. Kyoto: Kokusai Nihon Bunka Kenkyū Sentā.

Serafim, Leon A. 2004. "The Shuri Ryukyuan exalting prefix *myi*- and the Japanese connection." *Japanese Language and Literature* 38.2 (Oct.): 301–322. Special Issue: In Honor of Samuel E. Martin.

Serafim, Leon A. 2007. "Progressive stative predicate extensions in Ryukyuan, and their relation to Earlier Japonic." In: B. Frellesvig, M. Shibatani, and J.C. Smith, eds., *Current Issues in the History and Structure of Japanese*, 207–218. Tokyo: Kuroshio Shuppan.

Serafim, Leon A. 2008. "The uses of Ryukyuan in understanding Japanese language history." In: Bjarke Frellesvig and John Whitman, eds., *Proto-Japanese: Issues and Prospects*, 79–99. Amsterdam/Philadelphia: John Benjamins Publishing Company.

Serafim, Leon A. 2016. "Rendaku in Okinawan." In: Timothy J. Vance and Mark Irwin, eds., *Sequential Voicing in Japanese: Papers from the NINJAL Rendaku Project*, 139–172. Amsterdam: John Benjamins.

Shibatani, Masayoshi. 1985. "Passives and related constructions: A prototype analysis." *Language* 61.4: 821–828.

Shigeno Hiromi 重野裕美. 2010. "Amami sho-hōgen no keigohō: Keigo keishiki no bunpu to sono tenkai ni chakumokushite" [奄美諸方言の敬語法——敬語形式の分布とその展開に着目して——; Polite language systems of the dialects of the Amami islands: focusing on the distribution of polite forms and their development], *Kokubungaku Kō* 208: 1–18.

Shimabukuro, Moriyo. 2007. *The Accentual History of the Japanese and Ryukyuan Languages: A Reconstruction*. Kent, UK: Global Oriental/Brill.

Shimamura Kōichi 島村幸一. 1983. "*Omoro Sōshi* no fushi-na ni tsuite" [『おもろさうし』の節名について; Concerning the tune names in the *Omoro Sōshi*]. *Okinawa Bunka Kenkyū* 10: 304–345.

Shimamura Kōichi 島村幸一. 2010. *Omoro Sōshi to Ryūkyū Bungaku* [『おもろさうし』と琉球文学; The *Omoro Sōshi* and Ryukyuan literature]. Tokyo: Kasama Shoin.

Shimamura Kōichi 島村幸一. 2012. *Omoro Sōshi* [『おもろさうし』; The *Omoro Sōshi*]. Tokyo: Kasama Shoin.

Shimamura Kōichi 島村幸一. 2015. "Omoro Sōshi Sen, shōkai II" [『おもろさうし』選、詳解II; Selected songs from the *Omoro Sōshi* with detailed analyses, II]. *Risshō Daigaku Bungakubu Kiyō* 31: 161–213.

Shimizu Akira 清水彰, ed. 2003. *Hyō'on Omoro Sōshi Chūshaku* [表音おもろさうし注釈; The *Omoro Sōshi*, with pronunciations, annotations, and interpretations]. Tokyo: Izumi Shoin.

Shinzato, Rumiko, and Leon A. Serafim. 2013. *Synchrony and Diachrony of Okinawan Kakari Musubi in Comparative Perspective with Premodern Japanese*. Kent, UK: Global Oriental/Brill.

Shinzato, Rumiko. 2004. "Some observations concerning mental verbs and speech act verbs." *Journal of Pragmatics* 36: 861–882.

Shinzato, Rumiko. 2007. "(Inter)subjectification, Japanese syntax and syntactic scope increase." *Journal of Historical Pragmatics* 8.2: 171–206.

Shinzato, Rumiko. 2008. "From 'Emergence' to 'Ability': A Case of Japanese *naru* and *dekiru*." *CLS* 40: 365–379.

Shinzato, Rumiko. 2011. "Nominalization in Okinawan: From a diachronic and comparative perspective." In: F.H. Yap and J. Wrona, eds., *Nominalization in Asian Languages: Diachronic and Typological Perspectives*, II: *Asia Pacific Languages. Typological Studies in Language*, 445–472. Amsterdam/Philadelphia: John Benjamins.

Shōgakukan Kokugo Jiten Henshūbu 小学館国語辞典編集部, eds., 2000–2002. *Seisenban Nihon Kokugo Daijiten*; 精選版日本国語大辞典. Tokyo: Shōgakukan.

Smits, Gregory. 2019. *Maritime Ryukyu, 1050–1650*. Honolulu: University of Hawai'i Press.

SNKDJ, see Shōgakukan Kokugo Jiten Henshūbu, eds.

Takahashi Toshizō 高橋俊三. 1991a. *Omoro Sōshi no Kokugogaku-teki Kenkyū* [おもろさうしの国語学的研究; Studies in the *Omoro Sōshi* utilizing *Kokugogaku* research methods]. Tokyo: Musashino Shoin.

Takahashi Toshizō高橋俊三. 1991b. *Omoro Sōshi no Dōshi no Kenkyū* [おもろさうしの動詞の研究; A study of *Omoro Sōshi* verbs]. Tokyo: Musashino Shoin.

Takahashi Toshizō高橋俊三, comp. [n.d.] Bare electronic *Omoro Sōshi*, to be used in database searches, for example, with Sven Osterkamp's Sōshi Sāchā. Available, e.g., from the authors.

Tamaki Masami 玉城政美. 1976. Omoro no kōzō [おもろの構造; The structure of omoros]. *Okinawa Bunka Kenkyū* 3: 61–124.

Tamaki Masami 玉城政美. 1987. "Omoro no ⟨mata⟩ o megutte" [おもろの「又」をめぐって; On the "mata" of the omoro]. In: Ryūkyū Hōgen Kenkyū Kurabu 30 Shūnen Kinen Ronsō Kankō I'inkai, eds., *Ryūkyū Hōgen Ronsō*, 269–284. Tokyo: Daitō Insatsu Kōgyō Kabushiki Gaisha.

Tamaki Masami 玉城政美. 1991. "Omoro ni okeru shinjo no *mochīfu*" [おもろにおける神女のモチーフ; The motif of the shamaness in omoro]. In: Nakamatsu Yashū Sensei Sanju Kinen Ronbun-shū Kankō I'inkai, eds., *Kami, Mura, Hito* [Deities, villages, and people], 535–557. Tokyo: Dai'ichi Shobō.

Tanigawa Ken'ichi 谷川健一. 1999. *Nihon no Kamigami* [日本の神々; The deities of Japan]. Tokyo: Iwanami Shoten.

Thomason, Sarah Grey, and Terrence Kaufmann, eds. 1988. *Language Contact, Creolization, and Genetic Linguistics*. Berkeley and Los Angeles: University of California Press.

Thorpe, Maner L. 1983. *Ryūkyūan Language History*, Unpublished University of Southern California dissertation.

Torigoe Kenzaburō 鳥越憲三郎. 1968. *Omoro Sōshi Zenshaku* [おもろさうし全釈; A complete interpretation of the *Omoro Sōshi*], 1. Ōsaka: Seibundō Shuppan.

Toyota, Junichi. 2011. *The Grammatical Voice in Japanese: A Typological Perspective*. Cambridge: Cambridge Scholars Publishing.

Traugott, Elizabeth Closs, and Richard Dasher. 1987. "On the historical relation between

# REFERENCES

mental and speech act verbs in English and Japanese." In: Anna Giacalone Ramat et al., eds., *Papers from the Seventh International Conference on Historical Linguistics*, 561–573. Amsterdam: John Benjamins.

TOS, see Hokama and Hateruma, editors and authors. 2011.

Uchima Chokujin 内間直仁 and Nohara Mitsuyoshi 野原三義, eds. 2006. *Okinawago Jiten: Naha Hōgen o Chūshin ni* [沖縄語辞典: 那覇方言を中心に; Dictionary of Okinawan, focusing on Naha dialect]. Tokyo: Kenkyūsha.

Uchima Chokujin 内間直仁. 1994. *Ryūkyū Hōgen Joshi to Hyōgen no Kenkyū* [琉球方言助詞と表現の研究; A study of Ryukyu-dialect particles and expression]. Tokyo: Kasama Shoin.

Uemura Yukio, ed. 1963. *Okinawago Jiten* [A dictionary of the Okinawan language]. Tokyo: Ōkurashō Insatsukyoku.

Unger, J. Marshall, with Yōko Itō Tomita. 1983. "The classification of Old Japanese adjectives." *Papers in East Asian Languages* I: 52–65.

Unger, J. Marshall. 1993 [1977]. *Studies in early Japanese morphophonemics*. Yale University PhD dissertation. Bloomington: Indiana University Linguistics Club Publications. 2nd revised edition.

Vance, Timothy. 2005. "Sequential voicing and Lyman's Law in Old Japanese." In: Salikoko S. Mufwene, Elaine J. Francis, and Rebecca S. Wheeler, eds., *Polymorphous Linguistics: Jim McCawley's Legacy*, 27–43. Cambridge: MIT Press.

Vendler, Zeno. 1957. "Verbs and times." *The Philosophical Review* 66.2: 143–160.

Vovin, Alexander. 2005. *A Descriptive and Comparative Grammar of Western Old Japanese, Part I: Sources, Script and Phonology, Lexicon, Nominals*. Folkestone, Kent: Global Oriental.

Vovin, Alexander. 2009a. *A Descriptive and Comparative Grammar of Western Old Japanese. Part 2: Adjectives, Verbs, Adverbs, Conjunctions, Particles, Postpositions*. Folkestone, Kent: Global Oriental.

Vovin, Alexander. 2009b. "Ryūkyū-go, Jōdai Nihon-go to shūhen no sho-gengo: Saikō to setten no sho-mondai" [琉球語、上代日本語と周辺の諸言語——再構と接点の諸問題; Ryukyuan, Old Japanese, and the neighboring languages: Problems of reconstruction and point of contact]. *Nihon Kenkyū* 39:11–27.

Vovin, Alexander. 2012. "Ryūkyū sogo no gochū ni okeru yūsei shi'in no saiken ni tsuite" [琉球祖語の語中における有声子音の再建について; Concerning the reconstruction of medial voiced consonants in Proto-Ryukyuan]. Paper presented at NINJAL, 2012-8-7.

Wada Yoshikazu. 2007. "Senmyō no "kamunagara" to Ōtomo Yakamochi" [宣命の「かむながら」と大友家持; The word "Kamunagara" in the Imperial edicts, and Yakamochi's poetry]. *Fukui Kōgyō Daigaku Kiyō* 37: 115–124.

Whitman, John B. 2008. "The source of the bigrade conjugation and stem shape in pre-Old Japanese." In: Bjarke Frellesvig and John Whitman, eds., *Proto-Japanese: Issues and Prospects*, 159–173. Amsterdam/Philadelphia: John Benjamins Publishing Company.

Yamada Yoshio 山田孝雄. 1954. *Narachō Bunpōshi* [奈良朝文法史; A history of Nara-Period grammar], Tokyo: Hōbunkan.

Yoshida Kanehiko 吉田金彦. 1973. *Jōdaigo Jodōshi no Shiteki Kenkyū* [上代語助動詞の史的研究; A historical study of Old Japanese auxiliary verbs]. Tokyo: Meiji Shoin.

Yoshinari Naoki 吉成直樹 and Fuku Hiromi 福寛美. 2006. *Ryūkyū Ōkoku to Wakō: Omoro no Kataru Rekishi* [琉球国と倭寇――おもろの語る歴史; The Ryukyu Kingdom and the pirates: What the omoros tell us] Tokyo: Shinwasha.

Yuzawa Kōkichirō 湯沢幸吉郎. 1943. *Kokugoshi Gaisetsu* [国語史概説; An introduction to the history of the national language], Tokyo: Yagi Shoten.

# Index of Authors

Abe Minako    90, 124, 125
Akiyama Noriko    48
Anttila, Raimo    231, 233

Bentley, John    130(n70)

Drake, Chris    121(n48), 149, 214(n53), 224(n66), 251, 320(n140)
Dasher, Richard    3, 351, 374

Endō, Mitsuaki    124
Erickson, Blaine    85(n3)

Frellesvig, Bjarke    151
Fuji'i Misako    263
Fuku Hiromi    91(n21), 93, 93(n30), 125, 289(n64)

Greenberg, Joseph H.    268
Grice, H. Paul    351

Hagers, Steven    249
Handa Ichirō    365
Hashimoto Shinkichi    268
Hashimoto Shirō    122
Haspelmath, Martin    269
Hateruma Eikichi    11, 12(n20), 120, 131(n72), 325(n152)
Hattori Shirō    230(n79)
Higa Minoru    95, 96(n38), 264, 304(n103), 325(n152), 328
Hokama Shuzen    2–4, 4(n8), 6(n11), 9(n17), 10–12, 24(n10), 27(n16), 88, 95, 96(n38), 97, 98, 108, 114, 119(n43), 138(n93, n95), 152(n4), 161, 164, 164(n25), 165, 165(n28), 166(n30), 170(n39), 171(n42), 172(n44, n45), 177, 177(n56), 178, 182, 189(n118), 198, 206(n141), 207, 214(n152), 221, 221(n60), 222(n61), 223(n63), 247, 247(n100), 250(n106), 252(n114), 253(n115), 259(n127), 263(n9), 283, 284, 289(n61, n64), 299, 309(n110), 314, 314(n122), 316(n128), 321(n146), 325(n152, n153), 329, 330, 334(n168), 335(n170), 340(n177), 346(n190), 347(n191), 352, 352(n208), 358(n209),

358(n213), 361, 362, 367(n225), 370(n229), 385(n262), 386(n267)
Hopper, Paul J.    104

Ifa Fuyū    2, 6(n11), 9(n17), 95, 125, 135(n83), 141(n99, n100), 143(n106), 182, 266(n11), 275(n32), 290, 360, 362(n219)
Ikemiya Masaharu    1, 2, 4, 5, 9(n17), 11, 13, 14, 27(n16), 113, 114(n35), 120, 121, 121(n47), 128(n62), 134(n82), 137(n91), 167, 173(n47), 220(n59), 253(n115), 277, 278, 291(n67), 304(n103), 306, 368(n226)
Ishizaki Hiroshi    112, 194(n18)
Iwasaki, Shoichi    268(n17)

Jōdaigo Jiten Henshū Iinkai    3, 4, 4(n8), 23, 30(n20), 32, 38, 56, 66(n65), 67, 74(n73), 85(n2), 87(n9), 90, 105(n14), 119(n43), 140(n98), 150, 150(n1), 163(n22), 170(n41), 173–175(n52), 177, 179, 182, 195(n23), 229(n77, n78), 230, 235(n86), 240, 240(n92), 241, 242(n94), 268(n16), 271(n22), 274(n26), 276, 278(n35), 312(n114), 325(n152), 329(n159), 357(n208), 358(n209), 374(n233), 377(n238), 388(n268)

Kadekaru Chizuko    12, 110(n28), 111, 111(n30), 291, 292
Kamata Kunihiko (ESKR)    69
Katō Masaharu    359(n214)
Kaufmann, Terrence    234
Kimura Akira    112
Kindaichi Haruhiko    342, 343(n181), 344, 354(n205)
Kinjō Chōei    103, 134(n81)
Kojima Yōrei    103
Kokuritsu Kokugo Kenkyūjo (OGJ)    1(n1), 2, 2(n3), 3(n5), 5, 31, 33, 35–37, 40(n40), 41(n41), 44, 46(n44), 48(n48), 49(n51), 51, 51(n53), 52, 54–58(n58), 59, 62, 63, 65, 66, 69, 70–74, 74(n71), 78–82, 85(n2), 87, 87(n9), 88(n11), 90(n19), 92, 93, 99, 100, 100(n4), 101–103, 105(n14), 107(n20), 109(26), 111(n30), 123, 135(83), 136(n88), 137(n91), 142(n103), 154,

## Index of Authors

Kokuritsu Kokugo Kenkyūjo (OGJ) (*cont.*) 157, 158, 159(n15), 162, 163(n21, n22), 164, 167, 167(n34), 170(n39), 173(n46), 174, 174(n50), 175(n53), 181, 182(n64), 192(n10), 195, 195(n23), 197, 200(n25), 209(n45), 212(n47), 214(n50), 215(n54), 228(n75), 229(n76), 230(n79), 240, 241, 245(n96), 246, 251(n109), 252, 252(n113), 256(n119, n120), 260(n10), 269(n18), 272(n23), 280(n41), 285, 286(n58), 289(n62), 290(n65), 290, 291(n67), 300(n92), 301(n94), 304(n103), 306(n105), 307, 307(n107), 309(n109), 311(n113), 312(n115), 314(n120, n121, n123), 315(n124, n125, n126), 316(n127, n128), 317(n131), 318(n134, n136), 319, 325(n152), 334(n168), 344(n185), 348(n195), 353(n200, n201), 357(n208), 358(n210, n212), 359(n214, n215), 362(n218), 364(n221, n222), 367(n225), 374, 375, 378(n239), 379(n241), 382(n249), 382(n250), 383, 383(n254, n255), 384, 384(n257), 385, 385(n259, n261), 388(n268)

Lin, Chihkai 48(n48), 75, 75(n76), 76, 77

Mamiya Atsushi 55, 65, 95, 95(n34), 96, 96(n39), 108, 109, 109(n27), 110, 110(n29), 112, 193(n13), 359(n215)
Martin, Samuel E. 34, 72(n69), 142(n103), 151(n2), 158(n14), 172(n45), 179, 235(n86), 256(n119), 274(n26), 324(n151), 388(n268)
Matsumoto Hirotake 292(n73), 294(n77), 295, 296
Matsumura Akira 217(n56)
Minami Fujio 260
Miura Sukeyuki 110, 110(n29), 112
Murayama Shichirō 71(n68), 131(n73)

Nakahara Zenchū 1, 4, 27(n16), 88, 97, 138(n93, n95), 235(n86), 290, 299, 300(n91), 302, 302(n100), 304, 304(n103), 323(n148, n149), 328, 347(n191), 348(n195)
Nakamoto Masachie 59, 95, 123, 147, 359(n215)

Nakasone Seizen 71(n68), 105(n12), 115, 144, 145(n112), 173(n49), 242, 265(n96), 292(n73), 311, 328, 331(n162), 359(n215), 381
NHK Hōsō Bunka Kenkyū-jo 72, 158, 240, 243
Nohara Mitsuyoshi (OGJ2) 59, 256(n119), 290(n65), 314(n121)

Ōkawa Jun'ichi 69(n67)
Okazaki Tomoko 122
Ōno Susumu 118, 260
Onoe Keisuke 314
Orikuchi Shinobu 4, 4(n8), 93(n30), 141(n99)
Osada Suma 263(n8)
Oshiro, Tokiko 373, 374
Osterkamp, Sven (Sōshi Sāchā) 31, 388(n268)
Ōtomo Shin'ichi 112

Pellard, Thomas 230(n80)

Quinn, Charles J. 122, 159–161, 161(n18), 166

Saigō Nobutsuna 11, 12
Sakakura, Atsuyoshi 314
Sanada Shinji 95
Sawaki Motoei 292(n73), 295
Schuessler, Axel 69, 70, 123(n56, n57), 302(n100)
Serafim, Leon A. 17, 33(n24), 34, 59, 66, 73, 76, 102, 103, 107(n18), 118, 127, 128, 130(n70, n71), 133 (n166), 159(n15), 170(n39), 192(n11), 193(n13), 195(n19), 208(n44), 217(n56), 230(n80), 236(n90), 244, 248, 252(n113), 253, 255, 281(n43), 288, 308, 314(n122), 318(n133), 319, 328(n156), 335(n172), 339, 342
Shibatani, Masayoshi 268(n15)
Shigeno Hiromi 263(n8)
Shimabukuro Moriyo 37(n32)
Shimabukuro Zenpatsu 12, 12(21)
Shimamura Kōichi 6(n11), 9(n17), 71(n68), 88(n10), 93(n29), 105, 120, 125, 142(n102), 144, 299, 299(n89)
Shimizu Akira 274(n26), 316(n128), 326(n154), 365, 387

## INDEX OF AUTHORS

Shinzato, Rumiko   2, 3, 17, 76, 107(n18),
  118, 192(n11), 193(n13), 195(n19),
  208(n44), 244, 252(n113), 253, 255, 260,
  269(n18), 281(n43), 288, 308, 314(n122),
  333(n166), 337, 339, 372(n230)
Shōgakukan Kokugo Jiten Henshūbu
  (ENKDJ)   72, 134(81), 158, 377(n236),
  384(258)
Smits, Gregory   2(n2), 132(n74), 289(n64)
Suyama Nahoko   263(n8)

Tamaki Masami   11, 13, 177(n57)
Tanigawa Ken'ichi   93(n30)
Thomason, Sarah Grey   234
Thorpe, Maner L.   20, 22–24, 28(n17), 29,
  33(n24), 41(n43), 63, 101, 133(n76), 147,
  147(n114), 163, 182, 232(n82), 233, 235,
  235(n85), 243, 256(n119), 268(n14), 288,
  295, 296
Tomita, Yōko Itō   160(n16)
Tomosada Kenji   95
Torigoe Kenzaburō   137(n91), 269(n19), 276,
  278(n36), 283, 284, 284(n51), 287, 288,
  288(n60), 291(n69), 312, 321(n146), 329,
  330, 332, 356(n206), 360, 365
Toyota Jun'ichi   268, 268(n15), 269
Traugott, Elizabeth Closs   3, 104, 351, 374

Uchima Chokujin   306, 360
Unger, J. Marshall   109(27), 160(n16),
  235(n86)

Vance, Timothy   68
Vendler, Zeno   343(n181)
Vovin, Alexander   15, 72, 93, 93(n31), 94,
  94(n33), 112(n31), 122, 125, 141, 157,
  157(n12), 158, 177, 267, 267(n13),
  268(n16), 269, 270(n20), 270(n21),
  271(n22), 274(n27), 278(n35), 279(n37),
  283(n50), 288, 288(n60), 296(n81), 298,
  303, 306, 311, 312, 321, 322(n147), 355,
  356(n206), 363, 365, 387

Wada Yoshikazu   3

Yamada Yoshio   112(n31), 303, 332
Yasuda Naoko (ESKR)   69
Yoshida Kanehiko   177, 287, 302, 303, 332
Yoshinari Naoki   91(n21), 93, 93(n30),
  289(n64)
Yuzawa Kōkichirō   269

# Index of OS Examples

Note: The use of Italic script is to indicate the examples that are fully annotated, with textual presentation in Japanese and Roman scripts, phonological presentation, glosses, and translation. Those not italicized are missing one or two of those items.

| | | |
|---|---|---|
| OS 1 | 1 | *8, 9, 10, 11,* 68, 85, 86, *94, 94*(n33), *132, 134, 141, 218, 265* |
| OS 1 | 2 | *95, 147, 367* |
| OS 1 | 4 | *277, 368* |
| OS 1 | 5 | *87, 139, 209, 374* |
| OS 1 | 6 | 75, *123* |
| OS 1 | 7 | *7, 137, 216, 283,* 288 |
| OS 1 | 8 | 127, *349, 355* |
| OS 1 | 12 | 97 |
| OS 1 | 13 | *86, 381* |
| OS 1 | 14 | *388* |
| OS 1 | 16 | 88, 103 |
| OS 1 | 17 | 36, 67, *79, 89, 105, 128* |
| OS 1 | 18 | *123, 146, 373* |
| OS 1 | 19 | 48(n48), *171* |
| OS 1 | 20 | *210, 272,* 365(n222) |
| OS 1 | 24 | *376* |
| OS 1 | 25 | *352, 369, 380* |
| OS 1 | 26 | 75 |
| OS 1 | 28 | *110* |
| OS 1 | 29 | *126, 209* |
| OS 1 | 31 | *147, 148, 155, 306* |
| OS 1 | 33 | *94, 140, 148, 171, 210, 212, 280* |
| OS 1 | 34 | *57, 91, 130, 173*(n48), *222* |
| OS 1 | 35 | *226, 340* |
| OS 1 | 36 | *140, 304, 306* |
| OS 1 | 37 | *239, 283, 288, 350* |
| OS 1 | 38 | *148, 148*(n115), *201, 367,* 367(n255) |
| OS 1 | 40 | *228* |
| | | |
| OS 2 | 42 | 75, *139* |
| OS 2 | 44 | *238* |
| OS 2 | 45 | *303* |
| OS 2 | 47 | 69, *205, 224, 250* |
| OS 2 | 48 | 75 |
| OS 2 | 49 | 74 |
| OS 2 | 50 | *271* |
| OS 2 | 52 | *210,* 237(n91) |
| OS 2 | 53 | *325* |
| OS 2 | 54 | 66, *108, 199, 223* |
| OS 2 | 60 | *116* |
| OS 2 | 63 | *202* |

| | | |
|---|---|---|
| OS 2 | 66 | *316* |
| OS 2 | 69 | 52, *259* |
| OS 2 | 80 | 75 |
| OS 2 | 82 | 40(n39) |
| OS 2 | 83 | 148 |
| OS 2 | 86 | *111, 143* |
| | | |
| OS 3 | 88 | *369* |
| OS 3 | 89 | *61, 263* |
| OS 3 | 90 | *208, 373* |
| OS 3 | 91 | 104, *111,* 169, 211, 341, 365(n222) |
| OS 3 | 92 | *144* |
| OS 3 | 93 | 35, *152, 188,* 304 |
| OS 3 | 94 | 127(n60), 227, 264, 344(n184), *345* |
| OS 3 | 95 | 148(n115), *149,* 264, *264* |
| OS 3 | 96 | 113, 113(n33), 114, *115,* 148, *198,* 271 |
| OS 3 | 97 | 75, 113(n33), 114, 119, *280* |
| OS 3 | 101 | *226* |
| OS 3 | 103 | 62 |
| OS 3 | 107 | 26, 107(n22), 245, 248, *359, 382* |
| OS 3 | 108 | 79 |
| OS 3 | 110 | *355(n205)* |
| OS 3 | 119 | 10 |
| OS 3 | 125 | 288 |
| OS 3 | 132 | *388* |
| OS 3 | 139 | *324* |
| OS 3 | 151 | 36 |
| | | |
| OS 4 | 153 | 104 |
| OS 4 | 158 | 324 |
| OS 4 | 159 | 58, *120, 215, 340* |
| OS 4 | 173 | 104 |
| OS 4 | 179 | *329* |
| OS 4 | 180 | 24(n10) |
| OS 4 | 182 | *261* |
| OS 4 | 187 | 104 |
| OS 4 | 195 | 137(n91), *218* |
| OS 4 | 198 | 35 |
| OS 4 | 202 | *175* |
| OS 4 | 203 | *129, 239* |
| OS 4 | 205 | *203* |
| OS 4 | 206 | 104 |

# INDEX OF OS EXAMPLES

| | | |
|---|---|---|
| OS 4 | 208 | *104* |
| OS 4 | 210 | *104, 152* |
| | | |
| OS 5 | 212 | *122* |
| OS 5 | 214 | *95* |
| OS 5 | 216 | *161* |
| OS 5 | 217 | *137*(n91) |
| OS 5 | 223 | *72, 159*(n15), *290*(n66), *318*(n132) |
| OS 5 | 226 | *104* |
| OS 5 | 228 | *145* |
| OS 5 | 229 | *58*(n59) |
| OS 5 | 230 | *181* |
| OS 5 | 231 | *103* |
| OS 5 | 237 | *36, 272* |
| OS 5 | 239 | *269*(n19) |
| OS 5 | 240 | *347* |
| OS 5 | 242 | *42, 119, 139* |
| OS 5 | 244 | *173* |
| OS 5 | 246 | *251* |
| OS 5 | 248 | *276, 348* |
| OS 5 | 250 | *214* |
| OS 5 | 253 | *226* |
| OS 5 | 257 | *67, 117* |
| OS 5 | 260 | *109*(n26), *152, 171* |
| OS 5 | 261 | *47, 97, 204, 262* |
| OS 5 | 264 | *180, 365*(n222) |
| OS 5 | 266 | *255* |
| OS 5 | 268 | *74*(n74) |
| OS 5 | 272 | *246* |
| OS 5 | 273 | *148* |
| OS 5 | 284 | *72* |
| OS 5 | 289 | *385* |
| | | |
| OS 6 | 297 | *35* |
| OS 6 | 298 | *81* |
| OS 6 | 299 | *205* |
| OS 6 | 305 | *347* |
| OS 6 | 306 | *148* |
| OS 6 | 309 | *120* |
| OS 6 | 310 | *305* |
| OS 6 | 311 | *271* |
| OS 6 | 314 | *307* |
| OS 6 | 319 | *320* |
| OS 6 | 324 | *360* |
| OS 6 | 325 | *68* |
| OS 6 | 329 | *203* |
| OS 6 | 330 | *110* |
| OS 6 | 332 | *329*(n158) |
| OS 6 | 333 | *223* |
| OS 6 | 337 | *176* |
| OS 6 | 339 | *290* |
| OS 6 | 344 | *154, 168, 169* |
| | | |
| OS 7 | 348 | *66, 280, 297, 298, 360* |
| OS 7 | 349 | *221, 278* |
| OS 7 | 356 | *70, 274* |
| OS 7 | 357 | *137, 231* |
| OS 7 | 358 | *199, 255* |
| OS 7 | 362 | *386* |
| OS 7 | 363 | *368* |
| OS 7 | 365 | *267* |
| OS 7 | 367 | *124, 288* |
| OS 7 | 370 | *370*(n229) |
| OS 7 | 371 | *234, 327* |
| OS 7 | 372 | *349* |
| OS 7 | 375 | *269*(n19) |
| OS 7 | 378 | *117* |
| OS 7 | 380 | *52, 180, 313* |
| OS 7 | 385 | *221* |
| OS 7 | 386 | *339* |
| OS 7 | 391 | *201*(n28) |
| | | |
| OS 8 | 396 | *200* |
| OS 8 | 399 | *94* |
| OS 8 | 402 | *386* |
| OS 8 | 404 | *128*(n62), *386* |
| OS 8 | 411 | *277* |
| OS 8 | 418 | *3, 13* |
| OS 8 | 420 | *57, 344* |
| OS 8 | 421 | *170, 172*(n43) |
| OS 8 | 425 | *166* |
| OS 8 | 426 | *57, 314* |
| OS 8 | 430 | *321* |
| OS 8 | 442 | *175* |
| OS 8 | 443 | *329*(n160) |
| OS 8 | 447 | *383*(n252) |
| OS 8 | 449 | *208* |
| OS 8 | 454 | *357, 358* |
| OS 8 | 456 | *100, 363, 369* |
| OS 8 | 457 | *236, 358*(n211) |
| OS 8 | 458 | *206* |
| OS 8 | 465 | *172*(n43) |
| OS 8 | 472 | *88*(n11) |
| | | |
| OS 9 | 477 | *198* |
| OS 9 | 478 | *239* |
| OS 9 | 479 | *65, 85*(n2), *195* |
| OS 9 | 480 | *293, 304*(n103) |

| | | |
|---|---|---|
| OS 9 | 482 | 120 |
| OS 9 | 484 | *238* |
| OS 9 | 485 | 105 |
| OS 9 | 486 | 285 |
| OS 9 | 488 | *197, 330* |
| OS 9 | 490 | *181* |
| OS 9 | 491 | 113, 113(n330), *114, 177, 314, 315* |
| OS 9 | 493 | 290 |
| OS 9 | 505 | *282* |
| OS 9 | 506 | 62 |
| OS 9 | 507 | 262(n6) |
| OS 9 | 508 | 227, 344(n184), *345* |
| OS 9 | 510 | *134, 196* |
| | | |
| OS 10 | 512 | 148, *198*, 222, 342 |
| OS 10 | 513 | *272* |
| OS 10 | 515 | *196* |
| OS 10 | 518 | *204* |
| OS 10 | 519 | *317* |
| OS 10 | 520 | 329(n158) |
| OS 10 | 521 | *263* |
| OS 10 | 523 | 330(n161) |
| OS 10 | 524 | 103 |
| OS 10 | 525 | *197*, 230(n79), *252, 279* |
| OS 10 | 527 | *96* |
| OS 10 | 530 | *106* |
| OS 10 | 531 | *340* |
| OS 10 | 532 | *71, 158* |
| OS 10 | 534 | 68, *87, 136, 238* |
| OS 10 | 535 | *359* |
| OS 10 | 536 | 108, *350* |
| OS 10 | 538 | 68, 318(n133), *319* |
| OS 10 | 541 | 66, 137(n91), *201, 211, 250* |
| OS 10 | 543 | *196* |
| OS 10 | 545 | 66, *196, 256, 337* |
| OS 10 | 546 | 24(n10), *201, 255, 287, 288, 289, 314, 316* |
| OS 10 | 554 | 336(n171) |
| | | |
| OS 11 | 557 | 153, *296, 297* |
| OS 11 | 559 | *297, 298, 299, 361* |
| OS 11 | 560 | 40(n39) |
| OS 11 | 561 | 67, *211, 317*, 317(n131) |
| OS 11 | 562 | 56 |
| OS 11 | 564 | 264, *265, 335, 336* |
| OS 11 | 565 | 41(n43), 137(n91) |
| OS 11 | 566 | *245, 356* |
| OS 11 | 567 | 383(n252), *384* |
| OS 11 | 568 | *137* |

| | | |
|---|---|---|
| OS 11 | 571 | *348*, 348(n195) |
| OS 11 | 572 | 51(n53), 103, *228*, 253, 253(n115), *320* |
| OS 11 | 576 | 15, 62, *135, 195* |
| OS 11 | 577 | 265, *266* |
| OS 11 | 579 | 285 |
| OS 11 | 581 | 67, *275* |
| OS 11 | 582 | 172(n43) |
| OS 11 | 584 | 291(n66) |
| OS 11 | 586 | *189* |
| OS 11 | 593 | 105, 165 |
| OS 11 | 595 | 293(n103) |
| OS 11 | 596 | *294* |
| OS 11 | 598 | *219* |
| OS 11 | 604 | *205* |
| OS 11 | 608 | *189* |
| OS 11 | 610 | *142* |
| OS 11 | 617 | *372* |
| OS 11 | 618 | 148, *337* |
| OS 11 | 627 | *328*, 329(n158) |
| OS 11 | 628 | 344(n184) |
| OS 11 | 631 | *238* |
| OS 11 | 637 | 119(n43) |
| OS 11 | 639 | 137(n91) |
| OS 11 | 642 | 145(n111), 275(n31) |
| OS 11 | 643 | 66, *212, 282*, 365(n222) |
| OS 11 | 648 | *164*, 291(n66), 365(n222) |
| OS 11 | 650 | 29, 29(n19), 120, 121 |
| | | |
| OS 12 | 660 | *367* |
| OS 12 | 663 | 107 |
| OS 12 | 664 | 110 |
| OS 12 | 670 | 145, *154* |
| OS 12 | 671 | 146 |
| OS 12 | 672 | 80, *238* |
| OS 12 | 676 | 104 |
| OS 12 | 677 | 100 |
| OS 12 | 678 | *290* |
| OS 12 | 683 | *91* |
| OS 12 | 686 | *370* |
| OS 12 | 691 | *228* |
| OS 12 | 694 | 41(n43) |
| OS 12 | 697 | *143* |
| OS 12 | 700 | 265 |
| OS 12 | 703 | 329(n158) |
| OS 12 | 704 | *192, 202* |
| OS 12 | 708 | *194* |
| OS 12 | 709 | 40(n39) |
| OS 12 | 711 | *347* |

## INDEX OF OS EXAMPLES

| | | |
|---|---|---|
| OS 12 | 713 | 29, *195* |
| OS 12 | 721 | 222, *310*, 324 |
| OS 12 | 725 | 66, *192, 198, 203* |
| OS 12 | 727 | *127* |
| OS 12 | 730 | 35, *252* |
| OS 12 | 731 | 58(n60), *117, 216, 339* |
| OS 12 | 734 | 110 |
| OS 12 | 740 | 141, *143* |
| | | |
| OS 13 | 746 | *245* |
| OS 13 | 747 | 314, *315* |
| OS 13 | 748 | *203, 219, 237, 245* |
| OS 13 | 749 | *251, 336*, 337 |
| OS 13 | 750 | *320* |
| OS 13 | 756 | *129* |
| OS 13 | 757 | *310*, 365(n222) |
| OS 13 | 758 | *318* |
| OS 13 | 761 | 90(n19), *220* |
| OS 13 | 763 | *311* |
| OS 13 | 765 | *220* |
| OS 13 | 766 | *203* |
| OS 13 | 769 | *112* |
| OS 13 | 770 | *338* |
| OS 13 | 775 | *387* |
| OS 13 | 777 | 41(n43) |
| OS 13 | 778 | 153 |
| OS 13 | 780 | 104 |
| OS 13 | 785 | 324, 344(n184), *345*, 365(n222) |
| OS 13 | 788 | 329(n158) |
| OS 13 | 789 | 104, 153 |
| OS 13 | 792 | 36, 319 |
| OS 13 | 795 | 86(n4) |
| OS 13 | 797 | *337* |
| OS 13 | 798 | 172(n43), *252, 336* |
| OS 13 | 800 | 153 |
| OS 13 | 805 | 67, *292* |
| OS 13 | 807 | 104 |
| OS 13 | 808 | 291 |
| OS 13 | 809 | *199* |
| OS 13 | 814 | *327* |
| OS 13 | 820 | 48(n147), *91* |
| OS 13 | 822 | 120 |
| OS 13 | 824 | *284* |
| OS 13 | 828 | 26, *131* |
| OS 13 | 831 | *321* |
| OS 13 | 833 | 217 |
| OS 13 | 847 | 58 |
| OS 13 | 850 | 103 |
| OS 13 | 852 | 74 |

| | | |
|---|---|---|
| OS 13 | 853 | 36, *307* |
| OS 13 | 854 | 356(n206) |
| OS 13 | 855 | 189 |
| OS 13 | 858 | *229* |
| OS 13 | 859 | *346(n190)* |
| OS 13 | 864 | *353* |
| OS 13 | 865 | 329(n158) |
| OS 13 | 868 | 335(n171) |
| OS 13 | 873 | 110 |
| OS 13 | 878 | *148* |
| OS 13 | 879 | *293*, 293(n76) |
| OS 13 | 882 | 67 |
| OS 13 | 887 | 74 |
| OS 13 | 888 | 205(n39) |
| OS 13 | 889 | 104, 153 |
| OS 13 | 891 | *318*, 319 |
| OS 13 | 892 | *134* |
| OS 13 | 895 | *273* |
| OS 13 | 898 | *244, 357* |
| OS 13 | 899 | *119, 321* |
| OS 13 | 891 | *318*, 319 |
| OS 13 | 892 | *134* |
| OS 13 | 895 | *273* |
| OS 13 | 898 | *244, 357* |
| OS 13 | 899 | *119, 321* |
| OS 13 | 900 | 356(n206) |
| OS 13 | 901 | *148* |
| OS 13 | 902 | 68, 202, 218(n58), 224, 264, 265, *322(n146), 346* |
| OS 13 | 903 | 100 |
| OS 13 | 904 | *111* |
| OS 13 | 905 | *197* |
| OS 13 | 906 | *341* |
| OS 13 | 917 | *219* |
| OS 13 | 919 | 90(n19) |
| OS 13 | 920 | *202, 205*, 322(n146) |
| OS 13 | 925 | 107(n22), 109, 248 |
| OS 13 | 928 | *200, 363* |
| OS 13 | 937 | 335(n170) |
| OS 13 | 938 | 35 |
| OS 13 | 940 | *335, 342* |
| OS 13 | 948 | 74, *141* |
| OS 13 | 953 | 104 |
| OS 13 | 955 | *197, 358* |
| OS 13 | 957 | 137(n91), 250(n105) |
| OS 13 | 958 | 75, *305* |
| OS 13 | 961 | 172, *283* |
| OS 13 | 962 | *141, 275* |
| OS 13 | 968 | *344* |

| | | |
|---|---|---|
| OS 13 | 971 | *152, 165, 175* |
| OS 13 | 977 | *216* |
| OS 13 | 981 | 108, *287*, 314, *315* |
| | | |
| OS 14 | 982 | 69, 146, 178, *180*, 217, *318, 338,* |
| | | 344(n184) |
| OS 14 | 983 | 36, *122, 142, 143*, 172(n45), |
| | | 344(n184) |
| OS 14 | 987 | *264* |
| OS 14 | 991 | 110, *111* |
| OS 14 | 992 | *174, 267* |
| OS 14 | 993 | 79 |
| OS 14 | 994 | *108* |
| OS 14 | 995 | *357* |
| OS 14 | 996 | *343*, 347(n192), *362* |
| OS 14 | 998 | 113, *206* |
| OS 14 | 1000 | 154(n7), *167* |
| OS 14 | 1001 | *238* |
| OS 14 | 1005 | *208, 246* |
| OS 14 | 1006 | *119* |
| OS 14 | 1011 | 67, 104, *294* |
| OS 14 | 1013 | 21(n4) |
| OS 14 | 1020 | 101 |
| OS 14 | 1022 | *337* |
| OS 14 | 1027 | 100 |
| OS 14 | 1031 | 58, *215*, 218(n58) |
| OS 14 | 1034 | *209* |
| OS 14 | 1037 | 51(53), 329(n160) |
| OS 14 | 1040 | *247, 334* |
| OS 14 | 1042 | 47, *204* |
| OS 14 | 1043 | *202* |
| OS 14 | 1044 | 42, *213* |
| OS 14 | 1051 | 341 |
| | | |
| OS 15 | 1056 | *146* |
| OS 15 | 1058 | *206* |
| OS 15 | 1074 | *284* |
| OS 15 | 1079 | 344(n184) |
| OS 15 | 1085 | *92*, 238 |
| OS 15 | 1087 | *58* |
| OS 15 | 1095 | 104, *179* |
| OS 15 | 1096 | 104, *178* |
| OS 15 | 1100 | *162*, 255 |
| OS 15 | 1104 | 100 |
| OS 15 | 1105 | 55, *90, 120, 134* |
| OS 15 | 1110 | 65, *107* |
| OS 15 | 1114 | 104 |
| OS 15 | 1118 | 72 |
| OS 15 | 1122 | 38(n38) |

| | | |
|---|---|---|
| OS 15 | 1126 | *170* |
| | | |
| OS 16 | 1131 | *225* |
| OS 16 | 1133 | 45, 75 |
| OS 16 | 1134 | *206* |
| OS 16 | 1138 | 155, *374* |
| OS 16 | 1139 | *218* |
| OS 16 | 1144 | *116* |
| OS 16 | 1146 | 75 |
| OS 16 | 1148 | *357* |
| OS 16 | 1155 | 109, *261* |
| OS 16 | 1156 | 324 |
| OS 16 | 1157 | *116*, 145, 334 |
| OS 16 | 1158 | 45 |
| OS 16 | 1160 | *199* |
| OS 16 | 1164 | 99 |
| OS 16 | 1165 | 99 |
| OS 16 | 1167 | 41(n43), 357 |
| OS 16 | 1174 | 99 |
| | | |
| OS 17 | 1177 | *195, 261, 262* |
| OS 17 | 1180 | *112, 138*, 188(n6), 220 |
| OS 17 | 1181 | 110 |
| OS 17 | 1185 | 145 |
| OS 17 | 1204 | 100 |
| OS 17 | 1205 | *176*, 176(n56) |
| OS 17 | 1207 | 344(n168) |
| OS 17 | 1211 | 109, *297, 299, 300* |
| OS 17 | 1213 | *154* |
| OS 17 | 1215 | 100 |
| OS 17 | 1217 | 40(n39) |
| OS 17 | 1222 | 297, 299, *300* |
| OS 17 | 1234 | *211* |
| OS 17 | 1238 | 54 |
| OS 17 | 1240 | *93* |
| OS 17 | 1248 | 101, 137(n91) |
| | | |
| OS 18 | 1252 | *297* |
| OS 18 | 1256 | *170* |
| OS 18 | 1275 | 94 |
| OS 18 | 1278 | 101 |
| | | |
| OS 19 | 1284 | 329(n158) |
| OS 19 | 1285 | *216* |
| OS 19 | 1287 | *225* |
| OS 19 | 1288 | *211* |
| OS 19 | 1295 | *96*, 222, 324, *325* |
| OS 19 | 1297 | *226, 282* |
| OS 19 | 1300 | *92* |

# INDEX OF OS EXAMPLES

| | | |
|---|---|---|
| OS 20 | 1323 | *271* |
| OS 20 | 1332 | 309(n110), *311* |
| OS 20 | 1334 | 51 |
| OS 20 | 1339 | 74(n71) |
| OS 20 | 1345 | *172*, 172(n43) |
| OS 20 | 1346 | 341 |
| OS 20 | 1353 | 145 |
| OS 20 | 1364 | *221* |
| OS 20 | 1366 | *207, 314, 323* |
| OS 20 | 1367 | *353* |
| OS 20 | 1376 | *208* |
| OS 20 | 1377 | *244* |
| OS 20 | 1383 | 356(n206) |
| | | |
| OS 21 | 1394 | 41(n43), 153 |
| OS 21 | 1395 | 153, 335 |
| OS 21 | 1396 | 378 |
| OS 21 | 1397 | 41(n41) |
| OS 21 | 1401 | *295* |
| OS 21 | 1403 | 46(n44) |
| OS 21 | 1409 | 66, *180, 296, 297, 299, 301, 302* |
| OS 21 | 1411 | *297, 307, 308* |
| OS 21 | 1428 | *131* |
| OS 21 | 1434 | 344(n184) |
| OS 21 | 1443 | 41(n43) |
| OS 21 | 1446 | *349, 352* |
| OS 21 | 1451 | *307, 308, 334* |

| | | |
|---|---|---|
| OS 21 | 1454 | *265, 266* |
| OS 21 | 1455 | *210, 297, 301* |
| OS 21 | 1456 | 317(n131), 344(n184) |
| OS 21 | 1457 | 51(n53), 66, 103, *108*, 228(n74), 253(n115) |
| OS 21 | 1462 | *293*, 304(n103) |
| OS 21 | 1470 | *347* |
| OS 21 | 1472 | 153 |
| OS 21 | 1480 | 165 |
| OS 21 | 1483 | 335 |
| OS 21 | 1488 | 329(n158) |
| OS 21 | 1489 | *381* |
| OS 21 | 1492 | *347* |
| OS 21 | 1493 | *326* |
| OS 21 | 1497 | 119(n43) |
| OS 21 | 1501 | *164, 214* |
| OS 21 | 1502 | 56, 103 |
| OS 21 | 1506 | 67, *275* |
| OS 21 | 1507 | 172(n43) |
| | | |
| OS 22 | 1516 | *317* |
| OS 22 | 1524 | *203* |
| OS 22 | 1525 | *360* |
| OS 22 | 1543 | 91 |
| OS 22 | 1545 | *355* |
| OS 22 | 1546 | 201(n28) |
| OS 22 | 1550 | *245* |

# Index of Particles

## Case-Marking Particles

### ABLative
-*kʰara* 'after (V-ing)'   171, 312, 337
-*kʰara* 'from; more than'   180, 225, 305, 358
-*yuryi* 'from; more than'   117(n42)

### ADVerbial
-∅   239
-*N*   167
-*nyi*   95, 167, 175, 195, 204–206, 206(n41), 221,
        225, 228, 229, 266(n12), 267, 308, 327,
        333(n165), 338, 345(n189), 356, 363, 369
-*tʰu*   143

### APPlicative
-∅   279, 304, 312, 327, 362, 364, 368
-*nyi* (= ditransitive/double-object)   149
-*yu* (= ditransitive/double-object)   149

### 'By' (Passive Agent)
-*nyi*   97, 262, 264

### COMitative
-*tʰu* 'with, and'   16, 88, 294

### GENitive/(APPositive)
-∅   93, (100), 117, (140), 169, 170, (170), 176,
        178, 221, (224), (253), 271, (282), 291,
        304, 327, 329
-*ga/-gya*   8, 9, 16, 97, 107, 109(n26), 110, 111,
        114, 117, 120, 127, 136, 139, 152, 164, 165,
        167, 171, 180, 201, 204, 245, 253, 267, 280,
        294, 295, 298, 299, 305, 308–310, 319,
        321, 323, 330, 337, 338, 359–361, 373, 384
-*nu/ˣ-nyu*   16, 56, 71, 86, 87, 97, 106, 107, 116,
        117, 120, 121, 131, (134), 141, 148, 158, (162),
        165, (166), 170, 171, 175, (175), 177, 178,
        182, (182), 207, 218, 220, 221, 222, 224,
        225, 226, 228, 235, 245, 250, 261, 262,
        265, 266, 272, 276, 284, (289n64), (290),
        (292), 293, 294, (294), 300, (301), 305,
        (308), 309, (317), (325), 326, 327, (334),
        335, 336, 346(n190), 348, 356, 357, 358,
        359, 363, 364, 369, (374), 385, 386

### Direct Object
-∅   9, 14, 16, 87, 88, 91, 92, 96, 111, 112, 115, 119,
        124, 126–128, 130, 131, 138–140, 142, 143,
        148, 161, 164, 169, 170–173, 176, 189, 203,
        204, 210, 213, 215, 216, 219–223, 226,
        228, 236, 239, 245, 248, 251–253, 264,
        269(n19), 271–275, 275(n30), 276, 277,
        279–284, 287, 290–292, 294, 300, 308,
        311, 319, 320, 321(n146), 325, 330, 334,
        339, 340, 344, 346–349, 352, 353, 355,
        355(n205), 357, 359, 360, 362, 363, 368–
        370, 374, 386–388
-*ga/-gya*   16, 142, 177, 179, 311, 315
-*nu/ˣ-nyu*   175, 222
-*Qp°a* '[stressed DO]'   16, 106, 122, 130,
        137, 140, 217, 222, 265, 275, 310, 315,
        321(n146)
-*yu*   16, 115, 120, 248, 275(n30), 277, 280, 298,
        315, 340, 349
-*wo*   116(n38), 248

### Indirect Object
-∅   111, 117, 119, 143, 162, 172, 175, 176, 194,
        218, 219, 223, 225, 292, 298, 300, 317,
        364
-*nyi* (indirect object '(to)')   110, 116, 130,
        171, 178, 182, 188, 189, 194, 228, 263,
        269(n19), 271, 272, 329, 347
-*Nkayi*   273
-*(nyi)kʰac°yi*   225

### LOCative
-∅   86, 118, 139, 178, 181, 266, 272, 298, 312,
        317, 318, 339, 348, 360
-*nyi*   71, 121, 170, 218, 238, 280, 282, 301, 323–
        326, 331, 344, 345, 357, 361

### Purposive 'in Order to' (PRP)
-*ga/-gya*   120, 206, 215, 340

### Quotative Particle 'Quote, to Wit'
-*di-t°i*   145, 228, 252, 282, 336, 357

# INDEX OF PARTICLES

### Subject

-∅   86, 92, 93, 105, 111, 117, 121, 128, 138, 143,
152, 164, 165, 171, 175, 180, 207, 222, 225–
227, 246, 248, 253, 271, 272, 282, 287,
289(n64), 294, 299, 301, 302, 305–312,
313(n117), 315, 316, 319, 320, 334, 336,
337, 345, 346, 350, 355(n205), 362, 386

-*ga*/-*gya*   8, 9, 16, 41(n43), 86, 87, 108, 114,
117(n40), 129, 134, 141, 143, 147, 148, 164,
176, 177, 188, 201, 217, 218, 221, 223, 225,
245, 264–266, 266(n11), 267, 275, 293,
294, 301, 317–319, 334(n168), 337, 338,
340, 343, 353, 369, 373, 386, 387

### Focus Particles

#### TOPic

-∅   89, 112, 116, 119, 162, 173, 175, 180, 247, 256,
266, 310, 312, 317, 323, 327, 344

-*wa*/-*ya*   3, 16, 89, 91, 109(n26), 111, 112,
116, 118, 120, 128, 136, 143, 152, 164,
166, 170, 171, 175, 176, 178, 180, 201,
207, 214, 215, 217, 218, 225, 228, 238,
253, 265, 275, 281, 284, 289, 290,
294, 298–301, 303, 308, 312, 318, 320,
330, 331, 333, 334, 334(n168), 336–
340, 343, 355, 358–361, 367, 370, 373,
385

#### Non-final Focus *kakari* Particle (KP)

-*du*/-*dzyu*/-*ru* (KP) [focus]   16, 17, 42, 119,
120, 135, 147, 167, 170, 180, 227, 228, 251,
262(n6), 269(n19), 283, 294, 320, 328,
338, 339, 345, 359, 360

### Miscellaneous Sentence-Final Particle

*na* [question, prohibition, exclamation]
178, 271, 282(n148), 329, 338

*ya*(*a*) [exclamation]   146, 221, 226, 256, 266,
270(n21), 271, 290, 337

-*nu*/*ˣ-nyu*   16, 56, 95, 120, 147, 154, 165, 173,
175, 176, 194, 216, 224, 225, 226, 227, 246,
250, 267, 272, 273, 293, 300, 307, 311,
337, 340, 367

### Terminative (TRM 'Until')

-*gya*(*a*)*mi*   105, 123, 128, 146, 164, 175, 195, 227,
246, 274, 309, 310, 373

### Time 'at, on (Time)'

-*nyi*   118, 130, 158, 171

-*ga*/-*gya* (KP) [question]   16, 17, 90, 116,
116(n37), 117, 117(n40), 206, 214, 216,
253, 320, 333, 338, 339, 342, 384

-*si*/-*syu*/-*zyu* (KP) [sharp-focus]   3, 3(n3),
16, 17, 42, 97, 118, 123, 123(n55), 129,
139, 142(n105), 146, 148, 167, 179, 195,
195(n19), 204, 211, 222, 226, 245, 261,
262, 262(n6), 265, 267, 276, 306, 307,
310, 310(n111), 314, 314(n122), 321,
322(n146), 339, 357, 358, 367, 373, 384

### Sentence-Final *kakari* Particles (SKP/QP)

*do*(*o*)/-*ru* (SKP)   17, 118

-*ga*/-*gya* (SKP)   92, 118, 227, 253, 253(n115),
318, 338

-*syu* (SKP)   117

-*yi* (QP)   17, 210, 214(n50), 218, 226, 252, 254,
281, 281(n43), 282, 282(n48), 388

*yo*(*o*) [exclamation]   216, 221, 270, 319, 396

*yu* [exclamation]   87

# Index of Linguistic and Literary Terms

*-a.* → IA

AA (affective adjective [formative]) 142, 159, 160, 160(n16), 161, 164, 165, 165(n29), 166, 168, 175–180, 227, 296, 299, 301, 338, 345, 361

*-abir-.* → humilific auxiliary verb

*-ʔacʰir-u.* → emphatic locative

*-adana.* → NEG

ADJ.STEM (adjective stem) 157, 216

adjectival verb/noun/nominative. → AV

ADJective 14, 39, 150(n1), 151, 152, 166, 168–171, 181, 294, 334, 334(n168)

adjective derivational suffix. → ADS

adjective formative. → AF

adjective stem. → ADJ.STEM

ADS (adjective derivational suffix) 150–155, 159, 227, 261, 345

ADVerb(ial) 15, 94(n32), 95, 143, 151, 153, 158, 161, 162, 163(n21, n22), 165, 167, 170–172, 175, 192, 195, 206(n41), 215(n54), 221, 225, 227(n72), 228, 229, 239, 267, 276, 327, 330(n161), 333(n165), 338, 339, 345, 348, 355, 356, 363, 369

AF (adjective formative) 150, 151, 153, 165, 166

Affective Adjective (formative). → AA

*-(a)masyi.* → counterfactual (auxiliary)

*-(a)masyi.* → OPTative

*-ami.* → IA.IZ

*-aN.* → IA (archaizing)

*-an-.* → NEG

*-aN.* → NEG

archisegment (\*y) 22

*-ari(·r)-.* → passive

*-as-.* → CAUSative

*-as-.* → EAV (exalting auxiliary verb)

aspirated 3(n6), 28, 29, 33(n24), 38, 42, 43, 77(n79), 80–83, 86(n4), 89(n14), 98, 170(n40), 174, 194(n16), 266(n12), 306(n106), 327(n156), 345(n188), 353(n200)

aspiration 3(n6), 22, 28, 28(n17), 29, 33, 33(n24), 35, 40, 41(n41), 43, 49(n51), 55, 62, 74(n73), 75, 77, 77(n79), 78–82, 82(n83), 89(n14), 100(n3), 101(n7), 141(n101), 157, 158(n13), 194(n16),

236(n87), 266(n12), 282(n46), 291(n66), 345(n188), 353(n200)

AUXiliary, CONCessive. → CONCessive AUXiliary

auxiliary, counterfactual 296, 298, 303

auxiliary, POTential. → POTential

AUXiliary verb. → verbs

AV (adjectival verb/noun/nominative) 150

*-azi.* → NEG

BE (beautifying expression, *bishōgo/bishōji*) 99, 105, 105(n12), 126, 144, 154–156, 159(n15), 162–164, 170, 178, 179, 181, 182, 225, 261, 263, 279, 289(n64), 299, 308, 312, 316, 316(n28), 317, 318, 326, 334, 344, 349, 358, 360, 370, 373, 374, 386, 387

beautifying expression. → BE

beat. → meter

bigrade, lower. → lower bigrade

bigrade, middle. → middle bigrade

*bishōgo/bishōji.* → BE

boundary/boundaries 53, 54, 56, 64–66, 106(n16), 108(n24), 109(n27), 113(n23), 124(n58), 128(n62), 215, 223(n64), 224(n65), 250(n105), 291(n66), 300(n90), 318(n132), 380, 381, 385(n260)

*b*-stem/type 185

*-bu·sya.* → DSD1

Case and other nominal clitics and suffixes. → Index of Particles

case, COMitative. → COMitative case

CAUSative (*-as-*) 61, 126, 140, 160, 191, 196, 197, 209, 212, 213, 237, 245, 251, 266, 270, 270(n21), 271–275, 278–280, 291, 292, 297, 298, 304, 329, 347, 357, 371

coda, syllable. → syllable coda

ColloqOk. → Colloquial Okinawan

Colloquial Okinawan, Modern (CoOk, ColloqOk) 48(n48), 56, 85(n2), 242, 243, 325, 364(n221), 382

COMitative case (case, COMitative). → Index of Particles

# INDEX OF LINGUISTIC AND LITERARY TERMS

CONcessive AUXiliary (AUXiliary, CONCessive) 137, 216, 283, 300, 312, 356, 357(n208), 359

conditional. → TMP/CND

continuant, glottal. → glottal continuant (')

CoOk. → Colloquial Okinawan

copula? -n[-]ar- 96, 356, 361–366

COPula -yar- (→ -yar-) 14, 36, 89, 94(n32), 96, 106(n15), 119, 121, 122, 145(n111), 147, 150, 151, 219, 228, 244, 245, 252, 260, 298–300, 304, 304(n103), 305, 307(n107), 318, 328, 338, 345, 356–366

coronal 37, 42, 68, 70, 88(n13), 95, 131(n73), 143(n107), 163, 168, 209(n45), 259, 281, 368(n226), 382(n249)

counterfactual (auxiliary) -(a)masyi 279, 296–298, 298(n86), 299–303, 361

counterfactual auxiliary. → auxiliary, counterfactual

demonstrative(s) 118, 120–122

derivational suffix(es) (suffixes, derivational) 150–155, 159, 168, 193, 218(n58), 279

desiderative, 1st person. → DSD1

desiderative, 2nd/3rd-person. → DSD2/3

DEverbal 2, 66(n64), 99, 106, 110, 265, 301(n98), 348(n193), 368(n226), 388

DIG (destruction of incommensurate glides) 131(n73), 265(n10)

DIMinutive suffix(es) (suffix[es], DIMinutive) 140, 141(n99), 147, 147(n113, n114), 148, 155, 271, 310

diphthongs 21, 34, 36, 43, 44, 48, 107(n19), 335(n172)

direct-object marker. → DO

DO (direct-object marker). → Index of Particles

DSD1 (desiderative, 1st person) 176(n54), 177–179, 296(n83), 312

DSD2/3 (desiderative, 2nd/3rd-person) 176(n54)

*e. → mid vowel *e

Early Modern Japanese. → ENJ

EAV (exalting auxiliary verb) 91, 111, 139, 147, 176, 198, 201, 203, 204, 209, 211, 214(n50), 215, 218, 219, 222, 226, 239, 267, 271, 272, 274, 352, 353, 360, 363, 366, 367–383

EAV (exalting auxiliary verb). → -(u)wa·r/s-

EAV (exalting auxiliary verb) -as- 57, 270, 274–279

EMPHatic.LOCative (-nyi-ʔac°ir-u) 323, 324, 326, 331, 331(n162)

EMPHatic.LOCative (-ʔac°ir-u) 234, 323–325, 331, 331(n162), 332

ENJ (Early Modern Japanese) 99

EP.y (epenthetic y) 5(n9), 217, 333, 333(n167), 335–337, 342, 370, 379, 380(n243), 381(n246), 385, 385(n260)

epenthetic y. → EP.y

exalting auxiliary verb (-(u)wa·r/s-) 9, 95, 111, 139, 147, 203, 204, 209, 211, 218, 239, 274, 352, 366–372, 374–376, 378–382

exalting auxiliary verb. → EAV

EXalting prefix (prefix, EXalting) 107(n19), 126–130, 132, 133, 135, 136, 137, 137(n91), 138, 159(n15), 265, 309, 364(n221)

EXalting 3, 9, 23, 24, 65, 67, 86, 87, 92, 95, 106, 107, 112, 117, 119, 120, 123, 124, 126–139, 141, 144–147, 154, 166, 169, 172, 173, 175, 176, 179, 180–182(n64), 189, 203, 214, 217–220, 225, 227, 230, 235(n86), 238, 245, 246, 250, 251, 259, 260, 263–270, 274–279, 281, 282, 284, 287, 289, 290, 291, 291(n68), 292–295, 301, 303, 304(n204), 305, 306, 309, 311, 312, 314, 315, 317, 318, 318(n132), 321, 324(n150), 326–328(n156), 333, 336–338, 340, 346(n190)–350, 352, 355, 355(n205), 357–359, 363, 364(n221), 366, 367, 369, 372, 373, 377, 377(n238), 378(n240), 380–382, 388

EXCLamation 17, 121, 151, 165(n26), 214, 296, 302, 314, 315(n124), 333(165), 337, 338

focus 13, 15, 16, 192, 227, 227(n72), 244, 310(n111), 360(n216), 371

form. → PASSIVE

function. → passive

functional split 244

-ga ~ -gya (→ SKP sentence-final kakari particle). → Index of Particles

-ga ~ -gya (→ KP non-final focus kakari particle). → Index of Particles

-ga ~ -gya (→ GEN). → Index of Particles

-ga ~ -gya (→ SUB). → Index of Particles

GEN (-*ga* ~ -*gya*). → Index of Particles
GEN (-*nu*). → Index of Particles
GENitive marker. → Index of Particles
GER/PRFV (→ gerund/perfective) 190–194,
    196–200, 202, 204–206, 208–210, 212–
    217, 219–221, 224, 252(n112), 254, 257,
    280, 321, 321(n143), 322(n147), 330, 331,
    331(n162), 344, 353, 374, 376, 378, 380,
    381
GER/PRFV-derived forms. → T-form
gerund, development of 249, 249(n103)
GERund suffix. → gerund/perfective
glide (→ semivowel *w, y*) 21, 22(n7), 25, 26,
    35, 44, 48, 49, 52, 61, 63, 70, 77, 131(n72),
    145(n112), 153(n5), 172(n45), 221(n60),
    341, 379, 380(n243), 381(n246),
    382(n249)
glides, incommensurate, destruction of. →
    DIG
glottal continuant (') 21, 21(n3, n6), 22(n7),
    43, 44
glottal stop (ʔ) 21, 26, 35, 37, 43, 106(n16),
    145(n111), 241(n93), 364(n221)
*g*-stem/type 185, 255, 300

HAV (Humilific Auxiliary verb) 385–387,
    389
high vowel *\*yi*. → *\*yi*, high vowel
His Majesty's Ship. → HMS
HMS (His Majesty's Ship) 40, 156, 209, 219,
    220, 245, 293
honorifics 70–72, 115, 159(n15), 264,
    268, 268(n14), 269, 278(n350), 289,
    304(n104), 366, 375, 376(n234), 382, 383
hortative auxiliary. → IA
HUM (humilific/humble) 128(n62),
    137(n91), 201, 278, 376(n234),
    378(n238), 386(n262, n264), 387
humble/humilific. → HUM
humilific auxiliary verb -*abir*- 128(n62), 201,
    215(n54), 246, 385, 386, 386(n264), 387
humilific auxiliary verb. → HAV
humilific auxiliary verb -*tʰatʰimacʰir*- 387
humilific/humble. → HUM

IA (-*a*) 105, 116, 127, 128, 128(n62), 164, 178,
    191, 192, 194, 194(n18), 198, 200, 201, 206,
    208, 221(n60), 222, 227, 236, 236(n89),
    244–248, 271, 295(n79), 296, 303–

307, 307(n108), 308–311, 314(n122),
    315(n124), 333, 334, 349, 355, 356(n206),
    367, 376, 385, 386, 387, 388
IA (-*aN* [archaizing]) 194, 194(n18), 303–
    305, 307(n108), 356(n206)
IA.IZ (-*ami*) 57, 303–308, 314, 314(n122),
    388(n268)
indirect object marker. → IO
inferential auxiliary. → IA
INFinitive (-*yi*, -∅) 1(n1), 2, 2(n2), 3, 5(n9),
    21(n6), 23, 26, 60, 65, 67, 88, 89, 91,
    95, 106, 107, 107(n19, n22), 111, 128,
    128(n62), 131, 144, 147, 148, 167, 172,
    176, 177, 186, 187, 189, 191, 193–200,
    200(n26), 201–205, 205(n38, n39),
    206, 206(n40), 207–219, 221, 223, 224,
    224(n65), 225–228, 231, 235(n86), 237–
    239, 245–248, 251, 251(n109), 256–261,
    261(n2), 262, 263, 265, 267, 270–272,
    276, 277, 279–281, 284, 289(n64), 290,
    290(n66), 292–294, 299, 300(n92),
    305–308, 310, 310(n111), 314, 316, 317,
    320, 321, 321(n143), 322(n146), 327, 329–
    331(n162), 333, 335, 335(n172), 336–338,
    338(n176), 339–342, 344, 344(n184),
    345, 345(n187), 346, 346(n190), 347–
    349, 349(n196), 350, 351, 351(n197,
    n198), 352, 353, 353(n202), 354,
    354(n203, n204), 355, 355(n205), 356,
    356(n206), 357, 357(n208), 358–360,
    362, 365, 367–376, 378, 380, 381, 385–
    388, 388(n268)
INJ (interjection) 71, 111, 121, 136, 245, 315,
    340, 356
INSTRUmental case. → Index of Particles
INTensifier 61, 87
inferential auxiliary. → IA
interjection. → INJ
intransitive verb / intransitivizing suffix. → VI
IO (indirect object marker). → Index of Parti-
    cles
irregular verb. (→ verb, irregular)
ITERative 235, 252(n112), 346, 346(n194),
    350
*izenkei* (IZ) 3, 9, 16, 17, 42, 119, 120, 123, 134,
    137, 139, 142, 143, 146, 148, 157, 180,
    187–189, 190–202, 204–206(n40),
    207–212, 214–229, 231(n82), 232, 233,
    237, 238, 244–246, 261–263, 265, 267,

# INDEX OF LINGUISTIC AND LITERARY TERMS

270(n21), 276, 281, 283, 284, 294, 301, 303, 305–308, 310, 313, 314, 314(n122), 321, 321(146), 322, 322(n146), 333, 339, 340, 348, 356, 356(n206), 357, 358, 359, 359(n216), 360, 361, 362, 367, 368, 370, 372, 373, 377(n236), 378, 388, 388(n176)

Japanese    1(n1), 2, 3, 4, 6(n10), 14, 18, 20, 24, 25(n13), 28(n17), 32(n23), 33, 33(n27), 37, 38, 45, 47, 53, 68, 70, 71, 73, 78, 79, 87(n10), 88(n10), 90, 91, 91(n22), 95, 98, 102(n9), 105, 114(n35), 122, 122(n49), 123(n56), 124–126, 127(n59), 137(n92), 138, 141(n100), 142, 142(n103), 144(n108), 150, 154(n9), 157, 159, 162, 162(n22), 164(n23), 166(n31), 168, 169, 172(n49), 179, 182, 184, 186, 187, 190, 191, 194(n18), 195(n23), 203(n32), 205(n38), 217(n56), 221(n60), 229, 230, 235(n85), 241, 244, 247, 259, 269(n18), 270(n20), 274, 274(n28), 278(n36), 286(n58), 288, 288(n60), 289(n61), 294(n77), 295, 298(n87), 312, 319, 322(n147), 324(n150), 326(n154), 332, 333(n166), 335(n170), 342, 343(n181), 344, 346, 353(n200), 355, 355(n205), 362(n218), 363, 365, 366, 372, 377, 382(n249), 387

Japonic    57, 85, 85(n1), 99, 106(n15), 117(n39), 124, 147, 151, 154(n9), 160, 164(n22), 168(n36), 190, 191, 217(n56), 229, 230(n80), 235, 236(n90), 256(n119), 274(n27), 288, 342, 353(n200), 356, 377, 379, 386(n265)

Japonic, Proto- (PJ)    23, 47, 66(n65), 74(n73), 79, 85, 85(n2), 87, 90, 105(n14), 107(n18), 107(n21), 122, 122(n51), 126, 168(n36), 173, 174, 179, 188, 188(n56), 225(n6), 231, 232(n81), 249, 249(n104), 250(n104), 250(n104), 252(n111), 255, 256, 256(n119), 268, 274(n128), 277(n134), 329(n159), 342, 388

*kakari musubi.* → KM
*kakari* particle. → KP
kimi. → priestess
Kingdom, Ryukyu. → Ryukyu Kingdom
KM (*kakari musubi*)    16, 192, 193(n13), 202, 204, 211, 262, 265, 276, 306, 307, 333,

333(n166), 337–339, 345(n189), 357, 359(n216), 360, 360(n216)

KP (kakari particle). → Index of Particles
*k*-stem/type    185, 187, 213, 223, 255, 372

labial    21, 37, 38, 42, 51, 55–57, 59(n60), 70, 73(n71), 88(n13), 95, 100(2), 107(n20), 127(n61), 131(n73), 133(n76), 226(n71), 258, 281(n42), 300, 304, 348(n194), 382(n249)

linker (*rentai-shi*). → LK
Literary (→ LitOk)    64, 70, 120, 125, 134(n82), 135(n83), 194(n18), 209(n45), 215, 215(n54), 223(n63), 243, 307, 340(n177), 379(n241)

LitOk (Literary Okinawan)    1(n1), 48(n48), 58(n58), 81, 85(n2), 109(n26), 242, 243, 307, 362(n218), 364(n221, n222), 379(n241)

LK (linker [*rentai-shi*])    148, 310
loan    1(n1), 62, 85, 90, 91, 93, 123, 125, 142, 154(n9), 162, 169, 265, 272(n23), 274(n25, n26), 288(n60), 298, 311, 312, 332(n147), 326(n154), 355, 365, 365(n222), 385, 387, 388(n268)

LOCative. → Index of Particles
long vowel(s) (vowel[s], long)    5, 21, 34, 36, 37(n33), 50, 50(n51), 58, 70, 71, 77, 78, 80, 80(n80), 85(n2), 86(n4), 101, 101(n6), 102, 107, 119(n44), 123(n53), 138(n94), 153(n5), 201(n29), 205(n36), 241, 249, 249(n104), 250, 251(n109), 254, 256(n119), 274(n26), 275(n31), 283(n49, n50), 289(n62), 291(n67), 292(n72), 302(n99), 317(n131), 341(178), 348(n194), 371, 385(n261)

lower bigrade (bigrade, lower)    10(n19), 164(n22), 184, 187, 188, 189, 213, 217(n56), 223, 221, 229, 231, 234, 235, 237, 331, 331(n162), 376, 381

lower monograde (monograde, lower)    184, 185, 190, 213, 216

marker, PLural. → PL
MC (Middle Chinese)    69, 123(n56, n57), 302(n100)

*meireikei.* → MR

metathesis   57, 68–72, 95, 102(n9), 144,
      159(n15), 203(n33), 274(n25), 353(n201),
      382, 382(n249), 388(n268)
meter   3(n5), 64, 73, 107(n19), 214(n51),
      289(n62), 292(n72), 306(n106),
      318(n134)
metrical   3, 11, 62, 86(n5), 107(n19), 122(n53),
      145(n111), 146, 165(n27), 243, 289(n61),
      300, 307(n107), 309(n109)
mid vowel *e   20–22, 26, 48, 48(n48), 49,
      85(n2), 88, 122(n51), 130(n69), 182, 217,
      217(n56), 220, 230–233, 257, 379, 381
mid vowel *o   20–23, 26, 28, 29, 47–51,
      56, 61, 70, 101, 107, 128, 128(n62),
      129(n66), 130, 130(n71), 133, 133(n77),
      137(n91), 153(n5), 161(n20), 178, 188,
      190, 209(n45), 217(n56), 231(n81),
      235, 290(65), 291, 291(n68), 317(n131),
      318(n132), 326, 335(n172), 354(n203),
      372, 374–379, 381, 381(n248), 382,
      382(n251), 383(n254)
middle bigrade   217, 217(n56), 219, 220
Middle Chinese. → MC
Middle Japanese. → MJ
Middle Okinawan. → MOk
middle voice. → MV
miseeⁿ   132(n73), 366, 374
Mishōgo. → MO
mizenkei. → MZ
MJ (Middle Japanese)   22, 36, 67, 69, 70, 85,
      89(n16), 90, 92, 93, 95, 98, 104(n10),
      131(n71), 142(n103), 156, 157, 157(n12),
      163(n22), 169, 172(n45), 173(n49), 184,
      187, 223(n63), 226(n70), 228(n75),
      240, 241, 260, 265, 265(n10), 267–269,
      270(n20), 272(n23), 298, 302(100), 311,
      312, 312(n114), 322, 326(154), 353(n200),
      354(n203), 365, 365(n222), 366,
      374(n233), 377, 378, 382, 383, 384(n259),
      385, 385(n259)
Modern Japanese. → NJ
Modern Okinawan. → NOk
modifier   151, 169, 177, 178, 261, 265
MOk (Middle Okinawan)   10, 11(n19), 23,
      28, 40(n40), 48, 49(n51), 55, 70, 117,
      118, 119(n44), 122, 130(n70, n71), 135,
      135(n83), 138, 141(n100), 150(n1),
      228(n75), 274(n27), 307, 318(n136),
      325(n152), 366, 376, 383, 387

MO (Mishōgo, meaning obscure)   85, 97
monograde, lower. → lower monograde
monograde, upper. → upper monograde
mora   186, 200(n25), 214, 214(n51), 239, 242,
      243, 243(n95), 245(n97), 252(n114), 259,
      261(n1), 266(n12), 274(n26), 277(n33),
      292(n72), 301(n97), 309(n109),
      313(n116), 316(n128), 317(n130),
      318(n132, n134, n136), 319(n139),
      320(n142), 330(n161), 334(n168, n169),
      335(n171), 354(n204), 364(n221), 368,
      382(n249), 389
mora segments (M, N, B, G, K, Q)   51, 52, 63,
      74(n73), 135, 136, 281, 384
MR (meireikei)   9, 41(n42), 86, 92, 94, 111,
      112, 118, 137(n91), 138, 138(n94), 140,
      142, 143, 152, 157, 165, 171, 172, 175, 184,
      187, 188, 188(n5, n6), 189–192, 192(n11),
      193, 194, 196–199, 200(n26), 202–204,
      205(n40), 207–210, 212–214, 214(n50),
      215–217, 219–221, 223–225, 227, 229,
      231(n82), 233, 235, 235(n85), 236–239,
      245, 246, 250–252, 259, 261–263, 264,
      270, 270(n21), 271, 274, 276–280, 282,
      284, 290(n65), 291, 292, 329, 330, 336,
      347, 349, 357, 360, 363, 363(n220), 368–
      372, 374, 376, 383, 388
m-stem/type   185, 191
MV (middle voice)   117, 163(n22), 268(n15)
myi-ʔu-ya‖r-‖as-i   92, 259, 276–278, 347, 348,
      376
MZ (mizenkei)   41(n42), 107(n22), 111, 116, 127,
      128, 131, 140, 142(n105), 143, 155(n10),
      157, 160, 161, 163(n22), 184, 187, 188–194,
      196–200, 200(n26), 202, 204–206, 208–
      221, 221(n60), 224–227, 232, 233, 236,
      237, 237(n91), 244–246, 248, 250, 279–
      282, 282(n48), 283, 290, 292, 294, 295,
      295(n79), 296, 296(n80), 298, 302–304,
      306(n105), 307, 307(108), 308, 313, 314,
      315(n124), 322, 333, 334, 342, 355–357,
      367, 372, 377(n236), 385, 387, 388(n268)

Naha (dialect)   28(n17), 29, 167(n34),
      256(n119), 314(n120), 324, 345,
      365(n222), 375
Nakijin (dialect). → Nk
name(s), personal. → PN (personal name[s])
name(s), priestess. → priestess name(s)

# INDEX OF LINGUISTIC AND LITERARY TERMS

*-n*[*-*]*ar-.* → copula?

nasal   21, 22, 29, 45, 51, 65, 81, 82, 83, 87(n9),
   93, 215(n54), 259, 262(n6), 281, 287, 303,
   338(n176), 364(n221)

NDS (nominal derivational suffix)   153, 154,
   164, 227, 261, 345

NEG (*-adana*)   213, 287, 289, 290–296(n80),
   296(n81), 330, 338

NEG (*-an-*)   112, 123, 124, 124(n58), 126, 137,
   145, 191, 209, 210, 211, 216, 218, 226, 239,
   281, 282, 283, 296(n81), 301, 302(n99),
   366(n224)

NEG (*-aN*)   190, 211, 240, 252(n113), 281–283,
   305, 383(n254), 388(n268)

NEG (*-azi*)   222, 281, 284

NEG-inferential / -intentional (*-umazyi*)
   222, 309–311

NJ (Modern Japanese)   54, 56, 57, 62, 70,
   72, 86, 88, 95, 99, 100, 101, 104, 105, 107,
   118, 123, 128, 151, 156, 158, 161(n19), 162,
   163, 171(n42), 184, 188, 209, 209(n45),
   228(n75), 240, 241, 252, 260, 274,
   274(n26), 302, 316, 318(n136), 324,
   326, 342, 344(n185), 349, 353, 372, 375,
   382(n250)–384

Nk (Nakijin [dialect])   1, 3(n6), 18, 74(n73),
   79, 101(n7), 104(n11), 133, 141(n101),
   170(n40), 234, 245(n96), 256(n119),
   296, 306(n106), 335(n171), 353(n201),
   357(n208)

NOk (Modern Okinawan)   1(n1), 3(n5),
   5, 6(n10), 14(n22), 22, 23, 33, 35,
   36, 36(n31), 37, 40, 40(n40), 41, 44,
   46(n44), 48(n48), 49, 51, 52, 54–
   56(n65), 57, 59, 60, 62–64, 67, 69, 70,
   72, 72(n69), 73, 73(n71), 74, 74(n71), 78–
   80(n80), 81, 82, 86, 86(n7), 87, 87(n9),
   88(n11, n13), 90, 90(n19), 92, 92(n25),
   93, 99, 100, 100(n4), 101–103, 105,
   107(n20, n21), 109(n26, n27), 111(n30),
   115, 115(n36), 117, 118, 121, 122(n52), 123,
   128(n62), 129(n66), 133(n77), 135(n83),
   136(n88), 137(n91), 138, 140(n98),
   142(n103), 144(n109), 151, 153(n5), 154,
   157–158(n14), 159, 161(n19)–163(n21,
   n22), 167, 167(n34), 169, 170(n39),
   171, 172(n45), 173(n46, n49), 175(n53),
   176(n54), 177, 179–181, 181(n64), 188,
   191, 191(n10), 193(n13), 194(n14, n15),

195, 195(n23), 197, 199, 200(n25),
   207(n43), 209(n45), 213(n49), 214,
   215, 228(n76), 230(n79), 240, 241, 243,
   246, 247, 251, 251(n109), 252(n113),
   253, 254, 256(n119, n120), 257, 259,
   265(n10), 269(n18, n19), 270(n21),
   271(n22), 272(n23), 273, 274(n26),
   279, 280(n38, n41), 285, 286(n58),
   289(n62), 290(n65), 291(n67), 295,
   296(n83), 300, 301(n93), 301(n94),
   305, 306(n106), 307, 309(n109), 311,
   312(n115), 313(n117), 314(n120, n121,
   n123), 315(n124, n126), 316, 316(n127,
   n128), 317(n131), 318(n132–n134,
   n136), 319, 320(n142), 322, 325(n152),
   334(n168), 335(n170, n172), 341(n178),
   344, 344(n185), 347(n191), 348(n193,
   n195), 349(n196), 351(n197), 353,
   353(n200), 353(n201), 354, 354(n204),
   358(n210, n211), 359(n215), 364(n221,
   n222), 365–366(224), 374–376,
   378(n239), 379(n241, n242), 382,
   382(n249, n250), 383, 383(n254, n257),
   385(n261), 387, 388(n268)

nominal derivational suffix. → NDS

nominalize   106(n15), 166(n32), 319, 337

non-palatal   35, 43, 58, 61, 107(n20),
   108(n23), 131(n73), 251(n109), 376

non-palatalized   54, 251(n109)

noro/*nu*(*u*)*ru.* → priestess

noun(s)   2, 14(n22), 15, 56, 63, 66(n64), 85,
   87, 87(n10), 99, 105, 106, 106(n15), 108–
   110(n29), 123, 126, 129(n66), 130(n70),
   131, 133, 135, 136, 141, 143(n106),
   145(n112), 148, 150–154(n6), 155, 160,
   166(n32), 169, 173, 176, 181, 182, 192,
   212(n47), 223, 251(n109), 256(119), 261,
   265, 265(n10), 266, 274(n26), 285, 287,
   291(n66), 292(n70), 298, 304(n103),
   305, 310(n111), 314(n122), 318(n135),
   323, 324, 324(n151), 360, 368(n226),
   382(n250), 388, 389

*n*-stem/type   185

*-nu* (→ GEN). → Index of Particles

numerals   13, 122

*-nu* (→ SUB). → Index of Particles

*nu*(*u*)*ru*/noro. → priestess

*-nyi-ʔacⁱir-u* → EMPHatic.LOCative

*o. → mid vowel *o

OJ (Old Japanese)   4, 4(n8), 16, 23, 30(n20),
  31, 32, 34(n28), 36, 38, 54, 56, 57, 62,
  65, 66(n65), 67, 70, 72, 74(n73), 80,
  85, 85(n1, n2), 86(n8), 87(n9), 88, 90,
  94, 96, 105(n13, n14), 106, 107(n18),
  112, 115, 117, 118(n43), 120, 122(n51),
  127, 130(n70), 140(n98), 147(n116),
  149(n116), 150, 150(n1), 151, 151(n2),
  154(n9), 157, 158, 160(n16), 163(n22),
  168(n36), 170(n41), 173–175, 176(n54),
  177, 178(n60), 179, 182, 184, 186–190,
  195, 195(n23), 217(n56), 226(n70), 229,
  229(n77), 230, 231(n81), 234, 235(n85),
  240, 240(n92), 241, 242(n94), 248,
  251(n109), 265(n10), 267–270, 271(n22),
  274(n26, n28), 276, 277(n34), 278,
  278(n36), 279, 287, 288, 289(n62),
  291(n69), 296(n81), 302, 302(n100),
  303, 308, 311, 312, 321, 323, 329(n159),
  331, 332, 338, 339, 354, 355, 357(n208),
  358, 358(n209), 365, 366, 374(n233),
  377, 377(n236, n238), 378, 381(n248),
  388(n268)

Old Japanese (→ OJ)   4, 20, 32, 47, 229, 230,
  235(n85), 295, 387

Old Okinawan. → OOk

onset   24, 25, 35(n29), 44, 56, 58, 341(n178)

OOk (Old Okinawan)   10(n19), 15, 18, 20, 21,
  21(n3), 22, 22(n7), 23, 25, 25(n13, n14),
  28, 29, 32, 33, 33(n24), 34–36, 36(n31),
  37–39, 40(n40), 42, 43, 46(n44), 47–
  49, 49(n51), 51, 52, 54–57, 59–62,
  63(n62), 64–66(n65), 67–74, 74(73),
  75, 75(n76), 76–80, 80(n80), 81–85(n2),
  86(n7), 87(n9), 89(n16)–91(n22), 92,
  92(n25), 93, 96, 97, 99(n1), 100–102,
  105(n14), 107(n18, n20), 109(n27), 112,
  112(n31), 113, 115, 118, 119(n43), 122, 123,
  128, 130(n69), 131(n71, n73), 133(n76),
  135(n83), 137(n92), 141(n101), 142(n103),
  150(n1), 151–153(n5), 154(n9), 156, 157,
  157(n12), 159, 159(n15), 161(n20), 162,
  163, 163(n21), 167(n34), 168, 168(n36),
  169, 173(n49), 174, 177, 178(60), 179,
  182, 186–191, 193(n13), 194, 194(n14,
  n15), 196–200, 200(n25), 202, 204,
  205, 205(n38), 208, 209, 209(n45),
  210–213(n48), 214, 214(n51), 215, 217–

  221, 221(n60), 224, 226, 227, 229,
  229(n76, n78), 231, 233, 233(n83), 234,
  235(n85), 241, 243, 246(n99), 249,
  249(n103), 251, 251(n109), 252(n112,
  n113), 253–255, 255(n119), 257, 259,
  260, 265(n10), 267, 268, 268(n14),
  269, 269(n19), 270, 270(n20), 271(n22),
  273, 274, 276–280(n38), 281, 281(n42),
  285, 290, 295, 303, 308, 310(n111),
  311, 312(n114), 313(n116), 314(n120),
  315(n127), 316(n127, n128), 318,
  318(n134, n136), 319, 319(n139), 321,
  323, 323(n150), 324(n151), 325(n152),
  326(n155), 327, 331, 338, 338(n176),
  341–343, 343(n181), 344, 344(n185),
  345(n189), 346, 351(n197), 353(n200,
  n201), 354, 354(n203, n204, n205), 355,
  356, 356(n206), 357(n208), 362(n218),
  364, 364(n221), 365, 365(n222), 366,
  372, 374, 374(n233), 366, 377, 378,
  380–382(n250), 384(n257, n259,
  n268)

OPTative (-(a)masyi)   296, 296(n82),
  297(n85), 299, 303

PA (property adjective)   159–161(n18),
  165(n28, n29), 170(n41), 171

palatalization, progressive. → PP

paradigm(s)   41(n41), 58, 151, 157, 189, 214,
  217, 231, 291(n66), 323, 331, 341(n178),
  342, 344, 362(n218), 377, 385(n259)

passive   188(n6), 229(n78), 260–262, 264,
  267, 268, 268(nn14–16), 269, 270, 279

passive (-ari(·r)-)   97, 188, 191, 192, 195,
  202, 204, 252, 261, 261(n14), 262, 263,
  268(n15, n16), 269(n19), 279, 282,
  310(n112), 316, 336, 388(n268)

PASSIVE form   260, 261, 261(n4)

passive function (pass)   261(n4), 265(n10),
  268, 268(n14), 269, 270, 270(n20),
  278(n35)

passive (-(u)yi(·r)-)   8(n16), 11, 13, 88(13),
  91, 110, 116, 117, 124(58), 127, 130(n69),
  132, 176, 188, 218, 219, 260, 264, 265,
  265(n10), 266–268(n14), 269, 270, 284,
  317, 369–371, 373, 387

past. → PST

past -syi. → PST

perfect. → PRFT

# INDEX OF LINGUISTIC AND LITERARY TERMS

perfect. → -*Tar*-

perfective. → PRFV

Phonology  15, 18, 19, 22, 28, 29, 32, 51, 75, 76, 80(n80), 84, 99, 126, 145, 205(n37), 218(n57), 250(n108), 310(n112), 378

PJ (Proto-Japonic)  23, 47, 66(n65), 74(n73), 79, 85, 85(n2), 87, 90, 105(n14), 107(n18, n21), 122, 122(n51), 126, 147, 154(n9), 160, 164(n22), 168(n36), 173, 174, 179, 188, 188(n56), 191, 217(n56), 225(n6), 229, 230(n80), 231, 232(n81), 249, 249(n104), 250(n104), 252(n111), 255, 256, 256(n119), 268, 274(n28), 277(n34), 288, 329(n159), 342, 353(n200), 356, 377, 386(n265), 388

PL (plural marker/suffix)  109(n27), 111(n30), 124, 140, 141, 141(n99), 142, 143, 169, 272, 280, 283, 284, 284(n54), 294, 304, 336, 336(n173)

place name. → PLN

PLN (place name)  5, 41, 41(n43), 51, 53, 55, 70, 78, 99, 100–102, 104, 107, 121, 131, 138, 145, 146, 150, 162, 165, 170, 170(n39), 174–176, 178–182, 209(n45), 226, 228, 271, 277, 277(n33), 284, 301, 316, 319, 325–327, 329, 337, 339, 343–345, 347, 356, 358, 358(n210, n212), 359, 365(n222), 368, 373, 388

plural marker (→ PL)  141(n99), 283, 284, 284(n54)

PN (name[s], personal)  8, 41(n41), 67, 99, 107, 145, 146, 165, 166, 175, 176, 178, 182, 225, 247, 250, 261, 271, 290, 294, 295, 299, 311, 319, 320, 328, 333, 334, 334(n168), 335, 337, 338, 344, 353, 357, 358, 365, 369, 385

politeness  61, 384

potential (auxiliary). → POT

POT (potential auxiliary)  268, 269, 269(n19), 270, 312

PP (progressive palatalization)  9(n18), 10(n18, n19), 22, 23, 44, 54–57, 57(n57), 58, 59, 59(n60), 60, 61, 72, 75, 81, 81(n82), 85, 86(n4), 87(n9), 100(n2, n3, n5), 101, 102(n8), 107(n20), 117(n41), 120(n46), 123(n55), 124(58), 127, 127(n60), 130(n67, n69), 133, 133(n79), 142(n103), 154(n7), 155(n10), 158, 162, 164(n24), 167, 167(n35), 168, 201(n28), 204(34), 215, 215(n55), 217, 218(n58), 226(n71), 228(n74), 243(n96), 250(n105, n107, n109), 252(n112), 253(n115), 254, 255, 255(n117), 261(n1), 262(n5, n7), 275(n29), 282(n46), 283(n49), 285, 291(n66), 293(n74), 303(n102), 313, 314(n123), 315, 315(126), 320(n142), 321, 329, 337(n175), 338(n176), 341(n178), 345(n188), 348(194), 357(n208), 364(n222), 365(n222), 368(n226), 369, 382, 385(n261, n265), 388(n268)

P/P (PROG/PRFV)  352

predicate(s)  12, 14, 17, 150, 151, 163(n21), 166(n31, n32), 169, 171, 173, 177, 178, 181, 246, 247, 260, 265, 314, 345(n189)

prefix(es)  40(n39), 72, 75(n76), 77(n79), 105(n14), 107(n19), 126–128, 128(n62), 129(n66), 130(n70), 132, 133, 135–137, 137(n91), 138, 144, 156, 159(n15), 163(n21), 181, 183, 261, 265, 309(110), 318(n134), 364(n221)

prefix, exalting. → Exalting prefix

prefix, verbal. → VPFX

PRFT (perfect)  67, 119, 139, 202, 217, 228, 253, 287, 289, 300, 307, 311, 314–321, 321(n146), 323, 356(n206)

PRFV (perfective)  57, 66, 92, 117, 120, 122, 171, 172, 179, 180, 190–202, 204–206, 208–222, 224, 227, 249, 249(103), 251, 252, 252(n112), 253–255, 257, 271, 279, 280, 298, 312, 321, 321(n143), 322(n146), 323, 327–331, 331(n162), 332(n163), 336, 338–340, 344, 346, 350, 353–355, 355(n205), 369, 370, 374, 376, 378, 380, 381

priestess (kimi)  1, 5, 6, 8, 10, 11, 36, 41, 41(n41), 42, 67, 82, 87, 88, 91, 91(n21), 97, 99, 103–105, 120, 126, 132, 133, 140, 142, 142(n102), 143–145, 148, 156, 165, 178, 181, 188, 189, 192, 202, 203, 205, 207, 215, 216, 218–220, 222, 223, 228(n75), 239, 247(100), 248, 253, 263, 263, 271, 272, 278, 284–287, 290, 292–295, 300, 306–308, 317, 320, 321(n146), 323(n149), 324, 328, 330, 334, 336, 338, 338(n176), 339, 340, 349, 353, 355, 357, 363, 366, 367, 369, 370, 370(229), 371, 380, 387–389

priestess name(s)  41, 41(n41), 42, 99, 103, 104, 285, 286, 321, 338 priestess (noro/nu(u)ru)  1, 1(n1), 322

pRk (proto-Ryukyuan; → Ryukyuan)  20, 22, 24(n12), 28, 33, 41(n43), 56, 57(n57), 63, 74(n72), 105(n14), 122(n51), 147, 147(n113), 163, 163(n22), 217(n56), 225(n68), 230, 231, 235(n85), 241, 256(n119), 268(n14), 288, 295, 296(n80), 329(n159), 381(n248), 388

PRP (purposive)  120, 206, 215, 340

progressive palatalization. → PP

PROG/PRFV (→ progressive/perfective -yaaryi)  127, 346, 346(n190), 347–349, 349(n196), 350, 350(n196), 351–354, 354(n203, n205), 355

progresive -ur- (progressive -wur-)  17, 95, 107(n22), 116, 120, 129(n65), 131(n73), 142, 143, 170, 175, 177, 214, 216, 217, 219, 220, 221, 224(n65), 225, 234, 247, 248, 265, 294, 307(n108), 308, 331(n162), 332, 333, 333(n165), 334–345, 377

progressive -wur- (progressive -ur-)  247, 297, 299, 301, 305, 312, 335, 341, 342, 351(n197), 367

progressive/perfective -yaaryi (→ PROG/PRFV)

pronoun  108, 109, 112, 113, 115, 116

property adjective. → PA

proto-Japonic. → PJ

proto-. → proto-Japonic; proto-Ryukyuan

proto-Ryukyuan. → pRk

PST (past) -syi  180, 312

purposive. → PRP

QP  question particle (-ya, -yi). → Index of Particles

QT  quotative particle (-di-t°i). → Index of Particles

quadrigrade  62, 64, 185–187, 191, 194, 230–232, 234, 235, 235(n85), 236, 236(n88), 237, 239, 240, 242, 255, 257, 270, 277, 278, 322

quadrigradization, r-stem. → r-stem quadrigradization

question particle (QP). → Index of Particles

question marker, yes/no (YNQ). → Index of Particles

question, rhetorical. → rhetorical question

quotative particle (QT). → Index of Particles

ra-gyō henkaku katsuyō. → ra-hen = RH.

ra-gyō yodan-ka. → r-stem quadrigradization

ra-hen (RH = ra-gyō henkaku katsuyō = r-irregular conjugation)  186, 187, 313, 321, 331, 331(n162), 322, 333, 352, 354, 354(n205), 355, 356

reduplication  140, 148, 166, 350

religion/religious  1, 6, 95, 97, 103, 106, 129(n66), 137(n91), 177, 208, 274(n28), 285, 359, 366, 367(n225), 369

rendaku  53, 67–69, 72, 85, 85(n2), 94(n33), 103, 125, 158, 203(n31), 235(n86), 282(n45), 291(n68), 344(n183)

rentaikei. → RT

ren'yōkei. → RY

RH. → ra-hen

rhetorical question  293, 295

r-stem quadrigradization (ra-gyō yodan-ka)  184, 229, 231, 242, 277

r-stem/type  41, 42, 62, 185–187, 193, 213, 223, 231, 234, 235–237, 239–241, 251, 277, 322

r-stem verbs, (→ *(···)yir- in r-stem verbs)  60, 62, 63, 88, 115, 117, 123, 131(n73), 185, 212, 217, 257, 274(n28), 285–287, 292, 295, 329, 338(n176), 358(n210)

RT (rentaikei)  3, 9, 16, 17, 23, 36, 41(n42), 66, 67, 71, 86–88, 93, 96, 106, 108, 116–118, 122, 127, 136, 137, 139, 147, 150, 151, 153, 154, 154(n6), 157, 158, 160, 164, 170–173, 175–177, 180–182, 184, 186, 187, 188, 189, 190, 191, 192, 193, 194, 195, 196, 197, 198, 199, 200, 201, 202, 203, 204, 205, 206, 206(n41), 208–228, 231–234, 237, 238, 247, 248, 253, 255, 256, 264–267, 269–271, 278, 281, 281(n43), 281(n44), 283–287, 289, 290, 298, 300, 302–304, 307, 307(n108), 308, 309, 311, 312, 312(n114), 313, 314–324, 325–327, 331, 331(n162), 333, 333(n165), 334, 337–339, 345, 345(n187), 348, 356, 357, 357(n210), 359(n216), 361, 363, 364, 367–370, 372, 373, 377(n236), 381, 384, 385(n259), 388(n268)

RY (ren'yōkei)  3, 5, 9, 41(n41), 51, 60, 62, 63, 65, 66, 87–89, 91, 95, 106, 107, 107(n19, n22), 111, 116, 117, 120, 128, 128(n62), 131, 134(n81), 138, 138(n95), 139, 142–144, 147, 151, 151(n2), 152, 153, 157, 160, 161, 163, 165–167, 170–172, 175, 175(n52),

# INDEX OF LINGUISTIC AND LITERARY TERMS

176, 177, 179, 182, 184, 186–199, 200, 200(n25), 200(n26), 201–204, 205, 205(n38, n39), 206–229(n78), 231–234, 235(n86), 237–239, 245–248, 249, 249(n103), 250, 250(n104), 251, 256–261, 261(n2), 262, 263, 265, 267, 268(n14), 270–272, 276, 277, 279–281, 283, 284, 287–289, 289(n64), 290–296, 296(n80), 299, 300(n92), 302, 304–308, 310, 310(n111), 312(n114), 314, 315, 316, 317, 320, 321, 321(n143), 327, 329, 330, 331(n162), 332, 332(n163), 332(n164), 333–335, 335(n172), 336–345, 345(n187), 346, 346(n190), 347, 348–351(n197), 352–354, 354(n203), 355, 355(n205), 356, 356(n206, n207), 357, 357(n208), 358–363, 366–370, 372–377(n236), 377(n238), 378, 377(n240), 380–385, 385(n260), 386–388, 388(n268)

Ryukyuan (→ pRk [proto-Ryukyuan])  1, 2(n2), 4(n8), 18, 20, 22, 23, 24, 24(n12), 28(n17), 35, 37(n32), 53, 56, 57, 63, 68, 72, 76, 76(n77), 82, 101(n7), 102(n9), 122, 123(n56), 132(n74), 142, 147, 147(n114), 157, 158, 160, 163(n22), 182, 186, 191, 194, 230(n79), 233–235, 235(n85), 268, 274, 276, 279, 285, 288, 288(n60), 292(n73), 295, 298, 322(n147), 342, 355, 366, 375, 377, 387

Ryukyuan  2, 2(n2), 4(n8), 76, 132(n74)

Ryukyu Kingdom  1, 93

Ryukyus  1, 2(n2), 11, 19(n2), 28(n17), 29, 91(n22), 217

Sd (Shodon)  66, 319

semivowel (→ glide *w, y*)  38(n35), 45, 48

sentence-final particle (→ SFP). → Index of Particles

SE (stative EXTENSION -*ur*-)  95, 116, 120, 142, 143, 170, 175, 177, 214, 225, 248, 265, 294, 308, 332–344, 377

SFP (sentence-final particle). → Index of Particles

shaman(ess)  1, 2, 4, 62, 67, 93, 148, 149, 169, 194, 231, 266, 272, 275, 299, 320(n140), 358, 359(n214), 382

Shodon. → Sd

short vowels. → vowels, short

Shuri. → Sr

*Shūshikei*. → SS

SKP  sentence-final *kakari* particle (→ -*ga* ~ -*gya*). → Index of Particles

SOFTener -*wa* (-*wa* softener)  376

SPONtaneous -*uyi*(·*r*)-  8(n16), 11, 13, 88(13), 91, 110, 116, 117, 124(58), 127, 130(n69), 132, 176, 188, 218, 219, 260, 264, 265, 265(n10), 266–268(n14), 269, 270, 284, 317, 369, 370, 371, 373, 387

Sr (Shuri)  1, 1(n1), 2, 6, 9, 10, 28(n17), 29, 35, 37, 58(n58), 72, 90, 93, 94, 96, 100, 104, 107, 113, 122, 128, 129, 131(n71), 132(n73), 133, 135(n83), 137, 140, 158, 161, 167(n34), 181, 215(n53), 216, 218, 225, 231, 234, 245(n96), 256(n119), 259, 261, 262, 264, 269(n19), 279, 283, 307, 310, 311, 314(n121), 317–319, 324, 336, 337, 339, 347, 348, 357(n208), 358(n210), 359–361, 375, 389

SS (*shūshikei*)  41(n42), 89, 120, 128, 145, 150, 151, 157, 161, 161(n18), 165, 165(n26), 168(n36), 177, 179, 184, 186–188, 188(n5), 189–200, 202, 204, 205, 206, 208, 209, 210, 212–214, 214(n50), 215–217, 219–223, 225–228, 233, 237, 238, 244, 248, 250(n104), 251, 252(n113), 269(n19), 271, 271(n22), 273, 275, 279, 281, 281(n43, n44), 282, 287, 290, 291(n69), 293, 298, 303, 304, 304(n103), 305, 307, 308, 311, 312(n114), 313, 319, 321, 321(n146), 322, 322(n146), 323, 328, 329, 330, 331(n162), 332(n163), 333, 333(n165), 335, 335(n172), 336, 338, 340, 342–345, 345(n187), 346, 346(n190), 357(n208), 358, 360, 363, 369, 378(n238), 379, 380(n242), 385(n259), 386

*s*-stem/type  185, 213, 223, 278, 258, 377, 377(n236), 382

STATive  23, 96, 96(n36), 151, 151(n2), 153, 161, 162, 171, 177, 180, 192, 193, 193(n113), 201, 227, 228, 247, 250, 269, 288, 298, 299, 301, 304, 311, 312, 313(n117), 320, 322(n146, n147), 341, 343, 344, 345(n189), 351, 351(n197), 354, 354(n203), 355, 357(n208), 361

stative extension -*ur*-. → SE

stop, glottal. → glottal stop (ʔ)

SUB (-*ga* ~ -*gya*). → Index of Particles

SUBject. → Index of Particles

SUB (*-nu*). → Index of Particles

suffix(es), derivational. → derivational suffix(es)

suffix(es), DIMinutive. → DIMinutive suffix(es)

suffix(es)   14, 32, 33, 37, 70, 71, 86(n4), 111(n30), 121(n47), 126, 127, 140, 141, 141(n99), 142, 144(n108), 147, 147(n113), 150–153, 154(n8), 155, 156(n11), 157, 159, 161, 166, 168, 181, 182, 182(n65), 183, 193, 209(n45), 244, 249, 265, 267, 269, 270(n21), 271(n22), 275, 279, 279(n37), 290(n65), 296, 296(n81), 306(n105), 312, 321(n143), 331, 332(n164), 341–343

suprasegmentals   37, 73, 78, 80(n80)

*-syi* (PAST; → PST)   180, 312, 312(n114), 313(n116, n117)

syllable   11(n19), 12(n20), 25, 26, 29, 31, 33(n27), 34(n28), 35, 36, 40(n40), 44, 45, 49(n51), 53–55, 57, 57(n57), 59, 59(n60), 61, 62, 66(n65), 69, 73, 74, 74(n73), 78, 80, 81, 83, 93, 101, 101(n6), 102, 107(n20), 108(n23), 127, 130(n67), 130(n69), 134(n82), 152(n3), 186, 203, 206(n40), 218(n58), 220, 239, 241–243, 252(n112), 256(n119), 258, 266(n12), 283(n50), 306(n106), 314(n123), 315(n127), 316, 316(n127), 318(n134), 327(n156), 335(n171), 345(n187), 350(n196), 364(n221), 365(n222), 378–380

*-uyi*(·*r*)-. → SPONtaneous

vowels, short   5, 21, 34, 58, 58(n58), 61, 80(n80), 86(n4), 95, 109, 128(n64), 138, 138(n94), 174, 174(n50), 218, 256(n119), 259, 289(n62), 290(n65), 314, 317(n131), 341, 371, 378(n240), 382

ta bo re (⟨ta bo˚ re⟩)   383, 383(n252)

⟨ta bo˚ re⟩. → ta bo re

ta bo u (⟨ta bo† u⟩)   383, 383(n252), 384

⟨ta bo† u⟩. → ta bo u

*-Tar-* (perfect)   313, 314, 321, 322

*-tʰat˚imac˚ir-*. → humilific auxiliary verb

T-form (GER/PRFV-derived forms)   42, 58, 60, 66, 184, 194(n16), 203(n32), 251(n109), 253

TMP/CND (temporal or conditional)   9, 112, 191, 194(n17), 196, 206, 214, 237, 237(n91), 238, 244–246, 250, 284, 357, 358, 362, 387, 388

temporal. → TMP/CND

TOP (topic). → Index of Particles

topic. → TOP

transitive verb / transitivizing suffix. → VT

transitivity   24, 228, 230

TRM (terminative). → Index of Particles

terminative (→ TRM). → Index of Particles

*t*-stem/type   61, 185, 249, 249(n102), 250, 251, 257, 259, 316

Two-Mora Rule   63–65, 133(n78), 243, 243(n95), 320(n142)

*-umazyi*. → NEG-inferential/-intentional

upper monograde (monograde, upper)   62, 185, 189, 190, 213, 229, 380

*-ur-*, Progressive. → Progressive *-ur-*

*-(u)wa·r/s-* (EAV [exalting auxiliary verb] *-(u)wa·r/s-*)   9, 91, 95, 111, 139, 147, 176, 198, 201, 203, 204, 209, 211, 214, 215, 218, 219, 222, 226, 239, 271, 272, 274, 278, 352, 353, 360, 363, 366, 367–378, 378(n238), 379–382

*-(u)yi*(·*r*)-. → passive

VBZ (verbalizer)   142, 143, 168(n36), 240(n92), 250, 312, 313(n117)

velar   21, 21(n5), 37, 42, 43, 51, 52, 59, 63(n62), 72, 73, 73(n71), 88(n13), 107(n19), 159(n15), 167, 193, 194, 241(n93), 257, 257(n122), 258, 258(n124), 259, 327(n156), 372

verbalizer. → VBZ

verbal prefix. → VPFX

verb, irregular   160(n17), 184–186, 186(n1), 213, 223, 311, 322, 377

VI (intransitive verb / intransitivizing verbal suffix)   24(10), 41, 41(n41, n42), 72, 87, 158, 163, 163(n21), 194, 195(n23), 198, 214, 218, 220, 221, 224, 227, 228(n75), 230, 232, 235, 236, 238, 240, 241, 250, 251, 269(n19), 272, 306(n105), 310, 315, 317, 328, 370, 370(n229), 372, 384

VOCative. → Index of Particles

vowel(s), long. → long vowel(s)

VPFX (verbal prefix)   110, 262, 263, 317(131), 388(n268)

# INDEX OF LINGUISTIC AND LITERARY TERMS

VT (transitive verb / transitivizing verbal suffix) 23, 24, 24(n10), 72, 96(n37), 106, 111, 112, 116, 140(n98), 148, 152, 158, 163(n21), 165, 167, 175, 175(n52), 179, 194–197, 202, 213, 215, 217, 219–223(n64), 226, 230–232, 236, 237, 238, 240, 241, 250, 251, 259, 261, 269(n19), 272, 274, 279, 280(n38), 289, 289(n62), 291, 306, 309(n110), 315, 318(n134), 328, 348, 357, 372, 383, 384, 384(258)

*w*-stem/type 64, 200, 202, 203(n32), 239–243, 258

*-wa* 'SOFTENER'. → SOFTener *-wa*

wish 27(n16), 166, 175(n52), 177–179, 240, 291–296, 296(n82, n83), 297, 299, 299(n89), 302, 313, 371

*\*y.* → archisegment

*-yar-.* → COPula

*-ya, -yi.* → QP question particle

yes/no-question marker. → YNQ

*\*yi*, high vowel (high vowel *\*yi*) 11, 22, 23, 25, 26, 48, 55, 58, 59(n60), 61, 87, 100, 102, 130(n69), 218(n58), 258, 278, 314(n123), 385, 388(n268)

*-yi.* → INFinitive

*\*(··)yir-* in *r*-stem verbs (*r*-stem verbs, *\*(··)yir-* in) 57, 60, 63, 88, 185, 190, 212, 212(n46), 215, 217, 257, 274(n28), 287, 290(n66), 291(n67), 292

YNQ (yes/no-question marker). → Index of Particles

Yotsu-Gana (*dz* ↔ *z*; *dzy* ↔ *zy*) 44, 53, 64, 66, 67, 89(n16), 92(n28), 93, 100, 113(n33), 138(n96), 178(n58, n59), 192(n10), 228(n73), 317(n129)

Printed in the United States
By Bookmasters